Oracle UPK 12 Development

Create high-quality training material using
Oracle User Productivity Kit 12

Dirk Manuel

Oracle UPK 12 Development

First published: February 2015
Release 1

Cover image © Gerry McGlamery 2015
`http://photography.mcglamery.com`

ISBN-13: 978-0-692-39559-2

About the Author

Dirk Manuel is a Senior Consultant at Stefanini. He specializes in change management for large-scale ERP systems, in particular training and knowledge management activities. Dirk has been using Oracle UPK and its predecessor Global Knowledge's OnDemand for 10 years, during which time he has developed hundreds of quality UPK simulations for several SAP implementations and upgrades. Dirk has installed, customized, and administered several UPK environments, and has trained UPK authors in Europe, Asia-Pacific, and the Americas.

Dirk has a B.Sc. (Hons.) in Computer Science, and a City & Guilds in the Communication of Technical Information. He is a Fellow of the Institute of Scientific and Technical Communicators (ISTC).

Dirk can be contacted via LinkedIn, where he is a frequent contributor to the *Oracle UPK Community*.

```
http://www.linkedin.com/in/dirkmanuel
http://www.technicalauthoring.com
http://www.upkwiki.com
```

Acknowledgments

This book is a distillation of what is now 10 years' experience of using UPK, and of teaching it to other authors. I have seen many poor examples of simulations created using UPK, due primarily to a lack of knowledge on the part of the authors of the capabilities of UPK. My sole intention with this book is to show other authors of UPK content that it is not difficult to create truly impressive training simulations, with the correct knowledge and just a little effort. Less altruistically, I hope that by promoting a high level of quality and proving that this is eminently attainable, I can increase clients' appreciation of UPK, and consequently keep myself in a job.

I would like to thank my long-standing client, ExxonMobil, for giving me the opportunity to learn so much about UPK and OnDemand. I would like to thank Sjoerd DeVries and Tina Sasinowski for reviewing the previous versions of this book. I would also like to thank the many contributors to the LinkedIn *Oracle UPK Community*, along with the many UPK developers whom I've had the pleasure of 'guiding' on my various projects, all of whom continue to push my UPK skills and knowledge to their limits, driving me to keep on learning and improving.

Contents

ADDING VALUE IN THE PLAYER   419

INCORPORATING SOUND INTO YOUR TOPICS   445

Introduction

This book is an author's guide to Oracle User Productivity Kit. It has been written specifically for Version 12.1.0.1 ESP 1 of UPK (which was the latest release at the time of publication) but can also be used for the last several major releases of UPK, as much of the base functionality remains the same. This book covers all aspects of UPK's functionality, and—more importantly—explains how to get the most out of these features in order to build high-quality training exercises that will ensure the most effective knowledge transfer possible for your users.

Documentation on UPK has been (until the publication of Packt Publishing's *Oracle User Productivity Kit 3.5*, also by Dirk Manuel) almost nonexistent (consisting solely of the *Content Development Guide* shipped with the software), and formal training can be prohibitively expensive. This book fills the documentation gap by providing author-friendly, visually-appealing, and easy-to-read documentation on the functionality offered by UPK. It fills the training gap by taking a guided approach to this functionality, introducing new concepts and capabilities with each chapter, and building on the knowledge gained in the previous chapters. In this way, readers can start with the basics, and then progress to more advanced topics as needed, rather than being presented with "everything you need to know" all at once, in a dry and difficult-to-digest manner (as is the case with the Oracle-provided documentation).

Although it is primarily aimed at new or intermediate users, this book contains enough advanced information to keep all but the most hardcore of UPK authors happy. It includes tips on how to get the most out of UPK, suggested best practices for training material development with UPK, and advice on how to avoid some common mistakes.

What this book covers

This book provides a guided tour of UPK 12. Each chapter focuses on a specific task, based around specific functionality within UPK. Throughout the book, we will develop a sample simulation, and use this to introduce and explain new functionality by applying this functionality to the sample simulation.

By chapter, this book contains the following information:

Chapter 1   **An Introduction to UPK**
This chapter provides a high-level overview of what UPK is, and what its key capabilities are.

Chapter 2   **Recording a Simulation**
This chapter explains how simulations are recorded in UPK, and then jumps straight into productive work, providing instructions for creating the initial simulation that is built upon throughout the remainder of this book. Both the *Record It! Wizard* and recording via the UPK Developer are covered, along with both manual and automatic recording.

Chapter 3   **Working in the UPK Developer**
This chapter provides a first look at the UPK development environment. It starts by explaining the various components of the Developer screen, and provides some basic navigation techniques. It then provides guidelines on how to choose a suitable folder structure for your Library, and explains how to implement the chosen structure.

Chapter 4   **Editing a Topic**
This chapter provides a comprehensive description of the functionality provided by the Topic Editor. It does this by editing the simulation recorded in Chapter 2, changing the Bubble Text, providing Custom Text, inserting missing Frames, and editing or replacing screenshots.

Chapter 5   **Building an Outline**
This chapter introduces the concept of an Outline, and provides a full description of the capabilities of the Outline Editor. It explains the differences between Modules and Sections, and explains how best to use these to organize Topics into a structure suitable for presenting to your users.

Chapter 6   **Publishing Your Content**
This chapter explains how to preview and publish recorded Topics. It explains the various on-line and document-based output formats, provides instructions on how to generate them, and provides examples of each. This chapter also covers the quality assurance

activities that should be carried out prior to publication, including spell-checking and testing. Finally, this chapter explains how to integrate UPK's output with other applications.

Chapter 7   **Version Management**
This chapter is primarily aimed at authors working in a client/ server environment. It explains the check-in and check-out functionality of UPK, including the document history, reverting to prior versions of content objects, and restoring deleted content objects. The final sections of this chapter are applicable to both client/server installations and stand-alone installations, describing the importance of backups and explaining how to import and export content.

Chapter 8   **Allowing Alternatives**
This chapter is concerned with expanding the usefulness of recorded simulations by providing Alternative Paths, along with Branches and Decision Frames. It also explains how to improve the realism of simulations by providing Alternative Actions.

Chapter 9   **Adding Value to Your Topics**
This chapter is probably the single most important chapter in this book. It explains how to improve the quality of simulations by providing context through the use of Custom Text, Explanation Frames, and Web Pages, and including non-UPK content through the use of Packages.

Chapter 10   **Adding Value in the Player**
This chapter explains the various things that can be done to improve the quality of the user's interaction with the UPK Player. This includes using roles, jump-in points, and keywords.

Chapter 11   **Incorporating Sound into Your Topics**
This chapter explains the auditory capabilities that UPK provides, and discusses how best to utilize these. It explains how to record new sound files, as well as how to import and export sound files.

Chapter 12   **Testing Your Users**
This chapter explains how to use UPK 11's Assessment functionality to test that your users have retained the knowledge that they were given during training. It covers in-line Questions, Assessments, and the use of *Know It?* mode simulations in an Assessment.

Chapter 13   **Using UPK for Application Testing**
This chapter explains how UPK 11 can be used to test an application. It explains UPK 11's *Test It!* mode, and the output document types specific to tests.

Chapter 14 **Basic Administration**

This chapter is aimed at UPK Administrators in a client/server environment, explaining how to manage authors and control access to the Library. It also explains how to manage state values, and perform basic housekeeping activities.

Chapter 15 **Integrating UPK with other Applications**

This chapter explains how to make your published UPK training material available to your users by linking it to the recorded application and to other delivery mechanisms.

Chapter 16 **Customizing UPK**

This chapter covers the advanced topic of configuring UPK to meet your individual requirements. The chapter explains how to customize Template Text, and how to define new object types. It also explains how to customize the UPK Player, and how to update the standard document output formats.

Chapter 17 **Localizing Your Content**

This chapter explains how to convert your recorded Topics into another language. This includes using local language texts, deploying content in local languages, translating custom text, and replacing screenshots with localized versions.

Appendix A **Installing UPK**

This appendix explains how to install the UPK developer environment. It also explains how to create a UPK Profile, and how to work with multiple Profiles

Appendix B **User Options**

This appendix provides a consolidated list of all of the user options that can be specified for an author.

Appendix C **Object Types**

This appendix provides a list of all of the predefined object types in UPK, and shows the Template Text that is generated for each of these using the Standard Template and the Microsoft Template.

Appendix D **Toolbar Button Quick Reference**

This appendix provides a consolidated list of all of the toolbar buttons used in the UPK interface, describes their purpose, and provides a reference to the section in the book where this functionality is described.

What's new in UPK 12?

If you have previously purchased either of my books for prior versions of Oracle UPK, you are probably most interested in what has changed in version 12.1 For your ease of reference, the following list summaries all of the changes (from 11.1 to 12.1) that I have been able to identify, and specifies the page within this book on which these changes are explained.

- You can now create a **Style Sheet** to control the formatting of Web Pages (see page 571).

- You can now define a **Skin** to control the visual style of the Player (see page 623).

- You can now define default values for several Topic Properties (see page 701).

- It is now possible to specify a remediation level of "None" for Assessments (see page 479).

- IAS settings are now specified in an **IAS Configuration File**, which is selected at publishing time. Multiple IAS Configuration Files can be defined—but only one can be specified when publishing the Player (see page 539).

- Additional values can be specified for Player publishing—such as the initial size of the windowed *See It!* mode Player (see page 228).

- The 'non-windowed' *See it!* mode has been discontinued'; now, only the windowed *See It!* mode is available (see page 17).

- If a content object has been copied from another content object then the new **Derived From** feature can be used to identify this original source object (see page 69).

- You can search for content objects that have captured a specific Context (see page 92).

- The **Replace Fonts** feature has been enhanced to allow you to replace text formatting with a predefined text style, or to replace one style with another (see page 159).

- **Blank Frames** can be inserted into a Topic—similar to Explanation Frames, but with a blank image instead of a screenshot (see page 165).

- You can now cut and paste multiple Frames (see page 353).

- You can delete multiple Frames in a single action (see page 173).

- **Print Areas** can be used to select a different area of a screenshot to use as the thumbnail in printed output (previously, the Action Area was used) (see page 113)

- Jump-in points can be defined for Explanation Frames and Decision Frames (see page 431).

- Frame-level **Instructor Notes** now appear in the Instructor Manual publishing format by default (see page 267).

- The **Find In Library** function can be invoked directly from the *Related Documents* pane and the (new) *Derived Documents* pane (see page 69).

- When displayed in the *Outline Editor*, the *Properties* pane can be set to show the Properties of the selected Topic, the Properties of its Concept Page, or the Properties that are common to both Topics and Concept Pages (see page 191).

- You can now preview a Topic directly from the *Library* screen (see page 211).

- You can preview a Web Page directly from the *Library* screen, and independently of any content object to which it may be attached (see page 374).

- Concept Pages can be attached to Assessments (see page 486).

- The ability to convert Knowledge Pathways content to UPK has been discontinued (see page 316).

- The option to record a 'Test' from the Record It! Wizard has been discontinued (see page 36).

- You can define Assessments such that a user is required to answer a set number of questions, selected at random from the total number of Questions in the Assessment (see page 478). *

- You can define the specific play mode that a user will be required to complete when playing the simulation through an LMS that is tracking progress (see page 224). *

- You can convert published Player Topics to a video format for distribution as single, self-contained files for demonstration purposes (see page 290). *

* These features are only available in UPK 12.1 ESP1 (UPK 12.1.0.1).

Who this book is for

This book has been written with the following audiences in mind:

- New users of UPK 12, including those migrating from an earlier version of UPK, who want to understand the capabilities provided by UPK 12 and learn how they can best utilize UPK to meet their training goals.

- Intermediate users of UPK who want to improve the quality of their UPK training simulations.

- Experienced users of UPK who want to learn how to customize UPK to better match their own requirements.

Conventions used in this book

This book uses a number of typographic conventions to differentiate between different types of information, and uses specific terms to mean certain things. These are described below:

Formatting conventions

Code is formatted in a non-proportional font. An example of this is shown below:

```
<Class Name="PUSHBUTTON" ListName="Pushbutton"
  DisplayName="button"
  Gender="neutral">
  <Template Context="LClick1">
    <Text Sound="lclick1">Click on the</Text>
    <ObjectName />
  <ObjectType />
  <Text>.</Text>
  </Template>
</Class>
```

New terms and important words are shown in bold. An example of this is shown below:

The **Action Area** is the area in which the user is required to click during playback.

Words that you see on the UPK screen, in menus or dialog boxes for example, appear in bold navy (just like object names in UPK itself). This includes all button names (even if the name itself does not appear on the screen), field names, menu options, and so on. An example of this is shown below:

Clicking on the **Next** button moves you to the next screen.

Screen names (including dialog boxes, panes, views, editors, and toolbars) are shown in navy italics. An example of this is shown below:

Make sure that the *Deleted Documents* view is displayed.

Additional information appears in the outer margins of the page. The following icons are used differentiate between the various types of information provided:

● Additional information

■ Tips and Tricks

▲ Warnings

Specific terminology

UPK-specific entities are identified by initial caps, to differentiate them from more general nouns. Examples are Outline, Topic, Web Page, and so on.

"The Library" is the database in which UPK content is stored. "The *Library* screen" is the primary tab within the *UPK Developer* screen that shows the content of the Library, organized in folders.

A "Concept Page" is any content object that has been attached to a Module, Section, or Topic, so that it appears in the "*Concept* pane" of the Player. This could be a Web Page, an HTML file, or any other file housed within a Package.

The term "author" refers to a UPK developer. The term "user" refers to the people who will use the material that you develop.

Downloading the example code for the book

Throughout this book, we create and then edit a sample simulation A version of this simulation is available via the author's website, at:

```
http://www.technicalauthoring.com/UPK12Book/Samples.zip
```

Within this ZIP file is a single `.odarc` file that contains one Topic for the state of the sample simulation at the end of each chapter. For details of how to import this file into your UPK Library, refer to *Chapter 7, Version Management*.

Piracy

Please don't make illegal copies of this book. The author is an independent consultant, not a faceless corporation (not that *that* would make it any less wrong...). What little I make from this book (and I have endeavored to keep the price low) is unlikely to even cover the cost of the hardware and software I have had to buy and install just so that I could write this book. If you *have* obtained an illegal copy of this book, you can offset some of your guilt by making a PayPal donation to payee **donations@technicalauthoring.com**.

1

An Introduction to Oracle UPK

The things we have to learn before we do them,
we learn by doing them.
- Aristotle

In this first chapter, we will start with the absolute basics. We will look at what UPK is, and what it can do for us.

In this chapter, you will learn:

- What UPK is

- How UPK works and what it captures

- What delivery formats are available in UPK

- What to consider when embarking upon a training project using UPK

What is UPK?

UPK (User Productivity Kit) is a software application that can be used to create simulations of tasks performed in a software application, for use during training on that application. It can also generate various forms of documentation—such as job aids, test scripts, and business process procedures—based on these same recordings. UPK's deliverables can also be incorporated into an application's on-line help system to provide context-sensitive, in-application performance support.

UPK does all of this by capturing a person's interaction with an application (typically, to perform a discrete business task), and then repurposing this information to create the various delivery formats.

UPK has found a strong market in large corporations for developing training material for large-scale software implementations. Although it is most commonly-used for providing training on enterprise-level software applications, such as those offered by Oracle (including Agile, JD Edwards, PeopleSoft, Primavera, and Siebel) and SAP, UPK can be used to record and publish simulations for any Windows-based application.

A brief history of UPK

UPK has been around in one form or another for many years. Starting as an offshoot from SAP Tutor (now called iTutor), UPK began life as OnDemand, which was developed and marketed by OnDemand Software. OnDemand Software was eventually acquired by Global Knowledge Software (GKS), a division of Global Knowledge, Inc. In July 2008, GKS was acquired by Oracle Corporation. GKS was a long-time partner of Oracle, and OnDemand had been used extensively by Oracle and its customers for providing training on Oracle products.

● Rumor has it that this dependence on OnDemand its what fueled Oracle's purchase of GKS—Oracle did not want OnDemand falling into the hands of a competitor who possibly wouldn't continue support for Oracle products.

Because Oracle already had a product called On Demand (with a space), the decision was made to rename OnDemand to User Productivity Kit, or UPK. Concurrent with this, Oracle realigned the version numbering of UPK so that OnDemand version 9.1 (the last major release from GKS) was renumbered as UPK version 3.1. The next release (the first by Oracle) was UPK 3.5.0 which was, to all intents and purposes, a slightly enhanced version of OnDemand 9.1.7. The first significant release by Oracle was UPK 3.6, in which Oracle completely revamped UPK's sound functionality.

● Oracle refers to "pre-takeover" versions of OnDemand as "UPK 2.x". I interpret "UPK 2.x" as referring to OnDemand version 8.x, and treat UPK 3.5 and OnDemand 9.1 as generally the same product, save some minor differences in functionality highlighted as such in this book.

In 2011, Oracle released a new version of UPK, which they confusingly chose to number version 11.0. This was a relatively minor upgrade (versus UPK 3.6), and was followed in 2012 by a 'minor' version, UPK 11.1, which in fact contains more new functionality than the previous major version (11.0). Service Pack 2, which upgraded UPK to 11.1.0.2 was released in 2103 and provided a number of performance improvements and additional compatibility changes (most significantly compatibility with Internet Explorer 10).

In early 2014, Oracle released UPK version 12.1, bypassing UPK 12.0 entirely. Version 12.1 contained a number of significant performance improvements, and several new features, including screenshot overlays, and enhanced (almost native HTML) Web Page editing. Version 12.1 also introduced significantly improved functionality for customizing the visual look of the Player and content displayed in the Player, through Style Sheets and Skins. In September 2014, Oracle released Enhancement Service Pack (ESP1) 1, the most significant aspect of which was the 'publish to movie' (MP4) feature.

This book was written using UPK version 12.1.0.1 (UPK 12.1 + ESP 1) as the benchmark. However, any differences between UPK 12.1 and previous versions all the way back to OnDemand 9.1 are clearly highlighted as such. In this way, this book should be useful to authors using any version of UPK released in the past eight or nine years.

Why use UPK?

Despite Oracle (and Global Knowledge before it) championing the ability of UPK to generate multiple delivery formats from a single recording, the primary use of UPK is for the creation of interactive simulations for use in training. And for this, it can work very well—if the author is willing to put in the effort.

Simulations are captured in the application for which training is being developed. This means that the simulations have the 'look and feel' of the actual system. When these simulations are executed, the user gets the impression that they are interacting with a real system whereas, in reality, they are working within the safe confines of a training tool.

An example of a UPK simulation screen is shown in the following screenshot:

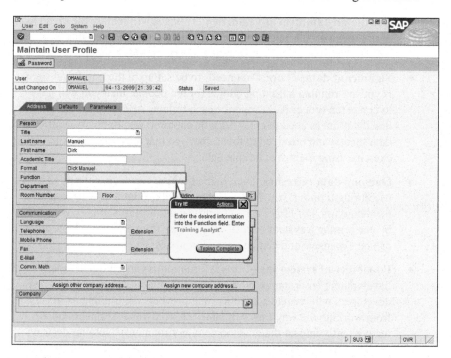

You will notice in this example that the simulation is played back in full screen (there are no Window borders), with the UPK-provided information overlaid on top of it. This information comprises a red rectangle indicating the area of the screen with which the user needs to interact (the 'action area'), and a 'bubble'

that provides the user with instructions. The user clicks in the area indicated, or types the information specified, just as they would with the actual system. Instead of interacting with the recorded application, they are in fact looking at a static screenshot and interacting with some clever JavaScript code that provides the 'look and feel' of the system. It is this 'look and feel' that provides the greatest argument for using UPK.

Instructor-led training

It is a generally accepted fact in learning theory that most people (certainly in the sphere of adult learning) learn more effectively by *doing* (practicing). In many large corporations, this practice has traditionally been achieved through the use of a training system (or a dedicated part of the 'development' system) in which trainees can carry out predefined training exercises.

However, there are a number of problems with this approach:

- **Additional capital costs:** A separate system needs to be provided to avoid having trainees interfere with the actual system. This can be costly both in terms of the capital cost of the hardware, and the need for ongoing maintenance.

- **Additional administrative burden:** Trainees will require the creation of training user IDs and passwords in order to access the training system, and these will need to be reset before every training conduct.

- **Significant data set up:** Data needs to be set up in the training system. If you are running a training course for ten people, then you will have to create ten sets of data—one for each trainee. Additionally, any values that the trainees need to enter must be captured separately (typically on data sheets) and provided to the trainees so that they can carry out the exercise using their own unique data.

- **Ongoing data refreshes:** Data in the training system is consumed by its use during training, which means that it will need to be set up again for the next class. For large, database-driven applications, this is achieved by performing a system refresh, or a restore from a backup. This, again, can be expensive and can be a lengthy process.

- **Possibility of system instability:** If training is carried out in a development environment, then there is always a danger that the developers will change something that prevents the training exercises from working the way they originally did (or, worse, trainees could inadvertently impact the development environment). Nothing destroys user confidence in a new system more than it 'not working' during training.

UPK solves these problems by capturing what is effectively a snapshot of the system, using a single set of data. This recording is external to the application, which means that once it has been captured the application is no longer required. Trainees do not need to log onto the system, and it does not matter if the developers change anything—or even crash the system. Additionally, any information that the trainee requires (such as data values) is built directly into the simulation, so there is no need for separate data sheets.

More importantly, because UPK generates a single, stand-alone simulation, every trainee can carry out the same simulation, at the same time, using the same data, and see the same result. Furthermore, a trainee can carry out a single simulation multiple times and see exactly the same result every time. This is important, as it means that the trainee can return to a simulation after the course conduct (for example, when they are back at their desk, performing the task for real) and see exactly what they saw during training, as a refresher.

Given this, UPK simulations are increasingly being seen as a good choice for providing exercises for classroom-based training. The classroom conduct still takes place, but instead of the instructor asking trainees to log on to the training system to carry out an exercise, they now ask the trainees to run a UPK exercise.

Self-paced learning

The fact that UPK simulations are self-contained, and do not rely on a system or instructor being available, means that they are well-suited to providing self-paced training (what used to be called *computer-based training* (CBT), before that term went out of vogue).

By placing all of the UPK output on a central server, or in a Learning Management System (LMS), users can access the training simulations on their own, and receive training at their own desks at a time that suits them best. This also removes the burden on trainers and other logistical resources (such as classrooms, and potentially travel to and from these), providing additional savings for companies.

However, it is important to understand that UPK does not automatically replace the need for a trainer. Yes, they *can* replace trainers, but doing so takes a significant amount of time and effort. In a classroom environment, the trainer is there to explain an exercise, point out interesting information, and provide additional business-specific information. They add *context* to the mechanics of the key-strokes and mouse-clicks captured in the recording.

If the trainer is not present to provide this information, then this information needs to be provided to the trainee through some other medium. Thankfully— as we shall see in this book—UPK works very well as this medium. But the information needs to be entered into UPK so that the trainee has access to it, and this takes time—and a little skill.

How does UPK work?

It is a common misconception that UPK simulations are 'recordings'. UPK (and this book, on occasion) uses the term *recording*, and although this is probably the most apt term, it is important to understand that a UPK simulation is not a 'recording' in the strict sense of the word. UPK does not capture 'live-motion' actions in the way that Camtasia or other video capture software does. Certainly, a UPK simulation may *look like* a recording (especially when you play it back in *See It!* mode, or convert it to MP4 format), but it isn't. What UPK captures when it 'records' are screenshots and the actions that trigger the transition from one screenshot to the next.

For example, if you use UPK to create a simulation of someone entering a text string into an input field on a screen, UPK captures the following:

- A screenshot showing the field before any text has been entered into it
- The action of typing the text, along with the text itself, and the coordinates of the location on the screen where this text is entered
- A screenshot of the field after the text has been entered into it

In terms of the actual files (or assets) created for this simulation, there will be two .png files for the screenshots, and a snippet of JavaScript that defines the text and the coordinates. There is no .wmf, .swf, .mp4, or any other movie-type file.

When this simulation is played back (in *See It!* mode) UPK displays the first screenshot, displays the text on the screen at the required coordinates one character at a time (so that it *looks* as though it is being typed), and then displays the second screenshot. Smoke and mirrors; that's all.

This simplicity has a couple of strong benefits. First, because the recordings consist purely of standard, browser-friendly assets (HTML files, .png image files, and JavaScript), the simulation can be played back in a simple web browser without the need for any add-ins, codecs, or proprietary players. Second, these assets all have very small individual file sizes, which means that they work well even over low-bandwidth connections.

But what is *really* clever is the way that UPK makes use of these assets. UPK allows exactly the same recording to be used to generate several different delivery formats, including two formats designed for on-line use, and eight formats for other uses.

Output formats

As noted above, UPK can provide output in two different formats designed for on-line use and eight formats designed for other purposes. *All* of the output formats are generated from the same, single recording. This provides true single-sourcing, but it also means that, for example, a Test Document can (by default) only contain the same content as the training simulation, which can only contain the same content as the Business Process Document, and so on.

Furthermore, what you want to teach a trainee during a classroom conduct (or in a self-paced training module) is not necessarily the same thing that you want described in your documentation. In training, you may want to look at certain scenarios. Maybe you want the trainee to hit a certain problem, and then explain how to overcome this. Maybe you want to take a bit more time and explain some related information on a screen, or point out how *this* ties in with *that*. In your documentation, and certainly for Business Process Procedures (a.k.a. work steps, user procedures, work instructions, and so on), you are more likely to want to provide clear, concise instructions on how to do something the single, correct way.

So yes, UPK *can* be used to generate additional output formats (over and above the interactive simulation), but this doesn't mean that you necessarily need to *use* these formats.

On-line delivery

For on-line delivery, UPK provides two different output formats. These are both variations on the same theme: on-line simulations with which a trainee interacts. These formats are:

- A **Player** format that provides access to a suite of simulations. The trainee can select a simulation from the list provided and run it in a number of modes (described below). This Player is generated in a format that is suitable for importing into an LMS. It is AICC and SCORM-compliant, which means that a trainee's progress and scores can be tracked within the LMS.

- An HTML **Web Site** that provides simulations with limited interactivity, in a format suitable for displaying in a limited-functionality web browser, such as the browser on a smartphone.

Both of these formats are explained in greater detail in *Chapter 6, Publishing Your Content*. Because the Player format is the most commonly-used format, and the Web Site is effectively a variation on the Player format, this book concentrates on the Player format.

An example of a UPK Player is shown in the following screenshot:

✚ Prior to UPK 11, the Player and the LMS package were separate deliverable formats; because 99.9% of the content is the same, they were combined in UPK 11.

✚ UPK 11 and earlier also allowed the generation of Standalone Topic Files (self-contained single-file versions of a simulation that required a proprietary player to view) was discontinued in UPK 12.

● This example shows the finished product of this book, using Web Pages, images, roles, hyperlinks, and a custom deployment format and Skin. If your first Player does not look like this, then don't worry; that's why this book was written—to get you there.

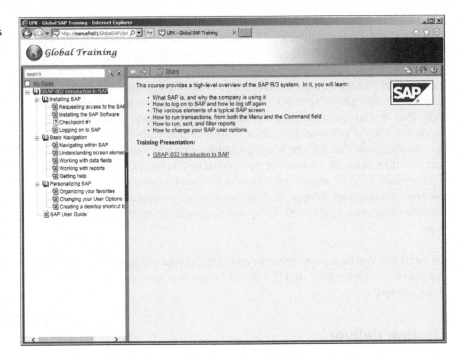

When a trainee selects a specific simulation from the list in the left-most pane of the Player, additional information about that simulation is displayed on the right-most side of the screen, along with option buttons for the six modes in which the simulation can be used (actually, five playback modes and a single document format). An example of this simulation-level screen is shown in the following screenshot:

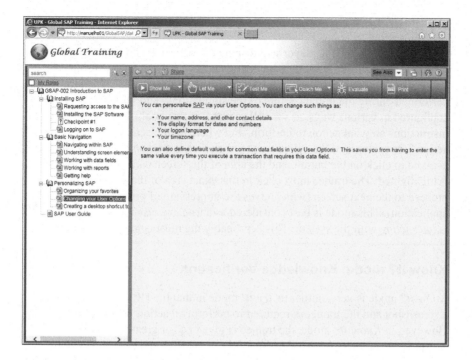

The six modes in which the simulation can be experienced are shown in the heading across the top of the rightmost portion of the screen. Each of these modes is explained separately, below.

Note that in reality you would probably not use all six of the modes shown above in the same player (for example, you would not include the *Test It!* mode in a Player that users will see, for reasons explained in *Chapter 13, Using UPK for Application Testing*), but all possible modes are included here for completeness. You can activate or deactivate specific modes for individual recordings, and only the buttons for the modes enabled for a simulation will appear when that simulation is selected.

See It! mode: Demonstrations

In *See It!* mode, the UPK player automatically displays the screenshots and carries out the required interactions. This looks like the playback of a video, and can be completely hands-free. This mode is best considered as a *demonstration* mode. When used in a classroom environment, the instructor could set this mode running and then provide additional commentary during the playback. Although this requires fairly close coordination between the instructor's speech and the playback, it does have the advantage (over the other modes) that the instructor does not need to interact with the simulation themselves, and can therefore better focus on the needs of the trainees.

✛ In UPK 11 and earlier, the *See It!* mode selected from the Player would always run in full screen mode, but a (re-sizable) 'windowed' mode was available via the kp.html file. In UPK 12, the full-screen *See It!* mode has been discontinued, and the Player launches the windowed *See It!* mode.

Try It! mode: Exercises

In *Try It!* mode, the UPK player will display a screenshot, and then wait for the trainee to perform the action, before advancing to the next screenshot. The trainee is required to carry out exactly the same action as the one that was performed during the initial capture of the simulation—although this can be configured in various ways, as we will see later in this book. The user is given instructions on what action to perform, and where on the screen to perform this action. For example, if the action was to click on a button on the screen, the user is asked to click on the button, and the area of the screen containing the button is highlighted. The trainee must click in this exact area of the screen in order to proceed to the next screen (which gives the impression of progressing through the application). This mode is best considered as a true *exercise* mode, in that the user is *interacting* with the system. This is probably the most commonly-used mode.

Know It? mode: Knowledge Verification

Know It? mode is very similar to *Try It!* mode in that the UPK player displays a screenshot and the trainee is required to perform an action on this screen. However, in *Know It?* mode, the trainee is given no (or greatly reduced) instructions and there is no indication of the area of the screen with which the trainee is required to interact. This is because the trainee is expected to *know* what they are doing. Another unique feature of the *Know It?* mode is that once they have completed the exercise, the user is presented with a 'score' that indicates what percentage of the exercise they managed to perform correctly, without assistance. This score can also be provided to an LMS, or some other system, for monitoring trainee progress. This mode is therefore best thought of as a *test* (or *knowledge verification*) mode.

Do It! mode: Performance support

Do It! mode differs from the first three modes described above in that it is specifically designed to provide assistance to *users* of the application (not trainees) while they are actually using the real application. With *Do It!* mode, the instructions for the actions are displayed in a help panel that floats above any other windows on the user's screen. The theory is that the user has the application open, and is working directly in it, with the UPK instructions being visible at the same time. This mode, therefore, is best thought of as *performance support* (or as providing an *electronic performance support* system, to use the latest buzzwords).

Test It!: System Testing

✛ *Test It!* mode was introduced in UPK 11.1. It is, for some reason, only available in a client/server environment. Test It! mode is described in detail in *Chapter 13, Using UPK for Application Testing.*

Test It! mode is similar to *Do It!* mode, in that it is designed to be used while the user is carrying out the activity in the actual application. However, the difference is that users are told what *should* happen as they perform each action, and they need to indicate whether or not they were able to carry out the specified action, and achieve the specified result. They also have the option to record their observations, and save the results of their testing (along with the steps performed) to a Microsoft Word document that can be sent to the support team. In this way, the user is *testing* that the application is working as documented (by UPK).

Print It!: Documentation

The sixth mode available through the Player is *Print It!*. This allows the user to print a hardcopy version of a simulation. This hardcopy can be one of the following three UPK document formats:

+ *Print It!* mode was introduced in UPK 3.5.

- Job Aid
- System Process
- Test Document

These three document formats, along with five further UPK publishing formats that cannot be used for *Print It!* mode, are discussed in *UPK-generated Documentation* on page 19.

Conditional texts

In order to provide the most appropriate text for each of the play modes described above, UPK makes use of *conditional texts*—that is, UPK has the ability to define in which specific modes the instructional texts will be displayed. You can also choose whether specific text will appear in the on-line publication formats (discussed above) and/or the 'printed' publishing formats (discussed below). Furthermore, for each of the 'printed' publishing formats, you can choose from which of the playback modes the text should be taken.

All of this provides a great deal of flexibility when providing text in UPK simulations. It is extremely important to know which publishing formats will be used, and what text modes will be used, when creating the simulation content— or specifically, when choosing the words to be used for describing (or not, depending on the mode) the actions that the user is required to carry out. These aspects are covered in detail in *Chapter 4, Editing a Topic*.

UPK-generated Documentation

As stated above, UPK can generate a number of different types of documentation. Again, these are all built from the same single recording, so the variation between them is extremely limited. Most of the uniqueness of a given document stems from a few small pieces of additional information that are entered outside of the actual recording, some minor formatting differences, and the display or suppression of certain elements of the recording.

The eight available documents are explained in brief below. A more detailed explanation of each document type, along with examples of each document, is given in *Chapter 6, Publishing Your Content.*

System Process Document

✛ Prior to UPK 3.5, the System Process Document was referred to as a Business Process Document, although the content is identical.

The **System Process Document** contains all of the actions carried out in the recording, including screenshots, plus some other developer-provided text describing the context of the process. The System Process Document is effectively a user procedure. This document format is sometimes referred to as a business process procedure, work instruction, job script, and so on.

Job Aid

The **Job Aid** is a scaled-down version of the recording. It does not (by default) include screenshots, and simply lists all of the actions as a single numbered list, formatted in a table. This format is often used as a 'quick reference'.

Training Guide

The **Training Guide** is effectively a hard-copy version of a training course for use by the trainee. Quite why they would want a two-dimensional printout when they have the full interactive version on-line is unclear, but some people like to receive handouts during training, and this will give them that. Additionally, because the Training Guide contains the full content of the simulation (all screenshots and all texts) it is useful for providing review copies of the training material to people who do not have access to the interactive, on-line version.

Instructor Manual

The **Instructor Manual** is, as the name suggests, designed to be a reference document for an instructor to use during the classroom conduct of a course. The content is largely the same as that of the Training Guide, but with (optional) simulation-level and step-level instructor notes. The instructor may find it useful to refer to this document during demonstrations, or prior to the trainees carrying out the exercise, in order to familiarize themselves with the content of the simulation.

Test Document

The **Test Document** provides the instructions from a simulation, but not the screenshots. It can also contain several additional pieces of information related to testing such as the purpose of the test, set-up instructions, expected time to complete, additional validation instructions, and so on. For each step in the procedure, the Test Document includes space to record the input (data entered or action taken), expected result, and whether the test (or step) was passed or failed.

Test Results

The **Test Results** document contains the instructions for a simulation, along with any Author Notes (explained in *Chapter 2, Recording a Simulation*) captured during recording or editing of the simulation. It is **not** the same as the Test Results document generated at the end of *Test It!* mode (see *Chapter 13, Using UPK for Application Testing*), and does not contain expected or actual results (despite the name). However, if the *Record It! Wizard* is used to record a test case being executed, and the tester enters their findings in the Author Notes, this document format could conceivably be used to provide the results of that test, in printable form.

Test Case

The **Test Case** format generates a file in a format that can be used with (typically, imported into) one of the more popular testing applications. The supported testing applications are:

- HP Quality Center (previously known as Mercury TestDirector)
- IBM Rational Quality Manager
- Oracle Application Testing Suite

You can also generate the Test Case format as a generic Microsoft Excel worksheet that may be usable in other testing applications.

✚ Prior to UPK 11.0, the Test Case document could only be generated in HP Quality Center format (and was called HP Quality Center, and not Test Case).

Presentation

The **Presentation** output format is a Microsoft PowerPoint presentation that contains one slide per screenshot/action pair. It can be used for presenting the steps to trainees, although obviously there is no interaction with this format.

✚ The Presentation format was introduced in UPK 3.6.1.

Stand-alone movies

There is one final 'output format' that is provided by UPK. This is the 'movie' format. UPK provides a companion utility (that is not fully integrated into the UPK publishing process) that can take simulations published (in *See It!* mode) to a Player, and convert each of these to a self-contained .MP4 'movie'/'video' format.

✚ The 'movie' format was introduced in UPK 12.1 ESP 1.

Deciding how you will use UPK

Now that you understand what UPK can do for you, you need to think about exactly what you *want* it to do for you.

Choosing delivery formats

Before starting any development, you should decide whether you are going to use your simulations as an integral part of classroom training conducts, or will be providing your training as stand-alone deliverables suitable for self-paced learning. Or both.

If you only plan on using your simulations to provide exercises within a classroom environment, then you may be able to get by with providing less business context in your simulations because the trainer will be able to provide this context during the classroom conduct. However, if you do this you will be selling yourself short. There will undoubtedly come a time when your UPK exercises will be used for self-paced training, even if this is not the initial intention. Providing this capability up-front will save re-work in the long run.

As explained above, UPK allows you to tag the text that is displayed to the users so that it appears only in specific playback modes. If you will publish to one of the true interactive formats (Player/LMS, Web Site), you should decide which of these playback modes you will use, and then tag the text appropriately for this. Tagging text so that it makes sense in several different modes takes time— especially if you are using Custom Text extensively (which you should, if you want to provide quality training). If there are certain modes that you know you will never use, then you can save yourself some development time by not tagging the text for these specific modes.

However, bear in mind that when you generate one of the document output formats, you need to tell UPK from which one of the playback modes the text for the document should be taken. You should therefore tag your text for the appropriate playback mode (that is used by the *Print It!* mode) during editing, even if you do not intend on making that particular playback mode available on-line. Tagging text for different modes is described in *Chapter 4, Editing a Topic.*

You should also decide which (if any) of the printed document formats you will use, before you start editing your recordings. As explained above, training is not the same as documentation; you can have high-quality, effective training simulations, but that does not necessarily mean that the documents generated from them will be as good.

Examine the available document formats and decide if you have a use for them. If you do not have a proven need for a document type, then do not generate it "just because you can". Don't initially worry about the *format* of the document (that can easily be changed, as we shall see in *Chapter 16, Customizing UPK*) – just determine which of the documents contain the information that you want to see (although, again as we shall see in *Chapter 16, Customizing UPK*, you can include or exclude information, within reason), and plan on using only these formats.

If you decide to use one of the document formats, then think about how these documents will be made available to the trainees or users. If you use only one document format, then you can provide access to this via the *Print It!* mode. If you provide more than one document format (which I'd question the need to do, as they all provide basically the same information), decide how you will deliver these. If they are not easily and immediately accessible to the people who need them, re-examine the wisdom of providing them at all.

Styles and standards

UPK does a very good job of ensuring consistency and adherence to styles and standards, via its built-in templates, which define the default texts shown in the yellow bubbles that are overlaid on the screenshots. One of the templates that it provides is even designed to be compatible with the terminology and formatting standards espoused by Microsoft's *Manual of Style for Technical Publications*.

You should check these default templates (both the **Standard** template and the **Microsoft** template) to determine if they meet your in-house standards. If neither of them seems suitable, then you may want to consider customizing one of the two provided templates in order to meet your requirements.

Over and above the Bubble Texts that are controlled by the template, you should develop your own style guide to specify the following things:

- The overall structure and content of your Outlines

- The information that should be provided in the Concept pane

- The type of information that should be provided via Custom Text

- Whether icons should be used, and which ones should be used in which types of Frames and/or Bubbles

- Fonts for Bubble Text and fills for Bubbles

- Word choice for Custom Text

- Whether external documents should be incorporated into your output, and how these will be accessed

- Whether you want to use images, and the allowed size and formats of these

Don't worry if most of these terms do not mean anything to you yet; you will be intimately familiar with them by the end of this book.

Developing an unequivocal style guide, and then ensuring that all authors adhere to this for all simulations, will ensure that your training deliverables are seen as forming a cohesive whole rather than just being "a bunch of stuff done by different people at different times".

In addition to providing a style guide, if you have multiple authors working in your Library, you should also set up all of your content defaults (see *Appendix D, User Options*), and then export these as an .ops file. You can then send this file to the other authors (and SMEs, if you are using SMEs for recording) for them to load into their UPK Profile. This will ensure that all simulations are at least captured consistently.

When to record

It is important to decide upon the stage during the application development cycle at which you will capture your simulations. Ideally, your simulations should be captured in the final version of the system.

The whole point of simulations is that they should have the 'look and feel' of the actual system. Specifically, they should match reality as closely as possible— there should be a willing suspension of disbelief on the part of the user that they are actually looking at static screenshots. This is a common fault with poor-quality UPK exercises: they do not allow for this suspension of disbelief because it is glaringly obvious that the user is not using an actual system. With a high-quality exercise, however, the user has the impression that they are using a 'live' system. One of the common complaints that users have with training conducted using UPK simulations is that they would rather have a 'real' system to play with. The easiest way to avoid such comments is by providing simulations that are as close to reality as possible.

That said, it is often impractical to wait until development for the entire application is complete before developing your training. Often, training development and application development will run in parallel. Fortunately, development is often gradual, with different parts of the application being completed over time (as opposed to *nothing* being ready until the whole thing is ready). You should therefore work closely with your development team to ensure that the training developers are informed as and when different pieces of the functionality are finalized, so that you can start developing training for these pieces, while the development teams work on the next piece of functionality.

What to record

Although you might think that determining *what* to record is obvious—just whatever the user will actually do—this is not necessarily the case. Consider whether you will demonstrate a specific scenario, provide general instructions, or show everything that the user *can* do in the application (or transaction), regardless of whether they actually *will* do this. Ask yourself: do you want to document "what the application does", or do you want to teach "how to use the application to complete an identified business task". This is an important distinction, especially when it comes to determining effort required, because if you take the latter approach, of documenting business tasks, you will likely end up with multiple recordings for some pieces of functionality (or transactions), where that functionality is used for multiple business purposes.

You should also decide whether you want to teach only one way to do something, or will provide *alternative actions* and *alternative paths* (both of which are covered later in this book). Ask yourself if you only want to teach the 'correct' way of doing something (sometimes referred to as the 'golden path'), or do you want to provide examples of common problems or mistakes, and how to identify and resolve them? Again, taking the latter approach will most likely result in more recordings (but a more complete training deliverable).

A useful technique when making these decisions is to produce a 'storyboard'—a simple flowchart of what screens you will use in the application, what you will do on each screen, and how you will get from one screen to the next. Having this information available beforehand will save you from having to decide these things during the recording itself, and potentially missing steps out. Storyboards are also useful if you have less-experienced developers who perhaps need some more guidance for their recordings.

Choosing a development model

As you plan your UPK development project, you should consider how the material will be developed. When developing UPK simulations, the initial recording (of the actions in the target application) is the easy part. Adding all of the bells and whistles, and turning this simulation into an effective training tool, is what takes time and effort. The former is best done by someone who knows the application being recorded (such as a Subject Matter Expert (SME)), but the latter is better performed by a skilled UPK author.

The ideal situation is for the UPK developer to also be skilled in the application, but this is not always possible. Your organization may not have a dedicated UPK development team, and may bring people into the organization purely for training development. In this case, they are unlikely to have the business knowledge of the application being recorded. In other cases, you may have a new application that is currently only understood by the application developers or designers, who do not know UPK at all. Teaching them how to use UPK effectively may be more effort than your organization or project is willing to commit. It is also likely to be met with resistance (most application developers do not *want* to be training developers) and the results are likely to be less than optimal. (Of course, there are exceptions, but in this author's experience, they are very few and far between.)

An alternative is to have simulations *recorded* by an SME who is an expert in the application, and then *finessed* by a skilled UPK author who can use the full power of UPK to turn this basic recording into an effective training simulation. Luckily, UPK includes functionality to support this 'split development' model— the *Record It! Wizard*. The SME can use the *Record It! Wizard* to record the simulation, without having to learn very much about UPK at all (especially if they use automatic recording). They can then pass this to the skilled UPK author, who will edit the recording in full UPK Developer Client, using the full functionality of UPK to create the finished, training-ready simulation.

● The *Record It! Wizard* is only available in a client/server environment. (Presumably, if you are working in a stand-alone (single-user) environment you are doing everything yourself anyway, so have no need for a 'split development' model.)

Summary

UPK captures a user's interactions with a software application. It can then generate a number of deliverables based on this recording.

Before creating training deliverables using UPK, you should decide which of these deliverable formats you want to use. Although you can choose the required deliverables at the time of final publication, knowing which deliverable formats you want to use, and in what modes, will allow you to better focus your editing of the simulations.

2

Recording a Simulation

In *Chapter 1, An Introduction to Oracle UPK* you received an overview of UPK, and now have a better appreciation of its capabilities. You're probably also impatient to get started, so now we will jump straight into recording our first simulation.

In this chapter you will learn:

- What UPK captures during a recording
- How to record a simulation via the *Record It! Wizard*
- How to record a simulation via the UPK Developer
- How to record drag-and-drop activities

The Record It! Wizard

One of the most significant pieces of functionality added to UPK in the last several releases is the *Record It! Wizard*, which was introduced in UPK 11.1. The *Record It! Wizard* ostensibly wrapped provides a simplified interface that guides a UPK author through the recording process, and exposes only enough of UPK's functionality to achieve that. At first glance the *Record It! Wizard* looks like a brand new piece of functionality, but in reality it is just a limited view of the existing UPK Developer functionality.

Because it is limited in scope, the *Record it! Wizard* provides an excellent way to allow less-skilled UPK authors to create recordings. In fact, it is a perfect way to allow Subject Matter Experts (SMEs) who may not really be UPK authors at all to create recordings, without having to endure the steep learning curve associated with the full UPK Developer product. Of course, the subsequent recording may not necessarily be ready for prime-time, but if your development process already

✛ The *Record It! Wizard* was introduced in UPK 11.1.

● The *Record It! Wizard* is only available in a client/server environment.

separates the 'recording' from the 'editing', the *Record It! Wizard* fully supports this approach.

The *Record It! Wizard* is really designed for casual users of UPK, and the chances are that if you are reading this book you are not (or do not anticipate being) a casual user of UPK. However, it does provide a useful—and immediate—introduction to the mechanics of UPK, so we will use the *Record It! Wizard* for our first recording, and then look at other methods of recording later in this chapter.

If you are not planning on using the *Record It! Wizard* (or are using a version of UPK prior to UPK 11.1, or are using a stand-alone installation of UPK) then you may want to skip the section *Recording using the Wizard* when we get to it, and go directly to the section *Recording via the UPK Developer* on page 53.

How UPK captures a recording

Recording a simulation is a relatively simple activity, but before we jump into it, it is helpful to know exactly what UPK is doing when you record a simulation.

It is important to understand that UPK does not *record*, in the traditional sense of the word. It does not create a video of what you do (in the way that, say, Camtasia does). Instead, it captures screen prints and the actions performed to move from one screen to the next.

Furthermore, UPK does not, by default, *automatically* capture these. You have to specifically tell it when to capture screen prints and actions by pressing the PRINTSCREEN key (or other nominated key or key combination; *Setting your User Options* on page 38).

This necessity of telling UPK when to capture a screenshot is both bad and good. It's bad in that you have to remember to press PRINTSCREEN, which can be distracting when you are trying to concentrate on what you are recording, but it is good in that you only capture exactly the screenshots you want. If an unexpected dialog box is displayed, you simply don't press PRINTSCREEN, and it is not captured (although you do need to be careful to ensure that the action is captured correctly; either that, or record the unexpected dialog box and then simply delete it from the recording, as we shall see in the next chapter).

When you press PRINTSCREEN, UPK will take a screenshot of the screen as it appears when you pressed PRINTSCREEN, and will capture the last action that you performed. This last action is effectively the thing that you did that caused the screen to look like it currently does in the screenshot that was captured. Often, this will be the key-press or mouse-click that moved you from the previous screen to the current screen, but it could also be the entry of a text string, or other action. Conceptually, therefore, UPK captures a set of action/screenshot pairs throughout a recording.

This order—action then screenshot—is important. Each capture records the action that was carried out on the *previous* screen, and a screenshot of the *current* screen (that is, the screen state once the action has been carried out). This is summarized in the following diagram, which shows what UPK captures for a recording of the user entering a text string into an input field and then pressing *ENTER*:

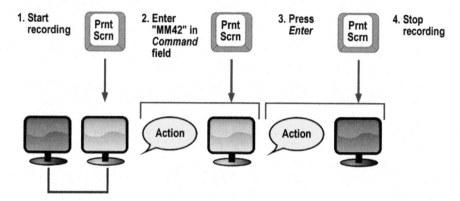

You will note, here, that we only performed two actions (the first one being the entry of the text string, and the second one being the key-press) but this has resulted in four screenshots being taken. Why? Because UPK will automatically insert a start screen and end screen and it uses the screenshots from the first and the last action/screenshot pairs to do this. Note that they are shown grayed out in the previous diagram; they are grayed out in the actual recording as well.

Automatic recording

UPK provides the ability to automatically record actions. If this feature is used, then you (the author) only need to press *PRINTSCREEN* twice—once to start the recording, and once to stop it. UPK will then automatically capture every mouse-click and key-press that you make, along with the resultant screenshots. However, this comes with a large caveat; the recording will capture *every time* the screen changes, regardless of whether this is in response to a specific action that you want to record. This may or may not be what you want, but the chances are that this approach will capture some unwanted screenshots that you will need to remove during editing.

That said, this option is extremely useful when you want to capture a demonstration by a non-UPK user, such as a Subject Matter Expert (SME). With manual recording, the SME will no doubt forget to press *PRINTSCREEN* from time to time, resulting in (typically, critical) steps being missed out of the recording, or else they will find the *Recorder* pane distracting and become frustrated with the whole recording process.

The automatic recording feature generally works well, and once you are comfortable with what UPK is capturing and understand what you will probably need to correct in the resultant recording, you may end up using it most of the

✛ The ability to record automatically, without you having to press *PRINTSCREEN* every time you want it to capture a new screenshot, was introduced in UPK 3.5.

■ There are some additional caveats to this approach. It is important that the Subject Matter Expert understands the limitations of automatic recording, and knows how to work around these. The main limitation is that pointing to an object will not automatically be recorded, so the SME should click on the object (and you will then need to change the action in the recording, which we explain in the next chapter).

time. Within this book, however, we will use the manual recording option partly because it gives us better control, and partly because it is like learning to drive: if you learn in a manual transmission, moving to an automatic is simple, but learning in an automatic does not mean that you'll successfully be able to drive a car with manual transmission!

Capturing actions

It is important to understand that (with manual recording) when you press *PRINTSCREEN* UPK will only capture the last *single* action that you performed—for example, a single mouse-click, a single key-press, or a single text entry. So if you enter text in Field A, then enter text in Field B, and then press *PRINTSCREEN*, your screenshot will show both Field A and Field B filled in, but the only *action* captured will be the entry of text into Field B (because this is the last action that you performed before pressing *PRINTSCREEN*). If you then played back this recording, text would suddenly appear in Field A, without warning, when you are asked to enter the string in Field B. Therefore, you must be careful to press *PRINTSCREEN* after **every** action that you perform.

● Thankfully, UPK does capture string input as a single action—so if you are typing one or more words, you don't have to press *PRINTSCREEN* after every letter.

For each action, UPK will capture the following things:

- The object against which the action was performed
- The action that was performed
- For text entry actions, the text that was entered

That's all. Nothing else. So it's not really that clever, after all! What *is* clever is the way that it uses this information, but we'll look at that later in this book.

Problematic actions

Although UPK will capture all of the (keyboard and mouse) actions that you perform, there are a few types of actions that cause problems. You should be aware of these before you start recording, so that you can compensate accordingly.

- **Clipboard actions**: UPK uses the Windows clipboard to capture the screenshot. This means that whenever you press *PRINTSCREEN*, UPK will replace the current contents of the clipboard with the screenshot, effectively losing anything that was previously on the clipboard. If you need to record a copy-and-paste (or cut-and-paste) action then you should copy the content, press *PRINTSCREEN*, re-copy the content, then paste, and then press *PRINTSCREEN* again.

- **Changing text values**: If you need to record the changing of a text field, then you should record the complete entry of the text. For example, if you are changing a text field from "1234" to "1235" but do this (during recording) by selecting the last digit and pressing *5* on the keyboard, or by positioning the cursor at the end of the text string and pressing *Backspace* and then *5*, then UPK will only capture the action of entering "5". You should therefore select the entire text, over-type it with the full, new text, and then capture this (action of entering the full text string). You can then use the **Implicit Text** option during editing to provide the current text that is changed.

Planning your recording

Before recording a simulation, you should always plan exactly what you want to record. This will save you the need to insert missing screenshots later, or to re-record the exercise, because you forgot to capture a particular screen and/or action.

Bear in mind that the actual recording is only one step in the process of producing an effective simulation. It is worthwhile remembering the term PREP:

- **P**lan
- **R**ecord
- **E**dit
- **P**ublish

Consider mapping out the screens that you want to navigate to, and the actions that you want to perform on these screens. An example of a simple plan for the exercise captured later in this chapter is shown below:

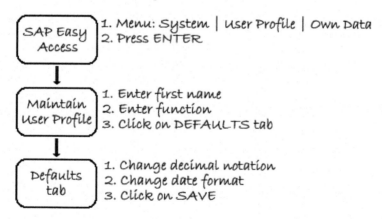

You should also make sure that any required data is available in the system, before you start recording. Bear in mind that the simulation should match reality as far as possible. This means that the screens should look exactly as they will when the end user sees them for the first time, that any data captured is correct and valid, and so on.

Preparing your PC for recording

Before recording a simulation, there are a number of things that you should do to prepare, or at least be aware of. Some of the things to watch out for are listed below:

- **Watch out for screen junk:** Make sure that there is no extraneous information on the screen. UPK will always capture full-screen images, so you may want to make sure that the application you are recording is in full-screen mode. If you do not want to (or cannot) record in full-screen mode, make sure that the application window stays in exactly the same position (to the nearest pixel) throughout the recording; otherwise, the playback will appear to 'jump'.

- **Set your screen to the correct resolution:** Set your screen to be the same resolution as the one to which your user's screens will be set. For example, if your company's standard screen resolution is 1024x768 pixels, then make sure that you also record your simulations at this resolution. UPK will always display screens full-size, as it cannot scale them. If you record at a higher resolution than the user can display, the user will need to scroll around the screen to see it all. If you record at a lower resolution, then the UPK Player will be centered on the screen and the surrounding area will be white, which will destroy the *illusion of reality*. If you do not know the resolution of the user's screens, or if there are several supported resolutions, either use the lowest common denominator, or explicitly state the recorded resolution up front (ideally, on the Concept Page for the simulation, and advise your users that they should switch to this resolution for the best playback results.

- **Hide the Windows Taskbar:** For Microsoft Windows, you may want to ensure that the Taskbar is auto-hidden so that you do not capture it in the recording (unless you are specifically recording interactions with the Taskbar). If you do include it, then make sure that you only have the application(s) that you are recording running—your user's don't need to see that you had Gmail running, or that you were flipping between the application that you were recording and checking Facebook. Note that UPK will automatically 'hide' itself, so your users will never see UPK in the Taskbar.

- **Close all other applications:** Close all applications apart from the one that you are recording, and UPK itself. You do not want unexpected interruptions—for example, by IM (Instant Messaging) clients, or other programs issuing alerts or pop-ups. Also, make sure that you have no other applications running that could interfere with the recording—especially screen capture applications, such as SnagIt, which also trap the *PrintScreen* key and/or make use of the clipboard.

- **Remove any personalization:** Make sure that you are not using personalized display profiles or color settings. If the application that you are recording allows users to change (for example) their color profile, make sure that you record using the default color profile. If users access an application for the first time and see a color scheme different than the one they saw in training, they may become confused and/or concerned (really, I've seen it happen). If a user has customized their own profile, then the chances are that they are knowledgeable enough to realize that this explains the difference between what they saw in training and what they see in the actual application, so always use the default, 'vanilla' settings.

- **Watch out for session data:** When recording a simulation, try to capture screens as data-neutral as possible. Some applications will remember the last values used, and automatically use these for subsequent tasks (similar to session cookies in the browser). Remove any data that will not be auto-populated for a user the first time that they carry out the task in the 'live' system. Similarly, remove all personal favorites, parameter defaults, and so on. Always ask yourself: "What would the user see if they were doing this for the first time?".

- **Record the complete task:** Related to this last point, endeavor to record simulations from a neutral starting point, for example, the initial screen of an application (although it would probably be excessive to require the user to log on to the application every time). Unless you are providing something such as advanced troubleshooting exercises that *start* from the premise of "If you see this…", you should not just drop the user into the middle of a task—always explain to them how to get there. Similarly, at the end of the task, always return to the same neutral screen, leaving the user ready to start the next task. There is nothing more annoying than being told how to navigate deep into an application's screens, and then just being left there.

- **Watch out for the cursor position:** When performing the actual recording, make sure that you pay attention to where the mouse pointer is located. Although UPK will automatically hide the pointer itself, it will not automatically hide any ToolTip text that may be displayed. If you have screen objects that change appearance when you hover over them, make sure that the cursor is not hovering over them when you capture the screen print—especially if this is the object that they will be clicking on, as this would give them too much of a clue to the action (especially in *Know It?* mode).

- **Maintain data continuity:** If you record your simulation in more than one go, or if (when!) you have to re-capture screen shots, watch out for data continuity. For example, if you record a topic on one day, and then replace a few screens the next day, make sure that any timestamps shown on the screens are consistent, that any data used is consistent throughout, and so on. If anything is inconsistent, then this will be evident in the Player—it may only be a quick flash as the user navigates from one screenshot to the next, but it could cause the user to question what they saw, and wonder whether they did something wrong, or worse, whether the system or training is incorrect.

- **Use realistic data:** Your simulations should look as close to reality as possible. This means that the data used in the simulations should, to the greatest extent possible, be realistic data. Avoid using customers called "Test Customer", products called "Dummy", and so on. Try to use valid number ranges, document types, and so on. This will better facilitate the trainees transitioning their knowledge to the actual system. However, you should also make sure that you do not use any sensitive or confidential data (use *realistic* data, not necessarily *real* data), such as actual customer names and addresses (unless, of course, you are recording a simulation on how to handle a specific customer). Although it may take longer to prepare before starting your recording, it is worthwhile setting up (or having the data team set up for you) your own set of data (such as products, customers, and suppliers) that is only used in training development.

- **Perform a test run before recording:** Finally, consider testing the activity before you record it. Make sure that the application works as expected, and that you can do what you need to capture. But when doing this, be careful not to 'consume' data that you will need for the actual recording.

Our first recording

Now that we have performed any necessary preparation, let's go ahead and record our first simulation. We will record a very simple simulation that covers a variety of actions, including text entry, screen navigation, and some option selections. For the purposes of this exercise, our simulation will teach users how to change their user options in the SAP application. Do not worry if you do not use SAP; the actual application is irrelevant—what is important is how we capture the recording.

Recording using the Wizard

● In fact, if you choose to install only the **Record It! Client** *shortcut* - the full software suite is still installed. This shortcut actually calls the same OdDev.exe executable as the full **UPK Developer Client**, but with a switch (/mode:recording) that opens the *Record It! Wizard* only.

When the UPK client software is installed (see *Appendix A, Installing UPK* for full details), there is the option to add shortcuts for the **UPK Developer Client** and/or the **UPK Developer Record It! Client** to the Windows Start Menu. The following screenshot shows the case where both of these shortcuts have been created:

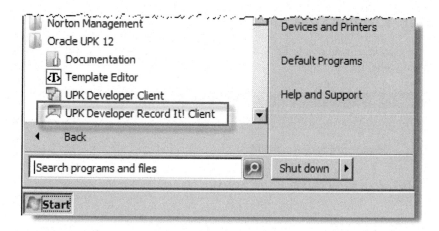

To record a simulation using the *Record It! Wizard*, select **UPK Developer Record It! Client** from the Windows Start Menu. Unless you have previously specified and saved them, you will be prompted to enter your Username and Password, as shown below:

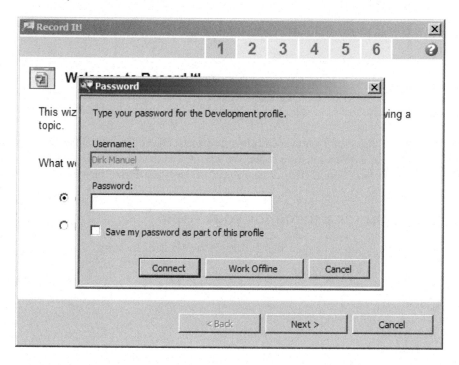

Specify your **Username** and **Password**, and then click on **Connect**. Note that you also have the option to work off-line, and the ability to save your password so that you do not need to enter it again.

Step 1: Select the recording option

Once you have logged in to UPK, the *Record It! Wizard* dialog box is displayed, as shown below:

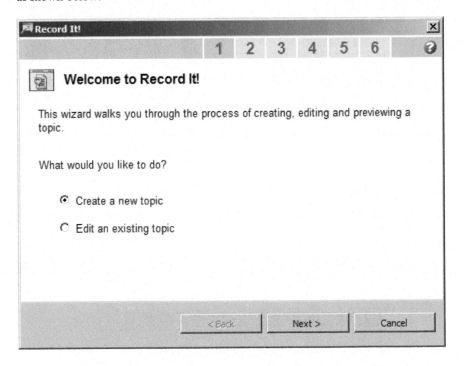

In Step 1 of the wizard, choose **Create a new topic**. The other option that is available is to **Edit an existing topic**. We will look at this option a little later. Click on the **Next** button. This causes Step 2 of the Wizard to be displayed.

Step 2: Enter a name for your Topic

An example of the screen for Step 2 of the wizard is shown below:

✦ UPK 11.1 also included the option to **Record a test**. However, this did exactly the same thing as the option to **Create a new topic**, so (thankfully) this option was removed in UPK 12.1.

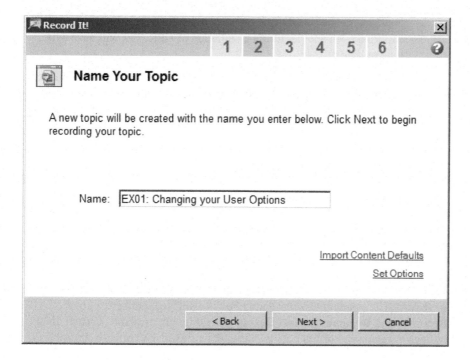

Enter a suitable name for your new recording, in the **Name** field. Although you can change this later, it is much easier to get it right here.

Before we continue with Step 3, you may have notice that there are a couple of links that in the bottom-right corner of this dialog box. These are **Import Content Defaults** and **Set Options**. Before we continue to the next step of the Wizard, let's take a look at these links and what they do.

Importing content defaults

There are a number of settings you can change that govern default fonts and colors to use in the recording. You cannot set these options via the *Record It! Wizard*. However, you can *import* a predefined set of defaults here. Although this may seem a little restrictive at first, bear in mind that one of the main purposes of the Wizard is to shield casual users from the complexity of UPK. If you have chosen to shield your SMEs in this way, the chances are that you also have also created a standard content defaults file that you want them to use. (In fact, you will likely have a single set of defaults that you want all of your authors and recorders to use, regardless of their UPK proficiency.)

To load a previously-saved set of defaults, follow the steps below:

1. From Step 2 of the *Record It! Wizard*, click on the **Import Content Defaults** link. The standard Windows *Open* dialog box is displayed.

■ For information on exporting your content defaults so that other users can import them, refer to *Sharing content defaults with other authors* on page 55.

2. Navigate to and select the content defaults file that you have previously exported from another user's installation of UPK (this will have a file type of .ops).

3. Click on **Open**. Your defaults are set based on the settings in the loaded file. Note that there is no confirmation message or other indication that anything has happened, other than the fact that you are returned to the *Record It! Wizard*.

Setting your User Options

The *Record It! Wizard* uses the same recording options as the full Developer Client application. However, because the Wizard tries to shield the (casual) author from the complexities of UPK as far as possible, the Wizard provides a shortcut to only the default settings that relate to activities that can be performed via the *Record It! Wizard*.

To set these defaults, click on the **Set Options** link from Step 2 of the *Record It! Wizard*. The standard *Options* dialog box is displayed, but here, only the **Recorder** and **Document > Test Results** categories are available. Change these settings as required. For full details of the options available, refer to *Appendix B, User Options*.

Once you have made any required changes, click the **OK** button in the *Options* dialog box to return to the *Record It! Wizard*. Back in Step 2 of the *Record It! Wizard* (which is where we were before we took a side-trip into the options settings), click **Next** to continue to Step 3.

Step 3a: Record your topic

When you advance to step 3 of the Wizard, the *Record It! Wizard* dialog box is hidden, and the *Recorder* window is displayed on top of the last application that you were using (before you made the *Record It! Wizard* the active window). If this is not the application that you want to record, then you can switch to the correct application, before you start recording.

■ You can choose whether to use automatic or manual recording via the **Set Options** link, explained above.

How the *Recorder* window looks, and how you perform your recording, depends on whether you are recording manually or automatically. Refer to the relevant subsection below, depending on your choice.

Manually recording a Topic

For manual recording, the *Recorder* window initially appears, as shown below, in the upper-right corner of the screen.

You can reposition this window by clicking on its title bar and dragging it to a new position on the screen. You may need to do this to see information on the screen behind the *Recorder* window. Don't worry; this window will not be captured in your recording and your users will be able to see the information behind it.

The title of the Topic (as entered by you in Step 2 of the Wizard) is shown in the title bar. On the upper right of the *Recorder* window is a **Context Capture** indicator, which indicates whether UPK will capture the context of the actions that you perform. This indicator may appear in one of the following forms:

Button	Mode	Description	
⊙	ExactMatch	You are recording a 'targeted' application, and UPK can capture the exact context of your actions.	▪ For more information on 'targeted' applications, refer to *Chapter 1, Integrating UPK with Other Applications*.
✪	SmartMatch	You are recording a 'non-targeted' application, and UPK will attempt to capture the context of your application based on information on the screen, and its own statistical engine.	
○	No Match	You are recording a 'non-targeted' application and UPK will not be able to identify the context for your actions.	

At the bottom of the *Recorder* window, there are a few additional buttons and icons. These are explained in the table below:

Button	Name	Description
▦	**Add or edit author notes**	Add or edit 'author notes' for a Frame. For more information on author notes, refer to *Adding author notes to your recording* on page 43, below.

Button	Name	Description
	Record Topic with / without sound	One or the other of these buttons will be displayed, depending on whether sound is currently being captured or not. You can click on whichever button is displayed to toggle to the other mode. For more information on capturing sound during your recording, refer to *Recording sound with your simulation on page 43*, below. For a full description of the sound recording capabilities of UPK and how best to utilize these, refer to *Chapter 11, Incorporating Sound Into Your Topics*.
	Sound tuning wizard	Click this button to launch the *Sound Tuning Wizard*, which can be used to adjust the sound capture and playback levels. Note that this button will be disabled if you are not capturing sound. It is also disabled after you start capturing sound (so that all sound is captured at the same level).
	VU Meter	This dynamic icon shows the current level of the captured sound (assuming that you are capturing sound). This is useful for confirming that sound is indeed being captured.
	Undo	Click on this button to discard the last action and screenshot that you captured (this action will be shown in the **Last recorded event** field). You can undo any number of past actions (and not just the last one) by clicking on this item multiple times, until you reach the last action that you want to keep. Note that this button will be disabled until you have captured at least one action.

To manually record a Topic, carry out the steps shown below:

1. Make sure that the application you want to record is the <u>active</u> application. Although UPK will display the application that you last used (as this is most likely to be the application that you want to record), the *Recorder* will still be the active application. You should click on a neutral area of the target application to make sure that it is the active application.

2. Press *PRINTSCREEN* (or other defined capture key) to indicate that you want to start recording. Technically, this will capture the **Start Frame** (this is explained in *Chapter 4, Editing a Topic*), and allow UPK to determine the application that it is recording against, for context capture purposes.

3. Perform a <u>single</u> action. This will typically be one of:

   • Clicking on a screen object or area of the screen

- Pressing a key or key combination on the keyboard

- Entering a text string

4. Press *PRINTSCREEN* again, to capture this action and the resulting screenshot. Each time that you press *PRINTSCREEN* to record an action, UPK hides the *Recorder* Window (so that it does not appear in the screen captures), and then re-displays it once the screenshot has been captured.

   ■ If the action results in a screen change or update (which it invariably will), wait for the new or updated screen to be displayed before pressing *PRINTSCREEN*.

5. Repeat Steps 3 and 4 for all additional actions that you want to capture in your recording

6. Click on the **Finish** button in the *Recorder* Window to stop recording. This will capture the **End Frame**.

Once you have finished capturing your recording, you are returned to the *Record It! Wizard*. Continue with *Step 3b: Edit your Topic* on page 47.

Automatic recording

If you are using automatic recording, then the *Recorder* Window that initially appears is slightly different with regard to the information shown in the Window. An example of the 'automatic' *Recorder* Window is shown below:

✦ The ability to record automatically, without you having to press *PRINTSCREEN* every time you want it to capture a new screenshot, was introduced in UPK 3.5.

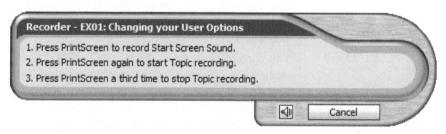

To record a simulation using the automatic recording function, follow the steps shown below:

1. Make sure that the application that you want to record is the <u>active</u> application. Although UPK will display the application that you last used (as this is most likely to be the application that you want to record), the Recorder will still be the active application. You should click on a neutral area of the target application to make sure that it is the active application.

2. Press *PRINTSCREEN* (or other defined capture key) to indicate that you want to start recording. The *Recorder* Window is hidden, and appears instead as a series of icons in the Windows Status Bar, just to the left of the System tray, as shown below:

These icons are described in the table below:

Button	Name	Description
	Add or edit author notes	Add or edit 'author notes' for a Frame. For more information on author notes, refer to *Adding author notes to your recording on page 43*.
	Pause / Resume recording	Click the **Pause** button to temporarily suspend the capture of actions and screenshots; click the **Resume recording** button to continue again. The ability to pause recording is very useful if you are interrupted in your recording, or if you need to perform some actions that you do not want to be included in the final simulation.
	Sound tuning wizard	Click this button to launch the *Sound Tuning Wizard*, which can be used to adjust the sound capture and playback levels. Note that this button will be disabled if you are not capturing sound. It is also disabled after you start capturing sound (so that all sound is captured at the same level)—although you can pause recording and then adjust it before resuming recording. For more information on the *Sound Tuning Wizard*, refer to *Chapter 11, Incorporating Sound Into Your Topics*.
	VU Meter	This dynamic icon shows the current level of the captured sound (assuming that you are capturing sound). This is useful for confirming that sound is indeed being captured.
	Context Capture	This is the same context capture indicator shown in the upper-right corner of the manual *Recorder* window. This is useful for confirming that your actions are indeed being captured – especially if you are recording sound (see below), as the default 'shutter click' sound effect is not played during sound recording.

✛ In UPK 11, the Context Capture icon would change to a 'camera' icon when a screenshot was being captured. In UPK 12, it was aligned to work the same way as manual recording.

3. Perform all of the actions that you want to be included in your simulation. Your actions and subsequent screenshots will automatically be captured (without the need for you to press *PRINTSCREEN* after performing each action).

4. Press *PRINTSCREEN* again, to stop recording.

Once you have finished capturing your recording, you are returned to the *Record It! Wizard*. Continue with *Step 3b: Edit your Topic* on page 47.

Adding author notes to your recording

You can add written notes to your recording, as you are capturing your actions in the target application. These can either be notes to yourself (for example, information that you want to remember when you are editing the simulation), or notes to the editor (assuming a 'split-development' model). These notes will be visible in the *Topic Editor* (which is described fully in *Chapter 4, Editing a Topic*), but will not appear in the final, published Topic (with the exception of the **Test Result** document, in which they do appear – see the section *Chapter 6, Publishing Documents* in *Chapter 6, Publishing Your Content*).

To add author notes, carry out the following steps:

1. During recording, click on the **Add or edit author notes** button () in the *Recorder* window (for manual recording) or in the Windows Taskbar (for automatic recording). The *Author Notes* dialog box is displayed, as shown below:

2. Enter your notes in the text area. There is no limit to the amount of text that you can enter, but you can only enter plain text. Note that you can resize and/or reposition this text box if necessary.

3. Click **Save**. Your notes will be stored with the Frame that is captured when you <u>next</u> press *PrintScreen*.

If you need to edit a note that you have previously entered, you can click on the **Add or edit author notes** button () again, and the notes that you have already entered (for that Frame) will be displayed. Note that once you capture the action, you will not be able to see the notes for the captured Frame. If you **undo** an action capture, you will lose any Author Notes that you have entered on the *current* frame (because they are only saved when you press *PrintScreen*), but the Author Notes on the *previous* frame (to which you have reverted) will then be available for editing.

Recording sound with your simulation

As noted above, UPK provides the ability to capture sound as you are recording your simulation. This does not refer to sounds generated by the application that

✦ The sound recording functionality in UPK was significantly overhauled in UPK 3.6. Prior to that version, sound could only be included within Topics, and relied heavily on the use of 'template sound files' to construct audio accompaniment.

you are recording, but instead is a way to provide an audio accompaniment for a simulation.

The intended purpose of the sound recording functionality is really to provide audio that can be heard by the user when playing the simulations. Typically, this would be a verbal reading of the information provided via the text on the screen or an explanation of what is being shown in the Topic. However, the ability to capture sound during the recording (as opposed to later, during editing) provides an excellent means for passing information from the recorder to the editor (assuming a 'split development' model – which is likely to be the case if you are using the *Record It! Wizard*).

Suppose you have a 'less-skilled' UPK resource such as a Subject Matter Expert recording the simulation, and they then pass the basic recording to the skilled UPK resource for editing and publishing. The recorder can record audio notes as they record their actions, just as if they were using a Dictaphone (younger readers may want to ask their parents!). These audio notes could be an explanation of what they are doing ("We are going to launch the application from the Start menu…"), additional information that they want to have included in the simulation ("Make sure you tell the users they can also use the desktop shortcut"), or any other information that cannot be captured by UPK ("Tell the users they need to have the physical invoice in their hand before they book it into the system"). When the skilled UPK resource starts editing the simulation, they can listen to these audio notes, and use the information provided by the recorder to enhance the simulation. Once the editor has incorporated the comments, they need to *delete* the sound recordings from the final simulation (or just publish without sound, if they want to retain the audio notes for future reference).

Using the recorded notes is really just an alternative to providing typed Author Notes, which are described above. The advantage of using audio notes is that it is easier for the recorder, and therefore more likely to get done. The advantage of Author Notes, by contrast, is that the text can be cut and pasted into the final simulation, if applicable. Most likely, some combination of the two will work best (they are not mutually exclusive).

Recording a simulation with sound

When you start to record a simulation and are also capturing sound, you need to press *PrintScreen* twice – once to start sound recording, and then once more to start action capture. This allows you to record sound for the Start Frame. The instructions in the *Recorder* window explain this, regardless of whether you are performing manual or automatic recording, although the difference (in recording sound over not recording sound) is easiest to see in the automatic *Recorder* Window, as shown below:

Recorder - EX01: Changing your User Options

1. Press PrintScreen to record Start Screen Sound.
2. Press PrintScreen again to start Topic recording.
3. Press PrintScreen a third time to stop Topic recording.

Cancel

Recording sound during automatic recording

To record sound when performing an automatic recording, carry out the following steps:

1. Press *PrintScreen* to start recording sound.

2. Record any sound that you want to be associated with the Start Frame.

3. Press *PrintScreen* to start recording your actions.

4. Perform the actions that you want to capture in the target application. Sound will automatically be captured.

5. Once you have recorded all required actions, press *PrintScreen* again, to stop recording (of both actions and sound).

■ Check that the **VU Meter** is registering your sound. If it is not, stop, check your settings, and then retry.

Recording sound during manual recording

To record sound when performing manual recording, carry out the following steps:

1. Press *PrintScreen* to start recording sound

2. Record any sound that you want to be associated with the Start Frame

3. Press *PrintScreen* to record the Start Frame.

4. Provide your verbal notes before, during, or after performing the action that you want to capture.

5. Press *PrintScreen* to capture the action/screenshot. Your sound recording will be saved at the same time. This will be all sounds captured between the previous press of *PrintScreen* and this press of *PrintScreen*.

■ Avoid pressing *PrintScreen* in the middle of providing your verbal notes, as this will cause them to be split across two frames. Instead, finish talking, and then press *PrintScreen*.

6. Repeat Steps 4 and 5 for all additional actions and sounds that you want to capture.

7. Once you have recorded all required actions, press *PrintScreen* again, to stop recording (both actions and sound).

When you have finished your record – regardless of whether this was automatic or manual, or whether or not you captured sound – you will be returned to the *Record It! Wizard*.

Our sample exercise

For the record, these are the exact steps that I carried out in order to record the sample exercise that we will use throughout the rest of this book:

1. Logged on to the SAP system and made sure I was at the start screen.

2. Pressed *PRINTSCREEN* to start the recording.

3. Clicked on the **System** menu to expand it. Pressed *PRINTSCREEN*.

4. Pointed to **User Profile** on the drop-down menu. Pressed *PRINTSCREEN*.

5. Clicked on **Own Data**. Pressed *PRINTSCREEN*. The *Maintain User Profile* screen is displayed.

6. Clicked in the **First Name** field. Pressed *PRINTSCREEN*.

7. Selected the existing text in the *First Name* field ("Dick") and typed "Dirk" on the keyboard. Pressed *PRINTSCREEN*.

8. Clicked in the Function field. Pressed *PRINTSCREEN*.

9. Typed "Training Analyst". Pressed *PRINTSCREEN*.

10. Clicked on the **Defaults** tab. Pressed *PRINTSCREEN*.

11. Clicked the drop-down list button for the Decimal Notation field. Pressed *PRINTSCREEN*.

12. Clicked on the entry for **X 1,234,567.89**. Pressed *PRINTSCREEN*.

13. Clicked the drop-down list button for the *Date Format* field. Scrolled up to the top of the list. Pressed *PRINTSCREEN*.

14. Clicked on the entry for **1 DD.MMYYYY**. Pressed *PRINTSCREEN*.

15. Clicked on the **Save** button. Pressed *PRINTSCREEN*.

16. Clicked on the **Finish** button in the recorder.

If you have access to SAP, go ahead and recreate this Topic by following the steps described above. If you don't have access to SAP, but still want to follow along with the exercises, then you can download all of the samples used in this book from the author's web site. All exercises are contained in a single `.odarc` file, which you can load into your Library using the **Import** function described in *Chapter 7, Version Management*. The sample exercise for this chapter is named **Changing your User Options (Chapter 3)**.

When you finish your recording, you are returned to the *Record It! Wizard*. Note that you are still at Step 3, but now the instructions on the screen are titled **Edit Your Topic**. Continue with *Step 3b: Edit your Topic* on page 47.

Step 3b: Edit your Topic

In the second part of Step 3 of the Wizard, you are given the option to launch the *Topic Editor* for the recording that you have just created. An example of the *Record It! Wizard* at this stage is shown below:

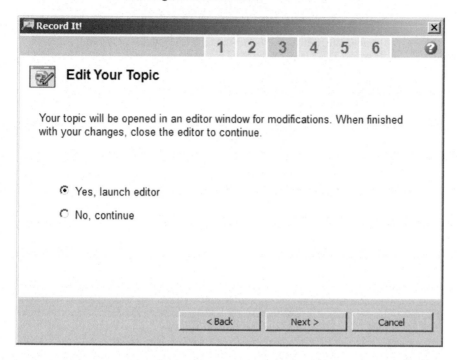

Although editing your Topic is *optional*, it is always a good idea to open your Topic in the *Topic Editor* to confirm that you have captured what you intended to. This applies just as much to recorders in a split-development model as it does to authors.

If you do not want to edit your Topic, select the **No, continue** option, click on the **Next** button, and continue with *Step 4: Preview your Topic on page 49*.

To edit your Topic, follow the steps shown below:

1. Make sure that the **Yes, launch editor** option is selected.

2. Click on the **Next** button. You are passed into the *Topic Editor*. Assuming that this is the first time that you have accessed the *Topic Editor*, a 'welcome' message is displayed, as shown in the following screenshot:

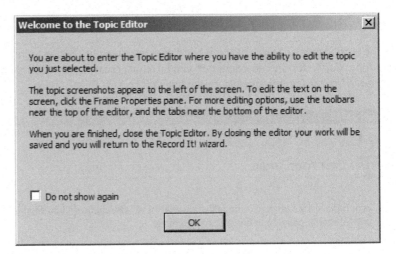

Welcome to the Topic Editor

You are about to enter the Topic Editor where you have the ability to edit the topic you just selected.

The topic screenshots appear to the left of the screen. To edit the text on the screen, click the Frame Properties pane. For more editing options, use the toolbars near the top of the editor, and the tabs near the bottom of the editor.

When you are finished, close the Topic Editor. By closing the editor your work will be saved and you will return to the Record It! wizard.

☐ Do not show again

OK

3. Select the **Do not show again** check-box, so that the welcome message is not displayed the next time that you use the *Topic Editor*.

4. Click **OK** to close the welcome message, and proceed to the *Topic Editor*.

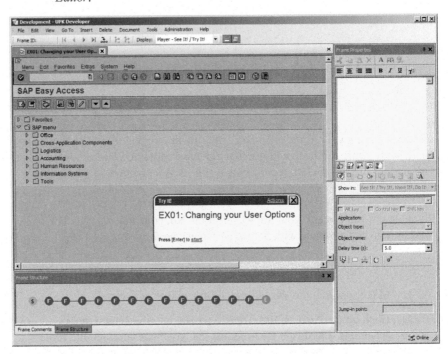

■ When you access the *Topic Editor* via the *Record It! Wizard*, you can click the **Close** button for the tab, the **Close All Tabs** button (on the far right of the tabs bar), or the **Close** button in the upper right of the *UPK Developer* window; they will all close the *Topic Editor* and return you to the *Record It! Wizard*.

5. The *Topic Editor* is fairly complex, and so a whole chapter is dedicated to it—see *Chapter 4, Editing a Topic*. For now, assume that you have confirmed that your simulation has been captured correctly. Click the **Close** button for the *Topic Editor* tab, to close the *Topic Editor* and return to the *Record It! Wizard*, where you will now be at Step 4.

Step 4: Preview your Topic

In Step 4 of the *Record It! Wizard*, you are given the opportunity to preview your simulation. The Wizard appears as shown below:

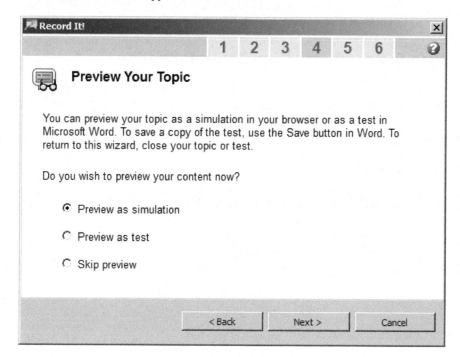

■ Although every step of the Wizard includes a **Cancel** button, you should not use this button from Step 4 onwards, If you do, the simulation (which was saved to your local repository in Step 3) will remain in the Library, as checked out to you. If you do not want to keep this recording, then continue through the Wizard until you reach Step 6, where you have the option to delete it.

Previewing the simulation allows you to see it as the user will see it. The Wizard allows you to preview the simulation in one of two ways:

- **Preview as a simulation**. This uses the Player *See It!* mode, and the *Do It!* mode texts (these things will make more sense once you have read *Chapter 6, Publishing Your Content*).

- **Preview as test**. This produces a Microsoft Word document in the **Test Results** document format, and uses the options specified in your user options (see *Setting the Recorder options* earlier in this chapter). Refer to section *Publishing a Test Document* in *Chapter 6, Publishing Your Content* for an example of this output.

You also have the option to skip the preview altogether. If you do not want to preview your Topic, select **Skip preview**, click **Next**, and continue with *Step 5: Specify the Workflow information* on page 50.

To preview your Topic, carry out the following steps:

1. Select the appropriate option, depending upon the format in which you want to preview your recording.

2. Click **Next**. The topic will be displayed in the selected format.

3. Once you have finished previewing your recording, close the preview application (either close the Player session, or close Microsoft Word, as appropriate). You will be returned to the *Record It! Wizard*, which will now be at Step 5.

Step 5: Specify the Workflow information

In Step 5 of the *Record It! Wizard*, you are prompted to provide some "optional" information. In fact, this information is not really *optional*, in that you must select a value for each of the two fields prompted. These two fields are what UPK refers to as its **Workflow** fields—they appear under the **Workflow** heading of the **Topic Properties**—and can be used to provide some very rudimentary workflow-like capabilities in UPK.

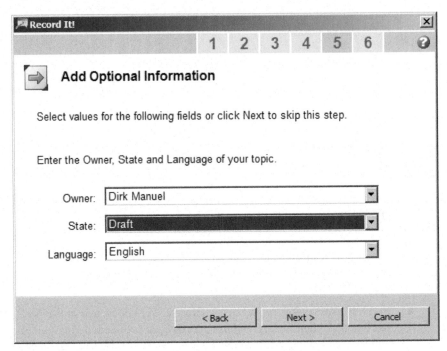

● If you want to edit an existing recording via the *Record It! Wizard* (see Step 1, above), you will only be able to access Topics for which you are specified as the **Owner**. Therefore, if you change the **Owner** to be another person, you will no longer have visibility on this Topic. If you do need to edit a Topic for which you are not the **Owner**, you will need to ask a UPK user who does have access to the *UPK Developer* client to set you as the **Owner**, first.

Specify values for the two prompted fields by carrying out the steps shown below:

1. In the **Owner** field, select the Userid of the UPK user to whom your new simulation should be assigned. This defaults to yourself, but depending on your development model, you may choose to assign the recording to another user for editing.

2. In the **State** field, select the current state of the Topic. Most commonly, the *State* field values are tied to your development process, and indicate the progress of the Topic through this process. UPK ships with five default states [**(blank)**, **Not Started**, **Draft**, **In Review**, and **Final**], although the Library Administrator can customize the list of permissible

States, to add or remove States, as required (see *Chapter 14, Basic Administration*).

3. Click **Next**. The *Record It! Wizard* moves on to Step 6.

Step 6a: Submit your Topic

In Step 6 of the *Record It! Wizard*, you are given a final chance to save or scrap your recording. An example of the Wizard window at this stage is shown below:

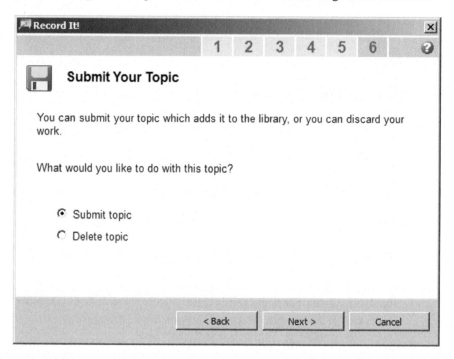

To cancel this recording and delete the simulation, select **Delete topic** and click **Next**, and you will be passed to the final step of the Wizard. Continue with *Step 6b: Complete the wizard* on page 53, below).

To keep your recording, and save it to the server, carry out the steps shown below:

1. Select the option **Submit topic**.

2. Click **Next**. You are prompted to enter a check-in comment, as shown in the example below (note that this example is taken from after a comment has been entered—initially, the input box is empty).

● Given that the values specified in the previous step are the 'workflow' fields, you might reasonably expect that choosing the "submit" option will cause your recording to 'flow' to the next step in your process. This is not the case. In fact, this option simply checks your recording in to the Library on the server. You may want to clarify this with your recorders, if you are using a split-development model.

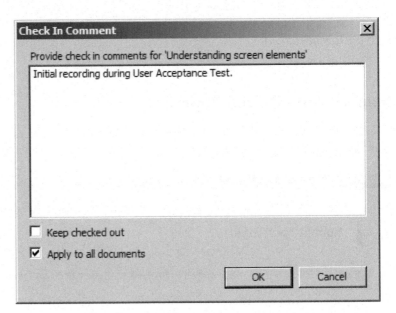

3. Enter a brief comment about your recording (or its current state) in the text box. Note that this is optional, but it is always a good idea to enter a comment every time you check in an object, as these comments appear in the *Version History* for the object (see *Chapter 7, Version Management*).

▲ If you assigned the Topic to another author in Step 5 of the Wizard (see *Chapter 2, Step 5: Specify the Workflow information* above), then you will not be able to edit the Topic via the *Record It! Wizard* (because the Wizard will only show you documents that are assigned to you). If you also select the **Keep checked out** option then the user you assign it to will not be able to edit the Topic (because it is checked out by you). You should therefore only keep the Topic checked out if it is still assigned to you, and only if you know that you will be the next person to edit this Topic.

4. If you know that you will be editing this file again, and do not want any other author editing it in the meantime, select the **Keep checked out** option. This will check the file in to the server (so that other users will be able to *see* it), but immediately check it back out to you (so that other users cannot *edit* it). See *Chapter 7, Version Management* for more details on working in a client/server environment.

When you check in a Topic via the *Record It! Wizard*, UPK will check in **all** Topics that you currently have checked out. Normally you will only be working on one Topic at a time, so will only have the Topic that you want to check in checked out. However, if you previously chose to keep a Topic checked out (by selecting the **Keep checked out** option – see Step 4, above), UPK will check in that Topic and the current Topic. If the option **Apply to all documents** is selected, then UPK will use the comment that you entered in Step 2, above, as the check-in comment for all of these Topics. If you want to specify a separate check-in comment for each Topic, then deselect this option. You will then be prompted to enter a comment separately for each Topic (note that the Topic for which you are currently entering a comment is shown at the top of the dialog box, for your reference).

5. Click **OK**. The document is checked in to the server, and you are returned to the main Wizard screen. Continue with *Step 6b: Complete the wizard* on page 53.

Step 6b: Complete the wizard

Once you have checked in your new recording, the final page of the *Record It! Wizard* is displayed, as shown in the example below:

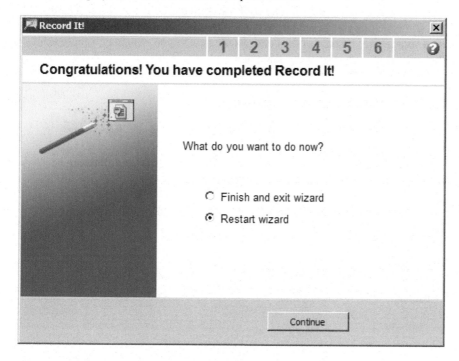

Here, you have a choice to close the Wizard, or start all over again, and record a new simulation.

To close the Wizard, carry out the steps shown below:

1. Select the option **Finish and exit wizard**.

2. Click **Continue**. The Wizard is closed, and you are logged out of the UPK Library (UPK is closed).

To record a new simulation, carry out the steps shown below:

1. Select the option **Restart wizard**.

2. Click **Continue**. You are returned to Step 1 of the Wizard. You can now record your next simulation, by repeating the steps described above, starting from *Step 1: Select the recording option* on page 36.

Recording via the UPK Developer

So far in this chapter, we have looked at using the *Record It! Wizard* to record simulations. This functionality is really designed for 'occasional' UPK authors— most likely Subject Matter Experts who are not skilled UPK authors. If you have shown enough interest in UPK to buy this book (for which I thank you), then the chances are you are more than a 'casual' UPK author. In which case, you are unlikely to use the *Record It! Wizard* to record your Topics. Instead, you are likely to record within the UPK Developer software itself. Although the *Library* screen isn't really discussed until *Chapter 3, Working in the UPK Developer Client*, this is the chapter for recording, so we will discuss how to record content from the Library here. If some of the concepts are new to you, you may want to skim through the next chapter at the same time.

Setting your content defaults

As we shall see in *Chapter 4, Editing a Topic*, there are many formatting changes that you can make to your recordings so that they better meet your individual (or client/project) requirements. Thankfully, most of these can be defaulted through your **Content Default**s options.

To change your **Content Defaults** options, select menu path **Tools | Options** from within the *UPK Developer* screen. The *Options* dialog box is displayed, as shown below.

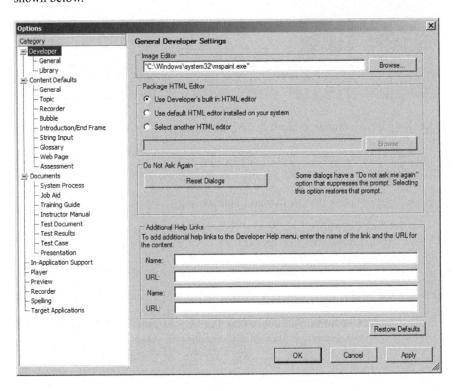

The *Category* pane on the left shows the categories and subcategories of options that can be changed. The pane on the right lists the options that are available for the category or subcategory selected on the left. Because these options relate to several different areas of UPK recording, editing, and publishing, they are all described together, in *Appendix B, User Options*. Refer to that Appendix for a full list of the **Content Default** options, and an explanation of what each of them does.

Sharing content defaults with other authors

If you have more than one author working on the simulations for an organization or project, you will most likely want to use a single set of content defaults, to ensure consistency of content. Although these defaults must be set per author, they can be shared between authors, as explained below:

To save your content defaults with another author (or SME), carry out the following steps:

1. Make sure that you have set all of your content default settings to the required values.

2. Select menu option **Tools | Export | Content Default Options**. The standard Windows *Save As* dialog box is displayed.

3. Navigate to the folder in which you want to save your content defaults, enter a suitable name for the file in the **File Name** field, and make sure that the **Save as type** field specifies **Options files (.ops)**.

4. Click on Save.

You can now distribute this (.ops) file to another author. Once the other author receives this file, they can import it as follows:

1. Select menu option **Tools | Import | Content Default Options**. The standard Windows *Open* dialog box is displayed.

2. Navigate to and select the .ops file passed to you by the other author.

3. Click on **Open**. Your content defaults are set from the loaded file. Note that you will not receive any confirmation message that this has happened (although you can check your user options to confirm that they have been changed).

Recording a Topic via the Library screen

Recording a simulation directly in the UPK Developer application (regardless of whether this is in a client/server environment or a stand-alone environment) is, in many ways, much simpler than using the *Record It! Wizard*. However, the Wizard wins over by stringing together the recording, editing, preview, and check-in activities into a simple set of steps. When you record via the *Library* screen, that's all you do – record. You then need to edit (as described in *Chapter 4, Editing a Topic*), preview (explained in *Chapter 6, Publishing Your Content*) and check in your Topic (covered in *Chapter 7, Version Management*), as separate activities.

That said, most 'serious' authors will probably create most of their recordings via the *Library* screen (because the *Library* screen is their natural habitat!), leaving the *Record It! Wizard* to the Subject Matter Experts and other 'occasional' UPK recorders.

To record a new Topic via the *Library* screen, carry out the steps listed below:

1. On the *Library* screen, navigate to the folder in which you want to store your recording.

2. Select menu option **File | New | Topic**. The UPK window is hidden, and the *Recorder* Window is displayed on top of the last application that you were using (before you switched to UPK). If this is not the application that you want to record, then switch to the correct application, before you start recording.

3. Record your Topic as described in *Step 4b, Record your Topic*, above.

4. When you have finished, click on the **Finish** button in the *Recorder* Window. You will be passed directly into the *Topic Editor*.

● This assumes that you have the option **Recorder > Open The Topic Editor** set to **At the end of each recording**. See *Setting your User Options* on page 38, for more information on this option.

5. Click on the **Save** button (🖫) to save your recording. (It is always sensible to save your Topic before you start editing it, just in case something goes wrong, or you need to revert to the 'as-recorded' version.) The standard Windows *Save As* dialog box is displayed, as follows:

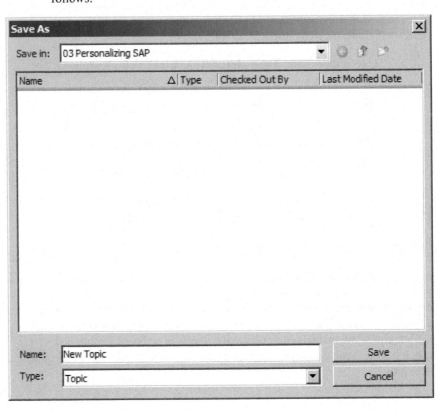

6. Enter a suitable name into the **Name** field, and then click **Save**.

7. If required, edit your recording as described in *Chapter 4, Editing a Topic*.

8. Once you have finished editing your Topic, save your edits by clicking on the **Save** button (🖫) again, and then exit from the *Topic Editor*.

<aside>
■ If you forgot to navigate to the correct folder in Step 1, then you can use the **Save in** drop-down field, and the buttons to the right of it, to navigate to and select (or even create) the correct folder.
</aside>

One more option for recording

There is a third way to record a Topic. This is by first creating an empty Topic in an Outline Element, and then recording this (either from within the Outline Element or from its containing folder on the *Library* screen). How to do this is described in the section *Inserting Topic placeholders* in *Chapter 5, Building an Outline*.

Recording drag-and-drop actions

Before we finish our examination of recording, it is worth looking at an area of recording that needs a bit more care and attention. This is recording drag-and-drop activities.

Most actions that you will record fall into one of the following categories:

*   Clicking on a particular area of the screen

*   Pressing a specific key or key combination on the keyboard

*   Entering a text string

These types of actions are relatively straightforward for UPK, with its philosophy of capturing screenshots and actions.

For mouse-clicks, UPK simply takes a screenshot before the mouse-click (as part of the *previous action)*, and a screenshot after the mouse-click. During playback, UPK simply displays the *before* screenshot, and then displays the *after* screenshot once the user has clicked on the correct area of the screen. Key-presses work in a similar way.

For text entry, UPK is slightly cleverer. In addition to taking the *before* and *after* screenshots, during playback it overlays a text box on the screen, to allow the user to enter the required text. It is still relatively straightforward, and (largely) based on static screenshots.

However, with drag-and-drop actions, things are not so simple. As the object is dragged across the screen, the screen image is changing constantly. Ideally, UPK would capture this as a video, but unfortunately UPK doesn't work like that. In fact, UPK sticks to its guns, and tries to capture this motion using static screenshots. To pull this off effectively, UPK would need to capture a new screenshot every time the object that is being dragged moves a single pixel.

<aside>
■ UPK's ability to record drag-and-drop activities does not work particularly well when dragging and dropping an object on the screen, and in these cases it may be more effective to just record the mouse-down action when selecting the object in its original location, and then record the mouse-up action when the object is dropped onto the target (that is, using standard action recording, and not true drag-and-drop. Where it does work well (or at least better) is when resizing objects by dragging their bounding handles. If there is a sufficiently-low distance between screenshots, this can appear almost true-to-life).
</aside>

However, this would be difficult to accomplish during playback. At best it would appear jerky, even on a fast network/processor, as the entire screen is being replaced each time. It would also be burdensome to work with in the *Topic Editor*.

Instead, UPK allows the object to be moved a predefined number of pixels before capturing a new screenshot. (Technically, UPK tracks the movement of the tip of the cursor, as this is easier to identify.) The number of pixels that the object moves before a new screenshot is captured is defined in your Options, under **Content Defaults | Recorder** (and not the **Recorder** category, for some reason).

To record a drag-and-drop action, carry out the following steps:

1. Click on the object that you want to drag-and-drop.

2. Press the *PRINTSCREEN* button on your keyboard to start the capture. The *Recorder* Window will disappear.

3. Drag the object in as straight a line as possible to where you want to drop it.

4. Drop the object at the destination, by releasing the mouse button. The *Recorder* Window reappears.

■ To ensure that you drag in a straight line (and do not 'veer off'), hold a ruler or other straight edge (a piece of paper works well) against your screen, between the drag-and-drop points, and drag along this line.

Let's look at how this manifests itself in the actual recording. The screenshot below shows a composite of all of the Frames captured for the drag-and-drop activity (in reality, each Bubble/Action Area pair is on a separate Frame/screenshot, but they have been combined here to more easily illustrate the progression):

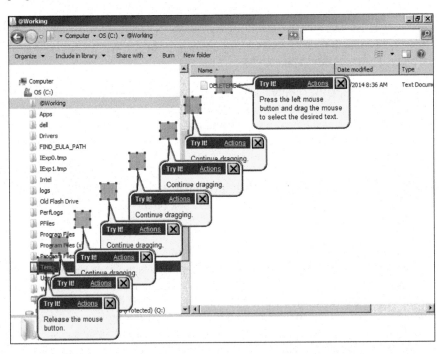

In the first Frame, the user is told to click on the object that is to be dragged. This is indicated by a (by default) red marquee, which is the standard way that UPK indicates Action Areas.

As soon as the user clicks on this object, the location (Action Area) to which the user needs to drag the object is highlighted. The user drags the mouse pointer towards the indicated area. Note that the object that they clicked on will not move – only the cursor will (which kind of ruins the illusion of reality, but it's the best that UPK can do). Once the user moves the mouse pointer into the indicated area, the next screenshot is displayed, showing the next Action Area and Bubble. The user then continues to drag the object into successive action areas.

● As long as the user keeps the mouse button held down, they can actually move the cursor all around the screen, but they will not progress to the next Frame until they move the cursor into the designated target area.

Finally, when the user moves the cursor over the position onto which the object was dropped during the recording, the last Bubble is displayed, telling the user to release the mouse button (the 'drop' action).

Note that during recording we only pressed *PrintScreen* once, and all eight of these screenshots were captured for us. This is because UPK treats the drag-and-drop as a single action (if you complete the drag-and-drop action in the Player and then select **Action | Previous step** from the bubble menu, UPK will return you to the first frame in the sequence). However, this single action consists of at least three frames in the recorder, as follows:

1. A single Frame with an Action Type of **Left begin drag**. This is the first screen print in the sequence above.

2. One or more Frames with an Action Type of **Drag**. In the example above, six such Frames were created.

3. A single Frame with an Action Type of **Left button up**.

■ Action Types are discussed in *Chapter 4, Editing a Topic*.

You must have these three frames, with these three specific actions (and not simply **Left button down** in Step 1) for the drag-and-drop to work correctly in the Player.

Play this exercise back (it is available from the author's web site, in the same `.odarc` file as before, as **EX99-03 Deleting a file**. You will note that the playback is a bit jerky, as the screens flip from one to the next. You could mitigate this effect by using a smaller capture interval in the **Distance between screenshots in pixels** option setting, but after a certain point this will become self-defeating as it will take the Player longer to load the screenshots than it takes to move from one to the next, resulting in more jerkiness.

Note also the size of the action area. The user has to move the cursor into this area in order to move onto the next frame in the sequence. You can cut the user a little slack by increasing the size of the action area (either in the **Action Area size in pixels** option before you start recording, or by manually adjusting the action area in the **Topic Editor** after you have captured the recording; how to do this is explained in *Chapter 4, Editing a Topic*) but be careful that your action areas do not become too close, or overlap, as this will cause problems during playback.

One last comment on drag-and-drop activities: In *Know It?* mode, there is no square around the action area to provide the user with a visual clue as to where to drag. It is unrealistic to expect the user to correctly follow an invisible path that is (by default) only 30 pixels wide. Therefore, during playback in *Know It?* mode, the user is not required to perform the drag-and-drop activity. Instead, the Player performs this activity for them. They are not scored on this action. You should therefore be wary of providing simulations in *Know It?* mode where the majority of the simulation consists of drag-and-drop activities.

Summary

UPK records simulations by capturing sets of action/screenshot pairs. Each pair consists of a screenshot of a screen, and the action performed to get to that screen. An action typically consists of a mouse-click, a key-press, or the entry of a text string, but it is also possible to capture drag-and-drop actions.

You can record a simulation via the *Record It! Wizard*, from a folder on the *Library* screen, or for an empty Topic in the *Outline Editor*. All three methods result in exactly the same kind of recoding.

UPK can capture simulations automatically or manually. If you choose the manual option, then you need to tell UPK when to capture each action/screenshot pair. With the automatic option, it will capture the action/screenshot pair every time that the screen changes.

3

Working in the UPK Developer Client

In Chapter 2, we created our first simulation. We did this via the *Record It!*
Wizard, which shielded us (or our SMEs) from the complexities of the full **UPK
Developer** screens. In this chapter, we will work directly in the UPK Developer
screen.

Any content objects that you create, change, or display within UPK are stored
within the Library. Technically, the Library is a database that contains the UPK
content objects and information about them. In a Client/Server environment,
the Library works just like a real, bricks-and-mortar Library - its contents are
available to many people, and if you want to work with one of these objects, you
'check out' the object, work with it, and then 'check in' the object when you are
finished with it. Even in a stand-alone (single user) implementation, the Library is
still stored as a database, just on your local PC and not on a server.

The *Library* screen is your main interface into the Library database. When you
access the UPK Developer application, it is the *Library* screen that you see. The
Library screen is also used to *organize* your content objects – that is, to arrange
your training material into a hierarchical folder structure that you (and/or other
authors) will use to organize your content. In this chapter, you will learn how to:

- Navigate around the *Library* screen

- Create folders, to organize your content

- Create and share Custom Views

- Set your content defaults and share these with other authors

Accessing the Library

● The very first time that you access UPK you will be required to create a Profile. How to do this is explained in *Appendix A, Installing UPK*.

● If you have access to multiple Libraries, you will need to create one Profile per Library.

When you start UPK (other than for the very first time—see the note below), the *Start Screen* window is displayed. This window allows you to open a **Module** that you most recently accessed, or create a new Module or Topic. You can also import content from another UPK Library. It also provides you with links to open the *Library* screen, and to open a specific content object. An example of the *Start Screen* is displayed in the following screenshot:

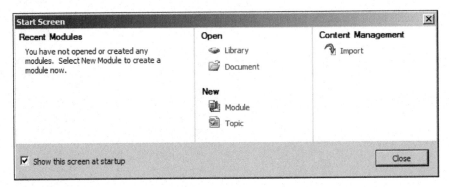

You can prevent the *Start Screen* from being displayed whenever you start UPK by deselecting the **Show this screen at startup** option at the bottom of the dialog box. If you do this, then UPK will start up from the *Library* screen.

To display the *Library* screen, click on the **Library** link in the *Start Screen* window. When you first display the *Library* screen (actually a tabbed page within the overall *UPK Developer* screen), it will appear similar to the example shown in the following screenshot:

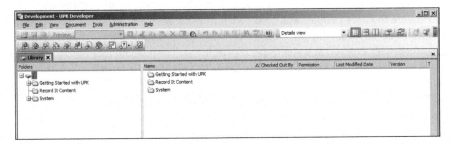

If you are working in a client/server environment and are accessing an existing Library for the first time, you will see all of the content to which you have been given access (although this may be only read access).

Refreshing the Library screen

In a client/server environment, UPK will automatically check the server every 60 seconds for new or updated content (for example, content objects that have been checked in by other authors since the last automatic refresh). However, if you currently have the *Library* screen or an Outline Element displayed on the screen then UPK will not automatically update your screen (because that would be too confusing, especially if you are in the middle of something). If you think that content has changed, you can manually refresh your screen by clicking on the **Refresh** button (🔁).

Working with the Library screen

The structure of the *Library* screen will be familiar to Windows users, as it is conceptually very similar to Windows Explorer. It consists of two panes: the leftmost pane contains a hierarchical list of all folders in the Library, and the rightmost side lists the contents of the folder selected on the leftmost side. You see from the previous screenshot that the Library is actually shown on a tabbed page within the main *UPK Developer* screen. If you double-click on a content object in the right-hand side of the screen, it is opened in a new tab; the *Library* tab remains open. You can open several content objects at the same time and can switch between them by clicking on the appropriate tab.

✛ Prior to UPK 3.6, Topics always opened in a separate window (the *Topic Editor*). Starting from version 3.6, the Topic Editor also opened in a tabbed page within the *UPK Developer* screen.

Changing the screen layout

The *UPK Developer* screen initially appears in a *single screen* layout. You can also display it in a split-screen layout - either horizontally or vertically. The following buttons on the *View Toolbar* control the layout:

Button	Name	Description
🔲	**Single view**	This is the default view, as shown in the previous screenshot
🔲	**Horizontal layout**	This splits the screen in two, horizontally (top and bottom)
🔲	**Vertical layout**	This splits the screen in two, vertically (left and right)

The split-screen layouts may be confusing at first, as you still have the folder/content panes within each split pane, and you will always have the same selection of tabbed pages in both of the split panes, regardless of the pane in which you opened them. However, you can select different tabs in each pane. Split screen is an extremely useful way of working when you are editing Outlines, as you can drag and drop Topics from the *Library* screen in one pane onto an Outline Element in the other.

The Properties Pane

✚ In UPK 12, the *Properties* pane appears slightly differently when viewed from within the Outline Editor. This is explained in *Chapter 5, Building an Outline.*

All content objects in the Library—Topics, Sections, and Modules, as well as Web Pages, Packages, Assessments, and Questions have a number of unique attributes. These attributes are maintained via the *Properties* pane, which can be displayed at any time by clicking on the **Properties** button (🖰) on the *View Toolbar*. Some of these attributes provide further information about the content object (such as the template used), whereas others define additional information that is used in different output formats.

Note that the *Properties* pane is independent of the split screen layouts - that is, you will only ever see one *Properties* pane. The attributes shown in it will be those that apply to the selected element in the *active* pane. An example of the *UPK Developer* screen, using the **Horizontal** layout, and with the *Properties* pane displayed, is shown below (you can see that the buttons for these two options are selected, on the rightmost side of the *View Toolbar*):

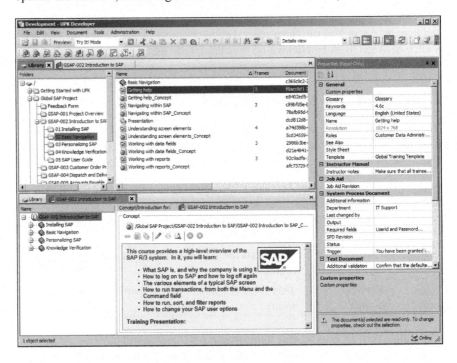

In this example above, there are two tabs open: The *Library* screen in the upper pane, and an Outline Element (**GSAP-002 Introduction to SAP**) in the lower pane. You will also note that the top pane is the active pane, so the details shown in the *Properties* pane are for the content object selected in this pane, and not the one selected in the lower pane.

Properties are categorized into expandable/collapsible categories, within the *Properties* pane. The categories that are available will depend on the type of object selected (such as Module, Section, Topic, and so on), as will the fields available within any given category. These categories are:

- **General**

  Available for all object types, but the fields available will depend on the specific document type. This category is described below.

- **Instructor Manual**

  Available only for Topics, and contains fields that apply only to the Instructor Manual printed document type. This category is described in *Publishing an Instructor Manual* on page 261.

- **Job Aid**

  Available only for Topics, and contains fields that apply only to the Job Aid printed document type. This category is described in *Publishing a Job Aid* on page 249.

- **System Process Document**

  Available only for Topics, and contains fields that apply only to the System Process printed document type. This category is described in *Publishing a System Process document* on page 241.

- **Test Document**

  Available only for Topics, and contains fields that apply only to the Test Document printed output type. This category is described in *Publishing a Test Document* on page 268.

- **Topic**

  Available only for Topics (obviously..) and contains fields that either control how the Topic can be used in the Player (or an LMS), or control how elements of the Topic appear (or sound). This category is described in *Creating a Player and LMS Package* on page 222.

- **Question**

  Available only for Questions, and contains fields that affect the question-level feedback provided to the user (who answer the question). This category is described in *Creating a Question* on page 463.

- **Assessment**

  Available only for Assessments, and contains settings that control how the Questions and answer feedback are presented to the user, and the required passing score. This category is described *Creating an Assessment* on page 477.

- **Workflow**

  Available for all object types. These fields allow you to assign an owner and a state to the object. These fields are described more fully in *Managing State values* on page 531.

General properties

The **General** category is shown in the *Properties* pane for all object types, although not all fields are available for all object types. The table below lists all of the available properties, lists the object types to which they apply, and explains their use. Note that most of these properties are explained elsewhere in this book, as they are used, but this table is provided here as a concise reference.

Property	Description
Assessments	Used to assign an Assessment to a Module or Section, where this Assessment is not already included in the Module or Section. This allows the Assessment to be used for a pre- or post-assessment in Knowledge Center. Assessments are explained in *Chapter 12, Testing Your Users*. Applies to: **Module, Section**
Background Color	Used to set the background color for a Web Page. Applies to: **Web Page**
Context	Used to assign a 'context' (which is normally captured in a Topic) to a Module or Section, so that the Module or Section is identified as applicable content for In-Application Help. How to do this is explained in *Adding context to non-Topic content objects* on page 549. Applies to: **Module, Section**
Custom properties	Used to define custom (non-UPK provided) properties for an object. These properties can be included in the printed document output formats, and their values searched on in the Player. Custom properties are explained in *Chapter 16, Configuring UPK*. Applies to: **Module, Section, Topic, Assessment, Question**
Description	Used to identify a Module or Section that is linked into an IN-Application Support Profile. See *Creating an IAS Profile* on page 550 for more information. Applies to: **Module, Section**
Glossary	Used to assign a Glossary to an object. Glossaries are explained in *Using a Glossary* on page 410. Applies to: **Module, Section, Topic, Web Page**
Group for LMS	Used to indicate that a Module or Section should be loaded into the LMS as a separate module to the Module or Section that contains it. Applies to: **Module, Section**

Side notes:

✛ The **Assessments** property is new in UPK 12.

✛ The **Background Color** property is new in UPK 12.

✛ The **Context** property was introduced in UPK 11.

✛ The **Custom properties** property was introduced in UPK 11.

✛ The **Description** property is new in UPK 12.

Property	Description
Keywords	Used to specify texts that do not appear elsewhere in the object, to facilitate keyword searches. See *Using Keywords* on page 434 for more information on using Keywords. Applies to: **Module**, **Section**, **Topic**
Language	Used to specify the language for the object. This is used both for spell checking and when exporting for localization. This property must be defined. Applies to: All objects in the Library.
Name	The name of the selected object. This property must be defined. Applies to: All objects in the Library.
Resolution	Used to define the screen resolution for a Topic. This must be set before the Topic is recorded, and cannot be changed once it has been recorded. Applies to: **Module**, **Section**, **Topic**
Roles	Used to assign defined roles to an object. This can then be used for role-filtering in the Player, or for publishing by role. Role assignment can also be shown in a column in the Library views, and included in the printed document output types. Refer to *Working with roles* on page 419 for more information on using roles. Applies to: **Module**, **Section**, **Topic**, **Assessment**, **Question**
See Also	Used to identify additional content objects related to the selected content object. These content objects appear on a drop-down list in the *Concept* pane for the selected object. Refer to *Identifying related material* on page 437 for more information. Applies to: **Module**, **Section**, **Topic**
Style Sheet	Used to assign a Style Sheet to a Web page. See *Putting Web Pages to good use* on page 356 for more information on this feature. Applies to: **Web Page**

✛ The **Style Sheet** property is new in UPK 12.

Property	Description
Template	Used to assign a content template to a Topic. The content template controls the Template Text for the Bubbles in a Topic. Every Topic must have a Template assigned to it. Refer to *Adjusting Bubble Text* on page 115 for additional information. Applies to: **Module, Section, Topic**

In addition to these **General** properties, properties in the **Workflow** category are also applicable to all object types. These properties are discussed in *Chapter 7, Version Management*. All other properties are publishing format specific, and are discussed under the relevant section in *Chapter 6, Publishing Your Content*.

The Broken Links pane

The *Broken Links* pane lists all of the content objects to which the selected content object (or any of its related documents) was initially linked, but that have now 'disappeared'. This will typically be because the linked content object has been deleted, but could also be because the linked object has been created by another author who has not yet checked that object in to the Library (assuming that you are working in a client/server environment). You should check for broken links periodically, and certainly before you publish your content.

An example of the *Broken Links* pane is shown below:

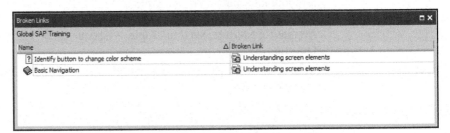

Note that for Outline Elements, the missing document is not necessarily linked to directly from the selected Outline Element, but may be linked to from any other document within the selected Outline Element. For example, in the above screenshot, the currently-selected object is a Module called **Global SAP Training** (you can't tell from this screenshot that it is a Module - just trust me on that). There are two broken links for this Module: one is a link from a Question that is included in an Assessment contained within the Module, and the other is a link from a Section within the Module.

Looking at the **Broken Link** column, you can see that these are both links to the same Topic, called **Understanding Screen Elements**. Quite likely, if we look in the *Deleted Documents* view we will find this Topic, and if we restore it, these broken links will be fixed. Alternatively, delinking the deleted Topic from both the Question and the Section will also resolve the broken link.

The Related Documents pane

The *Related Documents* pane consists of two sections. The first of these lists all of the content objects that are linked to *from* the selected content object. This will include Glossaries and Templates, as well as any Web Pages or Packages used in the *Concept* pane or otherwise hyperlinked to from the selected content object. It will also, perhaps unexpectedly, include any custom icons used in linked Web Pages (see *Chapter 9, Adding Value to Your Topics* for more information on using Web Pages). The second section of the *Related Documents* pane lists the opposite: all of the content objects in the Library that link *to* the selected content object. This can provide a useful means of checking whether it is OK to delete a content object.

An example of the *Related Documents* pane is shown below.

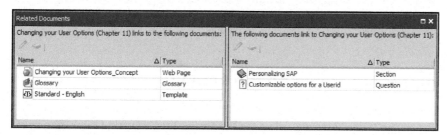

In this example, the selected item is a Topic. This links to a **Web Page** (used as the **Concept Page**), a **Glossary**, and a **Template**. In the other direction, two other documents link to this Topic - a **Section**, and a **Question**. (Don't worry if you do not know what these document types are yet—we will cover them later in this book.)

If you right-click on a document in the *Related Documents* pane (in either list), a shortcut menu is displayed, which contains two options, as follows:

- **Open in Editor**: This allows you to immediately open the document for editing in the relevant editor,

- **Find in Library**: This will switch to the *Details View* of the *Library* screen, open the folder in which the selected object is stored, and highlight the object by selecting it.

✚ Right-click functionality in the *Related Documents* pane was introduced in UPK 12.

The Derived Documents pane

The *Derived Documents* pane is similar to the *Related Documents* pane, but lists other documents that were created by taking a copy of the selected document

✚ The *Derived Documents* pane was introduced in UPK 12.

(or by using the **Save As** feature), and any 'source' document from which the currently-selected document was initially copied. This can be extremely useful, especially when you have localized content, to identify all additional documents that may need to be changed when you need to change a particular document.

An example of the *Derived Documents* pane is shown below.

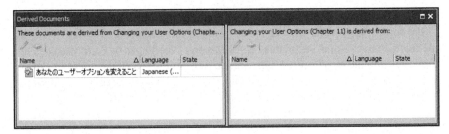

In the screenshot above, the currently-selected document is a Topic, which was created in the English language. We can see from the 'documents derived from this document' side that a copy was taken of this and then translated into Japanese. If we subsequently identify the need to change the original, English-language version of this Topic, we would be advised to also check the Japanese version, to see if this also needs to be changed.

Arranging panes on the screen

Let's look at how to display these four panes and arrange them on the screen. To display the *Properties* pane, select the **Properties** toggle button (🖼). To display the other panes you need to select menu option **View | Panes**, and then select the required view from the sub-menu list. The following screenshot shows all four of the 'sidebar' panes displayed and undocked:

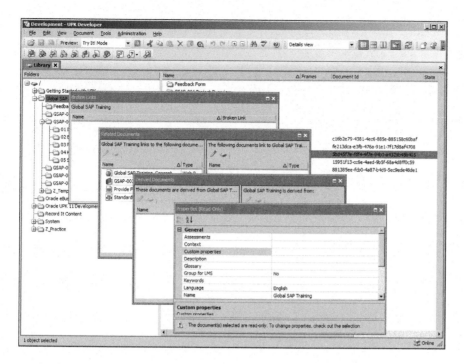

Each of these panes can be docked to any edge of the screen, as follows:

1. Click and hold the header of the pane that you want to dock.

2. Drag the pane toward the edge along which you want to dock it. As you start to drag the pane, a series of icons are displayed on the screen, one pointing to each edge, with a fifth icon appearing in the middle of the screen that features icons for all four edges.

3. To dock the pane against a particular edge, simply move the *cursor* over the icon (either on the perimeter of the screen or in the center) that is pointing to the required edge. Simply dragging the pane to the edge of the screen will not work. You must drag the *cursor* over one of the icons. As you do so, a shaded area appears on the screen, as seen in the following screenshot, showing where the pane will appear when it is docked.

4. Release the mouse button to dock the pane in the shaded area.

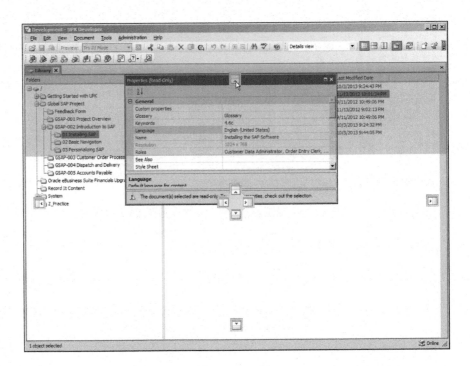

■ You can hide a docked side pane by clicking on the thumb-tack in its title bar. The pane will then slide out of view, with only the tab name(s) being displayed on the side of the screen. Hover the mouse over the tab names to slide the side pane out again.

Although each pane can be docked independently, and several panes can be docked separately against the same side, UPK also lets you dock multiple panes together, in a single, tabbed pane. To do this, dock one pane, and then drag the next pane over the already-docked pane. When you do this, a 'center' icon similar to the one in the previous screenshot is displayed. However, this time it has a further icon in the middle, as shown in the following screenshot:

Drop the pane onto this new icon (in the middle of the group), and the pane will appear as a tabbed page within the existing docked pane, as shown in the next screenshot:

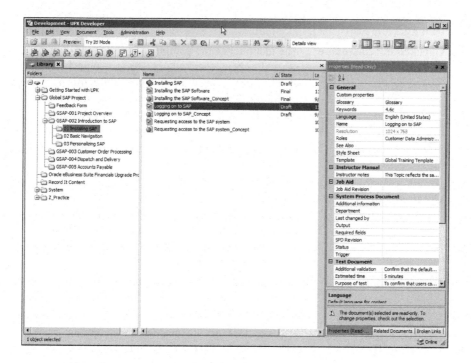

You can reorganize the order of the individual tabbed panes within the docked side pane, by dragging the tabs to the required position.

Changing the information displayed for objects

As explained in *Working with the Library screen* on page 63, the rightmost side of the *Library* screen displays the contents of the folder selected in the leftmost side of the *Library* screen. For each document, certain information is displayed in the pane's columns. This typically includes the name, last modified date, and object type of each object, but there are several other things that can be displayed. The full list of available attributes (in alphabetical order) is:

Column Name	Content
Checked out by*	If the content object is currently checked out of the Library, then this column shows the Userid of the person who has checked out the object.

Table 3-1 List of all Available View Columns

Column Name	Content
Checked out hostname*	The identifier of the computer to which the content object has been checked out. Because objects are checked out to the author's workstation, this is useful for determining on which workstation the checked out version can be found. This could be very useful to know if an author is in the habit of changing workstations, and sees an object in their Library appear as locked under their own Userid (which should never normally be the case).
Creation date	The date on which the content object was first created in the Library. Note that if you import content from another Library, or from a backup, then this date is the date that the content object was imported and not the original creation date.
Derived From	If the content object was created by copying (directly or via **Save As**) then this is the name of the content object on which it was based.
Derived From Document ID	If the content object was created by copying (directly or via **Save As**) then this is the Document ID of the content object on which it was based.
Document Id	UPK's own internal 32-character identifier for a content object. This identifier is used (by UPK) in exported files (including translation files) and can be seen in a few other places. Hopefully, you will never need this, but it is useful to know that it is there in case you do.
Frames	For Topics, this is the total number of Frames in the Topic. This is very useful for gaging the size of a Topic. Note that this count includes all Frame types and not just Action Frames.
Language	The language assigned to the content object. Note that this is only used for determining the spell-checker to use. It does not control the template that will be used, or the language in which the content will be published.
Last modified by*	The Userid of the person who last modified the content object.
Last modified date	The date and time on which the content object was last changed.

✛ The **Derived From** and **Derived From Document ID** columns were introduced in UPK 12.

Column Name	Content
Link count	The number of other content objects to which this object links. This corresponds to the number of objects listed in the *to* section of the *Related Documents* pane described above, and will always be at least 1 because every object must at least have a template attached to it.
Links to	The number of other content objects that link to this content object. This corresponds to the number of objects listed in the *from* section of the *Related Documents* pane described above.
Name	The display name of the content object. Note that this does not have to be unique—even within a single Library folder—because UPK uses the **Document ID** as the unique object reference. You will, however, find it much easier to differentiate between your objects if you use unique names for them.
Original Location	This property is only used in the *Deleted Documents* view, and specifies the location in the Library at which this document existed before it was deleted. If the document is restored, it will be restored to this location. This property will be blank for all documents currently in the Library. Refer to *Chapter 7, Version Management* for more information on deleted documents and how to restore them.
Owner*	If a particular author has been specified as the owner of the content object in the object's **Properties	Workflow	Owner** field, then this column shows the Userid of this author. Note that this is really just a static field—it does not 'control' anything—although it can be used quite effectively with custom views, which are described later in this chapter.
Path	The full path of the folder in which the content object is located. As the path is easily-discernible from the leftmost pane of the *Library* screen, this is of negligible use (unless you are using a view in which the hierarchical folder structure is not displayed at all).
Permission*	The access permission that you have for the object. For more information on access permissions, refer to *Chapter 14, Basic Administration*.

■ The Links To column provides a great way of finding 'orphan' content - that is, documents that are not linked to by anything. Simply use a 'flat' view, show this column, and then sort it in ascending order on this property and look for zero values.

Column Name	Content
Questions	The number of questions included in the selected assessment. Note that this only applies to Assessment content objects; for all other object types it will be blank.
Roles	The names of the Roles to which the content object has been assigned. Refer to *Chapter 10, Adding Value in the Player* for more information on Roles.
State*	The current 'workflow state' of the object. Note that this is simply the content of the **Properties	Workflow	State** field. You can sort, filter, and publish content objects based on their State.
Type	The content object type. As the icon for the object type is always shown to the left of the Name, this is of limited use – although it can be used to sort on.
Version*	This is the version number of the object. The version number is a simple integer that is incremented by 1 each time the content object is checked into the Library. Refer to *Chapter 7, Version Management* for more information on versions.

✚ The **Questions** column was introduced in UPK 11.0.

Note that columns marked with an asterisk (*) are applicable only to a client/ server environment. These columns will not be available in a stand-alone environment.

✚ In versions prior to UPK 12, the *Customization* dialog box was named the *Column Chooser* dialog box.

To add or remove columns from the display, right-click on any column header, and then select **Column Chooser** from the context menu. This will display the *Customization* dialog box, as shown below:

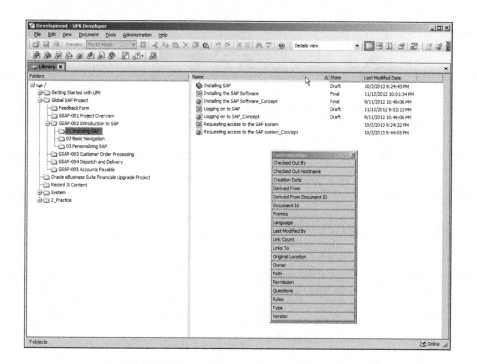

The *Customization* dialog box lists all of the additional columns that are available, but are not currently displayed on the screen. To add a column to the display, click (and hold) on the column name in the *Customization* dialog box and drag this onto a column header in the rightmost section of the Library screen. The column will be added to the left of the column onto which you drop it. To remove a column, simply click on the column header in the object list, drag the column off the header bar, and drop it anywhere on the screen.

You can re-order the columns in the object list by dragging them into the required order within the header bar. You can also sort the object list according to any of the displayed columns simply by clicking on the column header. Successive clicks on a column header will alternate between sorting in ascending order and sorting in descending order. More advanced ordering, sorting, and even filtering options are available when maintaining views, as described in *Working with views* on page 78.

The Library Toolbar

Whenever you display the *Library* screen, the *Library Toolbar* is displayed. This toolbar provides easy access to the most commonly-used actions for the Library. An example of this toolbar is shown below:

✦ The *Library Toolbar* is new in UPK 12. In prior versions, the functions accessed via this toolbar were only accessible via the menus.

We will cover each of the buttons on the *Library Toolbar* as we need them, throughout this book, but a full explanation can be found in *Chapter 3, Working in the UPK Developer Client*. As with all toolbars, the *Library Toolbar* can be undocked from the top of the screen and moved to wherever on the screen you want to place it.

Working with views

When you first access the *Library* screen, it displays the *Details View*, which is the view described above. Although this is the view in which you will probably work most of the time, there are other views that are available, depending on the type of UPK environment within which you are working. The current view is specified in the *View Toolbar*. You can select any other view via the **View** field's drop-down list button, as shown below:

■ Renaming the *Details View* to be all uppercase (as has been done in this example) makes it easier to find in the list of available views.

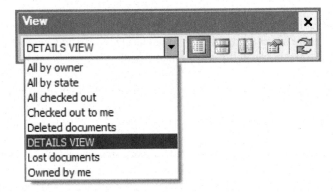

Note that most of these views are applicable only to a client/server environment. In a stand-alone environment, only the *Details view* and the *Lost documents* view are available. All possible views are described below:

- *All by owner*: This view lists all content objects, grouped and sorted by the Owner of the content object. This view displays the columns **Name, Owner, State, Checked Out By, Version**, and **Type**.

- *All by state*: This view lists all content objects, grouped and sorted by the current State of the content object. This view displays the columns **Name, State, Owner, Checked Out By, Version**, and **Type**.

- *All checked out*: This view lists only content objects that are currently checked out by any author, grouped and sorted according to the Userid of the author. This view displays the columns **Name, Checked Out By, State, Last Modified Date, Version**, and **Type**.

- *Checked out to me*: This view lists only content objects that you, personally, currently have checked out, sorted according to the object's name. This view displays the columns **Name, Checked Out By** (which is superfluous as it will always be your own Userid), **Last Modified Date, Version, Type**, and **Checked Out Hostname**.

- *Deleted documents*: This View lists all documents that have been deleted from the Library. Deleted documents will remain in the **Deleted documents** view until they are either restored by an author, or purged by an Administrator. This view displays the columns **Name, Original Location, Deletion Date, Deleted By**, and **Type**. For more information on deleting and restoring documents, refer to *Chapter 7, Version Management*.

- *Details View*: This is the default view, and lists the entire contents of the Library, organized by Library folder. In a client/server environment, this view displays the columns **Name, Checked Out By, Permission, Last Modified Date, Version, Type, Roles, State**, and **Owner**. In a standalone environment this view displays the columns **Name, Last Modified Date, Type**, and **Roles**.

- *Lost documents*: This view identifies any content objects that have become 'homeless'—typically because the folder in which they were stored has been deleted or has become corrupted, or because there is a problem with the folder's permission settings. You can select any of these lost documents and move them to the correct folder. In a client/server environment, this view displays the columns **Name, Original Location, Last Modified Date, Last Modified By**, and **Type**. In a stand-alone environment, this view displays the columns **Name, Last Modified Date**, and **Type**.

- *Owned by me*: This view lists only content objects for which you are specified as the **Owner** in the **Workflow Properties**, sorted according to the object's name. This view displays the columns **Name, Owner, State, Checked Out By, Version**, and **Type**.

Creating a Custom View

In addition to the pre-installed views listed above, you can define your own custom views. You can even change (and, in some cases, delete) the pre-installed views.

To define a Custom View, carry out the steps described below. By way of an example, we will create a new view that will list all of the documents that we have changed, most recent first.

1. Select menu option **View | Manage Views**. The *Manage Views* dialog box is displayed, as shown in the following screenshot:

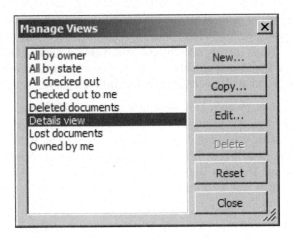

You can also base your new view on an existing view by selecting the existing view and then clicking on **Copy**, or change an existing view (even one of the default, pre-installed views) by selecting the existing view and then clicking on **Change**. If you change a pre-installed view, you can restore it to the default settings by selecting it and then clicking on **Reset**.

2. Click on **New**. The *View Editor* dialog box is displayed, as shown in the following screenshot:

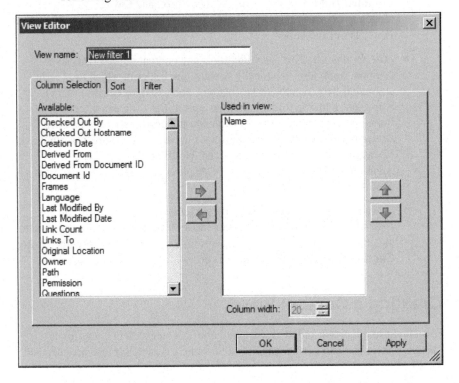

3. Enter a suitable name for your new Custom View in the **View name** field. In our example, we will use the name **Most recent by me**.

4. On the *Column Selection* tabbed page, choose the columns that you want to appear in the view by selecting them in the **Available** list and then clicking on the **Add** button. (You can also double-click on a column to add it to the **Used in view list**.) Use the **Up** and **Down** buttons to re-order the columns in the order in which you want them to be displayed (from left to right).

In our example, we will include the **Name, State,** and **Last Modified Date** columns, as shown in the screenshot below:

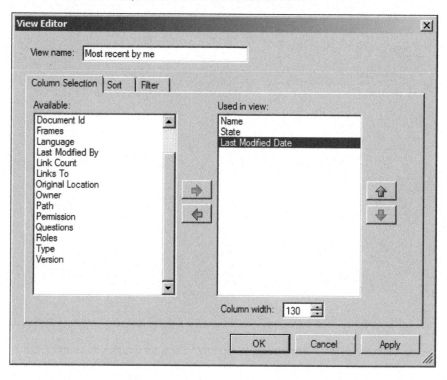

5. On the *Sort* tabbed page, choose up to three columns on which to sort the view. Note that you can sort on any column, and not just the ones chosen in Step 4. If you want your view to still be organized by folder, then select the **Organize by folders** option. Otherwise, make sure that this option is not selected.

    In our example, we are sorting in descending order on the **Last Modified Date** column. This will list the most recently-changed document first.

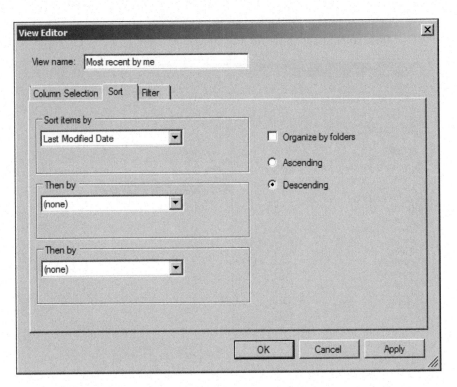

6. On the *Filter* tabbed page, select any values on which you want certain columns to be filtered. Again, you can filter on any column, not just the ones chosen in Step 4.

In our example, we are filtering on a **Last Modified By** value of our own Userid, as shown in the following screenshot:

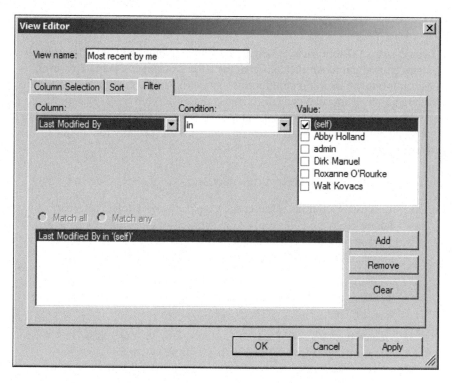

7. Click on **OK** to return to the *Manage Views* dialog box.

8. Click on **Close** to close the *Manage Views* dialog box.

You can now select this new view from the **View** drop-down, as shown in the following screenshot:

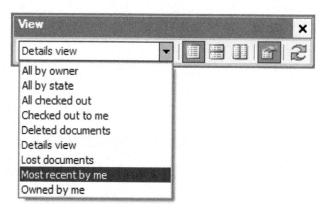

Note that if you have access to multiple Libraries, your new view will be available in all of these Libraries. That is, views are common to all of your Profiles.

Sharing views with other authors

If you create a Custom View, it will not be visible to other authors in the same Library (it is tied to *your* installation of the UPK Developer Client). However, you can locate the definition file for this view, and pass this to another author for loading into their installation. This is nowhere near as convenient as exporting and importing Developer Options, but may be worth doing if you want to ensure that all authors are using a consistent custom view – especially for complex custom views.

To share a custom view with another author, carry out the steps shown below:

✚ UPDev8 refers to UPK 12; UPK 11 is stored under UPDev7, and UPK 3.5 is stored under UPDev6.

1. In Windows Explorer, locate the `ViewFilters` folder for your language, in the UPK application data settings directory on your workstation. In my installation, this is `C:\Users\Dirk\AppData\Local\UPDev8\ViewFilters\en\`.

   Note that the `AppData` folder may be 'hidden' in Windows, in which case you may need to search for it, or type the above path into the Location bar.

2. Locate the `.xml` file for your Custom View, and copy this. The Custom View we created earlier in this chapter is shown in the following screenshot:

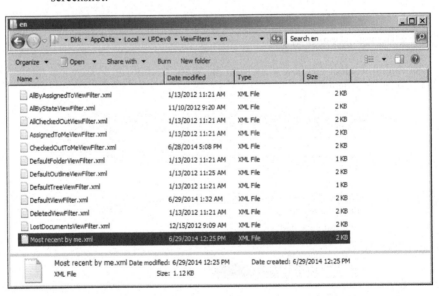

3. Send this file to the author with whom you want to share your Custom View, and tell them to save it to the equivalent directory on their own workstation.

Printing or saving a View

You can print the list of content objects displayed for a view (or the contents of the selected folder, if the view is organized by folder). To do this, carry out the steps described below:

■ You can use the same steps described below to print the contents of an Outline (once the Outline is displayed in the *Outline Editor*).

1. Select menu path **File | Print**. The *Preview* screen is displayed, as shown in the screenshot below:

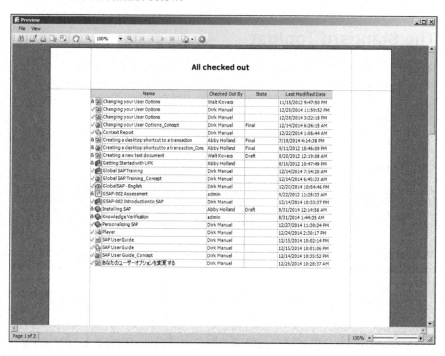

2. To print the view list:

    - To print to your default printer, using the default settings, click on the **Quick Print** button (▣) (or use menu option **File | Quick Print**).

    - To print to another printer or using other settings, click on the **Print** button (▣) (or use menu option **File | Print**) to display the standard Windows *Print dialog* box, change the print settings as required, and then click on Print.

3. To save the print list to a file on your workstation:

    i. Click on the **Save** button (▣) (or use menu option **Save**), and then select the appropriate file format from the drop-down menu. You can save as a PDF file, Microsoft Excel workbook, HTML file, or image file (JPEG, GIF, PNG, and so on). The standard Windows *Save As* dialog box is displayed.

    ii. Navigate to the location to which you want to save the list.

iii. Enter a suitable file name in the **File name** field.

iv. For image files, select the required image for mat in the **Save as type** field.

v. Click **Save**.

4. Back in the *Preview* dialog box, click on the **Close** button () to close the dialog box.

The Standard Toolbar

Regardless of which view you are in, or which Editor is open, the *Standard Toolbar* is always displayed. This toolbar provides access to a number of functions that are generally common to all areas of the UPK Developer (although some buttons will be grayed out if they are not applicable to the currently-selected object).

An example of the *Standard Toolbar* is shown below:

We will cover each of the buttons on the *Standard Toolbar* as we need them, throughout this book, but if you are impatient, you can find a full explanation of them in *Appendix D, Toolbar Buttons Quick Reference*.

Choosing an organization for your Library

The Library initially contains only a couple of folders: a set of help files in `Getting Started with UPK`, and the `System` folder. If you have recorded content via the *Record It! Wizard*, you will also have another folder, named `Record It Content`. It is into this folder that all Topics created via the *Record It! Wizard* are placed—regardless of who recorded them. However, it is extremely unlikely that you will want to leave all of your Topics in this folder. Instead, you will want a logical way of organizing your Topics and other content objects.

● Technically, content objects are not stored within this folder structure (or any folder structure). Instead, they are stored as objects in a database. It is the object's **Path** property that determines the folder within the Library screen in which it appears.

In essence, the *Library* screen shows a set of nested folders that conceptually works in the same way as the folder structure you see in Windows Explorer or similar file management systems. It should, therefore, be a very familiar concept to you.

The difficulty for authors who are familiar with OnDemand Version 8.x and earlier is in divorcing the Outline (which is covered in more detail in *Chapter 5, Building an Outline*) from the *Library* screen. The *Library* screen is just a set of folders into which content is stored by the authors; the Outline organizes this content into a structure that the users will see. The *Library* screen does not necessarily bear any relation to the Outline. So the first thing that you need to decide is how you want to arrange your content for the benefit of the author. As with Windows Explorer, there are an infinite number of possibilities, but some will make more sense than others. Some of the more commonly-used organizations are explained below:

- **An application-based structure**: If you (or all of the authors collectively) will be creating UPK simulations for a number of different applications, then you could choose to create a separate folder for each application and store all of the content for each application within its own folder.

- **A module-based structure**: With large ERP systems such as SAP, a company will typically implement several individual components of the ERP system. Here, it may be helpful to have separate folders for each functional area. So to use the example of SAP, you could have separate folders for FI, MM, SD, and so on.

- **A version-based structure**: If you will be creating UPK simulations for a single application, but need to provide separate simulations for different versions of the application (and retain all previous versions), then you could choose to have one folder for each version of the application.

- **A course-based structure**: Often, training programs will deliver a number of discrete training courses, possibly organized around the modules that the project is delivering, but more likely centered on the (business or system) roles of the users who are to be trained. Here, it may be sensible to organize the content into folders by course.

- **A content-based structure**: UPK recognizes several types of object, including the Module, Section, and Topic types of 'content', and Web Pages, and Packages. These are explained in more detail in *Chapter 9, Adding Value to Your Topics*. You could, therefore, choose to store each type of content in its own folder.

  ■ A content-based structure is useful if you only want certain authors developing Outlines, but want all authors to be able to create and maintain Topics.

- **A security-based structure**: In a client/server environment it is possible to define security for individual folders within a Library. In this case, you can choose to organize your content into folders based on who you want to be able to change those content objects. See *Chapter 14, Basic Administration* for more information on setting folder security.

● The folder structure that you choose for thew *Library* screen applies to all authors working in this Library. You should therefore take care to use an organization that makes sense to everyone, and communicate this structure and any standards and expectations to all authors when they first gain access to this Library.

In all likelihood, you will choose to have a hybrid structure. For example, you may choose to have separate folders per application, sub-folders below this for each course, and then further sub-folders for each type of content.

Whatever approach you choose, just remember that this is entirely for the benefit of the author(s)—do not concern yourself with the users, as they will never see the Library structure. Your sole objective should be to organize the content so that the authors can easily find what they are looking for when they need to change it. That said, there is a strong argument for having the structure of the *Library* match the Outline structure (assuming that you are publishing to a Player). The reason for this is that if someone identifies an object in the Player that needs to be changed, it is extremely easy to locate this object in the *Library* screen.

For our sample Library structure, we will use a hybrid structure. At the highest level, we will use a project-based structure with one folder per project. This will allow us to use folder-level security to limit access to project content to only those authors working on that project. Below this, we will have our content organized by course, and lessons within that course. Assuming that we publish a separate Player package per project, our Library structure will then match our Player Outline. This will drive us to store (only) one outline element (Module or Section) in each folder, which will keep things nice and simple. To reinforce this, we will name our folders to be the same as the Modules or Sections contained in them, prefixed with a number to reflect the order of the outline elements within the Player (otherwise they will be listed alphabetically, which can be confusing if you are trying to match the Player structure). This will give us a structure as shown in the following screenshot:

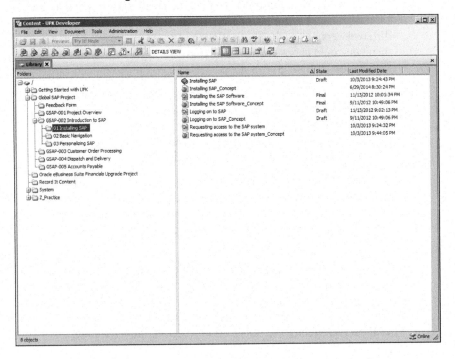

Creating folders

Now that you know how you want your *Library* screen to be structured, let's look at how to achieve this. To create a new folder, carry out the steps described below:

1. Click on the folder within which you want the new folder to be located. If this is the first folder that you are defining in your Library, then this will be the `root` folder, which is identified by a single slash (/).

2. Select menu option **File | New | Folder**. The *Create New Folder* dialog box is displayed, prompting you to specify a name for your new folder, as shown below.

● You can have as many levels of nested folder as you like—there is no limit (as there effectively was in OnDemand 8.7 and earlier, by virtue of only having Modules, Sections, and Titles within a Topic).

3. Enter the name of the folder, and then click on **OK**.

4. Repeat steps 1 to 3 to create all remaining folders.

Changing the Library structure

The folder structure that you create is not fixed. You can rename folders (right-click on them and then select **Rename** from the context menu), move them around (via drag-and-drop or cut-and-paste), and so on. So if you change your mind about how you want your content to be organized within the *Library* screen (as you inevitably will), don't worry about it.

Any changes that you make to your *Library* screen will not affect any links that you have created in your content. For example, if you create a link from a Topic in one folder to a Web Page in a sub-folder, and then move that sub-folder to be a parent of the Topic's folder, the link will not be affected at all. UPK will still find all of the content, and everything in the Player will work in the way that you originally designed it to. This is because UPK does not use the folder names or locations in any of the links. Instead, it uses its own unique (32-character) Document ID for each content object (as described in the section *Changing the information displayed for objects* on page 73, above).

Again, UPK can do this because the folder structure shown on the *Library* screen bears absolutely no reference to the structure that the user will see—as we shall see in *Chapter 5, Building an Outline*.

Searching for documents

Even with the best Library organization, there are occasions when you misplace a content object and need to find it. There are a few ways of doing this, as outlined in the following sections.

Searching via the Find and Replace function

UPK does not really have a search function. What it does have is a 'find and replace' function, which is accessed via the **Find** button ( ), but this is not particularly useful when trying to locate a specific content object, as it only identifies one object at a time, and there is no way to open or otherwise jump to this content object, other than making a note of the path (provided under **Location**) of the object in which the text was found, it does not take you to this object when you close the *Find and Replace* dialog box.

To locate a content object via the Find and Replace function, carry out the following steps:

1. Click on the folder within the *Library* screen in which you want to search in (all child folders will also be searched). To search in the entire Library, select the 'root' directory ('/').

2. Click on the **Find** button ( ).

3. In the *Find and Replace* dialog box, enter the text that you are searching for into the **Find what** field. Leave the **Replace with** field blank.

4. Set the **Find Options** as required.

5. Click **Find Next**.

6. Check name of the document found, and the context of the found text (which is shown in the large text area at the bottom of the dialog box. If this is the document you are looking for, make a note of the object path, click **Close**, then navigate to this path and object on the *Library* screen. Otherwise, return to Step 5.

An example of the *Find and Replace* dialog box is shown below:

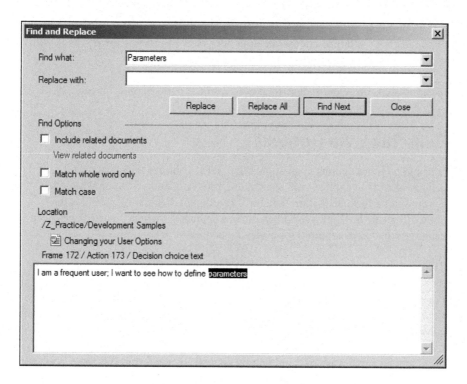

The advantage of using the **Find and Replace** function to search for content objects is that it will do a full search for any text string throughout the actual content of the objects. However, as you can see above, it does not provide an easy way of jumping to the content object that you locate.

Searching via a Custom View

A more useful option is to simply define a Custom View (perhaps called **Search**), and use the *Filter* tab in this to specify the search criteria. You will also need to deselect the **Organize by folders** option on the **Sort** tab, or else you will still need to search through all of the folders (most of which will appear empty).

The disadvantage of this approach is that you are limited to searching on columns that can be displayed in a view (and not the content of the document itself) but this includes the **Document Name**, and more often than not you will at least know some of the text in this. However, the advantages are that you can see a full list of all content objects that meet the search criteria, and (most importantly), you can open any of the found content objects simply by double-clicking on the content object in the Custom View.

You may also find it useful to include the **Path** column in your view, so that you can identify the folder in which the found content object is located. Alternatively, if you can open the Outline Element that contains the document that you are looking for (for example, by displaying the *Related Documents* pane and opening it from there), then the easiest way to locate the document is to select it in the *Outline Editor*, and then choose menu option **View | Find in Library**. This will take you directly to the folder that contains the document.

Creating a custom view is described in *Creating a Custom View* on page 79.

Searching via Context

✦ The **Find Context** function was introduced in UPK 12.1.

When you record actions in an application, UPK captures the context of these actions - that is, it captures the application, program, and screen on which the action was performed. Within the UPK Developer Client, UPK provides the ability to locate all Topics (or other content objects for which a context has been captured) that were captured for a specific context.

This is an extremely useful feature when determining what Topics need to be re-recorded (or have screens re-captured) in response to changes in an application. For example, if a specific screen within an application has changed to include new fields, you can use UPK's **Find Context** function to search for all Topics that contain this particular screen.

UPK provides two ways of searching by context: by capturing (via the recorder) the context you want to find, and by selecting the context from an existing Topic. Both of these methods are explained below.

Searching by capturing the context

This method is useful if you do not know which (if any) Topics contain the context that you want to search for. To use this method, carry out the steps described below:

1. Click on the folder within the *Library* screen in which you want to search (all child folders will also be searched). To search in the entire Library, select the 'root' folder ('/').

2. Click on the **Context Search** button (🔍) on the *Standard Toolbar*. The *Context Search* dialog box is displayed, as shown below:

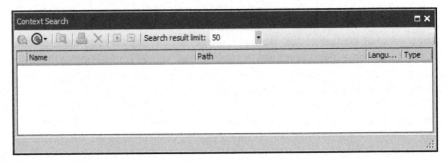

3. In the *Context Search* dialog box, click on the **Set Context** button (🔍▾), and then select **Capture and set Context** from the drop-down menu. The standard *Recorder* panel is displayed.

4. Click in the application in which you want to capture the context, and press *PRINTSCREEN* to identify the application to UPK (technically, this activates the context capture for this application). Navigate to the screen for which you want to capture the context, and then press *PRINTSCREEN* again to capture the context.

5. You are returned to the *Context Search* dialog box. The 'results' section of the *Context Search* dialog box now lists all of the documents that contain the captured context, showing their name, path, language, and document type. For instructions on how to process this information, refer to *Searching from within a Topic* on page 95.

Searching by selecting a context

If you can locate at least one Topic that contains the context for which you are searching, then you can search for other documents that contain the same context, directly from this identified Topic. To use out this method carry out the steps described below:

1. From the *Library* screen or from within an Outline Element, select the Topic (or other document to which context has been applied) that contains the context for which you are searching.

2. Click on the **Context Search** button (🔍) on the *Standard Toolbar*. The *Context Search* dialog box is displayed (for an example of this, refer to *Searching by capturing the context* on page 92).

3. In the *Context Search* dialog box, click on the **Set Context** button (🔍▾), and then select **Set Context from selected Document** from the drop-down menu. The *Find Context* dialog box is displayed, as shown below. This dialog box lists all of the contexts that have been captured in the selected Topic. You can click on each context to display a screenshot for that context in the rightmost side of the dialog box (and you can click on the **Enlarge to full resolution** link to display this screenshot full size).

■ You can also search for a context captured for non-Topic elements, such as Modules and Sections (see *Chapter 15, Integrating UPK with Other Applications* for more information on this).

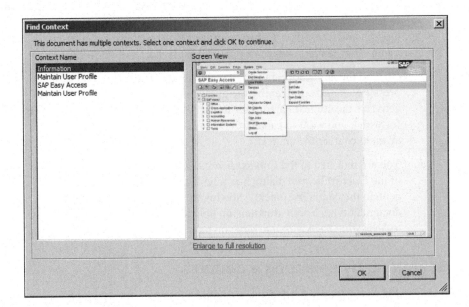

Enlarge to full resolution

4. Click on the context for which you want to search, and then click on **OK**. You are returned to the *Context Search* dialog box. This now lists the context details in the status bar at the bottom of the dialog box, as shown in the example below:

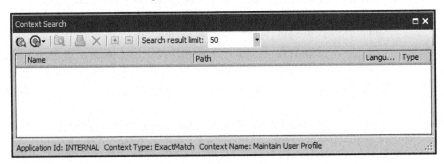

Application Id: INTERNAL   Context Type: ExactMatch   Context Name: Maintain User Profile

▲ Do not forget to select the folder within which you want to search. If you do not, then UPK will search only within the Topic selected in Step 1, and will return "No documents found" (because it ignores a match on the selected document).

5. Leaving the *Context Search* dialog box open, go back to the *Library* screen, and click on the folder within which you want to search (all child folders will also be searched). To search in the entire Library, select the 'root' directory ('/').

6. Go back to the *Context Search* dialog box, and click on the **Find Context** button (🔍). The 'results' section of the *Context Search* dialog box is populated with the results of the context search, listing all of the documents that contain the captured context, showing their name, path, language, and document type. For instructions on how to process this information, refer to *Searching from within a Topic* on page 95.

Searching from within a Topic

If you are editing a Topic within the **Topic Editor**, then you can search for other content objects within the Library that contain the same context as the context captured for the current Frame. This is useful if you have edited a specific Frame or recaptured the screenshot for this Frame, and want to see if there are any other Topics to which you need to make the same change.

To search for related context from within a Topic, carry out the steps described below:

1. From within the *Topic Editor*, click on the Frame that captured the context for which you want to search.

2. On *Topic Editing Toolbar*, click on the **Find Context** button (🔍). The *Context Search* dialog box is displayed, as shown below:

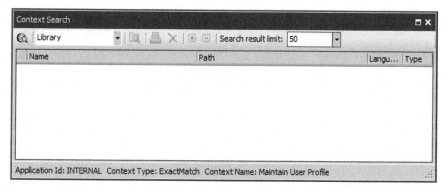

3. In the **Search Scope** field (to the right of the **Find Context** button), select the scope of your search. You can select **Library**, the Outline Element containing the Topic you are editing, or **Other** (for which you have to navigate to and select the required folder in the Library).

4. Click on the **Find Context** button (🔍). The 'results' section of the *Context Search* dialog box is populated with the results of the context search, listing all of the documents that contain the captured context, showing their name, path, language, and document type. For instructions on how to process this information, refer to *Searching from within a Topic* on page 95.

Processing the context search results

Once you have completed your search (via either of the two methods described), the *Context Search* dialog box lists all of the documents that contain the selected criteria. An example of this dialog box is shown below:

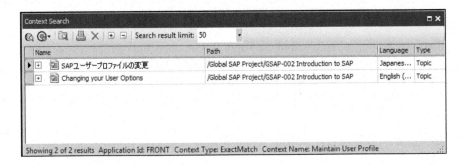

The **Context Search** dialog box initially shows one line per content object found. You can click on the **Expand** button ([+]) to the left of a document to list the specific Frames within this document on which the context was found. Click the **Collapse** button ([−]) to hide this information again. The screenshot below shows an example with the Frame information shown for one of the matches.

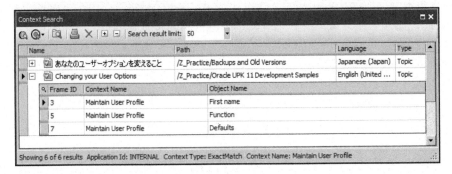

You can double-click on a document to open it in the relevant editor. The dialog box will remain open, and you will return to it when you close the editor.

You can also expand a single entry by clicking on the **Expand** button to the left of that entry. You can also collapse a single entry by clicking on the **Collapse** button to the left of that entry.

In addition to opening one of the documents, you can perform several other actions from within this dialog box, by using the available toolbar buttons. These are described in the table below.

Button	Name	Description
	View documents and folders included in search	List the folders and/or documents that were selected to be searched for the context. The list is displayed in the same results pane. Click on this button again to return to the search results.
	Print search results	Generate a printable version of the results list that you can print to your printer or save as a PDF, HTML, or Microsoft Excel file..

Button	Name	Description
✕	**Clear search results**	Clear the results of the current search, ready to perform a new search.
⊞	**Expand all**	Expand all of the search result entries, to list all of the Frames within that document that contain the context, along with the object acted upon.
⊟	**Collapse all**	Collapse all of the search result entries, to hide the list of Frames.

Checking for lost documents

Occasionally, UPK may 'lose' documents. Actually, it does not lose the *document*, it just loses track of where it thinks it should be in the Library. Typically, this is because you have created but not checked in a content object in a folder that has since been deleted by another user. In this case, UPK doesn't know where to put the document when you check it in, but it will keep hold of it so that you can locate it and put it in the correct place yourself.

● Lost documents only exist (or maybe they don't, depending on your existential viewpoint...) in a client/server environment. If you 'lose' a document in a stand-alone environment, it's gone.

If UPK detects that there are any 'lost' documents in the Library, it will display a warning message in the lower-right of the *Library* screen when you log on, as shown below:

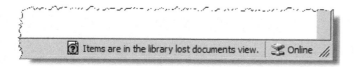

Click on this message to go to the *Lost Documents* view. (You can also select **Lost Documents** in the **View** field, at any time.) An example of the *Lost Documents* view is shown in the following screenshot:

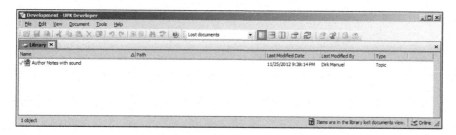

Note that the **Path** field is blank – this is why the document is considered 'lost'.

To retrieve this document, simply copy it and paste it into the correct folder in the Library (or drag-and-drop it in split screen mode).

Summary

The UPK Developer Client is the UPK application that you (as a 'full' author, as distinct from a SME who will likely only use the *Record It! Wizard*) use to access the content stored in the UPK Library. This content is typically organized into a hierarchical folder structure for display on the *Library* screen. The organization of the folders and their content does not impact or influence the structure in which these content objects will be arranged when they are presented to users.

The *Library* screen opens as a tabbed page within the *UPK Developer* screen. The various editors within UPK will also open as tabbed pages within this same screen. You can split the display of the *UPK Developer* screen to show two different tabbed pages at the same time. Separate panes exist for key information about content objects. These include the *Properties* pane, the *Related Documents* pane, the *Derived Documents* pane, and the *Broken Links* pane. Each of these panes can be displayed, hidden, or docked, independently, as per your personal preferences.

Several Views are available for the Library screen, each of which displays a predefined selection of information for each object. You can also define your own Custom Views, and apply sorting and filtering to these Views.

4
Editing a Topic

As exciting as the Library is, the core of your work (and certainly if you want to create *quality* exercises) will be in the *Topic Editor*. In this chapter, we will start by looking at the information that is shown on the *Topic Editor* screen. We will then edit the Topic that we recorded in *Chapter 2, Recording a Simulation*, looking at all of the tools and options that are available in the Topic Editor, as we go. This is a long chapter; you may not want to read it all in one sitting, but you will undoubtedly find it useful as an ongoing reference.

In this chapter, you will learn:

- What the *Topic Editor* is
- What the main components of the *Topic Editor* screen are, and how to interact with them
- How to change Bubble Text
- How to insert missing Frames
- How to delete Frames
- How to recapture screenshots

Throughout this chapter, we will build on the sample exercise that we recorded in *Chapter 2, Recording a Simulation*. If you want to follow along using the sample exercise, we will start with the Topic **Changing your User Options (Chapter 3)**. If you just want to skip straight the finished result, refer to **Changing your User Options (Chapter 4)**. Both of these Topics are available in the `.odarc` file downloadable from the author's web site.

Understanding the Topic Editor screen

The *Topic Editor* is where you edit your recorded Topics. You will automatically be passed into the *Topic Editor* either when you finish recording the Topic, or after each screen capture, depending on your options (see *Chapter 2, Recording a Simulation*). You are also passed into the *Topic Editor* whenever you double-click on a Topic on the *Library* screen or in an Outline Element. The following screenshot shows an example of a typical *Topic Editor* screen:

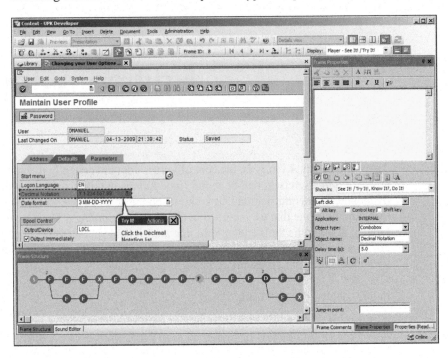

As you can see, the *Topic Editor* screen is composed of several distinct panes. Before delving into making any changes to our recorded Topic, let's look at each of these panes and what they do. Don't worry about the menus and toolbars; we'll get to them in good time.

The Screenshot pane

The largest portion of the *Topic Editor* screen is taken up by the *Screenshot* pane. This pane contains the screenshot that you captured during the recording. Note that this is not really a true 'pane', in that it is always displayed within the *Topic Editor*, and cannot be closed or moved as the other panes can be.

■ You can also click-and-hold the right mouse button on the screenshot, and then drag the screenshot around the Topic Editor window, to move the viewable area of the screenshot.

The screenshot is shown full-size, and UPK does not provide an option to scale this, therefore you cannot (for example) fit the entire screenshot into the viewable area. This means that you will need to scroll around using the vertical and horizontal scroll bars to see the different areas of the screenshot. (Or edit the

Topic on a screen that is set to a higher resolution than the resolution at which the Topic was captured.) This isn't *too* troublesome as you typically only want to see the area of the screenshot containing the **Action Area** (and therefore the Bubble) so you don't really need to scroll around that often.

The **Action Area** is represented by an opaque red box. In the example above, this is the rectangle overlaying the actual **Decimal Notation** input field (excluding the field name itself). The Action Area is the area of the screen that was clicked on, or into which text was entered, during recording. UPK generally does a pretty good job of correctly sizing this around the object, but it doesn't always manage it. In these cases, you can move or re-size the Action Area, as described in the section *Adjusting Action Areas* on page 111.

The **Print Area** is represented by an opaque magenta box. In the example above, this is the rectangle overlaying the **Decimal Notation** input field and the field name. The Print Area is the area of the screenshot that will be used as a thumbnail image in certain printed output types. By default, no separate Print Area exists and the Action Area is used as the Print Area, but a specific Print Area can be defined (separately from the Action Area) if necessary, as we shall see later in this chapter.

✦ Print Areas were introduced in UPK 12.1. In prior versions, the Action Area was used for thumbnails in printed output types.

Because the Action Area and the Print Area are often overlapping (in the example above, the entire Action Area is contained within the boundary of the Print Area), two buttons are available on the *Topic Navigation and View Toolbar* to allow you to display one or other of them at a time. These buttons are shown in the table below.

Button	Name	Purpose
	Show Action Area	Toggle the display of the Action Area (red box) off and on.
	Show Print Area	Toggle the display of the Print Area (magenta box) off and on.

The *Screenshot* pane also shows the Bubble for the Frame. This is the 'speech bubble' that (again, by default) points to the Action Area. The Bubble contains the instructions to the user carrying out the exercise, and is possibly the single most important component of UPK. By default, the Bubble is 'connected' to the Action Area, although you can move it to any other position on the screen that you like. However, when it is moved close to the Action Area, it will 'snap' to the Action Area (although you can hold down the *Ctrl* key to prevent this). You can also change the position of the 'pointer' on the Bubble, as explained below, under the section on the *Frame Properties* pane.

The Topic Editor panes

In addition to the *Screenshot* pane, there are a number of other panes that can be displayed in the *Topic Editor*. The table below lists the available panes and their use.

✥ In Version 3.6 and earlier, dedicated toolbar buttons were available to show or hide the *Action Properties*, *Bubble Properties*, and *Sound Properties* panes. However, with the proliferation of new panes in Version 11, these buttons have been discontinued and no longer appear. Note also that the *Action Properties* and *Bubble Properties* panes have now been combined into the single *Frame Properties* pane, which can only be shown or hidden as a single unit.

Pane	Purpose
Frame Properties	This pane is the most useful pane in the *Topic Editor*, and is displayed by default. This pane allows you to adjust the Bubble Text (explained in *Changing the Bubble Text* on page 147) and the action areas (explained in *Adjusting Action Areas* on page 111) for a frame.
Concept	This pane is the same as the *Concept* pane visible in the Outline Editor, and allows you to link a Web Page (or file within a Package) to the Topic, or display any currently-linked document. Being able to display this pane from within the *Topic Editor* is useful as it means that you can attach a content object to the *Concept* pane of the Topic without first having to include the Topic in an Outline Element. Concept pages are described in *Chapter 9, Adding Value to Your Topics*.
Frame Link	This pane allows you to link Library documents or external URLs to a bubble, via an icon. This functionality is described in *Chapter 9, Adding Value to Your Topics*.
Frame Structure	This pane provides a graphical representation of all of the Frames in the Topic, and shows how users progress from one Frame to the next (that is, the paths through the Topic). The *Frame Structure* pane is described in detail in *The Frame Structure pane* on page 103.
Sound Editor	This pane can be used to record sound for a Frame, or to play any existing sound for a Frame. The *Sound Editor* is explained in *Chapter 11, Incorporating Sound Into Your Topics*.
Frame Comments	This pane allows you to enter or display comments that can be provided in three categories: **Expected Results** (see Chapter 13, Using UPK for Application Testing), **Author Notes** (see *Chapter 2, Recording a Topic*), and **Instructor Notes** (see the section Entering Frame Comments, later in this chapter).

✥ Frame Comments were introduced in UPK 11.

You can show or hide any of these panes by selecting the appropriate option from the **View | Panes** menu. You can also hide or display the standard *Properties*, *Broken Links*, and *Related Documents* panes from the same menu. These panes are described in *Chapter 3, Working in the UPK Developer Client*.

By default (and as shown in the screenshot at the start of this section), the *Topic Editor* screen shows the *Frame Structure* pane docked at the bottom of the screen, and the *Frame Properties* pane docked on the right of the screen.

You can undock any of the panes, and position them anywhere on the screen, by clicking on the pane title bar and dragging the pane to a new location. If you drag a property pane to the left or right sides of the **Topic Editor** window, then it will snap back to a docked position. Refer to *Chapter 3, Working in the UPK Developer Client* for details of how to move and dock panes within the overall UPK window.

We will examine each of these panes—both their content and their purpose—as we use them to edit the example exercise that we recorded in *Chapter 2, Recording a Simulation*.

The Frame Structure pane

The *Frame Structure* pane provides a graphical representation of all of the Frames (almost exclusively screenshots) in the Topic, and the path(s) through them (that is, the order in which the Frames are replayed).

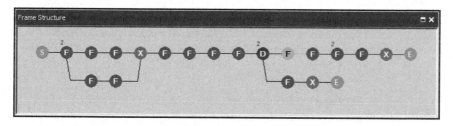

As you can see from the example above, there may be more than one path through the Topic. Don't worry about this for now; it is all explained in *Chapter 14, Allowing Alternatives*.

Each circle in the *Frame Structure* pane represents a Frame (which itself represents a screenshot that may be displayed during on-line playback or included in printed output, and its associated Action(s)). The table below lists the icons used in the *Frame Structure* pane, and describes the Frame types that they represent:

Table 4-2 Explanation of
Frame Icons

Icon	Description
	Start Frame: This is the first Frame in the Topic; a Topic can have only one Start Frame. The Start Frame is created automatically by UPK when you start recording, and uses the same screenshot as the Frame immediately following it (that is, the first **Action Frame** in the Topic). This Frame is sometimes referred to in UPK as the Introduction Frame (because it used to appear in the now-discontinued *Introduction* pane in the Outline). In this book we use the term Start Frame.
	End Frame: This is the last Frame in the Topic. Unlike the Start Frame, a Topic can have more than one End Frame—if the Topic includes a Branch. (Branches are discussed in *Chapter 14, Allowing Alternatives*.) Similar to the Start Frame, the End Frame is created automatically by UPK when you finish recording.
	Action Frame: Most Frames in a Topic are Action Frames. Action Frames are the ones that contain the recorded actions for your Topic, and are created each time that you press PRINTSCREEN (or other defined capture key) during recording.
	Decision Frame: A Decision Frame asks the user to make a choice from a number of options, and will direct playback down a specific path based on the choice made by the user. Decisions are discussed in more detail in *Chapter 14, Allowing Alternatives*. A Decision Frame can only be inserted from within the *Topic Editor* (it cannot be captured during recording), and initially takes its screenshot from the Frame immediately following it.
	(1) Explanation Frame: An Explanation Frame is a special kind of Frame, on which the user is not required to perform any specific action (such as a mouse-click or key-press). Explanation Frames are typically used to provide additional information to the user, or to draw the user's attention to specific elements on the screen. An Explanation Frame can only be inserted from within the *Topic Editor* (it cannot be captured during recording), and takes its screenshot from the Frame immediately following it.
	(2) Blank Frame: A Blank Frame is effectively an Explanation Frame without a screenshot. Instead, the 'screen' is plain white, but can be edited to display other information.

✛ Blank Frames were introduced in UPK 12, although you could achieve the same effect in earlier versions by inserting an **Explanation Frame** and then blanking out the screenshot in your **Screenshot Editor**.

When you hover the mouse pointer over a Frame in the *Frame Structure* pane, a thumbnail image of the screenshot is shown next to the pointer. This thumbnail also shows the unique identifier of this Frame within the Topic, in a yellow box. An example of this is shown in the following screenshot:

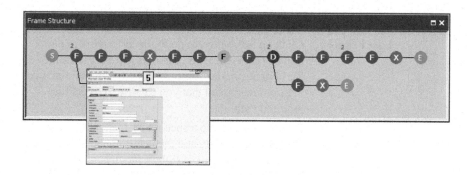

In this example, the mouse pointer is hovering over the currently-active Frame (which is highlighted), although in practice you wouldn't normally need to display the thumbnail of the currently-active Frame as you can already see the screenshot in the *Screenshot* pane. The identifier of this Frame is **5**, which is shown at the top center of the thumbnail (note that this does not necessary line up with the Frame icon). The Frame ID is also shown in the *Standard Toolbar*, to the left of the Frame navigation buttons. Note that the Start Frame and End Frame(s) do not have identifiers.

Knowing the identifier of a Frame can be useful for jumping directly to a specific Frame, as we will see when we look at the *Standard Toolbar*, below.

The currently-active Frame (that is, the Frame whose screenshot is currently displayed in the *Screenshot* pane) is highlighted, as shown in the previous example. You can click on the icon for any Frame in the *Frame Structure* pane to make that Frame the current Frame. You can also navigate between Frames by using the following buttons on the *Standard Toolbar*:

Button	Name	Purpose
⏮	**First Frame**	Click on this button to go to the first Frame in the Topic. This is the Start Frame.
◀	**Previous Frame**	Click on this button to go to the previous Frame (that is, the Frame immediately preceding the currently-active Frame). If the current Frame is at the convergence point of multiple paths, then focus will move to the previous Frame on the default path. (Alternative Paths are described in *Chapter 14, Allowing Alternatives*.)
▶	**Next Frame**	Click on this button to go to the next Frame (that is, the Frame immediately following the currently-active Frame). If the current Frame has multiple paths coming from it, then focus will move to the next Frame on the default path.

✛ Frame IDs are assigned internally, and fairly arbitrarily, by UPK. UPK does assign them sequentially, starting at 1, when you first record the Topic, but Frames inserted after that will start a new sequence that does not necessarily follow after the last Frame number used. You should therefore not read too much meaning into them.

■ You can hold down the *Alt* key and press the left arrow or right arrow key to move backwards or forward through the Frames. This is very useful when you are editing a Topic, and are adding to or adjusting the Bubble Text (as explained later in this chapter); you can keep the cursor focus in the Bubble Properties text field, and move through the Topic without having to move your hands from the keyboard to the mouse and click the navigation button and then back in the Bubble Text field.

Button	Name	Purpose
	Last Frame	Click on this button to go to the last Frame in the Topic. This is the End Frame. If there are multiple End Frames in the Topic, then the button will include a drop-down menu that you can use to select the required Path.
	Go To Frame	If you want to go to a specific Frame, then you can click on this button, and then enter the identifier of the Frame in the *Go To Specific Frame* dialog box that is displayed. This assumes that you know the identifier of the Frame; you can locate this as explained above, under the explanation of Frame thumbnails.

Displaying Frame IDs in the Player

One useful feature is the ability to have the Frame IDs displayed on the actual Frames during Player playback. By doing this, authors (or, more usefully – reviewers) who notice something that needs changing during playback can easily identify the specific Frame within the recording that needs to be updated. The author can then use the **Go To Frame** button ( ) (described above) to jump directly to this Frame in the *Topic Editor*.

To enable the display of Frame IDs during playback, carry out the following steps:

1. From the *Library* screen, open the Publishing Format Package for the Player, which is located at `\System\Publishing\Styles\<Category>\Player` (where `<Category>` is `User Productivity Kit` by default, or your own custom category).

2. Double-click on the file `config.xml`, to open it in Notepad (or other configured editor).

3. Locate the variable `ShowFrameID`. This can be found towards the bottom of the code, as shown in the following extract:

```xml
<?xml version="1.0" encoding="UTF-8"?>
<!--Copyright © 1998, 2014, Oracle and/or its
affiliates.  All rights reserved.-->
<config>
<configsection name="TreeConfig">
    <item name="AutoExpandLimit">100</item>
    <item name="SearchResultLimit">200</item>
</configsection>
<configsection name="PlayerConfig">

    .
    .

    <item name="ShowFrameID">"Off"</item>
</configsection>
```

```
    .
    .
    .
</config>
```

4. Change the value of this parameter as follows:

- To have the Frame ID always displayed, set `ShowFrameID` to **on**

- To have the Frame ID always hidden, set `ShowFrameID` to **off**

- To allow the user to dynamically choose showing or hiding the Frame ID, enter a key combination of *SHIFT+F1* to *SHIFT+F12*, in the format `ShiftF1`, `ShiftF2`, and so on. The user can press this key combination to toggle between showing and hiding the Frame IDs.

5. Save and close the `config.xml` file.

6. Save and close the Player Publishing Format Package.

7. Check in the Package (in a client/server environment only).

8. When enabled (either by setting `ShowFrameID` to **On**, or by dynamically toggling Frame ID display on), the Frame ID appears in playback in the upper-left corner of the screen, as shown in the partial screenshot below.

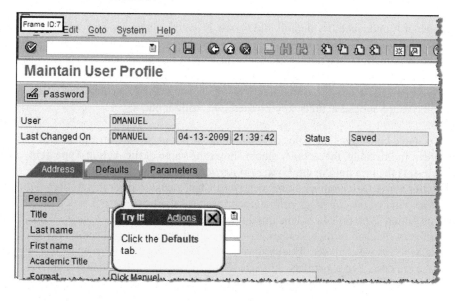

Alternatively, you can set this flag on for a specific published Player, by making the same change to the `config.js` file in the `PlayerPackage` folder (although you would then need to re-set it after each publish).

Adjusting Actions

In this section, we will look at how to work with Actions and Action Areas.

■ You would not want the Frame ID to be displayed for your users, so you may need to set the `ShowFrameID` parameter to `on` during the development and review stages, but set it to `off` for final publishing. Of course, if you use a two-Library set-up, you can set it on in your Development Library, and `off` in your Production Library, so that you don't have to keep changing the Publishing Format.

The Frame Properties pane

The *Frame Properties* pane contains all of the information related to the Action that was captured during recording, including the Bubble Text that will be displayed for this action. An example of this pane is shown below:

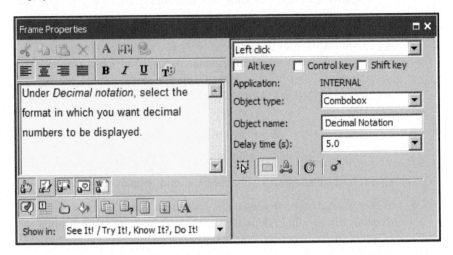

Note that the screenshot above shows the *Frame Properties* pane as it appears when it is undocked. By default, the *Frame Properties* pane appears docked on the rightmost side of the screen, with the Bubble properties shown above the Action properties (see the screenshot at the start of this chapter).

As explained earlier, there are effectively three categories of Actions that UPK can capture: mouse-actions, key-presses, and string input.

The table below lists the types of Action that UPK can capture, in alphabetic order. In this table, the *Action* column shows the value of the **Action Type** field, which is the first field in the *Frame Properties* pane (regardless of the type of Action). The *Description* column describes what is captured for this Action Type. Finally, the *Category* column identifies the broad category of action that this Action Type falls into. Unsurprisingly, the *Frame Properties* pane is slightly different for each of these categories—although there are several common elements, as we shall see. The various fields and buttons in the *Frame Properties* pane are described separately for each of these categories, later in this chapter.

Action	Description	Category
Drag	Dragging an object across the screen. A drag-and-drop action will typically consist of a **Left begin drag** action, followed by one or more **Drag** actions, and ending in a **Left button up** action. Refer to the section *Recording drag-and-drop actions* in *Chapter 2, Recording a Simulation* for more information.	Mouse
Keyboard	Pressing a single key or key combination on the keyboard.	Keyboard
Left begin drag	Clicking down with the left mouse button on an object on the screen, and beginning to drag it, while continuing to hold down the left mouse button.	Mouse
Left button down	Pressing down on the left mouse button, without releasing it. Normally, this would be followed by a Left button up action, indicating that the user is required to click and hold an object for a period.	Mouse
Left button up	Releasing the left mouse button after it has previously been held down (see also **Left button down**).	Mouse
Left click	A single click on an object with the left mouse button.	Mouse
Left double-click	Double-clicking on an object with the left mouse button.	Mouse
Left triple-click	Triple-clicking on an object with the left mouse button.	Mouse
Middle begin drag	Clicking down on an object with the middle mouse button, and beginning to drag it, whilst continuing to hold down the middle mouse button.	Mouse
Middle button down	Clicking down on the middle mouse button.	Mouse
Middle button up	Releasing the right mouse button, after it has previously been held down.	Mouse
Middle click	A single click on an object, with the middle mouse button.	Mouse
Middle double-click	Double-clicking on a screen object, with the middle mouse button.	Mouse
Middle triple-click	Triple-clicking on an object, with the middle mouse button.	Mouse

Table 4-3 Action Types and their Descriptions

Action	Description	Category
Point	Pointing to an object on the screen (effectively, hovering the cursor over it).	Mouse
Right begin drag	Clicking down with the right mouse button on an object on the screen, and beginning to drag it, whilst continuing to hold down the right mouse button.	Mouse
Right button down	Clicking down on the right mouse button.	Mouse
Right button up	Releasing the right mouse button, after it has previously been held down.	Mouse
Right click	A single click on an object with the right mouse button.	Mouse
Right double-click	Double-clicking on a screen object with the right mouse button.	Mouse
Right triple-click	Triple-clicking on an object with the right mouse button.	Mouse
String input	Entering a text string.	String input
Wheel	Scrolling the mouse wheel. Note that UPK does not distinguish between scrolling the mouse wheel up and scrolling it down.	Mouse

Let's look at the three varieties of the *Action Properties* pane, by way of a few examples.

Working with mouse Actions

When you record a mouse Action in a simulation, UPK identifies the screen element on which you clicked—most of the time. Sometimes it does not manage to identify the exact object, or captures an unrealistically large area around where you actually clicked (or simply identifies the entire screen as the Action Area). On rare occasions it identifies entirely the wrong object, or even thinks that you performed a different type of action. Let's look at an example of this.

Open up the sample Topic that we recorded in *Chapter 2, Recording a Simulation*, and navigate to Frame 1 (this is the first **Action Frame**). For your reference, this Frame, as it appears in the *Topic Editor*, is shown in the following screenshot:

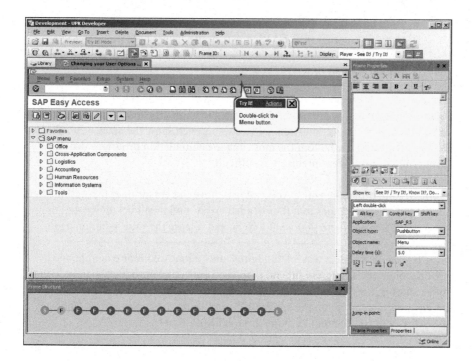

In this example, the action that we actually performed was a single-click on the **System** menu. Instead, the recording has captured a double-click somewhere on the menu bar, and identified it as a button and not a menu option. (To be fair, although UPK does occasionally make these mistakes, it typically doesn't make all of them at the same time—the example above has been "doctored" for the sake of illustration.)

Let's look at how to correct these mistakes.

Adjusting Action Areas

The first thing that we need to do is adjust the Action Area. There are three ways of adjusting the Action Area. These are:

- Click on the Action Area to select it, and then drag the 'handles' on the boundary of the Action Area to re-size it. This method is useful for making slight adjustments to the Action Area—for example, to set the edges of the Action Area closer to the object on which the user needs to click.

- Hold down the *Ctrl* key and click on where you want the upper-left corner of the Action Area to be. Then, with the mouse button and the *Ctrl* key held down, drag a marquee to where you want the bottom-right corner of the Action Area to be, and then release the mouse and the key. This method is useful if you want to just ignore what UPK captured, and define your own Action Area.

■ It is important to ensure that your Action Areas are correctly sized because in some of the printed output types a small graphic of that portion of the screenshot bounded by the Action Area is included in the Step/Action table, to show the area that should be clicked on. Refer to *Chapter 6, Publishing Your Content* for examples of the printed output types, showing these graphics.

- Hold down the *CTRL* key and double-click on the where you want the upper-left corner of the Action Area to be. Then, hold down the *SHIFT* key, and double-click on where you want the lower-right corner of the Action Area to be.

Unfortunately, UPK does not provide an easy way of absolutely resizing or repositioning an action area. It is not possible to explicitly specify the size and/or coordinates of the Action Area. UPK doesn't even show the size or coordinates in the status bar at the bottom (as most image manipulation programs do) so positioning Action Areas precisely is difficult.

If you need to move the entire Action Area, move the cursor over the Action Area so that the cursor changes to a four-headed arrow, and then click down and drag the Action Area to where you want it to be and release the mouse button again.

UPK does not provide a way of "nudging" an Action Area. For example, most applications—including the full suite of Microsoft Office products—allow you to move an object one pixel at a time by holding down the *CTRL* key (or sometimes the *ALT* key, depending on the application) and using the cursor (arrow) keys to move the object in the required direction. UPK does not.

These limitations mean that the only way to change the size or position of an Action Area is by using the mouse, and a mouse is not a great tool for pixel-perfect positioning (and a trackball or track pad is even worse!).

There are a few other buttons in the *Frame Properties* pane that are relevant to Action Areas. These are described in the table below:

Button	Name	Purpose
☐	**Action Area on/off**	Selecting this button will prevent the border around the Action Area from being displayed during on-line playback. This may be a useful option if you don't want to give the user too much in the way of clues. It is also useful if you want to give the appearance of automatically responding to a user's Action, and have several Alternative Paths (and therefore several Action Areas) defined for the same Frame. We look at this latter possibility in *Chapter 14, Allowing Alternatives*.
⬚	**Modify Action Areas**	If you click on this button, then a drop-down menu is displayed, with a further three buttons. These buttons are shown in the next three rows of this table.

In UPK 11.1 the **Modify Action Areas** button is annd the **Copy Action Area** button are only enabled if you navigate to the Frame by clicking on it in the **Frame Structure** pane. This has been partially fixed in UPK 12, as the **Modify Action Areas** button is now always available, but the **Copy Action Area** button is still only available if you navigate to the Frame by clicking on it..

Button	Name	Purpose
	Create Action Area	Select this option if you want to create one or more additional Action Areas for the same Frame. If you do this, then the user will be allowed to click on any of the Action Areas in order to progress to the next screen. Note that this is not something that you would normally want to do, as the Bubble can only point to a single Action Area, regardless of how many Action Areas you define. However, you may find it useful if (for example) you have a hyperlink over two (uneven-length) lines.
	Delete Action Area	Select this option if you want to delete an Action Area. Note that you must have at least one Action Area (for mouse or string input actions), so you would only want to do this if you had previously created an additional Action Area and then decided that you didn't want it after all. You need to make sure that you select the Action Area that you want to delete before you click on this option.
	Copy Action Area	Select this option if you want to replace the current Action Area on a Frame (or all Action Areas, if you have defined more than one) with a copy of the Action Area(s) from the previous Frame. This is useful where you record 'click-in'/'enter text' Action pairs, to ensure that the action areas are exactly the same (otherwise they can appear to 'jump' during playback, which is distracting at best). Another practical use of this feature is where you want the Action Areas on successive Frames to be exactly the same size and/or in the same position.

✛ The **Copy Action Area** function does not work correctly in UPK 11.1 – although the Action Area will be copied, this copy is lost as soon as you navigate away from the Frame. To make the copy 'stick' you need to click on one of the other action area buttons (for example, toggle the **Action Area On/Off** button off and then on again). This has been fixed in UPK 12.

Adjusting Print Areas

The **Print Area** for a Frame is the area of the screenshot that will be used as the 'thumbnail' image for the step in the printed output types (for example, the System Process document and the Job Aid - refer to *Chapter 6, Publishing your Content* for more information of these).

By default, the Action Area is used as the Print Area - because you want your users to see the area that is being clicked on. However, sometimes this is not particularly useful - for example, when clicking in an empty input field. We can see this example on Frame 5 of our initial recording, where we click in the **Function** field. The System Process step for this (once the Action Area has been resized as explained above) appears as follows:

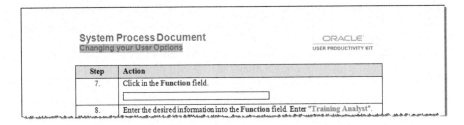

Step	Action
7.	Click in the **Function** field.
8.	Enter the desired information into the **Function** field. Enter "Training Analyst".

You can see that this does not really help the users identify the exact position on the screen. It would be better if the image showed some of the screenshot around the Action Area to allow the user to better locate it. To do this, we define a separate Print Area. How much of the screenshot you include in the Print Area is up to you, but for this example, we will include the input field label. We can do this by carrying out the following steps:

1. Go to the Frame for which you want to set the Print Area.

2. Because your Print Area will typically overlap the Action Area, you may find it easier to hide the display of the Action Area whilst you are making your adjustments. To do this, deselect the **Show Action Area** toggle button (⬚).

3. Make sure that the **Show Print Area** toggle button (⬚) is selected, so that you can see what you are doing.

4. Click on the **Modify action and print areas** button (⬚), and select **Create Print Area** (⬚) from the shortcut menu.

5. A magenta box with a dashed border is placed in the center of the screenshot. Move this to the required area, and resize it if necessary. You do this in exactly the same way as you would move and/or resize and Action Area (see *Adjusting Action Areas* on page 111 for instructions on how to do this).

● Unlike Action Areas, it is only possible to define a single Print Area for a Frame.

For our example, we have created a Print Area that includes the existing Action Area, and also takes in the field name. In the Topic Editor, this appears as follows (note that in this example, the Action Area is also visible, for comparison.

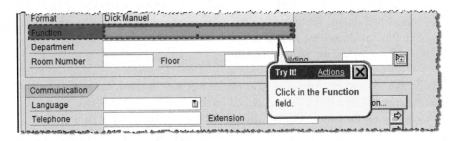

Now let's look at how this appears in the System Process document:

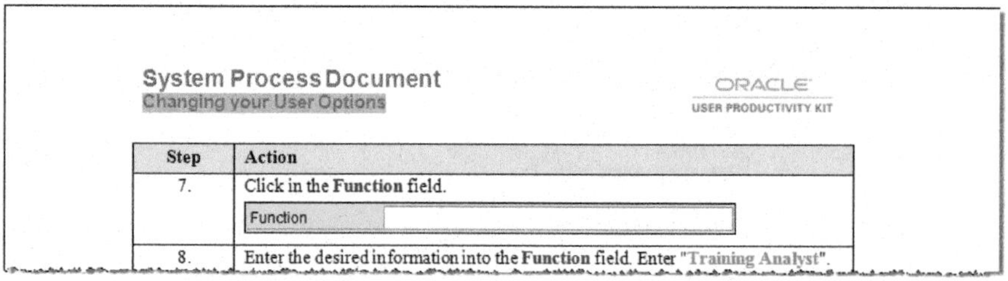

Now the 'thumbnail' image is a bit more useful, giving some context to the empty field in which the user is being told to click.

When you insert a Print Area, this tells UPK to stop using the Action Area as the Print Area. If you want to go back to using the Action Area as the Print Area, simply delete the Print Area by clicking on the **Modify action and print areas** button (🔲), and selecting **Delete Print Area** (🔲) from the shortcut menu.

Adjusting Bubble Text

The next thing that needs to be fixed in our sample exercise is the Bubble Text. In Frame 1 of our recording (which we looked at when adjusting the Action Area, on page 111), the captured text is "**Double-click the menu button**", which is clearly incorrect. So where does this text come from? The text comes from the Template attached to the Topic (see the section *Setting your content defaults* in *Chapter 2, Recording a Simulation*). The actual text generated by the Template is determined by what UPK considers to be the *context* of the action. During recording, UPK captures four things specific to the action:

1. The action that was performed
2. The application in which the action was performed (**Application**)
3. The type of object against which the action was performed (**Object type**)
4. The name of the specific object that the action was performed against (**Object name**)

These four things are shown in the *Frame Properties* pane. The diagram below shows an example of the portion of the *Frame Properties* pane that contains this information, along with the associated Bubble Text from the Player, and identifies the relationship between the two.

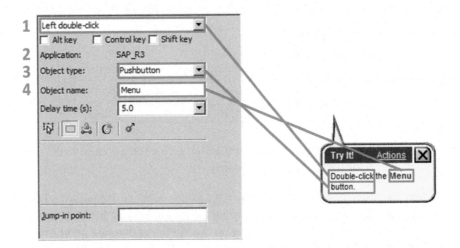

So if we want to change the Bubble Text, we can simply adjust the values of the context-related information in the *Action Properties* pane. Of these four, the **Application** cannot be changed, and the **Object name** is simply a text field that can be over-typed with any value that you like—regardless of whether this is the name of a valid object or not.

● With a little work, you can define your own Object Types, which we will do in *Chapter 16, Customizing UPK*.

The **Object type** is a little more restrictive. UPK only recognizes a certain set of Object Types, and it is only possible to select one of these predefined Object Types in the **Object type** field. *Appendix B, Object Types* lists all of the possible Object Types, and specifies the Bubble Text generated by the Template for each of these.

Many of the Template Texts are unimaginative. Some don't even make sense (such as "**Click the <ObjectName> sound**"). There is also little point in having separate Object Types that give exactly the same result (as all of the Pager ones do, and all of the Scrollbar Button ones do). However, bear in mind that UPK is doing its best to capture the context of what you do (that is, the actions that you perform during the recording), and uses the captured Action, Object Type, and Object Name to provide the most meaningful Template Text that it can. No, it's not always right, but it is acceptable more often than not. Additionally, providing multiple Object Types (even if it does not manage to correctly identify all of these all of the time) does allow for a good degree of flexibility. Firstly, you can change the Bubble Text simply by selecting a different Object Type in the *Action Properties* pane. Secondly, you can change the Bubble Text for a specific Object Type by customizing the templates themselves. (Customizing templates is covered in *Chapter 16, Customizing UPK*.)

Now that we understand the context a little better, let's look at how we can use this new-found knowledge to fix our example. You will recall that the Bubble Text generated from the Template was "**Double-click the Menu button.**". We can fix this by carrying out the following steps:

1. The **"Double-click"** text can be replaced by **"Click"** simply by changing the Action to **Left Click**.

2. The **"Menu"** text can be replaced simply by over-typing the **Object name** field with the correct menu name, which in our example is **System**.

3. The **"button"** text can be changed by selecting a new Object Type in the **Object type** field. Based on the table in *Appendix B, Object Types*, we will choose an Object Type of **Menu entry**.

After making these changes, our *Frame Properties* pane and the resultant Bubble Text are as shown in the following diagram (where the numbers correspond to the corresponding information for the *Frame Properties* pane shown in the illustration above):

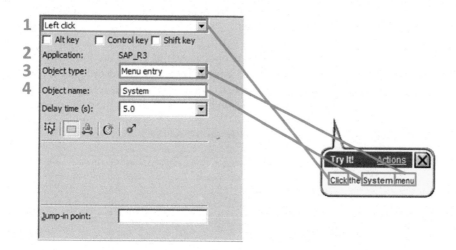

So there we have it. The Bubble Text now says just what we want it to and we didn't even need to revert to Custom Text (which we'll look at later in this chapter).

Ignoring context

In some circumstances, you may not to want to use UPK's context capture at all. In this case, you can select the **Ignore context** toggle button (ⓒ). This has two effects:

1. Template Text will not be used, because UPK has no context information on which to base it. However, there are other ways of removing the Template Text from a Bubble, as we will see in the section *Working with string input Actions* on page 121.

2. If you are using context-sensitive help links from your application, then the current Frame (for which you disabled the context) will not be

considered as a target for help. Context-sensitive help is described in *Chapter 15, Integrating UPK with Other Applications*.

For the sake of completeness, there is one final button in the 'Action' area of the *Frame Properties* pane that we have not yet looked at. This is the **Change end point** button (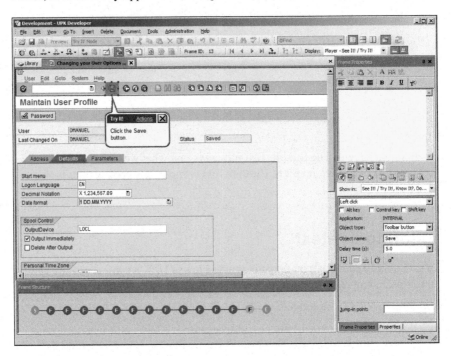). This is not strictly related to Action Areas, so we will not cover it here. Instead, we will describe it in *Chapter 14, Allowing Alternatives*.

Working with keyboard actions

The second category of action that we will look at is the **Keyboard** category. This category includes all actions that consist of a single key-press or key combination. However, it excludes the use of the keyboard to enter one or more characters into an input field on the screen; that is covered by the **String input** action category, which is explained later in this chapter.

Let's examine keyboard actions by way of an example. If you are following along with the sample exercises, open up the sample Topic that we recorded in *Chapter 2, Recording a Simulation*, and navigate to Frame **13**. For your reference, this Frame, as it currently appears in the *Topic Editor*, is shown in the next screenshot:

● Changing the Action Type in the *Topic Editor* also has the advantage that you do not need to go back into the application and record anything new. This can be useful if recreating the scenario that you originally captured is problematic.

In this Frame, we are asking the user to save their changes by clicking on the **Save** button on the toolbar. This is a mouse-click action. However, for the sake of variety, let's assume that we want the user to use the keyboard shortcut *CTRL+S* instead. We *could* do this by recapturing the action (via the **Recapture action** button (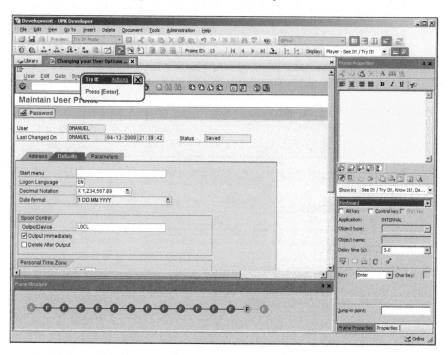), or via menu option **Edit | Recapture | Action**), but handily, UPK lets you change the type of action for a Frame directly from within the *Topic Editor*. You can change a mouse-click action into a key-press action (as we will do here); you can change a single-left-click into a double-right-click; you can even change a mouse-click action into a string input action. All you need to do is select the required action in the **Action Type** field of the *Frame Properties* pane.

In our example, we will change the **Left click** action to a **Keyboard** action. Once we do this, the Frame appears as follows, in the *Topic Editor*:

The first thing to notice here is that the Action Area (which was on top of the **Save** button) has disappeared. This makes sense, as keyboard Actions do not have Action Areas (they are the only category of Action that do not). The next thing to notice is that the Template Text has changed from "**Click the Save button**" to "**Press [Enter]**". Note that UPK assumes a default key of **[Enter]**, but you can specify any required key (or key combination) in the *Frame Properties* pane, as we shall see.

Now that we have an **Action Type** of **Keyboard** selected in the *Frame Properties* pane, the **Object Type** and **Object Name** fields are grayed out. This is because they (like the Action Area itself) are not relevant for keyboard Actions. Instead, two additional fields are now available in the *Frame Properties* pane. These are the **Key** field, and the **Char key** field. If they keyboard action is to press a single *character* key (*A-Z, 0-9, !@#$%^&*()_+,* and so on), select <**Character**> from the **Key** field's drop-down list, and enter the single character in the **Char key** field. If the keyboard action is to press a *special* key (*ENTER, ESCAPE, DELETE, F1-*

F12, and so on), then you would select this key from the **Key** field's drop-down list.

There are three additional options that are available in the *Frame Properties* pane that relate to **Keyboard** actions. These are the **Alt key**, **Control key**, and **Shift key** check-boxes. These are used for specifying key combinations. So if the action that you want the user to perform is to press *CTRL+ALT+DELETE*, then you would select **Delete** in the **Key** field, and select both the **Alt key** and **Ctrl key** check-boxes. Note that although these three options are most commonly used with keyboard Actions, they can also be used with mouse-click Actions so you can (for example) record a *SHIFT*-click Action.

For our exercise, we want the action to be pressing *CTRL+S*. We therefore need to enter *S* in the **Char key** field, and select the **Control key** check-box. Our Frame then looks like the example shown in the following screenshot:

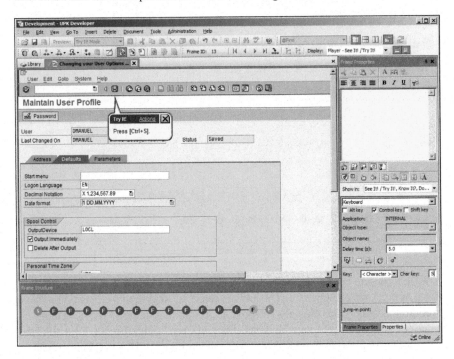

● What we have done here is fairly unrealistic and done purely for the purposes of demonstration. In this particular case, what we are more likely to do is leave the mouse-click action as it is, and add the key-press as an **Alternative Action**. Alternative Actions are covered in *Chapter 14, Allowing Alternatives*.

As you can see, our Bubble Text now correctly specifies "**Press [Ctrl+S]**". We have now completely changed the Action Type for the Frame. If we wanted to, we could change it back, but UPK will have forgotten our **Object type** and **Object name**, so we would have to capture these again. It would, however, have remembered the size and position of our Action Area, so at least we wouldn't need to recreate that.

That's really all there is to know about keyboard Actions. There are no further settings, and nothing else that we can do with them. So let's proceed on to the most interesting category of Action—string input.

Working with string input Actions

The last type of Action that we will adjust is the string input action, which is the most complex type of Action. Again, we will examine this type of Action by way of an example. If you are following along with the sample exercises, open up the sample Topic that we recorded in *Chapter 2, Recording a Simulation*, and navigate to Frame **4**. For your reference, this Frame, as it currently appears in the *Topic Editor*, is shown in the following screenshot:

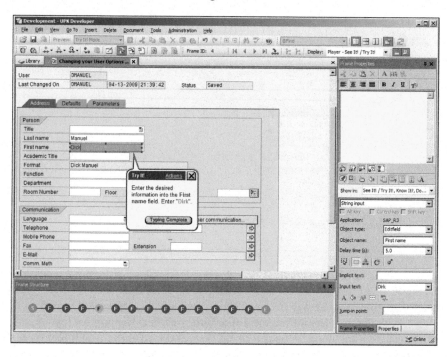

We will again be concentrating on the options available in the *Frame Properties* pane, which is located on the rightmost side of this screenshot. Some of the information in this pane is the same as for other categories of action, namely:

1. **Action type:** For string input actions, this will (unsurprisingly) always be **String input**.

2. **Application:** The application within which the action was recorded.

3. **Object type:** For string input actions, this will always be **Editfield**. This always creates a special type of Action Area, into which text can be entered.

4. **Object name:** The name of the input field into which the text is being entered.

For further information about these four properties, refer to the section *Working with mouse Actions* on page 110.

Now, let's go back to our example. In Frame 4, the action that we recorded was over-typing the value **Dick** with **Dirk**. There is a problem with this, as you can see if you play this exercise as-is. Here is a screenshot of the same Frame in the Player:

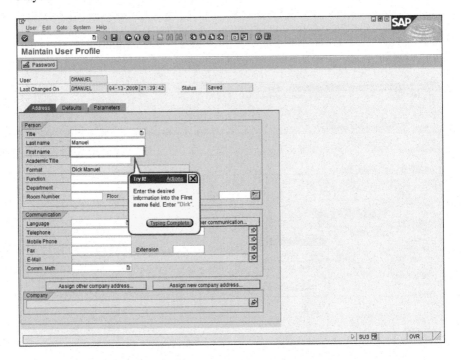

Notice anything missing? If you need a hint, compare this screenshot from the Player with the screenshot from the **Topic Editor** earlier. The original text of **Dick** that we want to over-type is missing. As mentioned above, an **Object type** of **Editfield** creates a special type of Action Area. In fact, it is a text box, with a solid background, that is overlaid onto the screenshot (unlike mouse-click Action Areas, which are rectangles with a transparent background). What you can see in the screenshot above is a white rectangle (with a red border) overlaid on top of the screen's input field. This is hiding the actual field, and making it appear empty. If we want the field to look correct (with the initial value in the field) then we need to explicitly specify this text (UPK is not clever enough to 'scrape' the screen and retrieve this value for us). You do this via the **Implicit text** field in the *Frame Properties* pane. For our example, we need to enter an **Implicit text** of **Dick**. This is shown in the following screenshot:

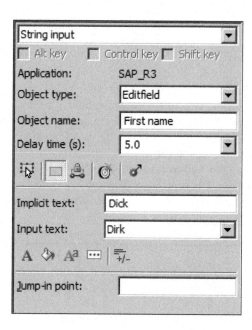

Now, the screen appears correctly in the Player, as shown in the next screenshot:

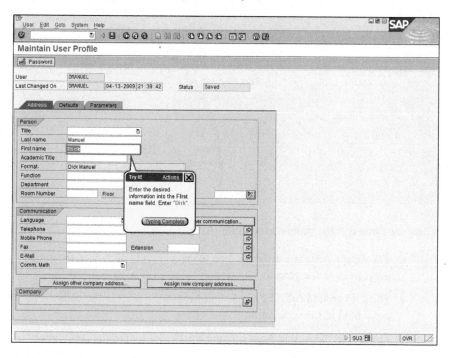

The screen now shows the current value of the field. This text is automatically selected, so the user can just start typing to replace it. Note also that this is a fully-functional text field. The user can click anywhere in the text string, use the cursor to move through the text character by character, and use the *DELETE* and *BACKSPACE* keys to delete some or all of the text. This is very useful as it means that the user will not be marked incorrect in *Try It?* mode if they happen to use a different way of editing the text than the one recorded by the author, as long as the final text is correct.

There are still a couple of other problems with this field that we need to fix. Firstly, the Action Area is larger than the actual field. This is not so obvious in the *See It!*, *Try It!*, and *Do It!* modes, where the border of the Action Area masks the problem, but if you play the exercise in *Know It?* mode, in which the border of the Action Area is not shown (or you can simply hide the border in the *Topic Editor* by deselecting the **Action area on/off** toggle button (▫), then the problem is easier to see. The screenshot below, taken from *Know It?* mode, with the area containing the input field magnified for clarity, illustrates this problem:

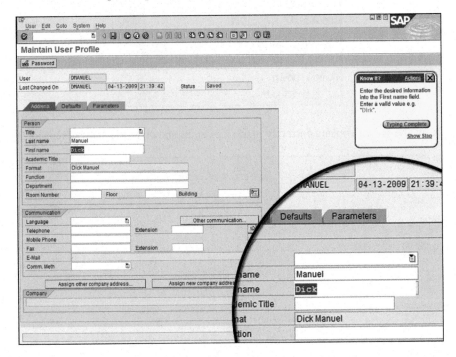

There are three specific problems with this Action Area:

- The Action Area is a different size (narrower and taller) than the actual input field on the screen.

- The background color of the Action Area is different to the color of the input field in the application.

- The text in the Action Area is using a different font to the application itself.

Let's look at how to correct each of these problems.

Adjusting the string input action area

An incorrectly-sized Action Area is actually one of the most common problems with UPK recordings (and one of the most jarring). Sadly, it is also something that often goes uncorrected. This is because adjusting Action Areas is a bit fiddly and, for string input Action Areas, requires a bit of trial-and-error. There are a couple of things that make it so fiddly.

Firstly, as described previously, UPK does not provide a way to precisely size and position an Action Area. Unfortunately, sizing and positioning a string input Action Area correctly requires pixel-perfect positioning.

A further problem is that the position set for the Action Area in the *Topic Editor* does not always translate directly into the Player. For some reason, string input Action Areas are tend to shift slightly. Normally only by a single pixel, and normally down and to the right, but one pixel is enough to destroy the 'illusion of reality', which is what you are trying to preserve. It doesn't help that UPK automatically aligns the text at the top of the Action Area, with zero space before it, so you often need to adjust the horizontal position of the Action Area so that the text appears in the correct position in the published Player.

▲ Frustratingly, UPK does not seem to position the String Input Action Area consistently in the various play modes: you get the Action Area in the perfect position for *Try It!* mode, only to find that it is then a pixel or two out in *Know It?* mode. There's no solution or workaround—you just need to pick the one mode you want to be perfect, and live with that.

You therefore need to identify the position of the Action Area relative to the borders of the field that will result in the 'best fit' for the field. This does, unfortunately, seem to be a matter of trial and error (which is why many authors never bother), but the good news is that once you work it out for one field, the relative positioning is the same for all string input Action Areas in all of your simulations (at least for the same application). For example, I have found that leaving space between the action area and the input field of zero pixels at the top, one pixel on the left, two pixels on the right, and three pixels at the bottom, results in a good fit in the Player. This is shown in the following screenshot, which has been scaled up to emphasize the spacing:

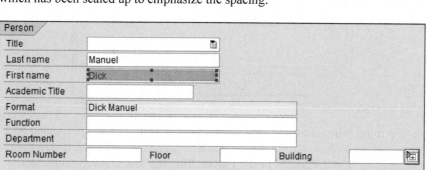

Yes, it is fiddly, but it does create a good fit in the Player (as you can see in the 'final version' screenshot at the end of this section). Besides, this book is all about creating *quality* training, right?

How to adjust the size and position of the Action Area was explained earlier in this chapter, in the section *Working with mouse Actions* on page 110. Refer to that section, and adjust the Action Area for the string input Action as described above.

In order to make the exercise as realistic as possible we also need to make sure that the background color of the Action Area is *exactly* the same color as the actual input field in the application. This is what we will look at adjusting next.

Adjusting the string input background color

As explained above, string input Action Areas are the only types of Action Areas that are not 'transparent'. They have a background color because the field may already contain text that would 'show through' if the action area was transparent. By default, the background color of a string input Action Area is white, but you can change this to any color you like, by clicking on the **String input background color** button (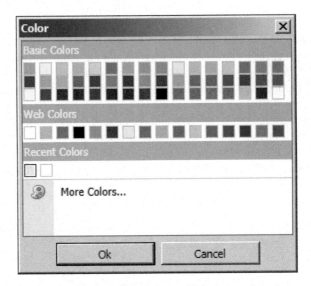), which is located below the **Input text** field. Clicking on this button displays the *Color* dialog box, where you can choose one of the predefined standard colors or, by clicking on the **More Colors** button, specify or select the exact color that you want to use. An example of this dialog box is shown below:

✦ The *Color* dialog box changed format slightly in UPK 12, with the addition of the 'web-friendly' colors palette, and renaming of **Define Custom Colors** to **More Colors**. Its use remains almost identical.

Bear in mind, when choosing a background color for the string input Action Area, that the background color must *exactly* match the color of the text field in the application **as it appears in the Player**. This last caveat is very important. UPK will (by default, although you can remove this option) down-sample screen prints to use only 256 colors. UPK does this because it makes the screenshot files (stored in .gif format) smaller, and therefore faster to load. This is not necessarily an issue in most Windows applications, although you may want to disable this option when recording color-sensitive applications such as photo editors. However, it does mean that there may well be slight differences between the colors in the actual application and the colors in the Player. You should therefore aim to match the color in the Player (as this is what your users will see) and not the color in the application. This means that you will need to publish (or preview) your first exercise, so that you can identify the correct color, before you can truly finalize the exercise.

Unfortunately, UPK does not include a *dropper*, which would allow you to select the required color by clicking on it. Thankfully, there are many free color dropper utilities (such as Colorzilla (`www.colorzilla.com`)) that you can use to identify the correct hue/saturation/luminescence or red/green/blue values, and then simply type these values into the input field in the *Colors* dialog box, shown below:

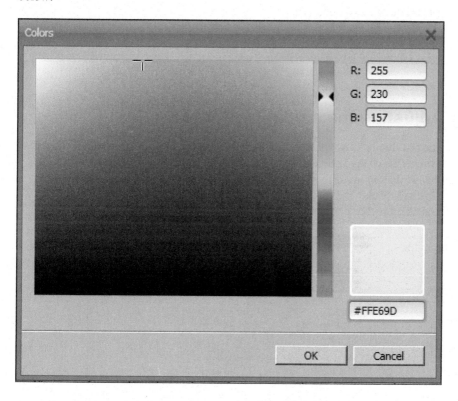

For our sample exercise, we are recording in the SAP application, and the background of the active field in SAP is a deep yellow color. In the Player, this is manifested as red **255**, blue **230**, and green **157**, as shown in the previous screenshot. We will change the background color of the Action Area for our string input Action to this value.

Some common applications and the default string input background colors are as follows:

- **Web applications, including SAP CRM, PeopleSoft, JDE (in Internet Explorer):**
  RGB 255, 255, 255 (White)

- **SAP R/3 Client:**
  Active field: 255, 230, 157 (Can vary slightly between SAPGui releases)
  Other: RGB 255, 255, 255 (White)

- **MS Office / Windows applications:**
  RGB 255, 255, 255 (White)

- **Oracle E-Business Suite:**
  Mandatory fields: RGB 255, 250, 156
  Non-mandatory fields: RGB 255, 255, 255 (White)
  Search fields: RGB 223, 234, 247 (Blue)

Adjusting the string input font

The last thing that we need to adjust in this example is the font used for the text string. This change will apply to both the **Input text** and any **Implicit text**. To change the font used for the text, click on the **String input font** button (A). This will display the *Font* dialog box, shown below, which lists all of the fonts available on your computer.

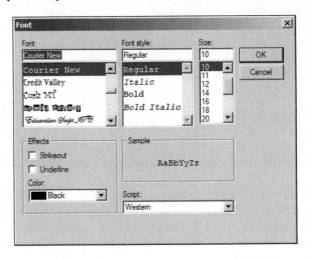

■ To save scrolling through the list of fonts (which may be quite long), you can simply start typing the name of the font that you are looking for to automatically scroll to that font. You can then use the *TAB* key to move to the **Font Style** column, use the cursor keys to scroll down to the required style, press *TAB* again to move to the **Size** column, cursor down to the required size, and then press *ENTER* to confirm your selections.

Select the required font from the **Font** list. You can also choose the font size, style and color, and set the font to be underlined or struck-through (you'd never do this for a string input field, but this same dialog box is re-used in other areas of UPK, where such options make more sense).

As with the background color, it is important that the font that you choose *exactly* matches the font used in the application. This might take a little trial and error, but once you find the correct font, it is normally the same for all input fields within the application.

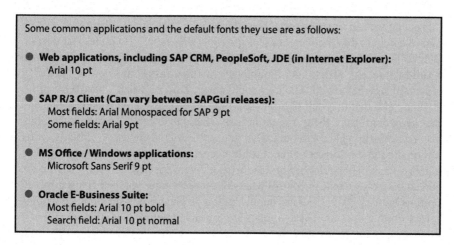

Some common applications and the default fonts they use are as follows:

- **Web applications, including SAP CRM, PeopleSoft, JDE (in Internet Explorer):**
  Arial 10 pt

- **SAP R/3 Client (Can vary between SAPGui releases):**
  Most fields: Arial Monospaced for SAP 9 pt
  Some fields: Arial 9pt

- **MS Office / Windows applications:**
  Microsoft Sans Serif 9 pt

- **Oracle E-Business Suite:**
  Most fields: Arial 10 pt bold
  Search field: Arial 10 pt normal

We've now fixed the Action Area size, the background color, and the font. Our Frame will now look like the example shown in the following screenshot (taken from *Know It?* mode, so that you can better appreciate the sizing and positioning of the input field):

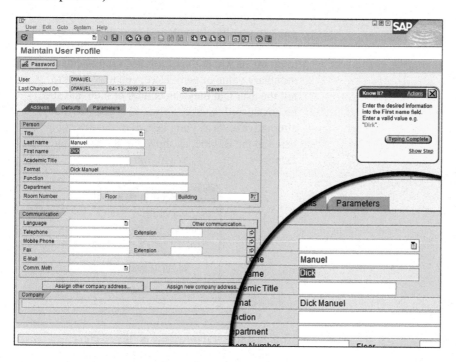

This is now perfect. You would be hard pushed to tell the difference between this Frame and the actual screen in the application. This is exactly the level of quality for which we are aiming.

Controlling what the user can enter

The *appearance* of the text field is now perfect. However, there are still things that we can improve (or at least that we could change—whether it is an improvement in this particular case, is possibly debatable). If you look at the Bubble Text in the example above you will see that the user is instructed to **Enter a valid value, e.g. "Dirk"**. As it turns out, "a valid value" in *Know It?* mode is actually anything at all. The user could enter "**Dirk**", "**Dork**", "**asdfgh**", or anything else that they felt like. These would all be considered equally valid, and the user would 'pass' the test regardless of what they entered. In some cases, this may be perfectly valid. After all, what you are testing is the user's ability to enter information in the correct fields; it is not necessarily a typing test. However, in other cases, it may be important that the user enters exactly the value specified and nothing else. You can control what the user can enter via the **String input options** button (⬚). Clicking on this button displays a pop-up menu containing several further options. These options are explained below. Note that several of these options can be combined.

The first two options directly relate to the actual text string that the user can enter:

Button	Name	Purpose
⬚	**Add new text**	By default, the user is told to enter the value captured during the recording. By using this option, you can specify alternative strings that the user can enter. A good example of when you would want to do this is where the user is required to enter a monetary value of zero. Here, you may want to tell the user that they can enter **0** or **0.00** and still be considered 'correct'. You can specify as many alternative texts as you like. All of them will be listed in the Bubble, as shown in the following example:

Note that if you remove the ability to enter 'anything' (see below) you will want to explicitly tell the user what values are valid. If you leave the 'anything' option then this is less important.

Button	Name	Purpose
	Replace text	This option allows you to change the **Input text** from the value captured during the recording (for some reason, the **Input text** field is not directly editable itself—although the **Implicit text** field, which is directly below it, is).
		Note that if you want to change an alternative string (added via the **Add new text** option), then you must first select the alternative string (by using the **Input text** field's drop-down list button) so that it is displayed in the **Input text** field, and then select the **Replace text** option.
	Add 'something'	Selecting this option will add <something> to the 'allowed' list. This will allow users in *Know It?* mode to enter any text (regardless of whether this is the recorded text), but they must enter something (that is, they cannot leave the field blank). Note that you cannot select this option if you have specified more than one text value (via the **Add new text** button).
	Add 'anything'	Selecting this option will add <anything> to the 'allowed' list. This will allow users in *Know It?* mode to either enter *any* text (regardless of whether this is the recorded text), or just leave the field blank. Note that you cannot select this option if you have specified more than one text value (via the **Add new text** button).
	Add 'blank'	Selecting this option will add <blank> to the 'allowed' list. This will allow users in *Know It?* mode to leave the input field blank and still progress to the next step. A key difference between this option and adding <anything> is that it is possible to specify multiple alternative texts in conjunction with this option.

● The last three options are mutually exclusive; if you add one of these options to the 'allowed' list, then you will not be able to add either of the other two options. Note that although these three options affect the appearance of the Bubble Text in all playback modes, they only affect the what the user can enter in *Know It?* mode.

These last three options can be a little difficult to understand. The names of the possible selections can be misinterpreted, and it is also possible (indeed, necessary, in some cases) to specify multiple options. It is therefore worth examining these options in more detail, by way of some examples.

The main 'possible value' for the **Input text** field is the actual value entered during simulation capture. In our sample exercise, we recorded the entry of a text string of "**Dirk**" in the **First name** field. The *Bubble Properties* pane for this initially appears as follows (with the **Input text** drop-down displayed, for easy reference):

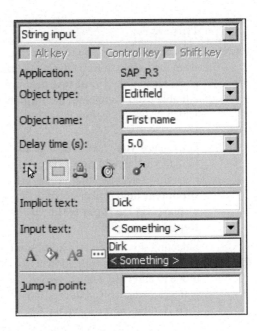

Note that the <Something> option is added automatically, along with the text that we explicitly entered. The option <Something> can be read as "The user must enter *something*" (that is, they cannot leave the field blank). Therefore, our Bubble Text (assuming that we are using the default Standard Template) will be as follows:

Mode	Bubble Text	Valid input
See It! / Try It!		"Dirk"
Know It?		Anything, but the field cannot be left blank.
Do It!!		n/a

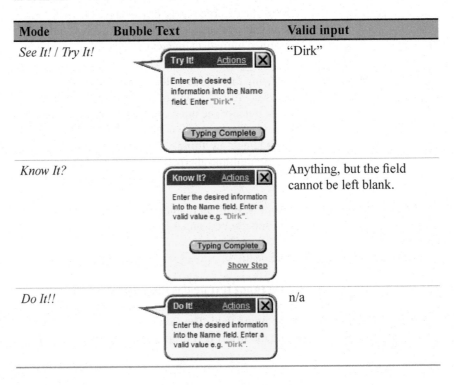

Now let's remove the <Something> option, and replace it with <Anything>. The *Frame Properties* pane then shows:

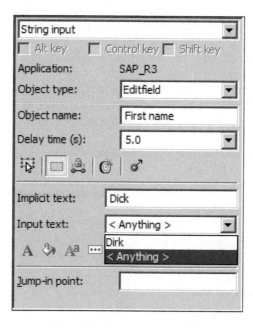

This will give us the following Bubble Text (again, assuming that we are using the default Standard Template):

Mode	Bubble Text	Valid input
See It! / Try It!		"Dirk"
Know It?		Anything, or the field can be left blank.
Do It!!		n/a

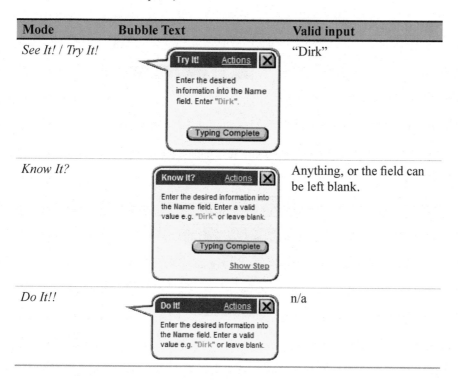

The only difference with these texts and the previous ones (using <Something>) is that the text "**or leave blank**" has been added for the *Know It?* and *Do It?* modes. Interestingly, you can see that in *See It!* and *Try It!* modes, the user is not given the option to leave the field blank, but they are in *Know It?* and *Do It!* modes. Maybe this is the way it is supposed to work; maybe it is just a bug. Either way, it is something to be aware of when choosing text input options.

In general, <**Anything**> can be read as "The user can either enter a value or leave the field blank". And just like <**Something**>, the value that they enter can be absolutely anything, and not just the explicit text(s) specified.

Now, let's remove <**Anything**> and add <**Blank**> instead. The *Frame Properties* pane in this case is as follows:

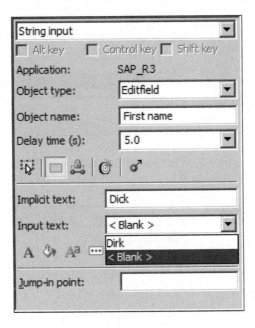

This will give us the following Bubble Text (again, assuming that we are using the default Standard Template):

Mode	Bubble Text	Valid input
See It! / Try It!	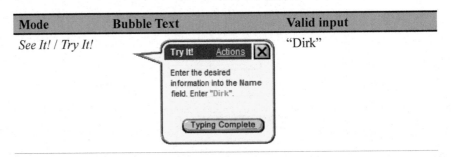	"Dirk"

Mode	Bubble Text	Valid input
Know It?	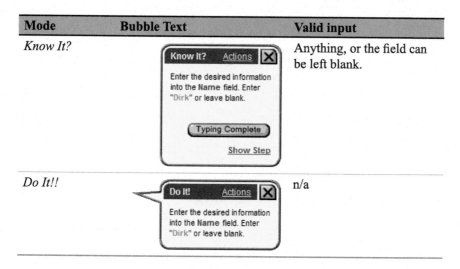	Anything, or the field can be left blank.
Do It!!	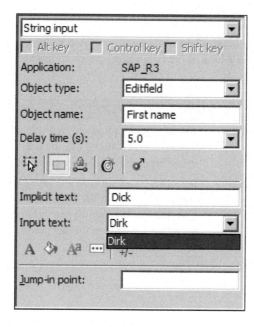	n/a

Again, the only difference is in *Know It!?* mode, where the user can either enter the specified input string, or they can leave the field blank. They no longer have the option to enter whatever they feel like entering.

Finally, for the fun of it, we'll remove all of the text input options apart from the original explicit text (captured during the recording). The easiest way of doing this is to select the **Clear list** option (▒) from the **String input options** context menu. The *Frame Properties* pane for this is shown in the next screenshot:

The Bubble Text is then displayed as follows:

Mode	Bubble Text	Valid input
See It! / Try It!	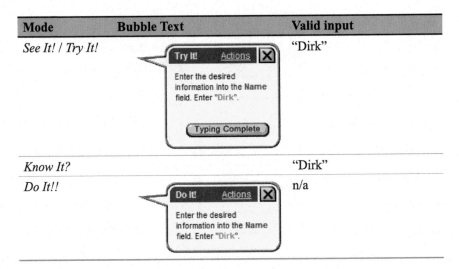	"Dirk"
Know It?		"Dirk"
Do It!!		n/a

Hmm, well that's interesting! In *Know It?* mode you get nothing? Well, by default, yes. If you look at the *Bubble properties* pane (which is described later), you'll see that the **Display template text in Know It? mode** toggle button ( ) has been deselected. This option is automatically selected when you include the <Something> option in the **Input text** options, but as soon as you remove this option, UPK (for some reason only known to its developers) deselects this option. Fortunately, all you need to do is manually re-select it, and the template text will appear in *Know It?* mode again (the text will be exactly the same as the text for *Do It!* mode, as shown previously).

Now that we have a better understanding of the <Anything>, <Something>, and <Blank> options, let's look at the remaining options in the **String input options** context menu:

Button	Name	Purpose
	Clear List	Selecting this option will remove all of the string input options, and require the user to enter **only** the string input text explicitly specified.
	Delete entry	Selecting this option will delete the entry that is currently shown in the **Input text** field. Note that if you delete the default entry (the first entry in the drop-down list) then the next entry in the list will become the default.

Button	Name	Purpose
	Set to default	If you define more than one valid string (for example, "0.00" and "0") then these will appear in the **Input text** field drop-down in the order in which you define them (starting with the string that was captured during recording). The option at the top is the *default option*. This is the string that will appear in the Bubble Text, although the user will be able to enter any of the texts in the list. To make another string the default option, select it from the **Input text** drop-down list, and then click the **Set to default** button. The selected option will then be moved to the top of the drop-down list, and will be used as the default.

Case sensitivity and password fields

There are two last options related to input fields that we have not yet looked at. We do not need to use them in our example exercise, but for the sake of completeness, they are explained here.

Button	Name	Purpose
	String input case sensitivity	By default, string input actions are case insensitive. So for our example, the user could enter "Dirk", "dirk", "dIRK", and so on, and still be considered correct. If you want the user to enter the text string exactly as given (but bearing in mind that in some circumstances they may not be given any examples in *Know It?* mode), then you can select the **String input case sensitivity** toggle button to force this.
	Set as password field	For applications that require the user to enter a password, the user's entry is usually masked so that their input cannot be seen. If your string input action is for such a password field, then you can select this option. The user's input will then be masked when they type it during playback. However, note that UPK chooses to mask the input using small circles ('bullets'), so if your application uses asterisks for masking (as is sometimes the case) then you will not be able to achieve a *perfect* match.

Changing the Bubble

In the previous section, *Adjusting Actions*, we looked at how to change Actions, and in the process influence the Bubble Text. However, this is only half of what we can do to change the Bubble. In this section, we will look at how to change the format of this Bubble and the text that it contains, and how to influence what text is displayed in which modes. As with adjusting the Action, all of this is controlled via the *Frame Properties* pane.

Bubble Properties

The upper portion of the *Frame Properties* pane contains information relating to the yellow 'speech bubble' that is overlaid on the screenshot. Although the Bubble is generated automatically, you can control the appearance and content of the Bubble via the *Frame Properties* pane. An example of the Bubble properties portion of the *Frame Properties* pane is shown in the following screenshot:

Changing the Bubble pointer

The Bubble pointer is the 'arm' that comes out of one corner of the Bubble, and points to a particular area on the screen. For Bubbles on Action Frames for mouse-click actions and string-input actions, UPK will create a Bubble with a pointer, and have this point to the Action Area. For keyboard actions, and Explanation Frames (discussed in *Chapter 9, Adding Value to Your Topics*), the Bubble will not have a pointer, and will (initially) be centered on the screenshot.

You can change the position of this pointer on the Bubble (that is, determine the location from which it extends from the Bubble), or remove the pointer altogether. This can be done for all Action Frames, and for Explanation Frames. You cannot add a pointer to a Decision Frame (discussed in *Chapter 14, Allowing Alternatives*). Additionally, note that Bubbles in *Know It?* mode do not have pointers in the published version (although they are visible in the *Topic Editor*), and are always positioned mid-way down the rightmost edge of the screenshot.

● *Know It?* mode is the only mode in which the user can reposition the bubble themselves.

To change the position of the pointer on a Bubble, carry out the steps described below:

1. Go to the Frame that contains the Bubble for which you want to change the pointer.

2. In the *Frame Properties* pane, click on the **Bubble Pointer** button (🖰). The following drop-down list appears below the button:

   🖰 Top left pointer
   🖰 Top right pointer
   🖰 Bottom left pointer
   🖰 Bottom right pointer
   🖰 Left top pointer
   🖰 Left bottom pointer
   🖰 Right top pointer
   🖰 Right bottom pointer
   ───────────────
   🖰 No pointer

3. Select the appropriate entry for the position at which you want the pointer to appear (or select the **No pointer** entry to remove the pointer altogether).

Note that UPK will automatically 'snap' and 'glue' the Bubble to the Action Area, and will therefore reposition the Bubble on the most appropriate edge of the Action Area, depending on the position of the pointer, and the amount of screen space available for the Bubble. If there is not enough space on the screen to attach the Bubble to the required side, then UPK will automatically change the pointer position and reposition the Bubble on another side of the Action Area. If you want to manually change the position of the Bubble, refer to *Repositioning the Bubble* on page 139.

Repositioning the Bubble

By default, UPK will 'attach' Bubbles for Frames that include an Action Area to the Action Area itself. If you move the Action Area, then the Bubble moves with it. For Frames without Action Areas (typically, Action Frames for keyboard actions and Explanation Frames) the Bubble is placed in the middle of the screen by default.

If the default position of the Bubble results in the Bubble obscuring a section of the screenshot that you want to be visible, or if you want the Bubble for an Explanation Frame to point to a specific area of the screenshot, then you can move the Bubble to a new location on the screenshot.

To move a Bubble on a Frame, carry out the steps described below:

1. Go to the Frame that contains the Bubble that you want to move.

2. Click on the Bubble header (which is blue, and contains the name of the mode for which it is being displayed), and drag it to the new location. Release the mouse button when the Bubble is in the required position.

3. If you are moving a Bubble for a Frame with an Action Area, then if you move the Bubble pointer into the proximity of the Action Area a light-blue marquee is shown around the Action Area. If you release the mouse button at this time, the Bubble will be snapped to the Action Area. You can stop the Bubble from snapping to the Action Area by holding down the *CTRL* key when moving the Bubble.

Note that you cannot move the Bubble for a Decision Frame. Note also that in *Know It?* mode, the Bubble will always be displayed in the vertical center of the rightmost edge of the Player screen, regardless of where you position it in the *Topic Editor*. The user has the ability to move the Bubble if it is obscuring key data or the action area, although if you know that the Bubble will obscure key data, you may want to include a text in the Bubble (and tag it for *Know It?* mode only, as explained later in this chapter) to inform the user that they should move the Bubble, as it is not immediately obvious that you *can* (let alone *should*) move it.

Changing the size of the Bubble

The Bubble is automatically resized to accommodate the amount of text (both Template Text and Custom Text) that is to be displayed in it. This is extremely useful because (as we shall see later) the amount of text in the Bubble may vary depending on the play mode being used.

The downside to this automatic resizing is that it is not possible to set a specific size or height-width ratio for the Bubble. Although UPK generally uses Bubbles of the same proportion (horizontal to vertical ratio), sometimes it will generate a short, wide Bubble, or a long, tall one. In other cases, the default shape may be obscuring key information on the screen that you could make visible if only you could resize the Bubble. Unfortunately, you can't.

What you *can* do is manually 'force' the shape of the Bubble by judicious use of non-breaking text (via the **Non-breaking Text** toggle button (![icon]) and/or line breaks). However, given that UPK may resize the Bubble depending on the mode in which it is displayed, this is extremely hit-and-miss. It is difficult to manually force a dimension that works well in every mode, so it is recommended that you do not even *try* to do this.

Adding an icon to a Bubble

You can add one of 35 built-in icons to a Bubble. You may want to do this to draw attention to a particular Bubble, or to identify specific types of information. In *Chapter 9, Adding Value to Your Topics* we use an icon to identify Explanation Frames. An example of a Bubble containing an icon is shown in the next screenshot:

To insert an icon into a Bubble, carry out the following steps:

1. In the *Frame Properties* pane, click on the **Bubble icon** button (▣), to display a drop-down list of available icons, as shown in the following screenshot:

● If you add an icon to a Bubble and then subsequently decide that you do not want to use an icon in the Bubble, then you can select the blank square in the upper-left corner of the icon drop-down list.

2. Click on the icon that you want to add to the Bubble.

You can add an icon to any Bubble, on any kind of Frame, with the exception of the Start Frame, End Frames, and Decision Frames. However, you should use icons sparingly and consistently (that is, always use the same icon to identify the same kind of information—both within a Topic and across all Topics in your Library). If every bubble contains an icon, your users will stop paying attention to them (especially as they are all the same size, and are all black and white) – and the whole point of using icons is to *draw* attention.

✛ The ability to hide the Bubble (for a Frame, or for the entire Topic) was introduced in UPK 3.6.1.

Hiding the Bubble

By default, the Bubble is always displayed on the screen during on-line playback. However, it is possible to hide the Bubble, so that it does not appear (in certain modes). To do this, simply deselect the **Display bubble in See It! and Try It! modes for this frame** toggle button (⊘). As the name suggests, this only

✛ In UPK11 the **Display bubble in See It! and Try It! modes for this frame** toggle button was renamed—from **Display bubble for this frame**— for clarity.)

applies to *See It!* mode and *Try It!* mode. It is not possible to hide the Bubble in *Know It?* mode or *Do It!* mode.

Note that although this feature hides the Bubble, it does not hide the Action Area, which will still appear, but with nothing pointing to it.

The ability to bide the Bubble is a particularly curious feature—at least with regards to the modes in which it takes effect. Being able to hide the Bubble in *See It!* mode is possibly useful, as it allows *See It!* mode to be used to present a 'clean' demonstration of the application without the distraction of little yellow overlays. However, the fact that using this option for *See It!* will also hide the Bubbles in *Try It!* mode makes it less useful – because typically you *do* want the Bubbles and their attendant explanations in *Try It!* mode.

Conversely, it would have been useful to be able to hide the Bubble in *Know It?* mode, where you don't necessarily want to give the user any information—and where, in cases where only the Template Text is provided, the bubble is empty anyway (so what is the point in displaying it at all?).

Note that hiding the Bubble altogether will override any mode tagging that you carry out for the text. That is, if you have text tagged as being visible in *See It!/ Try It!* mode, but have deselected the **Display bubble in See It! and Try It! modes for this frame** toggle button, this text (and the Bubble itself) will **not** appear during playback. Tagging text for different modes is discussed in the section *Tagging Custom Text for different modes* on page 153.

The **Display bubble in See It! and Try It! modes for this frame** toggle button applies to a specific Frame. It is also possible to hide Bubbles for an entire Topic in one fell swoop, via the Topic Properties. This is done via the **Show Bubbles** property in the **Topic** section, as shown below:

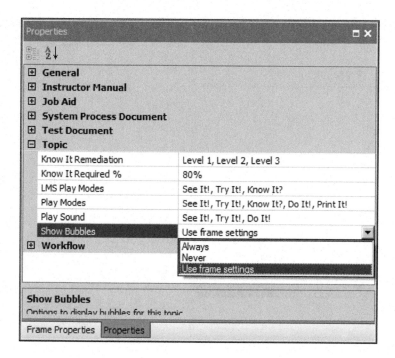

The following options are available:

- **Always**: *A*lways show all Bubbles, for all Frames, in all modes, regardless of the **Display bubble in See It! and Try It! modes for this frame** settings for individual Frames.

- **Never**: Hide all Bubbles, for all Frames, in all modes, regardless of the **Display bubble in See It! and Try It! modes for this frame** settings for individual Frames. Note that Action Areas are also hidden when you choose this option (at the Topic level). This is a little inconsistent with how the Frame-level function works.

- **Use frame settings**: Bubbles will either be displayed or not depending on the **Display bubble in See It! and Try It! modes for this frame** settings for the individual Frames. This is the default setting.

Note again that this setting only applies to *See It!* and *Try It!* modes.

- "All bubbles" literally means *all* Bubbles - including the Start Frame, End Frame, Decision Frames, Explanation Frames, and everything in between.

Hiding a Frame

In addition to hiding the bubble (for *See It!* and *Try It!* modes) on a specific Frame, it is also possible to hide an entire Frame during playback. Here, the functionality is a little more flexible (than that for hiding a Bubble) in that you can select the exact modes in which the Frame should be hidden. This is achieved by using the **Show in** setting in the *Frame Properties* pane, as shown in the screenshot below:

+ The ability to hide entire Frames was introduced in UPK 11.0.

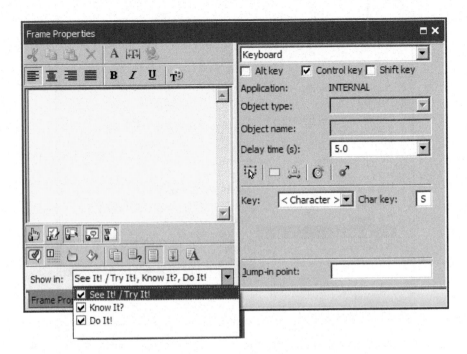

By default, all frames are shown in all modes. However, you can deselect **See It! / Try It!**, **Know It?**, or **Do It!** to hide the Frame in the associated modes, as required.

■ You can actually hide a Frame from *all* play modes, by deselecting all of the play modes in the **Show in** list. This could be useful if you **think** you want to remove Frames, but you're not sure if you'll need them again later. The Frames will still be saved in the Topic but will not appear in any play mode.

There are a number of reasons why you would want to hide a Frame in a specific playback mode. For example, you may be using the Topic in *Know It!* mode for knowledge verification purposes, but there may be some steps that you don't want to test the user on, such as routine or repetitive steps. Here, you can just deselect the **Know It?** check-box for the **Show in** option for these steps, so that you are only testing on the steps specific to the actions for which you need to verify knowledge. Alternatively, you may provide additional explanatory steps for *Try It!* mode and only want to provide a succinct set of steps in *Do It!* mode. Here, you would deselect the **Do It!** check-box for the **Show in** option for these additional steps.

✚ In UPK 11, If you wanted to hide a Frame that had a Alternative Actions, you needed to deselect the play mode for the Frame for every Alternative Action individually (actually, you had to go to the Alternative Action, then reselect the play mode and then deselect it again). This 'undocumented feature' has been corrected in UPK 12.

Note that the **Show in** settings apply both to the on-line Player formats and to the printed document formats.

Combining Frames

A further option for 'streamlining' playback—at least in *Do It!* mode—is the ability to *combine* Frames. Using this functionality, you indicate that the Bubble Text for a specific Frame should be combined with the Bubble text for the following Frame in *Do It!* mode (only). Let's look at this by way of a simple example.

In our example exercise, we require our users to click in the **Function** field in one step, and then enter their job title into this same field in the next step. In *Do It!* mode, these steps are displayed one after the other (as you would expect), as follows:

First Step:

Next Step:

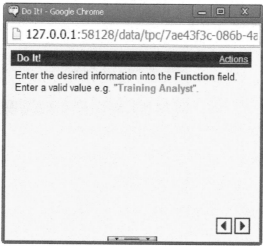

Here, the user is explicitly required to move from one step to the next in order to progress through the instructions. This can be disruptive to their work flow, especially as both of these actions are taking place against the same object in the application.

To rectify this, we locate the first of these Frames in the Topic Editor, and select the **Keep this action with next action in Do It** toggle button (⬚). (This button can be found in the *Frame Properties* pane, below the **Delay time (s)** option.) Now, when we play this Topic back in *Do It!* mode, our instructions appear as follows:

Note that although the two steps are combined into a single bubble, screenshots for both Frames are still available. If the user chooses to display the screenshots, a small 'picture' icon is shown to the right of each step, and the user can click on this icon for any step, to show the screenshot for that step in the screenshot area. The icon for the currently-displayed screenshot is highlighted. An example of this is shown below:

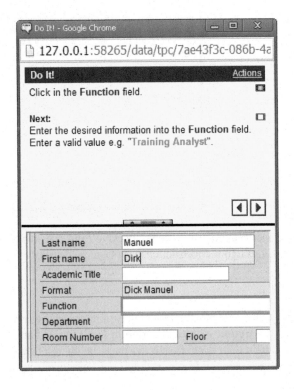

You can keep any number of Frames together in *Do It!* mode. The instructions for each subsequent Frame will simply be introduced by the text "**Next:**" and each step will have its own screenshot available as explained above.

Although you can use this feature to combine instructions in *Do It!* mode, you should be wary of using it to 'hide' Frames in *Do It!* mode. If you do not have any text tagged for *Do It!* mode for Frame, and combine that Frame with the previous Frame, the label "**Next**" will still be displayed, but will not be followed by any instructions, as shown below:

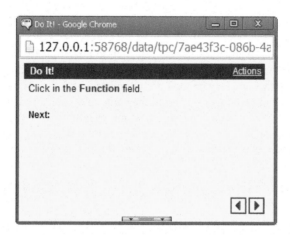

This looks slightly incongruous and may confuse your users. In this particular example, it would be better to hide the Frame (without any text tagged for *Do It!* mode) altogether, as explained in *Hiding Frames*, above. Of course then you also lose the ability to display the screenshot for this Frame, but if the screenshots on the hidden Frame is the basically same as the screenshot for the preceding (or next) Frame, then this may be acceptable.

Changing the Bubble Text

The most important aspect of the Bubble is the text inside it. This is what tells the user what they should be doing, or looking at. Fortunately, UPK provides a great deal of flexibility in determining what text is displayed, and how this text appears.

Template Text versus Custom Text

All of the examples of Bubbles that we have seen so far have contained **Template Text** - that is, text that is inserted automatically by UPK, based on the context of the action captured during recording (which we looked at in the section on the *Frame Properties* pane, earlier in this chapter), and the Template assigned to the Topic (which we will look at more closely in *Chapter 16, Customizing UPK*). This ability to capture the action and context correctly and generate useful instructions in the bubble is one of the strongest features of UPK. However,

Template Text is only the beginning - not the end - and there is so much more that we can do, by adding **Custom Text** to our recordings.

Consider the following bubble, that contains automatically-generated Template Text:

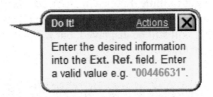

This is all well and good; a user referring to this Topic (in *Do It!* mode) will know that they have to enter something into the **Ext. Ref.** field, and they could perhaps infer that this needs to be an 8-digit number, but that's about it. What exactly is an Ext. Ref., and where do they find the value to enter? (And in my experience, if a user cannot determine the 'correct' value, they will enter the value that is shown in the documentation, which is potentially more damaging than them leaving it blank.)

This is where Custom Text comes in. Custom Text is really just any text that you want to appear in the Bubble, either as well as the Template Text, or instead of it. Custom text is incredibly useful for providing additional context to your recording, or to provide additional guidance or instructions on a step (or Frame).

Considering the example above again, it would be useful to explain exactly what an Ext. Ref. is, and to tell the users where they can find the correct value to enter. We can do this very easily, by adding some Custom Text that provides this information. Custom Text is entered into the large, yellow text box located at the top of the *Frame Properties* pane. Continuing our example, we want to enter the text shown in the following sample:

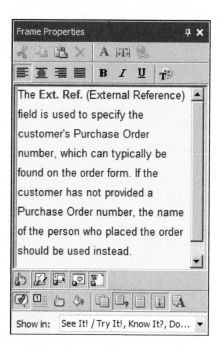

Now, our Bubble will appear as follows, in the Player (in *Do It!* mode):

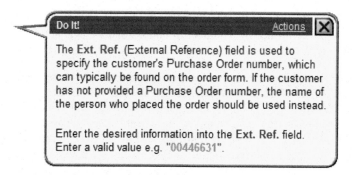

This is much more helpful (although not perfect - we will look at additional enhancements we can make, later in this chapter). The Bubble now contains two paragraphs: the first paragraph is the **Custom Text** that we entered into the *Frame Properties* pane, and the second paragraph is **Template Text** taken from the Template.

It is important to note that the Template Text exists in the template files, and not directly in the Topic. Effectively, this text is built 'dynamically' from the Template at preview or publishing time. If you change the template assigned to the Topic (as discussed in *Chapter 16, Customizing UPK*), then the Template Text that is displayed in the Bubble is automatically updated to use the new text from the Template the next time that you display the Topic in the *Topic Editor*, or preview or publish it.

● In this example, the **Use templates** button is selected. This indicates that the Template Text will be displayed in the Bubble, regardless of whether or not any Custom Text is specified. Deselecting this button will suppress the display of the Template Text in the Bubble.

Using Custom Text

To add Custom Text to your Bubble, carry out the steps described below:

1. Go to the Frame for which you want to add Custom Text.

2. Enter the required text in the **Custom Text** field (the big, yellow area) of the *Frame Properties* pane.

3. If you will also include the Template Text in your Bubble, then include an additional line break either before your custom text (if the Template Text is to be displayed first) or after your custom text (if the Custom Text is to be displayed first). This is necessary because by default UPK will show one text immediately after the other, on separate lines, but with no inter-paragraph spacing. Determining which texts will be displayed, and in what order, is explained under *Choosing which texts are displayed* on page 150.

The effective use of Custom Text is covered extensively in section *Providing business context through the use of Custom Text* of *Chapter 9, Adding Value to Your Topics*.

Choosing which texts are displayed

There are a number of possibilities for using the Template Text and/or Custom Text. These are controlled by a number of buttons that are available in the *Frame Properties* pane. The following table describes these buttons and their use:

Button	Name	Purpose
	Insert template text as user text	If you find that the Template Text doesn't *quite meet* your requirements then you can click the **Insert template text as user text** button to copy the Template Text into the Custom Text field, where you can change it as necessary. Note that this severs the link between the Template and this text, which means that any subsequent changes made to the Template will not be reflected in the Bubble Text. Furthermore, UPK will not be able to 'automatically' translate this text, which may be a concern if you are planning on translating your content into multiple languages. (Translating content is covered in *Chapter 17, Localizing Your Content*.)

Button	Name	Purpose
	Template text visible in Know It? mode	This toggle button allows you to choose whether the Template Text is visible during playback in *Know It?* mode or not.
		The Template Text describes the action that the user needs to perform in the exercise (such as, where to click, or what keys to press). *Know It?* mode is effectively a test, and so you would typically not want to give the user the exact instructions. However, in some cases this is not practical, for example, when the user is required to enter a specific value into a text field, and they cannot reasonably be expected to know or guess this. In this case, you probably want to give the user the same instructions in *Know It?* mode as you give them in *Try It!* mode (or any other mode). To do this, select the **Template text visible in Know It?** toggle button.
	Use templates	This toggle button allows you to choose between displaying the Template Text in the Bubble or not.
		As mentioned above, the default option is for the Template Text to be used in the Bubble. The **Use templates** toggle button is therefore selected by default. If you enter Custom Text and want to use *only* this Custom Text, then you can deselect the **Use templates** toggle button, and the Template Text will be suppressed.
		Another handy use of this option is where you have copied the Template Text into the Custom Text field (via the option **Insert template text as user text**), at which point the **Use templates** option is automatically deselected, but then decide to use the Template Text after all. In this case, you can delete all of the text in the Custom Text field and then (re)select the **Use templates** toggle button to go back to using the Template Text.

Button	Name	Purpose
	Show custom text first	If you choose to use Custom Text as well as the Template Text, then both of these text elements will be displayed in the Bubble. By default, the Template Text is displayed first, followed by the Custom Text. If you want the Custom Text to be displayed before the Template Text, then select the **Show custom text first** toggle button. For some reason best known to the UPK developers (actually, the OnDemand developers, before them) UPK places a single carriage return after the first text element (either Custom Text or Template Text, depending on whether the **Show custom text first** option is selected or not) and the second text element, and not a paragraph return. To make the Bubble Text more visually appealing, it is usually a good idea to insert an additional carriage return at the end of the first text element, as has been done in the previous example.

Editing Bubble Text

The following standard buttons can be used to edit the Template Text:

Button	Name	Purpose
	Cut	Cut the selected text to the clipboard.
	Copy	Copy the selected text to the clipboard.
	Paste	Paste the text currently on the clipboard into the Custom Text area. Note that if you have cut or copied Custom Text from another Frame, then any formatting or text tagging will be retained.
	Delete	Delete the currently-selected text.
	Left-aligned	Set the currently-selected paragraph(s) as left-aligned.
	Centered	Center the currently-selected paragraph(s).
	Right-aligned	Set the currently-selected paragraph(s) as right-aligned.
	Justified	Set the currently-selected paragraph(s) to be fully-justified.

Formatting Bubble Text

In addition to controlling what text is displayed, the *Frame Properties* pane allows you to control the appearance of the text itself. This includes the usual formatting options, plus a couple of options that are unique to UPK. All of these are explained in the following table:

Button	Name	Purpose
B	Bold	Select this toggle button to render the selected Custom Text in bold.
I	Italics	Select this toggle button to render the selected Custom Text in italics.
U	Underline	Select this toggle button to underline the selected Custom Text.
T	Font Color	Click this button to open up the standard *Color* dialog box, from which you can change the color of the selected Custom Text.
A	Custom Text Font	Click this button to display the **Font** dialog box, from which you can choose the font-family and size of the selected Custom Text. You can also select whether the text should be rendered in bold, italics, or underlined, but these options effectively duplicate the **Bold**, **Italics**, and **Underline** buttons also available in the *Bubble Properties* pane (as described above).
A	Template Text Font	Click this button to display the **Font** dialog box, from which you can choose the font family and size of the Template Text. Unlike Custom Text, you cannot choose whether Template Text is displayed in bold, italics, or underlined. This is controlled in the Templates itself.
⊢Γ⊣	Non-breaking Text	Select this toggle button to make the selected text non-breaking. This means that all of the selected text will be displayed on a single line in the Player.
🔗	Hyperlink	Click on this button to turn the selected text into a hyperlink. Hyperlinks are covered in *Chapter 9, Adding Value to Your Topics*.

● You can set the default font for Custom Texts and Template Texts in your author options (see *Chapter 2, Recording a Simulation*).

Tagging Custom Text for different modes

The previous sections explained how to control which texts are displayed in the Bubble, and the appearance of these texts. UPK offers a further level of customization by allowing you to specify exactly what portions of these texts will be displayed in the various modes in which the Topic can be played. In fact, UPK automatically does this (as best it can) for Bubble Text for string input actions. Consider the following examples:

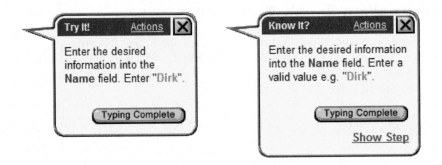

These two texts are both generated from the same Template Text. This is shown in the screenshot below. Note that in this screenshot the Template Text was copied into the **Custom Text** field so that we can see exactly how it is structured. Note also that this particular screenshot was taken with the **Display** property set to **Player-See It!/Try It!**:

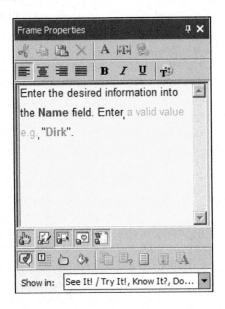

The first thing that you will notice is that one section of the text is 'low-lighted' in gray. Coincidentally, this is the same section of text that appears in *Know It?* mode but not *Try It!* mode. If you look closely at the previous example of the *Frame Properties* pane, you will see that there is a small 'tick' just underneath the baseline of the text, exactly at the point where the text changes from appearing in both modes to appearing in only the *Know It?* mode. This is because of **text tagging**.

The text "**a valid value e.g.**" in the *Frame Properties* pane above has been tagged to appear only in *Know It?* mode. As the *Frame Properties* pane is being displayed in **Player-See It!/Try It!** mode, the text is low-lighted—this can be interpreted as "this text appears in another mode, but not this one". The tick marks identify the points at which the tagging changes from one mode to another.

Tagging text for a particular more is done by selecting the text in the **Custom Text** field, and then clicking on the appropriate mode button, as shown below:

Button	Name	Purpose
	Visible in See It!/Try It!	Select the text and then select this toggle button if you want the text to appear in *See It!* mode and *Try It!* mode. Note that these two modes use the same formatting.
	Visible in Do It!	Select the text and then select this toggle button if you want the text to appear in *Do It!* mode.
	Visible in Know It?	Select the text and then select this toggle button if you want the text to appear in *Know It?* mode.
	Visible in Player	By default, all text will appear in the on-line deployment formats, in the relevant mode for which it has been tagged via the first three buttons. If you do not want the text to appear in *any* of the on-line deployment formats, then you should select the text and then *deselect* this toggle button.
	Visible in Print	By default, all text will appear in the printed deployment formats, in the relevant mode for which it has been tagged via the first three buttons. (Printed output is discussed in *Chapter 6, Publishing Your Content*.) If you do not want the text to appear in *any* of the printed output types (for example, because it refers to a "simulation"), then select the text and then deselect this toggle button.

Note that all text must be tagged to appear in at least one of the three selectable modes, and must be tagged to appear in either on-line deployment formats, or printed output, or both.

It is worth noting that you do not have to select entire sentences—or even entire words—when tagging text for different modes. For example, the following text tagging is perfectly acceptable (this screenshot was taken with the **Display** selection set to **Player - See It!/Try It!**):

■ You can enter your text and then tag it for the different modes, or you can position the cursor in the Custom Text field, select the relevant modes, and then start typing - the modes selected at the point you start typing will be applied to the text that you type. Personally, I find it easier to enter all of the text and then tag it for the correct modes, but you do need to be careful with this approach, as when you select text and then tag it for a specific mode, UPK will typically discard any existing tagging for that text—especially if different portions of the selected text are currently tagged for different modes (mode tagging is not cumulative).

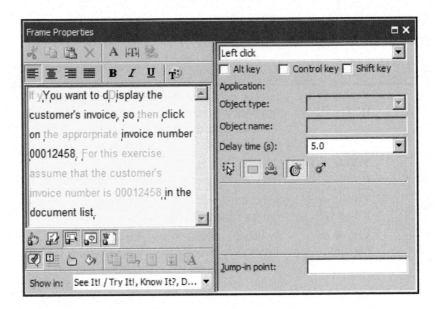

This will give us the following Bubbles in the various play modes (these screenshots are taken from within the *Topic Editor*, using the various **Display** modes):

See It!/Try It!

Know It?

Do It!

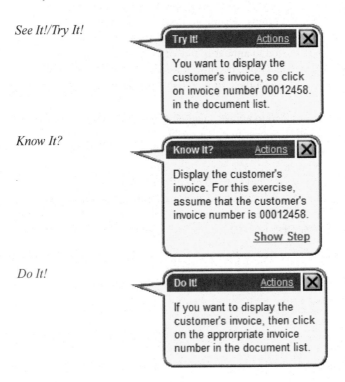

Of course, now the text in the **Custom Text** field makes little sense on its own, and the spell-checker will find a lot of fault with it, but the user's won't see anything wrong.

● Incredibly, this does not pose any problems for translation (covered in *Chapter 17, Localizing Your Content*) as UPK first identifies the full text for each mode, and then extracts this separately into the translation document.

A standardized approach to string input Bubble Text

In general, I advocate using the Template Texts as much as possible. This cuts down on development time, and also simplifies translation. However, the Template Text for string input actions leaves a lot to be desired. Although it is possible to customize this (as we do in *Chapter 16, Customizing UPK*) it is difficult to find a truly satisfactory solution using Template Text alone.

Given that I also advocate judicious use of Custom Text to provide business context, I usually end up completely replacing the Template Text for string input actions, and using all Custom Text. I lose some of the flexibility and convenience of using Template Texts, but this is an acceptable trade-off for being able to provide meaningful instructions to the user.

Although providing Custom Text takes time, especially if it has to be tagged for the various playback modes, if you consistently use the same words, and the same sentence structure, you will find that you can tag the text for the different modes fairly quickly. As an example, I always use the structure shown in the example below for string input Bubble Text:

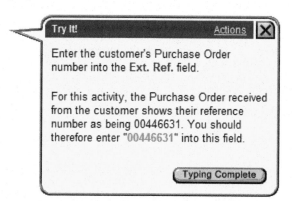

This includes business context, as well as the actual data required. Using this format also makes tagging the text for the various modes very simple, as explained below:

1. Select **all** of the text in the Bubble and tag it for *See It!/Try It!* mode (👍). Make sure it is **not** tagged for *Know It?* mode (🔲) or *Do It!* mode (🔲).

2. Select the first paragraph (in its entirety) and tag it for *Do It!* mode (🔲). (Make sure that you stop at the end of the paragraph and don't capture the carriage returns.)

3. Select the first sentence (only) in the second paragraph and tag it for *Know It?* mode (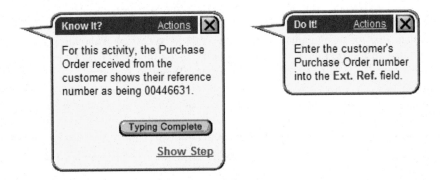).

This then leaves the *Try It!* mode text as shown in the example above, and provides text in *Do It!* mode and *Know It?* mode as shown in the following two examples:

This then provides three separate texts for the three selectable modes, and without having to tag individual words, mid-sentence (as the Template Text does). It also conforms to the following golden rules:

- In *See It!* and *Try It!* modes, the user is given the **instructions** and the **data**.

- In *Know It?* mode, the user is given the **data** only.

- In *Do It!* mode, the user is given the **instructions** only.

So we have now provided Custom Text for our string input action, and tagged it perfectly for the three selectable modes. And all in little more time than it takes to type the text into the **Custom Text** field.

Undo

At this point it is worth noting that the *Topic Editor* includes an **Undo** function (and a **Redo** function), which is very convenient if you do something by mistake and need to back out what you have done. Simply click on the **Undo** button ( ) on the *Standard Toolbar* and you are back to where you were.

However, it is worth noting that 'back to where you were' may be farther back in your edits than you thought. UPK thinks in terms of 'blocks of activities', and all of the changes that you make to the Bubble Text are considered as a single activity. For example, suppose you enter some Custom Text, then set a few words in bold, some other words in italics, and then tag text for different modes. If you then decide that you mode tagging is incorrect, clicking on the **Undo** button (or using the—thankfully standard—*Ctrl*+*Z* keyboard shortcut) will often back out **all** of these Custom Text changes (for the current Frame). This function should therefore be used with care—consider whether it is easier to manually reverse your last one change, or automatically reverse all of your changes for the Frame and then re-do the ones you want to keep.

Should you 'undo' more than you mean to, you can always click on the **Redo** button (🔁) to 'undo the undo'.

Replacing fonts

In *Chapter 2, Recording a Simulation*, we looked at how to set your content defaults. This included setting the default font family, size, and formatting of text in Bubbles, Web Pages, and String Input. Ideally, these defaults are set before you start recording. But what happens if you forget to set them before you record your simulation, or if you copy a simulation from another Library or project that used different standards? You *could* change the font on each individual Frame in each simulation, and/or in every attached Web Page, but this could take some time. Handily, UPK provides a much easier solution: the **Replace Font** feature.

The Replace Font feature allows you can change the font used for Custom Text, Template Text, Web Page text, string input text, and the text used in the Start Frame and the End Frame. Strictly speaking, you replace one specific font with another specific font, but as we shall see, it is possible to be a bit vague on the source font.

For text in Web Pages, there are additional options. It is possible to replace one Style with another, or even replace 'unstyled' text (that is, text with no Style applied to it) with a Style. This latter option is extremely useful where you have inherited content from a pre-UPK 11 version and want to apply Styles to this content.

✚ Styles were introduced to Web Pages in UPK 12. In prior versions of UPK, it was only possible to find and replace direct formatting (that is, text that has been formatted in a specific font face, size, and/or style).

To replace the fonts used in existing content objects, carry out the steps shown below:

1. Select the content object(s) for which you want to replace the font. You can do this from the Library, or from an Outline Element.

2. Select menu option **Edit | Replace Font**. The *Replace Font* dialog box is displayed, as shown below:

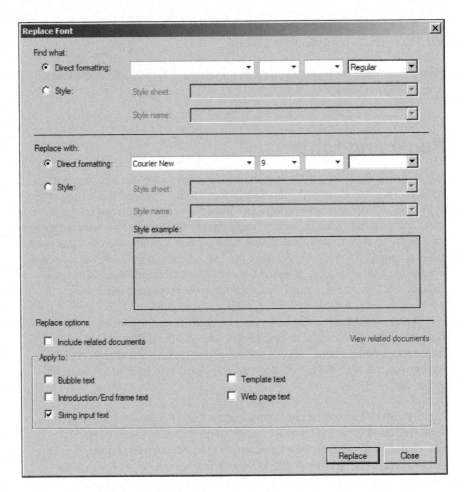

3. Under **Find what**, indicate whether you want to replace text with **Direct formatting** or replace a **Style**.

- If you are replacing direct formatting, then select the current font face, size, measurement (pixels or picas) and format that you want to replace. Unfortunately, UPK insists that you specify at least one of these (instead of just being able to replace all text regardless of the current formatting. However, you do not need to specify all three.

- If you are replacing an existing style, then select the **Style sheet** that contains the style to be replaced, and the **Style name**. Note that this will not change the style itself - just which style is applied to the text.

- You cannot replace a Style with direct formatting. As Styles are preferred over direct formatting, you would probably not want to do this anyway.

4. Under **Replace with**, specify the (new) format for the text, as follows:

- If you are replacing direct formatting with other direct formatting, then select the new font face, size, measurement (pixels or picas) and format that you want the text to be formatted with. Again, you do not necessarily have to specify all three.

- If you are replacing an existing style, then select the **Style Sheet** that contains the new style, and the new **Style name**. The **Style example** box will show you an example of text formatted in the new style, so that you can confirm you have selected the correct one.

- If you want to replace the font in the related documents for the selected content objects, then select the Include related documents option. As always, you can click on the **View related documents** link to display a list of these.

5. In the **Apply to** area, select the categories of text that you want to replace. Note that if you are replacing existing text (whether styled or unformatted) with a new Style, then only the **Web page text** option will be selectable, because styles only apply to Web Pages.

6. Click **OK**.

7. The fonts are changed, and the *Replace Successful* dialog box is displayed when this is complete. An example of this dialog box is shown below:

The dialog box specifies the number of text elements that have been changed, and (in a client/server environment) the number of documents that were checked out to you so that this change could be made (you can click on the **View activity log** link to list these).

8. Click **OK** to close the *Replace Successful* dialog box and return to the *Replace Font* dialog box.

9. Click **Close** to close the *Replace Font* dialog box.

Adjusting your recording

Beyond changing the actions that were captured during the initial recording, there are also a number of other things that you can do to adjust the simulation as a whole. This includes adding and removing Frames, replacing or editing screenshots, and even re-recording the entire simulation. These tasks are explained in the following sections.

Adding missing Frames

There may be occasions when you finish capturing a recording, and then realize that you missed out a couple of screens (or, as is more often the case, the developers forgot to tell you about some requirement). Never fear; there is no need to recapture the entire recording—UPK allows you to insert new Frames (screenshots) into an existing Topic.

Let's look at an example. In our sample exercise, we have explained how to use the **Address** tabbed page and the **Defaults** tabbed page. Now we look at it, we think that it would be useful to explain the last tabbed page, **Parameters**, as well. So we would like to insert some new Frames to explain this page.

To add new Frames to an existing Topic, carry out the steps described below:

1. Start up the application that you want to capture, and navigate to the exact point (screen) at which you want to start recording. In our exercise, this would be positioned on the **Defaults** tabbed page. It is important that the application screen *exactly* matches the screen in your recording from which you want to insert the missing frames, to ensure seamless continuity throughout your final recording.

2. Open the Topic into which you want to insert the additional Frames, in the *Topic Editor*.

3. Select the Frame after which you want to insert the new Frames. For our exercise, this will be Frame 12 (immediately prior to the 'save' Frame—Frame 12).

4. Select menu option **Insert | Missing Frame(s)** (🔏). (You could also click on the **Insert** button (⚏▾) on the *Standard Toolbar*, and then select **Missing Frames** (🔏) from the drop-down menu.) You are passed into the application, and the Recorder pane is displayed.

5. Record the missing actions and Frames, as explained in *Chapter 2, Recording a Simulation*. Once you have captured the last new screenshot, click the **Finish** button in the *Recorder* pane. Be careful about the Frame on which you stop recording. In our example, this would be immediately prior to clicking the **Save** button (because we already have this Action recorded, and this will be the next Frame after our newly-inserted Frames).

6. Once you have finished recording, you will be passed back into the *Topic Editor*, and can edit the newly inserted Frames as usual.

You now have an expanded recording, as you can see from the following screenshot. Note that in this screenshot the additional Frames that have been recorded are identified in this screenshot by a border around them:

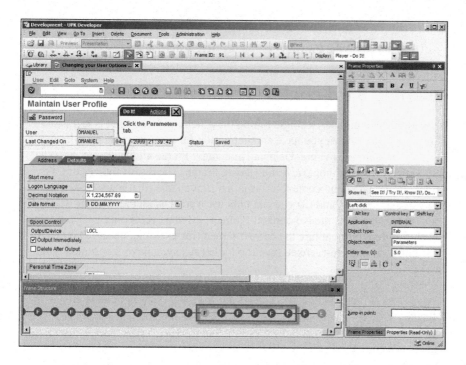

Note that the **Frame ID** for the first of these new Frames is **91**, even though we didn't previously have 90 Frames in the Topic, and they appear before existing Frame 13 . UPK's numbering system is a law unto itself, and there is little point trying to read a logic into it. The only surety is that Frames added later will have a higher number than Frames added earlier - just do not expect Frames to be numbered sequentially, or even in order, within a Topic.

For the record, I carried out the following steps to insert these missing Frames:

1. Logged on to SAP, and navigated to the **Defaults** tab in the **Maintain User Profile** transaction.

2. Switched to UPK, opened up the Topic in the *Topic Editor*, and selected the Frame that is immediately before the point at which I wanted to insert the missing Frames.

3. Selected menu option **Insert | Missing Frames**. UPK flipped me back to SAP, with the *Recorder* panel now displayed in the upper-right corner of the screen.

4. Pressed *PRINTSCREEN* to start the recording.

5. Clicked on the **Parameters** tab. Pressed *PRINTSCREEN*.

6. Clicked in the first free **Parameter ID** field. Pressed *PRINTSCREEN*.

7. Typed **VK0**. Pressed *PRINTSCREEN*.

8. Pressed *Tab*. Pressed *PRINTSCREEN*.

9. Typed **1001**. Pressed *PRINTSCREEN*.

10. Pressed *Enter*. Pressed *PrintScreen*.

11. Clicked on the **Finish** button in the **Recorder** pane.

Inserting a No-context Frame

If you only need to insert a single Frame for which the screenshot is identical to an existing Frame, then you have another option for inserting a missing Frame. This is a **No-context Frame**. Using a No-context Frame allows you to insert a new Action Frame without *recording* a new Frame. The disadvantages of this approach are that (1) no context information is available (that's why they call it a 'No-context' Frame), and (2) you can only use a screenshot that already exists in your Topic. That said, the No-context Frame is often a useful option if you do not have the ability to re-capture the correct screen (for example, because you were recording a difficult-to-recreate scenario, or because you have 'consumed' your data).

A No-context Frame will take its screenshot from the Frame immediately following it. This is a one-time copy, which means that you can insert a No-context Frame and then edit the screenshot that it uses (as described below), without affecting the Frame from which the No-context Frame originally took its screenshot. Note that this does not necessarily mean that you are limited to inserting a No-context Frame to immediately before the Frame that contains the screenshot that you want to use (although most of the time this will be the case). You can insert a No-context Frame before the Frame whose screenshot you want to copy, and then cut-and-paste the No-context Frame into the position where you really want it to appear. (How to cut-and-paste Frames is explained in *Chapter 9, Adding Value to Your Topics*.)

To insert a No-context Frame, carry out the steps described below:

1. Open the Topic into which you want to insert the No-context Frame, in the *Topic Editor*.

2. In the *Frame Navigation* pane, select the Frame before the Frame from which you want the No-context Frame to take its screenshot.

3. Select menu option **Insert | No-context Frame** (🖳). (You could also click on the **Insert** button (✴▾) on the **Standard Toolbar**, and then select **No-context Frame** (🖳) from the drop-down menu.) The No-context Frame is inserted into your Topic.

4. Adjust the Action Area as required.

5. Change the Custom Text as required (there will be no Template Text).

■ If you need context for the Frame (even if you will change the context fields) then you may find it easier to just copy the Frame from which the No-context Frame would take its screenshot) (assuming *that* has context) and paste this into your recording.

Any Custom Text on the source Frame will also be copied, but the Template Text will not be carried over (because there is no context, and UPK needs the context information to determine which Template Texts to use). You therefore need to use only Custom Text in the No-context Frame (or (re)capture the context for this Frame).

Inserting a Blank Frame

A **Blank Frame** is very similar to an **Explanation Frame** (see *Explanation Frames* on page 346), but does not have a screenshot. Actually, technically it does have a screenshot image associated with it, but this is entirely blank. The theory is that you can use your Screenshot Editor to edit this blank screenshot and insert whatever information you want to share with your users - maybe a process flowchart, or supporting information, and so on.

✛ Blank Frames were introduced in UPK 12.1.

To insert a Blank Frame into a Topic, carry out the steps described below:

1. Open the Topic into which you want to insert the Blank Frame, in the *Topic Editor*.

2. In the *Frame Navigation* pane, select the Frame after which you want the Blank Frame to appear

3. Select menu option **Insert | Blank Frame** (🔲). (You could also click on the **Insert** button (🔲) on the *Standard Toolbar*, and then select **Blank Frame** from the drop-down menu.) The Blank Frame is inserted into your Topic.

4. Use your Screen Editor to edit the 'screenshot' for this Frame as required.

Note that a Blank Frame will still have a Bubble associated with it. You can enter text into this as usual, but you cannot hide it by deselecting the **Display bubble in** *See It!* **and Try It! modes for this Frame** toggle button (🔲), as the Frame will not be displayed if the Bubble is not visible .

Replacing screenshots

Sometimes, you may find that you need to recapture a single screenshot in a recording. Maybe some extraneous information got captured by mistake, or you realize that not all of the required data was set up correctly. Given what you learned in the previous section, you could be forgiven for thinking that all you need to do is delete the Frame containing the incorrect screenshot, and then insert a missing Frame to capture the new screenshot. Sure, that would work; but UPK provides a much easier way of doing this: *replacing* a screenshot.

If we look back at our sample exercise, you will recall that we added several new Frames, to explain an additional tabbed page in the application. The problem with this is that when we recorded the initial exercise, we saved our changes when the **Defaults** tabbed page was displayed. Once we have added our missing Frames, the user should now be saving their changes from the **Parameters** tabbed page. However, because we inserted our new Frames *before* the 'save' action, the screen print for the 'save' action still shows the **Defaults** page, as shown in the following screenshot:

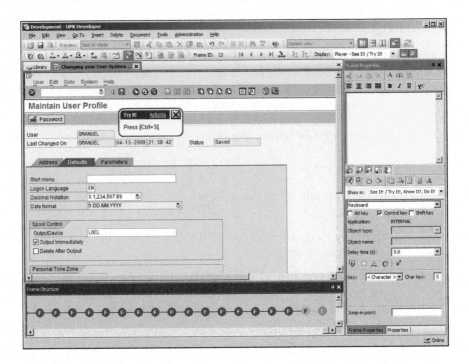

What we need to do here is replace this screenshot with a screenshot showing the **Parameters** page. Because the action is still exactly the same (and in exactly the same position), it is easier to just swap out the screenshot rather than re-record Frames.

To recapture a screenshot, carry out the following steps:

1. Go to the application for which you are creating the simulation, and position yourself on the replacement screen (that is, the screen that you want to use in your Topic).

2. Open the Topic in the *Topic Editor*.

3. Select the Frame containing the screenshot that you want to replace (Frame 13 in this example).

4. Select menu option **Edit | Recapture** (![icon]) | **Screenshot** (![icon]). (You could also click on the **Recapture** button (![icon]) on the *Standard Toolbar*, and then select **Screenshot** (![icon]) from the drop-down menu.) You are passed into the application.

5. Press the *PRINTSCREEN* button. The screenshot is recaptured, and you are returned to the *Topic Editor*.

Our Frame (Frame **13**) now appears as shown in the following screenshot. Note that the Action is still the same, and the Bubble is still in exactly the same place. These things do not change when we replace a screenshot.

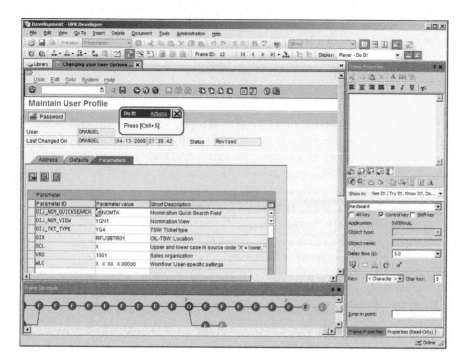

Note that you cannot replace the screenshot on the Start Frame. The Start Frame always uses exactly the same screenshot as the Frame immediately following it (which you *can* change, but the screenshots for these two Frames will always be the same).

Re-recording a Topic

In some cases, you may find that you need to replace **all** of the screenshots in a Topic. A few example scenarios for this are as follows:

- You have captured an entire simulation, but then noticed that you left the Windows Taskbar displayed when you do not want to include it in your exercise (or there was some other element that you did not want to be included in your training material).

- The software application that you have developed your training for is being upgraded, and the user interface has changed even though the basic functionality has not (this is a common occurrence in SAP, with upgrades to SAPgui).

- Your application's user interface is available in several languages. You have recorded the simulations in one language, and now want to provide exactly the same training in another one of the supported languages. (This scenario is covered in detail in *Chapter 17, Localizing Your Content.*)

✛ Users familiar with OnDemand 8.7 and earlier should note that the Re-record function in UPK is not the same as the Re-record function in OnDemand. In OnDemand, re-recording a Topic would effectively throw away the existing version of the Topic, and recapture the entire thing all over again. With UPK, only the screenshots and Actions are replaced, and any Custom Text, Explanation Frames, and so on are retained.

Whatever the motivation, UPK thankfully provides a very easy way of replacing all of the screenshots in a Topic: *re-recording* the Topic.

To re-record a Topic, follow the steps shown below:

1. Open the Topic that you want to re-record, in the *Topic Editor*.

2. Select menu option **Edit | Re-record topic**. You are passed back to the application that you want to record (actually, back to the last application that you had open; switch to the correct application if necessary), and the *Re-recorder* window appears in the upper-right corner of the screen.

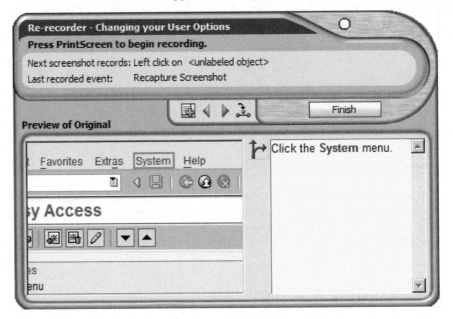

A portion of the screenshot for the current Frame is shown in the lower-left portion of the *Re-recorder* window, and the Bubble Text (Template and/or Custom) is shown in the lower-right portion of the window. This makes it very easy to recall exactly what you originally recorded in the exercise.

3. If you do not want to replace the screenshot for the current Frame, then you can use the **Next Frame** (▶) and **Previous Frame** (◀) buttons to move through the recording, to locate the next screenshot that you do want to replace.

4. When you are positioned in the *Re-recorder* window on the screenshot that you want to replace, and are positioned in the application on the screen that you want to replace it with, carry out the action specified and then press the *PrintScreen* button, as usual. The screenshot **and action** are replaced, and you automatically advance to the next screenshot in the Topic. Note that if there are multiple paths in the Topic then UPK will record one path before looping back to re-record the screenshots in the

■ If you do not want to replace the action—just the screenshot—then you can just press *PrintScreen* without performing the action.

Alternative Path. The *Alternative* icon (found between the screenshot and the bubble text) will be highlighted if you are in an Alternative Path.

5. If necessary, you can display (and optionally edit or augment) any Author Notes that exist for the Topic, by clicking on the **Add Notes** button (🖼). Author Notes are described more fully in *Chapter 2, Recording a Simulation*, and revisited in the section *Editing Frame Comments* later in this chapter.

6. Repeat Steps 3 to 5 for all additional Frames that you need to recapture (screenshot and/or action).

7. If you need to capture additional Frames not present in the original recording, then you can click on the **Insert missing frames** button (🔧), and proceed as described in the section *Adding missing Frames* earlier in this chapter.

8. When you have finished replacing the screenshots, click on the **Finish** button in the *Re-recorder* window.

Note that you would normally only want to use the **Re-record Topic** function if you have a non-trivial exercise, and want to replace all or most of the screenshots in the Topic. If you only want to replace one or two specific screenshots then it is easier to replace the screenshot as explained in *Editing screenshots* on page 169.

Editing screenshots

An alternative to recapturing a screenshot is to simply edit it (or "Photoshop" it, as common parlance now has it). Although this can be fiddly (and requires pixel-perfect precision), it can sometimes save you a lot of time when compared to recapturing the screenshot—especially if you would need to set up data all over again to get the application in a state where you can capture the screenshot that you need. Another case would be where you need to remove sensitive data.

Choosing an image editing application

Before you can edit a screenshot you need to tell UPK which image editing application you are going to use. Although you can use almost any image editor, you should make sure that it can handle bitmaps correctly. Although UPK saves screenshots in `.png` format, the screenshot is saved as a `.bmp` file for passing to the image editor, and then converted back to a `.png` file before being copied back into the Topic.

To specify your default image editor, carry out the steps described below:

1. From the main *Developer* screen, select menu option **Tools | Options**.

2. Select the **Developer | General** category of options. The *General Developer Settings* screen is displayed, as shown in the screenshot below:

■ I would advise against editing screenshots to 'pixilate' or 'blur' sections of the screen to obscure sensitive information. I would also advise against drawing borders around sections of the screen to which you want to draw the user's attention. Remember that you are trying to match reality as closely as possible. More judicious selection of data can eliminate the need to edit screenshots to remove unwanted or unwelcome data, and Explanation Frames can be used to draw the user's attention to specific information on the screen.

● In the absence of anything else, UPK will find **Microsoft Paint** on a Windows PC. Paint is suitable for basic editing, but you may prefer to use a more 'feature-rich' image editor., if you have one.

■ For a full list of the various developer settings, refer to *Developer category* on page 697.

3. Click on the **Browse** button to the right of the **Image Editor** field to navigate to and select the executable (`.exe` file) for the image editor that you want to use.

4. Click on the **OK** button to save your setting.

Editing a screenshot

Editing a screenshot is fortunately very easy, and can be done directly from the *Topic Editor*. Let's look at how to do this, by way of an example.

● This may seem overly nit-picky, but bear in mind that we are trying to create a quality exercise that matches reality as closely as possible. You, personally, may not think this level of attention to detail is entirely necessary, but don't say you weren't advised!

One of the problems with our sample exercise is that the screenshots taken by UPK include the bar cursor (which indicates the insertion point) in the input fields. This can be distracting, especially for string input actions, where the cursor may not be completely masked by the Action Area. If you look at Frame **4** in our original recording, you will see that the screenshot includes the cursor (immediately after the text "Dick" in the **First name** field), and that it protrudes out slightly below our Action Area, as shown in the screenshot below. It would look better if we removed this.

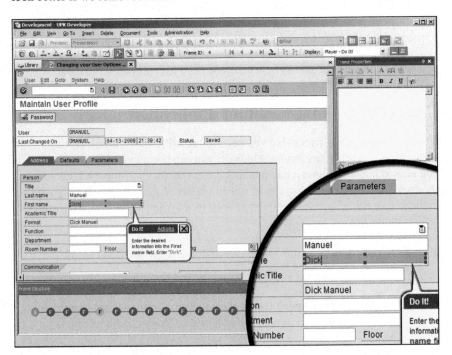

To edit a screenshot, carry out the steps described below.

1. Open up the Topic in the *Topic Editor*.

2. Select the Frame that contains the screenshot that you want to edit.

3. On the *Editing Toolbar*, click on the **Edit screenshot** button (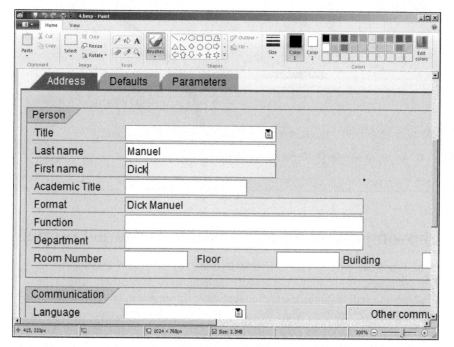). (You can also right-click on the screenshot and select **Edit Screenshot** from the shortcut menu.) Your image editing application is started, and you are passed into it, as shown in the following screenshot:

4. Edit the screenshot as required. How you do this will depend on your image editing software.

5. Once you have finished editing the screenshot, close your image editing application.

6. In response to the message asking you if you want to save your changes to the .bmp file, click on **Yes**. You are passed back into UPK.

You will now see that the screenshot has been changed in the *Topic Editor*. The example below shows our edited Frame **4**. The cursor is no longer visible.

■ Make sure that your image editing application is not open before you click on the **Edit screenshot** button, and that you close it again once you have edited the screenshot. If you do not close the image editing application then the updated image will not be saved back to UPK.

✚ In versions 11.1 and earlier, UPK would be 'hidden' when you opened the image editor, and would not appear until you closed the editor again. Because this caused problems if the image editor crashed (it would be difficult to get back to UPK), as of UPK 12, UPK itself stays visible, and a message is displayed stating that it will be available when you close the image editor. Most importantly, the message box includes a **Resume** button that you can click on in the event of a problem in the image editor, to return to UPK (your image edits may be lost but at least your Topic will not).

● Note that the file name in the window title bar shows a file name of xx.bmp file, where xx is the Frame ID. In pre-UPK 12 versions the file name would be a combination of the Document ID and the Frame ID. In UPK 12, only the Frame ID is used.

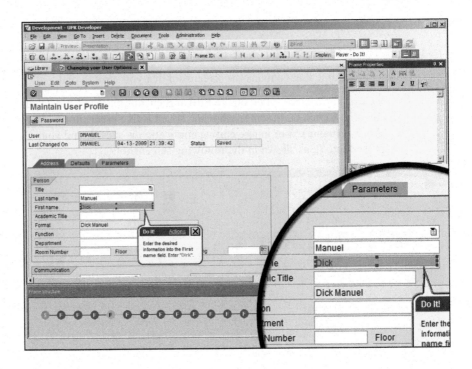

Showing or hiding screenshots in printed output

In the Word-based publishing formats (described in *Chapter 6, Publishing Your Content*), UPK will not necessarily include every screenshot. Instead, in an attempt to reduce 'unnecessary' or repetitive information, UPK typically only includes screenshots when there is a change of context. However, you can override UPK's automatic screen inclusion determination, and force it to include or exclude specific screenshots. This is achieved through the use of the following buttons on the *Standard Toolbar*:

Button	Name	Purpose
	Autoselect screenshot	If this button is selected, then UPK will decide itself whether to include or exclude the screenshot in printed documents. The icon used indicates whether UPK has decided to include the screenshot or exclude the screenshot, respectively.
	Include screenshot	Click on this button to always include the screenshot in printed documents.
	Exclude screenshot	Click on this button to always exclude the screenshot from printed documents.

Note that these settings can be overridden at publishing time, by the **Include screenshots** option. Refer to *Chapter 6, Publishing Your Content*, for more information about this.

Deleting Frames

It is generally advisable to 'over-capture' when recording. Capture every single thing that you do, regardless of whether you think that you will need it in the final recording. This is a useful tactic, especially if you are recording a difficult-to-reproduce scenario, or consuming data that is difficult to set up. Alternatively, you may have adjusted some element on the screen (such as resizing or repositioning a dialog box) to create a more effective screenshot, but do not want your adjustment actions to be included in the final recording.

In these cases (and no doubt in countless other cases), you may need to delete a Frame or two from your recording.

In our sample exercise, we have a further example of where it is desirable to delete a Frame. When we recorded the action to select a date format, the date format that we want the user to select is at the top of the drop-down list, and is initially not visible. We therefore had to scroll up in this list, and then select the required entry, as shown in the following screenshot:

✛ The ability to delete multiple Frames at once was included in UPK 12. In prior versions it is only possible to delete one Frame at a time.

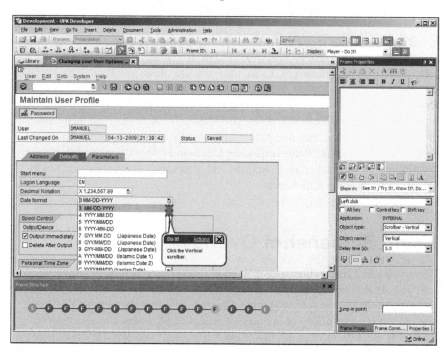

Our exercise would be more effective if the drop-down list showed the required entry when we first opened it, so the user can just click on the required entry.

Although this is not strictly 'as we did it', or 'true to life', this will not be evident in our final recording. It is important, when building exercises, to think about exactly what you need to teach your users. The chances are (in this example) that our users are already familiar with scrollbars, so having them scroll up is not really a 'value-add' learning activity. In addition, consider *Know It?* mode—do you really need to test your user's ability to correctly use the scrollbar, and grade them on this? Probably not.

So, for our sample exercise, we will remove this Frame (on which the user is required to scroll up) from our recording.

To delete a Frame from a recording, carry out the steps described below:

1. Open the Topic from which you want to delete the Frame, in the *Topic Editor*.

In versions prior to UPK 12.1 you can only delete one Frame at a time.

2. Select the Frame(s) that you want to delete. (To select a sequence of Frames, click on the first Frame, and then *SHIFT*+click on the subsequent Frames, to select them.) In our example, this is Frame **11**, as shown in the previous screenshot.

In versions prior to UPK 12.1, a message was displayed asking you to confirm the deletion. This has been removed in UPK 12.1 (although if you delete a Frame in error you can always **Undo**).

3. Select menu option **Delete | Frames** (⚡). (You can also click on the **Delete** button (⚡▾) on the *Standard* toolbar, and then select **Frames** (⚡) from the drop-down list.)

4. Save and then close the Topic.

If you now play our sample Topic through, it goes from selecting the drop-down button for the **Date format** field (Frame 10), straight to selecting option **1 DD.MM.YYYY** (Frame 12). To the user, it is seamless.

Note that you cannot delete a Frame that has Alternative Actions recorded for it. In this case, you need to first delete the Alternative Action(s) and then delete the Frame (once it has only one Action associated with it). The same applies to Frames with Alternative Paths (including Decision Frames); you must first delete the Alternative Path. Alternative Actions and Alternative Paths are described in *Chapter 14, Allowing Alternatives*.

Using Screenshot Overlays

Screenshot Overlays are a brand new feature added in UPK 12.1.

When you edit a screenshot, as explained in *Editing screenshots* on page 169, you are making a permanent change to the screenshot. So if you edit the screenshot to mask out some sensitive data, the area of the screenshot that you masked out is permanently obliterated - you can never go back to seeing what used to be there. In most cases, this is probably what you want. However, there may be times when you want to make a temporary change to a screenshot, or you may want to provide the option to revert to the unedited version. In this case, you should use a **Screenshot Overlay**.

A Screenshot Overlay is effectively an additional layer placed on top of the screenshot, onto which you can place objects such as text boxes or shapes (such as a solid rectangle used to mask sensitive data). This is very similar to layers in many image editing applications, but with UPK, this is actually implemented through the use of Microsoft PowerPoint.

Let's illustrate this by way of an example. Let's suppose that our current sample exercise was recorded using a specific software level—in our case, SAPGui 4.6c. We know that ECC 6.0 is gradually being rolled out to our users, but don't know exactly when, and different users will see the update at different times. We also don't know if this new version will materially affect the system screens. We therefore want to add a note to all of the screenshots in our recording informing the users that the recording shows a 4.6c version of the screen. If a user referring to our recording is using version 6.0, and their screen looks different to the recording, this note will tell them why. And if it turns out that the screens really look no different under 6.0, we can just come back, remove the note, and republish, without the need to recapture or re-edit our screenshots.

Adding a Screenshot Overlay to a Frame

To add a Screenshot Overlay to one or more screenshots in your Topic, carry out the steps described below:

1. Open the Topic to which you want to add the overlay in the *Topic Editor*.

2. Click on the **Create Overlay** button (🔲). You are passed into Microsoft PowerPoint, as shown in the following screenshot:

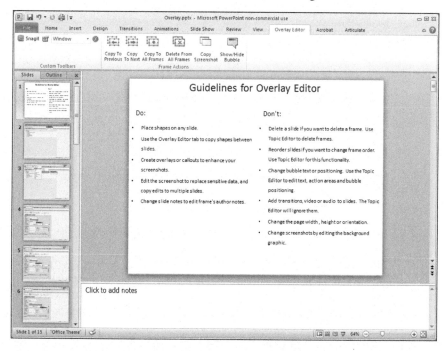

Note that all of the Frames in your Topic appear as individual Slides within the PowerPoint presentation (except the **Start Frame**, which doesn't have its own screenshot). Note also that a new category has been added to the Ribbon, called **Overlay Editor** - this contains all of the UPK-specific functions.

3. The first Slide in the overlay presentation (as shown in the example above) provides some initial tips for using the *Overlay Editor*. You may want to read these (at least the first time that you use the *Overlay Editor*), as they explain what PowerPoint features will and will not work with UPK overlays.

4. Go to the Slide for the Frame to which you want to add the overlay (the Frame ID is shown to the upper-left of the Slide image in the main PowerPoint window, for reference). If you want to add the same overlay to multiple Frames (or all of the Frames in the Topic) then select the first one - you can propagate the overlay to additional Frames later.

5. Use the standard PowerPoint functionality to add shapes or text boxes directly onto the Slide, as necessary. In the following example, we have added a semi-transparent Word Art text of "Screenshot for SAPGui 4.6" to Frame 1.

● Within PowerPoint, the Bubble is rendered as a separate object that can be moved within the Slide. This is purely for convenience in case you need to see what is behind it; when you return to UPK, the Bubble will be returned to its original position.

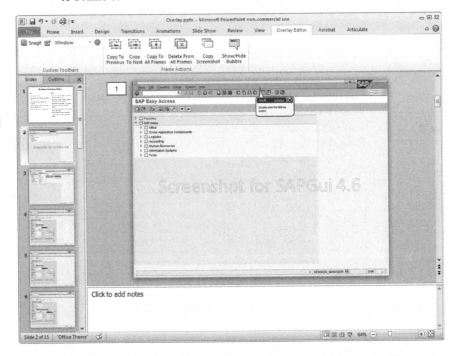

6. Once you have added the required overlay object(s), you can copy these object(s) to other slides (Frames/screenshots) within the presentation (Topic) by using the buttons in the **Frame Actions** group of the **Overlay Editor** ribbon. Refer to the table below for details of these buttons.

Button	Name	Purpose
	Copy To Previous	Copy the currently-selected overlay objects to the previous slide in the presentation.

Button	Name	Purpose
	Copy To Next	Copy the currently-selected overlay objects to the next slide in the presentation.
	Copy To All	Copy the currently-selected overlay objects to all slides in the presentation.
	Delete from All Frames	Delete the currently-selected overlay objects from all slides on which they currently appear. Note that if you want to delete all overlay objects from all Frames, then you may find it easier to use the **Delete All Overlays in this Topic** button within the UPK *Topic Editor*.
	Copy Screenshot	Take a copy of the screenshot on the current slide, and insert it as an overlay object. You can then crop and resize this copy, to draw attention to specific areas of the screenshot.
	Show/hide Bubble	Toggle between showing and hiding the Bubble image on the current slide. Note that this does not affect whether the Bubble appears in the Topic itself; it simply hides the bubble so that you can add overlays to the area of the screenshot that is underneath the Bubble.

■ If you place an overlay object on top of the Bubble, then you can move the Bubble to the front again by hiding the Bubble and then re-showing it.

7. Once you have made all required changes to the Topic, close PowerPoint, and in response to the message asking you if you want to save your changes, click on **Save**. You are returned to the **Topic Editor**, where you can see the overlays on the screenshots, as shown in the example below:

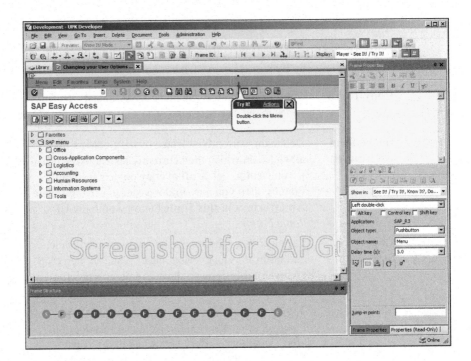

Note that this text is not a permanent part of the screenshot, although it will appear in the published output. You can confirm this by editing the screenshot (as explained earlier in this chapter); you will see that the overlay does not appear in your screenshot editor.

Editing an existing Screenshot Overlay

If you want to edit a Screenshot Overlay that you have previously added to a Topic, then you can do so as follows:

1. Open the Topic in the *Topic Editor*.

2. Click on the **Edit Overlay** button (![icon]( )). You are passed into Microsoft PowerPoint.

3. Edit your overlays as required (see the instructions above, on creating overlays).

4. Once you have finished making your changes, close PowerPoint and return to the *Topic Editor*.

Deleting all Screenshot Overlays from a Topic

If you have previously added overlays to a Topic, and now want to remove all of the overlays,on all Frames, then you can do so in one fell swoop, as explained in the steps below.

In the case of our sample exercise, assume that we have since checked the latest version of the software (SAP ECC 6.0) and determined that there are no visible changes to the screens captured in this recording. We therefore just want to remove the text overlay.

To remove all overlays from a Topic, carry out the steps described below:

1. Open the Topic in the *Topic Editor*.

2. Click on the **Delete All Overlays in this Topic** button ( ).

3. A message is displayed asking you to confirm the deletion. Click **Yes**.

All of the overlays are deleted—without you being passed into PowerPoint.

Editing Frame Comments

Authors can enter 'comments' for a Frame. Three categories of comments can be entered:

- **Author Notes**: These are designed to capture notes made by the author, or, in a split-development mode, to pass information from the recorder to the editor. Refer to *Chapter 2, Recording a Simulation* for additional information on capturing Author Notes.

- **Instructor Notes**: These are, presumably, used to capture information for the benefit of an instructor who will use the simulation as an integral part of a training conduct. However, they do not appear in the Presentation publishing format (where it would be reasonable to assume they would appear in the slide notes).

- **Expected Results**: These are designed to be used in Test It! mode, and most test document output formats, to specify what the expected result is of carrying out the specified action. Refer to *Chapter 13, Using UPK for Application Testing* for additional information on this functionality.

All three of these types of comments can be displayed, entered, and edited via the *Topic Editor*. This is done on the *Frame Comments* pane. To display this pane, select menu option **View | Panes | Frame Comments**. An example of the *Frame Comments* pane is shown below:

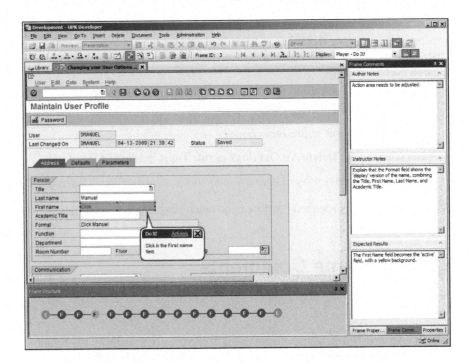

To edit any of the comment categories, simply change the text in the relevant text box. Note that comments are simple text only – you cannot use bold, italics, or any other formatting.

Where are Frame Comments used?

The following table identifies the output formats in which the various categories of comments appear.

Table 4-4 Where Frame Comments Appear

	Expected Results	Author Notes	Instructor Notes
Player / LMS			
Player – Test It! mode	●		
HTML Web Site			
Standalone Topic Files			
System Process			
Job Aid			
Training Guide			
Instructor Manual			●
Test Document	●		
Test Results		●	
Test Case – HP QC	●		
Test Case – IBM RQM	●		
Test Case – Oracle ATS	●		
Test Case - Other	●		●
Presentation			

✛ Instructor Notes only started appearing in the Instructor Manual in UPK 12.

Although these texts do not appear in many of the output document formats by default, they can be included in *any* Word document output by including the relevant bookmark at the relevant point. The relevant bookmarks are:

- FrameAuthorNotes
- FrameExpectedTestResults
- FrameInstructorNotes

Customization of the output documents is covered in *Chapter 16, Customizing UPK*.

There is one further place where Frame Comments (described in *Editing Frame Comments* on page 179) appear - this is in the *Overlay Editor*, where the **Author Notes** appear in the slide **Notes** section. An example of this is shown below:

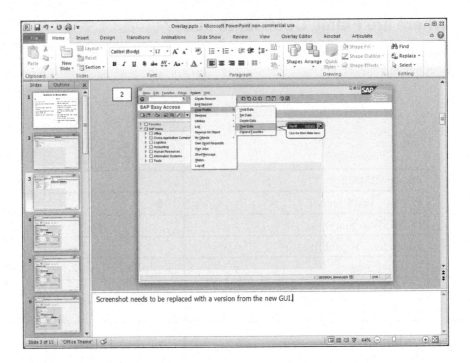

This is presumably done as the Author Notes may contain information that the Developer would find useful when creating or editing overlays (for example "Please mask customer name".

If you make any changes to the Author Notes from within PowerPoint, these changes are carried back into the Topic.

What is interesting, here, however, is that this clearly demonstrates that Frame Comments *can* be transferred to the Notes page of a Slide, yet the Instructor Notes are not transferred to the PowerPoint Notes page during publishing in the Presentation format—a feature that has been asked for since the presentation format was first introduced. Maybe we'll see it in the next release...

Summary

Although it is relatively quick to *record* a simulation, a simulation can hardly be called "finished" once it is recorded (despite what the Oracle salesperson may tell you). If you are lucky, the simulation will *work* as recorded, but even then, you will most likely want to edit it to improve the overall quality of the simulation. Fortunately, UPK makes it easy to change just about every aspect of a recording. Screenshots can be changed, Action Areas adjusted, Action Types changed, and just about every conceivable change can be made to the Bubble Text.

Much of this editing work is painstakingly detailed, but if we are to create *quality* training exercises, then this work is absolutely essential.

Editing takes place in the *Topic Editor*, which provides the following key components:

- The *Screenshot* pane, which shows the captured screenshot for the Frame that is currently being edited, and the content and position of the Bubble.

- The *Frame Navigation* pane, which shows the path(s) through the recorded Frames.

- The *Frame Properties* pane, which can be used to select Template Text, enter Custom Text, format these texts (and the Bubble containing them) and tag text for different modes. This pane is also used to specify the Action Type and Object Type captured during the recording. You can change these to influence the Template Text used.

- The *Sound Properties* pane (covered in *Chapter 11, Incorporating Sound Into Your Topics*), which can be used to assign sound files to Frames.

- The *Frame Comments* pane, which can be used to enter or change **Author Notes**, **Expected Results**, and **Instructor Notes**.

In the next chapter, we will look at how to insert our newly-edited simulation into an Outline, so that we can publish it.

5
Building an Outline

In *Chapter 3, Working in the UPK Developer Client*, we looked at the environment in which authors work. In this chapter, we will examine how to build an Outline, which is what your users will see.

In this chapter you will learn:

- The differences (and similarities) between Modules and Sections
- How to build an Outline by using Modules, Sections, and Topics

Outlines versus the Library

In *Chapter 3, Working in the UPK Developer Client*, we looked at how to organize our content objects within the *Library* screen. Although we organized our content into folders that were arranged in a hierarchy (by virtue of their being nested), the organization we chose was purely for the benefit of the author (or maybe for the Library Administrator) , and did not necessarily reflect the way in which our content would be presented to our users. Users (typically) access Topics through the Player, and within the Player, Topics are organized into an **Outline**.

The Outline is a hierarchical tree structure that uses Modules and Sections for branches, and Topics (and/or Questions and/or Assessments) for leaves. An example of an Outline, as it appears in the Player, is shown below.

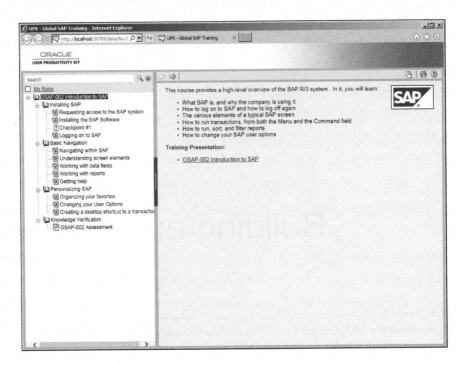

In UPK 8.7 and earlier, a Module could only contain Sections, and Sections could only contain Topics. This rigid three-level hierarchy was abandoned in OnDemand 9.1/UPK 3.5.

Prior to UPK 3.5, Sections appeared as blue books in the Player. The distinction was removed in UPK 3.5, when it became possible to nest Modules within Sections.

Starting with UPK 11, (only) empty Sections are once again displayed as blue books.

Functionally, there is no difference between modules and Sections—a Module can contain other Modules, Sections, Topics, Questions, and Assessments; a Section, in turn, can contain Modules, other Sections, Topics, Questions, and Assessments. The only difference between the Modules and Sections is the color of the icon that they use, although even that distinction is changing. On the *Library* screen, Modules are represented by purple 'books' (📕 / 📖) and Sections are represented by blue 'books' (📘 / 📖). However, this distinction largely disappears in the Player, where both Modules and Sections both appear as purple books. That is, unless they are 'empty' (they contain no 'children')— an empty Module is represented by a purple 'page' icon (📄) and an 'empty' Section is represented by a blue 'page' icon (📄)—both in the *Library* screen and in the Player!.

Therefore, because Modules and Sections function in the same way in the Library, and appear the same way in the Outline (assuming that you do not have any empty Outline Elements), the decision as to which one to use when building an Outline is largely an author (or Administrator) decision, and should be made based on what makes sense for you, and not what makes sense for the users. Personally, I tend to use Modules for my Player outlines, and Sections for Outlines that will be loaded into an LMS (as the two are seldom the same), just to make sure that I never confuse the two, or publish the wrong thing to the wrong place.

As we saw in *Chapter 3, Working in the UPK Developer Client*, authors can organize their content objects into folders in any way that they see fit. It is not necessary for Topics that are to appear within the same Outline Element in the Player to be stored in the same folder within the *Library* screen. Instead, an **Outline** can contain Modules, Sections, Topics, Assessments, and Questions organized in a structure for presentation to the user, regardless of the folder within the *Library* screen in which they are located. You could have the Modules in one folder, the Sections in another, and the Topics spread all over the place (although this would probably be a little confusing for the authors).

Organizing your Topics

Once are ready to publish your content objects, you need to decide how you want to structure your Outline (just as in *Chapter 3, Working in the UPK Developer Client* you decided on how to organize your *Library* screen).

There are a few key points to bear in mind while choosing your Outline structure. These are as follows:

- An Outline is for the benefit of the user. You should structure your Outline in a way that makes sense to your *users*, and certainly not for the convenience of your *authors*.

- You can have as many Outlines as you like. An Outline is really just a 'publishable unit', and if different users would benefit from different Players, then you should create different Outlines. There are some limits on the use of multiple Players if you choose to link your Player to an application (as described in *Chapter 15, Integrating UPK with Other Applications*), but it is perfectly acceptable to publish different Players for different groups of users.

- Any given Topic can appear in multiple Outlines. If you want to publish separate Players for each user group or training course, and want to include some common Topics in all every Player, then you can do this—and without having to duplicate the Topics.

- Although a single Topic can be included in a single Outline multiple times, it is strongly suggested that you have each Topic appearing only once in an Outline – otherwise, if a user uses the search function, role filtering, or context-sensitive help, the resulting list of 'applicable' Topics will include the repeated Topic multiple times, which may be confusing, especially if the user does not have an easy way to tell that these are all duplicates of the same, single Topic.

- You can include Outlines in other Outlines (strictly speaking, Outlines are just Outline Elements themselves). This means that if you create a separate Outline for each user group, you can also combine all of these individual Outlines into a single, 'master' Outline for integrating into your application help.

How you organize your Outline(s) is entirely up to you (or your client) and your individual requirements. Just be sure that you use a structure that makes sense to your users. Some options are:

- Having an Outline entry for each application and including everything to do with that application within this single Outline.

- Having an Outline entry for each of the application's functional areas. Note that if you want to provide context-sensitive help in Oracle or SAP, then you can only link to a single Outline. In this case, all of the content for the application needs to be in this single Outline.

- Having an Outline entry for each user group that contains only the content that those users need. (Note that you also have the possibility to publish by role, as explained in *Chapter 6, Publishing Your Content*, or filter your Topics based on the user's role, as explained in *Chapter 10, Adding Value in the Player*, so user group specific Players can actually be created from a single Outline.)

- Having an Outline entry for each training course. Given that role-based training is now almost taken for granted, this option and the preceding one (creating an outline for each user group) may well be the same.

It is worth consulting your user base to see which option they find most intuitive. Perhaps prototyping a few options for them to try out would help.

Although the Outline Elements can be nested to as many levels as you like, in any combination of Modules and Sections, and Topics can appear at any level in the hierarchy, some degree of restraint is advised. When the user first displays the Outline (for example, in the Player), all levels of the hierarchy will be collapsed. The user will be required to expand their way down the hierarchy to reach the required content. Having too many levels, or having Topics at inconsistent levels, will simply annoy your users. The flip-side of this is that you do not really want too many Topics within a single Outline Element —if you have more than around 20 then this may be an indication that you need to split the Outline Element.

In general, I advocate a three-level hierarchy for training content, where the first level of the hierarchy represents the course, the second level represents the lessons (or sections, or units, depending on your terminology) within the course, and the lowest level is the actual exercises (Topics) themselves. This works very well for relatively small, self-contained courses, although you may need to expand this model if you want to build out an entire training curriculum. We will be using this three-level, course-based structure when building our example Outline.

Building an Outline

Let's build an Outline to house the Topic that we recorded in *Chapter 2, Recording a Simulation*. We will create an Outline for a single course that contains three lessons, with a few simulations in each lesson.

Creating an Outline

An Outline is simply an Outline Element (either a Module or a Section) that contains Topics and (optionally) other Outline Elements. Creating an Outline, therefore, effectively consists of creating a Module or Section, and then inserting the Topics and additional Modules or Sections within it. For our sample exercise, we will use a Module for the highest level of the Outline.

To create an Outline, carry out the following steps:

1. On the *Library* screen, select the folder in which you want to create the Outline. As explained earlier, it is advisable to keep the outline elements in the same folder as the Topics that they contain, unless you have a good reason for not doing so (for example, if you have a habit of sharing Topics across Outlines, or because you want to provide different levels of security for Outline Elements and Topics). For our example, we have a folder named **GSAP-002 Introduction to SAP**, into which we placed our initial Topic. We'll store our Outline Elements in this same folder.

2. On the **Library Toolbar,** click on the **New Module** button (![icon]) (or select menu option **File | New | Module**). The *New Module* dialog box is displayed, as shown in the following screenshot (note that this example shows the dialog box after steps 4-6 have been completed):

   If you want to insert a Section instead of a Module, click on the **New Section** button (![icon]) instead (or select menu option **File | New | Section**). The resultant dialog box will be titled *New Section*, but will work in exactly the same way as the *New Module* dialog box, described below.

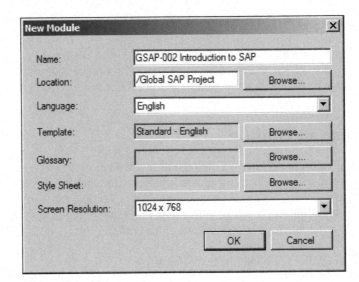

3. In the **Name** field, enter the name of the Module (or Section). For our example, because this is an Outline for a course we will give it the name of our course, which is **GSAP-002 Introduction to SAP**.

4. The **Location** field will default to the current folder. This is the one that you selected in Step 1, if you've been following along correctly. You can select any other folder by clicking on Browse and navigating to and selecting the required location, if necessary.

● You're probably wondering why we need to specify a Template for a Module (or Section) when the Template controls the Bubble Text and there is no Bubble Text in a Module. The simple answer is: inheritance. If you select a Template here, then this Template will automatically be used for any objects that are created from within this Module. This last point is significant. If you link an existing Topic into an Outline Element that uses a Custom Template, then the Custom Template will *not* automatically be applied to the existing Topic. The same inheritance applies to the Language, Glossary, and Screen Resolution settings. Note that you can change these settings for any element individually, so you do not need to keep the inherited value.

5. In the **Language** field, you can change the language of the spell-checker that will be used when spell-checking the Module—but not the content objects within the Module—they have their own language definition, as we shall see.

6. The **Template** field defines the Bubble Text Template that should be used with the Module. If you have a Custom Template, then you can select it here. Custom Templates are described in detail in *Chapter 16, Configuring UPK*. For now, we'll just accept the default of **Standard - English**.

7. If you have created a Glossary, then you can use the **Browse** button for the **Glossary** field to navigate to and select the required Glossary. Glossaries are covered in *Chapter 9, Adding Value to Your Topics*, so we will leave this field blank for now.

8. If you have created a Style Sheet (used for formatting Web Pages) then you can use the **Browse** button for the **Style Sheet** field to navigate to and select it. Style sheets are covered in *Chapter 16, Configuring UPK*, so we will leave this field blank for now.

9. The **Screen Resolution** should be set to be the same as the Topics that will be contained within the Module. Note that this only serves as a reminder or for inheritance (see the note above). A different resolution

can be specified for the Topics recorded from within this Outline Element.

10. Once you have specified all required information (Steps 3 to 9), click on **OK**. The Module is created and opened for editing in the *Outline Editor*.

The **Outline Editor** appears as another tab within the main *UPK Developer* screen, as shown in the example below. Note that a new toolbar—the *Outline Toolbar*—is available within this editor. We'll look at the various buttons on this toolbar as we need them.

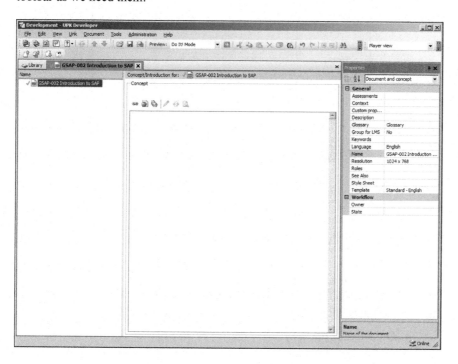

The Properties pane in the Outline Editor

If you display the *Properties* pane from with the *Outline Editor*, you will notice that it contains a selection field not present when the *Properties* pane is displayed on the *Library* screen. An example of this is shown below:

✦ The selection field was introduced to the *Properties* pane in UPK 12.1. In earlier versions, the only way to display the properties for a Web Page (used as a Concept Page) was to select the Web Page on the *Library* screen or open it in the *Web Page Editor*

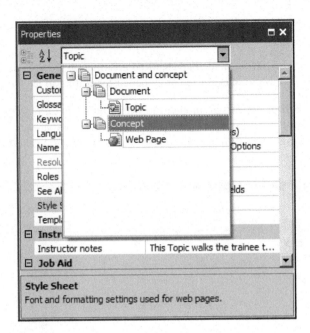

This field identifies the content object currently selected in the Outline and its associated Concept Page (if one is attached) in a hierarchical form. You can use this to choose the content object(s) for which the properties are displayed in the *Properties* pane. Although this will show (a maximum of) five entries, there are only really three that you need to use, as explained below:

- **Document and Concept**
  Clicking on this will display only the properties that are applicable to both the content object and its associated Concept Page.

- **Document**
  Clicking on this will display the properties for the content object (document) that is currently selected in the Outline.

  The entry hierarchically below this in the selection drop-down shows the type of document that is selected (typically a Module, Section, or Topic, but possibly a Question or Assessment). Clicking on this (document type) has the same effect as clicking on **Document** itself.

- **Concept**
  Clicking on this will display the properties for the content object that is attached as the Concept Page for the content object that is currently selected in the Outline.

  As with the **Document** level of the hierarchy, the type of this document is shown hierarchically underneath the **Concept** level, and works the same way as described above,

This is an incredibly useful feature for a number of reasons. Firstly, it means that you can display (and optionally change) the properties for the Concept Page without leaving the *Outline Editor*. Secondly, if you select the **Document and**

Concept option from the drop-down, only the Properties that are applicable to both the Document and the Concept Page are displayed. You can then change these properties for both of these at the same time. There aren't actually many properties that are shared by two different object types, but the **Workflow** ones are, so you can change the **Owner** or **State** for a Topic and the Web Page attached to it at the same time (as these two will normally be progressed through the content development process at the same time).

Adding content objects to an Outline

Next, let's insert some Sections into our Module.

To insert content objects into an existing Outline, carry out the steps described below. Note that these instructions explain how to create a **new** Outline Element within the Outline. How to insert an *existing* content object is explained later in this chapter.

1. Select the content object below which you want to insert the new Module, Section, Topic, Assessment, or Question. In our example, we currently have only one content object in our Outline—our initial Module.

2. Click on the appropriate button on the *Outline Editor Toolbar* depending on what type of content object you want to insert—for our example, we will use the **Link New Section** button (🔗) (you could also use the **Link New Module** button (🔗) to insert a new Module).

3. A new content object of the selected type is added below the selected element. This is given an initial name of **New Section** (or **New Module**, as appropriate). However, the name is open for editing. Change this to the name that you want to use for this content object. For our example, we will use **Installing SAP** for the name of our first Section.

4. Press *ENTER* to confirm your new name.

5. Repeat Steps 1 to 4 for all additional Outline Elements that you want to add to the Outline. For our example, we will insert another two Sections, named **Basic Navigation** and **Personalizing SAP**.

Our example outline now looks as follows:

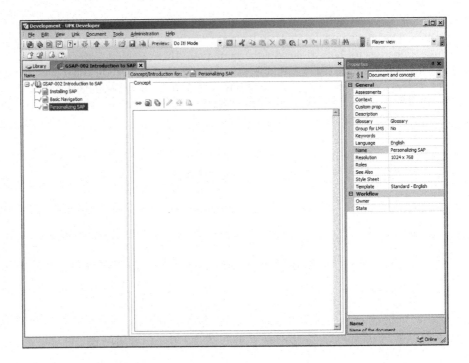

Note that Sections have exactly the same Properties as Modules. Because the Sections were created from within the Module, the values of some of these Properties (**Language**, **Template**, **Glossary**, and **Screen Resolution**) are inherited from the Module. You can change these Properties in the *Properties* pane, as explained for Modules, above.

Linking existing content objects into an Outline

Now that we have our Sections in place, we're ready to insert the Topic that we recorded in *Chapter 2, Recording a Simulation.*

To insert Topics (or any other *existing* content objects) into an Outline Element, carry out the steps described below:

1. Within the *Outline Editor*, click on the Outline Element below which you want the existing content object to appear. In our example, this is **Personalizing SAP**.

2. Select menu option **Link | Existing Document**. The *Link Existing Document* dialog box is displayed, as shown in the following screenshot:

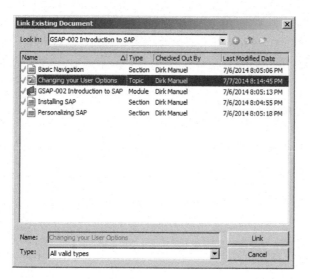

3. If the **Look in** field does not already show the folder into which you saved your Topic, then navigate to the required folder, by double-clicking on folders to navigate down, or clicking on the **Up One Level** button (🔼) to navigate up.

4. Click on the content object that you want to insert into the Outline Element, to select it, and then click on **Link**. For our example, we will insert the exercise we have been working on so far: **Changing your User Options**. The Topic is inserted into the Outline Element.

Our Outline now looks as shown in the following screenshot:

Note that the rightmost side of the *Outline Editor* is now split horizontally. The upper portion shows the *Concept* pane—exactly as it does for Modules and Sections. However, the lower section now contains the *Introduction* pane. This will contain any Bubble Text entered for the Start Frame (there is none in this example). This is only shown in the *Outline Editor* - the *Introduction* pane does not appear in the Player. This is explained in more detail in section *Using a Web Pages as the Concept Page* on page 356 of *Chapter 9, Adding Value to Your Topics*.

Inserting Topic placeholders

▲ If your authors are using the *Record It! Wizard*, then you must set the **Owner** property of the empty Topic to be the author who you want to record the Topic – otherwise they will not see it. Also, you will need to advise your authors to select the **Edit an existing topic** option, and not the **Create a new topic** option, in order to see the empty Topic. They will then be promoted to either create or delete the Topic; there is no other option—not even cancel.

Although we have technically done as much as we need to with our Outline, we'll finish things up by inserting placeholders for the remaining Topics that we will create for this course. Building the full Outline even before you have recorded the Topics is a good way of making sure that you don't miss anything. It also allows you to review the final structure of your Outline before you start work. If you are coordinating the work of several authors, this is also a useful way of identifying where everyone's work will go. You can also assign the empty Topics to specific individuals for recording.

To insert Topic placeholders, carry out the steps described below:

1. Click on the Module or Section within which you want the empty Topic to appear.

2. Click on the **Link New Topic** button (📄).

3. A new Topic is inserted, and given an initial name of **New Topic**. Change this name to the correct name of the Topic.

4. Repeat Steps 1 to 3 for all additional Topics that you want to add to the Outline.

Once you have finished, the Outline should look something like the example in the following screenshot:

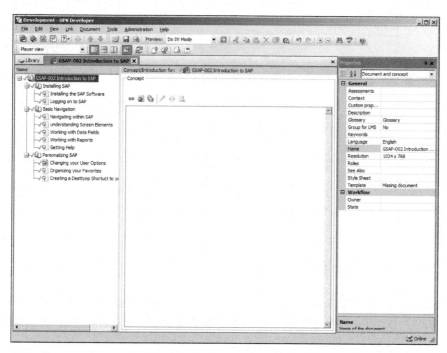

Note that the icon for an empty Topic ([image]) is different from the icon used for recorded Topics ([image]). This allows you to easily identify what is left to be done.

When you are ready to record the simulation for one of these empty Topics, simply select it and then click the **Record** button ([image]) on the *Standard Toolbar* (you can also double-click on the Topic). You'll then be taken directly to the **Recorder**. Refer to *Chapter 2, Recording a Simulation* for additional instructions on recording Topics.

For now, we are finished so we can click on the **Save** button ([image]) to save the Outline, and then close the *Outline Editor* tabbed page.

Adjusting the Outline

So, we now have a working Outline. Or do we? There is actually a problem with this Outline; however, this will not become apparent until we publish it. So for the sake of illustration, we will fast-forward several chapters and assume that we now have a fully-populated Outline. The following screenshot shows our finished Outline as it appears in the *Outline Editor* (so you're also getting a sneak peek of where we're going!):

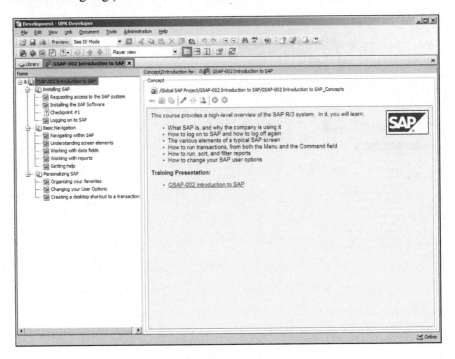

Now let's look at how this appears in the Player (assuming that we select the highest-level Module in the Outline for publishing):

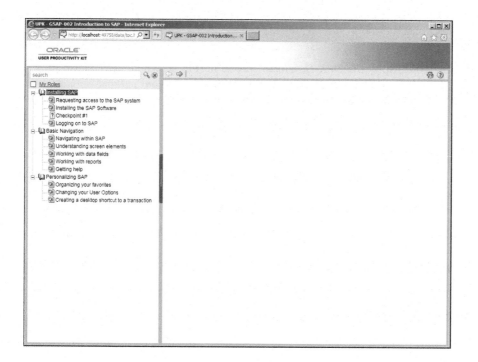

Notice anything missing? In the Outline we have a Module that contains four Sections each of which contains one or more sub-elements, but in the Player we only have the three Sections and their contents. What happened to the Module? Take a look at the Title bar of the Player window - you can see the text **GSAP-002 Introduction to SAP**. This is our Module. UPK has taken the highest-level Outline Element and used this as the Window title. What's more worrying is that the content of the Concept pane (which we will look at in *Chapter 9, Adding Value to Your Topics*) is no longer visible. This is because the Module to which the Concept has been attached is no longer a part of the hierarchy shown on the left.

So how do we resolve this? Simple: we just include our existing Outline within another Module or Section, and then that new Outline Element will be used as the Title. Let's take a look at how to do this.

First, we'll create our new high-level Module. Refer to *Creating an Outline* on page 189 for full instructions on how to do this. Because this Player will ultimately contain all of the training courses for our Global SAP Project, we will use a Module name of **Global SAP Training** for this high-level module. This Module name will appear in the Player Title bar, and a few other places in document output, as we shall see in *Chapter 6, Publishing Your Content*.

Once we have our new high-level Module, we need to insert our existing Outline into it. We can do this as explained above (in *Linking existing content objects into an Outline* on page 194) but for the sake of variety, and to introduce you to a

✦ In OnDemand 8.7 and earlier, where an Outline was limited to a three-level hierarchy (Module-Lesson-Topic), the Library was called a **Title** (OnDemand *Title*, Windows *Title* Bar— see, there's a kind of logic to it).

useful shortcut, we're going to use drag-and-drop. Carry out the steps described below:

1. Display the *UPK Developer* screen, in split-screen mode. You can split horizontally by clicking on the **Horizontal Layout** button ( ), or vertically by clicking on the **Vertical Layout** button ( )—it makes no difference for the purposes of this exercise (although the **Horizontal Layout** is used in the following screenshots).

2. In one pane (the upper one in the following screenshots) open up the Module that you just created, in the *Outline Editor*.

3. In the other pane (the lower one in the following screenshot) display the *Library* screen and navigate to the folder containing all of the content objects that we have created so far. Your screen should now look similar to the example shown next:

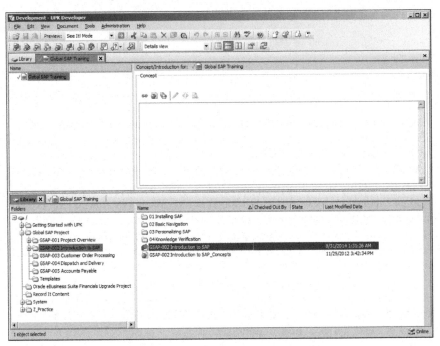

■ You can use this same drag-and-drop approach to insert any kind of content object (Module, Section, Topic, Assessment or Question) in an Outline. You can even drag from one Outline to another (this will *copy* and not *move* the element).

4. In the pane showing the *Library* screen, click on the original course Module (**GSAP-002 Introduction to SAP**) and drag this onto the *Outline* pane. As you hover the Module over its new location, UPK will indicate where it will be inserted, by the text **<documents will be inserted here>**, as shown in the example below. This allows you to make sure that you get your nesting correct.

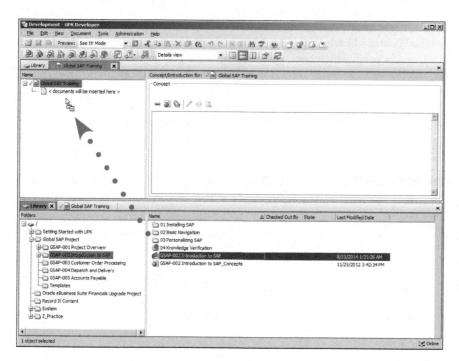

5. Click on the **Save** button ( ) to save your changes to the new Module, close the *Outline Editor* tabbed page, and then click on the **Single Layout** button ( ) to exit from split-screen view. Open up the new Module (**Global SAP Training**), and the Outline should now appear as shown in the following screenshot:

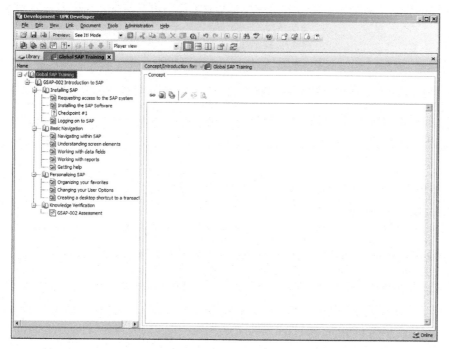

We have now created an additional Module that contains nothing apart from the original course Module. Note that this new Module does not contain anything in the *Concept* pane, which goes against our general guidelines outlined in *Chapter 10, Adding Value in the Player*. However, as this high-level outline will never really be seen by the users, this does not really matter.

What does matter is that all of our course elements are now displayed in the published Player, and our title bar contains a meaningful title. This is shown in the following screenshot:

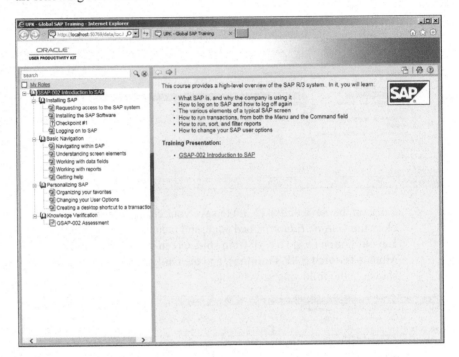

● Because the Concept Page for the highest-level Outline Element in our Outline will never be displayed, but it is this Outline Element that we select when publishing, you may find it convenient to attach a Concept Page that provides instructions to the person who performs the publishing – such as the URL to which the Player should be published, or a summary of the publishing process, or a list of things to check before publishing, and so on. However, do not use this approach if you publish any of the Outline-level printed formats, as they *do* include this Concept Page.

One last thing to note here: the **Introduction to SAP** Module and the four *Lesson* Sections use the same icon (a purple book), even though in the Outline Modules use purple books and Sections use blue books. In the Player, all Outline Elements are treated the same.

Inserting elements into an Outline via copy-and-paste

So far in this chapter we have looked at building an Outline by inserting new or existing elements via the menu. We have also looked at dragging and dropping elements into an Outline. There is one further way that we can add elements to an Outline: **copy-and-paste**. To use this method, follow the steps listed below:

1. From the *Library* screen, click on the element that you want to include in your Outline, and then press *CTRL+C* on your keyboard. (You could also right-click on the element and select **Copy** from the context menu.)

2. Open the Outline Element into which you want to insert the copied element.

3. In the *Outline Editor*, select the Outline Element into which you want to insert the copied element, and then press *CTRL+V* on your keyboard. (You could also right-click on the Outline Element and select **Paste** from the context menu.)

You can also use this method to insert multiple elements (within the same Library folder) into an Outline. To do this, simply hold down the *CTRL* key when selecting the subsequent elements (in Step 1 above). Interestingly, UPK will insert the elements *in the order in which they were selected*. By selecting the elements in the order in which you want them to appear in the Outline, you can save yourself from having to re-order the elements once they have been inserted into Outline Element.

Moving elements within an Outline

If you accidentally insert an element into the wrong place within an Outline (or you just want to change the order of the inserted elements) then you can this by either dragging and dropping the elements into the required order (even moving them from one Outline Element to another), or by selecting the element that you want to move and using the **Move Up** button (🔼) and the **Move Down** button (🔽) to move the elements to the correct position.

● Moving an element within the Outline will not move the actual content object within the *Library* screen—it will still remain in its original folder. If you are in the habit of arranging your *Library* screen folders to match your Outline, you should remember to move the content objects whenever you move them within Outline Elements in the Outline.

Deleting elements from an Outline

If you decide that you no longer want a particular element to be included in an Outline, then you can remove it by clicking on the element in the **Outline Editor** to select it, and then clicking on the **Delete Link** button (🔳). You can also remove an element simply by clicking on it to select it and then pressing the *DELETE* key on your keyboard. Note that this will not delete the element from the Library – it will only remove it from the Outline.

Summary

Whereas folders in the *Library* screen are used to organize content objects for the benefit of the author, **Outlines** are used to organize these content objects into a structure suitable for presenting to the users.

Modules and Sections are organizational objects (referred to as Outline Elements) that group **Topics**, **Assessments** and **Questions** (and other Modules and Sections) into a hierarchical structure. This hierarchy can consist of as many sub-levels (by nesting Modules and Sections—in any order or combination as necessary.

It is the **Outline** that is selected for publishing. This leads us nicely into the subject of our next chapter: publishing your content.

6

Publishing Your Content

In this chapter, we will look at how to publish an Outline. We will also look at some of the things that you should always do before publishing your content, in order to check that your deliverables are of the best quality possible.

This chapter takes a close look at the available publishing formats, and provides examples for each of them. If you are not sure which format best suits your needs, or you just want to see what else is available to you, then you may find this chapter to be a useful reference.

Bear in mind that although publishing will always be the last thing that you do, you will quite possibly publish your content at regular periods throughout the development process, to check your work, or to provide review copies to reviewers, and so on. Therefore, it helps to have a solid understanding of the options available when publishing your content, before you get as far as your final delivery.

Note that you can only publish content from an Outline. If you want to publish a Topic, you will first need to add it to an Outline Element. Refer to *Chapter 5, Building an Outline* for more information on Outlines and Outline Elements.

✦ However, you can *preview* Topics (and Web Pages) directly from the Library screen (in UPK 12.1).

In this chapter, you will learn:

- How to spell-check your content
- How to test your simulations
- How to publish to on-line formats
- How to publish your content as documents
- How to publish Topics to movie (video) format

Pre-publication checks

Before publishing your content, there are a few things that you should always do. These are summarized in the following list, and then explained in further detail in the sections following this list.

- Perform a full spell-check on the content that you will be publishing.
- If you have defined a glossary (see *Chapter 9, Adding Value to Your Topics* for details) then re-generate the glossary links.
- Test your content in all of the modes in which it will be made available.

You will typically do all of these things many times throughout the development process (especially the testing), but it is advisable to perform all of these tasks again, immediately prior to publication. This is particularly important if you are working in a multi-author environment and will be publishing content that may have been created or changed by other authors, whose checks may not be as thorough as yours.

Checking your spelling

To check the spelling of a content object, select the content object either on the *Library* screen or in the *Outline Editor*, and then click on the **Check Spelling** button (![icon]). Note that you can also select a folder, an Outline Element, and/or multiple content objects, depending on what you want to spell-check. Before publishing an Outline, it is recommended that you select the highest-level element in the Outline. The spell-checker will then include all sub-elements within this, as explained below.

Once you click on the **Check Spelling** button, UPK will determine if there are any other documents related to the document(s) that you selected, and, if it finds any, will display the following dialog box:

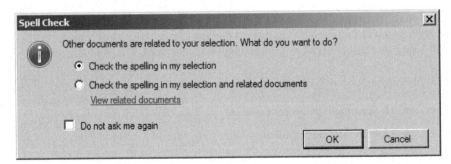

What are these related documents? Generally, they are documents contained within, or linked to by the selected element. To see exactly which content objects UPK has identified, you can click on the **View related documents** link. This will display a dialog box similar to the following one:

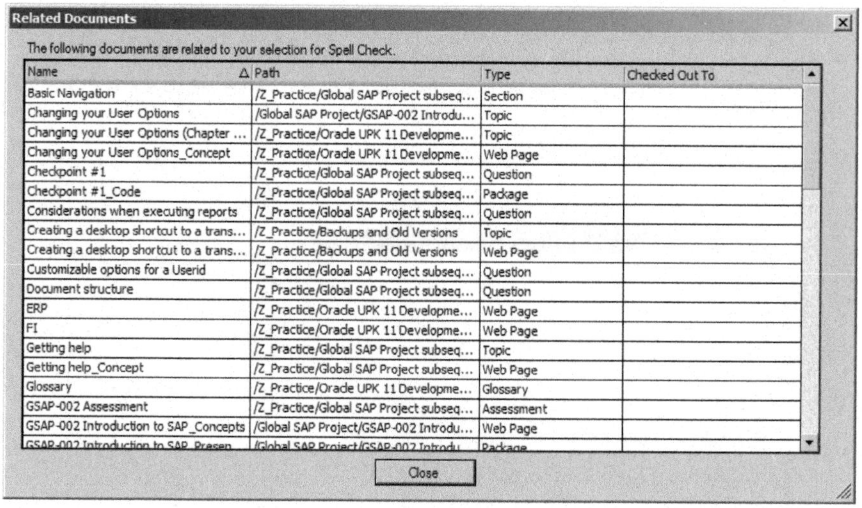

Related Documents ✕

The following documents are related to your selection for Spell Check.

Name	Path △	Type	Checked Out To	▲
Basic Navigation	/Z_Practice/Global SAP Project subseq...	Section		
Changing your User Options	/Global SAP Project/GSAP-002 Introdu...	Topic		
Changing your User Options (Chapter ...	/Z_Practice/Oracle UPK 11 Developme...	Topic		
Changing your User Options_Concept	/Z_Practice/Oracle UPK 11 Developme...	Web Page		
Checkpoint #1	/Z_Practice/Global SAP Project subseq...	Question		
Checkpoint #1_Code	/Z_Practice/Global SAP Project subseq...	Package		
Considerations when executing reports	/Z_Practice/Global SAP Project subseq...	Question		
Creating a desktop shortcut to a trans...	/Z_Practice/Backups and Old Versions	Topic		
Creating a desktop shortcut to a trans...	/Z_Practice/Backups and Old Versions	Web Page		
Customizable options for a Userid	/Z_Practice/Global SAP Project subseq...	Question		
Document structure	/Z_Practice/Global SAP Project subseq...	Question		
ERP	/Z_Practice/Oracle UPK 11 Developme...	Web Page		
FI	/Z_Practice/Oracle UPK 11 Developme...	Web Page		
Getting help	/Z_Practice/Global SAP Project subseq...	Topic		
Getting help_Concept	/Z_Practice/Global SAP Project subseq...	Web Page		
Glossary	/Z_Practice/Oracle UPK 11 Developme...	Glossary		
GSAP-002 Assessment	/Z_Practice/Global SAP Project subseq...	Assessment		
GSAP-002 Introduction to SAP _Concepts	/Global SAP Project/GSAP-002 Introdu...	Web Page		
GSAP-002 Introduction to SAP _Presen	/Global SAP Project/GSAP-002 Introdu...	Package		▼

Close

For the screenshot above, we had selected a Module. UPK has identified several other content objects as related documents. Most of these are the other content objects contained within the selected Outline Element. However, UPK has also identified a number of Web Pages. Where did these come from? Typically, they are Web Pages that have been attached to one of the Topics (or other elements) already identified—for example, Web Pages used as the Concept Page for the identified content object(s). Web Pages are discussed in detail in *Chapter 9, Adding Value to Your Topics*.

UPK will also include any Glossaries that have been attached to any of the content object(s) that you are spell-checking. As the check for related documents is recursive, it will also include *all* of the Glossary entries (Web Pages) included in the Glossary (and not just the Glossary entries actually *linked* to the content object). This means that if you separately spell-check three Topics that all use the same Glossary then you will end up spell-checking the Glossary, in its entirety, three times. You can mitigate this to some degree by adding the Glossary terms to the custom dictionary the first time that you spell-check the Glossary.

Choose whether or not you want your spell check to include these related documents, by selecting the relevant option in the dialog box (shown earlier), and then click **OK**. The *Check Spelling* dialog box is displayed, as shown below:

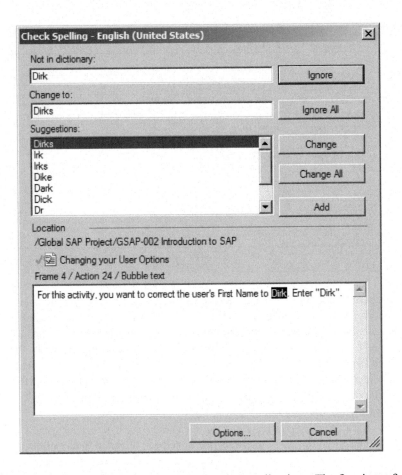

This is similar to the spell-checker in many other applications. The first input field in the dialog box is the text that the spell-checker thinks is spelled incorrectly. Below this, the spell-checker provides a suggested alternative (in the **Change to** field), followed by a list of other possible alternatives, in the **Suggestions** box. You can accept the proposal (click on **Change**), select any other suggestion (by double-clicking on it in the **Suggestions** list), or simply overtype the **Change to** field with your own value. Of course, you also have the usual options of **Ignore**, **Ignore All**, **Change**, **Change All**, and **Add** (to custom dictionary).

The **Location** section of the *Check Spelling* dialog box contains several items of useful information. The first line of this specifies the location (folder) in the Library in which the content object currently being spell-checked can be found. The line immediately following this specifies the name of the object itself. If you are spell-checking a Topic, then the third line specifies the exact point within the Topic at which the spelling mistake was found. This consists of up to three identifiers, separated by slashes ('/'). These are:

- **Frame identifier**: This is useful if you do not want to accept the spell-checker's suggestion as it is, but do want to go to this frame in the Topic Editor to manually adjust the text.

- **Action identifier** (for Action Frames): This is the sequential number of the Action within the Topic. This is almost useless as it is impossible to identify an Action within the *Topic Editor* based on this number.

- **Text type**: This specifies the type of text element in which the potential spelling mistake was found. This is normally **Bubble Text**, but could instead be the **Object Name**, **String input text**, **Author Comments**, and so on.

Finally, the *Check Spelling* dialog box contains a text area (at the bottom of the dialog box), that shows the full text of the element being spell-checked. This is extremely useful for seeing the text that the spell-checker objected to in its full context, so that you can determine if it really is invalid, or is acceptable.

Once the spell check is complete, a confirmation message is displayed. As you can see from the following example, this shows the number of changes made (across all checked documents).

If you are working in a client/server environment and corrected the spelling in any documents that were not currently checked out to you, then UPK will automatically check these out to you, and will inform you of the number of content objects that were checked out, as shown in the example above. If you are working in a standalone environment then you will not see this second message.

If you click on the **View activity log** link, UPK will display a list of what was changed. This is not as useful as it sounds, as the activity log contains one entry for each content object changed, and not one entry for each replacement. However, it is useful if you are working in a client/server environment, as you will be able to see exactly which documents were checked out. You will need to know this in order to check them back in again. (Although, of course, if you choose the **Check in related documents** when you check in the main content object that you selected for spell-checking, then once again UPK will identify these checked-out documents as related documents, and include them in the list of content objects to check in. Refer to *Chapter 7, Version Management* for more information on checking in content objects.) An example of the *Spelling Activity Log* is shown below:

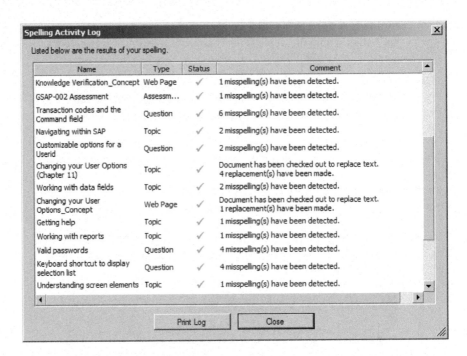

Note that the comment **x misspelling(s) have been detected** indicates that UPK found what it thought was a spelling mistake, but you chose to ignore it (by clicking on **Ignore** or **Ignore all** in the spell-checker). The comment **x replacement(s) have been made** indicates that UPK found a spelling mistake and you corrected this (by clicking on **Change, Change all**, or **Add**).

Changing your spelling options

At the bottom of the *Check Spelling* dialog box is the **Options** button. Clicking on this button displays the *Options* dialog box, with which you are no doubt familiar by now, but with only the **Spelling** category available. For details of the options provided in this and a description of their use, refer to *Appendix B, User Options*.

Updating the Glossary links

If you have assigned a Glossary to any of your content objects, then you should update the glossary links for all content objects in the Outline before publishing (at least before your final publication).

Update the Glossary links by carrying out the steps described below:

1. On the *Library* screen, select the objects for which you want to update the Glossary links. You can either select specific content objects, or you

can select a folder, in which case all of the objects within that folder (and any sub-folders) will be updated.

2. Select menu option **Edit | Update Glossary Links**.

For more information on Glossaries and the update process for Glossary links, refer to *Chapter 9, Adding Value to Your Topics*.

Previewing Topics

UPK provides the ability to play or display a Topic without first publishing the Outline Element in which it is contained. This is normally quicker than publishing (and more convenient, as the content is launched immediately), which makes it a good option for testing your content during development.

Setting your preview defaults

There are a number of user options in UPK that determine how Topics are previewed. To set these, choose menu option **Tools | Options**, and then select a category of **Preview**. For a list of the available options, and a description of their purpose, refer to *Appendix B, User Options*.

The **Document** and **Player** categories of options can be used to set the default preview values for the Player and the output document formats, respectively. The options available in these categories are exactly the same as the publishing options described later in this chapter, under each publishing format (albeit sometimes in a different order). They will therefore not be repeated here. The values selected under **Options** here will be used as the default settings for publishing, although they can be changed at publishing time.

Previewing a Topic

To preview a content object, carry out the following steps:

1. Click on the Topic (either on the *Library* screen or in the *Outline Editor*) that you want to preview.

2. In the **Preview** field on the *Outline Editor Toolbar*, use the drop-down to select the mode in which you want to preview the Topic.

3. Click on the green **Go** to button ( ) to the right of the **Preview** field.

Prior to UPK 12.1 it was only possible to preview a Topic from within the *Outline Editor* (which meant that you had to first link the Topic into an Outline). UPK 12 allows you to preview Topics or other content objects directly from the *Library* screen.

The Topic is displayed on the screen in the selected mode or document format. Once you close the Topic (or document), you are returned to the *Library* screen or *Outline Editor*, as appropriate. Note that (unlike published versions) the preview version of your Topic is not saved, and you will need to repeat the steps above if you want to preview it again.

Testing your content

Before you publish your content, you should *always* test your simulations. This may seem to be such a truism that it does not even need to be said. However, I have seen several 'final' simulations that simply don't work in one or more of the published modes, so apparently it *does* need to be said. Again: Before you publish your content, you should *always* test your simulations.

Note that testing does not mean simply running through the simulation once, in *Try It!* mode, with 'skip' enabled. It means making sure that every Frame in every path in every mode has the correct Bubble Text and the correct Action.

Here is a good set of steps for testing a single Topic:

1. Open the Topic in the *Topic Editor*.

2. In the **Display** field, select **Player - See It / Try It**.

3. Visit every Frame and check that the Bubble Text is correct and that the action area is in the correct place. Make sure that you go to every Frame, every Alternative Path, and every Alternative Action.

4. Repeat Steps 2 and 3 for all of the other modes (that you are using). A few things to watch out for in each of the modes, are:

    See It! mode:

    *   Check the speed of the transition from one Frame to the next.

    *   Check that **Explanation Frames** (discussed in *Chapter 9, Adding Value to Your Topics*) are displayed where necessary.

    *   Check that **Decision Frames** (discussed in *Chapter 14, Allowing Alternatives*) are not displayed (unless required).

    Try It! mode:

    *   Check that the user is provided with both the instructions and the data required to complete each Action (see also *Chapter 4, Editing a Topic* for a discussion of Bubble Text in different modes).

    *   Check that the **Action Area** is a realistic size, and that string input Action Areas look good (that is, it is correctly sized, and using the correct font and background color).

    *   Check that Bubbles are correctly positioned, and do not obscure information on the screen to which the user needs to refer.

    Know It? mode:

    *   Check that the user is provided with the data but not the instructions required to complete each Action.

    *   Check that the 'pass score' is realistic.

- Check that adequate Alternative Actions (discussed in *Chapter 14, Allowing Alternatives*) are provided, in order to give the user a sporting chance.

Do It! mode:

- Check that the user is provided with the instructions but not the data required to complete each Action.

- Check that linked Frames (where the **Keep this action with next action in Do It! mode** option has been used—see *Chapter 4, Editing a Topic*) are used appropriately.

Print **It? mode:**

- Check that only the required screenshots are included.

- Check that all additional information taken from the Topic Properties is specified.

- Check that appropriate Print Areas have been defined (typically, this is only necessary when the Action Area is unsuitable for use as the Print Area).

5. Close the *Topic Editor*, and go to the *Library* folder or an Outline Element containing the Topic.

6. Preview the Topic in *See It!* mode (see *Publishing your content* on page 214). Although *See It!* mode and *Try It!* mode use the same Bubble Text it is worth running through them separately so that you can check the timing of the auto-advance in *See It!* mode. Check that every Action works correctly, and that the Bubble Text correctly describes these Actions. If you have Alternative Paths and/or Alternative Actions, make sure that you test each of these, even if it means running through the Topic several times in each mode.

7. Repeat Step 6 for all of the other modes (that you are using).

It is a good idea, when testing your content, to have both the Player and the *Topic Editor* open at the same time. That way, as soon as you notice something wrong in the Player, you can flip to the *Topic Editor*, make the change, then flip back to the Player and continue testing. This is much easier than going through the entire Topic in the Player, and remembering or making a note of everything that needs to be fixed before going back and making any changes. This method of working is particularly effective if you have two screens attached to your computer (as is an increasingly common practice, especially with laptop users) as you can display the Player and the *Topic Editor* side-by-side, while you are working. Note that you can play the Topic either by publishing it (as explained in the next section in this chapter) and then opening the Player, or simply by using the **Preview** option (described above). Both methods will allow you to flip between the Player and the *Topic Editor*.

Publishing your content

UPK allows you to publish your content in a number of formats, as shown in the *Formats* pane of the *Publish Content* dialog box (see the screenshots later in this chapter). This includes two formats for on-line (interactive) use, and eight 'document' formats. The overall approach for publishing in any of these formats is the same, and so is described only once, under *"Publishing content—a generic approach"*, next. The options available, and the format of this output, obviously vary depending on the chosen format, and these are described separately, in subsequent sections.

Publishing content—a generic approach

To publish one or more content objects, carry out the following steps:

1. Open the Outline Element (Module or Section) that you want to publish, in the *Outline Editor* (refer to *Chapter 5, Building an Outline* for further details of the *Outline Editor*, if necessary).

2. In the *Outline Editor*, click on the Outline Element that you want to publish, to select it. Note that this does not have to be the same Outline Element as you opened in Step 1—you can publish at any level within the Outline. You can even select an individual Topic to publish only this Topic (although UPK will also include the Modules and/or Subjects within which it is contained—but not other content objects within them).

3. Click on the **Publish** button (🗐). (You can also select menu option **File | Publish**). The *Publish Content* dialog box is displayed, as shown in the following screenshot:

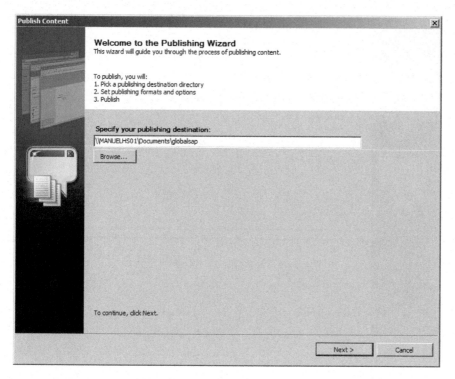

4. Specify (or navigate to and select, via the **Browse** button) the folder to which you want to publish your content. This can be on a local or remote drive (although publishing to your local PC will typically be faster).

5. Click **Next**. The *Select Publishing Options* settings are displayed, as shown below:

● The first time that you publish content to a specific location, UPK will remember all of your settings including the content objects that you selected for publishing. UPK will save these within that folder. The next time that you publish to the same folder, UPK will automatically load these settings (and will prompt you for confirmation if you are publishing different content objects to the same location).

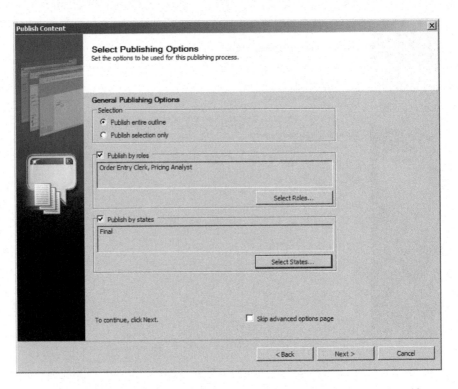

Select Publishing Options

6. Under **General Publishing Options**, in the **Selection** section, specify whether you want to publish the entire Outline selected in Step 1 (option **Publish entire outline**), or only the content object selected in Step 2 and everything under it (option **Publish selection only**).

■ Roles are described
*Chapter 10, Adding Value in
the Player.*

7. If you have defined Roles for any of the included content objects and only want to publish content that is tagged for specific Roles, then select the **Publish by roles** check-box and continue with Step 8. Otherwise, go directly to Step 11.

8. Click on **Select Roles**. The **Select Roles** dialog box is displayed, as shown in the following screenshot:

Note that you will only see Roles in this list that have been assigned to at least one of the content objects selected. This may not be the full list of Roles that you have defined in your Library.

9. Select all of the Roles for which you want to publish the content. Only content that has been tagged for the Role(s) that you have selected will be published.

10. Click **OK** to return to the *Select Publishing Options* screen.

11. If you are working in a client/server environment, and only want to publish content that has a certain State property, then select the **Publish by states** check-box and continue with Step 12. Otherwise, skip to Step 17.

12. Click on the **Select States** button. The *Select States* dialog box is displayed, as shown in the following screenshot:

■ States are described in *Chapter 7, Version Management*.

● The option to publish by state is only available in a client/server environment. This option is not available in the standalone (single user) environment, because the **State** Property is not available in a standalone environment.

✦ The option to publish by state was introduced in UPK 3.5, and is not available in earlier versions.

Note that (unlike the Roles list in Step 9) this list will include **all** States, regardless of whether the any of the selected content objects have these states. If you select (only) a State that does not apply to any content, then nothing will be published.

13. Select each of the States that an object can have in order to be selected for publishing. You can use this option to (for example) publish only Final content, or only content that is **In Review** (for example, for sending to a reviewer), and so on.

14. Click **OK** to return to the *Select Publishing Options* dialog box.

15. Make sure that the **Skip advanced options page** check-box at the bottom of the *Select Publishing Options* dialog box is not selected.

16. Click on **Next**. The *Advanced Publishing Options* settings are displayed, as shown in following screenshot:

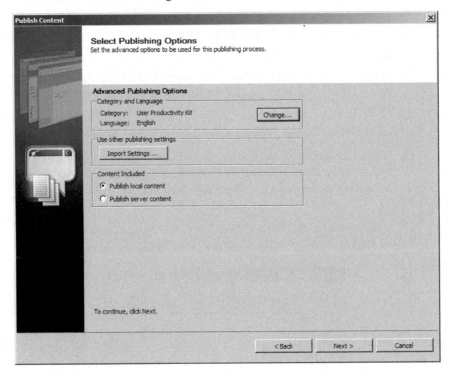

17. Under *Advanced Publishing Options*, select the appropriate settings as follows:

■ For more information on Publishing Categories, refer to *Chapter 16, Configuring UPK*. For more information on local language support, refer to *Chapter 17, Localizing Your Content*.

- To change the Publishing Category or language, click on the **Change** button, and then select the required category and/or language.

- If you are publishing to a new folder location, but want to use the publication options used when you previously published to another folder, then you can use the **Import Settings** button to navigate to and select the original publication folder. For more information on saved settings and their use, refer to *Automatic publishing* on page 287.

- If you are working in a client/server environment, then select whether you want to include only content that has been checked in to the server (select the **Publish server content** option) or want to include content that you currently have checked out (select the **Publish local content** option).

18. Click **Next**. The *Format Selection* screen is displayed, as shown below:

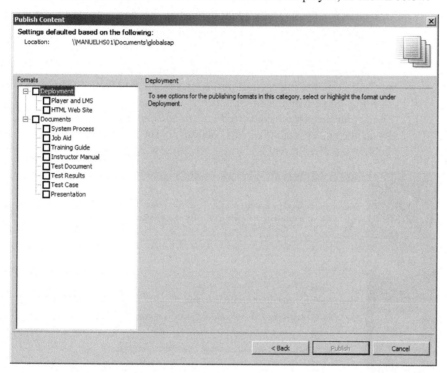

19. In the **Formats** pane on the leftmost side of the dialog box, select the check-box for the format in which you want to publish the content. Note that you can select multiple formats at the same time. You can also select the check-box for a category (**Deployment** or **Documents**) to publish in all of the formats in that category.

20. Depending on the format that you select, the pane on the rightmost side of the screen will be populated with the options available for the format. (Note that even if you click on the format name, the options will be grayed out until you select the check-box for that format.) The options for each format are explained separately, below. Refer to the relevant section and make any necessary adjustments to the options, before continuing with the next step.

21. Click **Publish**. Your content is published in the selected format(s). While this is happening, a *Publishing Progress* dialog box similar to the one shown in the following screenshot will be displayed:

✦ The ability to publish to multiple formats at the same time was introduced in OnDemand 9.1—in previous versions, you could only publish to one format at a time).

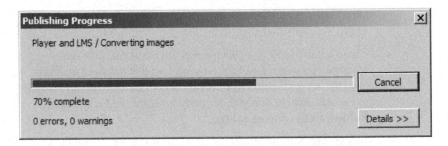

You can click on the **Details** button to show the messages for any errors or warnings generated during the publishing process (these messages will also be displayed in the *Activity Log* when publishing finishes.

Depending on the volume of content that you are publishing, the location of the destination folder (local or network), and the number of formats in which you are publishing it, this may take some time. Once the content has been published, the *Publishing Complete* dialog box will be displayed. An example of this dialog box (in this example for the publication of a Player) is shown in the following screenshot:

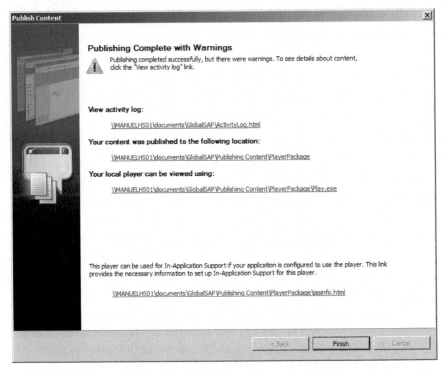

✛ Prior to UPK 12, the various links provided in the *Publishing Complete* dialog box were presented as a set of mutually-exclusive options; you could only choose one and then the *Publishing Wizard* would close so that you could not choose another.

22. Depending on the format into which you have published your content, and whether there are any errors during the publication process, links to one or more of the following links are provided:

    ○ A link to the *Activity Log*, which will list any errors found (such as broken links, and so on). This link is only available if there were Warnings or Errors during publishing.

o A link to the location to which the content has been published (which is useful if you need to rename or move the published content).

o A link to launch the Player from the publish location (this is only available if you published to the Player format).

o A link to instructions on setting up In Application Support (IAS). These are very basic instructions, and you're better off referring to the *In-Application Support* document in the Documentation folder for your installation.

Generally, you should display the local player, so that you can check the published content. Even if you have only made a very minor change, it is worth checking that the changes have been correctly implemented.

23. Once you have clicked on any links necessary, and reviewed everything you want to, close the *Publishing Wizard* by clicking on the **Finish** button.

Published folder structure

If you choose to display the folder into which the content was published, you will see a structure similar to the one shown in the following screenshot:

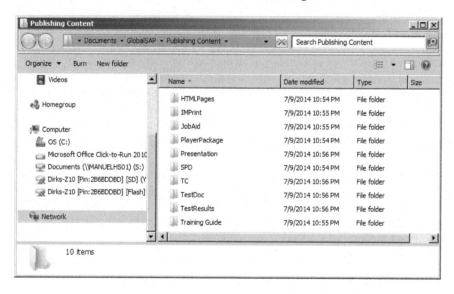

There are two sub-folders in the destination folder (which is \\MANUELHS01\ Documents\GlobalSAP\ in this example): Publishing Content and Publishing Data. The Publishing Content folder contains your actual generated output. The Publishing Data folder contains work files that UPK generated during the publication process. These files will be used by UPK for incremental publishing (for example, when republishing an existing

Outline within which only some of the content has changed), but should not be distributed with your content.

● The folder names that are used are defined in the Deployment Category Package for each output type. Refer to *Chapter 16, Configuring UPK* for more information on Deployment Categories.

Within each of these main folders there is one folder per publication format. The previous example shows all ten of the possible folders (compare this list with the list of publication formats shown on the final screen of the Publishing Wizard, above). The exact content of these folders will depend on the publishing format to which it applies. Refer to the relevant section below for additional information on the files generated for each publication format.

Publishing for on-line use

UPK provides two formats in which an Outline can be published for on-line use. These are listed under the **Deployment** category in the **Publish Content** dialog box. Each of these formats is described separately below.

Creating a Player and LMS Package

✛ Prior to UPK 11, the **Player** and the **LMS Package** were separate publishing formats and could be selected independently of each other. However, as the LMS format only requires a few small additional files over the Player, the two formats have since been combined, for simplicity.

The **Player** is the possibly the most common publishing format, and the one that we have been looking at throughout this book. The Player is effectively a self-contained browser-based application that contains one or more Topics, organized according to an Outline. The Player is entirely self-contained; no special software, add-ins, or **ActiveX** controls are required by the users. This makes it a great option for web sites, or for publication to (for example) CD-ROM. The downside of this format is that it generates a large number (typically, thousands for all but the most trivial of Outlines) of individual files in a specific folder structure that must be retained. This makes it unwieldy for emailing to users, or loading into a **Content Management System** (**CMS**) that manages content at the individual file level. That said, all of these files are very small (30 KB or less), which again makes this format suitable for web-based delivery.

A **Learning Management System** (**LMS**) – including UPK's own **Knowledge Center** – also provides the same interactive functionality as the Player, which may explain why UPK now bundles these two formats together. An LMS simply requires an additional handful of files to be generated (such as the **SCORM** manifest), so it is easier for UPK to just generate these at the same time.

Document properties

The **Properties** that are relevant for the **Player and LMS** format are shown in the following screenshot.

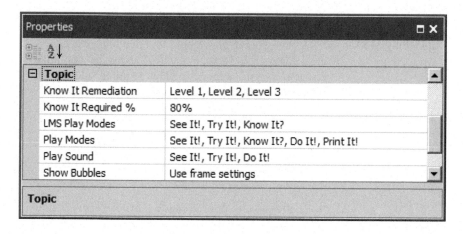

The table below describes the use of these Properties.

Property	Use
Know It Remediation	When a user performs an incorrect action in *Know It?* mode, there are three possible levels of assistance that may be displayed. These are: • **Level 1**: The user is asked to try again • **Level 2**: The user is given instructions (effectively, the *Try It!* mode texts) and asked to try again • **Level 3**: The user is given instructions and the Action Area is highlighted, and the user is asked to try again. The first time that the user gets the step wrong, Level 1 assistance is provided. If they get it wrong again, Level 2 assistance is provided. If they get it wrong a third time, the Level 3 assistance is provided. You can select or deselect any of these levels of help; for example, if you want UPK to go straight to displaying the instructions and the Action Area (Level 3) the first time that the user gets the step wrong, you would deselect the Level 1 and Level 2 remediation levels.
Know It Required %	Use this Property to specify the percentage score that the user must achieve in *Know It?* mode, to pass the 'test'. This applies to both the Player and the LMS.

● There is actually a fourth level of remediation, if the user does not carry out the correct action at Level 3. At that point UPK effectively performs the action itself, in *See It!* mode, before handing control back to the user. This level of remediation cannot be deactivated.

Property	Use
LMS Play Modes	Select the specific play modes that should be made available for this Topic, in the LMS. Note that the 'most restrictive' of these modes will be 'required' and used to determine if the user has 'completed' the learning activity. This is determined as follows 1. If *Know It?* mode is available, use this 2. Otherwise, if *Try It!* mode is available, use this 3. Otherwise, if *See It!* mode is available, use this 4. Otherwise, if *Print It!* mode is available, use this
LMS Required Mode	If your content will be accessed via an LMS, then by default, the mode that the user must complete a Topic in to be considered complete will be determined as the 'most restrictive' mode (see **LMS Play Modes**, above). If you want to require that a specific mode be used for this Topic, then select this mode, here.
Play Modes	Select the specific play modes that should be made available for this Topic, in the Player. If a play mode is not selected, the button for that Play mode will not be displayed.
Play Sound	Select the modes for which sound should be played. This applies to both the Player and the LMS.
Show Bubbles	Select whether or not the Bubbles should be displayed for the Topic as a whole. Possible values are: • **Use frame settings**: Defer to the individual Frame settings within the Topic to determine if Bubbles should be displayed, on a Frame-by-Frame basis. • **Always**: Display all Bubbles for all Frames, regardless of the individual Frame settings in the Topic. • **Never**: Do not display any Bubbles, regardless of the individual Frame settings in the Topic.

Publishing options

The following sections explain the publishing options available for the **Player and LMS** publishing format. Each category of options is explained separately.

In-Application Support

The following screenshot shows the options that are available in the **In-Application Support Configuration** category when publishing content in the **Player and LMS** format.

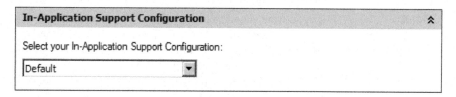

The following table explains the purpose of the options shown in the screenshot above:

Option	Use
Select your In-Application Support Configuration	If you have created a custom In-Application Support (IAS) configuration file, then select this file from the drop-down. Otherwise, the **Default** configuration will be used. For more information on IAS configuration, refer to *Chapter 15, Integrating UPK with Other Applications*.

Content

The following screenshot shows the options that are available in the **Content** category when publishing content in the **Player and LMS** format. .

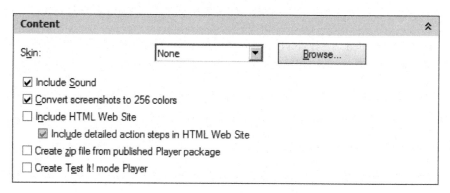

✛ The option **Create links for backward compatibility**, which allowed dhtml_kp.html links created for pre-9.1 versions of OnDemand has been discontinued as of UPK 12.

The following table explains the purpose of the options listed in the screenshot above:

✛ Prior to UPK 12, you could select the sound frequency (to use), or "None". With UPK 12, sound is always published at a standard hard-coded frequency of 96kbps in ACC format (or .flv files for Windows 2008 SP2).

Option	Use
Skin	If you have defined a custom Player **Skin**, then select this skin (use the **Browse** button to navigate to it and select it, if necessary). For information on creating your own Skin, refer to *Chapter 16, Configuring UPK*.
Sound	If you want sound to be included in your Player, then select this option. The use of sound tends to significantly increase the overall size of the Player package, so if you know your users will not listen to the sound (perhaps their workstations do not have speakers attached to them) then you can deselect this option and exclude the sound files altogether. The use of sound is described in detail in *Chapter 11, Incorporating Sound Into Your Topics*.
Convert screenshots to 256 colors	Selecting this option will result in all screenshots being down-sampled to 256 colors, which will result in much smaller files. For most applications this is sufficient, but for simulations for graphics-intensive applications (such as photo-editing software) you may want to deselect this option.
Include HTML Web Site	If you select this option, then additional files will be generated to provide a 'pure HTML' index to the Player (that is, without the JavaScript-enabled hierarchical outline). This HTML web site is exactly the same as the one generated by the **HTML Web Site** publishing format (see *Creating an HTML Web Site* on page 235), but is stored in a subfolder of the `PlayerPackage` folder called `htmlwebsite`.
Include detailed action steps in HTML Web Site	If you chose to Include **HMTL Web Site** then you can use this option to control whether or not the HTML Web Site includes the full details of all actions, with images.
Create zip file from published Player package	You may find it easier to zip all of the Player files (which will typically run into the thousands of individual files) into a single file that you can distribute or load into a Learning Management System. UPK will create this zip file automatically if you select this option. The zip file will be saved to the `Player Package` folder in the publication directory.
Create Test It! mode Player	As explained in *Chapter 13, Using UPK for Application Testing*, UPK can provide a *Test It!* mode that guides testers through a task and captures the results of this test. If you select this option, an additional playback button (**Test It!**) is included in the Player. It is not recommended that this is enabled for access by your users.

Player Preferences

The following screenshot shows the options that are available in the **Player Preferences** category when publishing content in the **Player and LMS** format.

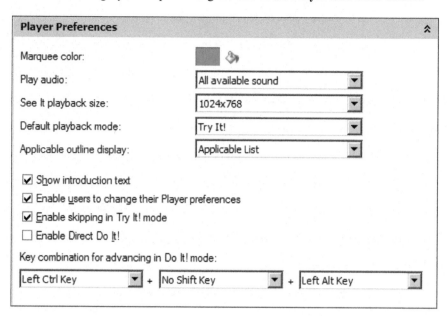

The **Enable outline navigation buttons** option was introduced in UPK 11, but then removed again in UPK12 (presumably because of the introduction of the **Previous** and **Next** buttons in the Player.

The following table explains the purpose of the options listed in the screenshot above:

Option	Use
Marquee color	This option defines the color of the rectangle that is shown around the action area during playback of the simulation. By default this is red, but if you need to (for example, if the application you are recording uses red prominently in its screens) then you can change this color by clicking on the **Fill** button ( ) to the right of this option, and selecting the required color.

Option	Use
Play audio	This option allows you to specify which sounds should be played during playback. The choices are: ● **None**: No sound will be played. ● **Keyboard and mouse-clicks**: Only the sounds for keyboard presses and mouse-clicks will be played. Sounds for Bubble Text will not be played. ● **All available sound**: All sound files used in the simulation will be played, including Bubble Text sound files. Note that the option **All available sound** is only relevant if the **Include sound** option under **Content** is selected. If you have chosen to not include sound files, then the **All available sound** option will have the same effect as the **Keyboard and mouse-clicks** option.
See It playback size	Use this option to select the default size for the (Windowed) *See It!* mode playback window (although it can be resized by the user).
Default playback mode	This option allows you to choose the mode in which the Topic will be launched when the user double-clicks on it in the Outline (as opposed to single-clicking on the Topic to select it and then clicking on the appropriate mode button). This defaults to *Try It!* mode.
Applicable outline display	If the Player is displayed in response to a context-sensitive help call, then you can choose whether the user initially sees a flat list of applicable content (**Applicable List**), a filtered Outline (**Applicable Outline**). or the full Outline with the option to switch to the applicable Outline (**All**).
Show introduction text	By default, the Bubble Text specified on the Start Frame of the simulation will be displayed on the first screen of the Topic playback. If this option is deselected, then the entire Start Frame will be omitted from playback. You would normally only choose this option if you do not have Concept Pages attached to the Topics, in which case the contents of the Start Frame are shown in the *Concept* pane (so hiding the Start Frame during playback avoids seeing it twice). For more information on this option and the Start Frame, see *Chapter 9, Adding Value to Your Topics*.

Side notes:

✦ Full-screen *See It!* mode was discontinued in UPK 12.

✦ The **Default playback mode** option was introduced in UPK 3.5.

✦ The **Applicable Outline** option was introduced in UPK 12.1. Previous versions displayed the flat list, with the option for the user to display the full Outline.

Option	Use	
Enable users to change their Player preferences	If this option is selected, then users will be able to change a number of Player options within the Player window itself. The options that they can change are: **Marquee color, Play audio, Show introduction text, Enable skipping in Try It! mode**, and **Key combination for advancing in Do It! mode**.	■ This is an 'all or nothing' option; if selected, users can change all of their preferences. I usually deselect this option, along with the next one, as I do not want users skipping in Try It! mode.
Enable skipping in Try It! mode	If this option is selected, then users can progress through the screens in *Try It!* mode simply by pressing the *ENTER* key on their keyboard. As the whole point of *Try It!* mode is that the users are trying it (!) allowing them to skip through the simulation is counter-productive. However, it can be useful when testing to be able to do this. I therefore always leave this option selected during development, and then deselect this option for the final publication. Note that this is just a default setting. If you deselect this option, but select **Enable users to change their Player preferences**, then although users will not initially be able to skip through a simulation, they will be able to go into their Preferences and re-enable it. Therefore, if you deselect this option, you should also consider deselecting **Enable users to change their Player preferences**.	
Enable Direct Do It!	If this option is selected, then if a user invokes context-sensitive help from within the application and only one Topic matches this context, then that Topic will automatically be launched in *Do It!* mode (versus being listed in the Player, for the user to select). This option applies only to targeted applications for which in-application performance support has been implemented (see *Chapter 15, Integrating UPK with Other Applications*).	✛ **Direct Do It!** was introduced in UPK 3.5.

Option	Use
Key combination for advancing in Do It! mode	In *Do It!* mode, the UPK window is displayed on top of the application with which the user is interacting. If the key combination specified by this option is pressed, then the instructions in the UPK window will advance to the next step (screen) in the UPK window, even though the user's application (and not UPK) is still the active window. (See *Chapter 1, An Introduction to Oracle User Productivity Kit* for a more detailed explanation of *Do It!* mode.) You can use any (one-, two-, or three-) key combination, but should choose one that is not used in the application to which the simulation applies. Note that you will have to educate your users on this key combination, especially if you deselect the **Enable users to change their Player preferences** option as the users may not know that this feature exists.

Print It!

The following screenshot shows the options that are available in the **Print It!** category when publishing content in the **Player and LMS** format.

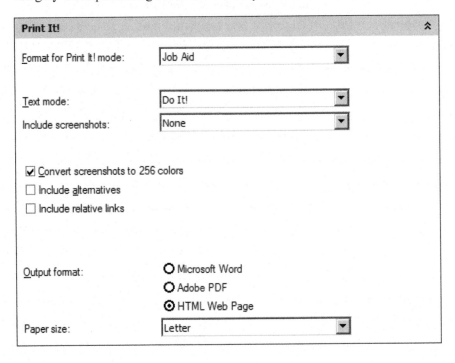

The following table explains the purpose of the options shown in the screenshot above:

Option	Use
Format for Print It! mode	Select the type of document that you want to be provide via the **Print It!** button in the Player. You can choose from: • **System Process Document** • **Job Aid** • **Test Document** • **None** (No Print It! document is generated; the **Print It!** button is not even available in the Player) Note that this selection is independent of any documents selected under **Documents** in the leftmost selection list—and the options selected for those documents. That is, you do not have to select the **Job Aid** publishing format (on the left) to be able to provide the Job Aid via *Print It!*. In fact, even if you do publish the Job Aid, then if you choose **Job Aid** for *Print It!* mode, then UPK will generate a *separate* Job Aid document for use with *Print It!* (in a subfolder of the `PlayerPackage` folder).
Text Mode	As we saw in *Chapter 4, Editing a Topic*, Bubble Text in Frames can be tagged to appear or not appear in different playback modes (**See It!/Try It!**, **Know It?**, and **Do It!**). This option allows you to choose which mode you want to use for the text in the *Print It!* mode document.
Include screenshots	Select whether or not screenshots should be included in the document. The available options are: • **Topic settings**: Use the settings in the Topic itself to decide which individual screenshots to include or not. Refer to *Chapter 4, Editing a Topic* for details of how to set this. • **One screenshot per topic**: Only include one screenshot per Topic. The first screenshot will be used. • **One screenshot per frame**: Include a screenshot for every Frame in each Topic. • **None**: Do not include any screenshots. This is independent of the any settings specified when generating a deployment type of the same type as the one used for *Print It!* mode (where, by default, the **System Process Document** and **Test Document** include screenshots, and the **Job Aid** does not).

Option	Use
Convert screenshots to 256 colors	Selecting this option will result in all screenshots being down-sampled to 256 colors, which will result in much smaller files. For most applications this is sufficient, but for simulations of graphics-intensive applications (such as photo-editing software) you may want to deselect this option.
Include alternatives	By default, the *Print It!* document will include any Alternative Actions and Alternative Paths recorded in the Topic. If you want to exclude these, then deselect this option.
Include relative links	If relative URLs are used for links in your content, and you are certain that the documents pointed to by these links will be in the correct location relative to the published *Print It!* document, then selecting this option will result in clickable relative links being included in the *Print It!* document. If you cannot guarantee that the targets of these relative links will be in the correct place then do not select this option, and clickable links will not be included in the *Print It!* document.
Publishing format	Select the file type to be generated. This can be **Microsoft Word, Adobe PDF**, or **HTML Web Page**.
Paper size	Choose whether you want the paper size of the Word or PDF document to be **Letter, A4,** or **Print template setting** (in which case whatever size is specified in the appropriate document format template is used).

➕ The **Microsoft File Type** option has been discontinued in UPK12. .docx is now used exclusively.

LMS Options

The following screenshot shows the options that are available in the **LMS Options** category when publishing content in the **Player and LMS** format.

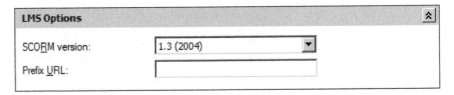

The following table explains the purpose of the options shown in the screenshot above:

Option	Use
SCORM Version	This option allows you to select the version of SCORM with which the generated package should be compliant. This will depend upon the version supported by your LMS. The options available are **1.2** and **1.3 (2004)**. 1.3 (which is also known as SCORM 2004 4th Edition) is the latest version, and so is selected by default. Note that there are no AICC-specific options. All versions of SCORM are also AICC compliant.
Prefix URL	If your content will be published to an external content server (and not the LMS) then you need to specify the URL of the location at which the package will be placed on the content server. This URL is prefixed to all of the assets in the LMS Package, to ensure that all links work correctly. If the content is imported into an LMS directly then relative links are used, in which case this option should not be used.

Knowledge Center Publishing

The following screenshot shows the options that are available in the **Knowledge Center Publishing** category when publishing content in the **Player and LMS** format.

The following table explains the purpose of the options shown in the screenshot above:

Option	Use
Publish content to Knowledge Center	If you want to publish your content directly to the UPK Knowledge Center then select this option, and then use the **Server Settings** button to specify the URL of the Knowledge Center, and your logon ID and workgroup.

Generated files

In the `PlayerPackage` folder, you will find several files and folders. If you will be making your Player available on a Web Server (or other file server) and did not publish directly to this server, then you will need to copy the complete contents of this `PlayerPackage` folder to your server.

In order to provide access to this Player package, you should provide a link to either the `index.html` file (for Apache servers), or the `default.html` file (for IIS servers). Alternatively, just provide a URL that includes the path up to `PlayerPackage`, and let the server resolve it.

If you chose to generate an HTML Web Site as part of the Player, then the `PlayerPackage` folder will contain an additional folder, called `htmlwebsite`, which contains the complete web site (again, with `index.html` and `default.html` files).

● If you try accessing the Player locally (for example, from the Publishing Content folder on your local workstation) and not from a server, then you need to run the `play.exe` file instead.

Example output

Although you are no doubt completely familiar with the Player by this stage in the book, for the sake of completeness (or in case you are flicking through this book as a reference), an example of the Player publishing format for our sample exercise is shown in the following screenshot:

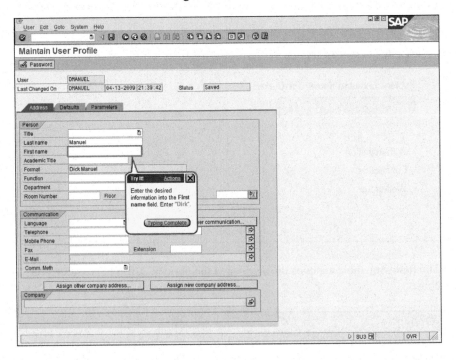

This example is taken from *Try It!* mode. For an explanation of the different play modes and the differences between them, refer to *Chapter 1, An Introduction to Oracle UPK*.

Note that this screenshot shows an example of the Player when displayed via a Browser. If you load the published output into a Learning Management System, your output may look slightly different (at least on the Outline screen), depending on your individual LMS.

Creating an HTML Web Site

The **HTML Web Site** format generates a version of the Player that is, in theory, better-suited for use as a web site. This is because for this format UPK generates only HTML, CSS, and PNG files. There is no JavaScript, as there is in the Player. However, in doing so, UPK sacrifices a good deal of its functionality. The HTML Web Site only allows the Topics to be executed in *Try It!* mode, Bubble Text is actually displayed below the Frames, string input is not possible, and Alternative Actions are not supported at all.

Given that almost all Web Browsers support JavaScript, the only real advantage to the HTML Web Site format is that it confirms to Section 508c accessibility standards. Section 508c mandates requirements to work with a *screen reader* (software that reads the content on a screen and outputs this via speech synthesis). It also requires that users be able to change the font size in the browser. However, unless you have specific accessibility requirements (that can't be met through judicious use of sound—see *Chapter 11, Incorporating Sound Into Your Topics*), it is better to use the Player package (see above), and load this to your web server, rather than use the **HTML Web Site** format.

Publishing options

The following screenshot shows the sole publishing option available for the **HTML Web Site** format.

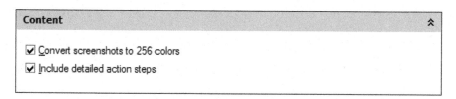

The following table explains the purpose of the options shown in the screenshot above:

Option	Use
Convert screenshots to 256 colors	Selecting this option will result in all screenshots being down-sampled to 256 colors, which will result in much smaller files. For most applications this is sufficient, but for simulations of graphics-intensive applications (such as photo-editing software) you may want to deselect this option.
Include detailed action steps	Use this option to control whether or not the HTML Web Site includes the full details of all actions, with images.

Generated files

In the generated `HTMLPages` folder, you will find several files and a single `tpc` folder. If you will be making your HTML Web Site available on a Web Server (or other file server) and did not publish directly to this server, then you will need to copy the complete contents of the `HTMLPages` folder to your server.

In order to provide access to the HTML Web Site, you should provide a link to either the `index.html` file (for Apache servers), or the `default.html` file (for IIS servers) in the main `HTMLPages` folder.

Example output

An example of the output for the **HTML Web Site** format is shown in the following screenshots. The first screenshot shows the main `index.html` file, which is the first screen that the users will see (this is the **HTML Web Site** equivalent of the *Player* Outline, which co-incidentally, is also called `index.html`):

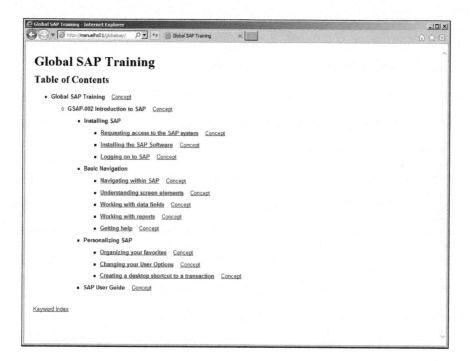

As you can see from the above example, the Outline structure is maintained, but there is only a single link available for each Topic, which leads to a limited version of the *Try It!* mode. Users can also see any information attached to the Concepts pane for a content element by clicking on the **Concept** link. Note that there is no ability to filter by Role, and there is no *Search* function. To compensate for this latter limitation, a new link, **Keyword Index**, is provided at the bottom of the page. The following screenshot shows the page that is displayed by clicking on the **Keyword Index** link:

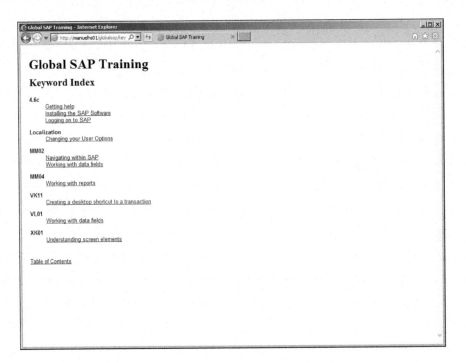

This *Keyword Index* page (above) provides an index to the Topics in the HTML Web Site organized according to the Keywords assigned to each Topic (if any). This could prove to be quite a useful page depending on the purpose that you have assigned to your keywords (it would actually be useful to have this feature in the Player). Given that the HTML Web Site format does not provide us with a Roles index, if you do organize your Topics according to Roles, you might want to consider using your Role names as Keywords. Your *Keyword Index* would then give access to your Topics organized by Role. Of course, the page would still be called "Keyword Index", but you could always change this, as explained in *Chapter 16, Customizing UPK*.

The **Table of Contents** link at the bottom of the *Keyword Index* page links back to the main index page, discussed earlier.

Clicking on the link for a Topic displays a page similar to the one shown in the following screenshot:

■ Keywords are explained in detail in *Chapter 10, Adding Value in the Player*.

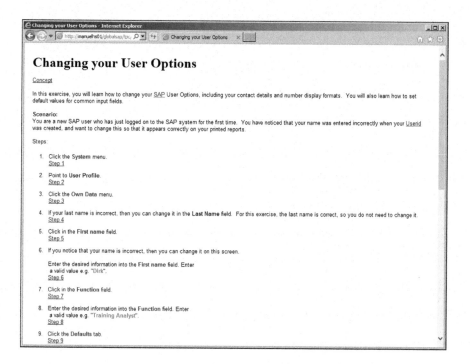

This initial page is very similar to the Job Aid document described below, in that it is a text-only version of the instructions. However, if the **Include detailed steps** option is selected, then for each step a hyperlink (of "Step x") is provided. Clicking on a hyperlink displays a page similar to the one shown in the following example. Note that this screenshot was taken from the middle of our sample exercise, for the purposes of illustration.

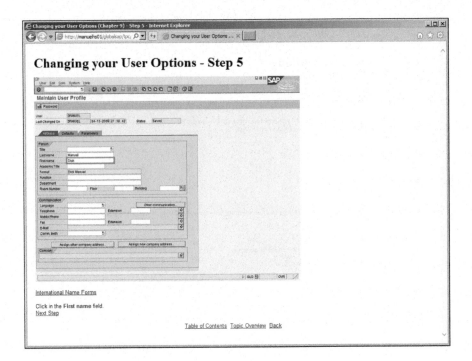

In this example, you can see that the Action Area is highlighted (and works; if you click on it, you will move to the next step—technically, UPK uses `imagemaps` in the HTML file to achieve this), but the Bubble Text is shown below the screenshot. You can also see that links are provided to any (UPK) Web Pages attached to the Frame, such as the link **International name forms**, in this example. (Web Pages are described in *Chapter 9, Adding Value to Your Topics*.) Finally, links are provided to the next step (**Next Step**), to the Web Site index page (**Table of Contents**), the initial page of this Topic (**Topic Overview**), and the previous step (**Back**).

Publishing Documents

● The term 'documents' is a bit of a misnomer, as this category includes PowerPoint presentations and Excel workbooks. Some authors use the term 'printed output' (which UPK also uses in some places) but that too is not strictly correct, as these documents may never actually be printed,

UPK provides the ability to publish content in a number of different 'document' formats. The information included in these documents is almost entirely the same as for the on-line output, with the addition of one or two specialized pieces of information that are defined via the Topic's Properties. The publishing process is exactly the same as above.

All of the additional information is pure text (that is, there is no *contextual* information associated with it), so in theory you could put whatever information you wanted into these Properties. However, the labels will still say what UPK wants them to say. You can customize the output documents (as explained in *Chapter 16, Configuring UPK*), but the labels in the **Properties** pane in the Library will still be the same.

You can choose to have any of the document output types output to Adobe PDF, Microsoft Word, or HTML (or any combination of the three). If you choose PDF or HTML, UPK simply outputs the content to Word anyway, and then creates a PDF and/or HTML file from that (before deleting the Word document if you did not choose this particular output type).

▲ If you use a version of Word older than Word 2010 (which includes its own PDF creator) you need either a full version of Adobe Acrobat (not just the Reader), or (for Office 2007) the Microsoft **Save as PDF or XPS** plug-in, in order to publish to PDF. UPK does not include its own PDF creator.

Publishing a System Process document

The **System Process** document is probably the most commonly-used UPK document format. This document can be thought of as a user procedure, work instruction, job step, and so on, and is designed to explain the steps required to complete a specified task in the application. The UPK-generated document contains all of the actions carried out in the Topic (screenshots and Bubble Texts), plus an additional page of *context* information. This includes the contents of any Concept Page linked to the Topic, plus other information taken directly from the Topic's Properties.

Document Properties

The **Properties** that are relevant for **System Process** documents are shown in the following screenshot.

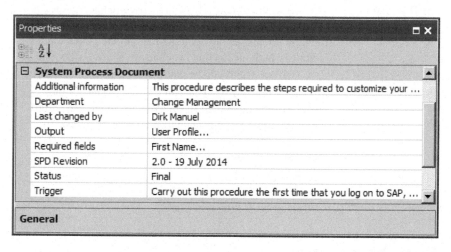

The table below describes some possible uses of these Properties, although it should be noted that they can really be used for any suitable purpose; there is no data validation against what you enter.

Property	Use
Additional information	A short block of text that is printed immediately prior to the actual instructions. Possible uses include specifying prerequisites, or providing additional information about the overall process of which this activity is a part.

Property	Use
Department	A single line of text. This can be used to specify the business function responsible for carrying out this procedure, or the group responsible for maintaining this document, and so on.
Last changed by	A single line of text. This can be used to specify the person who either made the change (that is, the content author), or the person who requested or authorized the change. The latter would be more useful.
Output	A two-column table, with column headings of **Result** and **Comments**. This can be useful for specifying what will change as a result of carrying out this procedure.
Required fields	A two-column table, with column headings of **Required Fields** and **Comments**. Most usefully, this can be used to specify the information that the user needs to know in order to carry out the procedure. The third column (**Bookmark Name**) contains an automatically-generated (but customizable) bookmark for the Required Fields/Comments pair, so that they can be included in a printed document. (Refer to *Chapter 16, Configuring UPK* for details of how to do this.)
SPD Revision	A single line of text. This can be used to specify the revision number of the document. This appears both within the text of the document and in the generated file name, which means that previous revisions will not be overwritten when you re-publish.
Status	A single line of text. This can be used to specify the status of the document (such as Draft, Final, and so on). Note that this is not related to the Topic State Property, and is not taken into account when publishing by state (see earlier in this chapter).
Trigger	A short block of text that is printed at the start of the document. This can be used to specify 'when to use' information for the procedure.

Publishing options

The following sections explain the publishing options available for the **System Process** publishing format. Each category of options is explained separately.

Content

The following screenshot shows the options that are available in the **Content** category when publishing content in the **System Process** format.

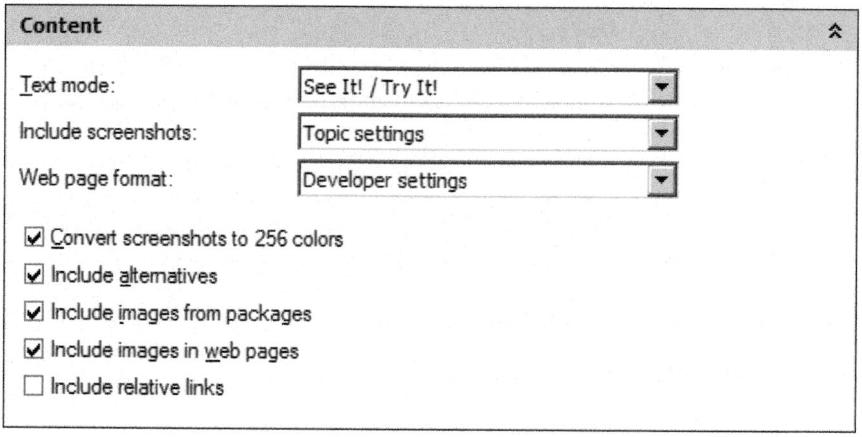

Content

Text mode:	See It! / Try It!
Include screenshots:	Topic settings
Web page format:	Developer settings

☑ Convert screenshots to 256 colors
☑ Include alternatives
☑ Include images from packages
☑ Include images in web pages
☐ Include relative links

The following table explains the purpose of the options shown in the screenshot above:

Option	Use
Text Mode	As we saw in *Chapter 4, Editing a Topic*, Bubble Text in Frames can be tagged to appear or not appear in different playback modes (**See It!/Try It!**, **Know It?**, and **Do It!**). This option allows you to choose which mode you want to use for the text in the *System Process* document.
Include screenshots	Select whether or not screenshots should be included in the document. The available options are: • **Topic settings**: Use the settings in the Topic itself to decide which individual screenshots to include or not. Refer to *Chapter 4, Editing a Topic* for details of how to set this. This is the default. • **One screenshot per topic**: Only include one screenshot per Topic. The first screenshot will be used. • **One screenshot per frame**: Include a screenshot for every Frame in each Topic. • **None**: Do not include any screenshots.

+ The **Web Page Format** option was introduced in UPK 12.

Option	Use
Web page format	Content in Web Pages that are directly linked to the Topic will be included in the printed output. Use this option to select whether this content should be formatted according to the formatting applied to the Web Page (whether this is direct formatting or formatting applied through the use of a Template), or whether all Web Page formatting should be overridden with the formatting defined in the document's Publishing Format Package. The latter option is preferable from a consistency point of view, but you should be careful not to discard any formatting that may have been specifically applied to the Web Page by the author.
Convert screenshots to 256 colors	Selecting this option will result in all screenshots being down-sampled to 256 colors, which will result in much smaller files. For most applications this is sufficient, but for simulations for graphics-intensive applications (such as photo-editing software) you may want to deselect this option.
Include alternatives	By default, the document will include any alternative paths recorded in the Topic. If you want to exclude these, then deselect this option.
Include images from packages	If any image files have been attached to the Topic via Packages, then by default the document will include these. If you do not want to include attached images, then deselect this option.
Include images in web pages	If any (UPK) Web Pages attached to the Topic include images, then (by default) the document will include these. If you do not want to include these images, then deselect this option.
Include relative links	If relative URLs are used for links in your content, and you are certain that the documents pointed to by these links will be in the correct location relative to the published document, then selecting this option will result in clickable relative links being included in the document. If you cannot guarantee that the targets of these relative links will be in the correct place then do not select this option, and clickable links will not be included in the document.

Output

The following screenshot shows the options that are available in the **Output** category when publishing in the **System Process** format.

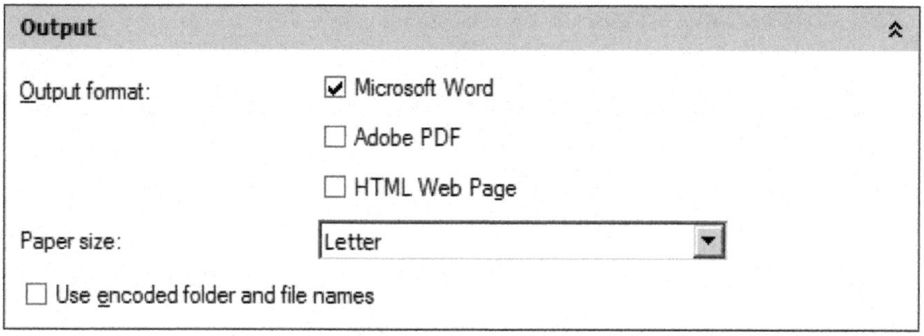

The following table explains the purpose of the options shown in the screenshot above:

Option	Use
Publishing format	Select the file type(s) to be generated. This can be one or more of **Microsoft Word**, **Adobe PDF**, and **HTML Web Page**.
Paper size	Choose whether you want the paper size of the Word or PDF document to be **Letter**, **A4**, or **Print template setting** (in which case whatever size is specified in the appropriate document format template is used).
Use encoded folder and file names	If you select this option, then the filename for each generated file will be UPK's internal 32-character Document ID for the Topic. Otherwise, the Topic name will be used as the filename.

✚ The **Microsoft File Type** option has been discontinued in UPK 12. .docx is now used exclusively.

Generated files

The following files may be generated in the SPD folder, depending upon the **Publishing format** selected in the publishing options:

- A docx file, for Microsoft Word output
- A .pdf file, for Adobe PDF output
- A .html file, and a subfolder containing the image files for the HTML page for HTML output

The screenshot below shows the case where all of the above files have been generated for a single document.

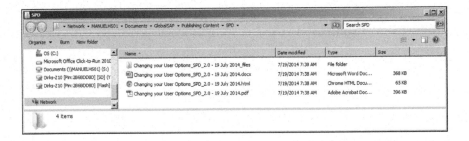

Note that in this example, the **SPD Revision** property was specified for the Topic, and so has been appended to the filename. The advantage of doing this is that the previous version is not overwritten (except the HTML subfolder - old versions are deleted). However, the disadvantage is that any links to the document will still point to the prior version, and will need to be updated to point to the new version.

Example output

Sample pages from the **System Process** document for our sample exercise, using the information shown in the *Properties* pane earlier, are shown next. The first example shows the first page of the System Process document, including some of the additional information that is pulled from the Properties settings:

Department	Change Management
Responsibility/Role	Customer Data Administrator
File Name	Changing your User Options_SPD_2.0 - 19 July 2014.docx
Revision	2.0 - 19 July 2014
Document Generation Date	7/19/2014 7:38:00 AM
Date Modified	7/19/2014 7:38:00 AM
Last Changed by	Dirk Manuel
Status	Final

Changing your User Options
Trigger:
Carry out this procedure the first time that you log on to SAP, to set your personal preferences.

Concept

You can personalize SAP via your User Options. You can change such things as:

- Your name, address, and other contact details
- The display format for dates and numbers
- Your logon language
- Your time zone

You can also define default values for common data fields in your User Options. This saves you from having to enter the same value every time you execute a transaction that requires this data field.

Required Field(s)	Comments
First Name	User's given name
Last Name	User's family name
E-mail address	Full internet e-mail: someone@company.com

Output - Result(s)	Comments
User Profile	Updated

Additional Information
This procedure describes the steps required to customize your SAP logon ID. It explains how to specify your contact details, change your date and number formats, and also how to set default values for commonly-used fields.

The second screenshot shows an example from further into the document. In this example, you can see a screenshot, the step table (listing the actions on that screen) and also the content of a Web Page that was linked to from one of the Bubbles for this screen.

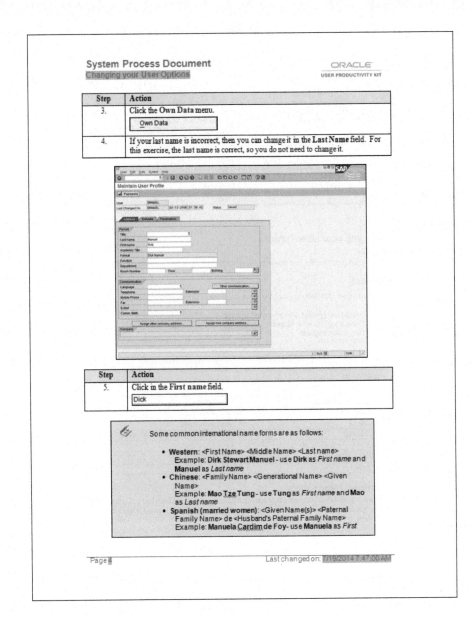

System Process Document
Changing your User Options

ORACLE
USER PRODUCTIVITY KIT

Step	Action
3.	Click the Own Data menu. Own Data
4.	If your last name is incorrect, then you can change it in the **Last Name** field. For this exercise, the last name is correct, so you do not need to change it.

Step	Action
5.	Click in the **First name** field. Dick

Some common international name forms are as follows:

- **Western**: <First Name> <Middle Name> <Last name>
  Example: **Dirk Stewart Manuel** - use **Dirk** as *First name* and **Manuel** as *Last name*
- **Chinese**: <Family Name> <Generational Name> <Given Name>
  Example: **Mao Tze Tung** - use **Tung** as *First name* and **Mao** as *Last name*
- **Spanish (married women)**: <Given Name(s)> <Paternal Family Name> de <Husband's Paternal Family Name>
  Example: **Manuela Cardim de Foy** - use **Manuela** as *First*

Last changed on: 7/19/2014 7:47:00 AM

If the **HTML File** output was chosen, then the generated file will look like the example shown in the following screenshot (taken from the same point as the example in the Word document above, for comparison):

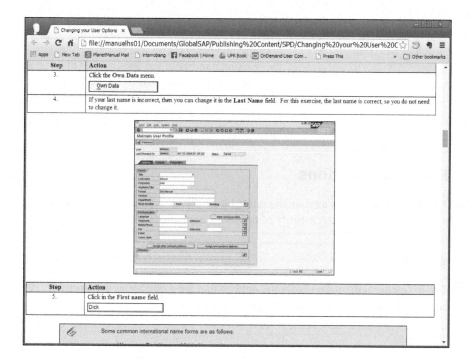

Publishing a Job Aid

The **Job Aid** is a very scaled-down extract of a Topic and simply lists all of the actions as a single, numbered list, formatted in a table. By default, screenshots are not included, but you have the option to include them if required.

The Job Aid format is often used as the document format for the *Print It!* mode.

Document Properties

The **Properties** that are relevant for the **Job Aid** document are shown in the following screenshot:

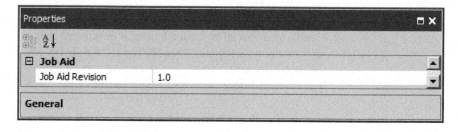

The table below describes possible uses of this Property:

Property	Use
Job Aid Revision	A single line of text. This can be used to specify the revision number of the document. This appears both within the text of the document and in the generated file name, which means that previous revisions will not be overwritten when you re-publish.

Publishing options

The following sections explain the publishing options available for the **Job Aid** publishing format. Each category of options is explained separately.

Content

The following screenshot shows the options that are available in the **Content** category when publishing content in the **Job Aid** format:

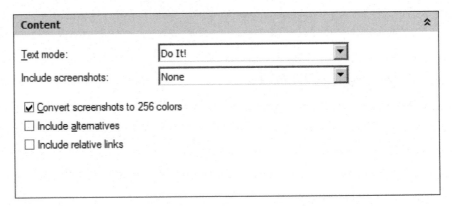

The following table explains the purpose of the options listed in the screenshot above:

Option	Use
Text Mode	As we saw in *Chapter 4, Editing a Topic*, Bubble Text in Frames can be tagged to appear or not appear in different playback modes (**See It!/Try It!**, **Know It?**, and **Do It!**). This option allows you to choose which mode you want to use for the text in the document.

Option	Use
Include screenshots	Select whether or not screenshots should be included in the document, and how many should be included if they should. The available options are: **Topic settings**: Use the settings in the Topic itself to decide which individual screenshots to include or not. Refer to *Chapter 4, Editing a Topic* for details of how to set this. • **One screenshot per topic**: Only include one screenshot per Topic. The first screenshot will be used. • **One screenshot per frame**: Include a screenshot for every Frame in each Topic. • **None**: Do not include any screenshots. This is the default.
Convert screenshots to 256 colors	Selecting this option will result in all screenshots being down-sampled to 256 colors, which will result in much smaller files. For most applications this is sufficient, but for simulations for graphics-intensive applications (such as photo-editing software) you may want to deselect this option.
Include alternatives	By default, the document will include any Alternative Actions and Alternative Paths recorded in the Topic. If you want to exclude these, then deselect this option.
Include relative links	If relative URLs are used for links in your content, and you are certain that the documents pointed to by these links will be in the correct location relative to the published document, then selecting this option will result in clickable relative links being included in the document. If you cannot guarantee that the targets of these relative links will be in the correct place then do not select this option, and clickable links will not be included in the document.

Output

The following screenshot shows the options that are available in the **Output** category when publishing content in the **Job Aid** format:

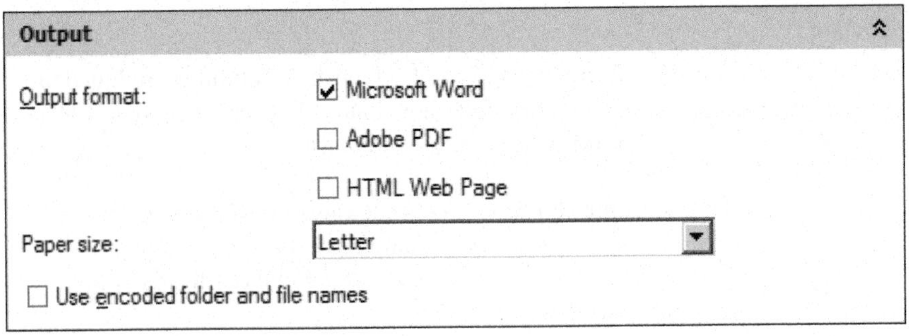

The following table explains the purpose of the options shown in the screenshot above:

Option	Use
Publishing format	Select the file type(s) to be generated. This can be one or more of **Microsoft Word, Adobe PDF**, and **HTML Web Page**.
Paper size	Choose whether you want the paper size of the Word or PDF document to be **Letter, A4**, or **Print template setting** (in which case whatever size is specified in the appropriate document format template is used).
Use encoded folder and file names	If you select this option, then the filename for each file will be UPK's internal 32-character Document ID for the Topic. Otherwise, the Topic name will be used as the filename.

✚ The **Microsoft File Type** option has been discontinued in UPK 12. .docx is now used exclusively.

Generated files

The following files may be generated in the JobAid folder, depending upon the **Publishing format** selected in the publishing options:

- A .docx file, for Microsoft Word output

- A .pdf file, for Adobe PDF output

- A .html file, and a subfolder containing the image files for the HTML page for HTML output

The screenshot below shows the case where all of the above files have been generated for a single document.

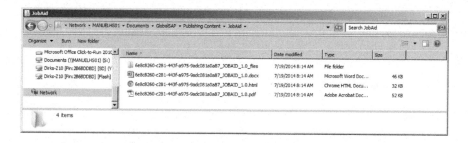

Note that in this example, the option **Use encoded folder and file names** has been selected.

Example output

A sample page from the **Job Aid** document for our sample exercise, using the information shown in the *Properties* pane earlier, is shown below. Note that the **Job Aid Revision** property is only used in the file name and not within the body of the document itself (which is why you do not see it here).

Changing your User Options

Step	Action
1.	Click the System menu.
	System
2.	Point to User Profile.
3.	Click the Own Data menu.
	Own Data
4.	If your last name is incorrect, then you can change it in the **Last Name** field. For this exercise, the last name is correct, so you do not need to change it.
5.	Click in the **First name** field.
	Dick
6.	If you notice that your name is incorrect, then you can change it on this screen. Enter the desired information into the **First name** field. Enter a valid value e.g. "Dirk".
7.	Click in the **Function** field.
8.	Enter the desired information into the **Function** field. Enter a valid value e.g. "Training Analyst".
9.	Click the **Defaults** tab.
	Defaults
10.	Under *Decimal notation*, select the format in which you want decimal numbers to be displayed. Click the **Decimal Notation** dropdown button to activate the menu. Y 1 234 567,89
11.	Click the **X_1,234,567.89** list item. X 1,234,567.89
12.	Click the **Date format** list. 3 MM-DD-YYYY
13.	Click the **1 DD.MM.YYYY** list item. 1 DD.MM.YYYY

Publishing a Training Guide

The **Training Guide** is effectively a complete print-out of all of the Topics in the selected Outline. This includes all screenshots and instructions, along with the content of any Web Pages used in the Concept panes or otherwise attached to any of the content objects in the Outline.

Document Properties

There are no **Properties** specific to the **Training Guide** document.

Publishing options

The following sections explain the publishing options available for the **Training Guide** publishing format. Each category of options is explained separately.

Content

The following screenshot shows the options that are available in the **Content** category when publishing content in the **Training Guide** format:

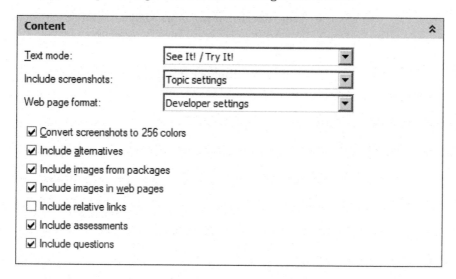

The following table explains the purpose of the options listed in the screenshot above:

Option	Use
Text Mode	As we saw in *Chapter 4, Editing a Topic*, Bubble Text in Frames can be tagged to appear or not appear in different playback modes (**See It!/Try It!**, **Know It?**, and **Do It!**). This option allows you to choose which mode you want to use for the text in the **System Process** document.

Option	Use
Include screenshots	Select whether or not screenshots should be included in the document, and how many should be included if they should. The available options are: • **Topic settings**: Use the settings in the Topic itself to decide which individual screenshots to include or not. Refer to *Chapter 4, Editing a Topic* for details of how to set this. This is the default. • **One screenshot per topic**: Only include one screenshot per Topic. The first screenshot will be used. • **One screenshot per frame**: Include a screenshot for every Frame in each Topic. • **None**: Do not include any screenshots.
Web page format	Content in Web Pages that are directly linked to the Topic will be included in the printed output. Use this option to select whether this content should be formatted according to the formatting applied to the Web Page (whether this is direct formatting or formatting applied through the use of a Template), or whether all Web Page formatting should be overridden with the formatting defined in the output document template. The latter option is preferable from a consistency point of view, but you should be careful not to discard any formatting that may have been specifically applied by the developer.
Convert screenshots to 256 colors	Selecting this option will result in all screenshots being down-sampled to 256 colors, which will result in much smaller files. For most applications this is sufficient, but for simulations of graphics-intensive applications (such as photo-editing software) you may want to deselect this option.
Include alternatives	By default, the document will include any alternative paths recorded in the Topic. If you want to exclude these, then deselect this option.
Include images from packages	If any image files have been attached to the Topic via Packages, then by default the document will include these. If you do not want to include attached images, then deselect this option.
Include images in web pages	If any (UPK) Web Pages attached to the Topic include images, then (by default) the document will include these. If you do not want to include these images, then deselect this option.

✛ The **Web Page Format** option was introduced in UPK 12.

Option	Use	
Include relative links	If relative URLs are used for links in your content, and you are certain that the documents pointed to by these links will be in the correct location relative to the published document, then selecting this option will result in clickable relative links being included in the document. If you cannot guarantee that the targets of these relative links will be in the correct place then do not select this option, and clickable links will not be included in the document.	
Include Assessments	If the selected Outline contains one or more Assessments, and you want these assessments (and the questions contained in them) to be included in the Training Guide, then select this option. Note that the answers will not be included in the document.	■ Assessments and Questions are described in *Chapter 12, Testing Your Users.*
Include Questions	If the selected Outline contains one or more in-line Questions, and you want these questions to be included in the Training Guide, then select this option. Note that the answers will not be included in the document.	

Output

The following screenshot shows the options that are available in the **Output** category when publishing content in the **Training Guide** format:

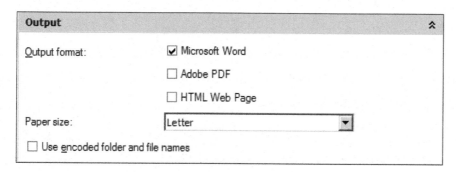

The following table explains the purpose of the options listed in the screenshot above:

Option	Use	
Publishing format	Select the file type(s) to be generated. This can be one or more of **Microsoft Word**, **Adobe PDF**, and **HTML Web Page**.	✛ The **Microsoft File Type** option has been discontinued in UPK 12. .docx is now used exclusively.

Option	Use
Paper size	Choose whether you want the paper size of the Word or PDF document to be **Letter, A4,** or **Print template setting** (in which case whatever size is specified in the appropriate document format template is used).
Use encoded folder and file names	If you select this option, then the filename for each generated file will be UPK's internal 32-character Document ID for the Topic. Otherwise, the Topic name will be used as the filename.

Generated files

Training Guides are published to the `TrainingGuide` folder. In this folder, you will find one or more of the following, for the entire published Outline (and not one per Topic in the Outline), depending upon the **Publishing format** selected in the publishing options.

The screenshot below shows the case where all of the above files have been generated:

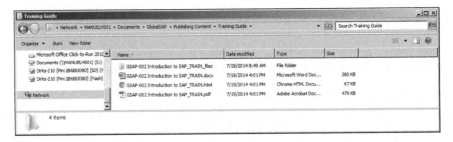

Example output

A few sample pages from the **Training Guide** document are shown below. The first screenshot shows the table of contents for the document, which confirms that a single document is generated for the entire Outline:

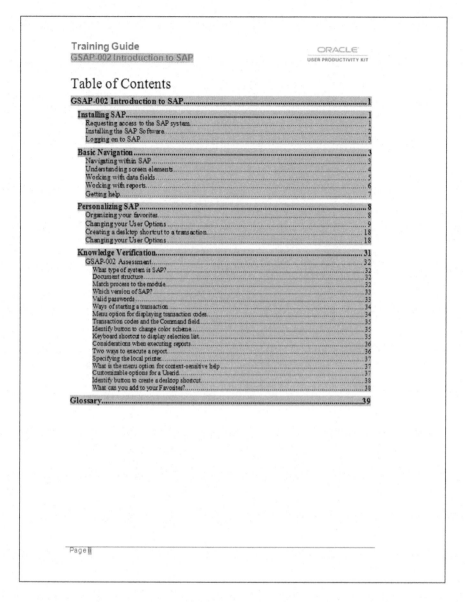

Table of Contents

The second screenshot (below) of the **Training Guide** document shows a page taken from our sample exercise. This is the comparable page shown for the System Process Document, allowing you to see that the actual content is effectively the same for these two document formats:

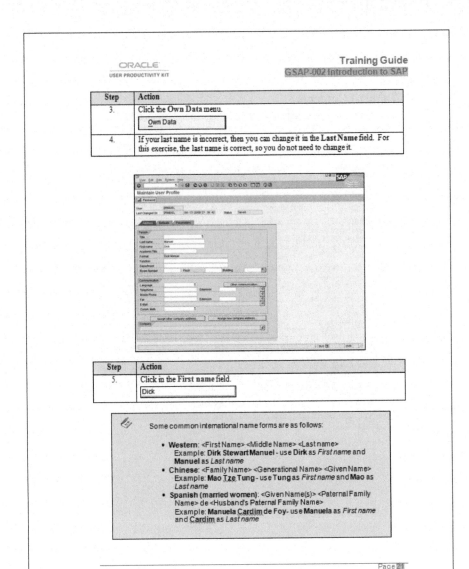

Step	Action
3.	Click the Own Data menu.
	Own Data
4.	If your last name is incorrect, then you can change it in the **Last Name** field. For this exercise, the last name is correct, so you do not need to change it.

Step	Action
5.	Click in the **First name** field.
	Dick

Some common international name forms are as follows:

- **Western:** <First Name> <Middle Name> <Last name>
  Example: **Dirk Stewart Manuel** - use **Dirk** as *First name* and **Manuel** as *Last name*
- **Chinese:** <Family Name> <Generational Name> <Given Name>
  Example: **Mao Tze Tung** - use **Tung** as *First name* and **Mao** as *Last name*
- **Spanish (married women):** <Given Name(s)> <Paternal Family Name> de <Husband's Paternal Family Name>
  Example: **Manuela Cardim de Foy** - use **Manuela** as *First name* and **Cardim** as *Last name*

The final screenshot of our **Training Guide**, below, shows the first page of the Assessment section of our course. This includes the full questions, but not the answers (compare this with the Instructor Guide, later in this chapter). Note that although our sample Assessment (built in *Chapter 12, Testing Your Users*— refer to that chapter for full details) contains two Topics in *Know It?* mode, these are simply omitted from the output (there is not even a reference to the name of the simulation).

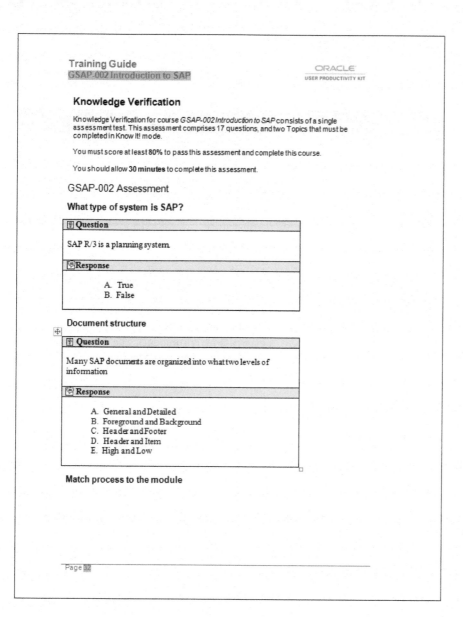

Knowledge Verification

Knowledge Verification for course *GSAP-002 Introduction to SAP* consists of a single assessment test. This assessment comprises 17 questions, and two Topics that must be completed in Know It! mode.

You must score at least **80%** to pass this assessment and complete this course.

You should allow **30 minutes** to complete this assessment.

GSAP-002 Assessment

What type of system is SAP?

🗊 Question
SAP R/3 is a planning system.
🖰 Response
A. True B. False

Document structure

🗊 Question
Many SAP documents are organized into what two levels of information
🖰 Response
A. General and Detailed B. Foreground and Background C. Header and Footer D. Header and Item E. High and Low

Match process to the module

Publishing an Instructor Manual

The **Instructor Manual** provides a simple run through the screens and actions in whichever mode you select for publication, but with the addition of the Frame-level Instructor Notes. It also includes any *Instructor Notes* defined in the Topic **Properties** immediately before the procedure itself.

✛ The inclusion of Frame-level Instructor Notes is new in UPK 12.

Document Properties

The **Properties** that are relevant for **Instructor Manual** documents are shown in the following screenshot:

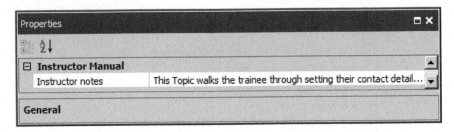

The table below describes possible uses of this Property:

Property	Use
Instructor Notes	This property can be used to provide information to the instructor (who will use this Topic in a classroom environment). These notes only appear in the Instructor Manual.

Publishing options

The following sections explain the publishing options available for the **Instructor Manual** publishing format. Each category of options is explained separately.

Content

The following screenshot shows the options that are available in the **Content** category when publishing content in the **Instructor Manual** format:

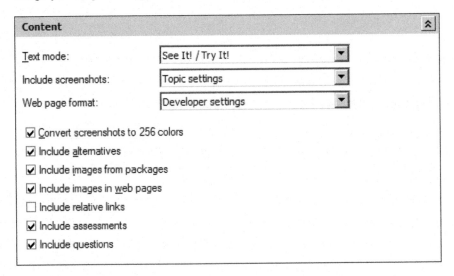

The following table lists the options that are available in the **Content** category when publishing in the **Instructor Manual** format, and explains their use:

Option	Use
Text Mode	As we saw in *Chapter 4, Editing a Topic*, Bubble Text in Frames can be tagged to appear or not appear in different playback modes (**See It!/Try It!**, **Know It?**, and **Do It!**). This option allows you to choose which mode you want to use for the text in the **System Process** document.
Include screenshots	Select whether or not screenshots should be included in the document, and how many should be included if they should. The available options are: • **Topic settings**: Use the settings in the Topic itself to decide which individual screenshots to include or not. Refer to *Chapter 4, Editing a Topic* for details of how to set this. This is the default. • **One screenshot per topic**: Only include one screenshot per Topic. The first screenshot will be used. • **One screenshot per frame**: Include a screenshot for every Frame in each Topic. • **None**: Do not include any screenshots.
Web page format	Content in Web Pages that are directly linked to the Topic will be included in the printed output. Use this option to select whether this content should be formatted according to the formatting applied to the Web Page (whether this is direct formatting or the use of a Template), or whether all Web Page formatting should be overridden with the formatting defined in the output document template. The latter option is preferable from a consistency point of view, but you should be careful not to discard any formatting that may have been specifically applied by the developer.
Convert screenshots to 256 colors	Selecting this option will result in all screenshots being down-sampled to 256 colors, which will result in much smaller files. For most applications this is sufficient, but for simulations of graphics-intensive applications (such as photo-editing software) you may want to deselect this option.
Include alternatives	By default, the document will include any alternative paths recorded in the Topic. If you want to exclude these, then deselect this option.

✛ The **Web Page Format** option was introduced in UPK 12.

Option	Use
Include images from packages	If any image files have been attached to the Topic via Packages, then by default the document will include these. If you do not want to include attached images, then deselect this option.
Include images in web pages	If any (UPK) Web Pages attached to the Topic include images, then (by default) the document will include these. If you do not want to include these images, then deselect this option.
Include relative links	If relative URLs are used for links in your content, and you are certain that the documents pointed to by these links will be in the correct location relative to the published document, then selecting this option will result in clickable relative links being included in the document. If you cannot guarantee that the targets of these relative links will be in the correct place then do not select this option, and clickable links will not be included in the document.
Include Assessments	If the selected Outline contains one or more Assessments, and you want these assessments (and the questions contained in them) to be included in the Instructor Guide, then select this option. Note that both the questions and the answers will be included in the document.
Include Questions	If the selected Outline contains one or more in-line Questions, and you want these questions to be included in the Training Guide, then select this option. Note that both the questions and the answers will be included in the document.

Output

The following screenshot shows the options that are available in the **Output** category when publishing content in the **Training Guide** format:

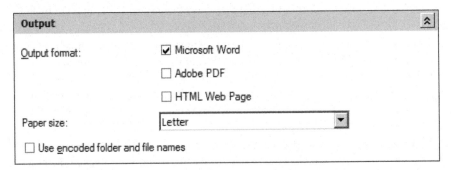

The following table explains the purpose of the options listed in the screenshot above:

Option	Use
Publishing format	Select the file type(s) to be generated. This can be one or more of **Microsoft Word**, **Adobe PDF**, and **HTML Web Page**.
Paper size	Choose whether you want the paper size of the Word or PDF document to be **Letter**, **A4**, or **Print template setting** (in which case whatever size is specified in the appropriate document format template is used).
Use encoded folder and file names	If you select this option, then the filename for each generated file will be UPK's internal 32-character object identifier for the Topic. Otherwise, the Topic name will be used as the filename.

✚ The **Microsoft File Type** option has been discontinued in UPK 12. .docx is now used exclusively.

Generated files

Instructor Manuals are published to the IMPrint folder. In this folder, you will find one or more of the following, for the entire published Outline (and not one per Topic in the Outline), depending upon the **Publishing format** selected in the publishing options:

- A .docx file, for Microsoft Word output

- A .pdf file, for Adobe PDF output

- A .html file, and a subfolder containing the image files for the HTML page for HTML output

The screenshot below shows the case where all of the above files have been generated:

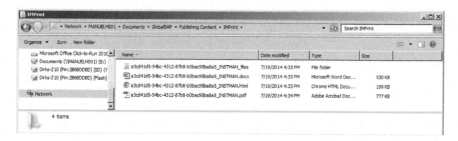

Note that in the example above, the option **Use encoded folder and file names** has been selected. In this case, the Document ID used in the filename is that of the Outline Element selected for publishing (our "Global SAP Training" element).

Example output

A few sample pages from the Instructor Manual document for our sample exercise, using the information shown in the **Properties** pane above, are shown in the following images.

The first image below shows the first page for our sample exercise. Here, you can see the *Instructor Notes* taken from the Topic Properties. Subsequent pages (for a Topic) are the same as for the Training Guide (see above).

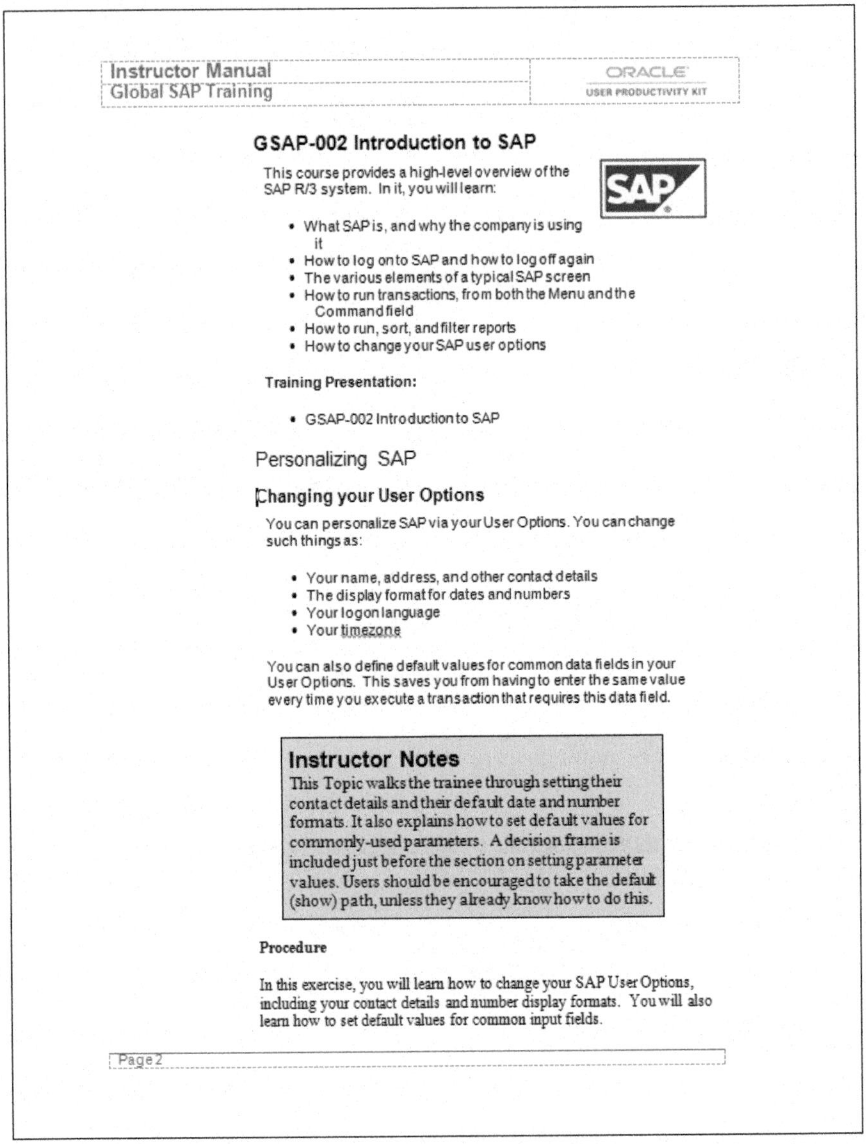

The next image shows a page from the middle of our example Topic, showing the Frame-level *Instructor Notes* (these are printed in italics, as the first paragraph in each step.

+ Frame-level *Instructor Notes* have only been included in the Instructor Manual since UPK 12.1.

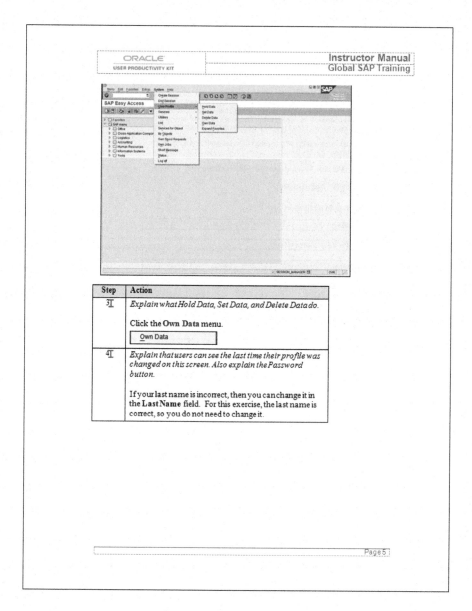

Step	Action
3	*Explain what Hold Data, Set Data, and Delete Data do.*
	Click the **Own Data** menu.
	Own Data
4	*Explain that users can see the last time their profile was changed on this screen. Also explain the Password button.*
	*If your last name is incorrect, then you can change it in the **Last Name** field. For this exercise, the last name is correct, so you do not need to change it.*

Page 5

The final screenshot , below, the first page of the Assessment section. Here, you can see that both the question and the answers are included:

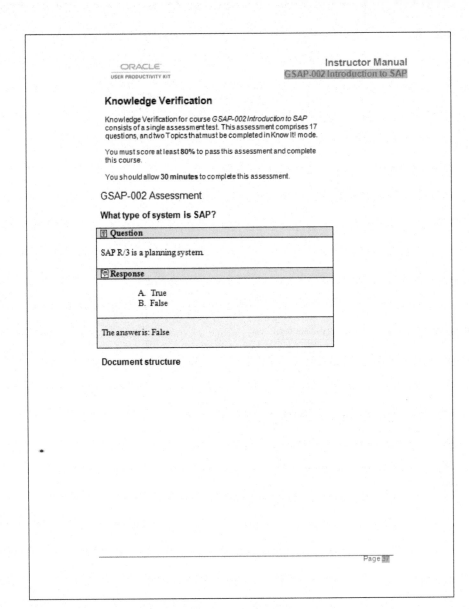

Knowledge Verification

Knowledge Verification for course *GSAP-002 Introduction to SAP* consists of a single assessment test. This assessment comprises 17 questions, and two Topics that must be completed in Know It! mode.

You must score at least **80%** to pass this assessment and complete this course.

You should allow **30 minutes** to complete this assessment.

GSAP-002 Assessment

What type of system is SAP?

Question
SAP R/3 is a planning system.

Response
A. True
B. False

The answer is: False

Document structure

Publishing a Test Document

A **Test Document** is designed to be used by testers of the application for which the simulation was recorded. It includes additional information about the test (recorded in the Topic **Properties**), and any expected results entered into the Frame Comments. This document also includes space for the tester to record the details of their test, including the results of the test.

If *Test It!* mode is used, then the results of the test (including steps passed/failed, tester notes, and so on) are recorded in this document format when you display or print the "detailed report". (See *Chapter 13, Using UPK for Application Testing* for additional details.) However, the recorded results are not stored anywhere, so the document must be manually saved separately, after entering these results, if the results are to be retained.

Document Properties

The **Properties** that are relevant for a Test Document are shown in the following screenshot:

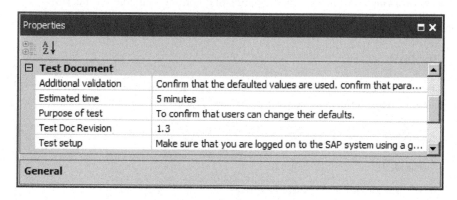

The table below describes possible uses of these Properties:

Property	Use
Additional validation	A short block of text that is printed at the end of the Test Document. This can be used to record any additional activities that should be carried out after the steps recorded by the Topic have been completed, to confirm whether or not the activity was successfully tested. For example, if the Topic records the creation of a document, the additional validation step could be to display this document.
Estimated time	A single line of text. This should be used to specify how long the test should take to complete. This is free-form text, so "5 minutes", "A couple of hours", and "All day" are all equally valid.
Purpose of test	A short block of text. This will be printed before the test instructions, and should explain what the steps in the document are testing.
Test Doc Revision	A single line of text. This can be used to specify the revision number of the document. Note that this is not used within the printed document, but does appear in the generated file name, which means that previous revisions will not be overwritten when you republish.

Property	Use
Test setup	A short block of text. This will be printed before the test instructions, and should specify any prerequisite activities that should be completed before the test is carried out.

Publishing options

The following sections explain the publishing options available for the **Test Document** publishing format. Each category of options is explained separately.

Content

The following screenshot shows the options that are available in the **Content** category when publishing content in the **Test Document** format:

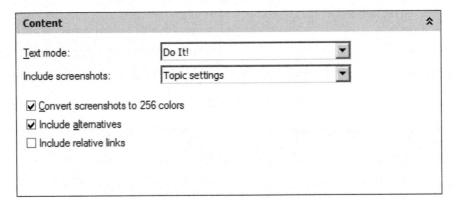

The following table explains the purpose of the options listed in the screenshot above:

Option	Use
Text Mode	As we saw in *Chapter 4, Editing a Topic*, Bubble Text in Frames can be tagged to appear or not appear in different playback modes (**See It!/Try It!**, **Know It?**, and **Do It!**). This option allows you to choose which mode you want to use for the text in the document.

Option	Use
Include screenshots	Select whether or not screenshots should be included in the document. The available options are: • **Topic settings**: Use the settings in the Topic itself to decide which individual screenshots to include or not. Refer to *Chapter 4, Editing a Topic* for details of how to set this. • **One screenshot per topic**: Only include one screenshot per Topic. The first screenshot will be used. • **One screenshot per frame**: Include a screenshot for every Frame in each Topic. • **None**: Do not include any screenshots. This is the default.
Convert screenshots to 256 colors	Selecting this option will result in all screenshots being down-sampled to 256 colors, which will result in much smaller files. For most applications this is sufficient, but for simulations for graphics-intensive applications (such as photo-editing software) you may want to deselect this option.
Include alternatives	By default, the document will include any Alternative Actions and Alternative Paths recorded in the Topic. If you want to exclude these, then deselect this option.
Include relative links	If relative URLs are used for links in your content, and you are certain that the documents pointed to by these links will be in the correct location relative to the published document, then selecting this option will result in clickable relative links being included in the document. If you cannot guarantee that the targets of these relative links will be in the correct place then do not select this option, and clickable links will not be included in the document.

Output

The following screenshot shows the options that are available in the **Output** category when publishing content in the **Test Document** format:

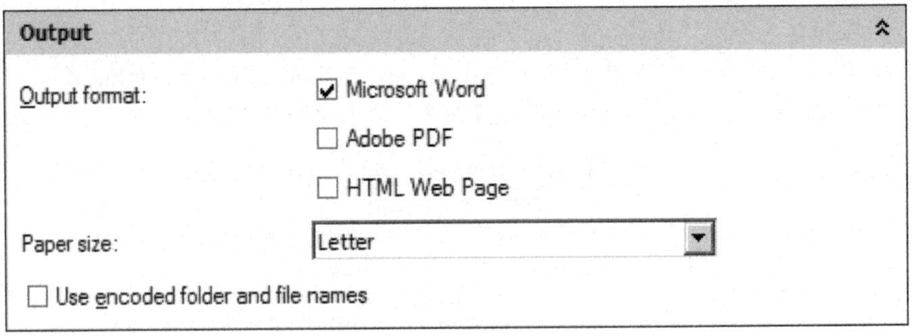

Output	⌃
Output format:	☑ Microsoft Word
	☐ Adobe PDF
	☐ HTML Web Page
Paper size:	Letter ▼
☐ Use encoded folder and file names	

The following table lists the options that are available when publishing to the **Test Document** format, and explains their use:

✛ The **Microsoft File Type** option has been discontinued in UPK 12. .docx is now used exclusively.

Option	Use
Publishing format	Select the file type(s) to be generated. This can be one or more of **Microsoft Word, Adobe PDF**, and **HTML Web Page**.
Paper size	Choose whether you want the paper size of the Word or PDF document to be **Letter, A4**, or **Print template setting** (in which case whatever size is specified in the appropriate document format template is used).
Use encoded folder and file names	If you select this option, then the filename for each file will be UPK's internal 32-character Document ID for the Topic. Otherwise, the Topic name will be used as the filename.

Generated files

Test Documents are published to the `TestDoc` folder. In this folder, you will find one or more of the following, for each Topic in the selected Outline:

- A `.docx` file, for Microsoft Word output
- A `.pdf` file, for Adobe PDF output
- A `.html` file, and a subfolder containing the image files for the HTML page for HTML output

The screenshot below shows the case where all of the above files have been generated:

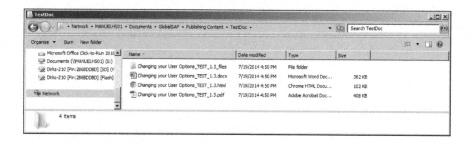

Example Output

The following screenshots show a few sample pages from the **Test Document** generated for our sample simulation. The first screenshot (below) shows the initial page. Here, you can see the first set of Topic Properties. The document also includes space for the tester to record the details of their test.

ORACLE
USER PRODUCTIVITY KIT

Purpose of Test
To confirm that users can change their defaults.

Test History

Date	Tester	Test Notes	Results

Time to Test

Estimated Time	5 minutes
Actual Time	

Test Setup
Make sure that you are logged on to the SAP system using a generic testing ID that currently uses the default user options.

Last changed on: 7/19/2014 4:50:00 PM   Page 1

The second screenshot (below), shows the last page of the **Test Document**. Here, you can see the **Additional validation** Property. You can also see that the **Expected Results** are included in the document, and there is space for the tester to record any notes, and also indicate the results for each step.

Step	Action	Expected Results	Test Step Notes	Results
26.	Click the Save button.	User is returned to the SAP Easy Access screen. Confirmation message is displayed at the bottom of the screen.		
27.	Your changes are saved, and a confirmation message is displayed at the bottom of the screen.			
28.	You have now completed this exercise. You now know how to change your SAP User Profile, including changing your contact details and number display formats. You also know how to set default values for common input fields. **End of scenario:** Your name is now correct, and numbers and dates will be displayed in the correct format. If you defined a default value for the Sales Organization, then the next time that you access a transaction that requires this field as an input field, the correct value of 1001 will automatically be pre-populated. **End of Procedure.**			

Additional Validation

Confirm that the defaulted values are used. confirm that parameter values are defaulted in correctly.

Publishing a Test Results document

The **Test Results** document is not really designed to be published in the way described in this section. Instead, if you record a simulation via the *Record It! Wizard* (see *Chapter 2, Recording a Simulation*) and then choose to "Preview as a test", then it is this document that is displayed. It contains the captured steps and screenshots, and any *Author Notes* entered (as these are the only types of comments that are captured during the recording).

✚ The **Test Results** document was introduced in UPK 11.

That said, you *can* publish to this document format as explained in this chapter, should you need to re-create the 'preview' document from the initial recording. If you are using UPK to *record* all of your tests (this is not the same as recording the *results* of pre-recorded tests via *Test It!* mode) then publishing these documents out at the end of testing provide a nice, easy way of generating all of your test results in one go.

Note that this document is not used for the output of *Test It!* mode—the **Test Document** is used for that.

Document properties

There are no document properties specific to the **Test Results** document, but several other content object Properties are used in this document, as follows:

- **General** Properties: **Name**
- **System Process** Properties: **Department, Last Changed by**
- **Workflow** Properties: **Owner, State**

Publishing options

The Properties that are relevant for **Test Results** documents are exactly the same as those for the **Test Document**. Refer to the section *Publishing a Test Document* on page 268 for details.

Generated files

Test Results documents are published to the `TestResults` folder. In this folder, you will find one or more of the following, for each Topic in the selected Outline:

- A `.docx` file, for Microsoft Word output
- A `.pdf` file, for Adobe PDF output
- A `.html` file, and a subfolder containing the image files for the HTML page for HTML output

The screenshot below shows the case where all of the above files have been generated:

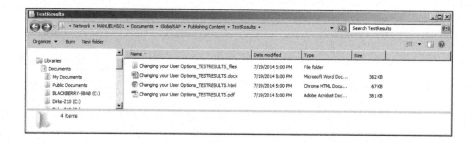

Example Output

The following screenshot shows the first page of the **Test Results** document generated for our sample simulation. Here, you can see the Properties that are included at the start of the document, and can also see the **Author Notes** entered in the **Frame Comments**.

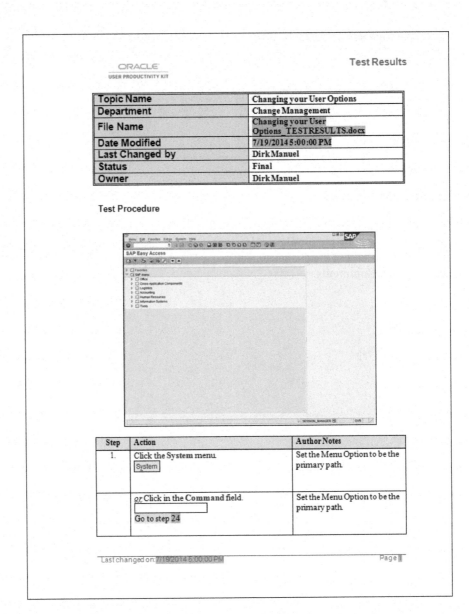

Note that this example above shows the same Author Notes in the first two rows in the step table. In fact, these are two actions for the same Frame (through the use of an **Alternative Action**), and as the Author Notes are entered for a Frame (and not an Action), the same Author Notes are repeated for each Action.

Publishing a Test Case document

⊹ In UPK 3.6 and earlier, the **Test Case** output type was called **HP Quality Center** and could only be used to generate files for that application. In UPK 11, three new output formats are supported.

The **Test Case** publishing format generates a file in Microsoft Excel format that contains the details of the steps carried out in a simulation and the expected results (plus a lot of other information taken from the Topic). This file can then be loaded directly into a testing software application to 'automatically' create test cases.

Document properties

There are no document properties specific to the **Test Case** document.

Publishing options

The following sections explain the publishing options available for the **Test Case** publishing format. Each category of options is explained separately.

Content

The following screenshot shows the options that are available in the **Content** category when publishing content in the **Test Case** format:

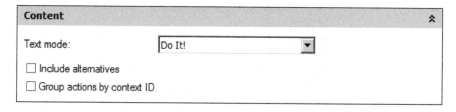

The following table explains the purpose of the options listed in the screenshot above:

Option	Use
Text Mode	As we saw in *Chapter 4, Editing a Topic*, Bubble Text in Frames can be tagged to appear or not appear in different playback modes (**See It!/Try It!**, **Know It?**, and **Do It!**). This option allows you to choose which mode you want to use for the text in the document.
Include alternatives	By default, the document will include any Alternative Actions and Alternative Paths recorded in the Topic. If you want to exclude these, then deselect this option.
Group actions by Context ID	When you record a simulation for certain targeted applications (see *Chapter 15, Integrating UPK with Other Applications*), UPK will capture the *context* of the action – the application, program, screen, and field acted upon). This context is included in the **Other** Test Case output file. By default, the rows in the file reflect the order the actions were carried out during recording. If you select this option, then all actions for a specific context are grouped together.

Output

The following screenshot shows the options that are available in the **Output** category when publishing content in the **Test Case** format:

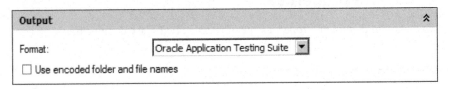

The following table lists the options that are available when publishing in the **Test Case** publishing format and explains their use:

Option	Use
Format	Select the file type to be generated. You can choose one of the following formats: • **Oracle Application Testing Suite** (this is the default) • **HP Quality Center** • **IBM Rational Quality Manager** • **Other** The **Other** option simply creates a spreadsheet containing **all** available information.
Use encoded folder and file names	If you select this option, then the filename for the generated file will be the UPK 32-character Document ID for the selected Outline. Otherwise, the Outline name will be used as the filename.

Generated files

The **Test Case** document is published to the `TC` folder. In this folder, you will find a single Microsoft Excel Workbook, which contains the test cases for **all** Topics contained in the selected Outline. For completeness, the screenshot below shows this file for our test Outline:

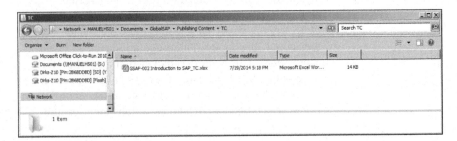

Example Output

The following screenshots show some samples of some of the file formats that can be generated by the **Test Case** publishing format. The first screenshot shows an example of the file generated in **Oracle Application Testing Suite** format:

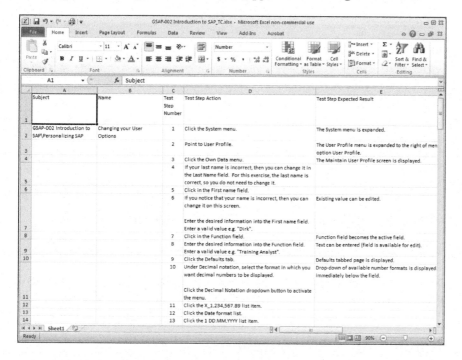

The next screenshot (below) shows an example of the file generated in **Other** format. For the sake of variety, this example was generated using the **Group By Context ID** option:

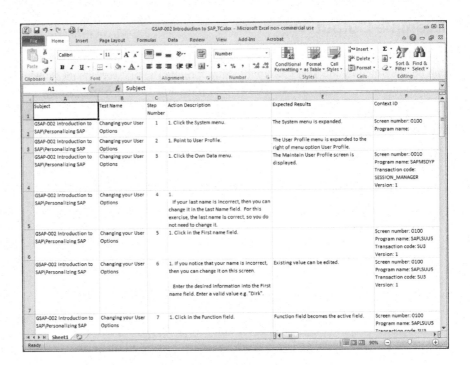

Note that in this example (above), the **Context** column has been moved from its original position at column **N** to column **F** for the purpose of illustration.

Publishing a Presentation

+ The **Presentation** publishing format was introduced in UPK 3.6.1

The **Presentation** publishing format generates a Microsoft PowerPoint presentation for each Topic in the selected Outline. The presentation will contain one slide per Frame in the Topic (even if you choose *Do It!* mode texts and have **Keep action with next action in Do It! mode**). Also note that the presentation will **not** include the **Instructor Notes** from the **Frame Comments** – and there is no way to configure this output type to include them.

Document Properties

There are no Properties that are specific to the **Presentation** publishing format.

Publishing options

The following sections explain the publishing options available for the **Presentation** publishing format. Each category of options is explained separately.

Content

The following screenshot shows the options that are available in the **Content** category when publishing content in the **Presentation** format:

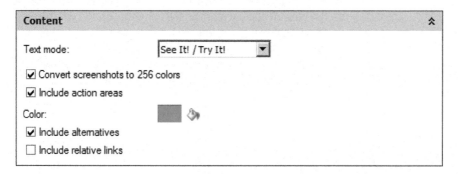

The following table explains the purpose of the options listed in the screenshot above:

Option	Use
Text Mode	As we saw in *Chapter 4, Editing a Topic*, Bubble Text in Frames can be tagged to appear or not appear in different playback modes (**See It!/Try It!**, **Know It?**, and **Do It!**). This option allows you to choose which mode you want to use for the text in the document.
Convert screenshots to 256 colors	Selecting this option will result in all screenshots being down-sampled to 256 colors, which will result in much smaller files. For most applications this is sufficient, but for simulations for graphics-intensive applications (such as photo-editing software) you may want to deselect this option.
Include action areas	If you want the action areas to be shown on the screenshots, then select this option. Otherwise, make sure that this option is deselected, and screenshots will be shown without action areas.
Color	If you chose to **Include action areas** then select the color in which you want the action area border to be drawn. It is recommended that you use the same color as you use when (if…) publishing the Player, for consistency.
Include alternatives	By default, the document will include any alternative paths recorded in the Topic. If you want to exclude these, then deselect this option.

Option	Use
Include relative links	If relative URLs are used for links in your content, and you are certain that the documents pointed to by these links will be in the correct location relative to the published document, then selecting this option will result in clickable relative links being included in the document. If you cannot guarantee that the targets of these relative links will be in the correct place then do not select this option, and clickable links will not be included in the document.

Output

The following screenshot shows the options that are available in the **Output** category when publishing content in the **Presentation** format:

+ The **Microsoft File Type** option has been discontinued in UPK 12. .pptx is now used exclusively.

The following table explains the purpose of the options shown in the screenshot above:

Option	Use
Use encoded folder and file names	If you select this option, then the filename for each file will be UPK's internal 32-character object identifier for the Topic. Otherwise, the Topic name will be used as the filename.

Generated Files

Presentations are published to the Presentation folder. In this folder, you will find one .pptx file per Topic. You will also find a set of files that group these PowerPoint files and the Topics' Concept Pages into a rudimentary website (or sub-site) that can be loaded to your web server to make accessing these files easier. The website consists of:

- An index.html file and a default.html file that acts as an index for this website
- A play.exe file that can be used for launching this website locally
- A forweb.css file that contains formatting for the website
- An img folder that contains the small_logo.gif image for use on the website index page

- A set of folders that each contains supporting documents required for web presentation of the Outline, such as the Concept Pane of an element in the Hierarchy, a linked UPK Web Page, an in-line Question, and so on. The name of the folder is the 32-character UPK Document ID of the element contained in the folder.

The screenshot below shows the files generated for our example Outline:

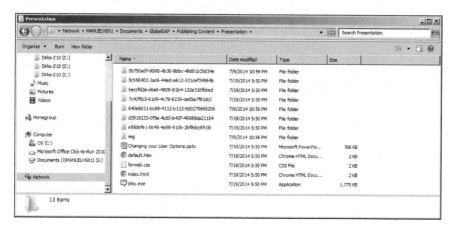

Example Output

The following screenshots show a sample of the generated output for the **Presentation** format. The first screenshot shows our sample exercise, opened in Microsoft PowerPoint.

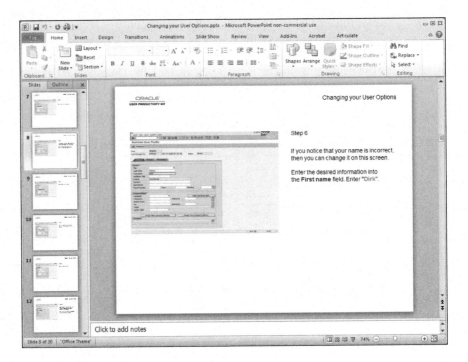

Here, you can see that each Frame appears on a separate slide. You can also see that the Notes are blank, even though some Instructor Notes have been entered into the Topic.

The next screenshot (below) shows the `index.html` file generated as part of the **Presentation** publishing format. This provides access to the generated presentations in a structure similar to the Outline that was selected for publishing.

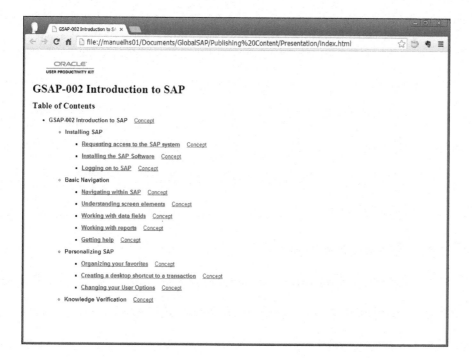

Note that although there is an entry for our **Knowledge Verification** Assessment, this only provides a link to the concept pane for the (Outline containing the) Assessment – the assessment itself is simply omitted. Refer to *Chapter 12, Testing Your Users* for more information on building Assessments.

Automatic publishing

UPK provides the ability to execute publishing tasks via the Windows command line. This is a useful feature, as it allows you to put the publishing commands in a batch file and submit this via a scheduled batch job—for example, during off-peak times. Let's look at how to do this.

Settings files

You may recall from the discussion on publishing options earlier, that UPK saves your publishing options to the destination folder along with the actual published output. It is the files that UPK saves here that are used during batch publishing. This means, of course, that you need to publish your content manually at least once, using the methods described earlier in this chapter, in order to initially create these files, before you can publish via a batch job. The important files are:

- `Selection.xml`: This file specifies the content objects that are to be published. It is this file to which the publication command must refer.

- `Publishing.project.xml`: This file defines the 'global' publishing options that apply to all publishing formats. It also contains a list of the individual configuration files for each of the publishing formats.

- `<format_guid>.config.xml`: There will be one or more of these configuration files, one for each of the chosen publishing formats. Each file contains the publishing options specific to that publishing format. Note that the `<format_guid>` variable specifies the 32-character Document ID of the deployment package that defines the publishing format. You can find these packages under **System | Publishing | Styles** in the UPK Library. (Refer to *Chapter 16, Customizing UPK* for more information on publishing packages.)

The command line command

The executable file that you execute via the command line is `CommandLinePublish.exe`. You can find this command in the program folder for your UPK installation (that is, the same folder that contains the `OdDev.exe` executable).

The format of the command is:

```
CommandLinePublish.exe <settings> /
profilename:<profile> /password:<password>
```

or:

```
CommandLinePublish.exe <settings> /profile:<profile>
/password:<password>
```

or (for a standalone implementation):

```
CommandLinePublish.exe <settings>
```

The following table explains the command-line parameters:

Parameter	Description
`<settings>`	This is the path to the `Selection.xml` file in the destination folder. This can be a relative path, as long as it is relative to the folder containing the `CommandLinePublish.exe` file.
`/profilename:<profile>` *	Use this parameter to specify the name of the user profile within the `UserProfiles` folder that should be used for the publication process. If the user's password is not stored within the profile, then the `/password` parameter must also be used.

Parameter	Description
`/profile: <profile>` *	If you want to use a user profile that is not stored within the `UserProfiles` folder, then use this parameter to specify the full path and file name of the user profile that should be used for the publication process. If the user's password is not stored within the profile, then the `/password` parameter must also be used.
`/password:<password>` *	If the password for the user profile that you are using does not contain the password, then use this parameter to specify the password.

Note that parameters marked with an asterisk (*) apply only to a client/ server (multi-user) environment. In a standalone implementation, only the `<settings>` parameter is used.

To execute the command, simply open a Windows command prompt, and enter the command. You should either do this from the same folder in which the `CommandLinePublish.exe` file is located, or prefix the command with the path to this file.

During the publishing process, a succession of status messages will be displayed, indicating the progress of the publishing activities. There are likely to be many of these messages (just as there are for online publishing); a selection of these is shown below:

```
Player and LMS / Getting documents [OK]
Player and LMS / Creating section and topic list
Player and LMS / Creating title list
Player and LMS / Importing section and topic list
...
...
...
Player and LMS / Copying static files
Player and LMS / Removing files
Player and LMS / Creating LMS files
Done
Publishing process completed successfully
```

Once you see the message `Done`, publishing is complete.

Note that in this example, we have mapped our destination publishing directory as our `S:` drive so that we can use it on the command line. We then navigate to the directory containing the `CommandLinePublish.exe` file (which in this implementation is `C:\Program Files (x86)\User Productivity Kit\UPK Developer 12_1Client`) so that we don't have to specify this full path in the command.

Publishing via a batch job

Publishing via a batch job is very simple, given the command-line functionality explained above. Simply place the command in a batch file (file type .bat), as shown below:

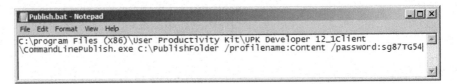

You can then publish your content simply by double-clicking on this file in Windows Explorer. Note that you can include multiple commands within the same batch file, as long as each command is on a separate line. Note also that if you include the path to the command executable, and this path includes spaces, then you need to enclose the full path/file specification in quotes.

● The Task Scheduler in recent versions of Windows allows you to specify the program, parameters, and the folder from which this will be executed for a task. This allows you to call CommandLine Publish.exe directly, saving the need to create a batch file.

You can now set this batch job to run at a specific time, or at regular intervals. How to do this will vary depending on your Operating System, but is likely to be some variation on the Windows Task Scheduler. Use your operating system's Help function to search for "Schedule a task" for details of how to set up batch jobs.

Publishing to video

Although the *See It!* mode effectively looks like video, in that playback is automatic and does not require user intervention, it is still not really video. It still requires a published Player, and still involves (typically) hundreds of individual files. This latter point makes it unsuitable for distribution as simple 'demo' videos—a gap which was (kind of) filled by the **Standalone Topic** format, until that was discontinued (in UPK 12).

✛ The ability to convert published Topics to video format was introduced in UPK 12.1 ESP 1.

Thankfully, UPK (now) provides the ability to generate true video files (in WM4 format) from Topics. However, this isn't quite 'baked in' to UPK—you won't find 'video' as a publishing format in the Publishing Wizard—and is actually implemented through a separate utility called **Player2Movie**. This utility effectively takes a recording of the *See It!* mode from a Player, which means that you first have to publish a Player, and then run the utility against this. However, this does have the advantage that you can generate videos for multiple Topics at the same time (as long as they are all in the same Player).

To publish one or more Topics in video format, carry out the steps shown below:

1. Make sure that you have already published the Player that contains the Topics that you want to convert to video format. Refer to the instructions earlier in this chapter for details of how to do this.

You should also make sure that *See It!* mode is enabled for the Topics that you want to convert to video.

2. Make sure that your Windows Desktop Theme is set to one of the 'Aero' themes.

3. In Windows Explorer, navigate to the installation folder for your UPK client software (for example, `C:\Program Files\User Productivity Kit\UPK Developer 12_1Client`), locate the file `Player2Movie.exe` (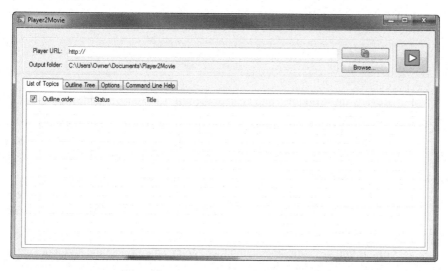) within this folder, and double-click on it to start the utility. The *Player2Movie* screen is displayed, as shown below:

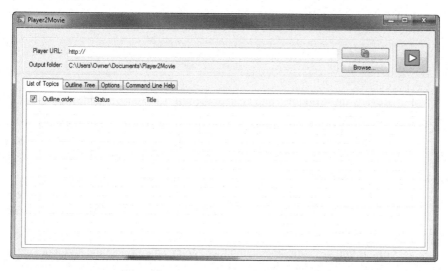

4. In the **Player URL** field, enter the full URL of the published Player that contains the Topics that you want to convert to video format.

5. Click on the **Refresh** button ( ) to the right of the **Player URL** field, to retrieve the list of available Topics from this Player. The *List of Topics* tabbed page is updated to list the Topics found in the Player (that are available in *See It!* mode).

   ■ The *List of Topics* in tabbed page provides a flat list of the Topics in the Player. If you would find it easier to review the Topics in the original Outline structure, then click on the **Outline Tree** tab to display this.

6. Click on the **Browse** button, and navigate to the folder into which you want the video files to be saved.

7. By default, all of the Topics in the Player are selected form conversion. If you do not want to convert specific Topics, then deselect the check-box to the left of these Topics.

8. If you want to review or change the video conversion options, then click on the **Options** tab. The following screen is displayed:

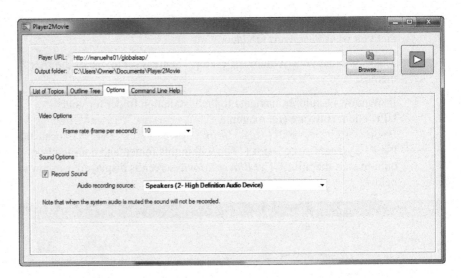

Review these options, and change them if necessary, as follows:

i.   The **Frame rate** field specifies the number of frames per second in the video. This defaults to **10**, but can be changed if necessary. Note that a larger number will create a more 'fluid' video, but at the cost of larger files.

ii. If you included sound in your published Player, and want to include this in your videos, then make sure that the **Record Sound** option is selected.

iii. If you are including sound (see Step ii) then select the audio device through which the sound will be captured. Note that this is actually the speakers through which the sound that would be played back during regular playback of the Topics in the Player—UPK simply 'intercepts' this sound; no new sound will be captured via the microphone or any other recording source.

9.   Click on the **Convert** button (this is the big, green 'play' button in the upper-right corner of the *Player2Movie* screen).

The Player2Movie utility will work its way through each of the selected Topics, playing them in See It! mode, and capturing this playback in video format. During this playback/capture, you will see a *Recorder* window similar to the following example:

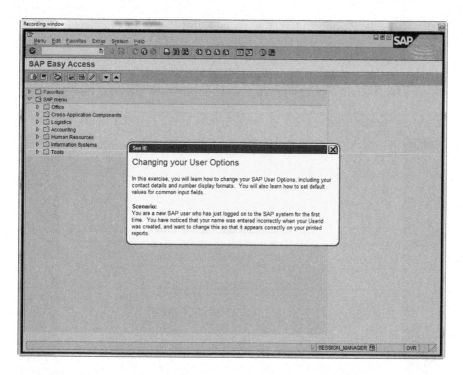

As each Topic is being recorded, a status of "**Recording**" will be shown in the *List of Topics* tabbed page. This changes to "**Done**" as each Topic is completed. An example of this is shown below:

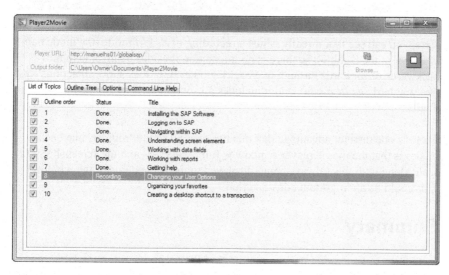

Once all selected Topics have been recorded, you can close the Player2Movie utility.

If you check the folder that you selected for the output, you will see one .mp4 file for each Topic. The file name will be the same as the Topic Name (there is no option to use the Document ID). You can now distribute or link to these files, as required.

If you open this .mp4 file, the 'video' will be played back in your default video player. The example below shows how it could appear in Windows Media Player

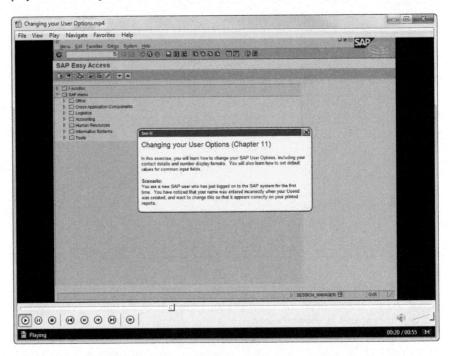

Here, you can see that it really is just a recording of *See It!* mode (the mode name is shown in the Bubble), so there is no interaction (besides being able to move backwards or forwards through playback). However, it does show all actions (just like standard *See It!* mode), and it includes all sound that has been included in the Topic.

There is one distinct advantage that this has over all of the 'regular' playback modes is that the movie player window is fully scalable - and the screenshot will scale along with this (always being displayed to the full extents of the window). This could be an important consideration.

Summary

In addition to generating the commonly-used Player package format, UPK provides the ability to deploy content in a number of other formats. UPK provides two on-line formats (including the Player), plus eight 'document' formats. These formats are:

- **Player and LMS**: A suite of interactive simulations suitable for loading onto a Web Server and/or into a Learning Management System.

- **HTML Web Site**: A limited-interaction version of the simulations, suitable for use with low-bandwidth/low-functionality browsers (such as those on mobile phones).

- **System Process**: A document that contains (by default) screenshots and action steps. This is suitable for use as a User Procedure.

- **Job Aid**: A 'slimmed-down' version of the Business Process, which (by default) does not contain screenshots. This is suitable for use as a quick reference.

- **Training Guide**: A printout of the full content of all Topics for a published Outline. This is suitable for use as a handout for users.

- **Instructor Manual**: A printout of the full content of all Topics for a published Outline, including the *Instructor Notes*. This is suitable for use as a 'teacher's edition' of a Training Guide, for use by an instructor during classroom training.

- **Test Document**: A test script that guides testers through the steps that they need to perform in order to complete a test, or a document that captures the results of a *Test It!* mode execution of a simulation.

- **Test Results**: A document that captures the results of a recording performed using the Record It! Wizard, and previewed in the Wizard.

- **Test Case**: A test script in Microsoft Excel format that can be used in conjunction with a number of testing software applications.

- **Presentation**: A simulation in Microsoft PowerPoint format.

Each of these formats has specific options that can be used to tailor the layout and content of the output. The overall publication process is largely the same for each format.

Which of the deployment formats you use will depend upon your individual requirements. Many corporations do not look beyond the Player package, but even though the document formats are not always pretty, and may take significant work to match in-house styles, they do have their uses, as described in *Chapter 1, An Introduction to Oracle UPK.*

You also have the ability to convert Topics that have already been published to a Player into a video format. This is useful if you need to distribute single, self-contained files for demonstration purposes.

7

Version Management

This chapter applies primarily to a *client/server* environment (sometimes referred to as a multi-user environment, although a client/server setup could technically still be used with only one user). If you are a lone author working in a *stand-alone* environment (sometimes referred to as a single-user environment), you may want to just skip straight to *Exporting and importing content* on page 309. Sorry, but version management in a stand-alone environment is almost nonexistent, so you're largely on your own.

In a client/server environment, all content objects are stored on a central server. authors create and edit content on their own workstation, and then send this content to a database on the central server for storage when they have finished with it. This is referred to as **checking in** a content object. If they subsequently want to change a content object (created by themselves or another author) that is on the server, they need to **check out** the content object, change it, and then check it back in.

In this chapter, you will learn how to:

- Check in a content object
- Check out a content object
- Display the version history for an object
- Revert to an earlier version of an object
- Restore a deleted content object
- Export content to a backup file
- Import content from a backup file
- Import content from a previous version of UPK

Client versus Server

When you create a content object in a client/server environment, the content object is initially stored in your **local repository** (that is, on the client side of the client/server environment). It is important to understand that your local repository is (by default) located on your *local* workstation. This means that if you have a content object in your local repository, and then move to another workstation, you will not see your local version of this content object on the new workstation. This is because the content object is located on the workstation on which you created it or checked it out. You should, therefore, always use the same workstation, or check in all of your content objects before moving to a new workstation.

✛ By default, your local repository is on your C: drive. Starting with UPK version 3.5.1, it is possible to choose a specific location for your local repository. You *can* create your local repository on a LAN drive or other location—but it is recommended that you still create it on your workstation so that you can still work in the event of a network failure.

Documents that are checked out to your local repository are identified by a green check-mark (✓) to the left of the object details on the *Library* screen. You will need to check in these objects if you want them to be accessible to other authors. Generally, you should do this whenever you have finished working on a content object. However, there are good reasons for checking in objects more frequently. Your local repository is (by default) on the C: drive of your workstation, whereas the Library is on a central server. Unless you are very fastidious about backing up your workstation, the chances are that the server is backed up more often than your PC, and is usually backed up automatically. Placing your files in the Library will, therefore, provide greater security in terms of having a backup that you can revert to in the event of a disaster.

In addition to this, whenever you check in a content object, a copy of the previous version is retained. Should you need to back out your changes, you can simply revert to an earlier version of the content object. Related to this, content objects are never really deleted from the server Library. Actually, they can be deleted, but only by an Administrator, and typically only as part of a clean-up. However, if you delete an object (that has never been checked in to the central server) from your local repository, it is gone. Forever!

Finally, it is not unheard of for a local repository to simply disappear when UPK crashes (which thankfully doesn't happen that often, but it has been known to happen). If this does happen to you, then you may lose all of the content that you currently have checked out (although the *Lost documents* view, introduced in UPK 3.5, may save you); the good news is that you won't have lost anything on the server.

For all of these reasons and more, it is recommended that you check in all of the content that is stored in your local repository to the server at least at the end of each work day. Fortunately, UPK provides a quick way of doing this. If you click in the **Check In All** button (📇), then all of the content objects that you currently have checked out will be checked in again. The down-side of this is that if you do check in all of the documents that you are currently working on at the end of the day, you need to remember which objects these are so that you can check them out again the next day. An easy solution to this is to select the **Keep checked out** option when you check in the documents (this option is explained

✛ The **Keep checked out** option was introduced in UPK 3.6.1.

later in this chapter). That way, the most recent version is saved to the server, but the content object remains checked out to you (so no other author can edit it), and stored in your local repository.

There is one further thing to bear in mind when deciding upon how often you are going to check in your content objects. As mentioned above, UPK retains every version of a content object that has been checked in. These are accessible via the *Document History*, as we will see later in this chapter. This means that if you check in a content object ten times, then UPK will retain ten versions of it. This can make it difficult to identify the 'released' versions of the content object versus the 'incremental saves' in the Document History, should you subsequently need to roll back to the last-released version.

UPK Workflow

The down-side to checking in content objects that you may not have finished working on is that these objects could be misperceived as being final, and actually used or published. In some cases, you may have checked some of them out not because you want to change them, but specifically to stop anyone else from changing them.

UPK does not provide you with a simple, automatic solution to these shortcomings, but there is a manual workaround that you can use. This is to use the **Workflow** properties of the objects.

UPK does not have a 'real' workflow. It does not have routing of content objects based on their status, or automatic email notification of content objects that are due for review, or any of the things that you'd expect from workflow functionality. Of course authors can use a View (as explained in *Chapter 3, Working in the UPK Developer Client*) to display content objects according to their Workflow properties, but this is still not really "workflow" as most people interpret it.

If you display the Properties for a content object, by clicking on the **Properties** button ( ), the last category of properties (at the end of the *Properties* list) is the **Workflow** category. Within this, there are two properties:

- **Owner**: This property allows you to select (from a drop-down list) the Userid of any author who is defined to the *Library*. If you select your own Userid in this field, then this should be an indication to the other authors that they should not work on this content object themselves.

  This property is particularly important if authors are using the *Record It! Wizard* (see *Chapter 2, Recording a Simulation*), as authors can only edit simulations via the *Record It! Wizard* for which they are identified as the Owner.

- **State**: This property can be used to specify the current status of a content object. The default values are (blank), **Not Started**, **Draft**, **In Review**,

● Administrators can add, remove, or rename statuses. How to do this is explained in *Chapter 14, Basic Administration*. It is recommended that a suitable set of statuses are established and defined prior to any development work starting, and that these statuses and their meaning are communicated to all authors.

and **Final**. If you select a status of **Draft**, then this is an indication that you have not finished with the object.

An example of the *Properties* pane, showing the **Workflow** category, is given in the following screenshot:

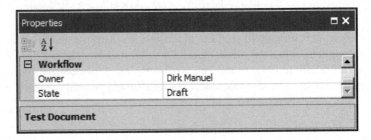

Of course, these **Properties** do not provide 'hard checks'. You still rely on the other authors seeing, and then paying attention to, these **Properties**, but it is a start. Some strong guidance from your Project Manager or Team Leader would help here. For information on making specific properties visible on the *Library* screen, refer to *Chapter 3, Working in the UPK Developer Client*.

Checking in a content object

To check in a content object, carry out the steps described below:

● You can also check in content objects by selecting them in the *Outline Editor*.

1. On the *Library* screen, select the content object(s) that you want to check in. Normally, you will want to check in one or more specific content objects, so you would only select these. As always, you click on a content object to select it. You can *CTRL*-click to select multiple objects, or *SHIFT*-click to select a contiguous set of objects. You can also select a folder in the *Library* to check in all of the content objects in that folder. Do not worry if some of the objects that are included in your selection are not checked out; UPK will simply ignore these objects during check-in (it will not "error-out").

2. Once you have selected all of the content objects that you want to check in, click the **Check In** button ([⬆]).

3. When you check in one or more specific content objects, UPK will automatically check for any content objects that are related to the object that you are checking in. You will be prompted to check these in, as well. An example of this prompt is shown in the following screenshot:

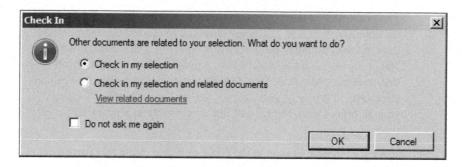

Click on the **View related documents** link to list the related documents. An example of the *Related Documents* dialog box is shown in the following screenshot:

■ For more information on related documents, refer to *What are related documents?* on page 302.

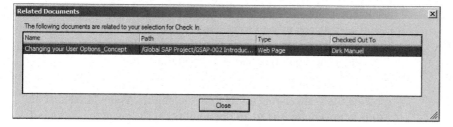

Click on **Close** to close the *Related Documents* dialog box and return to the *Check In* dialog box.

4. If you want to check in only the selected content object(s), then select the option **Check in my selection**. If you want to check in the selected content object(s) and all of their related content objects, then select the option **Check in my selection and related documents**.

5. You will be prompted to enter a short description of the change, as shown in the following screenshot:

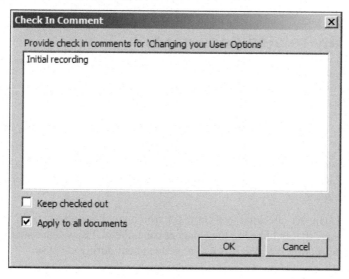

The title of the content object that you are checking in is shown above the comment text box. If you are checking in multiple content objects, then this will initially specify the first object in alphabetical order and (assuming that you deselect the **Apply same comments to all documents** option—see Step 8) will specify the next object when you click **OK**. In this way, you can provide separate comments for each content object, even though you are checking them all in at the same time.

■ Although it is (unfortunately) entirely optional, it is a very good practice to always enter a comment. This comment will appear in the *Document History*, and therefore serves as a useful audit log.

6. Enter a suitable comment in the space provided. Note that you do not need to specify the date and time of the change, or your Userid. These are captured automatically by UPK.

7. If you want to keep the content object(s) checked out to you then select the **Keep checked out** option. Why would you want to check a document in only to immediately check it out again? Because checking it in will save a copy to the server, and create a new version of the content object. Checking it in but keeping it checked out is therefore a good way of saving a checkpoint, or taking a 'backup'.

8. If you are checking in multiple objects, then UPK will initially suggest applying the same comments to all of the objects. You will see that the **Apply same comments to all documents** check-box at the bottom of the dialog box is selected. If you do not want to use the same comment for all objects that you are checking in, then deselect this check-box.

9. Once you have entered your description of the change (or reason for the change), click on **OK**.

10. When you click on **OK**, the *Check In Comment* dialog box for the next content object in the check-in selection will be displayed. You can then repeat the above processing from Step 1. Once you have specified a comment and clicked on **OK** for the last object, the content objects are checked in, and the *Library* screen is re-displayed.

What are related documents?

Related documents identified during check-in are generally Web Pages and Packages used by the content object that you are checking in, or Topics within the Outline Element that you are checking in. For example:

- If you are checking in an Outline Element (Module or Section) then UPK will automatically select all of the content objects (Modules, Sections, Topics, Assessments, and Questions) included in this Outline Element, along with any Web Pages used by any of these content objects.

- If you are checking in a Topic for which you have also created a Web Page that is linked to the Concept pane, then UPK will automatically select this Web Page as a related document during check-in.

- If you are checking in a Glossary, the related documents will be all of the Web Pages for the content definitions used by the Glossary.

This list of related documents shown in the *Related Documents* pane during check-in can be confusing, as it does not match the list that you see in the *Related Documents* pane for the content object that you are checking in. The (check-in) list will include Web Pages to which there are explicit links from the content object that you are checking, but will not include Glossaries, Templates, Packages, or icons, all of which are listed in the *Related Documents* pane.

This inconsistency is important to understand. If you update a Glossary and as a result UPK checked out several content objects during the glossary link regeneration, UPK will *not* identify all of these content objects as *related documents* during check-in of the Glossary. You will need to locate these and check them in separately (the All Checked Out view will help you with this),

Adding to the confusion, the list of related documents will include **all** of the explicitly-linked content objects, and not only those objects that are currently checked out to you. Do not worry about this – UPK will only physically check in the content objects that you have checked out (these are the ones that have your Userid in the **Checked Out To** column of the *Related Documents* dialog box). In the example above, we are checking in an Outline Element that contains one Topic, which in turn links to a Web Page. The Topic is currently checked out, but the Web Page is not. UPK will simply ignore the Web Page when checking in the Topic and related documents.

Checking out a content object

If you want to change a content object that is currently checked in to the Library on the server, you need to check it out from the Library.

To check out a content object from the server, carry out the following steps:

1. On the *Library* screen, click on the content object that you want to check out.

2. Click on the **Check Out** button ( ) on the *Versioning* toolbar. If there are other content objects related to the content object that you are checking out, then UPK will ask you if you want to check out these objects as well, as shown in the following screenshot:

✦ Prior to version 3.5.1, UPK did not warn you (other than a small text of "Read only" in the title bar – which was easily overlooked) if you edited a content object that you did not have checked out, and would simply prompt you to save the read-only content object as a *new* content object when you tried to save it. As from UPK 3.5.1, if you try to open a Web Page or Outline Element that you currently do not have checked out, UPK will ask you if you want to check it out first. For Topics, UPK will not ask you, but when you try to save your changes, you have the option to then check out the content object (your changes will be retained – as long as no-one else has checked out the Topic in the meantime). This is a significant improvement.

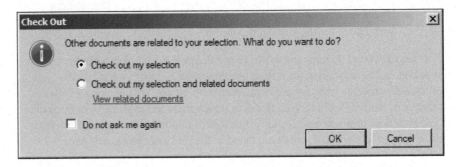

3. Select whether you want to check out only the selected document, or the selected document and all related documents. Then click on OK. Refer to *Checking in a content object, above,* for additional guidance on related documents, if necessary.

The document is checked out into your local repository. A green check-mark (✓) is shown to the left of the content object's name to indicate that the content object has been checked out. All other authors will see a lock symbol (🔒), indicating (to them) that another user has the content object checked out. If you have a content object checked out, then other authors can still display the currently checked in version of the content object. However, they will not be able to make any changes to it as this would necessitate them checking it out themselves, which they will not be able to do. They will also, obviously, not see any changes that you have made to the content object since you checked it out (as these changes exist only in your local repository).

You can now edit this content object as required. Once you have finished editing the content object, you should check it back into the server, as described above.

Canceling check-out

If you check out an object and then decide that you do not want to keep any changes that you may have made (or maybe you didn't make any changes after all), then you can cancel the check-out by carrying out the steps described below:

1. On the *Library* screen, select the content object for which you want to cancel the check-out.

2. Click on the **Cancel Check Out** button (🔲). If there are other content objects related to the content object for which you are canceling the check-out, then the following message is displayed (even if none of these related content objects have been checked out):

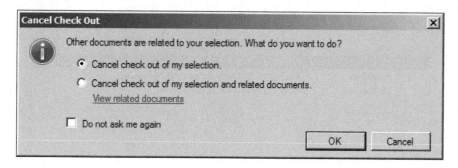

3. Select whether you want to cancel the check-out for only the selected document, or the selected document and all related documents, and then click on **OK**. Refer to *What are related documents?* on page 302, for additional guidance on related documents, if necessary.

4. If you have changed the content object since you checked it out, then the following warning message is displayed:

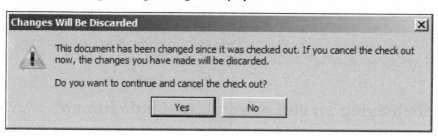

● Note that if you did not actually make any changes to the content object, then it is simply 'unlocked'— nothing is moved to the server, and no new version is created.

5. Assuming that you are happy to throw away your changes, click **Yes** to confirm the cancellation of the check-out.

The document is removed from your local repository (along with any related documents, if applicable) and will be available to other users for check-out. This will not create any entries in the version history.

Working with document versions

Every time that you check in a content object (and not every time that you save it in your local repository), UPK takes an archive copy of the previous version. You can list all of the previous versions of any content object by selecting the object on the *Library* screen (or in an Outline), and then selecting menu option **Document | History**. An example of the resulting *History* dialog box is displayed in the following screenshot:

● You can also display the *History* dialog box for a content object if you currently have it open in an Editor, via the same menu path.

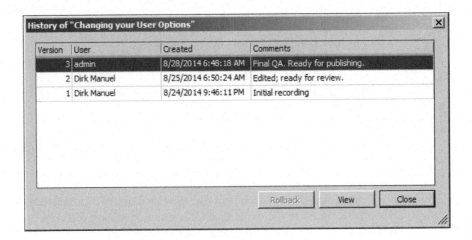

The *History* dialog box lists every checked-in version of the content object since it was first checked in to the server, along with the Userid of the person who created the version (that is, the person who checked in the content object) and the date and time at which this was done. The **Comments** field shows the comments that were entered when the document was checked in (this is why it is important to enter check-in comments, as described on page 301).

Displaying an earlier version of a document

You can display any version of a Topic, Web Page, or Package (but not Module or Section) from the document's *History*. To do this, follow the steps shown below:

1. Select the content object on the *Library* screen.

2. Select menu option **Document | History**.

3. In the *History* dialog box, click on the version that you want to display.

4. Click **View**.

■ You can use menu option **File | Save As** to save a copy of this earlier version—for example, if you need to retrieve content from it, or want to use it as the basis for a new document.

The document is opened in the relevant editor: *Topic Editor*, *Web Page Editor*, or *Package Editor*. The editor tab shows the version number that you are displaying (although for long titles, you may need to display the tooltip by hovering the cursor over the tab), as shown in the screenshot below.

In this example, we are displaying version **3** of the content object. Because this is a previous version, it always shows as being **Read-only**.

Reverting to an earlier version of a document

If you have checked in a content object, and then realize that you do not want to keep your latest changes (or you want to back out someone else's work because they made a poor job of it) then you can revert to an(y) earlier version of the content object. To do this, follow the steps shown below:

1. Select the content object on the *Library* screen. Note that the document must be checked in; you cannot roll back a document that is currently checked out (by you or any other user).

2. Select menu option **Document | History**.

3. In the *History* dialog box, click on the version to which you want to revert. This is shown in the following screenshot:

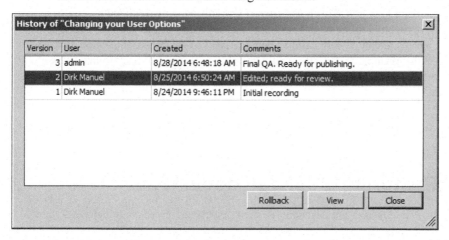

4. Click **Rollback**.

The version that you selected becomes the latest version again, with the **Comments** set to **Rolled back to version x**, as shown in the screenshot below:

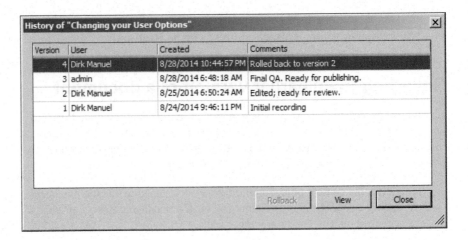

What has happened is that a *new* version has been created, by taking a full copy of the selected (historical) version. The version that you wanted to back out has not been deleted; it is still available, but it has just been superseded by the new (rollback) version. This means that if you subsequently realize that you *shouldn't* have reverted to the earlier version, and really do want to keep the previous changes, then you can simply select the last version before the rolled back version (in the example above, this would be version 3), and roll back to that (which will then create yet another version – version 5 in this example).

Note that the content object is not checked out to you when you revert to an earlier version.

Restoring a deleted document

In a client/server environment, content objects are never really deleted; they still exist on the server. Instead, they are removed from the *Library* screen so that they are not available within the *Library* screen itself. However, they will appear in the *Deleted documents* view, from where authors can display and restore them. The only way they can be truly deleted is by the Administrator purging them. The advantage of this is that you can always (up until the point that the Administrator has purged it) 'un-delete' a content object, if you realize that you (or someone else) deleted it by mistake.

■ See *Purging deleted documents from the Library* on page 536 for information on permanently deleting content objects.

To restore (un-delete) a content object, carry out the following steps:

1. From the *Library* screen, click on the drop-down button for the **View** field (which will normally indicate **Details view**) on the *View Toolbar*, and select **Deleted documents**. A list of all of the content objects that have been deleted (but not purged) is displayed, as shown in the following screenshot:

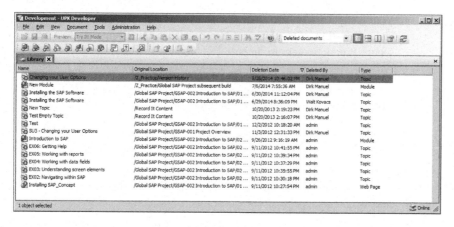

2. Right-click on the document that you want to restore, and select **Restore** from the context menu. This is the only option available on this context menu.

The document is restored, and placed back in the folder from which it was originally deleted. This location is also shown in the **Original location** column in the *Deleted documents* view, before you restore the document. This will create another version in the version history for the content object—just as deleting it did. This is shown in the screenshot below:

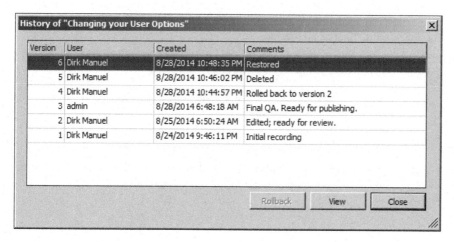

Exporting and importing content

If you are working in a stand-alone environment and want to share your developed content with another user, you will need to export it from your *Library* so that they can import it into their Library. If you are an author working in a client/server environment, it is unlikely that you will need to export your content because all users will be able to access it in the same Library. However, even then there may be a need to export your content, for example:

- Your company may use a 'staged' release strategy, whereby all content is developed in a Development library before being migrated to a more secure Production environment.

- You have developed content in one environment (for example, your personal stand-alone environment) and now want to bring it into your company's client/server environment.

- You want to take a copy of everything you have done, as a personal back-up.

- You are upgrading to a new version of UPK and want to export all of your content from the old version, so that you can import it into your new version.

Exporting content objects

■ Exporting sound is covered in *Chapter 11, Incorporating Sound Into Your Topics.* Exporting user options is covered in *Chapter 2, Recording a Simulation.*

You can use the **Export** function to export content objects as an archive, to export publishing options for sharing, and to export sound files for re-use. This section covers exporting content objects as an archive, although the approach is the same in each scenario.

You can export any type of content object to an archive: Modules, Sections, and Topics, as well as Web Pages, Packages, Assessments, and Questions. You can also export any of the objects in the System folder, such as Templates, Publishing Packages, Style Sheets, and Skins.

To export a content object, carry out the following steps:

1. On the *Library* screen, select the content object(s) that you want to export. You can select a single object, or multiple objects of various types. You also have the option of selecting a folder, which will export the entire contents of that folder.

■ If you are working with multiple libraries, then it is recommended that you always export/import from the Library screen, and not from within a Module or Section). This will reduce the possibility of elements that appear in multiple outlines being overwritten on successive imports.

2. Select menu option **Tools | Export | Documents**. The *Export* dialog box is displayed, as shown in the following screenshot:

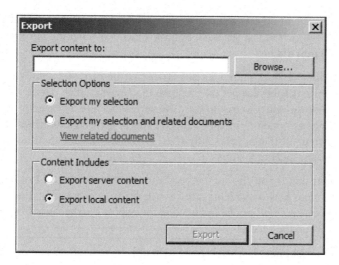

3. Click on the **Browse** button next to the **Export content to:** field. The *Save As* dialog box is displayed, as shown below:

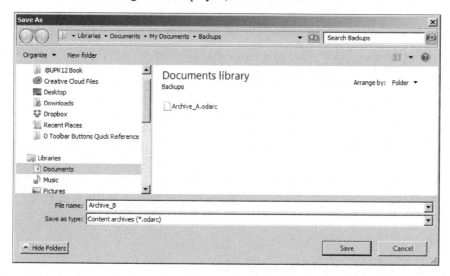

4. Navigate to the folder into which you want to save your export file.

5. Enter a suitable file name for your export file in the **File name** field.

6. Note that UPK will automatically select a file type of **Content archives (*.odarc)** and add the file prefix .odarc (for OnDemand Archive. Note the reference to OnDemand even though the product hasn't been called OnDemand in many years!).

7. Click **Save** to confirm the destination folder and file.

8. Back in the *Export* dialog box, under **Selection Options**, select whether you want to export only the specific content that you have selected (**Export my selection**), or the selected content and all related documents (**Export my selection and related documents**). Related documents

are content objects such as Web Pages that are linked to the selected object(s). You can see a list of these objects by clicking the **View related documents** link.

9. If you are working in a client/server environment then you will see the **Content Includes** option group on the *Export* screen. Here, you can choose whether to export only the versions of the documents currently that are stored on the server, or to export any copies of the selected documents that are currently checked out to you and are therefore stored in your local repository.

    Note that if you choose to export only server content, and your selection includes new documents that have never been checked in, then these documents will not be included in the export file (because they don't yet exist on the server).

10. Click **Export**. The selected content objects (and all related documents, if you chose that option) are exported to the specified file. While this is being done, a progress indicator is displayed showing the overall completion percentage of the export. The export may be very quick, especially if you are only exporting one or two Topics so don't blink or you'll miss it. An example of the progress indicator is shown below:

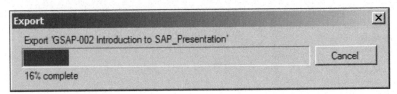

11. Once the export is complete, you are returned to the *Library*.

Because the content is exported to a single file, you can easily save the file to CD/DVD as a back-up, send the file to another author for importing into their UPK Library, and so on. How to import this file is described next.

Importing content objects

You can import UPK content that has previously been exported from another implementation of UPK. You can also import content that you have previously exported back into your own implementation.

To import content objects, carry out the steps described below:

1. Select menu option **Tools | Import | Documents**. The *Import* dialog box is displayed, as shown in the following screenshot:

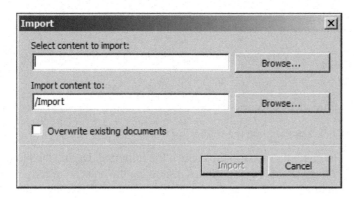

2. Click on the **Browse** button to the right of the **Select content to import** field. Navigate to, and select, the archive file that contains the content that you want to import. This must be a file with a file type of .odarc.

3. The **Import content to** field specifies the folder within your *Library* into which the imported content will be placed. This defaults to /Import, and UPK will create this folder if it does not exist already. If necessary, you can use the **Browse** button to navigate to, and select, any other folder within your *Library*. If you don't know exactly what content is contained within the archive, it is probably a good idea to not import it directly into your 'production' folders. In this case, consider accepting the default folder as you can always move the imported content into the correct folders, once the import is complete.

   If UPK finds that your *Library* contains versions of any of the objects contained in the archive, then the version in the archive will not, by default, be imported. If you do want to import this content, and are happy to overwrite any existing versions that you have in your Library, then select the **Overwrite existing documents** option in the *Import* dialog box.

   Note that UPK does not use the file name, or the folder into which it is being imported, to determine whether a file already exists. It uses 32-character Document ID, which is retained when the object is exported.

   Note also that if you are re-importing content objects that already exist in the *Library*, then the imported content will be placed in the folder in which a version already exists in the *Library*, and not in the **Import content to:** folder.

4. Click on **Import** to begin the import.

   If the folder that you specified in the **Import content** to field does not already exist, then a warning message similar to the one shown below will be displayed:

■ If you are importing new content from one Library to another and want it to be imported into exactly the same destination folder structure as the source Library, then select an **Import content to** value of "/".

▲ If you are importing content from one Library to another—for example, if you have separate Development and Production Libraries—then you should always select **Overwrite existing documents**. Otherwise, any changed content objects will not be re-imported.

✚ In UPK 3.x and earlier, the file is always imported into the folder in which it existed in the original Library.

▲ If the destination folder does not already exist, then you must have sufficient permissions in the Library to create it (for the default Import folder, you require **Modify** permissions on the root folder).

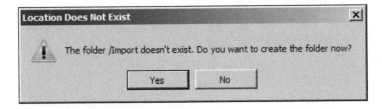

5. Click **Yes** to create the folder.

   The content objects in the archive file imported. During the import, a progress indicator is displayed showing the object currently being imported, and the overall percentage complete. The import may be very quick, especially if you are only importing one or two content objects. Again, don't blink or you'll miss it. An example of the progress indicator is shown in the following screenshot:

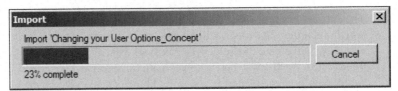

6. In some circumstances, UPK may not be able to import the content that you are trying to import. In this case, a warning message is displayed, as shown in the next screenshot:

   Always click on the **View activity log** link to display the *Import Activity Log* dialog box to check which files were and were not imported, and why. An example of the *Import Activity Log* dialog box is shown in the next screenshot:

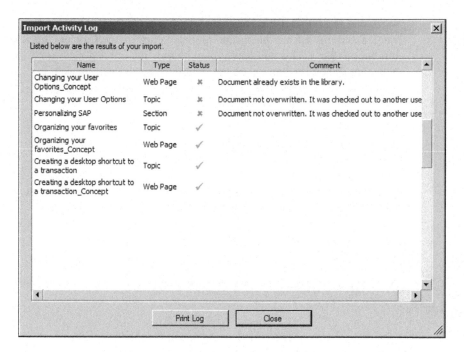

In this example, one Web Page could not be imported because it already existed in the Library (and the **Overwrite existing documents** option was not selected). In addition, a Topic and a Section could not be imported because they were checked out to another user (and are therefore locked).

Click on the **Close** button to close the *Import Activity List* dialog box. Back at the *Partial Import* dialog box, click on **OK** to close the dialog box.

Once the content has been imported, you are returned to the *Library*. You can now navigate to the /import folder and work with the imported objects the same way as you work with objects that you created yourself – although most likely you will want to move them to another directory once you have confirmed that they are correct.

Selective imports

When you import a .odarc archive file, UPK will import the entire contents of the archive. It is not possible to select only specific files within the archive (as you might want to, perhaps, if you needed to retrieve a single file from a backup). However, there is a workaround:

- In a client/server environment, make sure that you have nothing checked out, and then import the full archive. All of the imported files will automatically be checked out to you. Display these by selecting the *Checked out to me* view. Select all of the files that you do *not* want to keep (that is, all files apart from the specific content object(s) that you wanted to retrieve from the backup file), and click on the **Cancel Check-out** button (🗔). This will leave you with only the file that you want. Note that if the files that you do not want have never been checked in (that is, they are new to this *Library*) then you cannot cancel the check out, but should simply delete them, instead.

- In a standalone environment files are not checked out so you cannot use the above approach. Instead, make sure that the file you want to retrieve does not exist in your *Library* (the chances are that it won't if you are trying to retrieve it from a backup). Import the full archive, but make sure that the **Overwrite existing documents** option is not selected. Only the files that don't already exist in the *Library* will be imported, and these will be placed into the Import folder. Go to this folder and delete all of the files except for the single file that you wanted to retrieve.

Converting content from a previous version of UPK

✦ UPK 11.x also provided the ability to allow Administrators to convert Knowledge Pathways content (via menu option **Tools | Convert**), but this option has been removed in UPK 12.1.

In UPK version 3.x it was possible to convert content that had been created with a previous version (2.x, or OnDemand 9.x), via the menu option **Tools | Convert from 2.x | Content**. This option was removed from UPK 11.x. This is largely because you do not need to 'convert' content created in the previous version (for UPK 11.x, this is UPK 3.x) because it is already in the correct format (the database format did not change between UPK 3.x and UPK 11.x). Instead, you can simply export the content from your 3.x Library, and import it into your 11.x (or greater) Library, as explained earlier in this chapter.

If you need to import content created in UPK 2.x into your UPK 11.x or UPK 12.x Library, you can't. If you ask Oracle nicely they may be able to help you (possibly for a fee). Otherwise, if you still have access to a UPK 3.6 Library, then import the pre-3.6 content into that to convert it to the new database format. You can then export it from your 3.6 Library (in the new format) and import it into your new Library.

Summary

The need to make regular back-ups of your work is extremely important. In a client/ server environment, this is simplified by the fact that the server is typically backed up on a reasonably-regular basis. As long as you check in your content, it will be backed up as well. The other advantage of checking in your content is that each time that you check in a content object, UPK takes a copy of the previous version. You can display, or revert to, any of these previous versions should the need arise. A further advantage of a client/server environment is that content objects are not immediately deleted from the Library database when you delete them from the *Library* screen. This means that it is possible to un-delete a content object if necessary.

In a stand-alone implementation, there is no server so there are no regular backups, and no automatic versioning. It is therefore left to you, the author, to take your own backups. The best way of doing this is to use UPK's Export functionality, and use its Import functionality if you need to revert to an earlier version.

8

Allowing Alternatives

As we have seen in the previous chapters, UPK is good at capturing the execution of a task. The author simply executes the task, one action at a time, from beginning to end, recording as they go. What this gives you is a linear simulation, but this is not all that UPK can do. With a little more effort, it is possible to add alternative routes through the simulation. In this way, a simulation can cover multiple scenarios, or multiple outcomes. Adding alternative ways of doing something also makes the simulation more realistic, especially in *Know It?* mode—as we shall see.

In this chapter you will learn how to:

- Add Alternative Actions
- Add Alternative Paths
- Add Decision Frames
- Add Branches
- Respond automatically to user actions

Adding Alternative Actions

An **Alternative Action** (in UPK terms) is another way of doing the same thing on a single Frame. If you remember the description from *Chapter 1* of what UPK captures during recording, you'll recall that it captures a set of action/screenshot pairs—effectively, a screenshot and the action carried out to get there. With this in mind, an Alternative Action is another action that will also get you to the same (next) screenshot. This is probably best clarified by way of an example.

In the exercise that we have been working on throughout this book, we have a Frame where the user was required to refresh the screen by clicking the **Enter** button on the toolbar. In the *Topic Editor*, the Frame appears as follows:

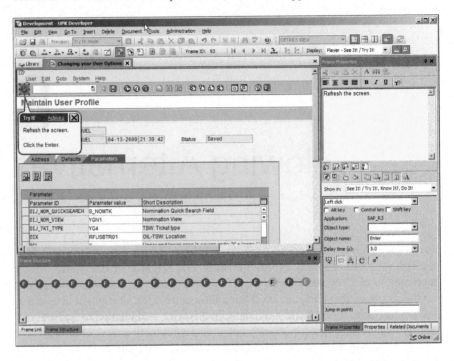

In reality (in this particular application), the user can either click the **Enter** button on the toolbar (as currently recorded), or press the *ENTER* key on the keyboard. Which option they use is largely a matter of choice. One could argue that it is best to teach people only one method so as not to confuse them. However, there is often strong feeling about mouse actions versus keyboard actions, and users seem to appreciate being given the choice of suffering from either repetitive strain injury or carpal tunnel syndrome.

There is also another strong driver for providing Alternative Actions: *Know It?* mode. Consider the example above. In *Know It?* mode, the user is asked to refresh the screen, but is not told how to do this (the *Template text visible in Know It? mode* toggle button ( ) is not selected, which is the default setting). You can see from the *Action Properties* pane that the Action is **Left click** on the **Toolbar button** object named **Enter**. If the user carries out this exercise and they press the *ENTER* key, which is a perfectly valid way of refreshing the screen, then they will be marked incorrect, and (depending on the required pass percentage, and their performance on the rest of the exercise) could fail the test. This is a bit harsh given that they did something that would have worked in the actual system.

One solution to this problem would simply be to display the template text in *Know It?* mode, but then it hardly seems like a test at all. A better solution would be to allow pressing the *ENTER* key as a valid Action as well. We can do this by recording the pressing of the *ENTER* key as an Alternative Action.

To record an Alternative Action for a frame, carry out the following steps:

1. Make sure that you are positioned on the correct screen in the application.

2. In the *Topic Editor*, select the frame for which you want to record the Alternative Action.

3. Select menu option **Insert | Alternative Action** (⟶). (You can also click on the **Insert** button (⟍⟋▾) on the *Topic Editor Toolbar*, and then select **Alternative Action** (⟶) from the drop-down menu.) You are passed back to the application, with the *Recorder* panel displayed, as usual.

4. Click in the application (from Step 1) to make it the active application.

5. Perform the Alternative Action and then press *PRINTSCREEN* to capture the Action. Note that you do not need to press *PRINTSCREEN* an initial time to start recording (even though UPK will always display a message stating that you need to press *PRINTSCREEN* to start recording). As soon as the Action has been captured, you are passed back into the *Topic Editor*.

● When you capture an additional Action, no screenshot is captured. The Alternative Action is applied to the same screenshot as the initial Action. However, the *context* is still captured—even though there is no Object type or Object name captured. You should, therefore, capture Alternative Actions on the correct screen in the correct application. Otherwise, the context-sensitive help would incorrectly identify this Topic as being relevant for another context (that is, for the one captured for the Alternative Action).

The screenshot below shows the result of recording the alternative action:

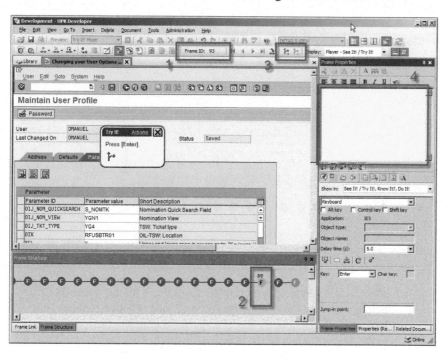

There are a few things worth noting here. These have been highlighted in the above screenshot, and are explained below:

1. The new Action (which is specified in the *Action Properties* pane) has been performed against Frame **93**. This is the same Frame as the

one against which the original Action was recorded (see the previous screenshot). This confirms that no new screenshot has been captured.

2.   In the *Frame Structure* pane, the indicator for this frame now has the text **2/2** displayed above it. This text indicates that there are two actions for the Frame, and the details of the second Action are currently being displayed. (For reference, the first digit is the number of this Action, and the second digit is the total number of Alternative Actions. The text can therefore be read as "action x of y".)

■ You can also press *Alt+Cursor Up* to move to the previous Alternative Action, and *Alt+Cursor Down* to move to the next Alternative Action.

3.   The **Previous action** button (⯈) is now 'active' (compare this with the previous screenshot, where it is not active because there was no previous Action). If you click on this button then the details of the previous Action are displayed, the **Previous action** button is deactivated (⯈), the **Next action** button (⯈) is activated, and the numbers above the frame indicator in the *Frame Structure* pane changes to **1/2**. The following screenshot shows this scenario:

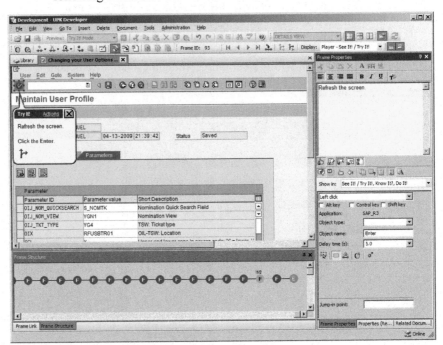

4.   The *Custom Text* field is empty (compare this with the screenshot from before we added the Alternative Action). This is because we are now looking at the Bubble for the *Alternative Action*, and Custom Text is tied to the *action* and not to the Frame.

Let's take a quick look at how this manifests itself in the Player. The following screenshot shows the same Frame in *Try It!* mode:

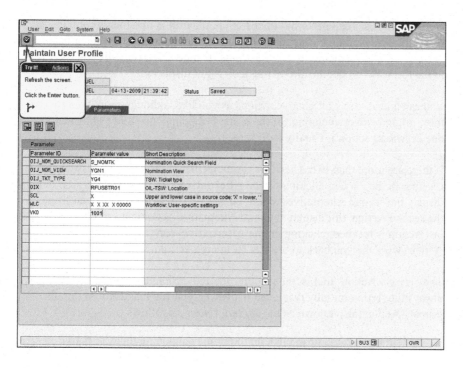

You will see that the bubble now contains an additional icon. This is the
Alternative icon. If you click on this icon, the Alternative Action is displayed.
This can be seen in the next screenshot:

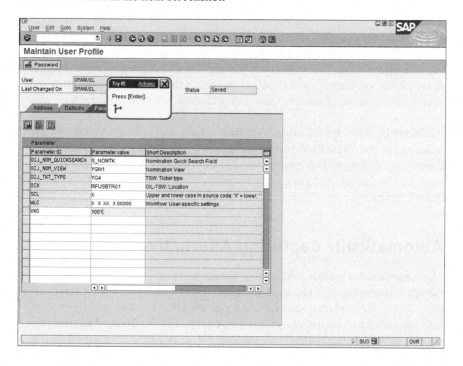

Note that the user can perform either Action, regardless of which Action is currently displayed on the screen. Although these screenshots are taken from *Try It!* mode, the same holds true for *Know It?* mode. The only difference is that in the *Know It?* mode, the alternative icon is not displayed.

You can add as many alternative actions as you like, although more than two or three might be overwhelming for the users. Providing one mouse-click action and one key-press action is usually sufficient.

If there are more than two Alternative Actions then these will be 'daisy-chained' together in the Player. Clicking on the **Alternative** icon from the first Action will display the second Alternative Action; clicking on the **Alternative** icon from the second Action will display the third Alternative Action; and so on. Once the last Action is reached, clicking on the **Alternative** icon (for the last Alternative Action) will take you back to the first (primary) Action.

The *primary* Action (that is, the Action captured during the initial recording) is always the Action initially displayed. However, you can make any Action the primary Action (also known as the *default Action*) as follows:

1. In the *Topic Editor*, click on the frame containing the Alternative Action(s).

2. Click the **Previous action** button (![icon]) or the **Next action** button (![icon]) to display the Alternative Action that you want to be the default action.

3. Select menu option **Edit | Set as default action** (![icon])

The original (mouse-click) Action had some custom text defined for it. This Custom Text is missing from the second (key-press) Action. This may, or may not be, what you want. In *Know It?* mode it makes no difference as the bubble text is never visible for Alternative Actions. However, in the other modes, you may want to provide the same, or similar, Custom Text for the Alternative Actions.

Additionally, if you have Custom Text for the (original) primary Action, but then make one of the Alternative Actions the primary Action (as just explained), then the primary Action will no longer have any Custom Text. In this case, you may want to copy (or cut) and paste the relevant portions of the custom text to the new default Action.

Automatically capturing Alternative Actions

Many applications include keyboard shortcuts for mouse actions. If UPK knows the application (that is, it can capture the context information), then it can usually also identify the keyboard shortcuts. You can ask UPK to automatically capture these shortcuts as Alternative Actions for you, by selecting **Record keyboard shortcuts** in your user options (see *Appendix B, User Options* for details of this setting).

Alternative Paths

An Alternative Action takes place on a single Frame (the Frame against which the original Action was recorded), and is another Action that has exactly the same effect as the original Action—meaning that it takes you to the same screen (the next Frame in the recording). But what if the Alternative Action should take you to an entirely different screen? What if the Alternative Action has an entirely different outcome to the primary Action? Or what if you just want to be able to describe two possible scenarios in the same single exercise? UPK can support all of these requirements through the use of **Alternative Paths**.

Inserting an Alternative Path

In our sample exercise, you may recall that we guide the user through the menu path in order to start the transaction that allows them to maintain their User Profile. It is also possible for users to reach this transaction by entering the transaction code in the input field in the upper-left corner of the screen (the **Command** field, in SAP terminology), and pressing ENTER. We will add this capability to our exercise.

To add an Alternative Path to a Topic, carry out the steps described below:

1. Start the application for which you want to capture the Alternative Path, and go to the first screen that you want to capture.

2. Switch to UPK, and open up the Topic in the *Topic Editor*.

3. Position the screen on the Frame from which the user should be able to select the Alternative Path. In our sample exercise, this is on the very first Frame, Frame **1** (the current Action for this screen is clicking on the *System* menu).

4. Select menu option **Insert | Alternative Path** (🔀). (You could also click the **Insert** button (✦▾) on the *Topic Editing Toolbar*, and then select **Insert Alternative Path** (🔀) from the drop-down menu.)

5. The pointer changes into an arrow, with a black "E" (for End) at the bottom (see the example in the next screenshot). In the *Frame Structure* pane at the bottom of the screen, navigate to the Frame at which you want this Alternative Path to re-join the main path, and click on it.

   Note that as you hover over a frame, its thumbnail is displayed. In addition, the thumbnail image includes the Frame ID (as shown in the example below), which will further help you to select the correct Frame. For our exercise, we will choose to rejoin the main path at Frame **3**.

● If you try to insert an alternative path to the next frame (for example, if you want the alternative path to have more Frames than the primary path), then UPK will insert the first captured action as an alternative action on the current Frame, and will then insert the remaining Frames/actions on the current path (that is, it will not create a branch-around for you, but will effectively insert the new Frames as 'missing frames'). The workaround is to record the alternative path as going around the next Frame (that is, to re-join the primary path at the next Frame +1) and then move the end point of this path back one Frame (as explained in *Changing the end point of an Alternative Path* on page 327) when you are done recording. (Of course, the cleanest thing to do is always record the 'longest path' first and then set the shorter, alternative path as the default action.)

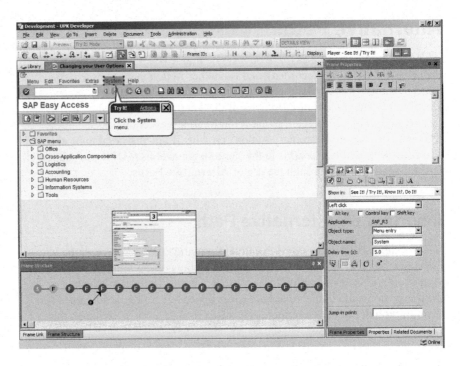

6. You are passed into the application for which you want to record the Alternative Path. Click in this application to make it the active application, and then press *PRINTSCREEN* to start recording. Record the actions for the Alternative Path as usual. (Refer to *Chapter 3, Recording a Topic* for additional guidance, if required.) For our sample exercise, we recorded the following actions:

    i. Clicked in the *Command* field, to make this the active field.

    ii. Entered the transaction code **SU3**.

    iii. Clicked the **Enter** button on the toolbar.

7. When you have finished (when you are positioned on the screen in the application at which you are rejoining the main path), click on the **Finish** button in the *Recorder* pane. You are passed back to UPK.

The Alternative Path has now been inserted, as shown in the following example:

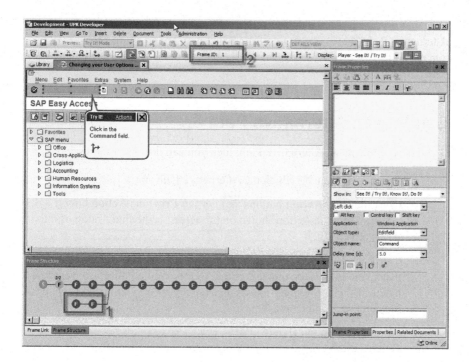

There are a few things to note in this screenshot. Firstly, although we recorded three actions there are only two additional Frames in the recording **(1)**. This is because the first Action that we recorded (clicking in the **Command** field) was recorded against the Frame from which we started our Alternative Path **(2)**. Secondly, the path that the Action is currently being shown for is highlighted in green in the *Frame Navigation* pane. This is useful for understanding what you are looking at on the screen (and which frame will be navigated to next if you click on the **Next Frame** button (▶), or press *ALT+RIGHT ARROW* on the keyboard).

Changing the end point of an Alternative Path

If you mistakenly select the wrong Frame at which you want to rejoin the main path, then you can rectify this by changing the end point of the Alternative Path.

To change the re-join point for an Alternative Path, carry out the following steps:

1. Select the last Frame in the Alternative Path (that is, the Frame immediately before the Alternative Path rejoins the main path).

2. Click on the **Change end point** button (✓) in the *Frame Properties* pane. The pointer changes to the **End arrow** we saw earlier when we were selecting the original end point for the Alternative Path.

3. Click on the Frame where the Alternative Path should now rejoin the main path.

✛ Prior to UPK 12 you could not change the end point of an 'empty' path (that is, an Alternative Path that contains no additional Frames - a 'bypass'). This limitation has been removed in UPK 12.

Note that if you have defined Alternative Actions for the last Frame in the Alternative Path (that is, the Frame from which you are changing the re-join point) then you will need to change the re-join point separately for each Alternative Action.

Deleting an Alternative Path

If you need to delete an Alternative Path, then you can do so as follows:

1. Select the Frame on which the Alternative Path starts.

2. Click the **Next Action** button (![icon]) or the **Previous Action** button (![icon]) so that the Action shown on the screen is the first Action of the Alternative Path.

3. Check which path is highlighted (in green) in the *Frame Navigation* panel, and make sure that this is the Alternative Path that you want to delete. This is extremely important as it is very easy to mistakenly select the main path and delete that.

4. Select menu option **Delete | Path** (![icon]). (You can also click on the **Delete** button (![icon]) on the *Topic Editing Toolbar*, and then select **Path** (![icon]) from the drop-down menu.)

5. In response to the message **Are you sure you want to delete the selected path?**, click **Yes**.

Decision Frames and Decision Paths

The Alternative Action and Alternative Path that we have seen so far are *benign* choices. The user can use any of the alternatives simply by carrying out the associated Action. What if we want to force the user to make a choice? What if we want to explain each of the Alternative Paths before the user makes their choice? This is where **Decision Frames** come into play.

A Decision Frame is a special kind of Frame where the user is presented with a question and two or more possible answers (technically, you could have only one answer, but what would be the point?), each of which directs them down a different path (called a **Decision Path**, in this context).

Decision Paths can be **Alternatives** or **Branches**. These are similar with one exception: an Alternative will always rejoin the main path (that is, both paths eventually share common Frames again), whereas a Branch does not (which means that the Topic will have two End Frames). Despite this difference, how they are created is largely the same. Let's look at this, by way of an example.

Inserting a Decision Frame

In our sample exercise, we describe the use of three tabbed pages: the *Address* page, the *Defaults* page, and the *Parameters* page. After consulting with our Subject Matter Experts, we learn that most casual users won't ever define any default parameter values and therefore don't need to be taught about the *Parameters* page. To support this, we'll use a Decision Frame to ask the user whether or not they want to learn how to maintain their parameters, and provide a Decision Path that bypasses the *Parameters* page entirely if they do not.

To insert a Decision Frame, carry out the steps described below:

1. In the *Topic Editor*, position yourself on the Frame after which you want the Decision Frame to appear. (This is the Frame before the first Frame in one of the paths resulting from making a decision.) In our sample exercise, we will select Frame **12**, because the following Frame, **91**, is the Frame containing the Action to click on the Parameters tab.

2. Select menu option **Insert | Decision Frame** ([icon]). (You can also click on the **Insert** button ([icon]) on the *Topic Editing Toolbar*, and then select **Insert Decision Frame** ([icon]) from the drop-down menu.) The *Create New Decision Path* dialog box is displayed, as shown in the following screenshot:

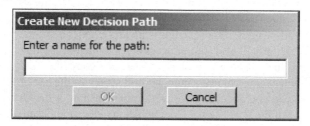

3. In the **Enter a name for the path** field, enter a short text description of the current path (this is the path that has already been recorded). In our sample exercise, this is the path that teaches the user how to maintain their parameters, so we will enter a description of "**I am a frequent user; I want to see how to define parameters.**".

4. Click on **OK** to save your description and create the Decision Frame.

The Decision Frame has now been inserted in the Topic, and is identified by a "**D**" icon in the *Frame Structure* pane, as shown in the following screenshot:

● If you subsequently need to change the text description for a path, select the path in the Path list, and then click on the **Rename path** button ([icon]). In the *Rename Decision Path* dialog box that is displayed, change the name as required, and then click on **OK**.

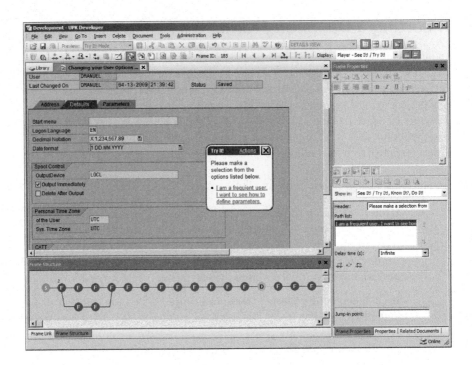

There are several things to note about this new Frame. First, the screenshot used for this Frame is a grayed-out version of the screenshot from the Frame immediately following it. This is actually the first Frame in our main path, but the same screenshot will also (out of necessity) be the first Frame in all other paths, so this is logical. However, this is a one-time copy (the Frames are not linked), so if you wanted to use a more neutral screen as the background for your decision, then you could recapture or edit the screenshot for the Decision Frame. The screenshot of the next Frame, from which the Decision Frame screenshot was initially taken, will not be affected.

Next, we have a new type of Bubble overlaid on the screenshot. This has an introductory sentence (the **Header**) about the decision, followed by a bulleted list of the options that are available (although at the moment there is only one option because we have not yet recorded any Alternative Paths for this decision).

Finally, you will notice that we now have a new set of fields and buttons in the *Frame Properties* pane. These are used to control everything to do with the Decision Frame. You can see that the **Header** field contains the introductory sentence that we can see in the Bubble, and the **Path list** lists all of the paths that are listed in the Bubble (again, there is only one at the moment).

The first thing we need to do is to change the introductory text. The default text is adequate, but if we are aiming for quality, we can make this a bit more meaningful. To change the introductory text, simply type over the current value in the **Header** field. There is no limit to the length of the text that you can specify here, but you cannot insert paragraph breaks (or use any other type of formatting) so you probably don't want to use a text string that is too long. Alternatively, you can remove the introductory text altogether by deleting all of the text in the Header field. This would be a useful option if all of your decision options are in the format "Click here to..." For our sample exercise, we will change the introductory text to "**Frequent users may find it useful to define default values for common input fields. Do you want to see how to do that?**".

Inserting a Decision Path

We are now ready to insert another Decision Path for this Decision Frame. For our sample exercise, we are providing the users with the option to bypass the description of the Parameters page entirely. Because the Parameters tab is the last thing described in the simulation, we will use a **Branch** that just exits from the transaction.

To insert a Branch, carry out the following steps:

1. In the application that you are recording, make sure that you are positioned on the screen from which you want to start your Decision Path.

2. In the *Topic Editor*, select the Decision Frame to which you want to add the Decision Path.

3. In the **Frame Properties** pane, click on the **Insert Path** button ( ). (You can also click on the **Insert** button ( ) on the *Topic Editing*, and then select **Decision Path** ( ) from the drop-down menu. The *Create Decision Path* dialog box is displayed, as shown in the next screenshot:

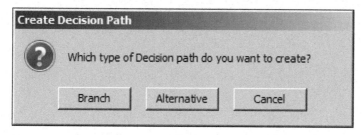

4. Click on the appropriate button, depending on whether your new path will rejoin the main path (**Alternative**) or will not (**Branch**). For our example, we will select **Branch**. Either the *Create New Decision Path* dialog box or the *Create New Branch* dialog box is displayed (as appropriate). The content and purpose of both is the same, so they are not described separately here, and only the *Create New Branch* dialog box is shown.

One could argue that it is the **infrequent** users who should set default values, as they are more likely to forget the correct values than a frequent user who enters them every day, but that's an entirely separate discussion.

This is actually the wrong choice in this case. The two choices (seeing and bypassing the *Parameters* page) do actually share a subsequent Frame. This is the very last Frame in the simulation where we see the save confirmation message. Therefore, it would be better to use an Alternative Path. However, for the sake of variety in our sample exercise, we'll use a Branch. This will also allow us to look at some other interesting functionality later in the book, and provide us with the interesting challenge of working around this mistake.

5. In the *Create New Branch/Create New Decision Path* dialog box, enter a short text name for your new path, and then click on **OK**. For our sample exercise, we will enter a path name of "**I am an occasional user; I don't need to know that.**".

6. If you are creating an Alternative Path (as opposed to a Branch) then you will be prompted to select the end point for the path in exactly the same way as you would for an Alternative Path without a Decision Frame (see *Inserting an Alternative Path* on page 325).

7. You are passed into the application for which you want to record the Alternative Path. Click in the application, to make it the active application, and then press *PRINTSCREEN* to start recording, and then record the Actions for the Alternative Path. (Refer to *Recording a Simulation* on page 27 for additional guidance, if required.) For our sample exercise, we recorded the following Actions:

   i.   Clicked the **Save** button.

8. When you have finished, which should be when you have completed the activity, as you are not re-joining the main path, click on the **Finish** button in the *Recorder* pane. You are passed back to UPK.

The Branch has now been inserted, as shown in the following screenshot:

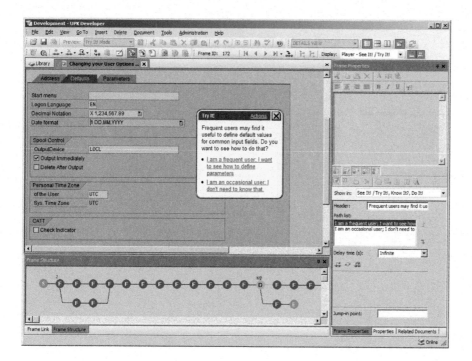

You can see that the Decision Frame now contains two options. These tie in with the paths shown in the **Path list** in the *Frame Properties* pane. You can also see from the *Frame Navigation* pane that we now have two end points for the Topic. This is because we used a Branch.

Let's look at how this manifests itself in the Player. The next screenshot shows what the user will see when they reach the Decision Frame:

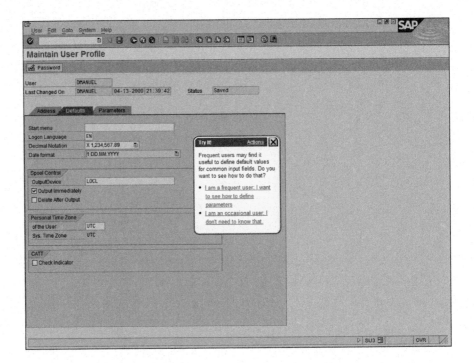

Note that you can add as many Alternative Paths or Branches as you like to a Decision Frame. You can even mix them, perhaps providing three Alternative Paths and two Branches, all from the same Decision Frame.

Changing the order of Decision Paths

Decision Paths will be listed in the Player the order in which they are recorded, but you can change this order if required. For example, you may want the path that you recorded second (for whatever reason) to be listed first. The order of the Decision Paths—or at least which one is listed first—also becomes important when considering *See It!* and *Know It?* modes (see below).

To change the order of the paths in a Decision Frame, carry out the steps described below:

1. In the *Topic Editor*, select the Decision Frame.

2. In the **Path list**, click on the path that you want to reorder.

3. Click on the **Move Up** button (🔼) or the **Move Down** button (🔽) to move the path to the required position. These buttons can be found to the right of the **Path list**.

Deleting a Decision Path

To delete a decision path, carry out the steps described below:

1. In the *Topic Editor*, select the Decision Frame to which the path that you want to delete is attached.

2. In the **Path list**, select that path that you want to delete.

3. Click on the **Delete Decision Path** button (🔀). (You can also select menu option **Delete | Decision Path**.)

Note that you cannot delete a path if it is the only path in the Decision Frame. In this case, you would first need to delete the Decision Frame itself, and then delete the path (which would effectively delete the remainder of the recording, which you probably wouldn't want to do).

Decision Frames in See It! mode

In *See It!* mode, the Decision Frame will (by default) be displayed until one of the options is selected. This may not always be desirable, especially if the simulation is being looped in kiosk mode. Whether UPK waits for a decision or not, and how long it waits for if it does, is controlled by the **Delay time (s)** field in the *Decision Properties* pane. As you can see from the previous screenshots, this is set to **Infinite** by default, which means that UPK will wait forever, if necessary, for the user to make a choice. If you want UPK to automatically continue down the primary path if a choice is not made within a certain period, then simply change the **Delay time (s)** field to specify how long (in seconds) UPK should wait before continuing. You can either choose one of the predefined options from the drop-down, or enter a specific number of seconds directly into the **Delay time (s)** field.

If you select a delay time of **Skip**, then UPK will act as though the Decision Frame does not even exist. The Decision Frame will not be displayed, and the playback will proceed immediately down the default path (this is the one listed first in the **Path list**).

Decision Frames in Know It? mode

Decision Frames effectively do not exist in *Know It?* mode. The user is required to carry out the actions for the default path (this is the one listed first in the **Path list**) only. This is in marked contrast to Alternative Actions and Alternative Paths, and is an important consideration when deciding whether to have an Alternative Path or a Decision Path.

If you recall the Alternative Path that we added (see *Inserting an Alternative Path* on page 325), we gave the users the choice of accessing the transaction either via the menu, or by entering the transaction code. In *Know It?* mode, the user can perform either set of actions. With our Decision Path (see *Inserting a Decision Path* on page 331), the user can only perform the Action for the default path (changing their parameters). If they try to take another path (assuming that they somehow know about it in advance—maybe because they have already carried out the simulation in *Try It!* mode—then they will be marked incorrect.

Stretching the envelope with Alternative Paths

What we have looked at so far has been fairly obvious uses of Alternative Paths. However, there are a few other interesting things that you can do with Alternative Paths. Note that the key word here is "interesting". These things may not be entirely practical, but explaining them here will at least open your mind to other possibilities.

Looping back

In our examples so far, Alternative Paths and Decision Paths have been used to move forward through the simulation. When selecting the end point for our Alternative Path, we have always selected a Frame that is further ahead in the simulation than the Frame where the Alternative Path starts. However, there is nothing in UPK that says that you have to go *forward*. You could quite easily go backwards to an earlier Frame. A good use of this would be where you have several decision options, and want the user to be able to go back to the decision and choose a different path. An example of such a scenario is shown in the following screenshot:

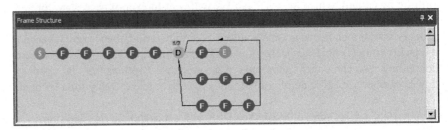

You can even rejoin the main path further back from where you originally started. This is illustrated in the following extract of the Frame Structure pane:

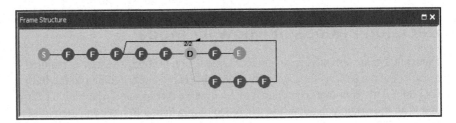

Quite under what circumstances this would be useful remains to be seen (possibly where one of the options is the 'wrong' thing to do and requires the user to re-do some of the steps), but the possibility is there, nevertheless.

Looping back in Know It? mode

There is an important consideration when using paths that loop back to earlier on the main path (regardless of whether this is to the Decision Frame, or to before the Decision Frame). As mentioned above, Decision Frames effectively do not exist in *Know It?* mode, and the user is automatically directed down the default path (the first path). If this default path lops back, then there is no way that the user can ever complete the simulation because they will be stuck in an infinite loop. Luckily, UPK watches out for this, and will not let you loop the main path backwards.

This does not mean that you can't have *any* paths looping back (as we have just seen, this is perfectly possible) – just that the first 'choice' in a Decision Frame cannot loop back. The easiest way to confirm you are doing things correctly is to confirm that both the Start Frame and the End Frame are on the same horizontal line (the uppermost one) in the *Frame Structure* pane.

However, this can be a limitation. For example, consider where you have a simulation that allows users to display several different pieces of information. They can do this in any order they like, so you choose to have a Decision Frame (with a header question of "**What do you want to display?**") that has a separate Decision Path for each piece of information, and loop each path back to the Decision Frame so that the user can choose to look at something else. Clearly, you need a way to get out of this, so you have one of the options on the Decision Frame be "**I do not want to look at anything else**", and have this lead to the End Frame. Because the 'exit' path must be the primary path, you need to have this option listed first in the Decision Frame. But then, in *Know It?* mode, this choice is selected automatically for the user, and they will be passed directly to the End Frame without actually doing anything! There is no easy solution to this (there *are* solutions, but they get very complicated), so you should think carefully about what you want to achieve, and in what modes, before you loop back in this way.

Automatically responding to user input

As was clearly stated at the outset of this book, UPK creates *recordings*. Users carrying out UPK simulations can only perform the actions that have been recorded; they can only follow along a predefined path. As we have seen in this chapter, it is possible to extend this slightly by recording multiple paths and allowing the user to go down any one of these paths, but the recording is not *automatically* responding to which Action the user has chosen.

If Alternative Actions (and Alternative Paths leading from these Actions) have been defined for a Frame, then the user can carry out any of these Actions on the screen. They do not have to click on the **Alternative** icon (⤵) to go to the specific Alternative Path to which the Action applies. You can use this capability to direct users down a certain path depending on where they click on the screen, by defining each of these clicks as Alternative Actions leading down Alternative Paths.

As an example, we will create a simplified version of our sample exercise. In this version, we will allow the user to click on any tab from any screen. They can also click on the **Exit** button to exit from the transaction (and therefore the simulation). We have done this by defining Alternative Paths on each of the tabbed screens that lead to the other tabbed pages. For the sake of simplicity, we have removed all of the intermediate frames where the user is performing actions on the tabbed pages. Our *Frame Structure* pane now looks like the example shown in the following screenshot:

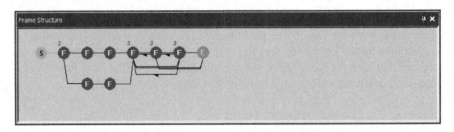

Despite having trimmed this back to only the navigational actions, this is still extremely complicated. However, it will *appear* to respond to user actions in that the user can click on any tab to move forwards or backwards through the simulation. In order to make this as realistic as possible, there are a few other things we need to do. First, we need to hide the Action Areas on all of the screens (by deselecting the **Action area on/off** toggle button (⬚) in the *Frame Properties* pane), so that the user has full flexibility of where to click. If you don't do this, then even though the user can click on any tab, the first tab will always be highlighted. Secondly, we need to remove any Bubble Text (custom or otherwise) that tells the user where to click, and replace it with some neutral text. For example, in our exercise we could say something like "**Click on any tab, or click the Exit button to quit.**" We need to do this for *every* Action on *every* Frame. Once we've done this, we'll have a simulation that appears to automatically respond to what the user does. If you have downloaded the sample documents for this book, you can find the Topic from which the above screenshot was taken, as **Exercise 4: Responding to user actions (Chapter 8)**.

As this is fairly complex to set up, it is probably not worth doing for every exercise, especially once you start including 'real' actions (and not just the navigation actions). However, there is certainly an argument to be made for using this approach for display-only activities, where users can roam around the various screens as they see fit.

Summary

Providing alternatives in a Topic will make the Topic more realistic and more flexible. There are three types of alternative:

- **Alternative Actions** provide another way of achieving the same result as an existing Action, on the same Frame. Alternative Actions are useful for providing such things as keyboard shortcuts for mouse-click actions (or vice versa).

- **Alternative Paths** provide different ways of progressing through the same simulation. In some cases, this may just be an extension of an Alternative Action, by providing an alternative that takes several screens – for example, navigating through more than one level of menu, versus the initial Action of clicking a button on the toolbar. Alternative Paths can also be used to provide alternative scenarios – for example, parking an entered invoice versus posting it.

- **Decision Frames** require the user to make a conscious decision about which **Decision Path** to take. Decision Paths can be either **Alternatives**—which rejoin the main path, or **Branches**, which don't.

- You can also use a Decision Path to allow users to bypass certain parts of the simulation that may be irrelevant to them.

9

Adding Value to Your Topics

In *Chapter 2, Recording a Simulation*, we recorded our first simulation. Some authors would have stopped there. In *Chapter 4, Editing a Topic*, we updated our simulation so that it worked a little better, and tidied up some of the Bubble Text so that it made a bit more sense. Most authors would have stopped *there*. In *Chapter 8, Allowing Alternatives*, we added some alternatives into our simulation, to make it match reality a bit more closely, and to extend the usefulness of the Topic. Not many authors even bother to go that far. But in *this* chapter, we will take our Topics to an entirely new level, adding a great deal of value to them, and significantly improving their quality. We will do this through the use of Custom Text, Explanation Frames, Web Pages, and Packages. We will also look at providing a Glossary, which we'll seamlessly integrate into our content.

These things are sometimes thought of as 'bells and whistles', because they are added after the recording has been done, and are sometimes perceived as purely being "nice to have" (which usually translates into "don't bother" in a project plan). However, these bells and whistles can make the difference between adequate training and outstanding training—and of course you always want to aim for outstanding.

Adding the bells and whistles is even more important when the simulations are to be used as 'stand-alone' learning objects (that is, simulations that will be used for self-paced learning and not necessarily within the context of a classroom conduct). In a classroom, the instructor is there to embellish on the information shown, to present additional information, explain new terms, and generally talk around the topic. If the user sits at their own desk, all of this has to be provided within the simulation itself—and this is where these bells and whistles prove essential. If you want your exercises to have a shelf-life beyond the first round of training (which is typically in preparation for the initial system implementation), then you really need to read this chapter.

In this chapter, you will learn how to:

- Provide context through the use of **Custom Text**
- Use **Explanation Frames**
- Use **Web Pages** in the *Concept* pane and beyond
- Incorporate non-UPK content into your material through the use of **Packages**
- Create a **Glossary** and attach this to your content

Providing business context through the use of Custom Text

The easiest and most effective way to add value to your Topics is to make good use of Custom Text in the Bubbles. We looked at how to influence the Template Text, and how to add Custom Text, in *Chapter 4, Editing a Topic*, so we will not go over the same information here. Instead, we will simply look at what you can (and should) do with Custom Text.

The Start Frame

You may recall that the very first Frame in a Topic is the **Start Frame**. This is often referred to as the **Introduction Frame**, which is largely a throwback to OnDemand, as we shall see shortly. Because this Frame is (by default) the first thing that a user will see when they play back a Topic, it is a good place to provide some additional scene-setting information to the user.

The first thing that you should explain in the Introduction Frame is exactly what the user will be learning in the exercise. Certainly the title of the Topic should give them a clue, but this is not really detailed enough. A good source of information for this is the learning objectives of the course for which this exercise has been built—or the competencies, depending on your curriculum development process. For our sample exercise, we could use the bubble shown in the following screenshot:

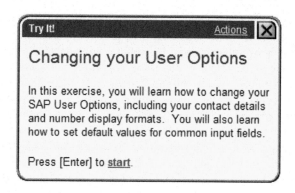

This is a good start, but we can do more.

It is always useful, with training exercises, to use realistic business scenarios to explain what the user is doing—to put the keystrokes and mouse-clicks into a business context. Users are much more likely to remember information to which they can relate. Consider telling a story and walking the users through that story as they carry out the exercise. Although it may be an oversimplification in this particular case, we will do this for our sample exercise. In this exercise, we will use the bubble shown in the following screenshot:

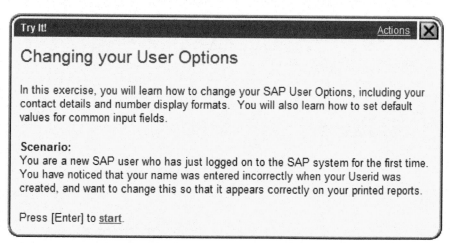

So now the user has a good idea of what they will learn, and they have an example that they can relate to. The text is also directed *at* the user (it is written in the *second person*, for the grammar buffs), so the user will feel actively involved. Note that we would likely tag portions of this text for display in certain modes only (for example, the 'scenario' would not normally be displayed in *Do It!* mode). Refer to *Chapter 4, Editing a Topic* for instructions on tagging text for different modes.

There is another strong argument for including a scenario in the form shown above. Consider the case where you are providing training for users in multiple locations (and possibly countries) or departments, each of which has its own set of customers, products, vendors, or other entities. Users will always want to see exercises using *their* data: orders for *their* products, placed at *their* location, and so on. To keep everyone happy, you would need to develop a separate, customized Topic for each location or user group. If the basic process (and, most importantly for us, the screens and Actions in the recording) is the same in each case, this is clearly inefficient. However, if you create a scenario, and say something like "You are a Customer Service Representative in the Tampa Service Center. Customer SunCo has phoned through an order for 1,000 gallons of regular gasoline. You need to record this order in the system so that it can be fulfilled by Fuel Services." then users who are not at the Tampa Service Center, or don't have a customer called SunCo, or don't sell regular gasoline will at least understand that this is *role play*; it is *make believe*, and they shouldn't be concerned that they see products that they don't necessarily supply from their own location. So set the scene with a scenario in the Start Frame, and then build on this throughout the exercise.

The Start Frame versus the Introduction pane

If you select a Topic within the *Outline Editor*, you will notice that the contents of the Start Frame are displayed below the (currently empty) *Concept* pane, under a heading of *Introduction*. An example of this is shown in the screenshot below:

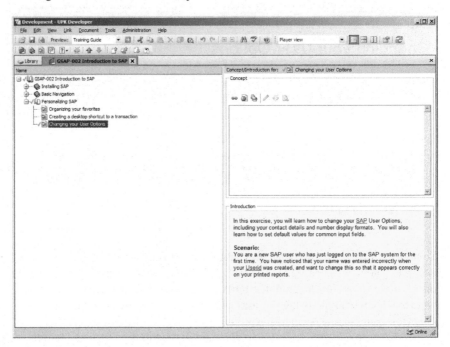

Generally, what you see in the *Outline Editor* reflects what your users will see in the Player. However, if we display the above Outline in the Player, we see the following:

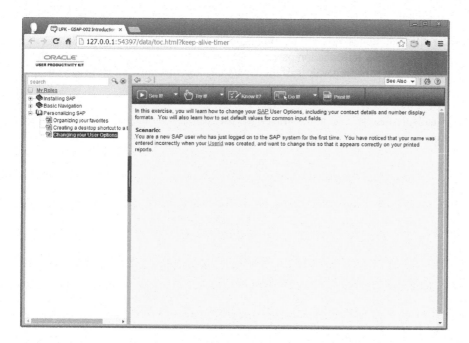

Here, we can see that the *Concept* pane (which we will look at later in this chapter) has been removed, and the *Introduction* pane (which is simply displaying the contents of the Start Frame) is displayed down the entire rightmost side of the Player window.

However, the problem that we now have is that the same text that is displayed in the Introduction pane is also displayed on the Start Frame during playback, which is a bit repetitive (and unnecessary). Luckily, UPK allows us to remedy this by not displaying the Start Frame during playback. This is done by **deselecting** the option **Show introduction text** when we publish. This option can be set in your defaults via the **Player** category of your **Options**, (see *Appendix B, User Options* for additional information) or specified during Publication (see *Chapter 6, Creating a Player and LMS Package*).

This feature (of displaying the Start Frame text in the *Concept* pane) is useful in that it does save you from having to create a separate Concept Page for display in the *Concept* pane (see *Using Web Pages in the Concept pane* later in this chapter). However, the **Show introduction text** setting is Player-wide. You should therefore decide whether you are going to use Concept Pages or just display the Start Frame in the *Introduction* pane before you start development, and then follow the chosen approach for *all* Topics.

Note that UPK gives you greater control over the formatting of Web Pages than it does over Bubble Text (especially in UPK 12, with the introduction of Style Sheets and the ability to include tables and nested lists) so you may find it more appealing to use Web Pages as Concept Pages, and not rely on the text on the Start Frame.

● It may seem counter-intuitive to *deselect* an option called **Show introduction text** when you *do* want the **Start Frame** text displayed in the *Introduction* pane, but don't want the Start Frame displayed, but that's the way it works (as from UPK 9.1). The option should really be interpreted as "Show the introduction text during playback of the exercise".

An additional consideration is that although you can tag text in the Start Frame for different modes, this text tagging is not used when the Start Frame is displayed as the Introduction pane: *all* text in the Start Frame is displayed in the *Introduction* pane, regardless of mode tagging, and this may not be what you want.

Finally, remember that in the Player, the user can display the Concept Page at the same time as the Topic, by using one of the following methods:

✦ The **Open concept in a new tab** feature was introduced in UPK 12.1.

- Select the Topic in the Player Outline and then click on the **Open concept in a new tab** button ().

- From within playback of the Topic (in *See It!*, *Try It!*, and *Do It!* modes), click on the **Actions** link in the upper-right of the Bubble, and then select **Display Concept** from the shortcut menu.

This is very convenient if the Concept Page contains information that they may want to refer to several times during playback of the Topic.

Action Frames

As we saw in *Chapter 4, Editing a Topic*, it is possible to add Custom Text to the Topic's Bubbles, either in addition to, or instead of, the Template Text. Using the Template Text has several significant advantages, especially when localizing your content (see *Chapter 17, Localizing Your Content*) or providing sound (see *Chapter 11, Incorporating Sound Into Your Topics*). However, the Template Text will only ever be able to describe the *mechanics* of what the user is doing, it cannot provide *business context*.

You should always try to teach more than just key-strokes and mouse-clicks. Specifically, you should always take the opportunity to add business context yourself, through the liberal use of Custom Text in Action Frames.

Consider the following example that uses solely the default template texts:

Certainly the user can *carry out* the required action and work their way through the exercise, but are they really *learning* anything? What is the **Ext.Ref** field, and what is the significance of the value **ZBW002342**? Should they *always* enter this value, or are other values possible, and if so, what is the nomenclature? Here, we should help the user out and *teach* them something by providing some more information through the use of Custom Text. A better version is shown in the following screenshot:

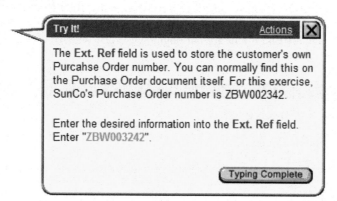

Now the user knows exactly what they are entering in the exercise, and understands the *business context* so they can perform the action correctly when they are doing their actual job.

Note that here we have retained the Template Text (we did not insert the Template Text as Custom Text) which will aid in the translation (although the Custom Text will still need to be manually translated). We simply added the first paragraph that you see in the Bubble above as Custom Text, and positioned it before the Template Text (the **Show custom text first** toggle button (🔳) is selected by default); you can deselect this toggle button if required, to have the Template Text displayed first.

● UPK will position the Template Text on the next line, immediately after the Custom Text, so you need to insert an extra line break at the end of the Custom Text if you want the two texts to appear as separate paragraphs.

Whenever practical, you should try to provide some relevant information in your exercises, whether this is business context, or a continuation of the scenario you are using. If you intend for your simulations to be used outside of a classroom environment, then you should consider providing exactly the same level of information as the instructor would provide in a classroom. Think about what you would say to the user—what additional information or guidance you would give them if you were sat next to them, talking them through the simulation, and then add *that* information into the Bubbles as Custom Text. Remember: training is the effective transfer of knowledge, and if that knowledge is incomplete, then the users have not been adequately trained.

The End Frame

The **End Frame** is always displayed as the final Frame in the simulation. There is no End Frame equivalent of the **Show introduction text** option to avoid having this Frame displayed. This is a good thing, as it means that we can use this Frame to provide some final information to the user. This should be seen as a companion to the Start Frame, and should confirm the information presented in that Frame.

In the Start Frame above, we told the user what they would learn. In the End Frame, we should confirm that they have learned this. (This much is standard learning theory.) If you have described a scenario in the **Start Frame**, and followed this through the Action Frames, then you should make reference to this, as well. A suitable End Frame for our ongoing exercise on SAP user options could be:

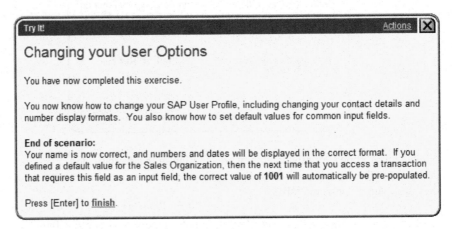

Although the scenario information is again fairly spurious in this example, it does at least give you an idea of the kind of information that can usefully be included in the End Frame. Again, this information should be tagged appropriately for the different playback modes.

Note that in this example we have also included a message of **You have now completed this exercise**. This is a nice courtesy, and confirms to the user that they have reached the end of the simulation.

Explanation Frames

In the previous sections, on the Start Frame, Action Frames, and the End Frame, we have looked at ways to provide additional information into the *existing* Bubbles. In this section, we will look at how to provide information on Frames that serve no purpose other than to provide information. These are **Explanation Frames**.

An Explanation Frame is a special type of Frame that does not have an associated Action. When you insert an Explanation Frame, it takes its screenshot from the Frame immediately following it (regardless of whether this is an Action Frame, a Decision Frame, or even another Explanation Frame. This makes Explanation Frames extremely useful for drawing the user's attention to particular information on that screenshot, or explaining things that are not explicitly covered by the Action Frames. Note that, unlike Decision Frames, the screenshot used in Explanation Frames is not grayed out.

■ If you are using the Explanation Frame as a transitional or scene-setting Frame, and not drawing attention to specific information on the screen, you may want to consider editing the screenshot for this Frame, to gray it out to match Decision Frames (and the Start Frame and the End Frame), so that the user knows they do not need to pay attention to the screenshot itself.

In our sample exercise, we will add two Explanation Frames. On the first of these we will inform the user that, although the simulation does not walk them through doing so, they can still change their last name. On the second Explanation Frame, we'll draw the user's attention to the message generated by the system when they save their user profile.

To insert an Explanation Frame, carry out the steps described below:

1. Open up the Topic to which you want to add the Explanation Frame, in the *Topic Editor*.

2. In the *Frame Navigation* pane, click on the Frame that is immediately before the point at which you want the Explanation Frame to appear. The screenshot of the *next* Frame will be copied into the Explanation Frame (this is a one-time copy; you can replace or edit either screenshot without the source Frame being affected). For our exercise, we want the Explanation Frame to show the initial view of the **Address** tabbed page, so we will select Frame **2**, as shown in the following screenshot:

■ This may seem counterintuitive at first, as you may assume that you should select the Frame on which your Explanation Frame should be based (and from which it will take its screenshot), but you can perhaps best visualize it as the Explanation Frame being inserted onto the highlighted green line in the *Navigation Pane*, (this holds true for inserting all Frame types) and that you want to draw the user's attention to something on the *next* screen that they see.

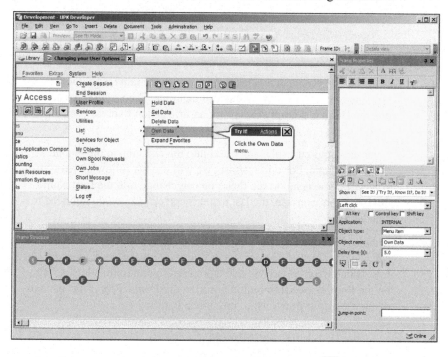

3. Select menu option **Insert | Explanation Frame** (▨). (You can also click on the **Insert** button (⊕▾) on the *Standard Toolbar*, and then select **Explanation Frame** (▨) from the drop-down menu.) A new Frame is inserted, as you can see in the next screenshot:

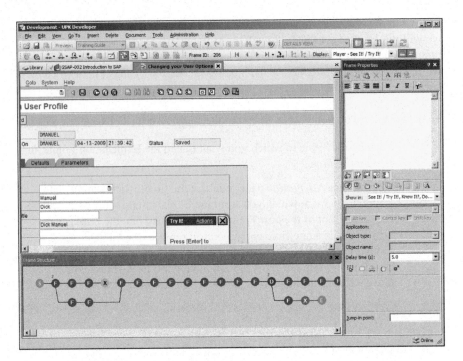

Note that the screenshot is taken from the *next* Frame, and not the previously selected frame. Note also that there is no Action Area, and that the Bubble is empty except for an instruction to press *ENTER* to continue.

4. Enter the required explanatory text into the text area in the *Frame Properties* pane. For our exercise, we will use the following text: "If your last name is incorrect, then you can change it in the Last Name field. For this exercise, the last name is correct, so you do not need to change it."

5. Bubbles in Explanation Frames do not contain pointers. However, you can add a pointer, if necessary. For our exercise, we are referring to the Last Name field, so we will add a pointer to point to this field. Click on the **Pointer position** button ( ) in the *Frame Properties* pane to display the drop-down list of possible pointers:

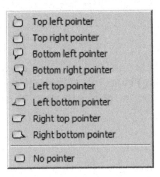

Select the appropriate pointer position from the drop-down list. For our exercise, we will use the **Left top pointer**. You will also have to move the Bubble so that the pointer is pointing to the required screen element. You can do this by clicking on the Bubble header, and dragging the Bubble to the required position.

6. Explanation Frames do not have an associated Action; the user is not required to do anything other than press the *Enter* button (or click on the **Continue** link in the bubble) to continue. However, it is worth emphasizing this to the user. We can do this by inserting an icon into the Bubble, which informs them that this Frame is for information only. To insert an icon, click on the **Bubble icon** button ( ), to display a drop-down list of available icons, as shown in the following diagram:

Click on the appropriate icon to select it. For our exercise, we will use the black "i" image in the top row. This icon will then appear in the upper-left corner of the Bubble (as shown in the finished Bubble for our exercise in the screenshot below).

7. Although there is no Action associated with this Frame, there is still one field in the *Action Properties* pane that is relevant: **Delay time (s)**. By default, in *See It!* mode, the Explanation Frame will be displayed for five seconds before the Player advances to the next screen. If you have a lot of text on your Explanation Frame, then this may not be enough time for the user to read it all. In this case, you should select or enter a longer period.

Our finished Bubble, in our Explanation Frame, now looks like the example shown in the next screenshot:

● You can change the pointer position (or remove the position altogether) for any bubble, on any kind of Frame, by using the **Pointer position** button. Refer to *Chapter 4, Editing a Topic* for more details.

● You can add an icon to any bubble, on any kind of Frame (except a Decision Frame), by using the **Bubble icon** button. However, you should use icons sparingly, and always consistently, as explained in *Chapter 4, Editing a Topic*.

● The **Delay time (s)** field contains a drop-down with values for 0, 5.0, 10.0, and Infinite. You can select one of these values, or simply enter any other value into this field (you are not limited to the drop-down selection).

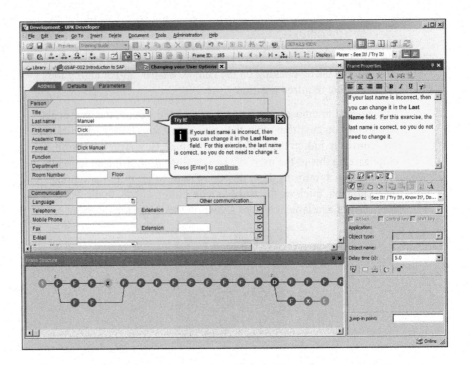

This icon isn't very eye-catching (none of the default ones are...) and is only in black and white (probably as a concession to printed output). In *Chapter 16, Customizing UPK*, we will look at how to replace these default icons with our own ones.

So far, so good, but inserting this Explanation Frame has introduced a new problem. Our Explanation Frame has been inserted *before* the re-join in our Alternative Path. This means that if a user chooses the Alternative Path (the lower of the two paths shown here) they will not see our new Explanation Frame.

We need to move the end point of this Alternative Path to re-join the main path on our new Explanation Frame. How to do this is explained in *Chapter 14, Allowing Alternatives*, under the section *Changing the end point of an Alternative Path* on page 325.

Once we have moved this end point, our *Frame Structure* pane now looks like the example shown in the following screenshot:

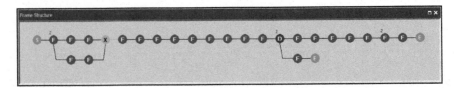

We are now ready to insert our second Explanation Frame. For this one, we are going to draw the user's attention to the message that is displayed when they save their changes. This message is visible only in the very last Frame, so we need to insert our Explanation Frame immediately before this.

Carry out the same steps as described above, to perform the following activities:

1. Insert an Explanation Frame as the penultimate Frame in the main path

2. Add the Custom Text "Your changes are saved, and a confirmation message is displayed at the bottom of the screen." to the Bubble.

3. Add a pointer, and point this to the message at the bottom of the screen.

4. Add the same 'i' icon as we used before to the Bubble.

Our new Explanation Frame appears as follows:

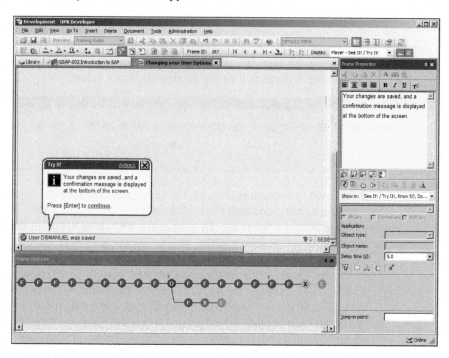

So far so good. But again, a new problem has been introduced. Now, users who follow the Branch will not see our new Explanation Frame. Unfortunately, this time there is no easy solution. Although UPK will let you change the re-join point of an *Alternative Path*, it is not possible to change the end point of a *Branch* to have it re-join the main path—that is, to change a Branch into an Alternative Path.

Copying and Pasting Frames

In the previous section, we had a problem where we had a Frame in our Main Path that we also wanted to be available in our Branch. Fortunately, UPK contains some functionality that we can use to resolve (or at least work around)

■ Although UPK does not provide a built-in way of changing a Branch so that it re-joins the main path, there is actually a way to do this. First, create an Alternative Path from the last Frame in the Branch to the point at which you want to join the main path. Then, select the existing path (which contains the End Frame for the Branch, and delete the path. Note that when recording the Alternative Path you need to use the same Action as the current (primary) Action for the Frame.

this problem. This is the ability to copy and paste (or cut and paste) Frames. For our exercise, we will simply copy our new Explanation Frame from the Main Path, and paste it into the Branch. This is fairly inefficient, as it means that if we want to change the Bubble Text for this Explanation Frame we have to do it in two places (or just re-copy-and-paste). However, it will save us from having to delete and then recapture the branch, and will be faster than inserting another Explanation Frame and re-entering our Custom Text.

➕ The ability to copy and paste Frames was introduced in UPK 3.5. The ability to *cut* and paste Frames was introduced in UPK 12.1.

To copy and paste Frames, carry out the following steps:

1. Open the Topic from which you want to copy the Frames in the *Topic Editor*.

2. In the *Frame Structure* pane, click on the Frame that you want to copy.

    Other options:

    *   If you want to copy multiple Frames, then click on the first Frame in the sequence, then *SHIFT*+click on the last Frame in the sequence. The selected Frames will be highlighted, as shown below:

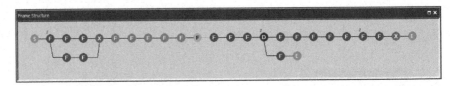

◼ This feature (of being able to copy an entire path) is extremely useful in cases where you have a simulation that includes multiple paths, but now want to split it out into separate Topics for each path.

    *   If you want to copy an entire path, then click on the first Frame that you want to copy, and then *CTRL*+click on any other Frame in the path. Be careful when using this option, as UPK will select *all* of the Frames that will be seen by users who follow this path even those frames in the main path. In the following example, we (i) clicked on the first Frame in the Alternative Path, and then (ii) *CTRL*+clicked on the second Frame in the Alternative Path. The result is that all of the Frames in the Alternative Path are selected, along with all of the Frames in the main path after the point where the Alternative Path rejoins the main path (as shown in the example below). If there are subsequent Alternative Paths, then the main path is selected. (If you want to force the use of a specific path, then simply make this the default path before you cut-and-paste.)

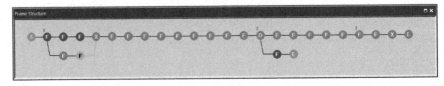

    *   You cannot copy non-contiguous Frames (that is, you can only copy a sequence of Frames). If you need to copy multiple individual Frames, then you need to perform multiple copy-and-paste actions, or copy and paste a sequence that includes all of the required

Frames and then delete the unwanted Frames from the pasted sequence.

3. To *copy* the Frames to a new location, either click on the **Copy Frames** button (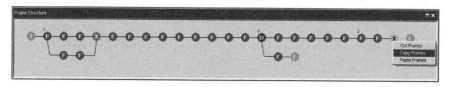), or select menu option **Edit | Copy Frames**, or right-click on any of the selected Frames, and select **Copy Frames** from the shortcut menu.

   To *move* the Frames to a new location, either select menu option **Edit | Cut Frames**, or right-click on any of the selected Frames, and select **Cut Frames** from the shortcut menu. (Note that there is no dedicated button for cutting Frames.)

4. If you want to paste the copied Frames into a different Topic, then open the destination Topic in the *Topic Editor.*

5. Right-click on the Frame immediately before where you want the copied Frames to be inserted, and select **Paste Frames** from the context menu.

   You can also click on the Frame immediately before the point at which the copied (or cut) Frames should be inserted into the Topic, and then either click on the **Paste Frames** button (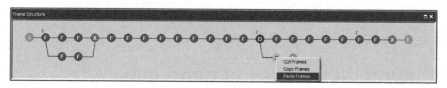), or select menu option **Edit | Paste Frames**).

■ Conceptually, the Frames will be inserted onto the green line connecting the selected Frame and the next one.

Our Topic now includes an additional copy of our Explanation Frame, as shown in the following screenshot:

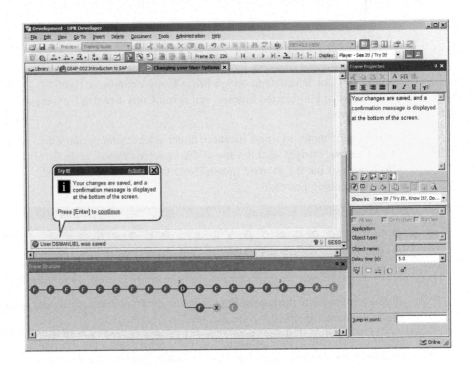

Note that the *entire* Frame and all of its contents have been copied. In our example, this is only the Bubble (including the Custom Text, icon, and pointer), but if you copy a standard Action Frame, then the Action Area (including any additional Action Areas that have been defined) and associated Action (including Alternative Actions, but not alternative paths) and any defined Print Area will also be copied.

Putting Web Pages to good use

✦ UPK 12 significantly improved Web Page formatting capabilities, by bringing them much closer to true HTML format, and introducing Style Sheets.

A **Web Page**, in UPK terms, is a single file that can contain text and images. They are not true web pages (in the sense of Internet web pages), but they do allow a reasonable level of formatting. Web Pages can be utilized within UPK in a number of ways, as described in the following sections.

Using a Web Pages as the Concept Page

✦ Prior to UPK 2.x (OnDemand 9.1) you could attach multiple *Infoblocks* to an Outline Element and they would be displayed sequentially in the *Concept pane*. In UPK 3.x and later, you can only attach a single Web Page to an Outline Element.

The most common use of Web Pages is to provide *conceptual* information for Topics via the *Concept* pane. Look at the following image of the Outline for our example course:

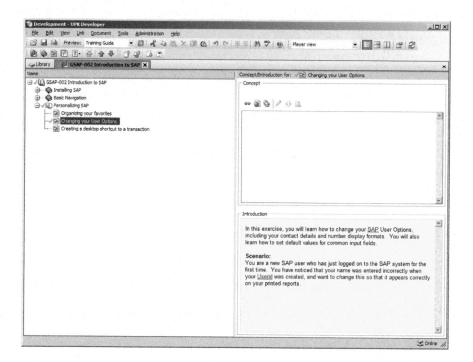

You will see that the upper-right section of the Outline window contains a pane labeled *Concept*. If you want any information to be displayed in this pane, then you need to create a Web Page (or file within a Package, as we will see later) and attach it to the content object.

To create a new Web Page and attach it to a content object, carry out the following steps:

1. Open the Outline containing the content object to which you want to attach the Web Page, in the *Outline Editor*.

2. Click on the content object to select it. Although in this example we are attaching a Web Page to the concept pane for a Topic, Modules and Sections also have *Concept* panes, so you can also attach Web Pages to these.

3. Check out the content object (if you are working in a client/server environment and it is not already checked out).

4. Click on the **Create new web page** button (🖼) in the *Concept* pane. The *Save As* dialog box is displayed.

■ If you leave the *Concept* pane empty, then the **Introduction** pane will be displayed across both the *Concept* and *Introduction* areas. This scenario is discussed in *The Start Frame versus the Introduction pane* on page 344.

■ You can also maintain the Concept Page assignment by displaying the *Concept* pane (by selecting menu option **View | Panes | Concept** from within the *Library* screen or in the *Topic Editor*.

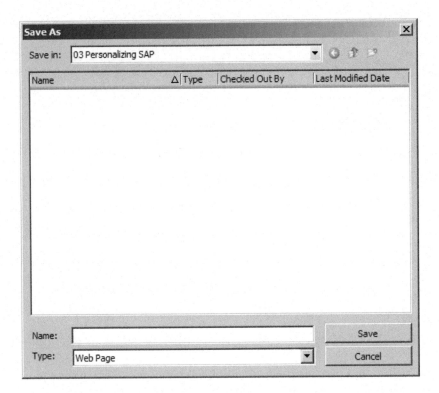

5. The **Save in** field defaults to the folder in which the object to which you want to attach the Web Page exists. If necessary, you can navigate to and select another folder (although as explained in *Chapter 3, Working in the UPK Developer Client*, it may be wise to store all Web Pages related to a Topic in the same folder as the Topic itself).

6. Enter a name for the Web Page in the **Name** field (again, as explained in *Chapter 3, Working in the UPK Developer Client* it makes sense to use the same name as the object to which it relates, appended with an indicator as to its use—in this case "_Concept")

7. Click on **Save** . The *Web Page Editor* is opened as a new tab within the *UPK Developer* screen, as shown in the next screenshot:

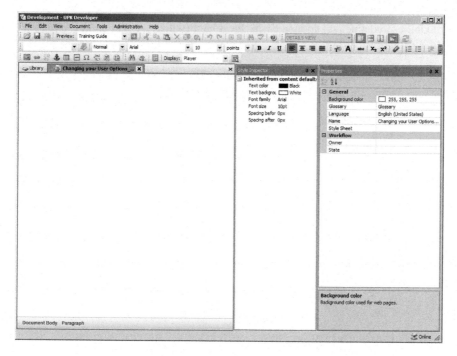

8. You can now enter the information that you want to appear in the *Concept* pane in the editor. How to do this is explained in *Using the Web Page Editor*, below.

9. Once you have entered the required text and formatted it as required, click on the **Save** button ( ) to save your changes, and then close the *Web Page Editor*. You are returned to the *Outline Editor*.

10. Close the *Outline Editor*. Note that you do not need to save your changes first - changes to Outline Elements take effect immediately.

Using the Web Page Editor

The *Web Page Editor* introduces four new toolbars: the *Appearance Toolbar*, the *Insert Toolbar*, the *Font and Formatting Toolbar*, and the *Tools Toolbar*. These are explained fully later in this chapter; we will also look at some of the features that they provide, as we enter content into the Web Page for our sample exercise.

Formatting your text

Before entering any text into your Web Page, it is worth considering how it will be formatted. You effectively have two options: apply direct formatting to your text, or use a Style Sheet to control the formatting. Of the two, using a Style Sheet is undoubtedly the best option for consistency (because you can apply the same Style Sheet to all of your Web Pages) but it does have the disadvantage that you need to set up the Style Sheet in the first place. For our sample exercise, we will build our Web Page to use UPK's built in styles. This will give us the

✛ The *Web Page Editor* underwent a significant upgrade in UPK 12, with the addition of named styles and the introduction of Style Sheets, plus the ability to include tables and other design elements.

flexibility to define and apply a Style Sheet later (which we will do in *Chapter 16, Customizing UPK*).

Style Sheets support style definitions for the following element types (which authors familiar with HTML will immediately recognize):

- Document Body
- Heading 1...Heading 6
- Paragraph
- Text
- Table
- Bulleted List
- Numbered List
- Image
- Link
- Horizontal Line
- Preformatted
- Address
- Block Quote

Some of these element types (such as numbered or bulleted lists) will automatically be applied to text when you apply certain formatting to the Web Page element. Others (such as Heading 1 to Heading 6) must be explicitly selected from the **Styles** field. This can be confusing, so it is probably best that we illustrate this by going through the various toolbars that are available in the *Web Page Editor* and explaining their purpose.

- There seems to be little logic to the grouping of features on the various toolbars. Commands applicable to element types influenced by a Style Sheet are split across three of the four *Web Page Editor* toolbars, commands for direct formatting appear on two separate toolbars, and so on.

The Font and Formatting Toolbar

The *Font and Formating Toolbar* is used to change character-level formatting, and apply built-in (Style Sheet supported) styles to text elements. This toolbar appears as follows in the Web Page Editor (note that in this screenshot the toolbar has been undocked and shown over three lines, for clarity):

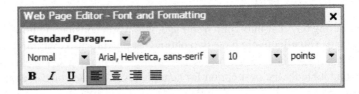

The following table explains the fields and buttons available on this toolbar, from left to right.

Button	Name	Use
(drop-down list)	Styles	If a Style Sheet has been assigned to the Web Page and it contains multiple style definitions for the element type of the currently-selected text element (such as Heading 1) then you can use this field's drop-down list to select the specific style variant to use. If a Style Sheet has not been applied to the Web Page, or there is only one definition for the current element type then this field's drop-down list will be empty. How to create a Style Sheet is explained in *Creating a Style Sheet* on page 571.
(icon)	Clear Style	If a style variant has been applied to the selected text (and this is not the default variant for the element type, then clicking on this button will re-apply the default style variant. You cannot remove the default style variant from the text.
(drop-down list)	Format	Use this field's drop-down list to select an element type to apply to the currently-selected text. The following element types are available via this field: **Normal**, **Heading1**...**Heading 6**, **Preformatted**, and **Address**. Other element types in the list given on page *page 360* are automatically applied when you format the text appropriately (for example, text is automatically assigned the **Bulleted List** element type when you format the text as a bulleted list (see below).
(drop-down list)	Font selection	Select the font family to apply to the text. All fonts installed on your PC are available.
(drop-down list)	Font Size	Select the font size for the text.
(drop-down list)	Font Unit	Select the unit of measure in which the font size is specified. This can be either **Points** or **Pixels**.
B	Bold	Set the currently-selected characters in bold.
I	Italics	Set the currently-selected characters in italics.
U	Underline	Underline the currently-selected characters.
(icon)	Left Align	Align the currently-selected paragraph(s) to the left.
(icon)	Center	Center the currently-selected paragraph(s).

✦ The **Styles**, **Clear Style**, and **Format** functions are new in UPK12..

● The toolbar options from **Font Selection** onwards (to the right on the toolbar, and below this point in this table) apply *direct formatting* to your text. You should avoid using these if you want to use a Style Sheet to control your Web Page formatting.

Button	Name	Use
	Right Align	Align the currently-selected paragraph(s) to the right.
	Justify	Fully-justify the currently selected paragraph(s).

The Appearance Toolbar

The *Appearance Toolbar* is used to apply various types of character formatting and text block level formatting. This toolbar appears as follows in the *Web Page Editor*:

The following table explains the fields and buttons available on this toolbar, from left to right:

✦ Of all of the features provided by this toolbar, only the **Numbered List** and **Bulleted List** were available prior to UPK 12.

■ To set the background color of the entire document, use the **Background Color** property, in the *Properties* pane for the Web Page.

Button	Name	Use
	Text Color	Set the color of the currently-selected text, via the standard *Colors* dialog box.
	Text Background Color	Set the background color of the currently-selected text, via the standard *Colors* dialog box.
	Strikethrough	Strike through the currently-selected text.
	Subscript	Set the currently-selected text as subscripted.
	Superscript	Set the currently-selected text as superscripted.
	Clear Formatting From Text	Remove any direct formatting applied to the currently-selected text. This is incredibly useful if you have copied and pasted text from another source, and want to remove any formatting that may have been copied with it.
	Numbered List	Turn the currently-selected paragraphs into a numbered list. Note that if a Style Sheet has been assigned to the Web Page then any (default) style defined for the Numbered List element type will automatically be applied to the list.

Button	Name	Use
☰	**Bulleted List**	Turn the currently-selected paragraphs into a bulleted list. Note that if a Style Sheet has been assigned to the Web Page then any (default) style defined for the Bulleted List element type will automatically be applied to the list.
⇤	**Decrease Indent**	Decrease the left-indent currently applied to the text by 40 pixels.
⇥	**Increase Indent**	Indent the currently-selected text by 40 pixels.
❞	**Block Quote**	Format the currently-selected text as a block quote. This will be indented from the left by 40 pixels and from the right by 40 pixels. Note that if a Style Sheet has been assigned to the Web Page then any (default) style defined for the **Block Quote** element type will automatically be applied to the list.
▲▼	**Spacing**	Clicking on this button will display the *Spacing* dialog box (shown below), which you can use to apply spacing before or after the currently-selected text.

Spacing		✕
Before:	6	points ▼
After:	6	points ▼
		OK Cancel

The Insert Toolbar

The *Insert Toolbar* is used to insert different types of objects into the Web Page. This toolbar appears as follows in the *Web Page Editor*:

The following table explains the fields and buttons available on this toolbar, from left to right:

Button	Name	Use
	Image	Insert an image. This is explained further in *Using images in Web Pages* on page 373.
	Hyperlink	Insert a hyperlink to an anchor within the current Web Page, to another object within the Library, or an external URL. You can also create an email link. Hyperlinks are explained further in *Linking via a hyperlink* on page 380.
	Unlink	Remove a hyperlink that was previously added.
	Anchor	Insert an anchor that serves as the destination of a hyperlink. This is a non-visible element.
	Table	Insert a table. This functionality is explained further in *Using tables in Web Pages* on page 365.
	Horizontal Line	Insert a horizontal line in the Web Page. Note that if a Style Sheet has been assigned to the Web Page then any (default) style defined for the Horizontal Line element type will automatically be applied to the list.
	Special Character	Insert characters with diacritics, or other special character.
	Page Break	Insert a page break into the text. This will cause the paragraph immediately following it to start on a new page in printed output, but will not affect on-line display of the Web Page.
	Paste as Text	Paste the content of the clipboard as pure text (that is, without any formatting). This is extremely useful if you are pasting text from a feature-rich editor, and do not want to retain the original formatting (especially for Word, which has a nasty habit of pasting hidden formatting that is almost impossible to remove).
	Paste from Word	If you have copied text from a Microsoft Word document then you can use this option to paste the text and retain the original formatting (or as close to it as can be achieved in a UPK Web Page).

● You cannot use the Special Character option to insert wingdings or characters from other font families.

■ I would advise against inserting a page break into a Web Page that is hyperlinked to from within a Topic, or used as a Glossary Definition, as this can disrupt formatting of document publishing formats in which Web Pages are set to appear.

The Tools Toolbar

The **Tools** *Toolbar* contains commands that are not directly related to the formatting of content in the Web Page. This toolbar appears as follows in the Web Page Editor:

The following table explains the fields and buttons available on this Toolbar:

Button	Name	Use
	Find	Search for a specific text string within the Web Page. This uses the same *Find* dialog box used elsewhere within UPK.
	Replace	Search for a specific text string within the Web Page, and replace it with another text string. This uses the same *Replace* dialog box used elsewhere within UPK.
	Show Blocks	Display the formating 'blocks' that make up the Web page. This is useful for seeing what element types have been applied to which sections of the Web Page (although here, UPK uses the HTML codes for the element types, and not the actual element type names used elsewhere within UPK). An example of this view is shown *Displaying the HTML blocks* on page 369
	Display	Choose whether to show the Web Page as it will appear in the Player or as it will appear in printed output. Note that this is only really relevant if you have assigned a Style Sheet that contains print-specific styles.
	Open In Browser	Preview the Web Page as it will appear in the browser. This is useful for checking how a Web Page will look, before attaching it to a Topic and publishing it.

● The *Find* dialog box and the *Replace* dialog box are actually two separate tabs within the same *Find and Replace* dialog box. Which tab is initially displayed depends on which button you click on the toolbar.

Using tables in Web Pages

The ability to insert tables into Web Pages is a long-requested feature that finally made its appearance with UPK 12. It is therefore worth looking at this functionality in a little more detail.

To insert a table into a Web Page, follow the steps described below:

1. Position the cursor in the Web Page at the position at which you want to insert the table.

2. Click on the **Insert New Table** button (▦) on the *Insert Toolbar*. The *Table Properties* dialog box is displayed, as shown below:

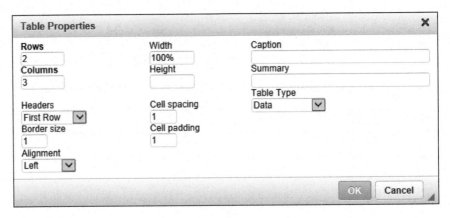

3. Specify the table properties, as follows:

   i. Specify the number of **Rows** and **Columns** in the table. Don't worry if you change your mind later—you can add or remove rows and columns via right-click functionality.

   ii. If necessary, specify the **Width** and **Height** for the table. You can specify this as a percentage (of the Web Page width), as an absolute number of pixels (**px**), or an absolute number of points (**pt**). It is fairly common to specify a width, but not a height.

   iii. If required, you can enter a title for the table in the **Caption** field. This will (by default) appear above the table. You can also enter a short description of the table in the **Summary** field. This is for information only and will not appear anywhere in your output.

   iv. Choose whether the **First Row**, **First Column, Both** (both the first row and the first column), or **None** (no row or column) should be considered to be the table **Headers**. Table header cells are often formatted differently to the table content itself (typically via bold text and/or a background color), and may be repeated in printed output if the table is split across pages.

   v. Specify the width (in pixels) of the table borders in the **Border size** field.

   vi. Use the **Cell Spacing** to indicate how much space (in pixels) should be left between the cells of the table, and use the **Cell Padding** to specify how much space (in pixels) should be left on the inside of the cell, between the cell edge and the cell content.

   vii. In the **Table Type** field, choose whether this table will be used to contain **Data**, or will be used simply for laying out content on the screen (**Layout**). This is important for Section 504 compliance: screen readers will not announce Data tables, but will announce Layout tables.

▲ The **Cell Spacing** and **Cell Padding** options did not seem to work correctly in UPK 12.1, but this has been fixed in ESP 1.

● Technically, a **Table Type** of **Layout** results in the role="presentation" tag being added to the HTML table definition. This tag is new to HTML5.

viii. Use the **Alignment** field to specify whether the entire table (not the contents of the cells) should be left-aligned, right-aligned, or centered on the Web Page.

4. Click on the **OK** button.

If you need to change any of the above details once you have inserted the table, you can right-click anywhere in the table and select **Table Properties** to re-display the *Table Properties* dialog box.

To change the formatting of an individual cell in the table, carry out the following steps:

1. Right-click on the cell and select **Cell | Cell Properties** from the shortcut menu. The *Cell Properties* dialog box is displayed. An example of this dialog box is shown below:

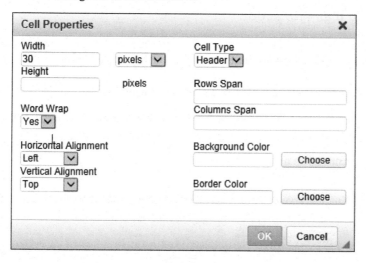

2. Specify the cell properties, as follows:

    i.   If necessary, enter the width of the cell in the **Width** field, enter the height in the **Height** field, and the select the unit of measure (**pixels** or **points**) from the unit drop-down.

    ii. If the cell content should wrap within the cell then select **Yes** under **Word Wrap**. Otherwise select **No**.

    iii. Select the required **Horizontal Alignment** and **Vertical Alignment**.

    iv. If the cell is a header cell (which is normally set in bold by the Style Sheet or browser) then select **Header** in the **Cell Type** field. Otherwise, leave this field as the default value of **Data**.

    v.   If the cell should span multiple rows then enter the number of rows it should span in the **Rows Span** field.

    vi. If the cell should span multiple columns then enter then number of columns it should span in the **Columns Span** field.

vii. If necessary, select the **Background Color** for this cell, via the field's **Choose** button (which will display the standard color chooser).

viii. If necessary, select the **Border Color** for this cell, via the field's **Choose** button (which will display the standard color chooser). Note that the border thickness is set at the table level.

3. Click on the **OK** button to close the *Cell Properties* dialog box and return to the *Web Page Editor*.

To insert or delete rows or columns, right-click at the relevant position in the table, and select the required option from the shortcut menu (these are all logically named, so there is no need to list them all here). You can also delete the entire table via the right-click shortcut menu.

Putting it all into action

Now that you know exactly what can be achieved in a Web Page, let's look at a simple example that puts some of this functionality into practice.

For our sample exercise, I made the following changes to our sample Web Page:

1. Entered a text of "Purpose" and chose the **Heading 1** format from the **Format** field on the *Fonts and Formatting Toolbar*.

2. Entered an introductory paragraph, which I left as using the default format of **Normal**.

3. Entered seven **Normal** paragraphs and then selected them all and clicked the **Bulleted List** button (▤) on the *Appearance Toolbar* to turn into a first-level bulleted list.

4. Selected the 2nd to 4th bulleted list items created in Step 3 and clicked the **Increase Indent** button (▤) on the *Appearance Toolbar*. This turned them into a second-level bulleted list.

5. Entered a text of "Timing" and formatted this as Heading 1, then inserted a Normal paragraph below it.

6. Inserted a text of "Version History" and formatted this as Heading 1.

7. Inserted a table by clicking on the **Insert New Table** button (▦) on the *Insert Toolbar*, and then specified the following information for this:

    - **Rows**: 3
    - **Columns**: 3
    - **Headers**: First Row
    - **Border size**: 1
    - **Width**: 100%

8. Adjusted the width of the first column in the table as follows:

    i.   Right-clicked in the header cell for the first column

    ii.   Selected **Cell | Cell Properties** from the shortcut menu

    iii.   In the *Cell Properties* dialog box, set the width of the first column to **30 pixels**. (I left the other columns with their default values.)

9.   Gave the header row a gray background, as follows:

    i.   Right-clicked on a cell in the header row

    ii.   Selected **Cell | Properties** from the shortcut menu

    iii.   Used the **Choose** button to the right of the **Background Color** field to select a gray background color

    iv.   Repeated steps i to iii for the remaining columns

10. Entered information into the header and data rows in the table.

After making all of these changes, the Web Page Editor appears as shown in the following screenshot:

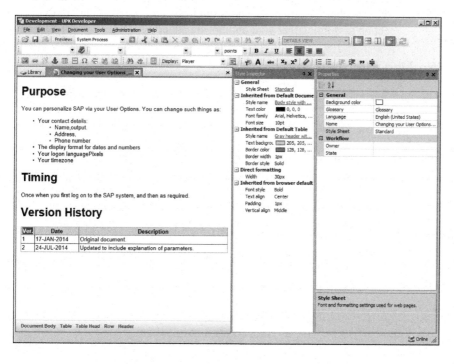

■ Consider using a different background color for Web Pages used for different purposes - for example, 'bubble-yellow' for Topics, light blue for Modules and Sections, light green for Assessments, and so on. This will provide your users with visual cues as to what they are looking at and what they can do with it.

There are a few interesting things to note in the *Web Page Editor*. The first is the *Style Inspector* pane, which is shown to the left of the *Properties* pane in the screenshot above. This shows the formatting styles that are applied to the currently-selected element for the element within which the cursor is currently located. These styles are grouped into the following categories:

■ You can dock the Style Inspector pane as a tabbed page within one of the other panes, as described in *Chapter 3, Working in the UPK Developer Client.*

- **General**
  This specifies the Style Sheet assigned to the Web Page. Initially, this

will be the **Standard** Style Sheet - we will assign a custom Style Sheet in *Chapter 16, Configuring UPK*.

- **Inherited from <category style>**
  This section lists all of the formatting applied to the selected content based on a style defined in the Style Sheet (if one has been applied).

- **Inherited from content defaults**
  This section lists all formatting applied to the selected content based on the author's content defaults (specified via **Tools | Options**).

- **Inherited from browser defaults**
  This section lists all formatting applied to the selected content based on the formatting settings in the default web browser on your PC (for example, [most versions of] Internet Explorer will format Heading 1 elements to be 24pt).

- **Direct formatting**
  This section lists all direct formatting that has been applied to the selected element within the *Web Page Editor*. If you opt to use a Style Sheet to control formatting you should expect to see nothing in this section (assuming that your authors are adhering to your standards...).

Working with the Element Path

The other interesting thing that you can see on this screen is the **Element Path** at the bottom of the Web Page. This shows the hierarchy of HTML elements for the currently-selected text. In the example above, the text in the first cell in the table header is selected. The element trail shows **Document Body - Table - Table Head - Row - Column**, which can be read as "the currently-selected text is in a Cell that is in a Row that is in the Table Head that is in a Table that is within the Document Body. This information can be useful for determining the style inheritance of the elements that the selected text or object is contained within, when troubleshooting why styles are not applied in the way that you expected.

If you hover the cursor over an element name in the Element Path, the HTML tag corresponding to this element type is shown, along with the formatting applied to the element. An example of this is shown below.

Clicking on an element in the Element Path will highlight the element in the Web Page itself, which will in turn display the formatting for this element in the *Element Inspector*.

Displaying the HTML blocks

Now that we have some content in our Web Page, let's display the element blocks by clicking on the **Show Blocks** button (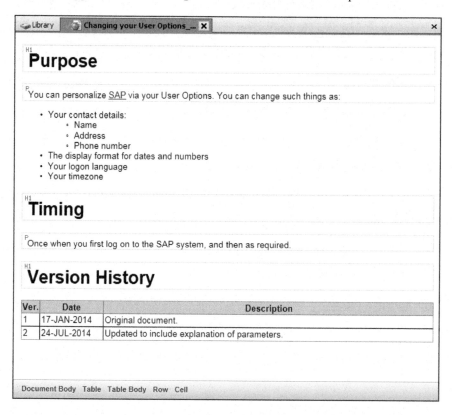) on the *Tools Toolbar*. The Web Page now appears in the *Web Page Editor* as shown in the example shown below:

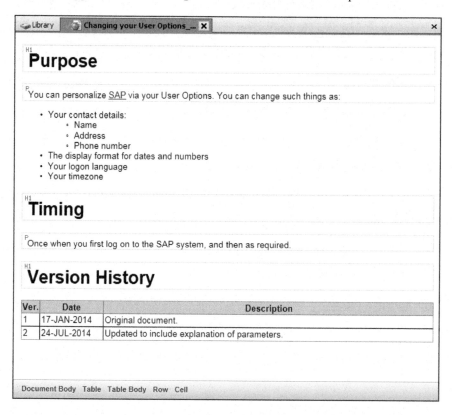

You can see that this isn't 100% perfect - lists aren't correctly shown, and nothing at all is shown for tables. However, this information can prove useful for identifying empty paragraphs (or other elements) that you can delete.

Web Page preview in the Browser

You can preview a Web Page from the *Web Page Editor*, to make sure that your formatting has been correctly applied. This is useful if you have not yet attached the Web Page to an Outline Element (because if you had, you could just preview it in the *Concept* pane within the *Outline Editor*).

To preview a Web Page as it will appear in the browser (or in print) carry out the steps described below:

1. On the *Web Page Editor - Tools Toolbar*, use the **Display** drop-down to select the mode in which you want to preview the Web Page. You can choose either **Player** or **Print**. The **Print** option is useful if you have

assigned a Style Sheet that includes print-specific formatting to the Web Page.

2. Click on the **Open in Browser** button (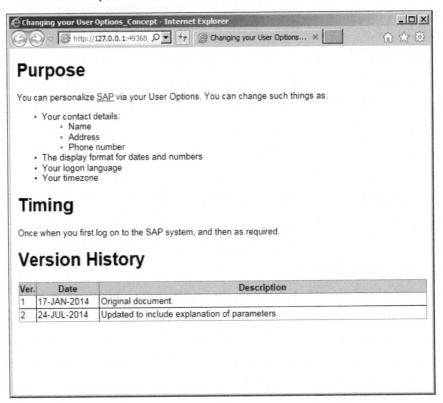). A browser window is opened, displaying the Web Page as it will appear in the selected format. An example of this is shown below:

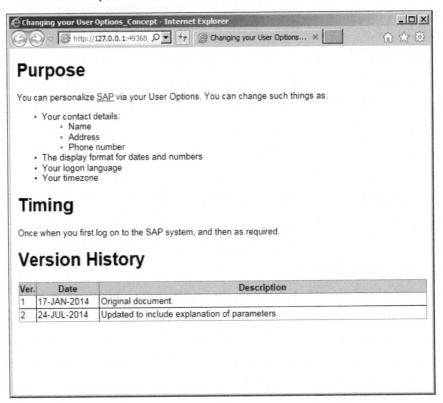

Web Page preview in the Outline Editor

Once you have created a Web Page to use as the Concept Page for a Topic, the content of this Web Page appears in the *Concept* pane of the *Outline Editor*, when ever this Topic is selected. An example of this, with our example Topic selected, and the Web Page that we just created displayed, is shown below:

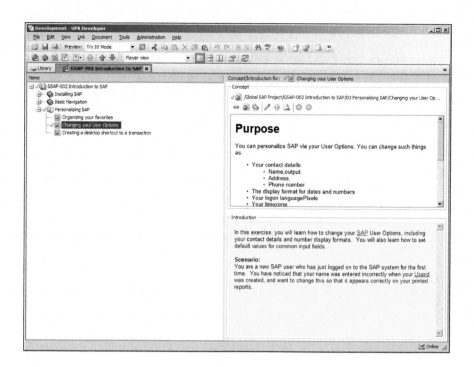

Let's take a quick look at how this is displayed in the Player. This is shown in the following screenshot:

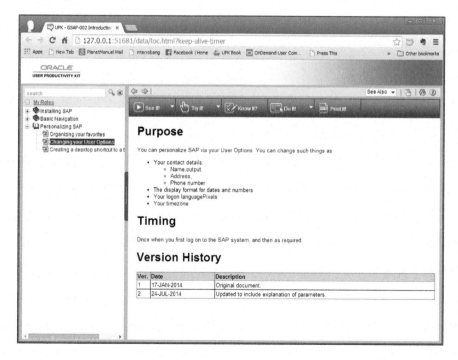

Web Page preview in a printed document

+ The ability to preview a Web Page independently of a Topic, and from the Library screen, is new in UPK 12.1.

You can preview any Web Page in any of the available printed publishing formats, directly from the *Library* screen. This useful for checking 'independent' Web Pages (that is, Web Pages that are not used as the Concept Page for a Topic) rather than previewing the entire Topic—and especially in cases where you are using a Style Sheet for the Web Page that has print-specific styles.

To preview a Web Page in a printed document, carry out the steps described below:

1. On the *Library* screen, click on the Web Page that you want to preview.

2. In the **Preview** field on the *Standard Toolbar*, select the appropriate (printed) publishing format from the drop-down list, and then click on the **Go** button ( ).

An example of a Web Page, as it appears when previewed in the Instructor Manual, is shown below:

Preview Topic

Some common international name forms are as follows:

- **Western**: <First Name> <Middle Name> <Last name>
  Example: **Dirk Stewart Manuel** - use **Dirk** as *First name* and **Manuel** as *Last name*
- **Chinese**: <Family Name> <Generational Name> <Given Name>
  Example: **Mao Tze Tung** - use **Tung** as *First name* and **Mao** as *Last name*
- **Spanish (married women)**: <Given Name(s)> <Paternal Family Name> de <Husband's Paternal Family Name>
  Example: **Manuela Cardim** de Foy- use **Manuela** as *First name* and **Cardim** as *Last name*

Procedure

Step	Action
1	
	End of Procedure.

Attaching a Web Page via the Topic Editor

In the last section, we saw how to attach a Web Page to the *Concept* pane for an exercise from within an Outline. Although this is done from the *Outline Editor*, the Web Page is attached to the Topic (or other element in the Outline) and not to the Outline itself. If you subsequently insert the same Topic in another Outline, the same Web Page will be used in the *Concept* pane of the new Outline.

You can also attach a Web Page to the *Concept* pane for an exercise from within the *Topic Editor*. This is a useful option if you want to create the concept Web Page but have not yet built an Outline to house the Topic (and therefore cannot create or attach the Concept Page via the *Outline Editor*). To do this, follow the steps described below:

1. Open the Topic in the *Topic Editor*.

2. Select menu option **View | Concept**. The *Concept Properties* dialog box is displayed. This is very similar to the *Concept* pane seen in the *Outline Editor*; it contains the same buttons.

3. Create and save the Web Page as described above.

4. When you have finished and closed the *Web Page Editor*, you will be returned to the *Topic Editor*.

Using images in Web Pages

As we saw when we looked at the toolbars available within the *Web Page Editor*, a Web Page can contain an image. This can be instead of, or in addition to, any text (although if you only wanted to include a single image (and no text) in the Web Page you could always use a **Package**, as explained later in this chapter).

Images are a nice way of adding interest to a Web Page (and therefore to your training), or of providing additional information that is better explained graphically (after all, a picture is worth a thousand words). However, if you are using images in the *Concept* pane, then you should consider the overall size of the image and the likely width of the *Concept* pane, bearing in mind that the user may run the Player in a smaller window than the one you design.

For our sample exercise, given that we are providing simulations for the SAP system, we will include a small logo in the Web Page that appears in the *Concept* pane for our course Module. For the sake of variety, we will do this from the Library, and not from the *Outline Editor*.

To add an image to a Web Page, carry out the steps described below.

1. On the *Library* screen, locate the folder containing the Web Page to which you want to add the image.

2. Double-click on the Web Page, to open it in the *Web Page Editor*. As before, this is opened in a separate tab in the main *UPK Developer* window, as can be seen in the next screenshot:

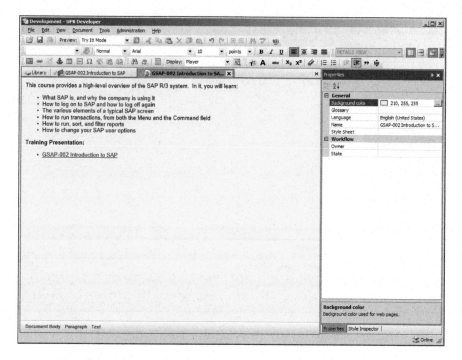

3. Within the Web Page, position the cursor at the position in the text where you want the image to appear.

4. Click on the **Image** button (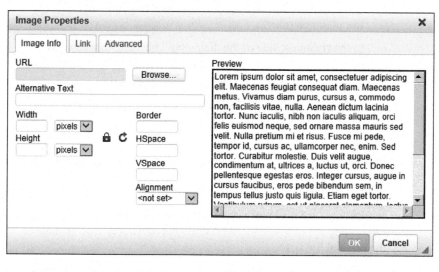) on the *Insert Toolbar* (or select menu option **Insert | Image**). The *Insert Image* dialog box is displayed, as shown in the next screenshot:

✦ The dialog boxes for images have undergone a significant change in UPK 12.1. In previous versions, inserting an image first displays the *Insert image* dialog box, in which you can only select the image file, and then you need to right-click on the inserted image to display the *Image Properties* dialog box in which you can change the image properties.

5. On the **Image Info** tab, click on the **Browse** button. The *Insert Image* dialog box is displayed, as shown below:

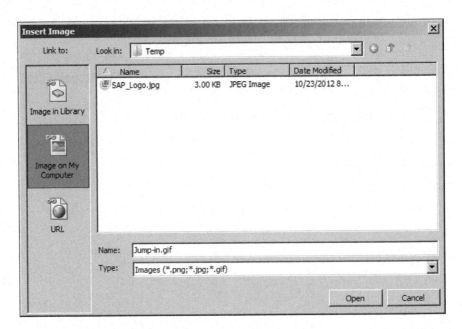

6. Select the image to insert into your Web Page as follows:

i. In the **Link to** bar on the leftmost side of the dialog box, select the location of the image file that you want to insert into the Web Page. You can insert an image that you have already imported into your Library (typically within a Package) (option **Image in Library**), an image that is located on your computer (or any attached drive) (option **Image on My Computer**), or an image from the Internet (option **URL**). For our sample exercise, we will insert an image from our computer.

ii. In the rightmost side of the dialog box, navigate to and select the image file that you want to insert into the Web Page.

iii. Click on **Open** to confirm your selection and return to the *Image Properties* dialog box. Note that the location of the image is now shown in the **URL** field, and the image is included in the **Preview** box, using its current sizing and positioning attributes.

7. In the **Alternative Text** field, enter a short text description of the image. This may be displayed in place of the image if the image itself cannot be displayed by the browser.

8. If necessary, use the **Width** and **Height** fields to resize the image. You can specify the new size in pixels or points (but not as a percentage of the original file size).

By default, the image will be resized proportionally (so if you change the width the height will automatically be adjusted accordingly, (and vice versa). If you want to resize each dimension independently, then click on the **Lock Ratio** icon (🔒) to disable this.

■ If you will use an image in more than one place (or are likely to update it) it will be more efficient to load the image into a Package within your library, and then link to it there. Packages are explained later in this chapter.

If you subsequently realize that you do not want to resize the image, clock on the **Reset Size** icon ($\boxed{C}$) to revert to the image's original size.

9. If you want to place a border around this image, then enter the width of this border in the **Border** field.

10. If you want to leave some space around your image (which is useful if you will run text around the image, then enter the amount of space (in pixels) to leave to the left and to the right of the image in the **HSpace** field, and enter the amount of space to leave above and below the image in the **VSpace** field.

▲ If you enter a value for **HSpace** or **VSpace** and then change your mind and want to remove it, you need to enter a value of **0**; simply deleting your initial input will not remove your original amount.

11. In the Alignment drop-down, select where the image should be aligned on the Web Page. Your choices are: **Left**, and **Right**.

12. If you want the image to act as a hyperlink, then click on the **Link** tab, and then enter the details of the target of this hyperlink as follows:

   i. Click on the **Browse** button. The *Insert Hyperlink* dialog box is displayed.

   ii. Either select **Document in Library** and navigate to and select the content object within the Library to which you want to link, or select **URL** and enter the URL of the destination in the **Address** field.

   iii. In the **Target** field, select the browser window into which the destination of the URL should be loaded. The choices are:

   ● The options available in the Target field are all standard HTML options available when inserting a hyperlink anywhere in UPK. However, it would not make sense to use **Same Window** or **Parent Window** from a Concept Page. Most of the time you would use **New Window** in this situation.

   - **New Window (_blank)**: Open a new browser window and display the content in that.

   - **Topmost Window (_top)**: Replace the entire Player with the target of the link (effectively leaving the Player).

   - **Same Window (_self)**: Replace the current content of the Concept pane (excluding the header bar containing the **Next** and **Previous** buttons, the **Help** icon, and so on) with the target of the link.

   - **Parent Window (_parent)**: Replace the HTML element that contains the Concept Pane (this is the entire rightmost pane in the Player, including the header bar) with the target of the link.

   iv. Click on **OK** to close the *Insert Hyperlink* dialog box and return to the *Image Properties* dialog box.

13. Click on the **Advanced** tab, and specify the following information if necessary:

   i. If you want to link to an external page that provides a description of the image, then enter the URL of this page into the **Long Description URL** field.

ii. If you want a specific text to be displayed as the ToolTip when the user hovers the cursor over the image, then enter this text into the **Advisory Title** field.

14. Click on **OK** button in the *Image Properties* dialog box. The image is inserted, as shown in the following screenshot:

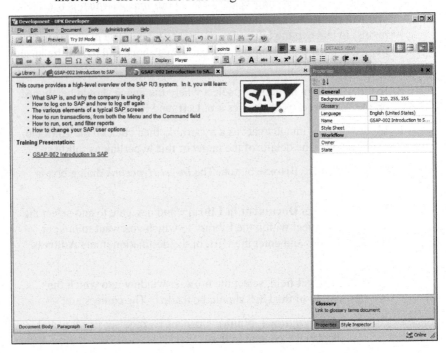

15. Save the Web Page, and close the **Web Page Editor**, if you have finished editing it.

This gives us a final Web Page as shown in the next screenshot. Note that this screenshot is taken from the Player, so that you can see how images are handled in the Player.

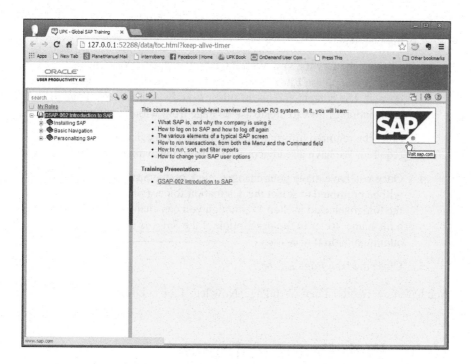

In the example above we have right-aligned the image, placed a border around it, and made it a hyperlink. The ToolTip (**Alternative Text**) for this hyperlink is set to "**Visit sap.com**". Note that the text flows *around* the image (this is not immediately apparent as the image is right-aligned and the text left-justified, but is proven by the fact that there is more than one line of text alongside the image).

Creating independent Web Pages

In the previous section, we looked at how to use a Web Page to add information to the *Concept* pane of a content object. In this section, we will look at how to use Web Pages to provide information in other areas.

Observant readers will have noticed that a Web Page is in fact an independent content object itself. When you created a Web Page to attach to a *Concept* pane, you edited this Web Page in its own tabbed editor and saved it as a separate content object within the Library. Hopefully, you also noticed that in addition to the **Create new web page** button ( ), the *Concept* pane also has a **Create link** button ( ) that can be used to attach an existing Web Page to the *Concept* pane. It should, therefore, come as no surprise to learn that Web Pages can be created independently of the *Concept* pane. In fact, the *Concept* pane is only one of several uses of Web Pages.

To create a Web Page that is independent of a *Concept* pane (or anything else), carry out the steps described below:

1. On the *Library* screen, navigate to the folder in which you want to store the Web Page.

2. Click on the **Create New Web Page** button (![icon]). (You can also select menu option **File | New | Web Page**.) The *Web Page Editor* is opened. The content and use of this is exactly as described above in the explanation of how to create a Web Page from within the *Outline Editor*.

3. Enter the required information into the Web Page, and format it as required. We have already covered most of the available options, above.

4. Once you have made your changes, click on the **Save** button (![icon]). You will be prompted to select the destination folder (which will default to the folder selected in Step 1, although you can change this) and specify a file name. Refer to the description of the *Save As* dialog box above for additional help if necessary.

5. Close the *Web Page Editor*.

You have now created a new Web Page. Now let's look at how to use it.

Using Web Pages in Topics

If you recall our long-running exercise on maintaining your SAP user profile, you will remember that we ask the user to enter their last name and their first name. These terms may be confusing in some countries—especially in countries where the 'family name' actually comes before the 'given name'—so we want to provide some extra explanation of some common name formats in different countries, and how these translate into a user's 'first name' and 'last name'. We'll provide this information in a Web Page, and then link to this Web Page at the relevant place(s) within our Topic.

First, we need to create the Web Page. How to do this is explained in the section *Creating independent Web Pages* on page 381. For our exercise, our created Web Page is as follows:

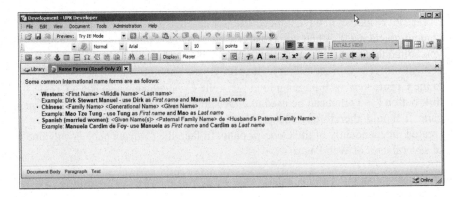

There are two ways in which you can link to a Web Page from a Topic. These are explained separately, below.

Linking via a hyperlink

With a hyperlink, the Web Page is linked from a word or phrase within the Bubble Text of a Frame. (Note that it is only possible to do this for Custom Text because you can't select the Template Text to hyperlink from.) To create a hyperlink to a Web Page from within a Frame in a Topic, carry out the steps described below:

1. Open up the Topic in the *Topic Editor*.

2. Navigate to the Frame from which you want to provide the hyperlink. In our exercise, we will link from the Explanation Frame describing the **Last name** field (this is Frame **185** in our sample exercise).

3. In the Bubble Text area of the *Frame Properties* pane, select the text that you want to form the hyperlink (that is, the text that the user will click on to display the Web Page).

4. Click on the **Bubble text link** button (🔖) in the *Frame Properties* pane. The *Bubble Text Link Properties* dialog box is displayed, as shown below:

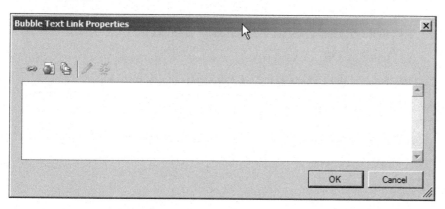

5. Click on the **Create link** button (🔗) to create a link to an existing Web Page. (You could also click on the **Create new web page** button (🔲) to create a new Web Page at this stage, if you have not yet created it, or click on the **Create new package** button (🔲) if you want to create a package and link to a file within it (as explained later in this chapter).) The *Insert Hyperlink* dialog box is displayed, as shown below:

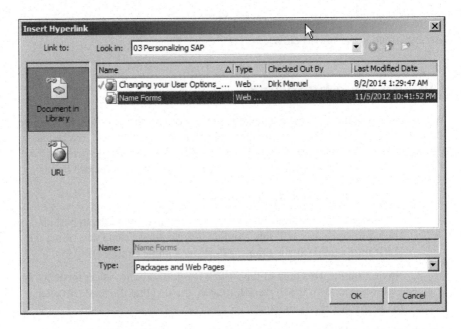

6. Make sure that the **Document in Library** option is selected in the **Link to:** bar.

7. In the **Look in:** field, navigate to the folder containing the Web Page.

8. In the file list, click on the Web Page to select it.

9. Click on **OK**.

10. Back in the *Bubble Text Link Properties* dialog box (which will now show the content of the selected Web page in the lower portion of the dialog box), click on **OK**.

This hyperlink will now appear as follows in the Player:

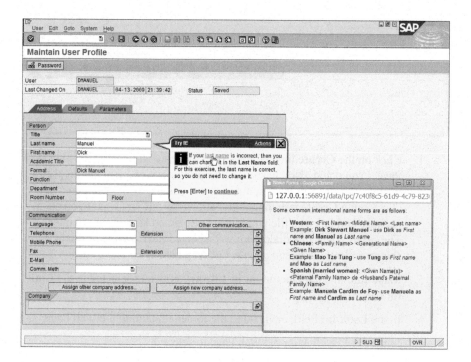

In the above screenshot, you can see the hyperlink that we inserted, within the bubble. Note that there is no ToolTip for this hyperlink—there was no opportunity to enter one in the steps above. The result of clicking on this hyperlink is that the *Name Forms* Web Page is displayed. This Web Page is also shown in the screenshot.

Linking via an icon

It is possible to link to a Web Page from an icon (a small image) that is displayed in the Bubble. The (primary) advantage of this approach is that you do not need to have custom text from which to link in the Bubble.

● Icons are not displayed in *Know It?* mode. If you want the Web Page to be available in *Know It?* mode, you must link it via a hyperlink.

To insert a link to a Web Page via an icon, carry out the steps described below:

1. Open up the Topic in the *Topic Editor*.

2. Navigate to the Frame from which you want to provide the hyperlink. In our exercise, we will link from the Action Frame in which we type our name into the **First name** field (this is Frame **3**).

3. Select menu option **View | Panes | Frame Link**. The *Frame Link Properties* pane is displayed, as shown below:

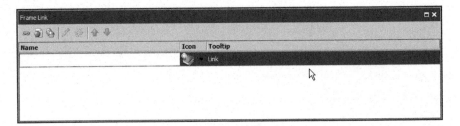

You can add multiple icon links to a single bubble; the icons will appear same order, from left to right, as they appear from top to bottom in the *Frame Link* dialog box (you can change this order via the **Up** and **Down** arrows).

4. Click on the **Create link** button () to create a link to an existing Web Page. (You could also click on the **Create new web page** button ( ) to create a new Web Page at this stage, if you have not yet created it, or click on the **Create new package** button ( ) if you want to create a package and link to a file within it (as explained later in this chapter).) The *Insert Hyperlink* dialog box is displayed (an example of this is shown under *Linking via a hyperlink* on page 383).

5. Make sure that the **Document in Library** option is selected in the **Link to:** bar.

6. In the **Look in:** field, navigate to the folder containing the Web Page.

7. In the file list, click on the Web Page to select it.

8. Click on **Open**.

9. Back in the *Frame Link* dialog box, click on the drop-down button for the **Icon** field, and select the icon that you want to use. There are several to choose from, as shown below:

You can also use your own images by adding them to the Custom Package contained in the `System/Icons/Custom` folder on the *Library* screen. Custom images must be 22 x 22 pixels in size.

10. In the **Tooltip** field, over-type the default (and unimaginative) "**Link**" with a suitable value (such as "**International name forms**", in our example). Your *Frame Link* dialog box should now look as follows:

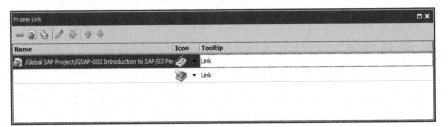

11. You can now close the *Frame Link* pane, if necessary.

This hyperlink will now appear in the Player as follows:

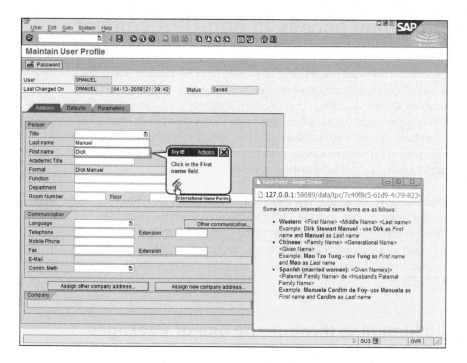

Note the ToolTip for the hyperlink. This now shows the text that was specified in the **Tooltip** field of the *Frame Link* pane.

Considerations for document Publishing Formats

When choosing whether to use a hyperlink or an icon for your link, and whether to reference this directly in the Bubble, you should consider how the Web Page will appear in the document Publishing Formats.

If you provide a link via an icon, then the full content of the Web Page will be included in the printed output, as shown in the example on *page 248*. However, if you provide the link via a hyperlink, then the hyperlink is omitted, and the content of the Web Page will simply not be included in the document.

If you use an icon, you may want to provide some textual reference to this in the Bubble itself—for example, by saying "Click on the icon below for additional information.". Here, you should bear in mind that in the document Publishing Formats, such an instruction will not make sense. Instead, you really want to say in the document is:"Additional information is provided in the box below", although then this won't make as much sense to users in the Player. Fortunately, UPK lets you use both texts, and tag one text for the Player, and one for print mode. Refer to *Tagging Custom Text for different modes* on page 153 for details of how to do this.

Providing access to non-UPK content

So far in this chapter, we have been looking at ways of enhancing our *Topics*. But what if we want our training to include learning content that is not strictly a Topic? Consider the case where you are using the UPK Player as your entire learning library, and this is the 'one-stop shop' for your users. Very few complete training packages consist of nothing more than a set of interactive exercises, regardless of how well-written or useful these are. Typically, you will have concepts to explain, processes to describe, and so on. It would be useful if we could also make this information available to our users.

Unfortunately, UPK does not allow you to add such content to the Outline. You cannot, for example, include a Microsoft PowerPoint presentation or a Microsoft Word process document as a node in the Outline. However, through careful use of Concept panes, you *can* make this information accessible to your users. In this section, we will look at a few ways of including a PowerPoint presentation in our UPK Player.

Linking files through the use of Packages

UPK allows you to import external files into your Library, so that you can then link to these files from your content objects. Technically, external files are imported into **Packages** within UPK, although the files within the Package are always referenced individually. That is, links to files are always to the individual file; you cannot create a link to a Package.

+ For authors familiar with OnDemand 8.x / UPK 2.x and earlier, Packages are the new, improved form of **File** *Infoblocks*.

Packages are conceptually similar to compressed ZIP files, in that they can contain multiple files. They can also contain only a single file. Whether you choose to store each external file in its own Package, or group all files (for example, for a course) into a single Package is your choice; it makes absolutely no difference to UPK. However, from a transparency of organization point of view, it makes sense to keep all external files that are linked to a specific content object in a single package within the same folder as that content object (and ideally with the Package using the same name as the content object, appended with "_External Files" or other suitable suffix).

External files can be used for a number of purposes, and in a number of places. Some of these options are described below:

- To provide a data sheet for a *Know It?* mode verification test. This is an interesting option if you also completely remove *Know It?* mode bubble text from the exercise. Note that here, you would need to make sure that the link to the external file is via a hyperlink in text that is tagged to appear in *Know It?* mode, otherwise the linked document will not be available.

- To provide an image of equipment related to a simulation.

- To provide a document that applies to the scenario covered by the simulation, for example, a vendor's invoice for a simulation that involves entering an invoice into the application.

- To provide the presentation for the training course to which the simulations relate.

For our example, we will use the last of these examples. We will provide access to the presentation for the course to which our sample exercise belongs. To make things interesting and to demonstrate the concept of having multiple files within a single Package, we will import a presentation that has been published to Flash format via Articulate Presenter. This published format consists of many files (at least one per slide, plus navigational elements) all of which are launched from a single file (`player.html`), which makes it an ideal candidate for using in a Package. There are three steps that we need to carry out:

1. Create a Package in UPK

2. Add the Articulate Presenter player to the Package

3. Link the Package into our content object(s)

Let's look at each of these steps in detail.

> ■ Linking to the course presentation from the exercises is back-to-front; logically, you should link to the exercises from the presentation (how to do this is discussed in *Chapter 15, Integrating UPK with Other Applications*). However, we'll do it this way round just for the sake of an example.

Creating a Package

In order to be able to link to a file from within UPK, you first need to create a Package to contain the file. To create a Package, carry out the steps described below:

1. From the *Library* screen, navigate to the folder in which you want to store the Package. For our exercise, this will be our GSAP-002 Introduction to SAP course folder.

2. Click on the **Create New Package** button ( ) on the *Library Toolbar* (or select menu option **File | New | Package**). The *Package Editor* is opened, as shown in the following screenshot:

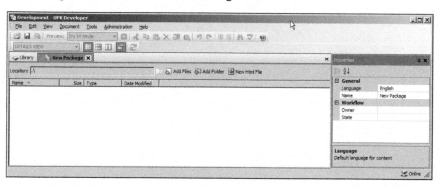

3. In the **Name** field of the *Properties* pane, over-type default name of **New Package** with an appropriate name for the Package. If you do not have

the *Properties* pane opened, then you can click the **Properties** button (🖻) now to display it, or you can just wait until the next step, where you will be prompted to specify a name when you save the Package. For our exercise, we will name the Package **GSAP-002 Introduction to SAP_Presentation**, so that it is easy to identify the (UPK) content to which it relates.

4. Click on the **Save** button (🖫) to save your changes to the Package, and then (if you are finished with the Package for now) close the *Package Editor*.

Adding files to a Package

We now have a package. The next thing to do is to add files to this Package. To do this, carry out the steps described below:

1. Make sure that the package to which you want to add the files is open in the *Package Editor* (see above).

2. You will notice that there are a few icons at the top of the *Package Editor*. These buttons, and their purpose, are explained in the table below:

Button	Name	Purpose
🔂	**Add Files**	Insert one or more individual files into the Package.
🔂	**Add Folder**	Insert an entire folder and its contents into the Package.
🔲	**New HTML File**	Create a new HTML file within the Package. (This is covered in the section *Using an HTML file as the Concept Page* on page 404).

■ You can also drag files from Windows Explorer and drop them directly into the Package. This is a useful method if you have many files and/or folders that you want to copy into the Package.

3. For this example, click on the **Add Folder** button (🔂). The *Browse For Folder* dialog box is displayed, as shown below:

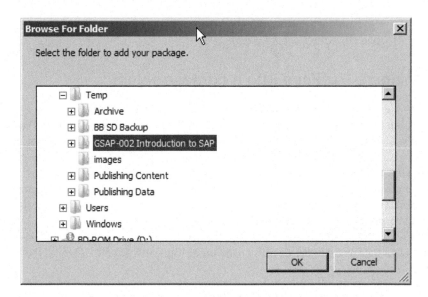

Note that if you choose to insert one or more individual files, then the standard Windows *Open* dialog box is displayed. Click on the required file to select it (or *S_HIFT_*+click or *C_TRL_*+click to select multiple files).

4. Navigate to and select the folder that you want to insert into the Package. For our example, we want to include the full Articulate Presenter version of our course, which consists of a `player.html` file and two folders containing the presentation itself. These are all contained in a single folder generated by Articulate. We will simply copy this entire folder into our Package

5. Click on **OK**. The folder is added to your Package. Our Package now looks like the following example:

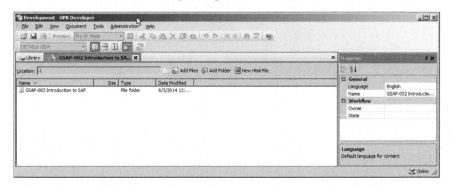

Note that the folder is imported as-is. That is, any existing folder structure and nesting of folders will be retained. This is important as it means that any relative links within these files will still work. This is extremely useful (in fact, essential) for importing entire web sites, or, as is the case in our example, a suite of interlinked files that make extensive use of relative links.

6. Click on the **Save** button (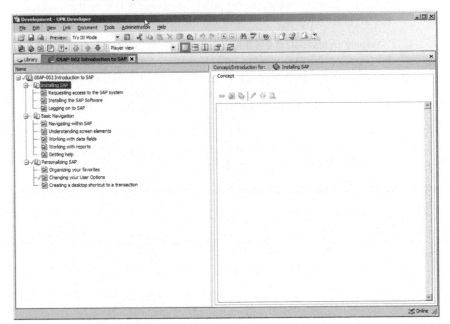) to save your changes to the package, and then close the *Package Editor*.

Linking a Package into a content object

The final step is to link the Package into a content object. You can link it via a hyperlink or an icon, just as we did for Web Pages above (see *Using a Web Pages as the Concept Page* on page 356), but there is something much more interesting that we can do. Essentially, we will link the Package itself (or, specifically, a *file* within the Package) as the Concept Page for the Outline Element. For our example course, we have put the entire presentation for our course in the Package. It would therefore make sense to link this into the *Concept* page of the highest-level course Outline Element. Let's look at how to do this.

To link a Package into the *Concept* pane for an Outline Element, carry out the following steps:

1. Open the outline element to which you want to add the Package, in the *Outline Editor*, as shown in the next screenshot:

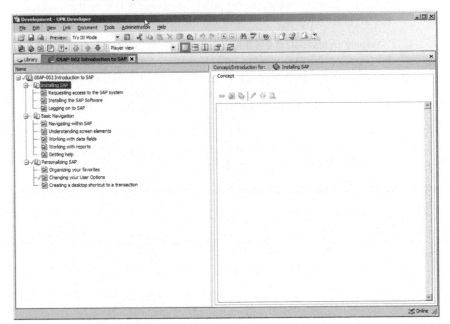

2. If you are working in a client/server environment, check out the outline element, by selecting it in the *Outline Editor* and then clicking on the **Check out** button ( ).

3. Click on the **Create link** button ( ) from the list of buttons in the *Concept* pane. The *Insert Hyperlink* dialog box is displayed, as shown below:

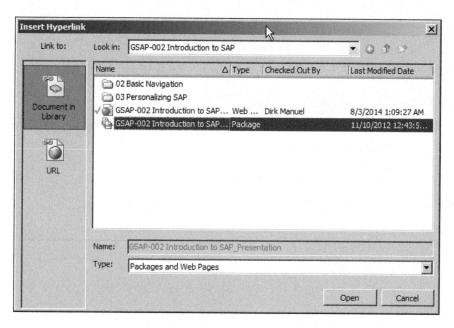

4. Make sure that the **Type** field at the bottom of the dialog box specifies either **Packages and Web Pages** or **Packages**.

5. Navigate to the Package that you created earlier. In our example, this is a Package named **GSAP 002 Introduction to SAP_Presentation**, in the same Library folder as the Module.

6. Double-click on the Package to open it (or click on it to select it and then click on **Open**). A list of all of the files and folders within the Package is displayed.

7. Select the specific file within the Package that you want to be displayed in the *Concept* pane. If your Package contains folders, you can double-click on a folder to open it and list its contents (and if you drill down too far, you can click on the **Up one folder** button ( ) or the **Go to the last folder displayed** button ( ) to go back. The screenshot below shows the contents of the main folder in our example package:

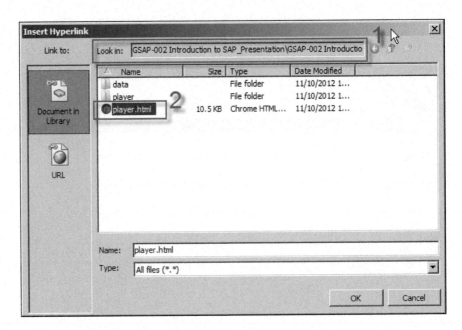

In this example, we have (1) navigated into the GSAP-002 Introduction to SAP folder within the GSAP-002 Introduction to SAP_Presentation Package, and (2) selected the file player.html. This is the launch file for our Articulate presentation.

8. Click on **OK**.

9. Back in the *Package Editor*, click on the **Save** button (🖫) to save your changes to the Outline Element, and then exit from the *Package Editor* tabbed page.

We have now successfully linked a file within a Package to an Outline Element. In case you missed that, we have linked *a file within a package* to a content object. You cannot link to a package as a whole, only to a specific, single file within a package. Now let's look at what this gives us in the Player:

■ If you absolutely need to link to an entire package then you can always bundle the Package as a ZIP file, add that ZIP file to a package, and then link to the ZIP file within the Package.

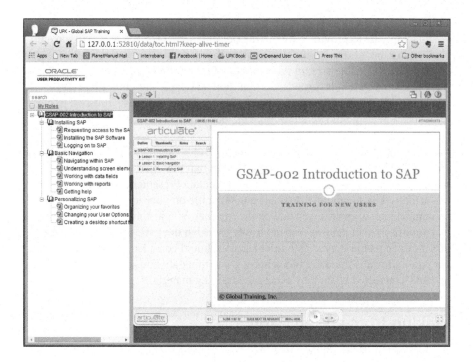

You can see that the complete Articulate Presentation has been incorporated into the UPK Player. This is fully-functional; you can use the navigation bar on the left (of the Articulate window) to locate and select slides; you can execute any Quizmaker learning activities included in the presentation, and so on. The only problem is that some of the text is a little small.

Although we have done so here, I would generally not advocate using a presentation (or similar external content) as the Concept Page of an Outline Element. Exercises are *components* of presentations, so presentations should link to exercises, and not the other way round. However, the above example does at least demonstrate the *possibilities* that UPK offers for improving the user's learning experience through the creative use of Packages.

Linking to a URL

In the previous section of this chapter, we looked at how to link to (a file included in a) Package, from the *Concept* pane of an outline element. We used an example in which we linked to a PowerPoint presentation that had been converted to Adobe Flash format via Articulate Presenter, and saw how this presentation would be launched within the *Concept* pane itself.

Although this initially seems like quite a cool thing to do, in fact the presentation is too small for effective use. In addition, we have the problem that if the presentation changes, we need to delete the old version from our Package, and then copy in the new version.

■ If you insert an Articulate Presentation (or similar package) into your Outline and this is set to auto-play, then it will start playing as soon as the user opens the Outline Element to which it is attached. In the example above, this is the first element in the hierarchy, so the package will start playing as soon as the user opens the Player. This may catch them unawares, and they may miss the start of the presentation. In this case, remove the auto-advance from the first slide in the presentation, and add a button called "Play" (or something equally obvious) that has an action of "Next Slide". The presentation will only start playing when the user clicks on the "Play" button.

If the presentation already exists outside of our UPK Library, then a better option would simply be to provide a link to the presentation. True, the user will have to click on the link to display the presentation, but at least the presentation will be displayed at a sensible size, in its own window. And if the presentation changes (on whatever server it is hosted), our link will automatically point to the latest version (assuming that the new version of the presentation was published to the same location as the old version). So let's look at how to do that.

In order to provide a link to an object that is located outside of the UPK server, you need to know the URL of the object. Although in this example we will be linking to the `player.html` file for an Articulate Presenter presentation, you can actually link to anything that has a URL: a file on your local LAN share, an intranet site, or even a web site on the Internet. You just need to make sure that your users will have access to the site to which the URL points at the time that they access the Player. In particular, you should consider interference from corporate firewalls that may block access, and think about users who may not be network-connected when they access the training material.

Linking from a Web Page

To create a link from within a Web Page to an external object via its URL, carry out the following steps:

1. Open the Web Page from which you want to provide the link in the *Web Page Editor*. This can be a Web Page used as the Concept Page for a Topic, or a Web Page attached (possibly via a hyperlink itself) to anything else. For our sample exercise, we will replace the Articulate presentation with a Web Page, and then link to the presentation from that Web Page.

2. Select the text that you want to form the link (that is, that the user will click on in order to display the linked object).

3. Either click on the **Hyperlink** button (🔗) on the *Web Page Editor - Insert Toolbar*, or right-click on the selected text and select **Edit Link** from the shortcut menu.

4. In the **Link Type** drop-down field, select **URL**. The dialog box is updated to show a **URL** field and a **Tooltip** field, as shown in the following screenshot:

5. Click on the **Browse** button. The *Insert Hyperlink* dialog box is displayed. Complete this dialog box as follows

   i.   Either select **Document in Library** and navigate to and select the content object within the Library to which you want to link, or select **URL** and enter the URL of the destination in the **Address** field.

   ii. Click on **OK** to close the *Insert Hyperlink* dialog box.

6. In the **Tooltip** field, enter any text that you want to be displayed as a Tooltip when the user hovers the cursor over the hyperlink.

7. Click on the **Target** tab. The Insert Hyperlink dialog box now appears as follows:

■ Although it is fairly common to enter the name of the object being linked to as the Tooltip, you may want to consider mentioning the type of object and its size, and/or how this will be displayed (for example, "PDF, 25kb, Opens in new window".

8. Select the browser window into which the destination of the URL should be loaded, in the **Target** field. The choices are:

   ● **<Not set>**: The browser will determine where to display the content.

   ● **<frame>**: The content will be loaded into the HTML frame that you specify in the **Target Frame Name** field. This is only really useful if your Player is being displayed within a Frameset that includes other frames into which content can be loaded.

- **<popup window>** The content will be loaded into a new, stand-alone dialog box. This is similar to the standard HTML _blank option (see below), but greater control is available as to what elements are included in this dialog box. These options are explained in *Using a popup window* on page 398.

- **New Window (_blank):** Open a new browser window and display the content in that.

- **Topmost Window (_top):** Replace the entire Player with the target of the link (effectively leaving the Player).

- **Same Window (_self):** Replace the current content of the Concept pane (excluding the header bar containing the Next and Previous buttons, the Help icon, and so on) with the target of the link.

- **Parent Window (_parent):** Replace the HTML element that contains the Concept Pane (this is the entire rightmost pane in the Player, including the header bar) with the target of the link.

9. Click on **OK** to confirm your URL specification.

Using a popup window

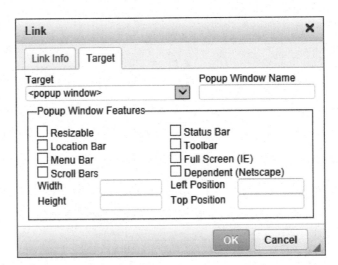

+ Popup windows are new with UPK 12.1 In prior versions of UPK, hyperlinks would always open in a new window.

If, when you insert a hyperlink from a Web Page, you choose a **Target** of **<popup window>**, the *Link* dialog box provides a number of additional options, as shown below:

The table below explains these options:

Option	Purpose
Resizable	In theory, this should allow you to choose whether the user can resize the popup window, but (in my testing with Internet Explorer 10) this just determined whether the Tab showing the page name was displayed, and the window was *always* resizable.
Location Bar	In theory this option will allow you to control whether the URL of the page is displayed in the Address bar, but (in my testing with Internet Explorer 10) the Address Bar is always displayed, unless you deselect this option and select the **Toolbar** option.
Menu Bar	Select this option to display the menu bar. In practice I never saw a menu bar at all, regardless of this setting.
Scroll Bars	If this option is selected then scrollbars will be displayed if the pop-up contains more content than can fit within the current size. If this option is not selected then scrollbars are never displayed.
Status Bar	Select this option to display the status bar at the bottom of the window.
Toolbar	Select this option to display the browser toolbar. In Windows Internet Explorer this contains **Home**, **Favorites** and **Tools** icons.
Full Screen (IE)	If this option is selected then the destination content will be displayed maximized to the full screen size (without an enclosing window). This option only applies to Windows Internet Explorer (IE).
Dependent (Netscape)	No idea. I didn't even know Netscape was still around.
Width, Height	Use these fields to specify the (initial) size of the pop-up window. If no values are specified, the browser's default window size will be used.
Left position, Right position	Use these fields to specify the (initial) position, in pixels, from the upper left corner of the screen, of the dialog box.

● Note that not all of these options may be supported by your browser. There also seems to be some problems with the implementation of these features, although it is unclear whether this is an error in UPK or in the browser.

The following image identifies some of the components that can be displayed or suppressed:

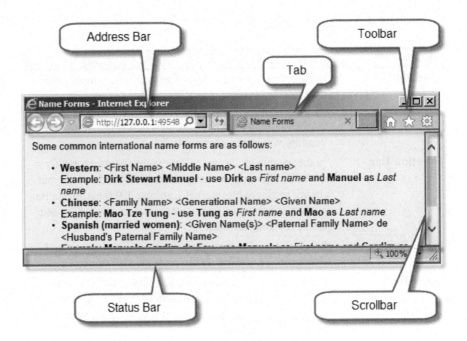

As explained above, the popup options may not work as expected, so you may want to test all the various combinations with your preferred browser before choosing your final settings.

Linking from Bubble Text

To create a link from within a custom Bubble Text to an external file via the URL of the external file, carry out the following steps

1. Open the Topic from which you want to provide the link, and navigate to the Frame that contains the custom text that you want to turn into a hyperlink.

2. Select the text that you want to form the link (that is, the text that the user will click on in order to display the linked object).

3. Click on the **Bubble text link** button (🔖). The *Bubble Text Link Properties* dialog box is displayed.

■ I have found the 'cleanest' display is obtained by deselecting everything except **Toolbar**.

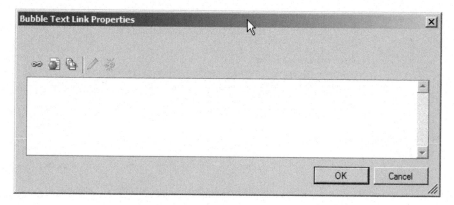

4. Click on the **Link** button (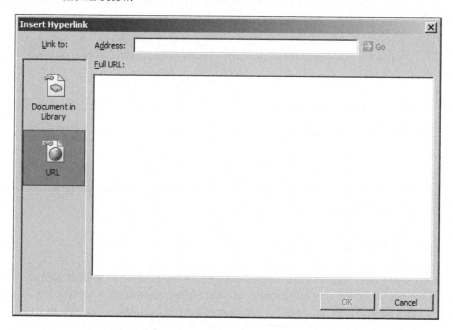). The *Insert Hyperlink* dialog box is displayed. Make sure that the URL option is selected on the left, as shown below.

5. Enter the URL of the site or object to which you want to link in the **Address** field.

6. Once you have entered the URL, you can click on the **Go** button ( ) to display the page to which you have linked in the lower portion of the dialog box (as shown in the screenshot below). This is useful for confirming that you have specified the correct URL – especially if you are using relative URLs. (See below for an explanation of absolute versus relative URLs.)

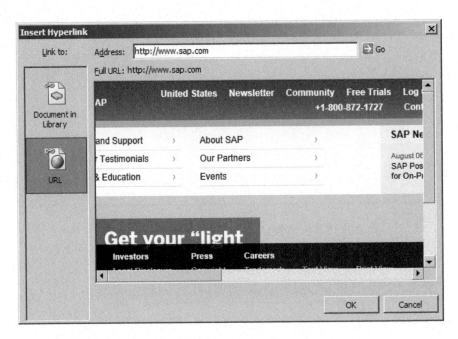

7. Click on **OK** to confirm your URL specification.

8. Back at the *Bubble Text Link Properties* dialog box (see Step 3), click on **OK** to return to the *Topic Editor*.

9. Save the Topic, and then close the *Topic Editor*.

● Unfortunately, the *Insert Hyperlink* dialog box does not provide a way to specify a ToolTip for a Bubble Text hyperlink. This is probably because Web Pages are stored as HTML which means that full HTML functionality can be supported, whereas Bubbles are not.

We now have a link to an external object: If the user clicks on this link, then the external object (in our case, the `sap.com` website) will be displayed in a separate browser window or tab:

Using Relative URLs

A relative URL specifies the location of the target file relative to something else, as opposed to specifying an absolute location. Most commonly, a relative URL specifies an address relative to the location of the file containing the link. In UPK, a relative URL specifies the location of a file relative to the Player's `index.html` file.

✛ Relative links were introduced in UPK 11.0

■ If you want relative URLs to be relative to a path other than the location of the `index.html` file, then you can specify a different base URL in the `baseurl` parameter in the `config.js` file in the root directory of your Player package, after publishing.

The advantage of using a relative URL is that if the location of your material changes (for example, if you move it to a new server, or replicate it across multiple servers) then your hyperlinks will still work (as long as the file(s) to which you are linking are still in the same location relative to your Player package (`index.html` file) and not to the actual file containing the link.

Specifying a base URL

When you preview a Topic, the Topic is published to a temporary location (typically on your C: drive. Therefore, relative links will not work. To resolve this, it is possible to specify a base URL to use specifically for previews.

The base URL is specified in your options (select menu path **Tools | Options**), under the **Content Defaults | General** category. Refer to the *General subcategory* of *Appendix B, User Options* for details of how to set this option.

Specifying a relative URL

To specify a relative URL, simply enter the location of the target of the hyperlink relative to your index.html file. When doing this, the following conventions can be used:

Convention	Meaning
.	
. .	Refers to the parent directory of the current directory
/	Refers to the root path of the host
/ /	Refers to an entirely different host

The following screenshot shows an example of the specification of a relative URL, when a base URL has been specified.

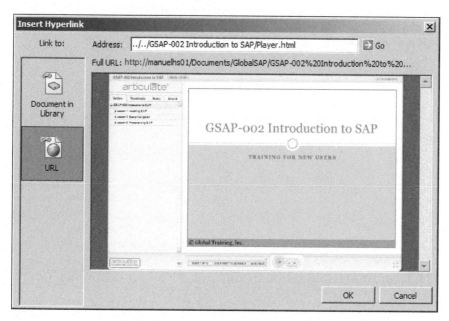

In this example, we are providing a hyperlink to our Articulate presentation, which is stored in a folder called GSAP-002 Introduction to SAP, located in the same folder on the server to which our content is published. This is 'two levels above' the `index.html` file (effectively backing up past `Publishing Content/PlayerPackage`). The full URL to which this relative URL will be 'resolved' during previews is shown below the **Address** field.

Using an HTML file as the Concept Page

Earlier in this chapter, we looked at using a Web Page as the Concept Page for a Topic (or Module, or Section). We also saw that although UPK calls this a 'Web Page', it is not a *true* HTML Web Page. Web Pages came a long way in UPK 12, with the addition of Style Sheets and the ability to enter tables and nested lists, but sometimes you want even greater control over the layout, or want to include some HTML features that just aren't supported by UPK's Web Pages. Thankfully, UPK provides you with the ability to do this, by attaching an *actual* HTML web page as the *Concept* pane. Doing so takes a little more work than attaching a UPK Web Page (notwithstanding the need to know HTML coding), but is well worth the effort. In this section, we look at how to do this.

Creating the Outline Element

One HTML feature that UPK Web Pages do not support is Forms. So by way of example, we will create a feedback form that users can use to provide us with comments on our training material. We will provide this via an entry in our Outline. To facilitate this, we will create a new (empty Module) called **Provide Feedback** that we include as the last entry in our **Global SAP Training** Outline. This is shown below:

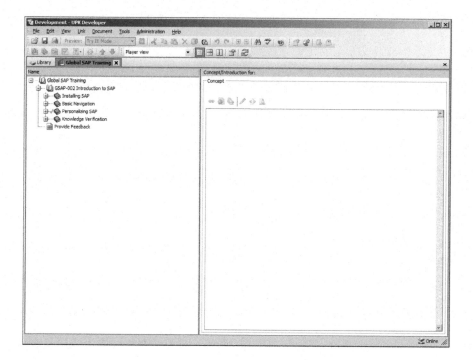

We will now use a Package as the Concept Page for this, and create a new HTML page within this Package.

Unfortunately, although UPK does provide a button (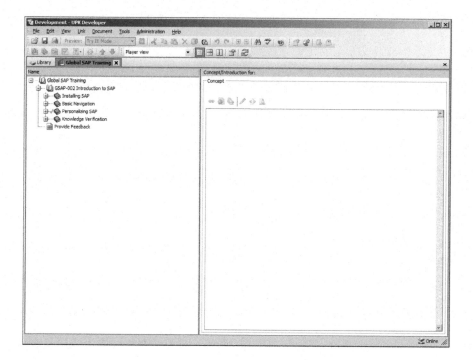) for creating a new Package directly from the *Concept* pane, you can only *add* files to a Package created in this way. For the purpose of demonstration, we want to create a new HTML file directly within a Package, and to do this we will need to create the Package from the *Library* screen.

✛ The ability to create a Package directly from the *Concept* pane was added in UPK 11.

Creating an HTML file within a Package

To create an HTML file within a Package, carry out the steps described below:

1. From the *Library* screen, navigate to the folder in which you want to create your Package.

2. Click on the **Create New Package** button (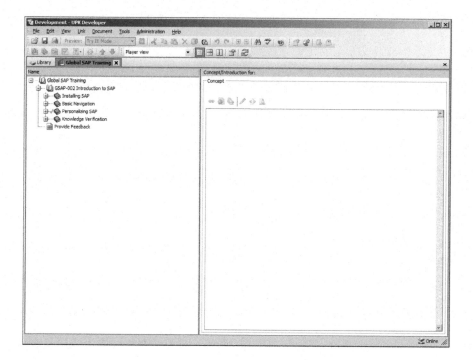) on the *Library Toolbar* (or select menu option **File | New | Package**). The *Package Editor* is opened, as shown in the following screenshot:

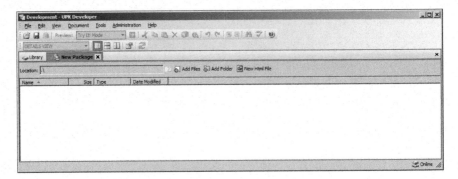

3. Click on the **New Html File** button (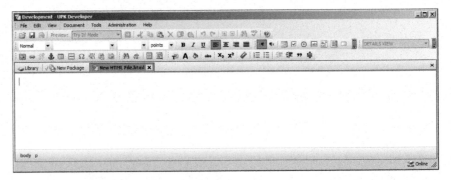). The *HTML Editor* is opened in a new tab within the *UPK Developer* screen, as shown in the following screenshot:

4. Create and edit the HTML file as required. For our exercise, we have created the following HTML file:

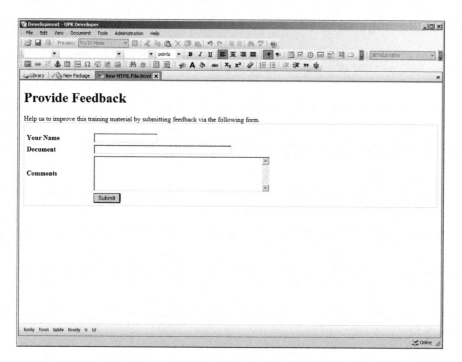

5. Once you have finished creating your HTML file, click on the **Save** button (🖫) to save your changes. The standard *Save As* dialog box is displayed.

6. Enter a suitable name for the file, and click **Save**.

7. Close the *HTML Editor*. and return to the *Package Editor*. You will see that your new file has been saved into the Package, as shown in the screenshot below:

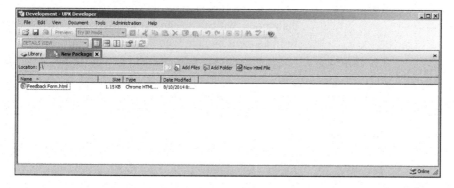

8. Click on the **Save** button (🖫) to save your changes to the package. The *Save As* dialog box is displayed again, this time for the Package.

9. Enter a suitable name for your new package, and then click on the **Save** button (🖫).

10. Close the *Package Editor*.

The Package Toolbar

✚ Prior to UPK 12.1, a separate toolbar containing most common HTML functions was available when editing text files. In UPK 12.1, this has been discontinued in favor of the five Web Page Editor toolbars mentioned here. This is unfortunate as there were some useful functions on the old *HTML Editor Toolbar*.

■ Most of the features accessed via the *Web Page Editor - Package Toolbar* require a knowledge of HTML to use. Such knowledge is beyond the scope of this book, bu if you need a decent reference, O'Reilly's *HTML & XHTML: The Definitive Guide* is as good a book as any on the subject.

If you are editing an HTML file within a Package, the same four toolbars available for UPK Web Pages are also available. These are:

- The *Font and Formatting Toolbar* (see page *page 360*)
- The *Appearance Toolbar* (see page *page 362*)
- The *Insert Toolbar* (see page *page 363*)
- The *Tools Toolbar* (see page *page 364*)

Inj addition to these four Toolbars, a further toolbar is available that provides access to features only supported in native HTML files (and not in UPK Web Pages). This is the *Package Toolbar*. An example of this toolbar is shown below:

The following table shows the buttons available on this toolbar, and explains their use.

Button	Name	Use
►¶	**Text direction from left to right**	Format the selected text for left-to-right reading (this is the default).
¶◄	**Text direction from right to left**	Format the selected text for right-to-left reading.
	Form	Click on this button to display the *Form Properties* dialog box, which you can use to insert an HTML form element into the Web Page.
☑	**Checkbox**	Insert a check-box form element into the form
◉	**Radio Button**	Insert an option button (commonly referred to as a radio button) form element into the form
abl	**Text Field**	Insert an edit field into the form
	Text Area	Insert a text input box into the form
	Selection Field	Insert a selection field form element into the form
▢	**Button**	Insert a button form element into the form

Button	Name	Use
[Image icon]	Image	Insert an image
[Hidden Field icon]	Hidden Field	Insert a hidden field
`<div>`	Create Div Container	Insert a HTML DIV container
[Show Source icon]	Show Source	Toggle between showing the HTML source for the page and the WYSIWYG view

Linking an HTML file to the Outline Element

We are now ready to link our newly-created HTML file to the Outline Element that we created earlier. We do this in the same way as described earlier in this chapter, but for ease of reference, the key steps are listed again, below:

1. Open the Outline Element to which you want to link the HTML file in the *Outline Editor*.

2. Make sure that the Outline Element is selected, and then click on the **Link** button ([icon]) in the *Concept* pane.

3. In the *Insert Hyperlink* dialog box, select **Document in Library**, and then navigate to the Package that contains the HTML file.

4. Double-click on the Package to open it, and then click on the HTML file within the package, to select it.

5. Click on **OK** to confirm your selection.

The HTML file will now be displayed in the *Concept* pane for the selected Outline Element. The screenshot below shows our sample outline, with the HTML feedback form that we created attached to our new **Provide Feedback** Module. Note that this screenshot shows the result in the Player, just for the fun of it.

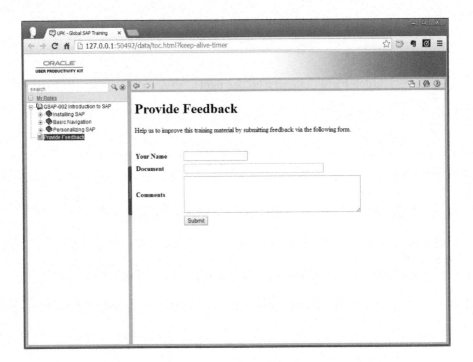

Using a Glossary

A **Glossary** defines terms that are unique to a project or system, or new to your users. A Glossary typically consists of a number of term/description pairs. The added value that UPK provides is that instances of each term in simulations can be hyperlinked to the relevant entries in the Glossary.

A Glossary in UPK effectively associates Web Pages to key terms. UPK will then turn any instance of that key term within a Topic (or other content object) to which that Glossary is assigned into a hyperlink to the associated Web Page. You could do this manually by creating Web Pages (as explained above) and then creating hyperlinks to these manually (also as explained above), but the advantage of using the Glossary functionality is that UPK will 'automatically' find each occurrence of the glossary term and create the hyperlink. I say 'automatically' in quotation marks, as UPK does not do this *completely* automatically. You have to *tell* it to go and create the hyperlinks, but once you tell it to do so, it will dutifully go off and find 'every' occurrence of all of the terms in the glossary and create the hyperlinks to the definition.

I say 'every' in quotation marks, because UPK won't necessarily link *every* instance of the term. UPK allows you to choose (at the Library level) whether it turns literally *every* occurrence of the term found in a location into a hyperlink, or only the first occurrence in the location. A *location* here is effectively a single Bubble or Web Page.

● One could well ask why UPK doesn't provide the option to create a Glossary link only for the first occurrence of the term in a Topic. The simple answer is that it does not necessarily know which occurrence is the first, because the Topic could include Alternative Paths and/or Decision Paths. So UPK takes an over-cautious approach, and considers each block of information separately.

This option is specified in the *Options* panel (menu option **Tools | Options**), under the **Content Defaults | Glossary** section. Refer to the section *Glossary subcategory* in *Appendix B, User Options* for full details of all user options relevant to Glossaries.

Creating a glossary

To create a Glossary in UPK, follow the steps described below:

1. From the *Library* screen, click on the folder within which you want to create the Glossary. You can create the Glossary in any folder, but it makes sense to have a single folder that contains the Glossary file itself and all of the Web Pages used for the Glossary terms.

2. Click on the **Create New Glossary** button (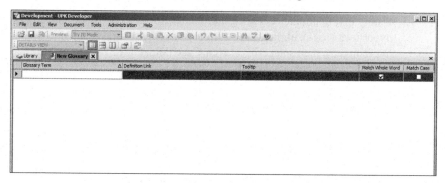) on the *Library Toolbar* (or select menu option **File | New | Glossary**). The *Glossary Editor* is opened in a new tab, as shown in the following screenshot:

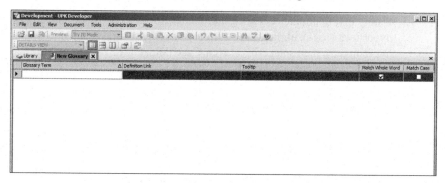

To create glossary entries from within the Glossary, follow these steps:

1. Enter the glossary term in the first free **Glossary Term** field.

2. Click in the **Definition Link** field on the same line. An ellipsis (...) is displayed on the rightmost side of the field.

3. Click on the ellipsis. The *Edit Definition Link* dialog box is displayed.

4. Click on the **Create New Web Page** field. The *Save As* dialog box is displayed.

5. Navigate to the directory in which you want to save the Glossary definition. Again, it makes sense to save these in the same folder as the Glossary itself.

6. The **Name** field will default to the glossary term specified in the **Glossary Term** field. It is recommended that you keep this default. You could use any other name, if you wanted to (UPK does not use this name to identify the definition Web Page; it uses the **Document ID**) but using the same name will allow you to easily locate the definition Web Page if you need to.

7. Click on the **Save** button. A new Web Page is created, and opened in the *Web Page Editor*.

8. Enter the glossary description into this page.

9. The Web Page will use the default font and colors. You can override these defaults, if required. You can also assign a Style Sheet to the Web Page, and control the formatting through that.

10. Close the *Web Page Editor*, saving your changes when prompted. You are passed back to the *Glossary Editor*.

11. Enter a suitable tooltip text for the glossary entry in the **Tooltip** field. This text will be displayed when the user hovers the mouse over the hyperlinked glossary term.

12. If only whole instances of the glossary term should be turned into hyperlinks (for example, if the term is Order then "Orders" and "Ordering" will not be hyperlinked), then select the **Match Whole Word** option. Otherwise, make sure that this option is not selected.

13. If only text that matches the case of the term should be turned into hyperlinks (for example, if the term is Order then "order" will not be hyperlinked), then select the **Match Case** field. Otherwise, make sure that this option is not selected.

14. Repeat Steps 1 to 13 for all additional terms that you want to add to the Glossary.

■ Just as you can use existing Web Pages for glossary entries, you can also use Web Pages created as Glossary entries anywhere you can use a Web Page (see earlier in this chapter).

To create a glossary entry that uses an existing Web Page for the glossary term, follow these steps:

1. Enter the glossary term in the first free **Glossary Term** field.

2. Click in the **Definition Link** field on the same line. An ellipsis (...) is displayed on the rightmost side of the field.

3. Click on the ellipsis. The *Edit Definition Link* dialog box is displayed.

4. Click on the **Create Link** button. The *Insert Hyperlink* dialog box is displayed.

5. Navigate to, and select, the Web Page that contains the glossary description.

6. Click on **OK**. The *Edit Definition Link* dialog box is redisplayed.

■ You can edit the Web Page directly from the *Edit Definition Link* dialog box, by clicking on the *Edit Web Page* icon. Editing Web Pages is explained in more detail earlier in this chapter.

7. Click on **OK**. You are returned to the Glossary tabbed page.

Once you have defined all required Glossary entries, save and close the Glossary by following the steps shown below:

1. Click the **Save** button (🖫) to save your changes to the Glossary. The *Save As* dialog box is displayed.

2. Navigate to the directory in which you want to save the Glossary.

3. Enter a suitable name for the Glossary in the **Name** field.

4. Close the *Glossary Editor*.

An example of a partially-populated Glossary is shown in the next screenshot:

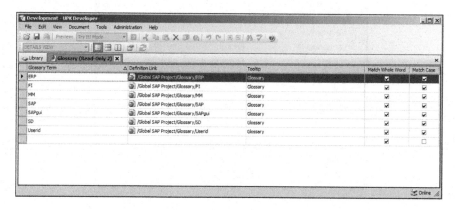

You can see from the **Definition Link** column above that all of the Glossary definition files are stored in the same, single folder, called `Glossary`. This is the same folder in which the Glossary object itself is stored. Personally, I find it useful to keep all of the content objects for the Glossary in the same single folder. This is not strictly necessary, but it does keep things organized.

You will also note that the *Tooltip* is the same in every case. I tend to always use the tooltip **Glossary** so that the user knows that the hyperlink links to the Glossary, and not to other content.

Assigning a Glossary to content objects

Creating a Glossary is only half the story. You need to manually assign the Glossary to each object that you want to use that Glossary (that is, for which you want the terms specified in the Glossary to be hyperlinked to the Glossary definitions). This assignment is done via the content object's Properties, as shown in the screenshot below.

Properties   □ ✕

☐ General

Custom properties	
Glossary	Glossary ...
Keywords	
Language	English (United States)
Name	Organizing your favorites
Resolution	1024 x 768
Roles	
See Also	
Style Sheet	
Template	Standard - English

Glossary
Link to glossary terms document

▲ There seems to be a problem in UPK 12 (at least as far as Build 12.1.0.33171) whereby it is impossible to remove a Glossary once one has been assigned to a content object. As a workaround, if you subsequently decide that you do not want to assign a Glossary to the content object, just create am empty Glossary object and assign that.

● The *Oracle UPK Content Development* manual states that you can "assign one or more glossaries to your content". This is misleading. Each content object can only have one Glossary assigned to it, although you can have different Glossaries assigned to different content objects.

The **Glossary** property is available for Modules, Sections, Topics, and Web Pages. This means that you could potentially assign one Glossary to a Module, another Glossary to a Section within this Module, and a third Glossary to a Topic within that Section. I'd question the wisdom of doing this, but I can certainly see the benefit of having multiple Glossaries available in a Library that contained (for example) simulations for multiple applications—you could create application-specific Glossaries (as you no doubt do at the moment) and then assign each Glossary to only the content objects for the relevant application.

The downside (for those of us who favor modularization and reuse) is that it is only possible to assign a single Glossary to any given object. So it is not possible to, say, create a company-wide Glossary and separate application-specific Glossaries, and then assign both the company-wide Glossary and the relevant application-specific glossary to a single Topic. However, more resourceful readers will have already worked out how to get around this limitation. Need a clue? Glossary entries are just Web Pages, and any given Web Page can be reused in multiple places. Need more help? A Web Page can be included in more than one Glossary. So you can define multiple application-specific Glossaries as required, and then just include all of the 'company-wide' glossary terms in each of these. Of course there is some slight duplication of effort as you need to define the Glossary term twice—once in once in each glossary—but you are reusing the individual Glossary definitions, so it could be worse.

Unfortunately, unlike Templates, it is not possible to specify a default Glossary in your user options. This means that this assignment must be done separately for each content object. However, there are a couple of shortcuts that UPK provides that avoid the need to assign the Glossary to content objects one by one. First, if you select multiple content objects (Modules, Sections, Topics, or Web Pages) and display the *Properties* pane, then you can assign the Glossary to all of the selected objects in one fell swoop. Second, if you assign a Glossary to a Module, then any new Sections (or other Modules) or Titles that you create *within* that

Module – that is, from within the *Outline Editor* – will inherit this Glossary assignment. However, it is important to note that this will only apply to *new* content objects. If you assign a Glossary to an outline element and then insert pre-existing content objects into this outline element, then these pre-existing content objects will not inherit the Glossary assignment.

Regenerating the Glossary links

Glossary links are not created (or updated) automatically. You need to tell UPK to go and search through your content objects and turn any instances of the Glossary terms into links to the Glossary definitions. This is good in that you can at least have control over when it does this, but bad in that it is easy to forget to do so.

Updating Glossary links after updating the Glossary itself

When you close (and not when you save) an existing Glossary, having just updated it (for example, to add or remove terms), UPK will prompt you to re-generate the Glossary links by displaying the following message:

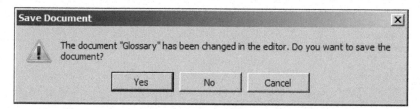

Click **Yes**. UPK will then update all of the content objects that the changed Glossary has been assigned to. It will hyperlink all occurrences of the Glossary terms to the associated Glossary definitions. Furthermore, if you have removed any Glossary terms from the Glossary, then UPK will also remove any hyperlinks for these terms. Once the Glossary has been updated, the following message is displayed:

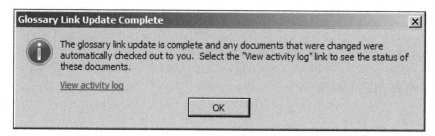

Note the text "**any documents that were changed were automatically checked out to you**". It is important to note that if you are working in a multi-author environment then any content objects that now include hyperlinks to your new glossary entries will have been checked out (in order to create the glossary links).

You will need to check all of these in again (typically, when you check in the updated glossary). You should, therefore, click on the **View activity log** link and make a note of the changed documents. Alternatively, you can choose to **Check in all** when you check in the Glossary, although you should be warned that this will check in all content objects that you have checked out—which may be more than just those objects changed by the Glossary link update.

An example of the *Glossary Link Update Activity Log* is shown in the following screenshot.

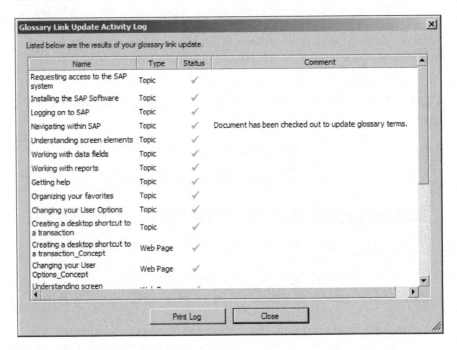

Note that the *Glossary Link Update Activity Log* lists all of the content objects that have been examined – even if they have not been updated. Also note the content objects identified the message "**Document has been checked out to update glossary links**". You will need to check back in all of these content objects.

It is also important to note that if UPK attempted to update the Glossary links in a content object that is currently checked out to another user, then it will not be able to. In this case, you will see a warning message similar to the one show ahead when the update completes:

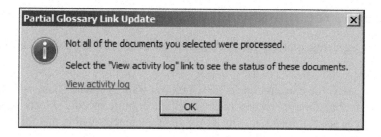

You can identify these documents in the *Glossary Link Update Activity Log*, as shown in the following screenshot:

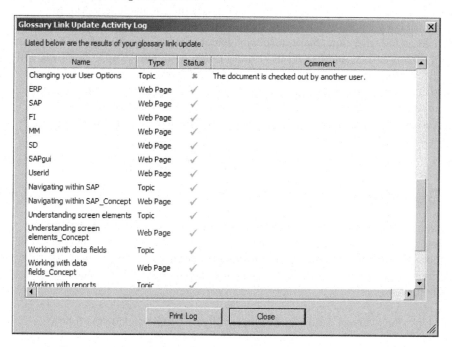

You should make a note of these unprocessed content objects. You will need to run the Glossary update again once they are checked in. Bear in mind that UPK will have identified the content object based on the most recently checked-in version of the object. The author could well have removed the text that would have been hyperlinked to the Glossary in their edits. Conversely, it is possible that UPK did not identify a content object for Glossary updates based on the most recent version, but an author had the object checked out and added the glossary terms (that are eligible for *hyperlinking*) whilst they had the object checked out. For these reasons, you should run the Glossary update periodically, and definitely run it immediately before publishing your content (when all of the content objects should be checked in, anyway).

Manually regenerating the Glossary links

You can regenerate glossary links whenever you want to, by following these steps:

1. Select the content objects for which you want to update Glossary links, in the Library. You can either select one or more specific objects, or you can select a folder, in which case all of the objects within that folder (and any subfolders) will be updated.

2. Select menu option **Edit | Update Glossary Links**.

It is advisable to always regenerate the Glossary links immediately prior to publishing your content. It certainly does no harm to regenerate the Glossary links at any other time, but bear in mind that it could take a while if you have a lot of content objects and/or a lot of glossary terms. Also, bear in mind that UPK will check out every object for which it updates the Glossary links, so you will need to manually check all of these back in again, which can also take time. This may also be inconvenient if you have authors working on the content objects (or are working on the content objects yourself at the time that you want to regenerate the Glossary links).

Summary

Although recording a simulation is just a matter of clicking the **Record** button and running through the task in the system, producing quality training material is not really this simple. Yes, the simulation may 'work', but it won't necessarily be 'training ready'. Producing high-quality training material in UPK requires a lot more work.

Things that you can do to improve the quality of a Topic include the following:

- Providing business context and additional explanations through the use of Custom Text and Explanation Frames
- Providing additional information via Web Pages
- Attaching relevant documents through the use of Packages
- Providing an on-line Glossary

These things are the *bells and whistles* that improve the user's experience. Because they are 'add-ons' to the basic recording, some authors may choose not to use them (or find that their project management has not allocated them enough time to add them). However, taking the time to add this level of features will greatly improve the overall usability of your exercises, and you will certainly see an increase in user satisfaction (assuming that you take post-training feedback— which you should).

10
Adding Value in the Player

In *Chapter 9, Adding Value to Your Topics*, we looked at things that you can do to your recordings to improve their quality (regardless of the deployment format). In this chapter, we will look at a few things that you can do to improve the user's interaction with the Player. These are all things that the user has control over, although as we shall see, it is you, the author, who allows them to have this control.

In this chapter, you will:

- Learn how to use roles to show users only those Topics that are applicable to their job

- Learn how to use jump-in points to allow users to start a simulation from a specific point

- Learn how to facilitate keyword searches

- Learn how to identify 'related documents' for content objects in the Player

- Learn how to allow (or deny) users the ability to change their Player options

- Examine some options for providing training on the Player to your users

Working with roles

It is likely that in any application there will be some features that are used by one set of users and other features that are used by a different set of users. Typically, the assignment of features is done on the basis of **roles** (or jobs, positions, department, or similar organizational criteria). Each user is assigned one or more roles, and based on this assignment they have a requirement to use certain functionality.

For example, your company or client may have a Sales department, a Finance department, and so on. Although these departments may use the same application (the application for which you are developing the training material), they are likely to use different features of the application, and will therefore need different training. This is the basis for *role-based training* (where each user is trained only on the functionality that they will use, rather than being trained on the whole application). This is, more often than not, the preferred training approach, especially with large (typically ERP) systems.

UPK *kind of* supports the concept of role-based training, in so far as it allows Topics to be *tagged* for different roles. This does not prevent users from accessing content that is not tagged for their specific role (as security roles may do in the application itself), but it does have two important uses:

- It allows users to filter the content that they see in the Player according to their chosen role(s).

- It allows authors to create Players for each role, each of which will contain only the Topics for that specific role (although for linking to in-application help you need a single player that contains all topics for all roles).

In this section, we will look at both of these uses.

Defining your roles

■ To lock down the roles list, so that individual content authors cannot create their own ones, simply make sure that only Administrators have Modify access to the `System/Roles` folder (see *"Chapter 14, Basic Administration"* for details of how to do this).

UPK does not *require* you to maintain a list of roles before you can assign them to content. You can simply define the roles as you assign them to Topics. However, from a *control* (and consistency) point of view it is probably wise to pre-define all roles prior to tagging content for these roles.

To define a list of master roles from which your authors can select when assigning roles to Topics, carry out the steps described below:

1. On the *Library* screen, open the folder `System/Roles`. Within this folder, you will see one role list per supported language, as shown in the next screenshot:

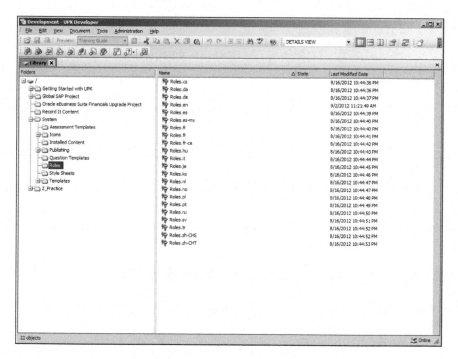

2. Double-click on the role list for your language. The *Role Editor* is opened in a new tabbed page, as shown in the following screenshot:

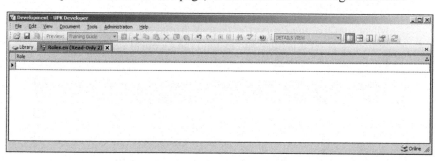

As you can see, there is nothing clever about roles (when compared, say, to Glossaries); the master role list is simply a one-column table containing the role names.

3. Enter the role name in the first (or next) free entry in the table, and press *ENTER* to confirm it. Repeat this step for all required roles. The following screenshot shows the finished role list for our example:

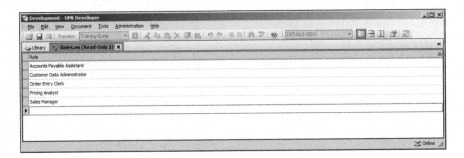

4. Once you have entered all of the required role names, click on the **Save** button (![save icon]), and then close the *Role Editor*.

You can now assign any of these roles to your Topics (or Modules, or Sections).

Assigning roles to content objects

To assign a role to a Module, Section, or Topic, carry out the steps described below

1. On the *Library* screen, click on the content object that you want to tag as being applicable to specific roles. Note that you can select multiple content objects if you want to assign the same role(s) to all of them at the same time.

2. Make sure that the *Properties* pane is displayed (click the **Properties** button (![properties icon]) if it is not), and expand the **General** section, as shown in the following screenshot:

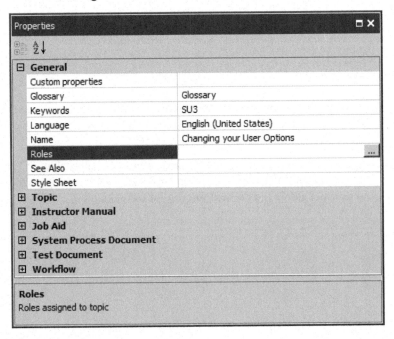

3. Click on the ellipsis (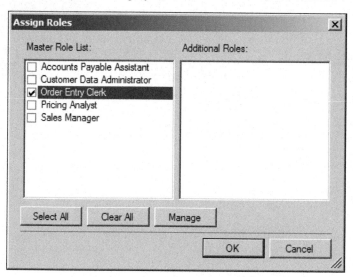) on the far right of the **Roles** field. The *Assign Roles* dialog box is displayed, as shown in the next screenshot:

- The **Additional Roles** pane on the rightmost side of the *Assign Roles* dialog box will list any roles that have been assigned to Topics in your Library but that do not exist in your master role list. How can this happen? Typically, it is because you have imported content from another Library, and the additional roles exist (and were assigned to the imported Topics) in that Library.

- If you want to identify the content objects that have one of these **Additional Roles** assigned to them, you can use one of the Views that include the **Roles** column (or add this column to any other View).

- If the role that you want to assign to the Topic does not appear in the **Master Role List**, then you can click the **Manage** button and add it now.

4. In the *Master Role List*, select the check-box to the left of all of the roles that you want to assign to this content object. In the previous screenshot, we have assigned the **Order Entry Clerk** role to a Topic.

5. Click **OK**.

That's all there is to it. Now let's look at how these roles are used in the Player, and during publication.

Selecting roles in the Player

If roles have been assigned to any of the Topics in a published Outline, then the Player for that Outline will contain an additional link, **My Roles**, in the Outline pane (below the **Search** box), as shown in the following screenshot:

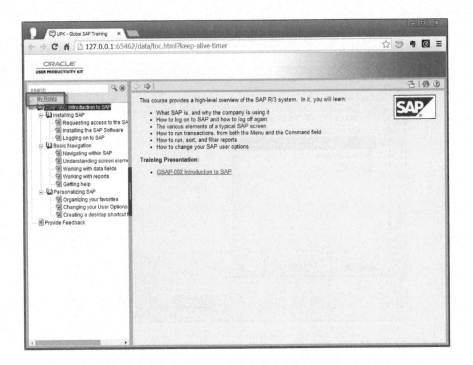

For our purposes, we will assume that the 11 Topics shown in the previous screenshot have been assigned to the five roles that we defined in the *Assigning your roles* section, as follows:

Topic	Accounts Payable Asst.	Customer Data Admin	Order Entry Clerk	Pricing Analyst	Sales Manager
Requesting access to the SAP system	X	X	X	X	
Installing the SAP Software	X	X	X	X	
Logging on to SAP		X	X		
Navigating within SAP			X		
Understanding screen elements					
Working with data fields		X		X	
Working with reports		X			
Getting help	X	X	X	X	
Organizing your Favorites			X		
Changing your user options		X			
Creating a desktop shortcut to a trxn		X	X		

Note that this is entirely fictitious, and has been done purely for the purposes of illustration.

Clicking on the **My Roles** link in the Player will display the *My Roles* dialog box. For our example, the *My Roles* dialog box appears as follows:

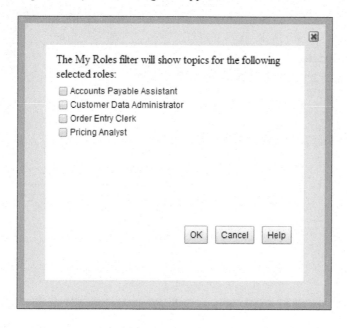

Note that there are only four roles listed, versus the five that we defined in our master role list. Why? Because the **Roles** list contains only those roles that have been assigned to the Topics included in the Outline. This may well be a subset of all of the roles that have been defined in the Library; obviously, the ability to select a role for which no content has been tagged would be both pointless and confusing. If you look at the role/exercise mapping table above, you will see that we did not assign any exercises to the **Sales Manager** role, so this role is not available for selection in the Player.

A user can select one or more roles, and then click the **OK** button to confirm their selection. The list of Topics in the Outline will then be filtered to include only content that has been specifically tagged for the selected roles. For our example, we will select the **Customer Data Administrator** role. Our Outline then appears as shown in the following screenshot:

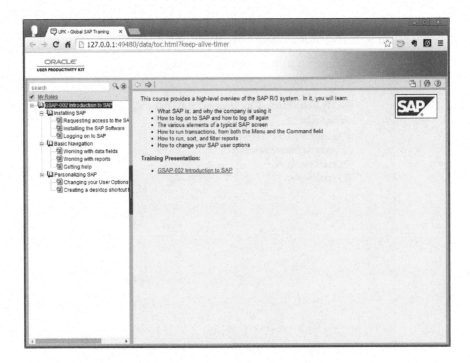

In our example, we can see only eight simulations (versus the 11 in our Outline). Cross-checking this against our role/exercise mapping table, we will see that only these eight Topics that have been tagged for the **Customer Data Administrator**. So, no surprises there.

It is important to understand that the Outline will include only content that has been explicitly tagged for the selected role. It will not include content that has not been tagged for *any* role (you will note that *Understanding screen elements* has not been included). The implication of this is that "untagged" does not mean "applicable to all roles". If you want a Topic to be available to all roles, then you need to explicitly tag it for all roles.

Once you have selected one or more roles and returned to the Overview, the check-box to the left of the **My Roles** link is selected (as shown in the example above). This indicates that role filtering is active. Deselecting this check-box will deactivate role selection, without the user having to go back into the *My Roles* dialog box to deselect all of the roles.

Remembering a user's selection

The user's role selection is saved in a browser cookie, and this cookie has (by default) a retention period of one year. The content of the cookie is similar to:

```
OnDemandPlayerFiltering:true&Roles:Role1+Role2
```

If a user defines their roles, and then disables role filtering, then UPK will still know what the user's roles are, because this is saved in the cookie. Should the

---

✛ OnDemand 8.7 and earlier used an obtuse combination of "always display" and "never display" in addition to the individual role tagging, to determine what would be displayed to the user. "Always display" meant that the Topic would be included even if it wasn't tagged for the selected role, and "never display" meant that the Topic would only be included if role filtering was not activated. Starting with UPK 3.5 the approach was simplified to that described above, but because of this, it is not as flexible.

user re-activate role filtering (by clicking the check-box to the right of the **My Roles** link) then the Outline will be filtered according to the roles that the user has previously selected. That is, the check-box simply toggles filtering *off* and *on*. Using the same example as above, if the user has selected two roles, but has disabled role filtering, their choices are still saved in a cookie, but now the cookie will appear as:

```
OnDemandPlayerFiltering:false&Roles:Role1+Role2
```

An implication of using browser cookies is that if multiple users are sharing the same workstation, and are not required to actively log on to it under a unique user ID, then any role selection made by the previous user of the workstation will apply to all subsequent users (unless they actively change it themselves). This can cause some confusion to users if they are not expecting this. Of course, in most corporate environments, users have unique, password-controlled Userids, and so this shouldn't be an issue.

Publishing for a role

As mentioned at the start of this section, in addition to allowing users to filter the Outline according to their role(s), it is also possible to publish an Outline that includes only Topics that have been tagged for specific roles. Let's look at how to do this.

> ● The following explanation assumes that you are already familiar with the publishing process. If you are not, then please refer to *Chapter 6, Publishing Your Content* for additional instructions.

1. Open the Outline that you want to publish, in the *Outline Editor*.

2. Click on the outline element (Module or Section) that you want to publish, to select it.

3. Click on the **Publish** button (📥).

4. On the *Welcome to the Publishing Wizard* screen, specify the publishing destination, and then click on **Next**.

5. On the *Select Publishing Options* screen, select the **Publish by roles** check-box (as shown in the following screenshot), and then click on the **Select Roles** button.

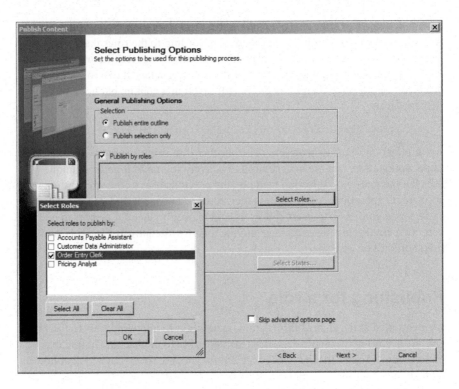

● You can only select roles that have been assigned to at least one content object in the Outline Element being published.

6. In the *Select Roles* dialog box, select the check-box to the left of the role(s) for which you want to publish the content, and then click on **OK**. In our example, we are going to publish only content tagged for the **Order Entry Clerk**.

7. Back on the *Select Publishing Options* screen, click on **Next**.

8. If the *Advanced Publishing Options* screen is displayed (depending on your selection on the previous screen), make any required changes, and then click **Next**.

9. On the *Formats* screen, select the appropriate deployment format (we will select **Player**), and then click on **Publish**.

Now let's look at what this gives us in the Player. (I assume that by this far in the book you know how to launch the Player.) The following screenshot shows the Player generated for the selection that we made.

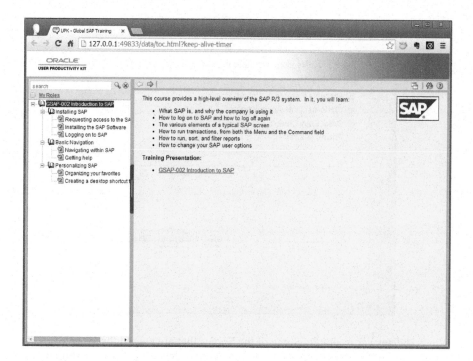

If you compare this screenshot with the earlier table that shows the roles assigned to the various exercises, you will note that (and as we would expect) the Player now only includes those Topics that were specifically tagged for the role(s) that we selected during publishing (in this example, the **Order Entry Clerk**). Success!

But wait! Why is the **My Roles** link still available? Surely if we have only published content for a specific role, then there is no need for this link? If you click on the **My Roles** link, you will see the following selections:

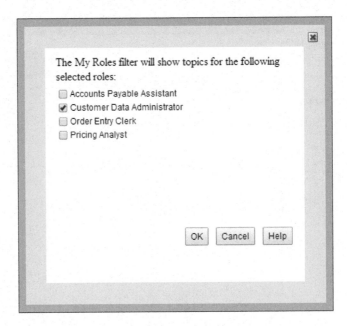

Why? The answer is simple. Some of the Topics that are tagged for the role that we selected for publishing are also tagged for other roles. So, even though we only selected a specific role for publishing, this does not mean that no other roles will be included in the published output. Furthermore, if you then select another role – other than the role specified during publishing, then the Player will show only those Topics that are tagged for both the role selected for publishing *and* the role selected in the Player. This is perhaps a minor point, but one that is worth bearing in mind if you have content that is tagged for multiple roles, and is something that you may need to explain to your users if they are expecting to see only (and all) content for their role (true role-based training).

Thinking beyond roles

Roles are really nothing more than *tags*. True, the tags will typically correspond to various (business) roles, but this does not necessarily have to be the case. Conceptually, this functionality is simply providing keywords on which to filter. In practice, these keywords could be the type of content, the product (or version of the product) to which the content applies, and so on. From an *information design* perspective, it is worth looking for other opportunities to use this functionality. That said, the functionality is called "Roles", and the option in the player is labeled "My Roles". Should you choose to co-opt this functionality for other purposes (say, to tag content as being applicable to specific releases of a product) you should also consider configuring this label and the associated dialog boxes, help topics, and so on, to match your new purpose. *"Chapter 16, Configuring UPK"* explains how to perform such configuration.

Jump-in Points

Most of the time, you will want your users to start a simulation at the beginning, and work their way through it to the end. However, there may be cases where you want to provide the flexibility to start a simulation at some other point. For example, say you have a task that consists of three separate stages. You could allow the simulation to be started from the beginning of any of these stages. Granted, during the initial training you will probably want your users to go through the entire exercise, but consider the case where the user has completed training and is now performing their actual job. They remember how to carry out the first two stages of the task, but need a reminder on the last part. They would find it very frustrating if they had to run through the first two-thirds of the simulation just to get to the stage with which they need help. UPK provides a solution to this problem in the form of jump-in points.

A **jump-in point** is little more than a bookmark defined for a specific Frame in a Topic. The user can see the defined jump-in points in the Player, and can select one of these to start the playback of the Topic from the Frame for which this bookmark has been defined.

The beauty of jump-in points is that they take very little time or effort to set up. You just enter the label on the relevant Frame in the *Topic Editor*, and UPK does the rest. The disadvantage is that they are not immediately visible in the Player. Unless the user knows that they are there (or has used jump-in points before, on another Topic) then they will not even know that they exist for a Topic. This is because (unfortunately) whereas the availability of role filters is indicated by the presence or absence of the **My Roles** link in the Player, the 'jump-in point selection button' is present all of the time, regardless of whether jump-in points have actually been defined for the Topic or not. This means that if you do use jump-in points, you will need to educate your users in what they are and where to find them. And if you use jump-in points for *some* exercises, then you should consider using them for *most* (if not *all*) of your exercises. If users check for jump-in points and find that they have not been defined in the majority of cases, then they will stop checking for them. And if that happens, you may as well not define them at all.

> ■ I find it helpful to place a small 'jump-ins available' icon in the Concept Page for Topics for which jump-in points have been defined.

Defining jump-in points

By way of an example, we will add some jump-in points to the exercise that we have been working on throughout this book. You will recall that the exercise takes the users through three separate tabbed pages within the same transaction. We will add jump-in points to each of these pages.

To define jump-in points in a Topic, carry out the following steps:

1. Open up the Topic for which you want to define jump-in points, in the *Topic Editor*.

2. Select the Frame to which you want to add a jump-in point (that is, the Frame to which the user should be able to jump).

3. Enter the text for the jump-in point in the **Jump-in point** field located at the bottom of the *Frame Properties* pane. This is the text that will be displayed in the jump-in list in the Player, so you should use a text that will make sense to the users. Note that you are limited to only 39 characters, so your text should be concise and to the point.

4. Repeat Steps 2 and 3 for all additional jump-in points that you want to create.

5. Save your Topic and exit from the *Topic Editor*.

✤ In UPK 11 and earlier, you could not specify a jump-in point for an Explanation Frame. UPK 12 lifted this restriction.

Note that you cannot provide a jump-in point for a Decision Frame, or for the Start Frame or End Frame (although that wouldn't make any sense, anyway...).

The following screenshot shows a jump-in point definition for a Frame in our sample exercise.

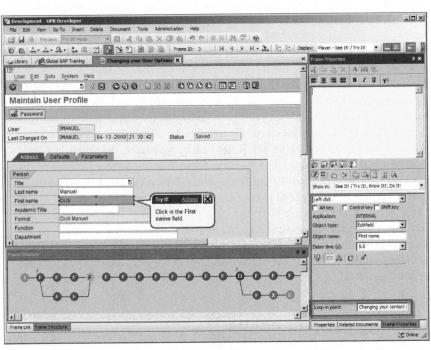

Selecting jump-in points in the Player

Let's now look at how the jump-in points appear in the Player. In the following screenshot, we have defined three jump-in points for our exercise: one for each of the tabbed pages.

Once the user clicks on the jump-in button (which is the small, downward-facing arrow on the right of the "mode" button), a drop-down menu is displayed, showing the available jump-in points (plus a standard "**Beginning of topic**" jump-in point, which is available whether you have defined any other jump-in points or not). The following screenshot shows this drop-down menu for our sample exercise:

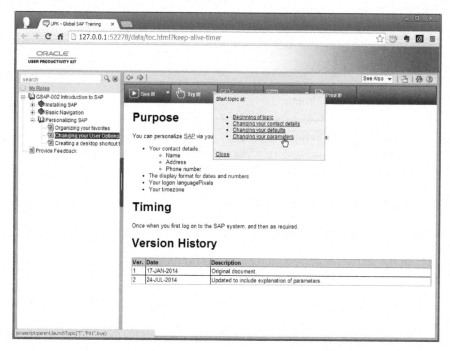

The user simply clicks on a jump-in point (which is actually a hyperlink) and the Player immediately jumps to the Frame within the Topic for which that jump-in point was defined.

Facilitating effective searches

UPK comes with a built-in full-text search function that is available in the Player. To use the search function, enter your search term in the **Search** box (highlighted in the following screenshot), and then click on the **Search** button (🔍). UPK then displays a list of all Topics that contain the specified text (either in the bubble text or an attached Web Page).

● For the technically-minded, there is one more thing of interest here. In this example, we are pointing to the last of our jump-in points (**Changing your parameters**). If you look in the lower-left corner of the browser window, you will see the actual hyperlink for this link. This is `Javascript: parent. LaunchTopic ("T","F91")`. Here, the "`T`" means *Try It!*, because this is the mode for which we selected the jump-in point. The "`F91`" is a reference to the specific Frame that the Player should jump to (Frame **91**, in this case). This matches the Frame ID of the Frame on which we select the *Parameters* tab, which you can see in the previous screenshot of the *Topic Editor*). Okay, so maybe it wasn't that interesting, but this could come in useful if you want to start creating your own hyperlinks to the middle of your exercises…

■ You can also use the Boolean operators AND and OR in the Search box.

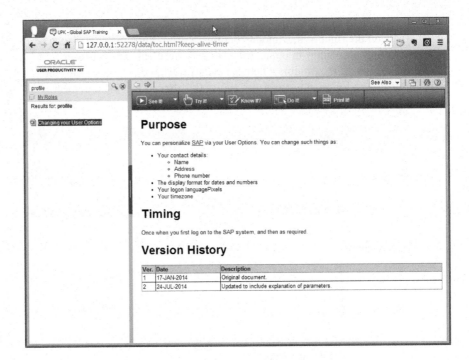

+ The **View Filtered Outline** option, which in UPK 11 and earlier versions allowed users to display the search results within the context of their containing Outline Elements, has apparently been discontinued in UPK 12. Which is a shame, as it was quite useful.

To clear the search results and return to the full Outline, simply click on the **Clear Search** button (⊗).

Although the availability of a built-in search function that you (as an author) don't need to set up, or otherwise configure, sounds like a great thing, it's not actually that useful. True, UPK will identify all of the Topics that contain the search term, but that is as far as it goes. UPK does not highlight, or otherwise identify, the search term within the Topic itself, or even identify the specific Frame(s) on which the search text was found. So, the user will still have to hunt for the actual location of the search text within the Topic.

Using Keywords

As stated above, UPK allows users to locate Topics that contain a specified text string. It also provides the ability to locate Topics based on a text string that does *not* appear in the Topic. This actually makes more sense than you'd think. UPK lets you assign **keywords** to Topics, and then these keywords are included in the list of the things that UPK will search when the user uses the **Search** function. So, if you assign a keyword of "XYZ" to a Topic that does not otherwise include the text "XYZ", then if the user searches for this text, that Topic will be identified and listed in the search results.

Still not convinced that this is useful? Consider the following possibilities:

- You have developed a generic Topic explaining how to run a report. You can specify the report identifiers as keywords for this Topic so that users are directed to this Topic when they search on the report identifier.

- You have a Topic for a customized version of a standard transaction. You can specify the standard transaction as a keyword for this Topic so that if users search for the standard transaction they will be directed to the Topic for the customized version.

- You want to allow users to search on old terminology that is no longer used.

- And so on.

Assigning keywords to a Topic

As an example, we will add a keyword to our sample exercise. We will add the word "Localization" as a keyword, so that if a user is searching for details of how to localize their number display formats, they will find our exercise.

To define keywords for a Topic, carry out the following steps:

1. On the *Library* screen, select the Topic for which you want to define the keywords.

2. Make sure that the *Properties* pane is displayed, as shown in the screenshot below.

3. Expand the **General** category.

4. In the **Keywords** field, enter your keyword(s). In our example, we will enter "Localization", as shown in the following screenshot:

■ You can be very creative with Keywords. These days, most people are familiar with *hashtags*. Consider prefixing 'unofficial' Keywords with "#" - users will remember them, and they are unlikely to appear in your actual content. For example, you could use a Keyword of **#2014UPGRADE** to allow users (or project members) to easily identify all (and only) Topics that were created or changed for the 2014 upgrade project.

● You can enter multiple keywords, separated by commas. There is a 1,024 character limit on the total length of the Keywords field, but this should be sufficient to meet most requirements.

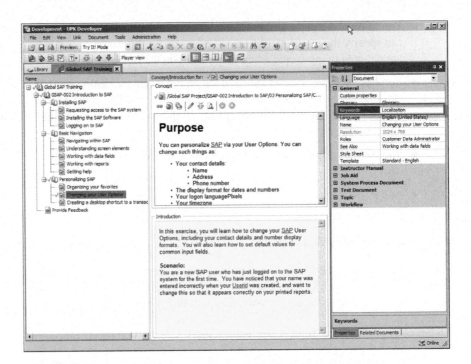

Note that you can also specify keywords for outline elements (Modules and Sections). In this case the search results will include only the outline elements (showing any concepts defined for them), and not the Topics within these outline elements.

Let's confirm that this works by going to the Player and searching for the text "Localization". The result is shown in the following screenshot, which proves that it is indeed working as expected.

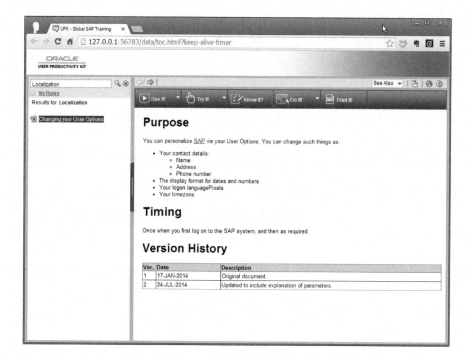

Identifying related material

UPK allows authors to identify additional content objects that are related to the content object that the user has selected in the Outline. This then allows the user to display this related content directly, via a hyperlink.

For example, for a 'create' simulation, you may choose to identify the 'change' and 'display' simulations as related documents. Or if you have several simulations for the same transaction but different business purposes, you may want to relate all of them to each other, so that the user can quickly jump from one to another in case they have selected the wrong one in the Outline.

✛ The **See Also** option, which provides this functionality, was introduced in UPK 11.

Identifying related documents for a content object

To identify one document as being related to another, carry out the steps described below:

1. On the *Library* screen, select the content object from which you want the related documents to be referenced.

2. Make sure that the *Properties* pane is displayed.

3. Under **General** properties, click the ellipsis button (![...]) on the far right of the **See Also** field.

4. In the *See Also* dialog box (an example of which is shown below), click on the **Add** button (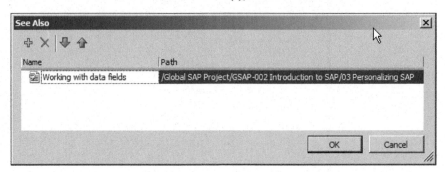). The *Add See Also Link* dialog box is displayed.

5. In the *Add See Also Link* dialog box, navigate to and select the content object that you want to reference. Note that you can reference Modules, Sections, and Topics.

6. Click **Open**. You are then returned to the *See Also* dialog box, which will now list the referenced document(s), as shown below:

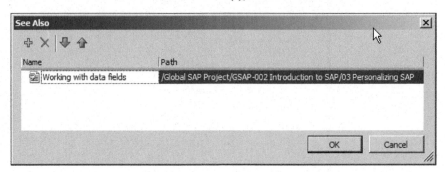

7. Repeat steps 4 to 6 to reference additional documents.

8. If necessary, you can use the **Up** button ( ) and the **Down** button ( ) to adjust the order of the documents in the list. In the Player, the documents will be listed in the order selected here.

9. If you want to remove a referenced document, click on the document in the *See Also* dialog box, and then click on the **Remove** button ( ).

10. Once your list of referenced documents is complete, click on **OK** to close the *See Also* dialog box and return to the *Library* screen.

Note that this is a one-way link. If you have two documents and want both documents to reference each other, you will need to perform the above steps for **both** documents. That is, linking from Document A to Document B will not automatically create a link from Document B to Document A. However, Document A will appear in the *Related Documents* pane for Document B (and vice versa).

Related documents in the Player

So how do **See Also** references manifest themselves in the Player? If (and only if) **See Also** links have been specified for a Topic, then when that Topic is selected in the Outline, a drop-down list containing (appropriately enough) the text **See Also** will appear on the rightmost side of the content area header bar (immediately above the play mode buttons). An example of this is shown below:

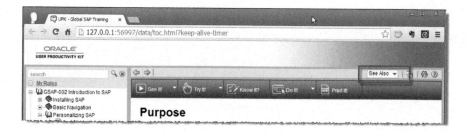

If the user clicks on this link, then they will see a drop-down list of all of the referenced documents. The screenshot below shows our sample Player, with the Topic to which we added the See Also links selected, and with the **See Also** link expanded:

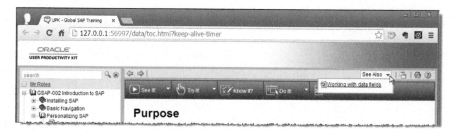

If the user clicks on a link in the **See Also** list, then a new browser window (or tab, depending on the browser settings) is opened, showing an Outline containing only the selected content (whether this is a Module, Section, or Topic).

Allowing users to change their Player options

Within the Player, there are a number of options that the user can configure (in addition to selecting their role(s), as explained previously). These are accessed by clicking on the **Preferences** button ( ) in the Player. This will display the *Interface Options* dialog box, as shown below:

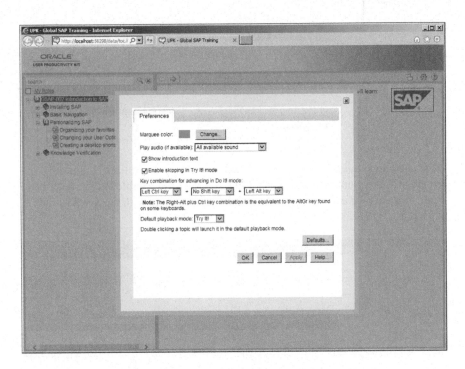

You will notice that all of these options are available to the author when publishing, in the **Presentation Options** for the Player output format (see *Chapter 1, Publishing Your Content*). When the author sets them, they are default values; the user can change any of them, via the *Interface Options* dialog box above.

However, the options available to the author include one option that is not available to the users. This is **Enable users to change their Player preferences**. If this option is deselected, then the **Preferences** button (⎇) will not be available to users in the Player, and therefore the users will not be able to change any of these options. Why would you want to deny the users the ability to perform this level of personalization? Because there is one very contentious option: **Enable skipping in Try It! mode**.

If the **Enable skipping in Try It! mode** option is selected, then users will be able to advance from one screen to the next in *Try It!* mode simply by pressing the *ENTER* key on their keyboard. Specifically, they will not be required to carry out the action itself. This means that they do not need to *try* in *Try It!* mode, which reduces this mode to a kind of 'manual advance' *See It!* mode. This isn't exactly *teaching* the users. I therefore recommend disabling this option (after you, the author, have done all of your testing—it is a useful option for being able to quickly run through a simulation).

● It is possible to customize the Player to remove only the **Enable skipping in Try It! mode**, but this is a fairly complex task and requires a working knowledge of HTML and JavaScript.

However, it is not possible to disable only this one option; it is necessary to disable the complete ability to change a user's preferences in the Player. So unfortunately the choice is all-or-nothing, and given that most of the other options are harmless (being able to change them adds no real *value)*, I'd recommend choosing nothing.

Providing training on the Player

Most of the improvements that we have made to our simulations in the preceding chapters of this book are largely intuitive to the users. The improvements that we have discussed in *this* chapter are less intuitive. If you choose to add value by using these less-intuitive features, you may want to consider providing training on the use of the Player. You may choose to do this anyway (intuitive features or not), but the use of jump-in points, keywords, 'see also' links, and roles is a much stronger driver for the need for training on the UPK Player itself.

What to explain

Should you choose to train your users on the use of the Player, exactly what you need to teach the users will depend on the functionality that you use. A list of things that you should consider training on is given below:

- *See It!* mode: How to pause playback; how to resume playback; using the ENTER key to advance

- *Try It!* mode: How to go back to the previous step, restart playback, and display the Concept Page

- *Know It?* mode: Remediation levels; how to move the bubble if it is obscuring required information

- *Do It!* mode: How to use the keyboard shortcut to advance to the next step without leaving the application

- Role filtering: How to select roles, and activate/deactivate role filtering

- The **Search** function: Boolean operators; switching between search results and the full Outline; switching between the results list and the filtered outline; any specific (hashtag) Keywords that you are using

- The **See Also** link

- The **Share** link

- Jump-in points

- In-application context-sensitive help; how to return to the full Outline

How to train on the Player

There are a number of ways that you can provide training on the Player. Some of these options are described below. There are certainly other options—this section is really just to get you thinking.

Explain the UPK Player during classroom training

UPK exercises can be used for stand-alone computer-based training (or "self-paced learning" as current fashion dictates), especially if they are developed to the standards suggested by this book. However, often they are not used in this way—or at least not initially. It is increasingly common for UPK exercises to be used as an alternative to providing an actual training system. In this way, they are seen as a direct replacement for the exercises that would normally be carried out in a training system during classroom-based training.

Assuming that this is the case, it is advisable to provide some brief training (perhaps in the form of a demonstration) during this classroom training—ideally, immediately prior to the users carrying out their first exercise in UPK. This has the distinct advantage that you can explain all of the relevant bells and whistles covered in this chapter and the last one, and also affords you the opportunity to gauge the user's understanding of the Player, and help them through their first exercise (or two) if necessary.

Conduct a UPK "show-and-tell"

If classroom-based training will not be used, then another alternative is to conduct some form of "show-and-tell" session for the users, prior to them actually using UPK. This could be done in person (perhaps during "site visits" where you are explaining the overall training approach, or during team meetings or employee forums), or remotely by using NetMeeting, WebEx, Centra Symposium, or a similar technology. The difficulty here is making sure that all of the users attend this session. If you cannot enforce this, then try to at least get some key personnel (such as local trainers, 'power users', or other knowledgeable 'go-to' people) to attend, and then make sure that the users know that they can get assistance from these key people, should they need it.

Create a UPK simulation on using the UPK Player

Inevitably, some bright spark will say "Hey! Here's a crazy idea—why don't we use UPK to *train* on UPK!". That's right; it's a crazy idea. Think about it—to be able to run the simulation on using the Player, the user needs to know how to use the Player, and to learn how to do that they need to run the simulation on using the Player, but to be able to do that... etc., etc., in ever decreasing circles. That said, in some circumstances, this may be the only option. In this case, consider the carrying out the following steps:

1. Create a simulation on using the UPK Player, call it "Double-click on me second", and have this in its own Module, called "Click on me first".

2. Include a Web Page in the Concepts pane for the Module that also tells them to click on the Module and then double-click on the Topic. Give this a nice, bright background, and a big heading of "READ ME FIRST".

3. In the Topic itself, hide the Action Areas on all Frames. The action areas will still appear on the example that you walk them through (that is, the recording that you play back when recording the simulation that demonstrates how to play a simulation), and having two sets of Action Areas would be confusing.

4. Select only *See It!* mode as available for this Topic, in the Topic's **Properties**.

Do nothing

Really. Doing nothing is a valid option. The UPK Player does come with perfectly adequate built-in help. And if you find this to be inadequate for your users, you can always provide your own specific help. If your users are in any way computer literate they should be able to work their way through the on-line help. In fact, if your users have mobile phones, then their phones are quite likely more difficult to use than the UPK Player, and if they can use their phones, they can probably use the Player.

That said, if you are expecting your users to rely on the Player help, you probably want to provide some text in the *Concept* pane of the first outline element in the Player (as this is the first thing that the user will see when they start the Player) to direct them to the Player help.

Summary

There are a number of things that you can do to provide your users with a little control over the way that they interact with the Player, and to *personalize* their 'learning experience'. This includes:

- Providing the ability to filter content in the Player based on the user's role

- Providing jump-in points so that users can start the playback of a simulation from a number of different points

- Using keywords to provide a more effective search facility

Although providing these things will undoubtedly improve the usefulness of your training, and increase the users' satisfaction, they are not things that are immediately obvious (or intuitive) to the users, who may be blithely ignorant to the fact that they exist, despite the hours that you painstakingly put into providing them. You may therefore want to consider providing some form of training on the UPK Player to your users, if you provide these features.

11
Incorporating Sound Into Your Topics

In this chapter, we will look at a less-used feature of UPK: sound. UPK provides the ability to incorporate sound recordings into your Topics and Web Pages. Generally, you would want to do this to provide 'voice-overs' of the text in these content objects, so that users can hear this when they play the simulation. This may be an important consideration for Section 502 accessibility compliance.

In this chapter, you will learn:

- How to record sound for a Frame

- How to record sound for a Web Page

- How to import and export sound files

How sound is provided in UPK

Each Frame in a simulation can have a sound file associated with it. This sound file can be created during recording of the initial simulation, captured during Topic editing, or even imported from an external file. We will look at each of these in turn.

Recording sound during editing

The cleanest and easiest way of providing sound is to record it during the editing process. Most likely, the sound will be added as the last thing, once the simulation

✦ Up to version 3.5, UPK made use of Template Sound to automate (or at least simplify) the provision of sound in a Topic. This proved difficult to do well (as sound for Template Text in a Frame was effectively pieced together from several sound files), and so starting with version 3.6, sound is recorded at the Frame level (that is, each Frame has a single sound file associated with it).

✦ Up to version 3.6, UPK required an external sound editor. From version 11 onwards, UPK includes its own, built in sound editor (that you *have* to use for editing sound – you cannot choose another application).

is 'finalized'—that is, once the Bubble Text, on which the sound will more often than not be based – is fixed.

All sound processing is done via the *Sound Editor*. Within the *Topic Editor*, this is displayed as a dockable pane. To display the *Sound Editor*, select menu option **View | Panes | Sound Editor**. If this pane is not already docked, you can dock it to any edge of the screen, or as a tabbed page on another pane (see *Chapter 3, Working in the UPK Developer Client* for more information on how to position dockable panes). In the following screenshot, the *Sound Editor* has been docked at the bottom of the screen, where it is in a tab group with the *Frame Structure* pane:

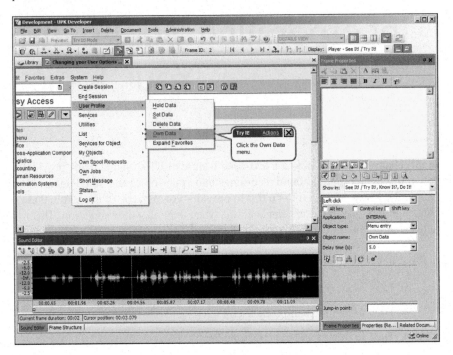

Note that in this example, sound has already been recorded for the Topic. If sound has not yet been recorded for a frame, the *Sound Editor* will show a flat, horizontal (blue) line.

The *Sound Editor* shows the sound amplification for the selected period (which can be the current frame, the current Frame and the preceding and following Frames, or a specific selection within the current Frame. The numbers immediately below this show the timing of the sound (starting the display at zero, and extending for as long as the sound lasts – but scaled to fit the full sound file within the width of the pane. The sound for the current Frame is delineated by solid, vertical yellow lines. The current playback position is identified by a dashed, vertical yellow line. Below the timeline, the current frame duration and current playback position (within the overall Topic timeline – not necessarily within the current Frame) are shown.

The colored scale to the left of the timeline provides an indication of the 'loudness' of the sound. Sound within the central, green section is at an acceptable level, but sound that peaks in the yellow or red sections on the outside risks sounding distorted during playback. When recording, it is best to ensure that your sound is within the green area (you can adjust this, within the *Sound Editor*, if necessary).

The *Sound Editor* has its own suite of buttons for working with sound. We describe some of these as we use them throughout this chapter, but for the sake of convenience and completeness, all of the *Sound Editor* buttons are listed below.

Button	Name	Purpose
	Import sound	Import a sound file from your PC into this Frame. This will remove any sound already recorded (or imported) for the Frame.
	Export sound	Export the existing sound for the current Frame (in its entirety—regardless of the selection).
	Record sound	Record new sound for the Frame. This will replace any existing sound already recorded (or imported) for the Frame.
	Insert sound	Record new sound and insert it at the current playback position (which is identified by the vertical dotted yellow line in the timeline).
	Play / Pause	Play the section of sound currently selected in the timeline, and pause the currently-playing sound, respectively.
	Stop	Stop the sound playback.
	Cut	Cut the currently-selected portion of sound to the sound clipboard. The remaining sound will be closed up so that there is no gap. Note the difference between this and **Delete**.
	Copy	Copy the currently-selected portion of sound to the sound clipboard.
	Paste	Paste the sound currently on the sound clipboard into the timeline at the current playback position, or in place of the currently-selected snippet (as applicable).
	Delete	Delete the currently-selected portion of sound. The deleted sound will be replaced with silence, so that the length of the sound clip for the Frame remains the same.
	Select frame	Select all of the sound for the current frame.

Button	Name	Purpose
	Deselect all	Cancel any current selection.
	Select start of frame sound	Extend the current selection backwards to the start of sound for the current Frame.
	Select end of frame sound	Extend the current selection forwards to the end of sound for the current Frame.
	Crop to selection	Crop the sound for the Frame so that it consists only of the current selection. Note that this applies to the Frame for which the sound is selected in the timeline – even if this is not the current Frame.
	Zoom	Change the scope of the timeline so that it includes sound for a specific period. The following options are available from the button's drop-down:

- **Zoom to current frame**: Reset the timeline so that only the sound for the current Frame is shown.

- **Zoom to previous and next frame**: Reset the timeline so that the sound for the preceding Frame, current Frame and next frame are all shown.

- **Zoom to selection**: Reset the timeline so that only the currently-selected portion of sound is shown.

Button	Name	Purpose
	Modify length or amplitude	The drop-downs for this button allow you to change the duration of a portion of sound, or change its amplification ('loudness'). The following options are available from the button's drop-down:

- **Extend timeline**: Extend the sound period for the current Frame (not the visible timeline) by a specified period. You will be prompted to enter this duration (which defaults to five seconds). The extension will consist of silence. This option is useful if you want to increase the amount of time between the sound for the current Frame and the next Frame

- **Add silence**: Insert a specified period of silence at the current playback position. You will be prompted to enter the duration of the silence (which defaults to five seconds).

- **Amplify**: Increase or decrease the volume of the currently-selected portion of sound. This is useful if the sound is too loud for a portion of the sound file (for example, if it peaks in the red areas of the scale on the left of the timeline) and you want to reduce this to avoid distortion.

Button	Name	Purpose
	Sound Tuning Wizard	Launch the *Sound Tuning Wizard*, which will guide you through setting your sound levels for optimal recording and playback. The *Sound Tuning Wizard* is covered in more detail below.

Using the Sound Tuning Wizard

The *Sound Tuning Wizard* can be used to adjust your sound settings. Typically, you will want to do this before you start recording any sound, but you can also use it at any stage during recording to adjust the sound recording settings.. To use the *Sound Tuning Wizard*, carry out the following steps:

1. From the **Sound Editor**, click on the **Sound Tuning Wizard** button ( ). The first step of the Wizard is displayed, as shown below:

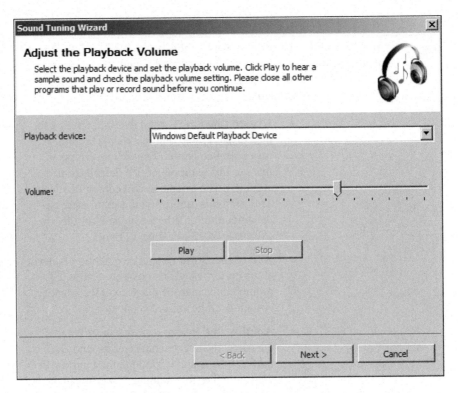

2. In the **Playback device** field, select the device (typically, speakers) through which you want to play sound from UPK. Note that this applies only to the playback of sound while you are editing, and does not apply to the playback via the Player—for either you or your users.

3. Use the **Volume** slider to select the default playback volume. Note that any volume control on the playback device itself will override this setting. You can click **Play** to play a sample sound that you can use to determine the correct playback level. Click **Stop** to stop playback of the sample sound.

4. Click **Next**. The second step of the Wizard is displayed, as shown below:

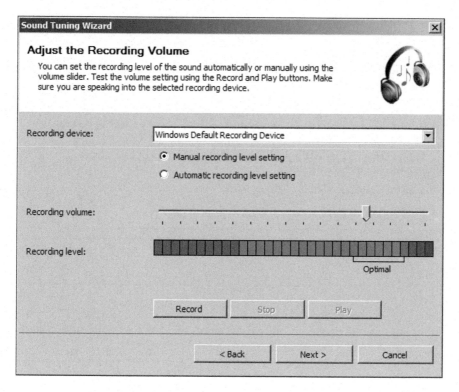

5. In the **Recording device** field, select the device (typically a microphone) that you will use for recording sound.

6. If you want UPK to automatically adjust the recording level for you, then select the **Automatic recording level setting** option. Otherwise, select the **Manual recording level setting** option, and then use the **Recording volume** slider to adjust the sound to an optimal level. Click **Record** and talk into your microphone to test the recording levels, and then (assuming you are setting the levels manually), adjust the slider until your sound peaks in the **Optimal** area of the **Recording level** indicator. Click **Stop** to stop recording. You can click **Play** to play back your recording and check for distortion.

7. Click **Next**. The final step of the Wizard is displayed, as shown below:

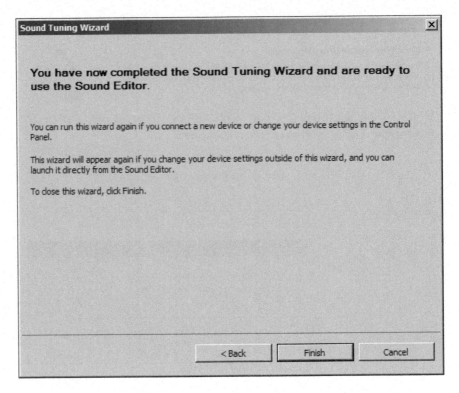

You have now completed the Sound Tuning Wizard and are ready to use the Sound Editor.

You can run this wizard again if you connect a new device or change your device settings in the Control Panel.

This wizard will appear again if you change your device settings outside of this wizard, and you can launch it directly from the Sound Editor.

To close this wizard, click Finish.

8. Click **Finish** to close the *Sound Tuning Wizard* and return to the *Topic Editor*.

Recording sound for a Frame

To record sound for a Frame, follow the steps shown below:

1. In the *Sound Editor*, make sure that the playback position is within the current Frame, and then click on the **Record sound** button (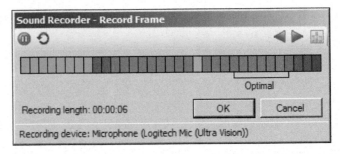). Sound recording starts *immediately*, and the *Sound Recorder* dialog box is displayed, as shown below:

2. Record your required sound, keeping an eye on the volume meter, to keep your volume within the **Optimal** range.

3. If you need to pause recording for this Frame, then click on the **Pause** button (⏸) in the upper-left corner of the *Sound Recorder* dialog box. Click on the **Record** button (⏺) again to continue recording.

   Note:
   Any time that recording is paused, you can click on the **Sound Tuning Wizard** button (▦) to launch the *Sound Tuning Wizard* and adjust your recording and playback options (as described above).

4. If you want to re-capture sound for a Frame, then click on the **Restart** button (⏺) to return to the start of sound recording for the Frame, and then click on the **Record** button (⏺) to restart recording.

5. Once you have finished recording your sound, click **OK** to stop recording and close the *Sound Recorder* dialog box. Alternatively, you can click **Cancel** to discard your recording(s).

6. You can use the remaining buttons in the *Sound Editor* to make adjustments to your recorded sound, if necessary. Refer to the table given earlier in this chapter for a full list of these buttons and their uses.

■ If you are recording sound for multiple Frames at the same time, you may find it easier to click the **Pause** button at the end of sound recording for one Frame, click the **Go to next frame** button to go to the next Frame, and then click the **Record** button to restart recording.

Recording sound during Topic recording

An alternative to recording sound during editing, is to record the sound during the actual recording of the simulation. This has the advantage that everything is done all at once, but has the disadvantage that if anything changes during editing (and it likely will), the recording will need to be re-done.

How to record sound during Topic recording is explained in *Chapter 2, Recording a Simulation.*

Recording Sound for a Web Page

In addition to providing sound at the Frame level, it is also possible to provide sound for a Web Page—regardless of whether this is a Web Page used as the Concept Page for a Module, Section, Topic, Assessment, Question, or a Web Page used for other purposes (such as a Glossary Entry).

✛ The ability to record sound for a Web Page was introduced in UPK 3.6.

To record sound for a Web Page, carry out the following steps:

1. Open the Web Page in the *Web Page Editor*.

2. Make sure that the *Sound Editor* is displayed. (Select menu option **View | Panes | Sound Editor** if it is not.)

3. In the *Sound Editor*, click on the **Record sound** button (⏺). Sound recording starts *immediately*, and the *Sound Recorder* dialog box is displayed, as shown below:

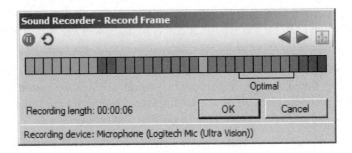

4. Record your required sound, keeping an eye on the volume meter, to keep your volume within the **Optimal** range.

5. If you need to pause recording, then click on the **Pause** button (⏸) in the upper-left corner of the *Sound Recorder* dialog box. Click on the **Record** button (⏺) again to continue recording.

   Note:
   Any time that recording is paused, you can click on the **Sound Tuning Wizard** button (⊞) to launch the *Sound Tuning Wizard* and adjust your recording and playback options (as described above).

6. If you want to re-capture the sound, then click on the **Restart** button (↻) to return to the start of sound recording, and then click on the **Record** button (⏺) to restart recording.

7. Once you have finished recording your sound, click on **OK** to stop recording and close the *Sound Recorder* dialog box. Alternatively, you can click on **Cancel** to discard your recording(s).

8. You can use the remaining buttons in the *Sound Editor* to make adjustments to your recorded sound, if necessary. Refer to the table provided earlier in this chapter for a full list of these buttons and their uses.

Importing and exporting sound files

In addition to recording sound files from within the **Topic Editor**, you can also create sound files outside of UPK, and then import these into the **Topic Editor**. There are some good reasons for doing so (apart from the fact that recording from within UPK just doesn't seem to work with some software and/or hardware set-ups). The most significant of these reasons is that you may choose to use external 'talent' to record all of your sound files. Perhaps you don't personally have the most engaging voice (as you will see if you play the sample exercise for this chapter, I include myself as one of those); perhaps you have someone within your organization who sounds like Richard Burton or Don LaFontaine (now *that* would make for an interesting exercise!); or perhaps you can afford to hire a professional voice-over person.

Alternatively, you may already have sound files that you want to use. Perhaps these are sound files from another Library, or a previous installation of UPK. Or you may have recorded a classroom demonstration of the exercise and want to use the sound files extracted from this in your recording.

Yet another possibility is that you may have already recorded sound files for one Frame or Topic, and want to re-use these sound files in other Frames or Topics. In this case, you can export the sound files from the original Frame, and then import them into your new Frame. However, you can also copy and paste sound snippets from one Frame to another, and even from one Topic to another, so unless you are copying across Libraries, there is little need to export and then import your own sound.

Note that if you export and then import a content object, the sound will automatically be included. You should therefore only need to export sound separately if you are moving it from one Topic or Web Page to another.

✚ In UPK 3.5 and earlier, there was no way to copy sound from one Frame to another. Therefore, the *only* way to re-use sound recordings (even within the same Topic) was to export the sound from one Frame and then import it into another Frame.

Exporting sound files

To export a sound file, preform the following steps:

1. Open the Topic or Web Page from which you want to export the sound file, in the **Topic Editor** or *Web Page Editor*, as appropriate.

2. For Topics, select the Frame from which you want to export the sound file.

3. Make sure that the *Sound Editor* pane is displayed. (Select menu option **View | Panes | Sound Editor** if it is not.)

4. In the **Sound Editor**, select the portion of sound that you want to copy. You can either click on the **Select frame** button (⊞) to select all of the sound for the Frame, or click and drag on the timeline to select a specific area. You can also use the drag-handles on the currently-selected area to increase or decrease your selection.

5. Click on the **Export sound** button (⊞). The *Export Sound* dialog box is displayed, as shown below. Note that this is effectively the standard Windows *Save As...* dialog box (which has been collapsed here, to hide the folders).

6. Navigate to and select the location to which you want to save the sound file, enter a suitable file name, and then click **Save**.

The sound file is exported. You can now import it into another Topic or Web Page, as explained in the next section, *Importing sound files*.

Importing sound files

To import an existing sound file (either one that you exported from another Topic or Web Page, or a sound file that you have obtained from another source), carry out the following steps:

1. Open the Topic or Web Page into which you want to import the sound file in the *Topic Editor* or *Web page Editor*, as appropriate.

2. For Topics, select the Frame into which you want to import the sound file.

3. Make sure that the *Sound Editor* is displayed. (Select menu option **View | Pane | Sound Editor** if it is not.)

4. Click on the **Import sound** button (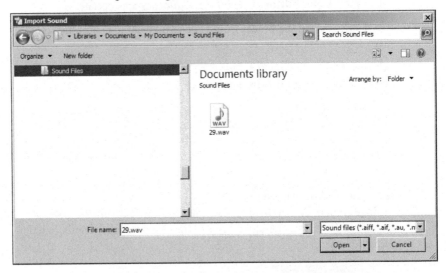). The *Import Sound* dialog box is displayed, as shown below. Note that this is effectively the standard Windows *Open* dialog box.

5. Navigate to, and select, the sound file that you want to import.

6. Click **Open**.

The sound file is imported into the current Frame or Web Page, replacing any (and all) existing sound for the Frame. Note that you cannot insert imported sound into the existing recorded sound for the Frame or Web Page.

Publishing sound

There are a number of options that are relevant to providing sound in your Player. These are: Topic Properties, and publishing options. These are described separately, below.

Sound options in the Topic Properties

One of the Topic Properties is the **Play Sound** option. This allows you to select the specific play modes in which sound should be provided (subject to the publishing options discussed in *Sound options in the Topic Properties* on page 457). The following screenshot shows this option, with the drop-down expanded so that you can see the individual options:

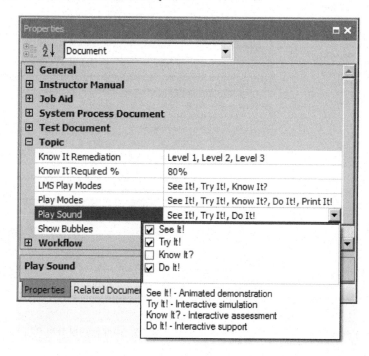

Here, you can see that you can choose to play or suppress sound in any of the four play modes. This is exceptionally useful, as you typically wouldn't want instructional sound played in *Know It?* mode (which is why this mode is deselected by default—as shown in the example above).

Note that these options are specified per Topic, although if you want to apply the same settings to multiple Topics, you can select all of the applicable Topics and then change these settings for all of them at once.

The Topic-level **Play Sound** option is new in UPK 12. In earlier versions, sound could only be made available in *See It!* and *Try It!* modes, and was either enabled for all Topics or no Topics, depending upon the settings chosen during publishing.

Sound options in the Publishing Wizard

In order to ensure that your sound files are available to the users, there are a few settings for the **Player and LMS** deployment format that you need to pay attention to, in the *Publishing Wizard*.

In the **Player and LMS** format, there are two settings, highlighted in the screenshot below:

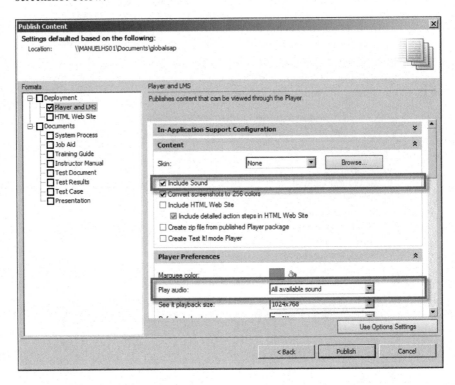

✦ UPK 12 replaced the previous **Sound** selection field, which allowed you to choose the sound frequency (and therefore quality), with a single check-box, to determine whether sound is included or not. All sound is now published at a default bit-rate.

To include sound in the Player, select the **Include Sound** check-box.

The **Play audio** setting is used to determine exactly what sound will be played during execution of the simulation. The choices are:

- **None**: No sound will be played.

- **Keyboard and mouseclicks**: UPK will play sounds to indicate keyboard presses and mouse-clicks during *See It!* and *Try It!* modes, but Frame or Web Page sound will not be deployed.

- **All available sound**: UPK will play sounds to indicate keyboard presses and mouse-clicks during *See It!* and *Try It!* modes, and will also play all available Frame or Web Page sound will be available.

Note that even if sound is included, the user can still disable sound playback if they want to, by changing their user preferences in the Player. By default, sound will be played if it is included, and the user must explicitly disable it if they do not want to hear it. Unless you provide sound for all of your simulations and the users know what to expect, you may want to provide some kind of an alert to the fact that a simulation includes sound (maybe a note in the Concept Page for the Topic), so that unsuspecting users aren't caught unaware by Don LaFontaine suddenly booming out "EXERCISE *ONE!!!*".

Sound in the Player

There are a few considerations with regard to how embedded sound is handled in the Player. Firstly, sound is played automatically as soon as the Frame is displayed. There are no sound controls available during playback.

Secondly, if you specify a **Delay** value in the *Action Properties* pane for a Frame that is less than the length of the sound file for that Frame, then the sound file takes precedence. That is, sound will not be 'cut short' by UPK going to the next Frame after the defined delay interval.

Finally, for sound in Web Pages, the sound is automatically played as soon as the Web Page is displayed. For Web Pages used as Concept Pages, this is as soon as the user selects the Outline Element (that has this Concept Page attached to it it) in the Outline. Again, this may be a nasty surprise for users (especially those in a shared office environment) so you may want to provide a warning on the entry screen. An example of the Concept Page for a Topic that includes sound, showing the sound playback controls (immediately below the play mode buttons), is shown in the screenshot below:

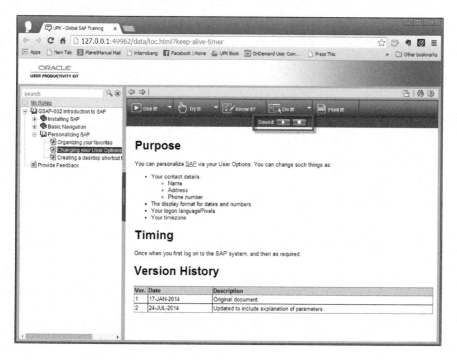

Summary

UPK allows you to include sound in your Topics and Web Pages so that this sound is heard by the user when they play the Topic or display the Web Page. Sound files can be recorded during Topic recording, recorded from within the *Topic Editor*, or recorded outside of UPK and then imported into UPK.

Although providing sound may initially seem like a good idea, doing it effectively is timely, costly, and sometimes difficult to achieve. It also makes maintenance much more difficult as you will need to re-record the sound (and ideally using the same 'voice talent') if anything changes. You should therefore be absolutely sure that a genuine requirement exists for sound before including it in your Topics.

12
Testing Your Users

So far in this book we have created our training material, and published it out to a Player that our users can access to carry out the training simulations. We have also created a number of documents to which they can refer. In this chapter, we will look at ways of confirming that our users have actually learned what we intended them to.

In this chapter, you will learn:

- How to create Questions

- How to create Assessments

- How to use *Know It?* mode in Assessments

- How to verify Assessment coverage for a Module or Section

Why use Questions?

Given that UPK utilizes *Know It?* mode to 'test' users, one could reasonably wonder why Oracle thought it necessary to add Questions and Assessments to UPK. The simple answer is that sometimes it is necessary to test the *theory* or *concepts* behind the activities that are captured in the Topics—to test beyond the mechanics of keystrokes and mouse-clicks.

✚ Questions and Assessments were introduced in UPK 11.0.

This becomes even more pertinent if you are choosing to use UPK as a complete *training library* – regardless of whether or not you are using UPK's Knowledge Center. There may be some courses that do not include simulations—perhaps introductory or conceptual courses. If you want to test our users' understanding of the content of these presentations, you cannot use *Know It?* mode; you need something else. Questions and Assessments fulfill this need.

Types of questions available

In common with many 'assessment-creation' applications and Learning Management Systems, UPK allows you to create several different types of questions. The question types supported by UPK are as follows:

- **Fill-in**: The user is required to enter a specific value into an input field. It is possible to define multiple 'correct' answers (for example, to cater for abbreviations, alternative terms, and so on).

- **Hotspot**: The user is required to identify an area of an image. This type of question is useful for having the user identify a specific object or information on a screen.

- **Multiple Choice (Single Answer)**: The user is required to pick the correct (one) answer from a list of possible answers.

- **Multiple Choice (Many Answers)**: The user is required to pick the correct combination of options from the list provided. Typically, this is used for 'all that apply' questions.

- **True/False**: The user is required to state whether a given statement is true or false.

- **User-Defined**: This type of question can be used to include a question that has been created outside of UPK.

We will look at examples of each of these question types, in the following sections.

Question-specific Properties

There are a few Properties that are unique to Questions (regardless of the type of Question). These are shown in the table below:

Property	Description
Associated Content	This property can be used to associate this Question with the content object to which it relates (that is, the learning activity that the Question is testing). You can associate a Question with a single Module, Section, or Topic. This association can then be used to check how much of a Module or Section is being assessed by your Assessments, Questions, and *Know It?* mode Topics. See the section *Checking Assessment coverage* on page 492. In addition, the user may have the opportunity to display this associated content after answering the question (depending on the **Remediation** setting).

Property	Description
Remediation	This property specifies the level of feedback that the user receives after answering the Question. This is one of:

- **Results only**: The user sees only the text "**Correct**" or "**Incorrect**".

- **User Asks**: The user sees the text "**Correct**" or "**Incorrect**", but this text is a hyperlink that the user can click on to see the correct answer along with any remediation text specified for the Question.

- **Incorrect**: If the user specifies the correct answer, they see the text "**Correct**" (not hyperlinked). If they specify the incorrect answer, then the correct answer is displayed, along with any remediation text specified for the Question.

- **Always**: The user sees the text "**Correct**" or "**Incorrect**", along with the correct answer and any remediation text specified for the Question.

- There is also a **Remediation** property for Assessments. The Assessment-level property takes precedence, and will be applied to all Questions within the Assessment. This means that the Question-level setting will only be used when the Question is used in-line in an Outline Element, and not when it is used within an Assessment.

Creating a Question

Questions are types of *content object* and, in common with all content objects, they can be created and stored in any folder in the Library. You may choose to store Questions with the content to which they apply, or you may choose to create a 'Question bank' folder that contains all of your Questions.

For the sample course that we have been working on throughout this book, we will create our Questions within the same folder structure as our course, but we will create a new sub-folder called **04 Knowledge Verification**, to keep things organized.

To create a Question, carry out the steps shown below:

1. On the *Library* screen, navigate to the folder within which you want to store the Question. As with all content objects, this does not necessarily have to correlate to the position within the Player in which this Question will appear.

2. On the *Library Toolbar*, click on the **Create New Question** button (![button]) (or select menu path **File | Create | Question**), and then to display the drop-down of possible question types, and then click on the required type of Question.

3. The *Question Editor* is displayed, along with the *Question Editor Toolbar* (this toolbar is explained below). The contents of the *Question*

Editor screen itself will vary depending on the type of Question being created. Refer to the relevant section below for specific instructions.

4. Make sure that the *Properties* pane is displayed (select menu option **View | Panes | Properties** if it is not), and then specify any required Question-related information (see *Question-specific Properties* on page 462):

5. In the lower section of the Question definition screen, click on **Click to add remediation text**, and enter any explanation that you want to provide in order to explain why the correct answer is correct.

● Whether or not this text is displayed depends upon the **Remediation** property of the Assessment or (if not specified at the Assessment level) of the Question.

6. Once you have entered all required information, click on the **Save** button (🖫).

7. When prompted, enter a suitable name for your Question. Your Question name does not have to be the same as the Question text, but you should choose your Question name carefully – although the name of the Question file will not be visible to the user in the Player, it will be used in the Outline if the Question is inserted into the Outline as an **In-line Question**, and it will also be visible in the Training Guide document and the Instructor Guide document.

8. Close the *Question Editor*, to return to the *Library* screen.

The Question Editor Toolbar

The *Question Editor Toolbar* is displayed as soon as you open the *Question Editor*. The table below explains all of the buttons that may appear on this Toolbar. Note that not all buttons will be available for all Question types.

Button	Name	Description
	Add Option	Add an answer option below the currently-selected option (or at the bottom of the list if an option is not currently selected).
	Delete Option	Remove the selected answer option.
	Move Up / Move down	Re-order the answer options within a Question.
	Update Image	Insert an image into the Question. Note that you can include an image in any type of Question.
	Delete Image	Remove an image that you have previously inserted (select the image first).
	Reset Layout	Return all elements within the Question Editor window to their original location.

Button	Name	Description
  	Edit / Preview	Toggle the Question area between edit mode (which allows you to create or change the Question) and preview mode (which allows you to attempt the Question)

Specifying a Fill in Question

Fill-in Questions require the user to enter a specific value into an input field.

Assuming that you have already opened the *Question Editor* for a **Fill-in** Question as described above, specify the required information for this Question type by following the steps shown below. An example of a Fill-in Question is given below these steps.

1. Under **Question**, click the text **Click to add question text**, and enter your question.

2. Under **Response**, enter the correct answer in the input field. Note that, unlike some quiz creation systems, you cannot enter multiple valid responses (for example, to cater for punctuation differences or abbreviations). In our example (see below), the user must enter "ECC 6.0" – they cannot enter "ECC 6" or "6.0".

The following screenshot shows an example of a completed Fill-in Question.

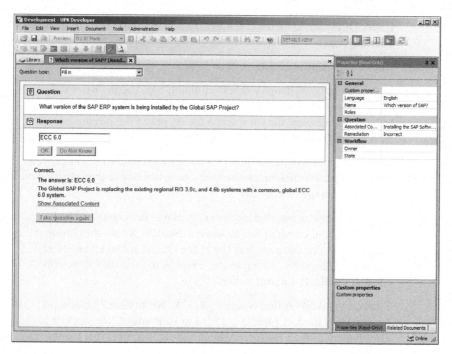

Note that the **Show Associated Content** link is displayed because we have specified **Associated Content** in the Question **Properties**. If the user clicks on this link, the associated content (in this example, the Module **Installing SAP**) will be displayed in a new window.

Specifying a Hotspot Question

Hotspot Questions require the user to identify the correct area on an image. This type of Question is useful for requiring the user to identify specific information on a screen or in a photograph.

You must have already loaded the image into a Package within UPK, so that you can select it when editing the Question. Refer to *Creating a Package* on page 389 for details of bow to do this.

Unlike 'hotspot-type' Questions in some quiz creation applications, the UPK Hotspot Question does not require the user to click on the correct area of an image (which would be similar to mouse-click actions in *Know It?* mode). Instead, the user is required to select the identifying number of the correct hotspot from several numbered hotspots identified on the image.

Assuming that you have already opened the *Question Editor* for a **Hotspot** Question as described above, specify the required information for this question type by following the steps shown below. An example of a completed Hotspot Question is given below these steps.

1. Under **Question**, click the text **Click to add question text**, and enter your question.

2. Click on the **Update Image** button (🖼).

3. In the *Background Image Properties* dialog box, use the **Browse** button to navigate to the Package that contains the image that you want to use, and select the image file (or select a file on your PC). If required, enter an **Alternative text**, and then click on **OK**.

   If you subsequently decide that you do not want to use the image, you can remove it by clicking on the image to select it, and then clicking on the **Delete Image** button (🖼).

4. The image will be inserted immediately above the Question block. If required, you can drag this to another position within the *Question Editor* pane. You can also drag the entire Question block to another position, if necessary. To return these blocks to their default position, click on the **Reset Layout** button (📋).

5. Click on the **Add Option** button (🖼). A 'hotspot area' (similar to Action Areas used in Topics) is added to your image. The hotspot is identified by a small number in the lower-right corner. This number is selected by the user to answer the question. Drag the hotspot area to the

■ You can actually add an image to any of the six built-in question types, although the Hotspot Question is the only type of question where an image is required.

● You can only insert one image into a Question. If you want the user to choose between several images you must first combine them into a single image via an image-editing application, and then inset this one, consolidated image.

correct location on the image. You can also resize the hotspot area by dragging the area's handles, if necessary.

Repeat this step to add more hotspot areas to the image. You need to identify multiple hotspot areas, as the user will be required to identify the 'correct' hotspot from all of the available hotspots. Note that these hotspots are (obviously) visible to the user (unlike Action Areas in *Know It?* mode.)

6. If you want to remove a hotspot area, select it and then click on the **Delete Option** button ( ).

7. In the **Response** area, select the number of the hotspot area that represents the correct answer, in the drop-down field.

The following screenshot shows an example of a complete Hotspot Question:

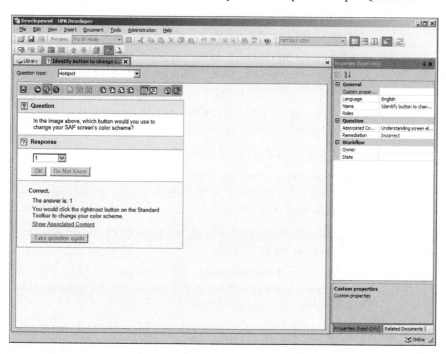

Specifying a Matching Question

With a **Matching** Question, the user is presented with two sets of information, and must match each item in one set with an item in the other set. Note that these are not necessarily 'pairs' – you can have more terms in one set than the other. This type of Question is well suited to term/definition matching or categorization. In the instructions below, we use a term/definition Question, simply to differentiate between 'set one' and 'set two'.

■ You can also use Matching Questions to provide 'ordering' activities (by specifying the activities in one set and the step numbers in the other.

Assuming that you have already opened the *Question Editor* for a Matching Question, as described above, specify the required information for this question type by following the steps shown below. An example of a Matching Question is given below the steps.

1. Under **Question**, click the text **Click to add question text**, and enter your question. It is important that you describe exactly how the user expected to answer the question. The user can either enter the number of the term in the rightmost list in the input field for the corresponding item on the left, or they can drag the 'definition' onto the 'term', so you may want to explain this. If you have a different number of terms than definitions (or vice versa), or items are repeated or not used, then you may also want to mention this.

2. Specify the first set of text values, as follows:

   i. Under **Response**, click on the <u>leftmost</u> text **Click to add choice text**, and enter the first 'term'.

   ii. Click on the **Add Option** button (🖳) (you can also press *ENTER*, if your cursor is still in the 'term' field from Step i). An additional row is added to the leftmost column.

   iii. Click on the newly-added text **Click to add choice text**, and enter the *next* 'term'

   iv. Repeat Steps ii and iii to add as many 'terms' as necessary.

3. Specify the second set of values, as follows. Make sure that you do not enter these in the 'correct' order for the terms, as they will be displayed in the order that you enter them.

   i. Under **Response**, click on the <u>rightmost</u> text **Click to add choice text**, and enter the first 'definition'.

   ii. Click on the **Add Option** button (🖳) (you can also press *ENTER*, if your cursor is still in the 'term' field from Step i). An additional row is added to the rightmost column.

   iii. Click on the newly-added text **Click to add choice text**, and enter the next 'definition'

   iv. Repeat Steps ii and iii to add as many 'definitions' as necessary. Again, you do not need to have the same number of terms as definitions.

4. Match the terms to the definitions, as follows:

   i. In the input field to the left of each 'term', enter the number of the 'definition' in the rightmost column that matches this term.

The following screenshot shows an example of a completed **Matching** Question:

■ If you want to remove an option after you have entered it (in either column) you can do so by clicking in the option text, and then clicking on the **Delete Option** button.

■ You can use the **Move Up** button and the **Move Down** button to re-order the 'terms' and/or 'definitions', if necessary.

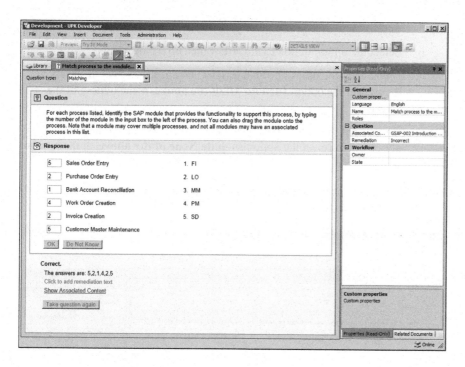

Note that in this example, we have more 'terms' than 'definitions', some 'definitions' have multiple 'terms', and not all 'definitions' are used.

Specifying a Multiple Choice (Single Answer) Question

With a **Multiple Choice (Single Answer)** Question, the user is presented with a list of possible answers, and has to select the one correct answer from this list.

Assuming that you have already opened the *Question Editor* for a Multiple Choice (Single Answer) Question, as described above, specify the required information for this question type by following the steps shown below. An example of a Multiple Choice (Single Answer) Question is given below these steps.

1. Under **Question**, click the text **Click to add question text**, and enter your question.

2. Under **Response**, click the text **Click to add choice text**, and enter your first answer option.

3. Click on the **Add Option** button (🖳) (you can also press *ENTER*, if your cursor is still in the 'term' field from Step 2). A new 'choice' line is added to the Response area.

4. Enter your next answer option in the new 'choice' line.

■ With a The Multiple Choice (Single Answer) Question, the answers are listed with option buttons (so that only one is selectable). With Multiple Choice (Multiple Answer) Questions the answers are listed with check-boxes. If you want to make this more challenging for your users, use only Multiple Choice (Multiple Answer) Questions—even when there is only one correct answer.

■ If you want to remove an option after you have entered it, you can do so by clicking in the option text, and then clicking on the **Delete Option** button.

■ You can use the **Move Up** button and the **Move Down** button to re-order the answer options, if necessary.

5. Repeat Steps 3 and 4 for all required answer options.

6. Select the option button to the left of the correct answer.

7. If you want the user to be able to select an answer of "All of the above", then select the option **Include All of the above**, at the bottom of the screen.

8. If you want the user to be able to select an answer of "None of the above", then select the option **Include None of the above**, at the bottom of the screen.

The following screenshot shows an example of a completed Multiple Choice (Single Answer) Question:

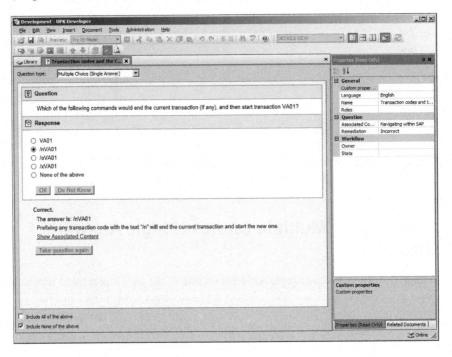

Note that in this example we have also included the **None of the above** option.

Specifying a Multiple Choice (Many Answers) Question

With a **Multiple Choice (Many Answers)** Question, the user is presented with a list of possible answers, and has to select all of the answers that apply from this list.

Assuming that you have already opened the *Question Editor* for a Multiple Choice (Many Answers) Question, as described above, specify the required information for this question type by following the steps shown below. An example of a Multiple Choice (Many Answers) Question is given below these steps.

1. Under **Question**, click the text **Click to add question text**, and enter your question.

2. Under **Response**, click the text **Click to add choice text**, and enter your first answer option.

3. Click on the **Add Option** button (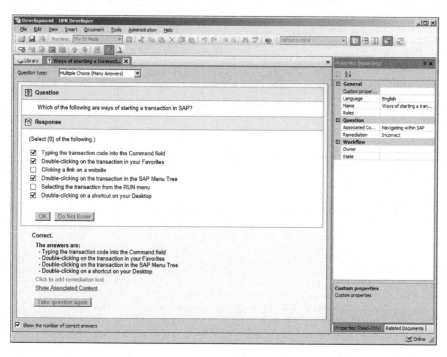) (you can also press *ENTER*, if your cursor is still in the 'term' field from Step 2). A new 'choice' line is added to the **Response** area.

4. Enter your next answer option in the new 'choice' line.

5. Repeat Steps 3 and 4 for all required answer options.

6. Select the check-box to the left of all of the correct answers.

7. If you want to tell the user exactly how many of the answer options should be selected, then select the option **Show the number of correct answers**, at the bottom of the screen (in which case you do not need to explain this in the question text).

■ If you want to remove an option after you have entered it, you can do so by clicking in the option text, and then clicking on the **Delete Option** button.

■ You can use the **Move Up** button and the **Move Down** button to re-order the answer options, if necessary.

The following screenshot shows an example of a completed Multiple Choice (Many Answers) Question:

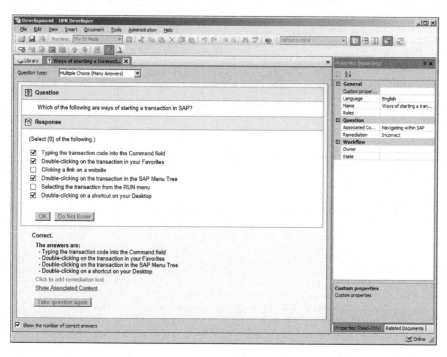

Note that in this example, we have selected the **Show the number of correct answers** option, which results in the text "**(Select x of the following.)**" being displayed above the response options. If this option is not selected, the text "**(Select all that apply)**" is displayed, instead.

Specifying a True/False Question

With a **True/False** Question, the user is shown a statement and then has to choose whether this statement is true or false.

Assuming that you have already opened the *Question Editor* for a True/False Question, as described above, specify the required information for this question type by following the steps shown below. An example of a True/False Question is given below these steps.

1. Under **Question**, click the text **Click to add question text**, and enter your question (the statement that the user has to judge as being true or false).

2. Under **Response**, select either **True** or **False**, as the correct answer.

The following screenshot shows an example of a completed Multiple Choice (Many Answers) Question:

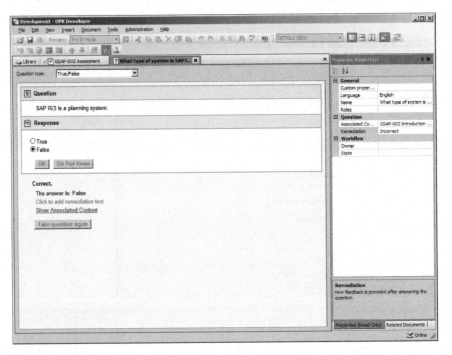

Specifying a User-Defined Question

The **User-Defined** Question type allows you to include a question developed externally to UPK. This may have been created in another application, or hand-coded, but must contain the necessary JavaScript to communicate the user's score back to UPK.

Assuming that you have already opened the *Question Editor* for a Multiple Choice (Many Answers) Question as described above, specify the required information for this question type by following the steps shown below. An example of (the preview of) a User-Defined Question is shown below the steps.

1. Create a new Package in your Library. Although you can store this Package anywhere, and name it what you want, it is recommended that you save it in the same folder as the content to which it relates (or the Assessment, if it will be included in an Assessment). You may also want to give it the same name as your UPK Question (possibly appended with "**_Question**") to make it easier to locate.

2. Copy the external file(s) containing your question into the Package, and save it. It does not matter what this file is called.

3. In the **Question Editor**, click on the **Update Link** button ( ).

4. In the **Insert Hyperlink** dialog box, click on the **Document in Library** button, and then navigate to and select the question launch file in the Package that you created earlier.

5. Click on **OK**. The question is displayed in the *Question Editor*.

The following screenshot shows an example of a User-Defined Question. Note that in reality this question could be implemented as a standard True/False Question (or a Multiple Choice (Single Answer) Question). This question has been created as a User-Defined Question purely for the purpose of illustrating the functionality through a simple example.

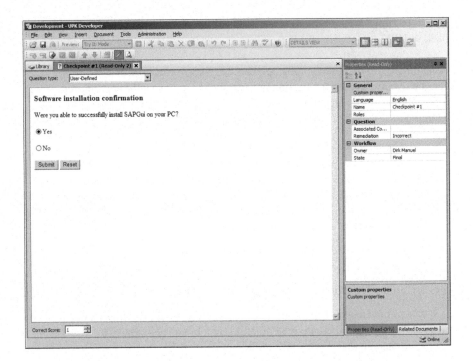

Note that with User-Defined Questions, there is no remediation text, and no **Show Associated Content** link (even if the **Associated Content** Property has been specified). If you want to provide these things, they must be included in the source file.

If you have downloaded the sample code for this book, then you can find a working User-Defined Question as question *Checkpoint #1*.

Including your Questions in an Outline

There are two ways in which Questions can be included in an Outline (so that they can be selected and answered by users). These are:

- As in-line Questions
- As part of an Assessment

In-line Questions are inserted directly into the Outline, and appear alongside the Topics (assuming that you also have Topics in your Outline…). The user clicks on the Question in the Outline, and the question text is displayed in the *Concept* pane in the Player, and can be answered within that pane. In-line Questions are useful for checking understanding before moving on to the next Topic, but this approach does assume that the user will take a linear path through the contents of the Section or Module.

An **Assessment** is a collection of Questions, and is comparable to a longer test. The user clicks on the Assessment in the Outline (which is not expandable to see the Questions), and the Questions are displayed, one after the other, in the Concept pane. Once the user has progressed through all of the Questions, their *overall* score is displayed.

Note that it is helpful if you know in which way you will use the Questions before you create them, as your choice can affect the naming of the Question object in UPK (which is not the same as the question text itself).

Both ways of using Questions are explained more fully in their own sections, below.

Using in-line Questions

If you want to insert a Question into an Outline as an in-line Question, you have two possibilities: you can either create the Question from the *Library* screen and then insert it into the Outline, or you can insert a blank Question into the Outline (just as you would an empty Topic), and then edit the Question.

Inserting an existing Question into an Outline

To insert an existing Question into an Outline Element, carry out the following steps:

1. Open the Module or Section in the *Outline Editor*, and make sure it is checked out (in a client/server implementation).

2. Select the element below which you want to insert the Question. Note that if you select a Module or Section, the Question will be inserted as the last element in the Module or Section. If you select a Topic, then the Question will be inserted immediately below that Topic.

3. Select menu path **Insert > Existing Document**. The standard *Link Existing Document* dialog box is displayed.

4. Make sure that the **Type** field at the bottom of the dialog box specifies **All valid types** or **Questions**.

5. Navigate to the folder containing your Question, and select the Question content object.

6. Click on the **Link** button. The Question is inserted into the Outline.

7. If you have finished changing the Module or Section, check it in and then close the *Outline Editor*

● As with all content objects, you can also drag-and-drop a Question into the Outline in split-screen mode, or copy the Question from the *Library* screen and then paste it into the Outline.

The following screenshot shows an example of an in-line Question, as it appears in the *Outline Editor*.

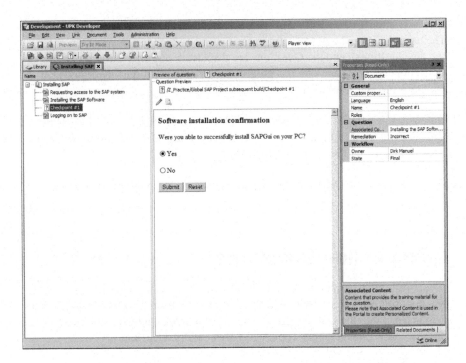

Note that in this example we have used the User-Defined Question created earlier in this section. Also note that we have chosen to call the Question **Checkpoint #1**, even though the actual question text is "Were you able to successfully install SAPGui on your PC?" (or "Software installation confirmation", depending on how you look at it).

Creating a new Question in an Outline

To create a new Question within an existing Outline, carry out the following steps:

1. Open the Module or Section in the *Outline Editor*, and make sure it is checked out (in a client/server implementation).

2. Select the element below which you want to insert the Question. Note that if you select a Module or Section, the Question will be inserted as the last element in the Module or Section. If you select a Topic, then the Question will be inserted immediately below that Topic.

3. Click on the **Link New Question** button ([?▾]) and select the required question type from the button's drop-down menu (or select menu option **Link | New Question | <Question Type>**). You are passed into the *Question Editor*.

4. Specify the Question's details as described earlier in this chapter.

5. Save your Question and close the *Question Editor* to return to the *Outline Editor*.

6. Check in the Outline Element (if applicable) and close the *Outline Editor*.

Creating an Assessment

An Assessment is a collection of Questions—and possibly Topics, as we shall see later in this section. You can either create the Questions first and then insert them into the Assessment, or you can create the Assessment and then create the Questions within that.

To create a new Assessment into which you can insert your (new or existing) Questions, carry out the following steps:

1. Navigate to the folder in which you want to store your Assessment.

2. On the *Library Toolbar*, click on the **Create New Assessment** button (⊡) (or you can select menu option **File | New | Assessment**). You are passed into the *Assessment Editor*.

3. Specify any required Properties, as explained under *Specifying Assessment Properties* on page 477.

4. Include your Questions as described in *Inserting an Existing Question*, or *Inserting a new Question*, below. Note that you will need to make use of the *Assessment Editor Toolbar*, which is described in *The Assessment Editor Toolbar on page 480*.

5. Once you have finished editing your Assessment, save it, and then close the *Assessment Editor*.

The above steps apply to the creation of an Assessment within the Library. It is also possible to create an Assessment directly from within a Module or Section via menu option **Link | New Assessment**.

Specifying Assessment Properties

Like all content objects, Assessments have a set of Properties that you can specify. Some of these are common to all content objects (those Properties in the **General** and **Workflow** categories), but some are specific to Assessments (those Properties in the **Assessment** category). These Assessment-specific Properties are explained in the table below.

Property	Description
Answer order	If you want the answers within each Question to be displayed in the order in which they are defined in the Question itself, then select **As authored**. If you want the answers to be shuffled each time the Question is displayed, then select **Random order**. Choosing **Random order** is useful if you think there is a risk that users will simply remember the position of the correct answer within a Question, from one attempt to the next.
Question order	If you want the Questions within the Assessment to be presented to users in the order in which they appear within the Assessment, then select **As authored**. If you want the Questions to be shuffled each time the Assessment is launched, then select **Random order**.
Question Limit	This Property can be used to require the user to answer a specific number of Questions, chosen at random from the Questions available in the Assessment, at the time the Assessment is launched by the user. Enter the number of Questions that the user will be required to answer. If you do not enter a value in this field, then the user will be required to answer all Questions in the Assessment. This feature is extremely useful for providing a more random assessment (effectively, selecting Questions from a 'Question bank'), but if you are using the Assessment for Knowledge Verification you should ensure that the learning objectives are still being effectively measured.
Passing Score	Specify the percentage score that the user must achieve in order to pass the Assessment. This defaults to 100%. Note that this is the overall pass mark for the Assessment (based on the number of Questions answered correctly versus the total number of Questions and does not affect any *Know It?* mode passing score specification for any Topics included in the Assessment.

✦ The **Question Limit** property was introduced in UPK 12.1.0.1 (this is ESP 1 for UPK 12.1).

● A Topic is considered to be a single question; there is no 'weighting'.

Property	Description
Remediation	This property specifies the level of feedback that the user receives after answering a Question. This is one of: • **Results only**: The user sees only the text "**Correct**" or "**Incorrect**". • **User Asks**: The user sees the text "**Correct**" or "**Incorrect**", but this text is a hyperlink that the user can click on to see the correct answer and/or any remediation text specified for the Question. • **Incorrect**: If the user specifies the correct answer, they see the text "**Correct**" (not hyperlinked). If they specify the incorrect answer, then the correct answer is displayed, along with any remediation text specified for the Question. • **Always**: The user sees the text "**Correct**" or "**Incorrect**", along with the correct answer and any remediation text specified for the Question. • **None**: No feedback is displayed at all, regardless of whether the user gets the question right or wrong - only the **Continue** button is displayed when they answer.
Show Associated Content	If this Property is set to **Yes**, then if a user answers a Question incorrectly a link (named **Show Associated Content**) is provided in the feedback to allow the user to launch the content object to which this Question has been associated (via the Question's **Associated Content** Property). If this value is set to **No** then no link is provided, and (obviously) if there is no associated content defined for the question, then no link is provided.
Summary	If you want to display details of the user's score – including whether each Question was answered correctly or incorrectly, and their final score – then select **Show Summary**. Otherwise, select **Hide Summary**, and the user will only see a message informing them that they have completed the Assessment.

● There is also a **Remediation** property for Assessments. The Assessment-level property takes precedence, and will be applied to all Questions within the Assessment.

✦ The **Remediation** level of **None** is new in UPK 12.1. It only appears on the Assessment-level **Remediation** property, and not the Question-level **Remediation** property.

You specify values for these Properties, as for all other Properties, in the *Properties* pane. Note that in a client/server environment, the Assessment must be checked out in order to change these Properties.

The Assessment Editor Toolbar

The *Assessment Editor Toolbar* is displayed automatically when you open an Assessment for editing. The following table describes the buttons that are available on this toolbar:

Button	Name	Description
[?]▼	**Link New Question**	Add a new Question to your Assessment.
⇔	**Link Existing Question**	Link an existing Question into your Assessment.
⚡	**Delete Link**	Remove a Question from your Assessment. Note that this will not delete the Question object – it will simply delete the link to the Question from this Assessment
⬆ ⬇	**Move Up / Move down**	Move the selected Question up or down within the Assessment.

Inserting an existing Question

● As with all content objects, you can also drag-and-drop a Question onto the Assessment in split-screen mode, or copy the Question in the Library and then paste it into the Assessment.

To insert an existing Question into your Assessment, carry out the following steps:

1. In the *Assessment Editor*, either click on the Assessment itself to insert your Question at the end of the Assessment, or click on an existing Question (to insert your Question immediately below the selected Question.

2. Click on the **Link Existing Question** button (⇔). The *Link Existing Question* dialog box is displayed.

3. Navigate to the folder containing the Question that you want to include in this Assessment, and click on it to select it.

4. Click on **Open** in the *Link Existing Question* dialog box. The Question is inserted into the Assessment.

Inserting a new Question

To insert a new Question into your Assessment, carry out the following steps:

1. In the *Assessment Editor*, click on the **New Question** button ([?]▼), and then select the required type of Question from the button's drop-down menu. The standard *Save As* dialog box is displayed.

Note:

This will insert the new Question below any existing Questions in the Assessment (assuming that there are some). If you want to insert your new Question into the middle of an existing set of Questions, first select the Question that you want the new Question to appear below.

2. In the *Save As* dialog box, navigate to and select the folder into which you want to save your new Question.

3. Enter a name for your new Question, and then click on **Save**. The Question is inserted into the Assessment.

4. Assuming that you are ready to define your new Question, double-click on the Question in the Assessment. The Question is opened in the *Question Editor*.

5. Define the Question as described *Creating a Question* on page 463.

6. Once you have finished editing the Question, close the *Question Editor*. You are returned to the *Assessment Editor*.

7. Insert additional Questions by repeating Steps 1 to 6.

8. Once you have added all required Questions, save your Assessment, and then close the *Assessment Editor*.

Using Topics in an Assessment

In addition to including Questions in an Assessment, you can also include Topics. An Assessment can contain a mixture of Questions and Topics, only Questions, or even only Topics. If you include a Topic in an Assessment, then only *Know It!* mode will be available for the Topic (when the Topic accessed from within the Assessment) – regardless of the actual Topic's settings.

● Even if *Know It?* mode is explicitly disabled for a Topic, it will be enabled if the Topic is used in an Assessment—and only when the Topic is launched from within the Assessment; the modes available for the same Topic in the Player will be unchanged..

Why would you want to include Topics in an Assessment, given that *Know It?* mode can be made available for any Topic in the Outline, anyway? Well, the advantage of housing your 'test' Topics in an Assessment is that it provides the users with a clearer and more logical indication that they will be assessed against these Topics.

Suppose you have some 'non-transactional' (that is, non-Topic-related) elements in your Training and therefore have created Questions to test this knowledge, but you also want to test the user's transactional knowledge by requiring that they carry out a selection of your Topics in *Know It?* mode. If the Assessment contains only Questions, you will need to instruct your users to answer the Questions in the Assessment, and then go back and carry out one or more identified Topics in *Know It?* mode. Grouping the *Know It?* mode Topics and the Questions together into a single 'container' (the Assessment) provides a nice, self-contained test.

Even if you will not use Questions for knowledge verification, and will only be using Know It! mode topics, there are good reasons for using an Assessment to house them. Consider the following scenarios:

- You only want to test your users' ability to carry out certain activities (for example, key ones that they absolutely must be able to perform on day one of system availability), and so want to enable *Know It?* mode only for these selected Topics.

- You want to make *Know It?* mode available for all of your Topics, so that users can 'self-test' their knowledge (unlikely though it sounds, I have seen this happen on multiple occasions), but you only want to use selected Topics for 'knowledge verification'.

- You have Topics that you are only providing in *Know It?* mode. This is a useful tactic when you want to provide a more realistic 'blind test' that the users have not had the chance to practice to their heart's content in *Try It!* mode first.

In each of these cases, grouping the *Know It?* mode Topics into a separate 'container' makes the whole test more logical to the users.

This becomes even more important if you are loading your UPK content into a Learning Management System. If you only want to use selected Topics in an Outline for knowledge verification purposes, you *could* simply activate *Know It?* mode only for these Topics and not for the others in the same Outline, but then, if you loaded that Outline into an LMS as a lesson, the user would be required to carry out all of the 'non-*Know It?* mode Topics – in (for example) *Try It!* mode – before this lesson is considered 'complete'. In addition, with this approach you would need to have some way of indicating to the user which simulations must be carried out in *Know It?* mode (and it is unwise to assume that they will infer this from the mode buttons available in the Player).

Don't forget that it is possible to include a Topic within a single Outline multiple times. You can include a Topic in the main Outline, and also include it within an Assessment under that main Outline. In previous versions of UPK, you could have just used a separate Module or Section called "Assessment" and re-linked the required Topics into that, but the play modes are defined at the Topic level, so if you enable *Know It?* mode for a Topic for its inclusion in an Outline Element used as an Assessment, *Know It?* mode would also be enabled wherever else the Topic appears in the 'main' Outline – which could be confusing to users. The advantage of using Assessments is that you can disable *Know It?* mode for a Topic, so that this mode will not be available in the 'main' Outline, but as soon as you include that Topic in an Assessment, *Know It?* mode is automatically enabled – and only when the Topic is accessed from within the Assessment.

There is another interesting side-effect of using Topics in Assessments – the Topics included in the Assessment are not listed under the Assessment in the Outline. This means that the user has no idea of which Topics are included in the Assessment (or even whether it is Topics that they have seen before in other modes elsewhere in the Outline) until they start the Assessment. This could be a good thing or a bad thing, depending upon how you look at it, and how 'strict' you want to be in the testing of your users.

Caution is advised if you are including Questions and Topics in the same single Assessment – especially if you are interspersing your Topics amongst the Questions. Because there is no indication of when (or even if) a Topic will be launched, users can be caught entirely unawares. In our example Assessment shown below, as soon as the user completes Question 4, the Topic *Logging on to SAP* will be launched in *Know It?* mode, seemingly *without warning*. Furthermore, if you have multiple Topics in succession in your Assessment, the user will be passed from one to the next, without a pause. If you have ten Topics and have not warned the user that this will happen, the user is likely to become very frustrated, wondering when it will ever end. It is therefore suggested that you specify the number of questions and Topics that are included in the Assessment— and possibly an indication of how long the Assessment should take to complete— in the Concept Page for the Assessment content object.

+ The ability to attach a Concept Page to an Assessment was introduced in UPK 12.1.

It is also important to note that every 'question' in an Assessment is given equal weighting - regardless of whether this is a Question or a Topic. So if your Assessment contains nine Questions and one Topic, each of these will be worth 10% of the final grade. If your Questions are simple True/False questions, and your Topic is 100 Actions long, this may be a little unrealistic.

LMS considerations

When you load a published Package into a Learning Management System (LMS), the user will be required to complete *all* of the content in that Package before the Package (a **Learning Activity** in the LMS) is considered complete. If you have a Package that contains both 'regular' (not *Know It?* mode) Topics and an Assessment, then the user will need to complete *both* (the Topics and the Assessment) before any of it is marked as complete.

However, you may not want a user's execution of possibly dozens of simulations in *Try It!* mode to factor into their overall 'test score', which you want to be based purely on the Assessment. Or perhaps you want to benignly track users' review of the training material (including *Try It!* mode executions) separately from formally tracking their Assessment results. In these cases, you effectively have two options:

- Publish the Assessment to a separate Player and load that into the LMS as a separate Lrearning Activity. To do this, you need to include the Assessment in its own Module or Section, so that you have something to publish (remember, you can only publish an Outline Element, from within the *Outline Editor*.

- Tell the LMS that the Assessment should be tracked separately from the rest of the Outline, even though everything is included in a single Learning Activity. To do this you need to place the Assessment into its own Module or Section within the main 'learning object' Outline, and then set the **Group for LMS** property for that Module or Section to **Yes** in the Module or Section's Properties.

Note that in both of these cases you need to include the Assessment in an Outline Element. When we include our sample Assessment into our course outline, below, we will use this approach.

There are a lot more considerations for the use of UPK Assessments, and the use of UPK in general, when using a Learning Management System, than the very brief points made here. However, this is best left to another book, where these considerations can be given the full attention they deserve.

Including a Topic in an Assessment

To include a Topic in an Assessment, carry out the following steps:

1. Open the Assessment in the *Assessment Editor*.

2. If the Assessment already contains Questions or Topics, click on the existing Question or Topic below which you want this Topic to appear, to select it.

3. Click on the **Link Existing Question** button (🔗). (Don't worry that this says "...Question".)

4. In the *Link Existing Question* dialog box, make sure that the **Type** selection field at the bottom of the dialog box specifies either **Questions and Topics** or **Topics**.

5. Navigate to and select the Topic that you want to include in the Assessment.

6. Click on the **Open** button to close the *Link Existing Question* dialog box and return to the *Assessment Editor*.

A sample Assessment

The screenshot below shows an example of an Assessment, which has been built to test users who take our sample course *GSAP-002 Introduction to SAP*.

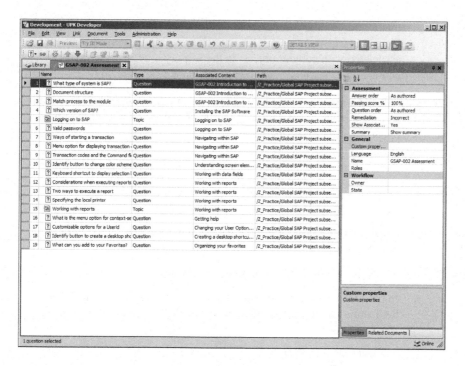

In this example, there are 19 'Assessment objects': 17 Questions and 2 Topics. These are distinguishable both by the icon to the left of the object **Name**, and by the value in the **Type** column. The **Associated Content** column shows the content object to which each Assessment Object has been associated. The first three of these have been associated with our highest-level course Module and not with a specific Topic. This is because these Questions relate to concepts that are covered in the training presentation that we attached to the Module in *Linking a Package into a content object* on page 392.

Note that we have named our Assessment as **GSAP-002 Assessment** both to make it easier to identify the course to which it relates, and also to provide us with more logical names in our Outline in our next step.

Incorporating your Assessment into an Outline

You can use an Assessment in one of two ways:

- By including it in an Outline Element that contains other content objects. For example, if you have a course that contains one or more lessons, each of which contains one or more Topics, you may want to include an Assessment at the end of the course. When you publish the course, the Assessment will appear as another 'lesson-level component'.

- By including it in its own Outline Element, and publishing that separately. Doing this creates a stand-alone Assessment (in its own Player) that does not directly relate to any other content objects. Note that if you do this, you will not be able to use the **Show Associated Content** property – even if the Questions within the Assessment are associated with content objects in the Library – because these associated content objects are not included in the Player.

Note that an Assessment can only be previewed from the *Outline Editor* (which means that it must be included within an Outline Element). You cannot preview an Assessment from the *Assessment Editor*.

To include an Assessment within an Outline Element, carry out the following steps:

● As with all content objects, you can also drag-and-drop an Assessment onto the Outline Element in split-screen mode, or copy the Assessment in the *Library* screen and then paste it into the Outline Element.

1. Open the Outline Element in the *Outline Editor*.

2. Click on the Outline Element within which you want to include the Assessment.

3. Select menu path **Link | Existing document**.

4. In the *Link Existing Document* dialog box, make sure that the **Type** field at the bottom of the dialog box specifies either **All valid types** or **Assessments**.

5. Navigate to and select the Assessment that you want to include within the Outline Element.

6. Click on the **Open** button to close the *Link Existing Document* dialog box and return to the *Outline Editor*.

7. The Assessment will be inserted as the last element within the Outline Element selected in Step 2. If necessary, you can change its position within the Outline Element by using the **Move Up** button (🔼) and the **Move Down** button (🔽). You can also drag and drop the Assessment into a new position within the Outline Element.

8. Save and close the Outline Element, and then check it in if necessary.

Attaching a Concept Page to your Assessment

✚ The ability to attach a Concept Page to an Assessment is a welcome addition to UPK 12.1. In UPK 11, this is not possible and instead the Assessment needs to be included in its own Outline Element that itself has a Concept Page.

Just like other things that can appear in the Outline (Modules, Sections, and Topics), you can link a Concept Page to an Assessment, so that this appears in the *Concept* pane during Playback. I recommend that every element in the Outline has a Concept Page, and this is especially important for Assessments. Without a Concept Page, your Assessment will appear as follows:

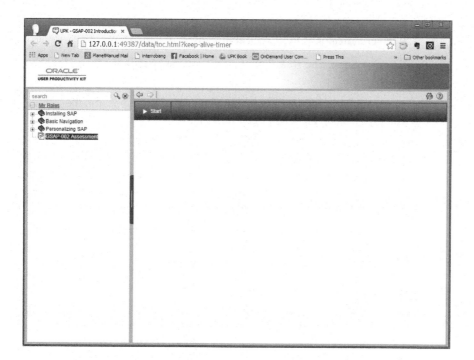

In the example above, you can see that the *Concept* pane just appears as a blank screen with a **Start** button on it. Clearly, here, it is better to provide some information about the Assessment, such as the number of questions, pass mark, and so on. I also like to 'warn' the user if the Assessment contains Topics, so they don't panic and wonder what's going on when they are suddenly launched into *Know It?* mode.

Adding a Concept Page to an Assessment is effectively the same as for adding any other document (refer to *Chapter 9, Adding Value to Your Topics* for instructions on adding Concept Pages):

1. Open the Outline Element that contains the Assessment (the Assessment must be contained in a Module or Section to be previewed or published).

2. Click on the Assessment in the Outline.

3. In the *Concept* pane (which will look slightly different for Assessments - an example of this is shown in the next section), click on the **Create new web page** button (🖼). The *Save As* dialog box is displayed.

4. The **Save in** field defaults to the folder in which the object to which you want to attach the Web Page exists. If necessary, you can navigate to and select another folder (although as explained in *Chapter 3, Working in the UPK Developer Client*, it may be wise to store the Concept Page in the same folder as the content object to which it relates.

5. Enter a name for the Web Page in the **Name** field (again, as explained in *Chapter 3, Working in the UPK Developer Client* it makes sense

> ■ You can also display the *Concept* pane from the Library screen and attach a Concept Page to the Assessment from there, but it is not as convenient to do so.

to use the same name as the content object to which it relates, appended with an indicator as to its use (in this case "**_Concept**")

6. Click on **Save**. The *Web Page Editor* is opened within the Developer screen:

7. You can now enter the information that you want to appear in the *Concept* pane in the *Web Page Editor*. How to do this is explained in *Chapter 9, Adding Value to Your Topics*, section *Using the Web Page Editor*).

8. Once you have entered the required text and formatted it as required, click on the **Save** button (🖫) to save your changes, and then close the *Web Page Editor*. You are returned to the *Outline Editor*.

9. Close the *Outline Editor* (there is no need to save), and then check in the Assessment if necessary.

Previewing an Assessment

As noted above, you can only preview an Assessment from the *Outline Editor*. Once you have included the Assessment in an Outline Element, and have opened that Outline Element in the *Outline Editor*, you can preview the Assessment by clicking on it in the Outline. The Assessment is then displayed in the area of the screen normally reserved for the Concept Pane. An example of this is shown in the following screenshot:

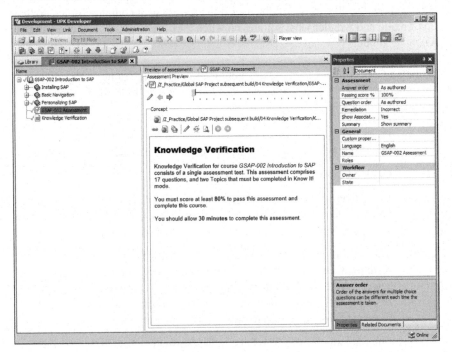

The first thing to notice here is that there is a new area of the screen, called *Assessment Preview*, immediately above the *Concept* pane. This contains a 'slider' control that allows you to navigate between the questions in the Assessment. The slider contains 'tick marks'—one for each Assessment Object in the Assessment (regardless of whether this is a Question or a Topic), and an initial tick for the Concept Page.

You can navigate between questions, as follows:

- Click on the **Next question** button (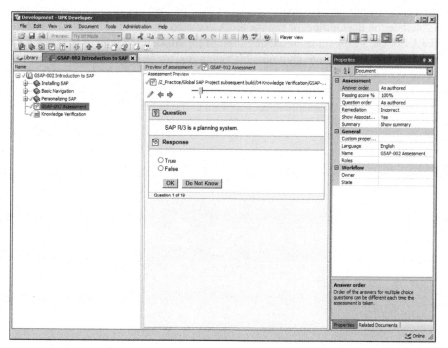) to advance to the next Question, or click on the **Previous question** button ( ) to go back to the previous Question.

- Drag the pointer on the Question slider to another Question.

- Click on the 'tick mark' on the slider for another Question.

When you navigate to an Assessment Object (or the Concept Page) using any of these methods, that Assessment Object (or Concept Page) is shown in the *Concept* area of the screen. the example above shows the Outline Editor when the Concept Page (the first element in the Assessment) is selected. The example below shows the same Assessment when the first Question (the second element) is selected):

■ You can open the Assessment in the *Assessment Editor* by clicking on the **Edit** button in the *Assessment Preview* area (or by double-clicking on the Assessment in the *Outline*).

● You can set the *Properties* pane to show either **Properties** for the Assessment itself, or for the Concept Page assigned to the Assessment. You cannot choose to display the properties for a Question.

The Assessment is functional; you can try any of the Questions (and can attempt a question multiple times without the need to re-start the Assessment), and check that the correct level of remediation is shown. The only thing that doesn't work in the Outline Editor (apart from *Know It?* mode Topics - see below) is the **Show Associated Content** links.

● If you navigate to a *Know It?* mode Topic within the Assessment, the Topic is not displayed in the Assessment Preview pane. Instead, you see only an informational message informing you that the Topic cannot be previewed from within an Assessment.

Publishing an Assessment

Once an Assessment is included in an Outline Element, it can be published as described in *Chapter 6, Publishing Your Content*. However, there is one additional point that is worth noting. If you have set the **Show Associated Content** Property to **Yes**, then UPK will check to see that the Associated Content for every Question (set via the Question's **Associated Content** Property) is also included in the same published Outline. If any of the Questions has Associated Content that is not included in this Outline, then the user will not be able to access the Associated Content, so a warning message is displayed during Publishing, as shown below:

If this error occurs, locate the Question specified in the **Name** field, check its **Associated Content** field, and either make sure that the document specified there is included in the Outline, or change the Associated Content field to dis-associate the Associated Content from the question. More information on how to check for missing associations and other possible errors is provided in *Checking Assessment coverage* on page 492.

An example of our Assessment, as it appears in the published Player, is shown below:

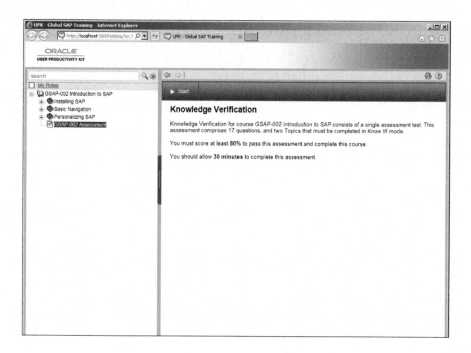

For the sake of completeness, the following screenshot shows how a Question will appear. Note that in this example, we have answered the question incorrectly, in order to show the remediation information.

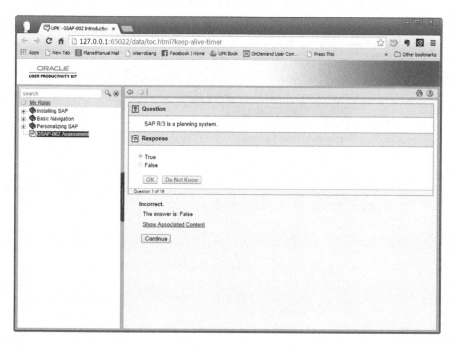

Checking Assessment coverage

● Each Question can only be associated with a single content object (Module, Section, or Topic), but a single content object may have multiple Questions associated with it.

As described in *Creating a Question* above, you can identify the content object to which a Question relates (that is, the content object that teaches the knowledge that the Question is verifying). This is done via the **Associated Content** property of the Question.

If an Assessment is intended to verify retention of the knowledge taught in a course or lesson, it is useful to be able to confirm that the Assessment adequately covers that course or lesson. This is where UPK's *Assessment coverage* view comes in to play.

The *Assessment coverage* view is a selectable view within the *Outline Editor* that checks the displayed Outline Element (Module or Section) against a selected Assessment, and identifies, for each content object (Module, Section, or Topic) in the Outline, the number of items (Questions or Topics) in the Assessment that are associated with each of the objects. This is best explained by way of an example. Let's take the *GSAP-002 Introduction to SAP* course that we have been assembling in this book. We will check this against the *Knowledge Verification* Assessment that we built earlier in this chapter.

To check the Assessment coverage of a Module or Section, carry out the steps shown below:

1. Open the Module or Section in the *Outline Editor*.

2. In the **View** field of the *Outline Editor Toolbar*, select **Assessment coverage view**, as shown below:

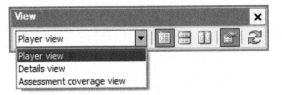

The *Concept* pane is replaced with the *Assessment* pane, and a new column, **Questions**, is shown on the right of the *Navigation* pane, as shown in the sample screenshot below:

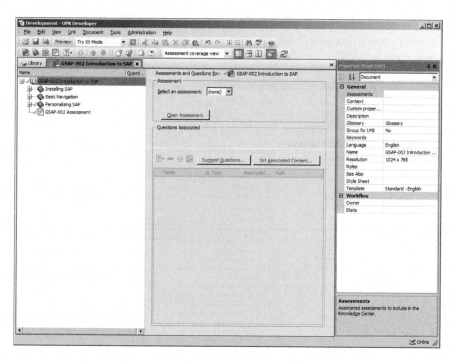

3. In the *Navigation* pane, click on the Module or Section for which you want to assess the coverage. Once you select a Module or Section, its name is shown to the right of the text **Assessments and Questions for:** at the top of the *Assessment* pane.

4. Click on the **Expand All** button (⊞) on the *Standard Toolbar*. This will allow you to check Assessment coverage down to the lowest level of the Outline (typically, the Topic level).

5. Click the drop-down for the **Select an assessment** field.

6. If the Outline Element selected in Step 3 contains one or more Assessments, then these will be listed in the field's drop-down, and you can select the required (or only) Assessment from this list.

   If the Assessment that you want to check against the selected Outline Element is not included in this Outline Element (and is therefore not listed in the **Select an Assessment** field's drop-down), then select it as follows:

   i.   In the **Select an Assessment** field's drop-down list, select **Other**.

   ii. In the *Open Assessment* dialog box, navigate to and select the Assessment that you want to use.

   iii. Click on the **Open** button to close the *Open Assessment* dialog box, and return to the *Outline Editor*.

Once an Assessment has been selected (to verify against the selected Outline Element), the *Assessment Coverage view* appears as shown in the following screenshot:

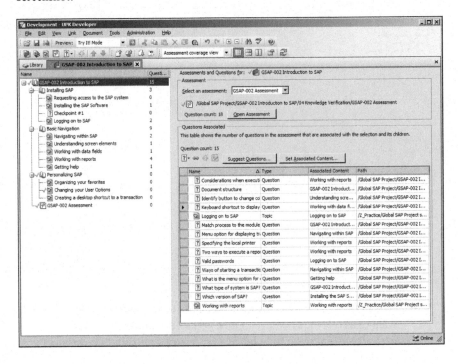

The screen contains three sections of useful information. These are

- The **Questions** column on the right of the Outline Hierarchy

- The *Assessment* area in the upper portion of the *Assessment Coverage view* (which is normally the '*Concept* pane' area)

- The *Questions Associated* area in the lower portion of the *Assessment Coverage view*.

These three sections are explained separately below.

In the *Assessment* area, you can now see the name of the Assessment, and its path within the Library. You can also see, in the **Question count** field, the number of Questions in the Assessment.

In the *Questions Associated* area, you can see, in the **Question count** field, the number of Questions in the Assessment that are associated with content objects in the selected Outline Element. The *Question Associated* area also includes a table listing all of the Questions that are associated with the content object selected in Outline Area (including all of its children). This information will change as you click on different content objects (Modules, Sections, and Topics) within the overall Outline. For each Question, the following information is given:

- **Name**: The file name of the Question object within UPK. Note that this is not the same as the question that is being asked within the Question object itself.

- **Type**: Either **Question** or **Topic**, depending on the type of the Assessment Object.

- **Associated Content**: The name of the content object to which this Question has been associated.

- **Path**: The path within the Library at which the Question content object can be located.

The most useful information on this screen is the **Questions** column on the left of the Outline structure. Once you select an Assessment, this shows the number of Questions that have been associated to each of the content objects in the Outline. This is the *Assessment coverage*. It is this information that allows you to determine whether the Assessment provides a reasonable test of the content of the Outline.

Note that the Question count for a Module or Section includes all Questions within the selected Assessment that are associated to that Module or Section, along with any Questions assigned to its direct children (this applies recursively, all the way down the Outline hierarchy). For example, the *Basic Navigation* Section in the example above has 9 Questions associated to it: 2, 1, 1, 4, and 1 Questions respectively associated to the five Topics within this Section. By contrast, the main *GSAP-002 Introduction to SAP* Module has 15 Questions associated to it, even though the sum of the Questions associated to its three child Sections is only 12 (3+9+0). Why is this? Because there are also 3 Questions associated to the Module itself. You can confirm this by checking the **Associated Content** column in the list of Questions in the rightmost portion of the screen.

Adjusting the Assessment coverage

After reviewing the count of Questions associated with each content object, you may determine that you need to make some adjustments to the Assessment.

You can make several adjustments to the Assessment within the *Assessment Coverage* view, by using the buttons above the *Question List* in the *Questions Associated* block. The types of adjustments you are likely to need to make, and the buttons that you would use to do this, are explained below.

- If you decide to create an additional Question that you can then associate with an 'under-represented' content object in the Outline, click on the **Link New Question** button (🔽), and then select the required question type from the drop-down list. You will be prompted to select a save location and specify a file name for your new Question, and can then define the Question as explained in *Creating a Question* on page 463. The new Question is inserted at the end of the Assessment.

- If you decide to include and associate an additional, existing Question within this Assessment, then click on the **Link Existing Question** button (☞). You are then prompted to navigate to and select this Question. Once the Question has been inserted, if it is not already associated with a content object in the Outline Element, you can click the **Set Associated Content** button and associate it now, as explained in *Fixing missing Question associations* on page 497.

- If you determine that the Assessment contains too many Questions that are associated with a specific content object, then you can remove one or more Questions from the Assessment. To do this, select the Question in the Question List, and then click on the **Delete Link** button (🗱).

   Note that this will remove the Question from the Assessment, but will not delete the Question from the Library. Note also that removing the Question from the Assessment will not remove the association of the Question with the content object. However, because the Question is no longer included in the Assessment, the Question will no longer be included in the Question Count of the *Assessment Coverage* view.

- An alternative way of reducing the number of individual Questions associated to a specific content object is to simply remove the content association. To do this, select the Question in the *Questions List*, and then click on the **Clear Associated Content** button (🗹).

   This will clear the **Associated Content** Property of the Question, which will then reduce the Question Count for the content object to which it was originally associated. However, it is important to note that this will not remove the Question from the Assessment. This will then create a discrepancy between the **Question Count** in the *Assessment* block and the **Question Count** in the *Questions Associated* block, which you may want to resolve as described in explained in *Fixing missing Question associations* on page 497..

- If you want to add more Questions to your Assessment, but are not sure if suitable Questions that you could include already exist within the Library, then you can have UPK identify and suggest existing Questions that are potential candidates for inclusion in this Assessment, by clicking on the **Suggest Questions** button and then following the steps described in *Identifying potential Questions for inclusion in an Assessment* on page 498.

- If the **Question Count** in the *Assessment* block is greater than the **Question Count** in the *Questions Associated* block, then this indicates that there are Questions in the Assessment that are not associated with Content objects in the Outline. This could be adversely affecting the Assessment coverage (in that the Questions with missing associations are not being counted in the **Question Count** when they probably should be). You can identify and correct such issues by clicking on the **Set Associated Content** button and then following the steps described in *Fixing missing Question associations* on page 497.

Note that the buttons in the *Questions Associated* area are simply shortcuts to functionality that is also accessible via the *Assessment Editor*. If you decide that it would be easier to simply edit the Assessment directly, then you can click on the **Open Assessment** button in the *Assessment* area, and edit the Assessment as described earlier in this chapter. If you add Questions to the Assessment via the *Assessment coverage* view, and want to change the position of these Questions within the Assessment, then you will need to do this via the *Assessment Editor*, anyway.

Fixing missing Question associations

If you have selected the highest-level Outline Object within the Outline, then the **Question count** field in the *Questions Associated* block (the number of Questions in the Assessment) should equal the **Question count** in the *Assessment* area (the number of Questions that are associated with the selected Outline Element). If they are not equal, then this means that there are Questions in the Assessment that are not associated with a content object in the selected Outline. This will generate a warning during Publishing (as described above, in *Publishing Your Assessment*), and will need to be resolved. Luckily, UPK provides us with an easy way of checking and fixing this: the **Set Associated Content** button.

To identify Questions within the Assessment that are not associated to any of the Outline Elements within the Outline Element that you have selected, carry out the following steps:

1. Click on the Outline Element that you are currently checking. Normally this is the highest-level Outline Element to which this Assessment relates (although in practice you can select any Outline Element in the overall Outline Hierarchy).

2. Click on the **Set Associated Content** button in the *Questions Associated* block. The *Set Associated Content* dialog box is displayed, as shown below:

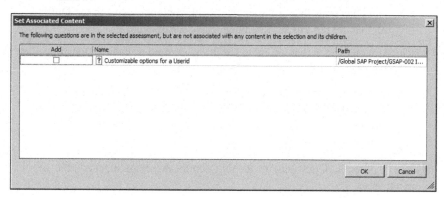

3. This dialog box lists all of the Questions that are included in the Assessment, but are not associated to a content object in the Outline.

4. Make a note of the Question that you want to associate with a content object. Do not associate it yet, or it will be associated to the Outline Element selected in Step 1.

5. Click on the **Cancel** button to close the *Set Associated Content* dialog box and return to the *Outline Editor*.

6. In the *Outline Editor*, click on the content object (Module, Section, or Topic) to which you want to associate the Question.

7. Click on the **Set Associated Content** button again. The *Set Associated Content* dialog box is displayed again. This time it will likely contain more Questions, as it will now list all Questions in the Assessment that are not associated with the content object selected in Step 6.

8. Select the check-box to the left of the Question that you want to associate with the content object selected in Step 6. (This is the Question that you made a note of in Step 4.)

9. Click on the **OK** button to make the association. The **Associated Content** property for the selected Question is updated to specify the content object selected in Step 6.

Note that if you are working in a client/server environment, the Question will be checked out to you (if it is not already). You will need to check it in to save your changes.

Identifying potential Questions for inclusion in an Assessment

If you decide that you want to include additional Questions in your Assessment, and think that there may be existing Questions within the Library that you could use, you can have UPK identify suitable Questions for you. UPK will consider the following objects as potentials for inclusion:

- Any Questions that are associated with content objects in the Outline, but that are not already included in the Assessment.

- Any Questions that are included in the Outline as in-line Questions, but that are not already included in the Assessment.

- Any Topics that are included in the Outline, but that are not already included in the Assessment. UPK's theory is that any Topic in the Outline can be played in *Know It?* mode and therefore used to assess knowledge retention.

To identify potential Questions for inclusion in the Assessment, carry out the following steps:

1. In the *Assessment Coverage* view, click on the Outline Element for which you want to identify potential Questions. This can be any Module, Section, or Topic within the Outline.

2. In the *Questions Associated* area, click on the **Suggest Questions** button. The *Suggest Questions* dialog box is displayed, as shown below:

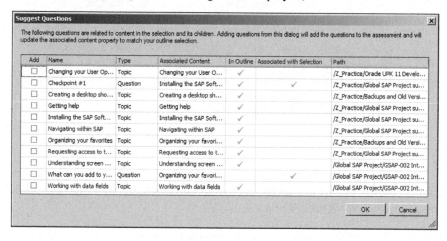

3. The following information is shown for each of the identified Questions or Topics:

Column	Description
Add	Select the check-box in this column to include the proposed Question in your Assessment (when you click OK). The Question will be added to the end of the Assessment.
Name	The name of the Question content object. Note that this is not necessarily the same as the question text.
Type	Indicates whether the suggested 'question' is a Question, or a Topic (which will be included with *Know It?* mode only activated).
Associated Content	Specifies the name of the content object that this Question has been associated to (if any). This is taken from the **Associated Content** property for the Question.
In Outline	If this column contains a green check-mark, then UPK has suggested this Question because the Question is already included in the Outline that you are processing. This will include <u>all</u> Topics in the Outline that are not currently included in the Assessment, and all in-line Questions that are not currently included in the Assessment.
Associated With Selection	If this column contains a green check-mark, then UPK has suggested this Question because the Question is associated with a content object that is included in the Outline. Note that this only applies to Questions (and not Topics).

Column	Description
Path	The path within the Library at which the Question or Topic can be found.

In the example above, UPK has suggested nine Topics and two Questions. Ignoring the Topics, one of these Questions has been suggested because it is associated with Content objects that are in the Outline, and one Question has been suggested because it is included in the Outline as an in-line Question.

4. Select the check-box in the **Add** column for all of the suggested Questions and Topics that you want to include in your Assessment.

5. Click on the **OK** button. The Questions and Topics are added to the end of the Assessment. (Note that if you want to reorder these, you will need to edit the Assessment itself.)

If you are operating in a client/server environment and the Assessment is not currently checked out to you, it will have automatically been checked out to you, and you will need to check it back in.

Summary

In this chapter, you have learned how to create Questions to verify that users have learned what you have taught them in your Topics and attached material. You have also learned how to make these Questions available either within an Outline, or as part of an Assessment (which can be published separately, or as a part of a broader Outline). Finally, you have learned how to check that your Assessment provides a realistic Assessment for an entire Outline.

The example Assessment built in this chapter for our sample course is included in the .odarc file available from the author's website (refer to the front of this book for the location of this).

13

Using UPK for Application Testing

UPK's *raison d'etre* is the creation of training simulations for software applications. However, it can also facilitate the testing of these software applications. UPK contains a number of 'test' output types, and also features a 'play' mode—*Test It!* mode—specifically designed to be used when testing an application.

In this chapter you will learn:

- How to use *Test It!* mode

- How to use the *Record It! Wizard* to capture application test results

- Which document publishing formats can be used to facilitate testing

Why use UPK for application testing?

Testing an application typically involves performing a set of actions in an application and confirming that they generate the desired result. More often than not, these actions are documented in a *test case* that (hopefully) specifies what to do, and what to expect as a result, step by step. In essence, UPK is capturing a set of step-by-step instructions on how to do something in an application. It is not really a great leap of faith to assume that these steps, captured in UPK, can be used as a *test case*. In fact, that is precisely what the **Test Case** and **Test Document** publishing formats provide.

One could reasonably ask exactly what exactly you are testing by following the steps in the Test Case or Test Document. You already know that the system works; it must have worked in order for you to record the UPK simulation in the first place. A good question, but UPK is not really designed to be used for the *initial* testing of an application (although it can be, as we shall see later in this chapter)—it is designed to be used on *subsequent* tests of the same functionality. This may be user testing that takes place after the initial developer testing, or could be 'regression testing' of an application. In these scenarios, having a document of the exact steps carried out in the first round of testing is extremely helpful for subsequent rounds of testing. And this is where UPK steps in.

● Regression testing is where one part of an application has been changed, and all of the other parts of the application are re-tested, even though they have not changed, to make sure that the new changes have not inadvertently affected the existing functionality.

Specifying the expected results

For a test document to be effective, the expected results must be defined for the test case. UPK allows the expected results of every Action to be recorded in a Topic. These expected results are not captured automatically during recording, and cannot be entered at recording time as **Author Notes** can – even if you are recording a 'test' via the *Record It! Wizard*. Therefore, they need to be entered manually.

Expected results are entered per Frame, into the **Expected Results** field, which can be found in the *Frame Comments* pane within the *Topic Editor*. How to display this pane, and enter comments, is explained in *Chapter 4, Editing a Topic*, but the location of the **Expected Results** field is highlighted in the following screenshot, for your reference.

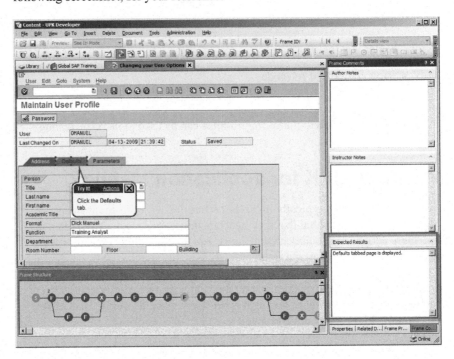

This screenshot shows the *Topic Editor* with the *Frame Comments* pane displayed (if it is not, select menu option **View > Panes > Frame Comments**) and anchored to the right of the workspace (see *Chapter 3, Working in the UPK Developer Client* for more information on positioning and anchoring panes).

Although the expected results *can be* entered per Frame, this does not necessarily mean that you *have to* enter expected results for **every** Frame—or even for *any* Frames at all. You may find it sufficient to only enter expected results for key Actions, or for steps where you want the tester to explicitly check something (versus assuming that an action was successful simply by virtue of being able to progress to the next step).

Now that we know how and where these expected results are entered, let's look at where they appear, and how they are used to facilitate application testing.

Testing using Test It! Mode

As described in *Chapter 1, An Introduction to Oracle User Productivity Kit*, *Test It!* mode is a specific playback mode that can be used to guide a user (tester) through the required steps in the application. In practice, it works very similarly to *Do It!* mode, but provides the ability to record the result of each of these steps.

✦ *Test It!* mode was introduced in UPK 11.1. It is only available in a client/server environment.

Publishing a Test It! mode Player

If you want *Test It!* mode to be available, you need to enable it. Unlike the other on-line modes, *Test It!* mode is not enabled via the Topic Properties. Instead, it is selected in the Player options of the *Publishing Wizard*, and will then apply to *all* Topics in the Player. This option is described in *Chapter 1, Publishing Your Content*, but is highlighted again below, for ease of reference:

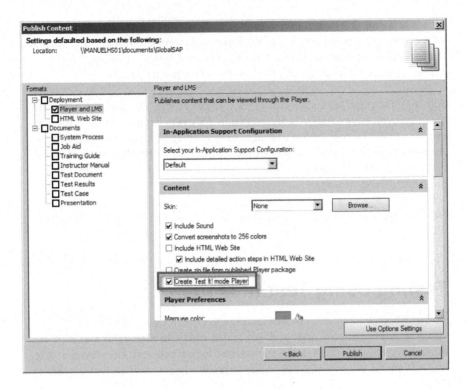

▲ In UPK 11, there
is a problem with the
Test It! Player in that it
cannot be created using a
custom publication format
(only the standard User
Productivity Kit publication
format can be used). This
was resolved in UPK 12.

To enable *Test It!* mode, simply make sure that you have selected the **Player
and LMS** publishing format, and then select the **Create Test It! mode Player**
option. Note that this option applies to both `kp.html` and the Player itself (see
Accessing a simulation in Test It! mode on page 504). If *Test It!* mode is made
available then <u>all</u> simulations in the published Player will be available in *Test It!*
mode.

All other steps and options for publishing are the same as those described in
Chapter 6, Publishing Your Content, and so are not repeated here.

It is important to note that *Test It!* mode is not designed for use by most users; it is
specifically designed to be used by *testers*. It is therefore strongly recommended
that if you want to make *Test It!* mode available to your testers, you publish an
entirely separate Player (with the **Create Test It! mode Player** option selected),
and—more importantly—make sure that the version of the Player that you
publish for your users does not include *Test It!* mode (make sure that the **Create
Test It! mode Player** option is **not** selected).

Accessing a simulation in Test It! mode

According to Oracle's official *User Productivity Kit Content Development*
document (E55345-01), "Test It! mode cannot be launched from a published
Player package like other playback modes. It must be launched from `kp.html`".
However, this is incorrect (it would be odd to have an option called "**Create Test**

It! mode Player" and then not actually have Test IT! mode. If the **Create Test It! mode Player** option is selected during publishing (see above), then *Test It!* mode is accessible via both kp.html *and* the Player.

Access via kp.html

As described in *Chapter 15, Integrating UPK with Other Applications*, a file called kp.html is created during publishing. This file can be used to directly access any Topic in any mode—including *Test It!* mode. An example of how kp.html appears when displayed in the browser is shown below:

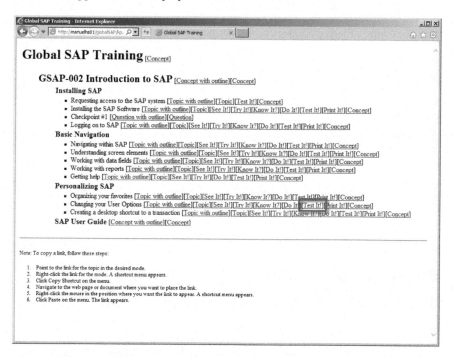

To access a simulation in *Test It!* mode via kp.html, click on the **[Test It!]** link to the right of the Topic name, and then proceed as described in *Running a simulation in Test It! mode* on page 506.

Access via the Player

If the **Create Test It! mode Player** option was selected during publishing, the **Test It!** mode button will be visible for **all** Topics in the published Player. An example of this is shown in the screenshot below:

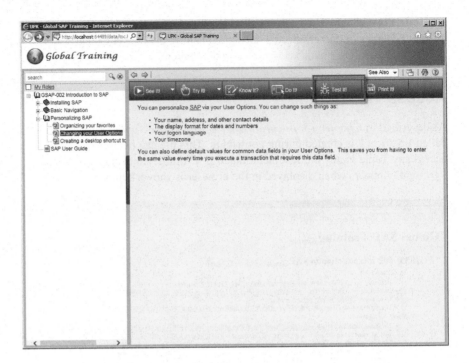

To access a simulation in *Test It!* mode via the Player, select the Topic in the Outline hierarchy, click on the **Test It!** button, and then proceed as described in *Running a simulation in Test It! mode* on page 506.

Running a simulation in Test It! mode

To run a simulation in *Test It!* mode, carry out the steps listed below:

1. Start the application that you want to test.

2. Start playback of the simulation in *Test It!* mode as described above. The *Test It!* window is displayed, overlaid on the last application that you accessed (hopefully this is the application started in Step 1—if it is not, switch back to the relevant application).

3. An example of the *Test It!* window is shown below. Note that for brevity we have hidden the screenshot, although this can be displayed in the same manner as for *Do It!* mode.

● Unlike *Do It!* mode, the *Test It!* window will not always remain on top, so if you switch to another application, you will need to switch back to the *Test It!* window to continue the test.

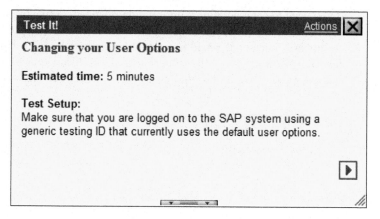

Note that in this initial window, you see the estimated time required to complete the test (taken from the Topic's **Test Document > Estimated time** property) and the test set-up instructions (taken from the Topic's **Test Document > Test setup** property).

4. Click on the **Next** button (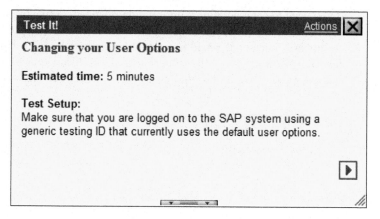) to continue. The Concept Page text and Start Frame text are displayed.

■ You can also use the same keyboard shortcut to advance as you would use in *Do It!* mode.

5. Click on the **Next** button ( ) again, to go to the first/next step in the test. Once you reach the first Action Frame, the *Test It!* window changes, as shown in the following screenshot:

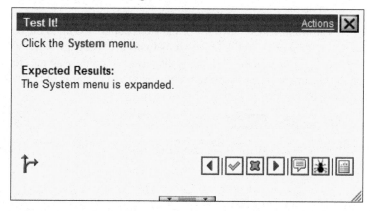

Now, the instructions (Bubble texts) are displayed, followed by the expected result (of carrying out the action described). These 'expected results' are taken from the Frame-level Expected Results in the Topic (see *Specifying the expected results* on page 502). In addition, a new set of buttons is displayed in the lower-right corner of the window; these are what you use to record the results of the test. Each button, and its use, is described in *Test It! Window buttons* on page 512.

6. Click on the **Passed** button ( ) to indicate that the step was successful, or click on the **Failed** button ( ) to indicate that the step failed, as appropriate.

7. If you want to enter additional information relating to a step (perhaps to explain what has happened, or suggest improvements to the application developers), click on the **Add notes to this step** button (🖳). The *Test Step Notes* window will be opened, as shown below (note that this example shows the window after comments have been entered; initially it will be empty):

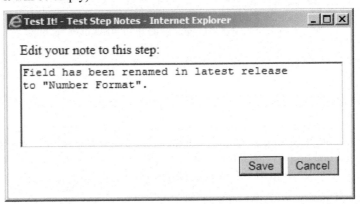

Enter your comments into the text field and then click on **Save**. Note that these comments will appear alongside the current step (displayed in the *Test It!* window); if you want to enter comments for the action that you just performed, then you should return to the previous step and enter them there.

■ The ability to generate a list of the steps taken so far is extremely useful if the application you are testing has crashed or otherwise terminated unexpectedly—you can provide this list to the developers to show them exactly what you did to make the system crash.

8. If you want to generate a list of the steps completed up to the current point, then click on the **Open steps to create webpage** button (🖳). The *Steps to recreate* window is displayed, summarizing the steps taken so far (this is taken from the Frame texts). An example of this window is shown below.

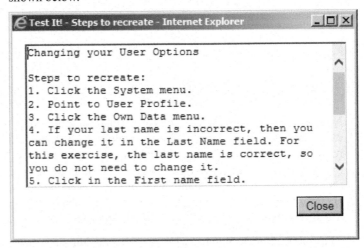

You can copy these steps and paste them into an email to the support team, or into your testing software, or other suitable place. Once you have finished with this information, close the window.

9. If the simulation contains a Decision Frame then you will be required to choose a path, and will only test the selected path. All Frames (even those in the path not taken) will be included in the Test Report generated at the end of testing, but the **Results** column for steps in the path not taken will be blank (not **Skipped**, **Passed**, or **Failed**). In this scenario, I would suggest that you specify the path chosen in the Test Notes - there will be no automatic indication of the path chosen in the Test Report, and it may not be obvious to the person reading the Test Report which path was chosen.

10. Repeat Steps 5 to 9 until you have completed all of the test steps, and have reached the End Frame.

11. Click on the **Next** button (▶) one last time. The *Results summary* is displayed, as shown in the example below.

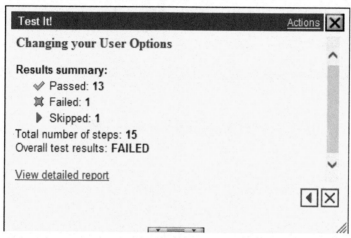

This shows the number of steps passed, failed, and skipped, along with a final result of "**PASSED**" or "**FAILED**". Note that if any step fails, the entire test fails (there is no 'pass percentage'). However, a test can still be passed if steps are skipped (as long as all of the steps that weren't skipped were passed).

12. Click on the **View detailed report** link. The report is displayed in a new window, showing all steps, expected results, and actual results. An example of the report is shown in the next two screenshots. The first screenshot shows the report header, which includes the following additional test information:

- **Purpose of Test**: Taken from the Topic's **Test Document | Purpose of test** property.

- **Test History**: Specifies the date on which the test was carried out, and the final result of the test (passed or failed), It also includes two additional fields (highlighted in the screenshot below) for you to enter your name (**Tester** field) and enter any additional information that you want to record (**Test Notes** field). This information is not captured via the *Test It!* window – and in fact, you cannot edit it directly on the web page output. Instead, you will need to save (or cut and paste) this Test Report to another format (for example, paste it into Microsoft Word), and then enter this information there.

- **Time to Test** – Specifies the estimated time required to complete the test (taken from the Topic's **Test Document | Estimated time** property), and the actual amount of time taken to complete the test,

- **Test Setup** – Taken from the Topic's **Test Document | Test setup** property.

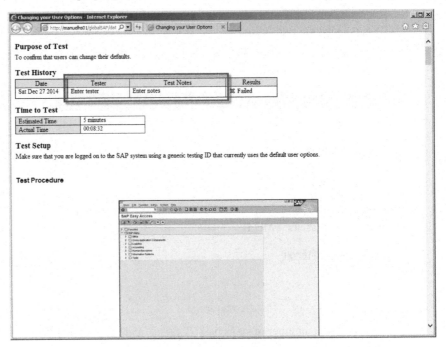

The next screenshot shows an example from further down the report (further into the test). Here we can see a failed test step. The **Test Step Notes** are shown (in our example, we entered these against the failed step) to the right of the expected results.

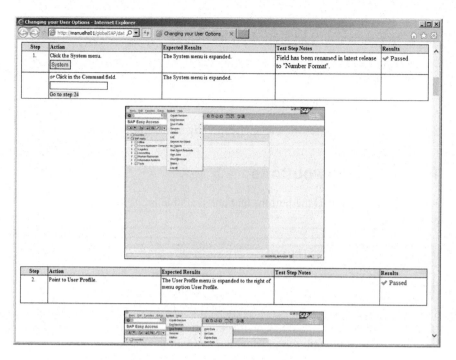

At the very bottom of the *Test Report*, the **Additional Validation steps** (taken from the Topic's **Test Document | Additional validation** property are displayed. Note that these did not appear in the *Test It!* window, and there is no indication of whether this additional validation has been performed (either successfully or not).

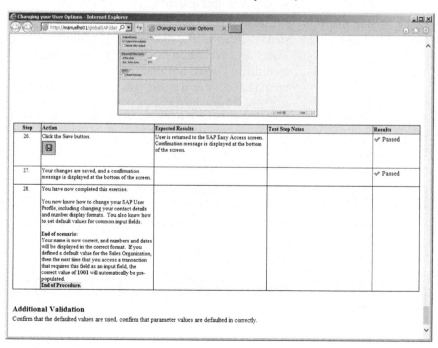

▲ The Test Report will not be automatically saved (either within UPK or anywhere else). If you do not save it yourself, it will be discarded as soon as you close the *Test It!* window.

13. If required, you can save the Test Report, or print it or email it (depending on your browser's capabilities).

14. Once you have finished reviewing the Test Report, close the *Test Report* window.

15. Click on the **Close** button to close the *Test It!* window.

You have now finished testing the application by using *Test It!* mode.

Test It! Window buttons

The following table lists the buttons that are available in the *Test It!* window, and explains their use.

Button	Name	Purpose
◀	**Previous step**	Click on this button to return to the previous step. You can change whether the previous step passed or failed, and display or change any entered notes
✓	**Mark this step as passed**	Click on this button if you were able to successfully complete this step (with the expected results, if specified). You will automatically advance to the next step as soon as you click on this button.
✗	**Mark this step as failed**	Click on this button if you were not able to complete this step with the expected result. You will automatically advance to the next step as soon as you click on this button.
▶	**Skip this step**	Click this button if you do not want to perform this step. The step will be recorded as "SKIPPED". Note that if you return to a step that you previously recorded as Passed or Failed, and then click this button to go forward again, you will simply advance to the next step; the revisited step will not be recorded as "SKIPPED".
💬	**Add notes to this step**	Click on this button to open a text window into which you can enter any notes relating to the currently-displayed action.
🐞	**Open steps to create webpage**	Click on this button to open a new window that will provide a summary of all of the actions carried out to reach this step. This is useful if you have hit an error, and want to provide the application developers (or support team) with the steps that you carried out, so that they know how to re-create the error.
📄	**Results Summary**	Display the *Results Summary* in a separate window.

✚ The **Results Summary** button is new in UPK 12. In prior releases, a *Close* button that would close the *Test It!* window was available instead, and the Results Summary could only be accessed once you had reached the end of the test.

Testing using the Record It! Wizard

The *Record It! Wizard* is designed for easy creation of simulations by non-expert UPK users. This could conceivably include testers. With a little training, there is no reason why a tester (whether they are an application developer or an application user) could not record a simulation as they are carrying out their test—especially if they use automatic recording. In fact, having the testers record their testing in order to capture a simulation has a couple of distinct advantages:

- If the test is successful then you have a 'working' simulation that can then be passed to a Training Development Team for turning into a training-ready Topic.

  However, there is a potential concern with using the recording of a test as the basis for training content development. This is that what a tester needs to test may not necessarily be the same thing that you want the users to be taught how to do. Perhaps the test case is designed for break testing (that is, deliberately trying to make the application fail), or stress testing (trying to overload the application) – and you wouldn't want your users thinking that this is the 'normal' way to use the application! It is therefore important that you look very carefully at which test cases could be used as input to training development, as it is unlikely that all of them will be suitable.

- If the test fails, then you have captured all of the steps required to reproduce the error, along with screenshots of the error itself, and this information will be helpful to the application developers for problem resolution.

The use of the *Record It! Wizard* is covered in detail in *Chapter 1, Recording a Simulation*, and so will not be repeated here. However, there are a few additional points to note when using the *Record It! Wizard* specifically for testing. These are discussed below.

- There is no option to specify whether a step was performed as expected or not.

- Any comments entered during the recording are saved as **Author Notes** and not **Expected Results** (as you might expect).

- If you preview your recording by selecting the **Preview as test** option, the simulation is displayed in the Test Results document format.

- The final recording is saved as a standard Topic in the Library (as distinct from the Test Report generated at the end of *Test It!* mode).

Testing outside of UPK

For the sake of completeness, it is worth mentioning in this chapter the three document publishing formats that are designed to facilitate testing. These do not work interactively, in the way that *Test It!* mode or the *Record It! Wizard* does, but they do guide the tester through the required steps, and provide a place to enter the results of the test. These three document formats are explained below. Examples of each of these documents can be found in *Chapter 1, Publishing Your Content*.

Test Document

The **Test Document** provides the tester with the test steps, but does not include screenshots. It includes the following standard test information taken from the Topic's **Test document** properties:

- **Purpose of test**
- **Test setup**
- **Estimated time**
- **Additional validation**

For each step, the Test Document includes the action, and the expected result, which is taken from the Frame's **Expected Results** field, and includes space for the tester to provide any notes and indicate whether the step was passed or failed.

Test Results

The **Test Results** document provides the tester with the test steps, and also includes screenshots (depending on the options specified in the Topic for including or excluding screenshots). None of the Topic's **Test Document** properties are included.

For each step, the Test Results document includes the action and any Author Notes, taken from the Frame's **Author Notes** field. The **Expected Results** are not included.

Given the lack of test-relevant information included in this document, its usefulness for *driving* testing is relatively limited. It is better considered as way of documenting the *results* of a test execution via the *Record It! Wizard* (as described earlier in this chapter).

Test Case

The information and input fields included in the **Test Case** format will depend on the application for which the file is being generated, but they all include the following standard test information taken from the Topic's **Test document** properties:

- **Purpose of test**

- **Estimated time**

In addition, the **IBM Rational Quality Manager** compatible file also includes the Owner name, taken from the Topic's **Workflow | Owner** property.

At the 'test level', the '**Other**' format file includes just about every Topic property.

For each step, the Test Case file includes the action, and the expected result, which is taken from the Frame's **Expected Results** field. Several input fields are provided, depending on the test application.

At the 'step level', the '**Other**' format file includes the **Context** information (**Application, Object type,** and **Object name**), **Author Notes**, and **Instructor Notes**, all taken from the frame properties.

Document cross-reference

The following table summarizes what (testing-specific) information is available in which document format. You may find this useful when deciding which document format to use.

Information	Test Document	Test Result	Test Case			
			HP QC	IMB RQM	Oracle ATS	Other
Test-level information – Taken from the Topic's properties						
Purpose of test	●		●	●	●	●
Test set-up	●					●
Estimated time	●		●	●	●	●
Additional validation	●					●
Test Doc Revision						
Step-level information – Taken from the Frame's properties						
Action	●	●	●	●	●	●
Screenshots		●				
Expected Results	●		●	●	●	●
Author Notes		●				●
Instructor Notes						●
Context						●

Summary

UPK can be used to facilitate application testing, either interactively via *Test It!* mode, by using the *Record It! Wizard*, or manually via one of several possible output document formats.

It is important to consider whether test recordings can be leveraged for training simulations, or whether the training recordings can be leveraged for testing, as often these are two separate activities requiring separate information.

14

Basic Administration

In this chapter we will look at some of the basic activities that may need to be carried out by a UPK Administrator. This is effectively everything behind the **Administration** menu option (plus a few other things that can only be done by an Administrator).

Note that these activities apply only to a client/server environment, and not to a stand-alone implementation of UPK. You will also only be able to carry out these activities if you are defined as an Administrator for the Library—if you are not an Administrator, you will not even *see* the options described in this chapter.

In this chapter, you will learn:

- How to grant authors access to your UPK Library
- How to control access to specific folders on the Library screen
- How to manage content object state values
- How to override the check-out of a content object
- How to purge deleted documents from the Library

Defining Access Groups

Unless you want everyone to have complete access to everything (which is a **very** bad idea!) you will want to limit author access to specific folders within the Library. You can do this by granting authors access to only selected content as you add the authors to the Library (see below), but if your authors will generally require similar accesses, it is much more efficient to create 'groups' that have specific access, and then assign users to these groups. This has the advantage that if you need to change access for your authors, you only need to make the change once—to the group's access—instead of to each author's access.

You can either define the groups first and then assign users to these groups as you define the users to UPK, or you can define the users first and then assign the users to the groups as you define the groups. Either approach works, but in this book we will define the groups first, as this forces us to consider our access control approach before we start providing users with access.

Deciding upon an access control approach

Before you define your groups, you should decide what you want to control access to. Hopefully, when you defined the structure of your Library's folders (in *Chapter 3, Working in the UPK Developer Client*), you also thought about your access control requirements and defined your folders accordingly.

For example, you may have organized your folders by project, and want to ensure that developers from one project cannot change content objects from another project. Alternatively, you may have split your development model so that one group of authors is responsible for creating and editing Topics and another group is responsible for maintaining Outline Elements and building the Outline.

Whichever approach you use, it is important that your folder structure is consistent with your group definitions, because access control (both at the group level and the individual author level) is predicated on the folder structure in the Library.

By way of example, we will define an access control structure for our Library that segregates access by project and by type of author. We will create the following access groups:

- **Recorders**: We will use this for our SMEs who will always use the *Record It! Wizard*. We will grant this group access to the Record It Content folder only.

  Note that we cannot separate access to this folder by project – there is only one Record It Content folder for the entire Library – so unfortunately we will have to take it on trust that authors from one project do not interfere with recordings from another project. Luckily, this risk is mitigated to some extent by the fact that authors using the *Record It! Wizard* can only see Topics for which they themselves are identified as the 'owner' via the Topic's **Owner** property, so the only way one author could change another author's content (via the *Record It! Wizard*) is if the other author set them to be the Owner. Of course, they could still access the Library via the *Topic Editor* and then locate and change someone else's Topics there, but the risk is much smaller.

  There is a further consideration with this particular approach (of limiting some authors' access to only the Record It! Content folder—or any other single folder). If a recording is moved from this folder to another folder (for example, once your main authors have picked up the recording, edited it, and moved it into a 'final' folder in the Library) the 'recorder' (SME) will no longer be able to change it – even if they can see it because they are still the Owner – because they will not have access to the 'final' folder. This may or may not be what you want.

- **<Project> Developers**: We will define a separate 'Developer' group for the main UPK authors (that is, not SMEs) for each project, and limit the access of each group to only the folders for that project.

Once you have chosen an access control approach, you can define your required groups, as explained below.

Changing the default Access Groups

UPK comes with two pre-installed groups: **Everyone** and **Administrators**. The **Administrators** group initially contains only the 'admin' user defined when you first installed the UPK server software, although you can assign additional users to this group if necessary. The **Administrator** group has **Modify** access to the entire library (so be careful who you assign it to). You are unlikely to want to change this Access Group.

The **Everyone** group automatically contains **all** of the users that have access to your Library—they are added to this group automatically when you define them to the Library. You cannot add users to this group, remove users from this group, or delete this group. Critically, this group is, by default, given **Modify** access to the entire library. **It is therefore strongly recommended that you change this group before you do anything else.**

To change the **Everyone** group, carry out the steps shown below:

1. Select menu option **Administration | Manage Groups**. The *Group Management* dialog box is displayed, as shown below:

▲ Actually, a SME working in the *Record It! Wizard* will be able to change content objects for which they are the owner and that they are the Owner of—they just won't be able to save their changes, which could be extremely frustrating for them as they will not know this until they try to save their changes, typically *after* they have done all the hard work.

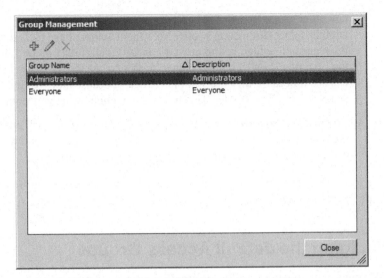

2. Double-click on the **Everyone** group to open it. (You can also single-click on the group to select it, and then click on the **Edit selected group** button (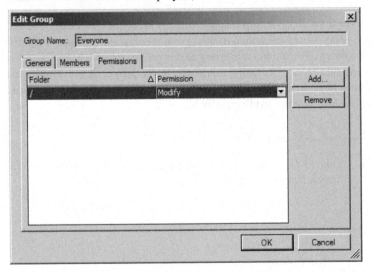)). The *Edit Group* dialog box is displayed.

3. Click on the **Permissions** tab. An example of the *Edit Group* dialog box, with the **Permissions** tab displayed, is shown below:

4. You can see here that the **Folder** to which the group has **Modify** permission is "/". This is the 'root folder'. Everything on the *Library* screen is under this root.

5. *Click on the* **Permission** field to display the drop-down list of possible values, and select **Read**.

Note:
The group will need **Read** access so that members of this group can use

the files in the `System` folder, which they will need to do in order to preview or publish content, select roles, and so on.

6. Click on **OK** to save your changes to the Access Group.

7. Click on **Close** to close the *Group Management* dialog box.

Defining a new Access Group

To define a new Access Group, carry out the following steps:

1. Select menu option **Administration | Manage Groups**. The *Group Management* dialog box is displayed, as shown below:

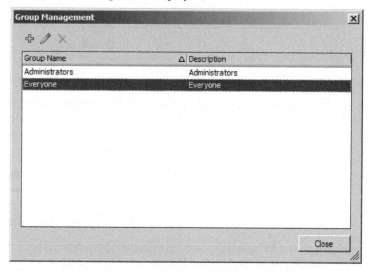

2. Click on the **Add new group** button (⊕). The *Add Group* dialog box is displayed, as shown below. (Note that this screenshot shows the dialog box *after* steps 3 and 4 have been completed.)

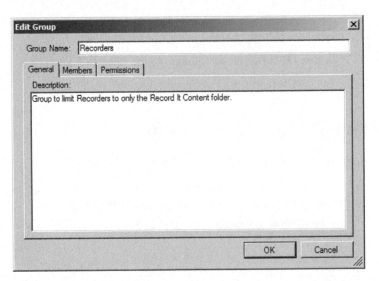

3. Enter a suitable, unique name for this group in the **Group Name** field.

4. Enter a short text description of this group in the **Description** field. It is always worth including an explanation of the intent of this group, for future reference—especially if you have multiple Administrators, and/or the Administrator is likely to change in the future.

5. If you have already defined users, and want to assign one or more of these users to the group now, then you can click on the **Members** tab, and then select the required members of this group from a list of all users. For our purposes, we will define and assign the users later.

6. Click on the **Permissions** tab. An example of this tab, before any permissions have been defined, is shown below:

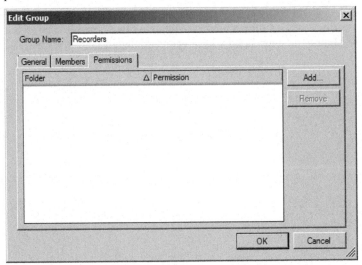

7. Click on the **Add** button. The *Select Location* dialog box is displayed, as shown below:

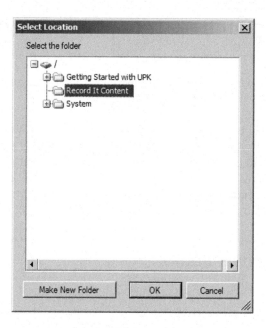

8. Navigate to and select the folder to which you want members of this group to have access (regardless of the level of access that you want them to have—we will define that in step 10).

9. Click on the **OK** button to confirm the folder selection and return to the *Add Group* dialog box.

10. Click the drop-down button for the **Permission** field, and select the required level of access. Available access levels are:

  ● **List folder contents**: Group members can list the contents of the folder, but cannot open any of the objects within it – not even in 'read only' mode.

  ● **Read**: Group members can open any objects in the folder in 'read only' mode. They cannot change objects or create new ones.

  ● **Modify**: Group members can create, change, and delete objects within the folder.

11. Click on **OK** to save your changes to the group.

12. Click on **Close** to close the *Group Management* dialog box.

We have now defined our first Access Group. We can define our additional groups by repeating the above steps. Once we have defined all of our required Access Groups we can move on to defining our users and assigning them to our Groups.

■ If you need to change an Access Group that you have previously created, you can do so as described in *Chapter 14, Changing the default Access Groups*.

Providing authors with access to your Library

Before an can even create a Profile for your UPK Library, they must be defined to the Library.

When you (or your tech people) installed the UPK server software, you were asked whether you wanted to use **Windows Authentication** or **Standard Authentication**. Regardless of which method you chose, granting access to your UPK Library is almost the same process. The steps below explain the use of **Standard Authentication**; any differences between that and **Windows Authentication** are clearly stated.

Defining a new author

To provide a new author with access to your Library, carry out the steps shown below:

1. Select menu option **Administration | Manage Authors**. The *Author Management* dialog box is displayed, as shown below:

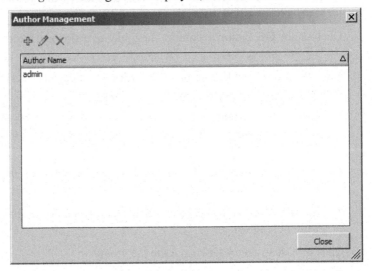

2. Click on the **Add new author** button (⊕). The *Add Author* dialog box is displayed, as shown below:

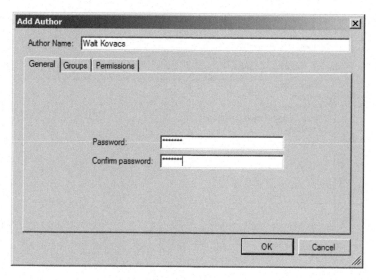

3. Enter the user name that this author will use when accessing the UPK Library, into the **Author Name** field.

- For **Standard Authorization**, this can be any suitable identifier, but as this name will appear in the Library (as **Last Changed By**, **Created By**, **Owner**, and so on) it is recommended that you use the author's actual name.

- For **Windows Authorization**, this **must** be the author's Windows ID (including domain name, where appropriate – so, "DOMAIN\USERNAME").

4. If you are using **Standard Authorization**, then enter a password for the author into both the **Password** field and the **Confirm password** field (obviously, these must be exactly the same).

   If you are using **Windows Authorization**, no password is required and the **General** tab will not be available,because in order for an author to access UPK they must have first logged on to their Windows account, and this same authorization is used for UPK (single sign-on).

5. Click on the **Groups** tab. A list of all currently-defined groups is displayed, as shown in the sample screenshot below:

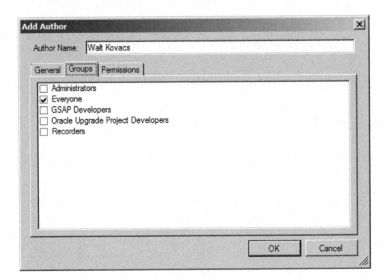

6. Select the check-box to the left of all groups to which you want to assign this author. Note that the author will automatically be assigned to the **Everyone** group; you cannot change this. If you have not yet defined the required groups, then you can ignore this tab now, and come back to it later (via the **Change an author** button (🖉)).

7. If you want to grant this user access to specific folders (in addition to accesses granted via the assignment of the user to specific groups) then you can select these folders, and the required level of access granted, via the **Permissions** tab.

▲ It is not recommended that you provide direct access (or denial) to specific folders; doing so makes it much more difficult to manage overall control, and to troubleshoot problems when they inevitably arise.

8. Click on **OK** to close the *Add Author* dialog box.

9. Click on **Close** to close the *Author Management* dialog box.

Changing an author's password

If you are using **Standard Authorization** then authors will be required to specify their password when they first access the UPK Library (unless they select the option **Save my password as part of this profile** option when they log on). They can change their password at any time, via menu option **Tools | Change Password**.

● Passwords in UPK never expire, and users are never required to change them. There are also no limits on length, characters used, or on being able to re-use prior passwords.

If an author forgets their password, then you can reset it for them by following the steps described below:

1. Select menu option **Administration | Manage Authors**.

2. In the *Author Management* dialog box, click on the author for whom you want to reset the password.

3. Click on the **Edit selected author** button (🖉).

4. In the *Edit Author* dialog box, enter a new password for the author in both the **Password** field and the **Confirm password** field.

5. Click on **OK** to close the *Edit Author* dialog box.

6. Click on **Close** to close the *Author Management* dialog box.

You can use the same approach to change an author's name, group assignments, or permissions. Note, however, that if you change an author's name, this will *not* change their name in the **Document History**, which will continue to show the name they had when the version was created.

▲ If you use **Standard Authorization** and change an author's name, they will lose access (and all content) associated with any Profile that they have created on their workstation under their old name.

Deleting an author

If you need to delete an author from your Library, then you can do so as follows:

1. Select menu option **Administration | Manage Authors**.

2. In the *Author Management* dialog box, click on the author for whom you want to reset the password

3. Click on the **Delete** button (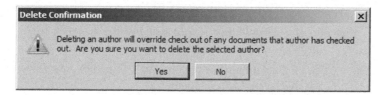). A confirmation message is displayed, as follows:

▲ Deleting an author will remove the author from being the Owner of any documents in the Library (the **Owner** property will be set to (blank). Because there is no indication as to which content objects this has been done for, it is recommended that you first take a print of all of the content objects for which the author (being deleted) is the Owner, in case you need to reassign these to another author.

4. Click on **Yes**. The author is deleted.

5. Click on **Close** to close the *Author Management* dialog box.

Managing folder permissions

When you define an Access Group, you specify the folders that members of that group can access, and the rights that they have on these folders. If Access Groups already exist, then you can define the access rights that these groups will have on the various Library folders as explained in this section (which way round you do this—assigning folders to groups, or assigning groups to folders—makes little difference). Note that in this book we assigned folder permissions when we created the group, so there is no need to do this now.

Assigning folder permissions

To assign specific permissions for a folder to an Access Group or to an individual author, carry out the steps described below:

1. On the *Library* screen, click on the folder for which you want to assign specific permissions.

2. Select menu option **Administration | Folder permissions**. The *Folder Permissions* dialog box is displayed.

3. Make sure the **Assigned Permissions** tab is selected, as shown below:

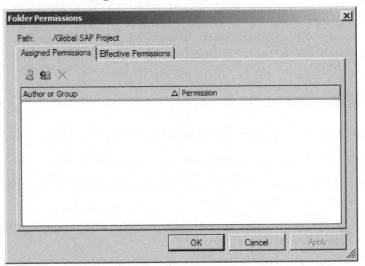

4. To grant a specific author permissions on this folder, carry out the following steps:

    i. Click on the **Add author** button (). The *Author Selection* dialog box is displayed, as shown below:

    ii. Click on the name or Userid of the author who you want to provide access to this folder, and then click **OK**.

    iii. Back at the *Folder Permissions* dialog box, select the level of access to this folder that you want to grant to this user, in the **Permission** column. Available access levels are:

- **List folder contents**: The author can list the contents of the folder, but cannot open any of the objects within it—not even in 'read only' mode.

- **Read**: The author can open any objects in the folder in 'read only' mode. They cannot change objects or create new ones.

- **Modify**: The author can create, change, and delete objects within the folder.

5. To grant a entire Access Group permissions on this folder, carry out the following steps:

   i.   Click on the **Add Group** button (). The *Group Selection* dialog box is displayed, as shown below:

   ii. Click on the name of the Access Group that you want to grant access to this folder, and then click **OK**.

   iii. Back at the *Folder Permissions* dialog box, select the level of access to the folder that you want to grant this group, in the **Permission** column. Available access levels are:

   - **List folder contents**: Group members can list the contents of the folder, but cannot open any of the objects within it – not even in 'read only' mode.

   - **Read**: Group members can open any objects in the folder in 'read only' mode. They cannot change objects or create new ones.

   - **Modify**: Group members can create, change, and delete objects within the folder.

6. To remove assigned folder permissions, carry out the following steps:

   i.   Click on the author or Access Group whose access to this group you want to remove.

   ii. Click on the **Delete** button ().

iii.   Click on **OK** to close the *Folder Permissions* dialog box.

Reviewing folder permissions

Given the multitude of ways of providing access to folders, and the way that these permissions can overlap (and even conflict) with one another, it is sometimes difficult to identify specific permissions for a folder. Handily, UPK provides a nice, easy way to see what permissions are currently effective for a given folder.

To display the effective permissions for a folder, carry out the following steps:

1.   On the *Library* screen, select the folder for which you want to review the currently active permissions.

2.   Select menu option **Administration | Folder permissions**. The *Folder Permissions* dialog box is displayed.

3.   Click on the **Effective Permissions** tab. An example of this tabbed page is shown below:

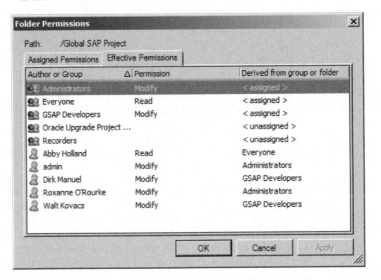

The *Effective Permissions* tabbed page lists all of the Access Groups and authors defined within the Library, and for each of these shows the level of permissions that the group or author has on the folder. More usefully, it also shows how this permission was determined, in the **Derived from group or folder** column. The table below explains the meanings of the various possible values for this column:

Value	Meaning
A folder name	The group's or user's permissions on the folder were inherited from the permissions assigned to the higher-level folder specified here.

Value	Meaning
A group name	The user belongs to this group, and this group has the specified permissions on this folder.
<assigned>	The user or group has been explicitly assigned the specified permissions on this folder, via the Folder permissions menu option.
<unassigned>	The user or group does not have any permissions on this folder.

In the event of conflicting authorizations (for example, where a user inherits certain permissions via a group, but has explicit permissions defined for the same folder), priority is determined as follows:

- A permission defined for a lower-level folder will take precedence over a permission defined for a higher-level folder

- A permission on a folder assigned to a specific author will take precedence over a permission on the same folder derived from a group to which the author belongs

- A lower-level folder permission that is derived from a group to which an author belongs will take precedence over a higher-level folder permission assigned to that specific author

This priority is independent of the level of permission (that is, more-restrictive permissions do not automatically take precedence over less-restrictive permissions—and vice versa).

Managing State values

As explained in *Chapter 3, Working in the UPK Developer Client*, UPK provides very rudimentary 'workflow' capabilities via the **Owner** and **State** properties available for all content objects. Although this falls some way short of true workflow (in that these properties do not *drive* anything), the **State** property can at least provide you with the ability to identify a document's progression through the development process. To facilitate this, UPK includes the following State values, which are designed to reflect a document's process through the development cycle:

- (blank)
- **Not Started**
- **Draft**
- **In Review**
- **Final**

It is possible to rename or remove any of these (with the exception of (blank), which cannot be deleted because that is the initial State of all documents), and/or add your own State values. Note that State values are Library-wide; you cannot have a separate set of State values for different folders or content types – so if you have multiple projects in the same Library, all projects need to agree on and use the same, single set of State values.

Before you change the set of State values, you should consider carefully how you will use them—or even *if* you will use them. State values must be set manually, and there is little point in having developers change the State of their documents for every little progression through the development process (1st edit, 2nd edit, and so on) if you are not going to track and report on each of these states. For example, if you have a fairly linear development process, and want to track the number of documents at each stage of the process, you could use the following set of State values:

- (blank)
- Recorded
- Edited
- Reviewed
- Published

By contrast, if all you are tracking is the number of completed documents, you only really need two States, as follows:

- (blank)
- Complete

To change the State values, carry out the following steps:

1. Select menu option **Administration | Manage** state values. The *Manage State Values* dialog box is displayed, as shown below:

2. To add a new State value:

 i. Click on the **Add** button (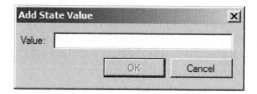).The *Add State Value* dialog box is displayed, as shown below:

   ii. Enter your new State in the **Value** field.

   iii. Click on **OK** to close the *Add State Value* dialog box.

3. To remove an existing State value:

 i. Click on the State value, to select it.

 ii. Click on the **Remove** button (☒).

4. To change an existing State value:

 i. Click on the State value, to select it.

 ii. Click on the **Edit** button (✎). The *Edit State Value* dialog box is displayed, as shown below:

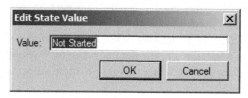

   iii. Change the State value, as required.

iv.   Click on **OK** to close the *Edit State Value* dialog box.

5.   To change the order of the State values (so that they reflect the correct progression through your process):

i.   Click on the State value, to select it.

ii. Click on the **Move Up** button (⬆) to move the value up in the list, or click on the **Move Down** button (⬇) to move the value down in the list.

6.   Once you have made all required changes, click on **OK** to close the *Manage State Values* dialog box.

Once you have defined all of your State values, you will likely want to define Custom Views to select content objects based on their state. Refer to *Chapter 3, Working in the UPK Developer Client* for details of how to define Custom Views.

Overriding check-out

In a client/server environment, authors must check out content objects before they can modify them. As long as a content is checked out to an author, no other authors can change it; they will still be able to see (in read-only mode) the last version of the content object that was checked into the server, or include it in an Outline Element, but they will not be able to edit it.

If the author who currently has a content object checked out is unable to check it back in (due to resignation, termination, death, and so on), an Administrator can override the check-out. This will discard any changes that the author has made to the object since it was last checked in, but at least the document is recoverable.

Checking who has a content object checked out – and where

As described in *Chapter 7, Version Management*, a content that is checked out to an author other than yourself is shown with a lock (🔒) to the left of the object name. The name of the author who has the content object checked out, and the workstation on which they have the object checked out are also available for display, although you may need to use the *Column Chooser* to display the **Checked Out By** and **Checked Out Hostname** columns, respectively, to see these values. (See *Chapter 3, Working in the UPK Developer Client* for more information on how to display these columns.) The following screenshot shows an example of the *Details view* where this information is displayed:

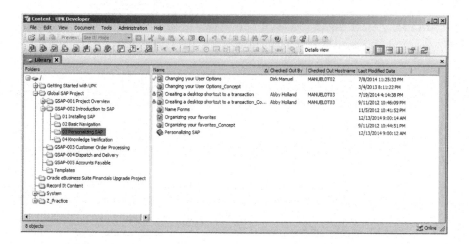

You can see from this example (above) that the Topic *Changing your User Options* is checked out to Dirk Manuel on workstation MANUELDT02, and the document *Creating a desktop shortcut to a transaction* is checked out to Abby Holland on workstation MANUELDT03.

Why is the workstation significant? Well, when a document is checked out by an author, it is saved to the author's local repository. This local repository is (by default) on the C: drive of their workstation; the Hostname is the machine name of this workstation. Checked out documents are therefore tied to a specific machine – and not just to the author. This means that if an author checks out a content object on one workstation, and then moves to another workstation they will not be able to access the content objects on the first workstation – even though the content object will be listed as being checked out to them. Therefore, before overriding a check-out, it is worth checking both that the author's Userid is no longer available (and if you are using standard authorization you can always reset an author's password and access their account yourself) and that their workstation is no longer accessible.

■ You can also use the *All checked out* view to list all documents that are currently checked out, although by default this view does not include the **Checked out Hostname** column (but you can edit the view to include this column, as described in *Chapter 3, Working in the Library*).

Overriding the check-out of a document

To override the check-out of a document, carry out the steps described below:

1. On the *Library* screen, click on the object that is currently checked out to another author, to select it.

2. Select menu option **Administration | Override Check Out**. The *Override Check Out* dialog box is displayed, as shown in the following screenshot:

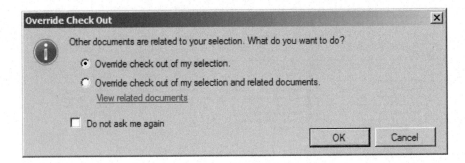

3. As with all such messages, you can choose to perform this action only for the selected document, or for the selected document and all related documents. You can also display the related documents by clicking on the **View related documents** link. Make the appropriate selection, and then click on **OK**. A warning message is displayed, as shown below:

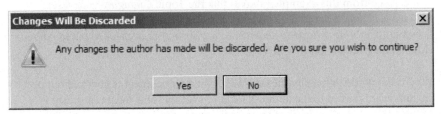

This message is simply warning you that any changes that the author has made to the document since it was last checked in will be lost. This is unfortunate, but unavoidable.

4. Click **Yes**. The lock on the content object is released, and the content object can now be checked out by another author.

Purging deleted documents from the Library

As explained in *Chapter 7, Version Management*, when an author deletes a document from the Library, the document is not deleted from the UPK database – it is simply hidden from view. You can list all deleted documents by selecting the *Deleted documents* view on the *Library* screen. An example of this view is shown below:

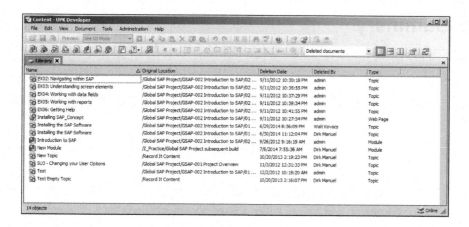

Because these documents are still taking up space in the database, it is a good idea to periodically purge them. Note that you should only purge deleted documents once you are absolutely sure that they will never be needed again (for example, at the end of a project, once all content has been approved)—once they are purged they can no longer be restored; they are truly gone.

To purge one or more documents that have previously been deleted, carry out the following steps:

1. On the *Library* screen, select the *Deleted documents* view. (See the screenshot above for an example of this.)

2. If you do not want to purge all deleted documents then click on the document that you want to permanently remove from the database. In common with many Windows applications, you can use *CTRL*+click or *SHIFT*+click, to select multiple documents.

3. Select menu option **Administration | Purge** to purge the selected documents, or menu option **Administration | Purge all** to purge all deleted documents. The following warning message is displayed:

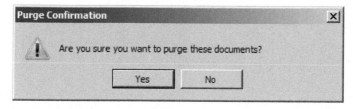

4. Click **OK** to purge the documents. The documents are purged from the database. As far as UPK is concerned, they no longer exist (and never did, if anyone asks…).

5. You can now return to the *Details view* (or other view, as appropriate).

Summary

In this chapter you have learned to perform some basic administrative tasks in a client/server environment.

- You have learned how to control access to your Library by defining authors, and have learned how to control access to specific folders within this Library through the use of Access Groups and folder permissions.

- You have learned how to define State values to support your UPK development process.

- You have also learned how to cancel an author's check-out of a document, and how to purge deleted documents from the UPK database.

15
Integrating UPK with Other Applications

Most likely you will publish your Topics to a content server or Learning Management System (LMS), and then have your users carry out the simulations from there. However, you may want to provide access to Topics in other ways. This chapter explains some of these ways. Note that this is certainly not an exhaustive list of possibilities, but it will hopefully provide you with some food for thought.

In this chapter, you will learn how to:

- Implement Integrated Application Support for UPK
- Link directly to a Module, Section, or Topic from a non-UPK document
- Link your UPK Library to a targeted application

Integrating UPK into a targeted application

UPK can be used to provide an online help library for just about any Windows application. However it really comes into its own when integrated with an application for which UPK can capture context information (referred to as *targeted applications*). In UPK 12.1, these applications are:

- Oracle Agile
- Oracle CRM On Demand
- Oracle E-Business Suite
- Oracle Enterprise Performance Management (Hyperion)

✛ Support for Microsoft Dynamics CRM was discontinued in UPK 11. Support for Oracle (Hyperion) EPM, Oracle Fusion Applications, Oracle Knowledge Center, Primavera was added in UPK 11. Support for Oracle CRM On Demand was added in UPK 12. Both SAPGui for Windows and Oracle Knowledge Center were listed separately as supported in UPK 11 but do not appear in UPK 12.

- Oracle Fusion Applications

- Oracle JD Edwards EnterpriseOne

- Oracle JD Edwards World

- Oracle Knowledge Center

- Oracle PeopleSoft

- Oracle Primavera

- Oracle Siebel CRM (On Premise)

- SAPGui for Windows and SAPGui for HTML)

What is context capturing, and what does it do?

You may recall from *Chapter 4, Editing a Topic* that the *Frame Properties* pane contains a few fields that are specific to the application being recorded. For reference, an example of the *Frame Properties* pane for a Frame in our sample exercise is shown in the following screenshot:

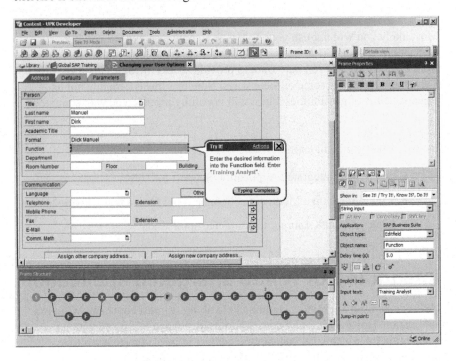

This information (highlighted in the previous screenshot) is part of the *context* that UPK captures—the actual object that has been acted upon, and the application to which it belongs. In the example above, UPK has captured the following information:

- **Application**: The targeted application that was recorded (**SAP Business Suite**, in this example).

- **Object name:** The name of the object that was clicked or the field into which text was entered (the **Function** field, in this example).

In addition to this information, UPK also captures some other, 'under the hood' context information. You can see this additional information if you click on the **Context ID** button (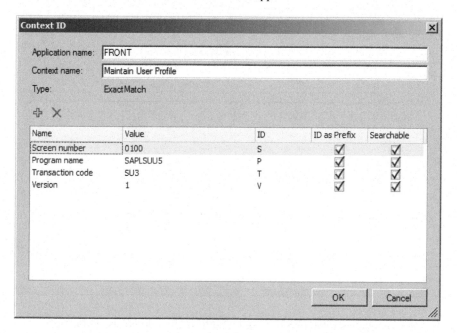) on the *Topic Editing Toolbar* (or select menu option **Edit | Context ID**). The screenshot below shows the context information for the same screen to which the frame shown above applies:

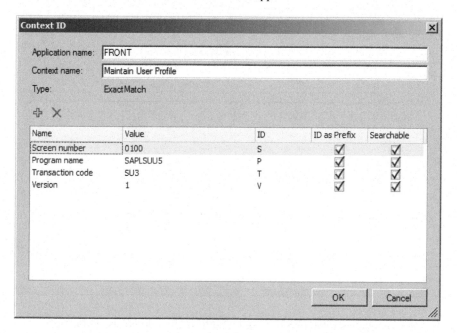

This information is the true *context* of the action—it identifies the exact screen within the application that was captured. Note that the information shown in the example above is for the SAP application (which UPK identifies as **FRONT**, for some reason...). Other information may be captured for other applications.

If we display the technical information for our application, we will find this same information. In the following screenshot, we see the technical information for the screen to which the context information shown previously relates. This information will obviously vary depending on the specific application that you are recording. This example is taken from SAP, but that is largely irrelevant. The point of this screenshot is simply to show that UPK *is* capturing the context from the application.

● In addition to being able to change any of the information in the *Context ID* dialog box, you can also recapture the context for any Frame within the *Topic Editor*. To do this, select menu option **Edit | Recapture Context ID**, then re-perform the action in the correct context within the application, and press PRINTSCREEN to recapture the context.

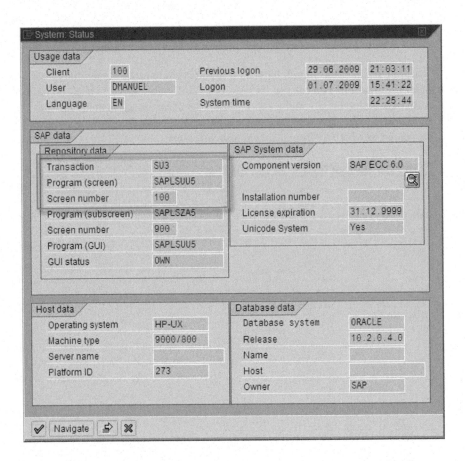

So far so good, but what does this context information do for us? Put simply, context information provides the ability to support *context-sensitive help* in our application. With context-sensitive help, if a user in the application selects the on-line help option, the application will pass details of the *context* within which the help option was selected (typically, the program, screen, and/or field) to the help system. The help system (UPK, in our case) can then see if it has help for this particular context, and display that context-specific help topic. In this way, users get help on exactly what they need, rather than being presented with the main index page of the help system and having to find what they are looking for themselves.

Adding context to non-Topic content objects

As noted earlier in this chapter, context is automatically captured for a Topic as you record it. This will ensure that the Topic is identified as applicable content when the user invokes the Help function from within that same context in the targeted application. But what if we have content that we also want to be identified as 'applicable content', but that does not have this context captured? Handily, UPK provides the ability to specify the context for non-Topic content, via the **Context** property (which exists only for Modules and Sections). Let's examine this by way of an example.

The sample course that we have been working on throughout this book is for general navigation within the SAP application. Say we have a User Guide that we have developed for SAP, and we have included this in our UPK Player by linking it into a Section of its own within our Outline. This scenario is illustrated in the following screenshot:

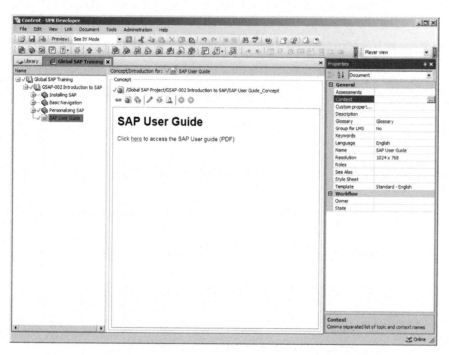

Now, suppose that we want this Section (containing our *SAP User Guide*) to be identified as 'applicable content' when we invoke the help function in our application for a specific context. To do this, we need to assign this context to the Section. There are two ways that we can do this: we can co-opt the context already recorded for a Topic, or we can record the context for this Section independently of our Topics. This latter option is useful if we do not have a Topic that covers the exact context that we want to assign to our non-Topic content. We will look at both of these options, below.

Copying context from an existing Topic

Say we want our *SAP User Guide* Section to be displayed as applicable help— along with our sample exercise—any time a user invokes Help from within transaction SU3. We can do this by assigning the same *context* to this Section as has already been recorded for our sample exercise (which was recorded for—and therefore captured the context of—transaction SU3).

To assign a Topic's context to a non-Topic content object, follow the steps shown below:

1. Select the Module or Section to which you want to assign the context.

2. Make sure that the *Properties* pane is displayed (select menu option **View** | **Panes** | **Properties** if it is not).

3. Click the ellipsis button (...) on the right of the **Context** field in the **General** category of the Properties. The following dialog box is displayed:

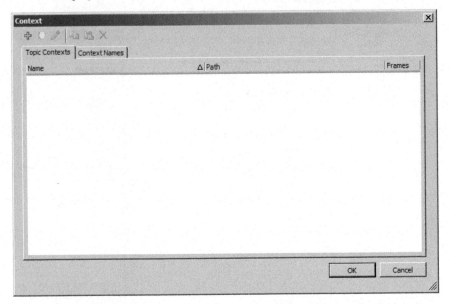

4. Click on the **Add topic contexts** button (✛). The *Add Existing Topic Contexts* dialog box is displayed, as shown below:

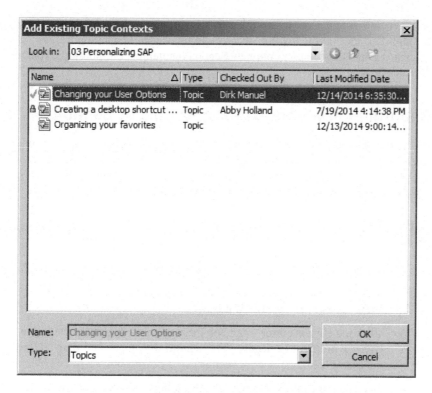

5. Navigate to and select the Topic whose context you want to assign to this Module or Section, and then click on **OK**. The Topic is now listed in the *Topic Contexts* list, as shown below:

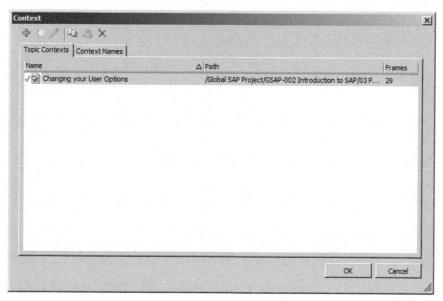

6. Click on **OK** to close the *Context* dialog box.

We have now assigned the context that exists within the selected Topic to our Section. This means that any time that this Topic is identified as applicable content via the Help function, our new Section (containing our non-topic content) will also be identified.

Recording new context for a Module or Section

If you do not have a Topic from which you can copy the context, you can capture (record) the required context for a Module or Section directly from the target application. This uses the same Recorder that we have been using to record our Topics, but does not capture a screenshot or an Action.

To capture the context for a Module or Section, carry out the steps described below:

1. Select the Module or Section to which you want to assign the context.

2. Make sure that the *Properties* pane is displayed (select menu option **View | Panes | Properties** if it is not).

3. Click the ellipsis button ([...]) on the right of the **Context** field in the *General* properties category. The *Context* dialog box is displayed (see the example in the previous section).

4. Click on the **Context Names** tab. The following screenshot shows an example of the *Context* dialog box showing this tabbed page:

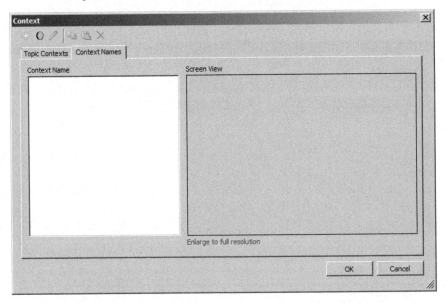

5. Click on the **Create New Context button** ([◉]). The standard *Recorder* panel is displayed, as shown below:

6. Click in the target application (to make it the active application), and then press *PRINTSCREEN* to allow UPK to identify the application that you are recording against.

7. Navigate to and click on the screen (and/or button or field) whose context you want to assign to the Module or Section.

8. Press *PRINTSCREEN* to capture the context.

9. Repeat steps 7 and 8 for all additional contexts that you want to assign to the Module or Section. Once you have captured all required contexts, click on the **Finish** button in the *Recorder* panel. You are passed back to the *Context* dialog box, where the primary context(s)—in this case the screen—along with a screenshot for the context are now displayed, as shown in the following screenshot:

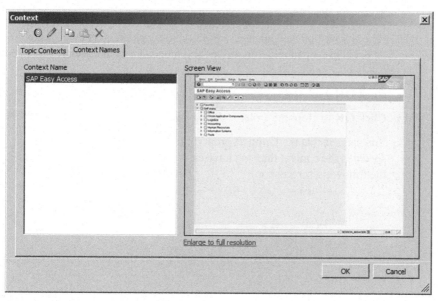

10. To confirm that context has been captured correctly, select the context in the *Context Name* list, and then click on the **Edit** button ( ). The *Context ID* dialog box is shown, as follows:

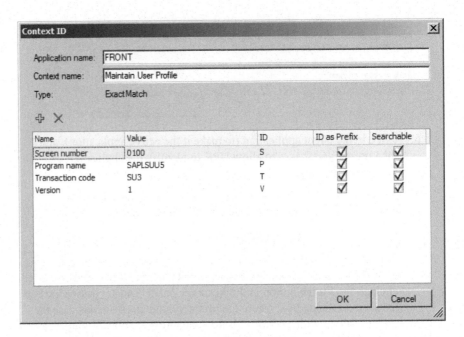

You can see that this is the same information that is captured for a Topic during recording (see the example on page 541).

11. If necessary you can delete any of the context parameters by clicking on the context parameter in the list and then clicking the **Delete** button (☒).

12. Click **OK** to close the *Context ID* dialog box.

13. Click **OK** to close the *Context* dialog box.

14. You can see that the **Context** property for the content object now specifies the context that you have captured for the object, as shown in the following screenshot:

Now, if a user invokes help from within the context that we have just captured, the non-Topic content object (the Section containing our User Guide) will be identified as applicable help.

Providing context sensitivity links from your application

Assuming that you have captured context in your recordings (and possibly assigned context to your Modules and Sections), the next step is to link your application to your UPK Player. This involves the following activities:

1. Create an In Application Support (IAS) Profile

2. Publish your Player using this IAS Profile in order to the include files required to support calls from your application in your published Player

3. Update your application to include the relevant functionality to issue context-sensitive help calls to UPK

How to update your application to provide context-sensitive help calls to your UPK Player will depend in your specific action, and is beyond the scope of this book. Instead, you should refer to the *Oracle User Productivity Kit In-Application Support Document* (E55349-01), which you can find in your UPK installation folder (typically /User Productivity Kit/{version}/ Documentation/{language}/Reference). However, the first two steps listed above are more-or-less common to all applications, so we will describe them here.

Creating an IAS Profile

✚ IAS Profiles are new in UPK 12. In prior versions, UPK would simply include all of the files required by any of the target applications in the Player.

When you integrate UPK into your targeted application, whenever a user selects your configured help option (see *How IAS appears in your application* on page 559), your targeted application will place a specific call to your UPK Player. To be able to understand and respond to this call, your UPK Player needs to have some specific files in place. An IAS Profile (which is actually just a specific type of file in your UPK Library) tells UPK which files to include in your Player, depending on the target applications specified in this IAS Profile.

To create a new IAS Profile, carry out the steps described below:

1. On the *Library Toolbar*, click on the **Create New IAS Configuration** button ([icon]). The *New IAS Configuration* screen is displayed, as shown below:

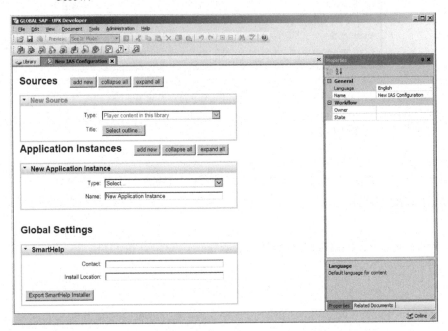

Specifying the sources

The first step in setting up an IAS Profile is to specify the UPK content objects that should accessible from within your application. This is done in the *Sources* section of the *New IAS Configuration* screen.

✚ Prior to UPK 12, you could only link application help to a single player.

Typically, you will have only one UPK Player, that contains all of your content, and will want to link this single Player to your application. However, as we shall see below, it is possible to link multiple Players and—in some cases—additional, non-UPK help content to your application.

To specify the UPK 'sources' for your context-sensitive help calls, carry out the steps described below.

1. The first (and possibly only) source that you specify must be content in the Library within which you are creating the IAS Profile. Therefore, the **Type** field defaults to **Player content in this library**, and you can only change this field for subsequent sources.

2. Click on the **Select Outline** button to the right of the **Title**, and then navigate to and select the Outline Element that you want to link to your application's help system. This must be the same as the Outline Element that you select when you publish outline.

    As soon as you select an Outline Element, the *New IAS Configuration* screen is updated to show additional fields. For the first source that you define, it will appear as follows:

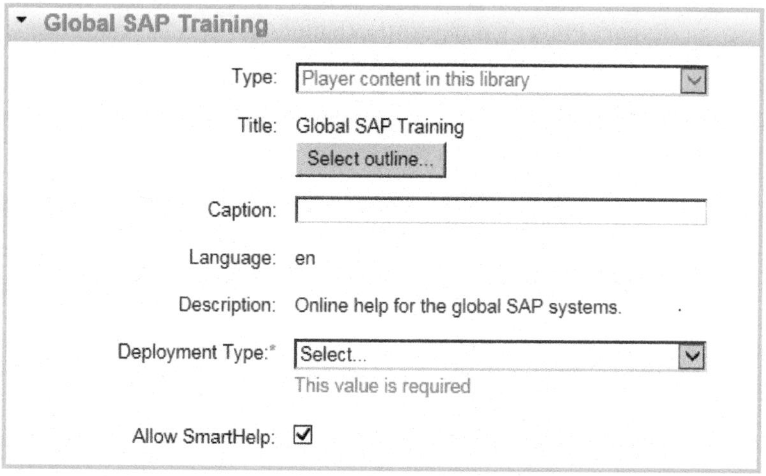

    There are a few points to note here. Firstly, the text "New Source" in the panel header has now been replaced with the name of the Outline Element that you selected. This name also appears in the **Title** field. Next, the **Language** field and the **Description** field show the content of these respective Property fields for the Outline Element (see *The Properties Pane* on page 64). You cannot change any of these values, here.

3. In the **Caption** field, you can enter a short(er) or alternative name for this Outline. This name may be used in the application's help links, depending upon the application. If you enter a name in this field, the specified name will then appear in the panel header.

4. In the **Deployment Type** field, select whether your application help will link to a Player deployed to a **Web Server** or an instance of the **Knowledge Center**.

5. If you selected **Web Server** in Step 4, then the source pane is updated again, this time to include two additional fields. The first of these is

Deployed Content URL (the second is covered in Step 7) . Specify the URL of your published Player in this field.

6. If you want SmartHelp to be activated for this Player, then make sure that the Allow SmartHelp option is selected. Otherwise, deselect this option.

7. If you selected a deployment type of **Web Server** (in Step 4) and SmartHelp is enabled (see Step 6), and your users require authentication to access the Web Server (or folders) on which your Player is deployed, then enter the URL of a publicly-accessible location at which users can find an access request form, in the **Public Subscription URL** field. This form is actually provided by the cdd.html file, which must be copied from your published Player to the location specified in this field.

8. If you have already published your Player, and don't want to publish it again, then you can create the required fies now, by clicking on the **Export Player Configuration** button, and then manually copy the generated files into your Player.

To specify additional sources, carry out the following steps before continuing to the *Application Instances* panel

1. Click on the **add new** button above the *Sources* panel. The *Sources* panel is updated to show the following choices:

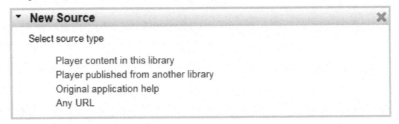

2. To link to an additional Outline Element located in the same Library, carry out the following steps:

   i. Click on the **Player content in this library** link, and then specify the remaining details as described above.

3. To link to content that has been published to another Player, carry out the following steps:

   i. Click on the **Player published from another library** link. The *New Source* pane is updated to include additional fields, as shown below:

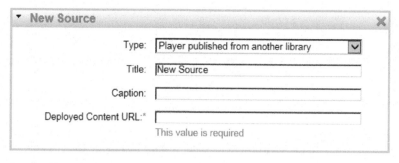

ii. In the **Title** field, enter the name of the Outline Element for the other Player.

iii. In the **Caption** field, enter a short text description of the additional content.

iv. In the **Deployed Content URL** field, enter the URL of the additional published Player.

4. For some Oracle applications, pre-built help content is available, and can be linked into your UPK IAS help. To include this content, carry out the following steps:

i. Click on the **Original application help** link. The *New Source* pane is updated to include additional fields, as shown below:

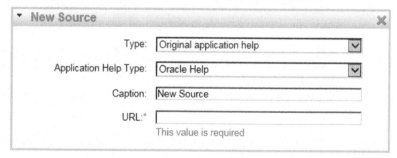

ii. In the **Application Help Type** field, select the application for which you want the help to be included. Your choices are **Oracle Help**, **PeopleBooks**, or **Siebel Help**.

iii. In the **Caption** field, enter a short text name for this suite of help documents.

iv. In the **URL** field, enter the URL at which the additional help can be found. Note that this field is not available if you select **Siebel** as the application in Step ii.

5. If you want to link to any other source of help, then carry out the following steps:

i. Click on the **Any URL** link. The *New Source* pane is updated to include addition fields, as shown below:

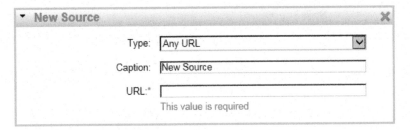

ii. In the **Caption** field, enter a short text name for this help.

iii. In the **URL** field, enter the URL at which the additional help can be found.

Specifying the applications

The next step is to specify the applications for which you want to use your Player (and any other specified sources) as the application help. This is done in the *Application Instances* pane.

For each application that you specify, UPK will generate the fields required by the Player package in order to support calls from that application. To specify these applications, carry out the steps shown below:

1. In the *Application Instances* pane, select the target application from which you want to provide in-application support via UPK.

    As soon as you select an application, the *New Application instance* pane is updated to show additional fields. The exact fields that are included will depend upon the application selected. The screenshot below (and the steps that follow) apply to SAP Business Suite,

Note that not all of the fields will necessarily be shown to start with; additional fields may be displayed as you select certain options within the pane.

2. Complete the appropriate fields for your application.

The fields that you see, and what you can (or should) enter into these will depend entirely on your targeted application, They are therefore not described here. Instead, you should refer to the relevant section of the *Oracle User Productivity Kit In-Application Support Document* (E55349-01). You may need to contact your application administrators for much of this information.

Complete the Global settings

At the bottom of the *New IAS Configuration* page is a section titled **Global Settings**. These are settings that apply to your IAS configuration across all sources and applications. Depending upon the options selected above, there may be a *SmartHelp* panel and/or a *Knowledge Center* panel. Complete these sections as follows:

1. If you have selected **SmartHelp** for at least one of the sources specified, then complete the *SmartHelp* details, as follows:

    i. In the **Contact** field, enter the details of the person or organization that a user should contact if they have problems installing the SmartHelp software.

    ii. In the **Install Location** field, specify the URL of the location from which users can install the SmartHelp software (you can generate this software in the next step).

    iii. To generate the SmartHelp installer software, click on the **Export SmartHelp Installer** button. Once the export completes, copy this software to the location specified in Step ii.

2. If you have selected a deployment type of **Knowledge Center** for any of your sources, then complete the *Knowledge Center* details, as follows:

    i. Enter the URL of the content root in Knowledge Center into the **Content Root URL** field.

Save your IAS Profile

Once you have specified all of the sources, target applications, and global settings, save your IAS Profile by carrying out the steps described below:

1. On the *Standard Toolbar*, click on the **Save** button (🖫). The standard *Save As* dialog box is displayed.

2. Navigate to the folder in which you want to save your IAS Profile. This can be in any folder within the Library.

3. In the **Name** field, enter a suitable name for your IAS Profile.

4. Click on **Save**.

5. Close the *IAS Configuration* window.

You can now use this IAS Profile when you publish your Player. How to do this is explained in the next section.

Using an IAS Profile

To use your IAS Profile, you need to specify it in the **In-Application Support Configuration** section for the Player publishing format, within the last step of the *Publishing Wizard*.

■ You can only select an IAS Profile that specifies the Outline Element being published as its source.

Complete instructions on how to publish a Player are given in *Chapter 6, Publishing Your Content*, but an example of the relevant screen, showing the selection of a custom IAS Profile, is included below, for your reference.

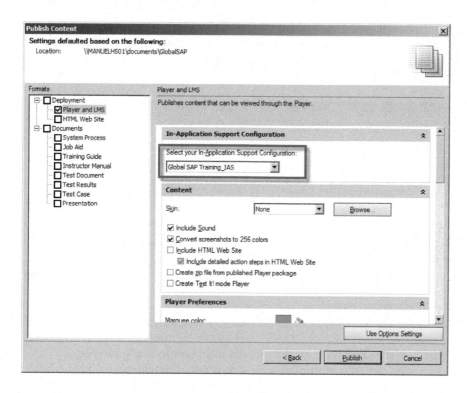

Once your Player has been created, the final page of the *Publishing Wizard* will be shown. An example of this is shown below:

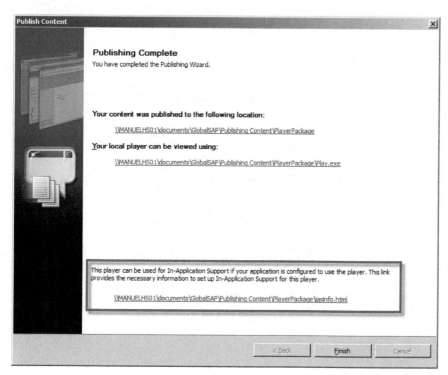

Note the highlighted box at the bottom of the *Publishing Wizard* screen. This informs you of the location of the key information for the implementation of IAS within your application(s). Clicking on this link will display a screen similar to the following:

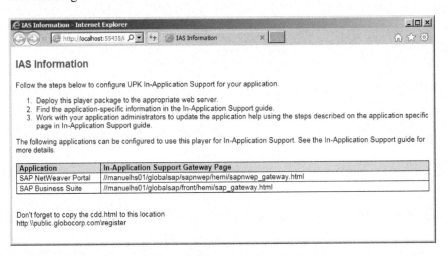

Here, you can see some basic information about how to configure your application (actually, more of an indication of where to find this information). You can also see the applications for which the required IAS files have been created within the Player. The 'gateway pages' specified are the pages that need to be specified in the application. You can see from the URLS listed that UPK effectively creates a separate subfolder within the `PlayerPackage` folder, for each of the target applications. Compare the URLs included on the *IAS Information* page, with the list of folders in the PlayerPackage:

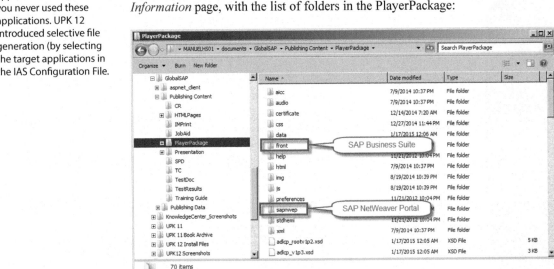

✛ Prior to UPK 12, UPK would simply create all of the required files for all of the possible target applications—even if you never used these applications. UPK 12 introduced selective file generation (by selecting the target applications in the IAS Configuration File.

Also note, at the bottom of the *IAS Information* page, a reminder that you should copy the cdd.html file to the specified location. This is important if you are using SmartHelp.

How IAS appears in your application

How your IAS help links appear in your application will depend upon the specific application. Our sample exercise was recorded for SAP, and in the SAP application screens, custom help is provided by way of another option on the **Help** menu, as shown in the next screenshot:

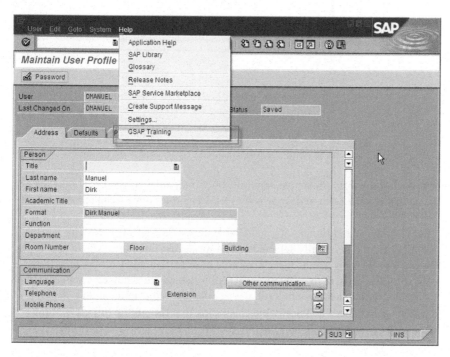

The menu option **GSAP Training**, above, is configured within SAP to point to a UPK Player on a server. If a user selects this help option, then the specified UPK Player is opened in the browser. The clever part is that the content of the Player is automatically filtered to show only Topics that apply to the exact context that was passed by the application. In our example, we selected **Help** from the initial screen of SAP transaction **SU3**. The context-sensitive Player then appears as shown in the screenshot below.

● If the option **Enable Direct Do It!** was selected during publishing, and there is only one Topic applicable to the current context, then this Topic will automatically be launched in *Do It!* mode (and the Player screen will not even be displayed). In order to capture the example above, this option was not selected, so that the filtered outline could be seen.

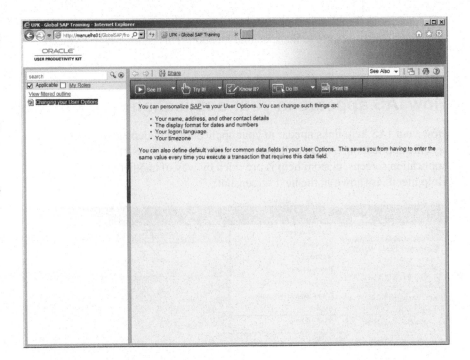

As you can see from the above example, only one Topic is listed – this is the only Topic that has the context of transaction **SU3** and the screen **0100** recorded for it.

There is now an additional option available above the Outline hierarchy. This is **Applicable**, and is initially selected (when we access the Player via the context sensitive help). This means that the outline has been filtered to show only the content that applies to the context from within which we accessed the Player (that is, from within which the help option was invoked in the application). The user can always deselect the **Applicable** check-box to return to the full view of the Outline.

■ It is highly recommended that each Topic appears only once in the Outline (that you link to the application). Although UPK will quite happily let you link a single Topic into an Outline multiple times, the (applicable) Topic will appear in the filtered outline as many times as it appears in the unfiltered Outline. This can be confusing to users, especially if they do not realize that they are multiple instances of exactly the same simulation.

Note that the list of topics is displayed as a simple list, as opposed to in the actual Outline hierarchy. This is to simplify access where multiple applicable Topics are found in several places within the hierarchy. The user can click on the **View filtered outline** link to display the *applicable* Topics (only) within their respective Outline Elements. This is useful if additional information is provided in the **Concept** panes of the Outline Elements. An example of this is shown in the next screenshot:

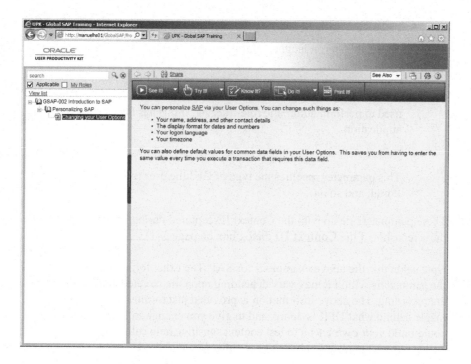

Technically, the application simply opens a browser window and passes it a URL in the following format:

```
http://<server>/globalsap/publishing%20content/
playerpackage/front/hemi/sap_gateway.html?TSU3&PSAPLSU
U5&S0100&LEN&R&GG&
```

You can see that this is calling a file named `sap_gateway.html` within the `front/hemi` folder within the `PlayerPackage` folder, and passing it a set of parameters that are define the context from within which help was invoked. Note that `front` is the identifier that UPK uses for SAP Business Suite, and `hemi` is the subfolder containing the scripts that handle the **H**elp **M**enu **I**ntegration (context-sensitivity) for SAP. There are similar folders for other targeted applications, where these are used. The parameters used (for SAP) are as follows:

- `T<transaction>`

  This is the transaction from which help was invoked.

- `P<program>`

  This is the program behind the transaction.

- `S<screen>`

  This is the identifier of the specific screen within the transaction from which Help was invoked.

■ Knowing the format of this URL is useful if you need to test your context-sensitive help links before the target application has been fully configured to support IAS. Note that you do not need to specify all parameters; if you just need 'proof of concept', the 'T' parameter (for SAP) is sufficient.

- L<language>

  This is the log-on language for the user.

- R<roles>

  This parameter specifies the roles assigned to the user. This can be used to perform automatic role-filtering, if this has been enabled in the application.

- G<gui>

  This parameter specifies the type of GUI the user is using (SAPGui, SAP Portal, and so on).

These parameters tie up with the Context ID captured during recording (refer to the screenshot of the **Context ID** dialog box on page 541).

Note again that the above example is for SAP. The exact format of the URL and the parameters within it may vary depending upon the targeted application you are recording. The above information is provided just to show you that there is no magic behind what UPK is doing, and to give you enough information that you could build your own URLs to test context sensitive help calls even if the help option in target application hasn't been fully-configured yet.

So now you know how it all works. Most of this is just 'for your information', as the set up and configuration is beyond the scope of this book. But it does highlight the need to correctly capture the context in your Topics (and to avoid the use of No-context Frames). The reverse side of this is that you should provide Topics for all of the screens for which you want to be able to provide context-sensitive help.

SmartMatch versus SmartHelp

The context sensitivity described above applies only to the "targeted applications" listed at the start of this section. This functionality is sometimes referred to as **ExactMatch**, because it provides *exact* context matching. UPK provides similar functionality for an increasing number of browser-based applications (that are not targeted applications). This functionality is called **SmartMatch**, and works in a similar way to context-sensitivity in targeted applications, but uses analytics similar to those used by search functions to identify the context within the application.

SmartHelp is a way of providing help menu integration for web-based applications. SmartHelp adds a new button to the browser toolbar that can be used to call up UPK simulations relevant to the user's (browser) screen, in a similar way to how the help menu integration for targeted applications works, by using the SmartMatch capabilities of UPK.

The implementation of SmartMatch and SmartHelp is something that is best left to the system administrators, and is therefore beyond the scope of this book. For more information, refer to the UPK *Content Deployment Guide.*

Linking directly to content from a non-UPK document

In this section we look at how to provide a link to a specific published Module, Section, or Topic from any source that is not within the UPK Player itself. This could be from a Microsoft PowerPoint presentation, or from an e-mail, or from a company website, or anywhere else you could have a hyperlink. The key consideration is that, upon clicking the link, an individual Topic is immediately launched, possibly in a specific play mode, rather than the user being directed to the Player and having to select the Topic and play mode from there.

Automatically launching a Topic in a specific play mode

When you publish to a Player, UPK also creates an additional, 'hidden', HTML page that can prove extremely useful to you as an author. This page is `kp.html`, and can be found in the `Publishing Content/PlayerPackage` folder (that is, exactly the same folder as the `index.html` and `default.html` pages). This file was initially developed as part of Global Knowledge's Knowledge Pathways application (which has now been superseded by Knowledge Center) as a way of providing easy access to individual Topics from within an e-learning environment, but it has its uses for authors.

If you open this `kp.html` file in the browser, you will see something like the example shown in the following screenshot:

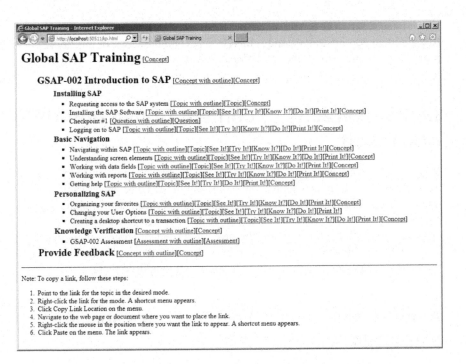

As you can see, this page provides a very basic way of accessing each of the Topics in the published outline, along with the Concept Pages attached to the Topic or any of the Outline Elements. If the published Outline includes in-line Questions or Assessments, then links are provided to these as well.

The original intention of `kp.html` was that provides direct links to any of the Player modes available for that Topic. Clicking on any of the standard mode links (`[See It!]`, `[Try It!]`, `[Know It?]`, `[Do It!]`, and `[Print It!]`) will launch the Topic just as if you had selected it in the Player Outline and clicked on the button for that mode. Similarly, clicking on the `[Assessment]` or `[Question]` links will launch that object as if it had been launched from within the Player.

Obviously, this is not really an interface that you'd want to give to your users, but for the author, it is indispensable, because what this page is really doing is providing you with *direct URLs* to the Topics.

Why is this useful? Well, consider the case where you are building a standalone course designed to be used for self-paced learning (as opposed to instructor-led classroom conduct). You have built a presentation in Microsoft PowerPoint, and want to integrate your UPK simulations into this. You *could* simply provide instructions telling your users to go and access the UPK Player, select their course, navigate to the correct exercise, and then run it in the required mode. All of which they *may* bother to do, and all of which they *may* actually do correctly. However, wouldn't it be better if they could just click on a link within the presentation and immediately be taken to the correct exercise, in the required mode? To do this, all you need to do is get the URL of the specific Topic/mode combination, and use this as a link in the presentation. And the `kp.html` file provides this link.

However, the `kp.html` file also contains another few useful links. For each Topic, the file contains a link named `[Topic]`. Clicking on this link will display the Concept Page for the selected Topic, including all of the play mode buttons along the top (for the modes in which the Topic is available). Effectively, this is the Player without the Outline, and with the selected Topic shown. An example of this is shown in the screenshot below:

● This is exactly the same as the link provided via the **Share** link in the Player, explained in *User-shared links* on page 568

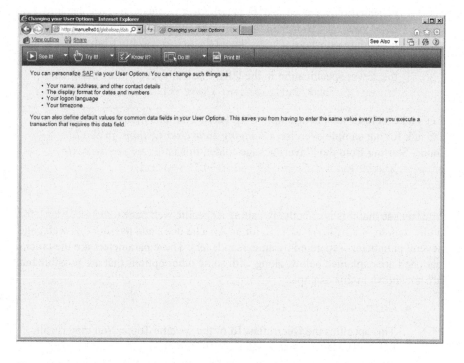

Here, the user can access any of the available play modes for the Topic (versus the play mode links, each of which gives access to only that mode. However, note that there is a new link, **View Outline**, available in the upper-left of the Player. Clicking on this displays the Outline, just as if the full Player had been launched and the user had navigated to the selected Topic.

✤ The ability to directly access Outline Elements (via the '...with outline" links) was introduced in UPK 12.

`kp.html` also includes a "...with outline" link for each content object (Module, Section, Topic, Assessment, and Question). This link will display the entire Player Outline in a new browser window, but will automatically expand to, and select, the Topic whose "...with outline" link you clicked. Effectively, if you provide a user with this link it will save them the trouble of having to locate the Topic in the Outline themselves, but will still provide them wit the full functionality of the Player (including access to all play modes, visibility of the Concept Page, and the ability to navigate through and select other elements in the Outline.

✛ In UPK 11 and earlier, the web page dhtml_kp.html was called, The link system has been completely overhauled in UPK 12, and now all links are handled directly by index.html or default.html, depending upon your server type. Note that the dhtml_kp.html file still exists for legacy support (so any Pre-UPK 11 use of it will not break), but it is deprecated and should not be used going forward.

To copy the link for a specific Topic/mode combination, carry out the steps described below:

1. Open the kp.html file in your web browser.

2. Locate the Topic to which you want to provide a link.

3. Right-click on the link for the relevant mode, and then select **Copy shortcut** from the context menu. (The option name may be different in browsers other than Internet Explorer.)

4. You can now use this URL in any link you like. You can use it in a presentation, as discussed, or email it to a reviewer, or even use it to build your own front-end for your UPK training exercises. Note that depending on where you displayed the kp.html file from (for example, the final content server, or your local machine), you may need to change the server specification in the URL (basically, everything between "http://" and "Publishing Content").

Let's take a closer look at a sample URL taken from this file. We will choose the link for our sample exercise, *Changing Your User Options*, in *See It!* mode. Starting from the PlayerPackage folder, this is: PlayerPackage/ index.html?Guid=0f76eb19-931b-4396-acbd-ed916ac526fe&Mode=S&Back

● The question mark (?) in the URL means that there are one or more parameters after the URL. This is standard web functionality. However, some applications may not support the use of a question mark in a URL, and interpret it differently. If you find that you cannot successfully call this URL from within your application, then try replacing the question mark with a hash mark (#), sometimes referred to as a pound or hex sign. This is also standard web functionality. Both are supported by all standard web browsers.

You can see that this is effectively calling a specific web page (index.html for an IIS server, or default.html for an Apache one), and passing this web page several parameters separated by ampersands (&). These parameters are the crucial part, and are explained below, along with some other options that are possible but are not shown in this example:

● Guid=<DocumentID>

This specifies the **Document Id** of the specific Topic. You may recall that UPK uses its own 32 character identifier to refer to all content objects; this is that identifier. For reference, a view of the *Library* screen, showing the same identifier, is shown below:

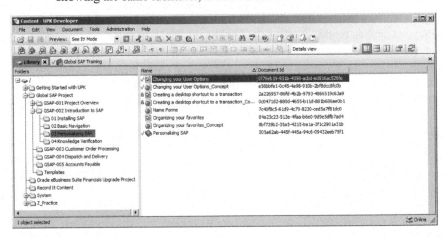

- `Mode=<Mode>`

  This parameter specifies the mode in which the Topic will be played. The following values are possible:

  - ♦ S: See It! mode
  - ♦ T: Try It! mode
  - ♦ K: Know It? mode
  - ♦ D: Do It! mode
  - ♦ E: Test It! Mode
  - ♦ P: Print It! mode

- `Frame=<Frame ID>`

  This parameter can be used to start playback from a specific Frame within the Topic. You probably wouldn't normally want to do this (why build a simulation and then allow users to bypass some of it?), but consider the case where you have Jump-in Points (covered in *Chapter 10, Adding Value in the Player*. There, you do want the users to be able to start playback from a certain frame. In fact, it is probably this requirement that led UPK to build this *entirely undocumented* feature into the URL – although using this parameter, you can jump to *any* Frame, and not just those with Jump-in Points.

- `Back`

  This parameter does not take a value, and simply means that once the simulation has completed, the browser returns to the previous page displayed—typically, the web page from which the link was called.

- `Back2`

  This parameter is similar to `Back`, but the browser goes back two pages (that is, to the page before the one from which the simulation was called). This is useful in cases where the link opens the "Launch" page which then opens the simulation, as a way of returning to before the "Launch" page.

- `Close`

  If this parameter is used, then the once the simulation has completed, the browser window from which the simulation was called is closed. This is useful if the simulation was called from an application (and not another web page). This parameter does not take a value.

- `Windowed`

  In versions of UPK prior to UPK 12, this parameter is used in the [**See It! (In Window)**] link to indicate that playback should take place in a resizable window and not full-screen. Starting from UPK 12, See It! mode is always played back in 'windowed' mode, and full-screen is no longer available, so this parameter is not used. However, it is still

■ The `Back` parameter is a good choice if the Topic is called from another web page in the browser, but for links from other applications this will simply re-display the "Launch" screen, so `Close` (see below) should be used instead.

supported, for backwards compatibility. This parameter does not take a value, and was only used in conjunction with *See It!* mode.

- `ConceptOnly`

  This parameter does not take a value. It is used in the **[Concept]** link to indicate that the Concept Pane for the Topic should be displayed.

- `BypassToc=`

  If this parameter is set to anything other than **0** then the Outline is suppressed in the browser window. This parameter/value is used in the "...with outline" links, to display the Outline.

✛ The `BypassToc` parameter was introduced in UPK 12 (see also the **Link** option below).

By using all of this information, you can manually build your own hyperlinks to Topics (without displaying the `kp.html` file), as long as you know the **Document Id**. This can be useful if you need to provide hyperlinks (for example, for use in an external access mechanism) before you have even published your content to its final location.

● There are four additional parameters: `name`, `owner`, `kpfeedbk`, and `kpnextpage`, but these are reserved for Knowledge Center and are not useful when building application links.

User-shared links

Although the `kp.html` file is accessible to all of your users (it is present in the published Player)—if they know to look for it—it is not really what you would call an 'end-user tool'. Handily, UPK does provide a more user-friendly way for your users to share links with other users (or embed into documents of their own). This is via the 'Share' feature in the Player.

✛ The Share feature was introduced in UPK 11..

The Share feature is available both from the Outline, and also from within a Topic, and works slightly differently in each case. Both options are discussed separately, below.

Sharing from the Outline

● The **Share** button is only available if you are accessing the Player via a web server. Presumably, this is because there is little point in sharing a link to content on your local drive.

In the published Player, a **Share** button is available on the upper-left of the **Concept** pane area. This is shown in the following partial screenshot:

The purpose of this feature is to allow a user to share a link to a specific Topic (or Module or Section) with other users. When the user clicks on this button, a dialog box containing a hyperlink to the currently-displayed content object is displayed. An example of this is shown below:

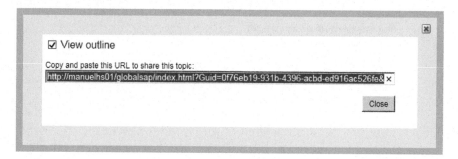

The user can copy and paste this link into an email, or save it to their favorites, and so on. The format of this link, again starting from the `PlayerPackage` folder, is as follows:

```
/playerpackage/index.html?Guid=0f76eb19-931b-4396-
acbd-ed916ac526fe&bypasstoc=0
```

You can see that this is, like the links in `kp.html`, a call to `index.html`, passing the **Document Id** of the specific Topic as a parameter. An additional parameter of `bypasstoc=0` is passed if the **View outline** check-box is selected in the link dialog box (and is omitted if it is not). The presence of this parameter causes the link to display both the Topic and its position within the Outline.

Sharing from within a Topic

If a user is currently playing a Topic (in *See It!*, *Try It!*, or *Do It!* mode), the Share feature is available from the Actions link in the upper-right corner of the Bubble. An example of this, with the drop-down menu expanded to show the Share link, is shown below:

✚ The ability to share from within a Topic was added to UPK 12.1. In UPK 11, it was only possible to share an 'entire' Topic, from the Outline.

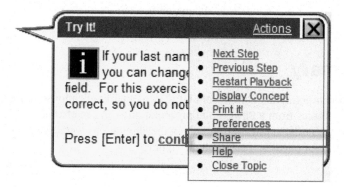

Clicking on the **Share** link in the **Actions** drop-down menu displays the following dialog box:

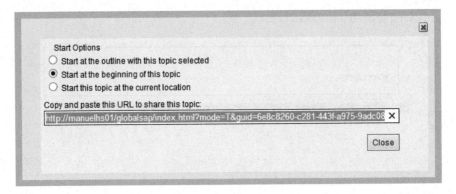

This is similar to the dialog box shown when accessing the Share feature from the Outline—in that there is a URL that can be copied—but there are a number of additional options. These are explained below:

- **Start at the outline with this topic selected**

  This is effectively the same as the Share function when invoked from the Outline, assuming that the **View outline** option has been selected/

- **Start at the beginning of this topic**

  This option creates a link that is comparable to the links obtained from the `kp.html` file, in that the link will immediately launch the Topic (in the mode from which the link was generated), without the Outline.

- **Start this topic at the current location**

  This option creates a similar link to the **Start at the beginning of this topic** option (where the Topic is immediately launched), but will start playback from the exact Frame from which the Share link was accessed.

As before, the user can select the relevant option (which will dynamically update the URL), copy the URL, and then paste this URL into an email, add it to their favorites, embed it in another document, and so on.

Summary

You can incorporate the output from UPK into other applications—for example, linking to Topics from a PowerPoint presentation. You can also link UPK to the help system for the application for which the simulations were recorded, in order to provide in-application performance support.

16
Customizing UPK

In this chapter we will look at some of the things you can do to make UPK better meet your company's or client's specific requirements. These things are not for the faint-hearted, as some of them involve digging around in the bowels of UPK and tinkering with the delivered files. However, as we will see in this chapter, a little effort can lead to some big improvements for your users—and that should always be the benchmark on whether or not something is worth doing.

In this chapter, you will learn how to:

- Create a Style Sheet

- Customize the Template Text

- Replace the default Bubble icons with your own icons

- Define a new Object Type

- Customize the Player publishing format

- Customize the Word Document publishing formats

Creating a Style Sheet

As discussed in *Chapter 9, Adding value to your Topics*, **Style Sheets** are used to define the way in which the content of your Web Pages appear. You do not **have** to define a Style Sheet, but there are a few distinct advantages in using them (versus the alternative of just relying on your individual Developers to apply direct formatting to the elements within their Web Pages). These are:

+ Style sheets were introduced in UPK 12.1.

- Using a Style Sheet will ensure consistent formating across all Web Pages (to which that Style Sheet has been applied)

- It is much faster to apply a single style to a text element in a Web Page than it is to apply several types of direct formatting (one for the font family, one for the font size, one for bold, one for spacing, and so on).

- You can define a separate Style Sheet for each client (or project, application, and so on) to provide client-specific formatting, within the same Library.

- You can define a separate Style Sheet for each specific *use* of Web Pages—for example, one for Web Pages used as Concept Pages for Modules or Sections, one for Web Pages used as Concept Pages for Topics, one for Web Pages used for Glossary definitions, and so on.

- If you change your mind on how something should look (or some manager assumes that they know better and wants everything formatted to his or her personal preferences) you only have to change this on one place—the Style Sheet—and the change will automatically be applied to all Web Pages that use this Style Sheet.

It is important to note, however, that UPK Style Sheets are not the same as Cascading Style Sheets (CSS). You can only apply a single UPK Style Sheet to a document, and one UPK Style Sheet cannot include references to other Style Sheets.

Available elements

UPK allows you to define the appearance of the following content elements. For authors familiar with HTML, the equivalent HTML elements are also shown.

Category	Defines the format of:	HTML
Document Body	Design elements that apply to the overall style of the entire Web Page (such as background color, font family, font size, and text color).	`<BODY>`
Paragraph	Text paragraphs.	`<P>`
Text	A text selection within a paragraph.	`<SPAN>`
Table	Data tables (including row header and column header formatting, borders and shading).	`<TABLE>` `<TR>` `<TD>`
Bulleted List	All levels of bulleted lists.	`<UL>`
Numbered List	All levels of numbered lists.	`<OL>`
Heading 1..6	Headings (separately for all six available headings).	`<H1>..<H6>`
Image	Embedded graphics.	`<IMG>`
Link	Hyperlinks (including hover and visited).	`<A>`

Category	Defines the format of:	HTML
Horizontal Line	Horizontal lines.	<HR>
Preformatted	Text that should be interpreted as pure text (and not as HTML characters).	<PRE>
Address	Address blocks.	<ADDRESS>
Block Quote	Sections of text to be formatted as block quotes.	<BLOCKQUOTE>

We will look at how to use several of these style categories by way of a practical example, as we build our own Style Sheet, in the sections below.

Defining a new Style Sheet

To define a new Style Sheet, carry out the steps described below:

1. Navigate to the folder into which you want to store your new Style Sheet. This can be any folder (to which you have **Modify** permission), but if you are performing client-level or project-level customization, it makes sense to store the Style Sheet in the same folder as your other customized templates (for example, any customized Bubble Text Template).

2. On the *Library Toolbar*, click on the **Create New Style Sheet** button (🖼). (You can also select menu option **File | New | Style Sheet**.) The *Style Sheet Editor* is displayed. An example of this is shown below:

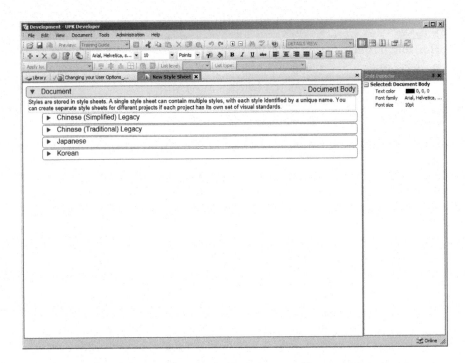

The Style Sheet initially a single style, called **Document** (shaded in blue, in the screenshot above), and some initial descriptive text. This descriptive text is used to show how the style that they appear under will appear (and also sometimes provides additional guidance). As you change the style definition, this text will be updated to reflect the style changes, so that you know how text using this style will appear (kind of like a pseudo-WYSIWYG editor).

Below the style definition (name and text sample) are any language-specific variants of this style. Initially, there are four variants (one for each of the main character set variants), but these can be deleted, and/or new language variants added instead. You can also define a 'Print' variant (which will be used when the Web Page is printed, as we shall see later in this section).

3. For our sample, we remove the local-language information. These are actually defined as styles, so in doing this we will learn how to delete a style:

   i. Click on the style definition or variant that you want to delete, to select it.

   ii. Click the **Delete** button (☒) on the *Style Editor - Styles Toolbar*.

   iii. Repeat these steps for all additional style definitions or variants that you want to remove from the Style Sheet.

4. To insert a new style definition, click on the **Add Style** button (⊞▾), and then select the text element for which you want to define the style

from the drop-down list. In the screenshot below, we have added a new style for **Heading 1**.

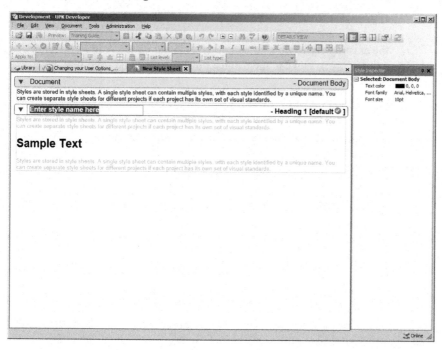

5. Replace the default style name of **Enter style name here** with a suitable name for your style. This does not need to be the same as the type of element that it is formatting (so you can have multiple styles for the same text element, and allow the author to choose which one to use in any particular circumstance), but it should be indicative of its use, and meaningful.

6. If you have created more than one style for the same text element, then you need to identify which one of these will be used by default. To do this, make sure that the default style is selected, and then click on the **Make Default** button (⊘) (you can also right-click on the style, and select **Set As Default** from the shortcut menu). Alternatively, if you do not want to set a default (in which case the author will always need to select which one to use), right-click on the current default, and select **Remove Default** from the shortcut menu.

7. Make sure that your style is selected (it is highlighted with blue shading), and then use the buttons on the various *Style Editor* toolbars to set the appropriate styles and formatting. See *The Style toolbars* on page 577 for an explanation of the available toolbar buttons and their purpose.

Note that for some object types (such as tables and lists), you may need to select the specific element within the object type that you want to format, before applying the formating.

You can use the *Style Inspector* pane to review the current definition, and refer to the sample text block to review how this style will look.

8. If you want to define a specific format to be used for an element when the document is printed, then you can define a 'print style' by selecting the existing style definition and then clicking on the **Add Print Style** button (⊞). You can then adjust this print version as required (see Step 7).

9. If you want to define a style to be used for a specific language, then you can define a 'language-specific' style by selecting the existing style definition and then clicking on the **Add Language** button (⊞). You can then adjust this print version as required (see Step 7).

10. Once you have made all required style definitions, click on the **Save** button (⊟) to save your new Style Sheet. The standard *Save As* dialog box is displayed. Make sure that you are in the correct folder, enter a suitable name for the Style Sheet, and then click **Save**.

11. If you are working in a client/server environment, check in your Style Sheet.

In the example below, we have defined a number of text styles, and have set the background color for the document to be blue. We have also defined a print-specific version of the Document Body style that removes the blue background. Finally, we added a table with some basic formatting. Note that some of the styles in the image below have been collapsed (by clicking on the arrow to the left of the style name) for simplicity.

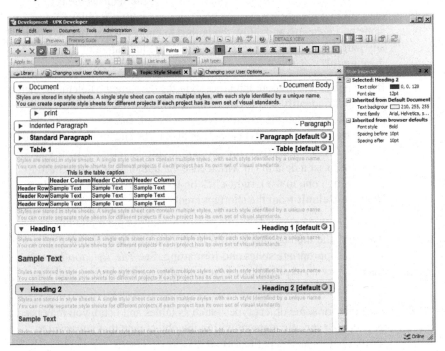

The Style toolbars

There are an additional three toolbars available when you are in the *Style Sheet Editor*. Most of the buttons on these are self-explanatory, but a few of them require further explanation. For completeness, all buttons on all three toolbars are explained below.

The Styles Toolbar

The *Style Editor - Styles Toolbar* is used to control the contents of the style sheet itself (as opposed to the formatting of individual elements). This toolbar appears in the *Style Sheet Editor* as follows:

The following table explains the buttons available on this toolbar, from left to right.

Button	Name	Use
	Add Style	Click on this button and then select the element for which you want to add style definitions to your Style Sheet. For a list of elements, refer to *Available elements* on page 572.
	Delete Style	Select a style definition and then click on this button to delete it from the Style Sheet.
	Make Default	Use this toggle button to make the currently-selected style definition the default style (or not) for the element (for which it is defined). Note that you do not have to have a default style definition for an element.
	Add Print Style	Select a style definition and then click on this button to define a print-specific variant of the style definition.
	Add Language	Select a style definition and then click on this button to define a language-specific variant of the style definition.

The Text/Paragraph Toolbar

The *Styles Editor - Text/Paragraph Toolbar* is used for formatting text elements within the Web Page. It appears in the *Style Sheet Editor* as follows (note that this screenshot shows the toolbar undocked, and with a reduced width for clarity):

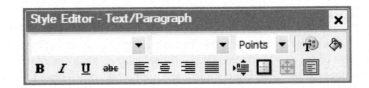

The following table explains the fields and buttons available on this toolbar, from left to right, top to bottom.

Button	Name	Use
(drop-down list)	Font Family	Select the font family to use for the text element from the drop-down list. The most commonly-used fonts are listed first, followed by all fonts in alphabetic order.
(drop-down list)	Font Size	Select the size of text from the drop-down list. The units are specified in the next field, so you may need to select the units first, and then select the text size.
(drop-down list)	Font unit	Select the unit in which the font size is specified (**Points** or **Pixels**).
	Text Color	Click on this button to display the standard *Color* dialog box, from which you can select the text color for the element.
	Background Color	Click on this button to display the standard *Color* dialog box, from which you can select the background (fill) color of the element
B	Bold	Format the element text in bold
I	Italic	Format the element text in italics
U	Underline	Underline the element text
	Strikethrough	Strike through the element text
	Align Left	Set the element text as left-aligned
	Align Center	Set the element text as centered
	Align Right	Set the element text as right-aligned
	Align Justify	Set the element text as fully justified

Button	Name	Use
	Spacing	Click on this button to display the following pop-up box, in which you can specify the amount of space that should be left around the text element.

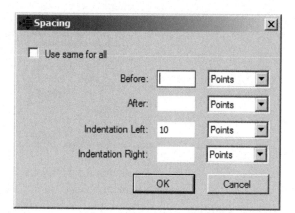

You can specify the spacing separately for **Before, After, Indentation Left,** and **Indentation Right,** or select the **Use same for all** option and then specify only one value that will be applied to all sides.

	Border	Click on this button to display the following pop-up box, in which you can assign a border to the text element.

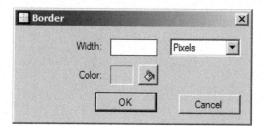

Here, you can specify the width of the border (in **Points** or **Pixels**) and can select the color of the border. Note that there is no option to specify the sides on which the border should appear.

● **Spacing** is analogous to the CSS Margin property.

● The difference between **Spacing** and **Padding** only really comes into play if you are using a background color for the element. With **Spacing**, space will be left outside of the background color; with **Padding**, space will be left within the background color.

Button	Name	Use
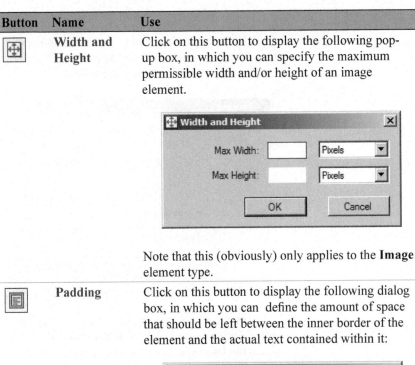	**Width and Height**	Click on this button to display the following pop-up box, in which you can specify the maximum permissible width and/or height of an image element.

Note that this (obviously) only applies to the **Image** element type.

Button	Name	Use
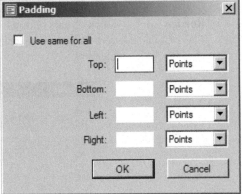	**Padding**	Click on this button to display the following dialog box, in which you can define the amount of space that should be left between the inner border of the element and the actual text contained within it:

You can specify the spacing separately for **Before**, **After**, **Indentation Left**, and **Indentation Right**, or select the **Use same for all** option and then specify only one value that will be applied to all sides.

The Table and List Toolbar

The Styles Editor - Table and List Toolbar contains buttons and options for formatting table elements and list items. It appears in the *Style Sheet Editor* as follows (note that this screenshot shows the toolbar undocked, and with a reduced width for clarity):

The following table explains the fields available on this toolbar, from left to right, top to bottom.

Button	Name	Use
(Drop-down list)	**Apply to**	Select the table element for which you want to define the formatting. All changes made using the toolbar buttons will apply only to the selected table element, until you select another table element from the drop-down.
(icon)	**Align Top**	Align text within the selected table element to the top of the cell.
(icon)	**Align Middle**	Align text within the selected table element to the center of the cell.
(icon)	**Align Bottom**	Align text within the selected table element to the bottom of the cell.
(icon)	**Align Baseline**	Align all text within the selected table element to the baseline.
(icon)	**Caption Top**	Position the table caption above the table
(icon)	**Caption Bottom**	Position the table caption below the table
(Drop-down list)	**List Level**	Select the list level to which you want to define the formatting. You can define up to five levels for both numbered lists and bulleted lists.
(Drop-down list)	**List Type**	Select the type of number or type of bullet that you want to use for the selected list level.

■ It only really makes sense to set the **Align Baseline** option for an entire row, to ensure that the text in all cells on the row are aligned along the same 'line'. For single cells, this has the same effect as **Align Bottom**.

Assigning a Style Sheet to a Web Page

Once you have defined a Style Sheet, you need to assign it to the Web Pages that you want to format according to this Style Sheet. By way of example, we'll assign the Style Sheet that we just created to the Web Page that we are using as the Concept Page for our sample exercise. For reference, this currently appears as shown in the screenshot below.

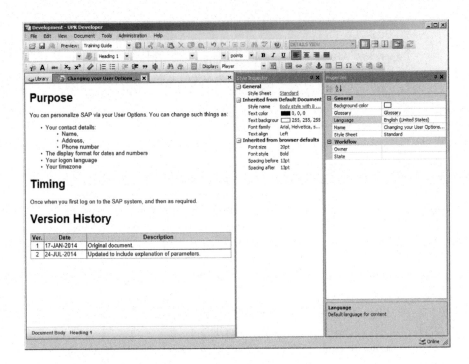

To assign a specific Style Sheet to a Web Page, follow the steps shown below:

1. Display the **Properties** pane for the Web Page in one of the following ways:

   - Select the Web Page in the *Library* and make sure the *Properties* pane is displayed.

   - Select the content object to which the Web Page is assigned in the **Outline Editor**, and make sure the *Properties* pane is displayed with the **Web Page** display option selected.

   - Open the Web Page in the *Web Page Editor* and make sure the *Properties* pane is displayed.

2. Click in the input field for the **Style Sheet** property, and then click on the ellipsis button (...) on the right of the field.

3. Navigate to and select the Style Sheet that you want to assign to the Web Page, and then click on **Open**. The Style Sheet is applied immediately.

By way of an example, we will the Style Sheet that we created earlier in this chapter to the Web Page that we are using as the Concept Page for or sample Topic. Our Web Page now looks like the example in the following screenshot:

■ If you apply a **Style Sheet** to a Web Page after the Web Page was initially created, you can remove all non-Style Sheet controlled formatting by selecting the entire contents of the Web Page and clicking on the **Clear Formatting from Text** button.

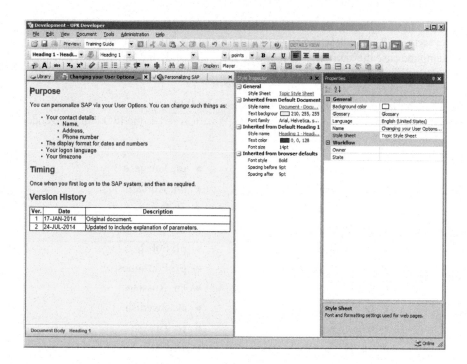

So there you have it: a Style Sheet that controls the formatting of your Web Pages. You can define as many Style Sheets as you like for your Library—maybe one per project, one per application, or one per Web Page use, depending on your (or your clients') individual needs.

Configuring Template Text

The text that appears (by default) in a Bubble is controlled by the Template attached to the Topic. In many cases the Template Texts will be adequate for your purposes. However, these may not match your in-house styles, or you may not like these default texts. In this case, you could just use Custom Text instead (as described in *Chapter 4, Editing a Topic*), but this can quickly turn into a lot of work if you have to do this for every Frame in every Topic. Luckily, you can make all of your changes only once, by changing the Template that controls the Template Texts.

All of the Template Text is contained in a single (per language) Template. Actually, the 'template' is really a **Package** that contains three separate files—a file named `template.xsl` that takes care of stylistic considerations, a file named `language.xsl` that provides some language-specific transformation functions, and a file named `template.xml` that contains the actual Template Text. It is this last file with which we are primarily concerned.

In fact, UPK ships with two templates per language—a "standard" one which is used by default, and an alternative one that conforms to the *Microsoft Manual of*

■ *Appendix C, Object Types* provides a side-by-side comparison of the Template Text that is generated by each of these templates.

Style. In this chapter, we will be working with the **Standard** template, although everything that we describe is also applicable to the **Microsoft** template. Both templates use the same tags in the same way—it is only the text within these tags that is different.

The template files can be found in the following folder: `System > Templates > {language}`, where `{language}` is the ISO language code of the supported language, as follows:

- **cs**: Czech
- **da**: Danish
- **de**: German
- **en**: English
- **es**: Spanish
- **es-mx**: Mexican Spanish
- **fi**: Finnish
- **fr**: French
- **fr-ca**: French Canadian
- **hu**: Hungarian
- **it**: Italian

- **ja**: Japanese
- **ko**: Korean
- **nl**: Dutch
- **no**: Norwegian
- **pl**: Polish
- **pt**: Portuguese
- **ru**: Russian
- **sv**: Swedish
- **tr**: Turkish
- **zh-CHS**: Simplified Chinese
- **zh-CHT**: Traditional Chinese

● For more information on supporting local languages, including using local-language templates, refer to *Chapter 17, Localizing Your Content*.

■ See *Chapter 9, Adding Value to Your Topics* for more information on Packages.

Within the appropriate language folder, you will find two Packages—one for each of the templates, Standard and Microsoft, as shown in the following screenshot:

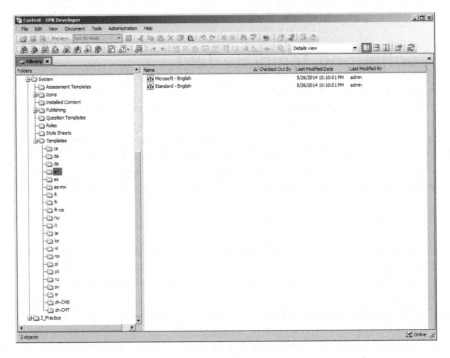

So what tells UPK which one of these two templates to use? Each Module, Section, and Topic has a **Template** Property that specifies which template file should be used for that object. By default, this is set to the **Standard - English** template, as shown in the following screenshot:

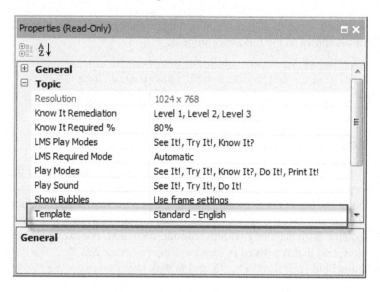

Although this Property is in the **Topic** group in the *Properties* pane, you will also find this Property—in fact, the entire **Topic** group—in the *Properties* pane for Modules and Sections. In case you are wondering why you would assign a Template to a Module or a Section when there is no Bubble Text in Modules or Sections, the simple answer is *inheritance*. If you assign a template to a Module and then create a new Section or Topic from within the *Outline Editor* for that Module, then the new Section or Topic will inherit the Module's template. (However, if you attach an existing Section or Topic to a Module, then the Section or Topic will not automatically inherit the Module's template setting.)

The **Topic** group is new to UPK 12. In UPK 11 and earlier, most of the Properties in this group were spread among the remaining groups (mostly in the **General** group), although some are new in UPK 12. See *The Properties Pane* on page 64 for additional information on the *Properties* pane.

Because the Template takes effect at the Topic level you could, in theory, assign different Templates to different Topics within the same Player. However, this could be very confusing for users, and at the very least will reduce consistency, which is never a good thing. That said, you may want to define separate Templates for each client or product—assuming that you are creating separate Players for each of these. A further advantage of using custom Templates—especially if you have several of them—is that you can easily change the Bubble Text in a Topic just by changing the Template that is assigned to it.

Understanding the template file

In order to gain a thorough understanding of the template file, we will look at each of its sections in detail. Don't worry, you don't need an in-depth knowledge of XML for this (although a basic appreciation of XML conventions will help); the XML file is really just a set of definitions, and these are fairly easy to understand once you know what they are defining—which is what this section will tell you.

The first few lines of code in the template simply identify the file as an XML format file, and include a couple of standard XML templates. You don't need to worry too much about these lines; you will never change them. An example of these lines is shown in the following snippet:

```
<?xml version="1.0" encoding="utf-8"?>
<TemplateSet xmlns:xlink="http://www.w3.org/1999/xlink"
xmlns:xsi="http://www.w3.org/2001/XMLSchema-instance"
xmlns="urn:template-v1">
```

The <Styles> section

The first section in the Template is the <Styles> section defines some basic formatting for some common elements used in the Template Text; specifically (from top to bottom in the following example), Bubble Text, Object Names, Object Types, text that is entered, keyboard keys, and hyperlinks. For each style, the style name is given, along with the format of the text. For example, in the code below, text that is entered (<Style Name="Content" />) will be displayed in bold (Bold="True"), and in dark blue (Color="#ff0000").

The default <Styles> section is shown below:

```
<Styles>
<Style Name="Text" />
<Style Name="ObjectName" Bold="true" Color="#000080" />
<Style Name="ObjectType" />
<Style Name="Content" Bold="true" Color="#ff0000" />
<Style Name="Key" Bold="true" Color="#000080" />
<Style Name="Link" Bold="true" Color="#0033cc" />
</Styles>
```

Note that these examples make use of **attributes**. The following table summarizes the attributes that are available:

Attribute	Description
Bold	Set to true if the text is to be formatted in bold. If omitted, or set to false, the text is not formatted in bold.
Italic	Set to true if the text is to be formatted in italics. If omitted, or set to false, the text is not formatted in italics.
Color	Set to the hexadecimal RGB value for the color in which the text is to be formatted.

Note that these are *default* values that are used in all of the class and context definitions (which are explained below). You can override any of these (should you need to, although you probably won't) at the class level.

The <Events> section

The next block of code is the `<Events>` set. This defines all of the different types of Actions that can be captured by UPK during recording. This list corresponds to the Actions that can be selected in the *Frame Properties* pane in the *Topic Editor*. For reference, a selection of these is shown in the next screenshot:

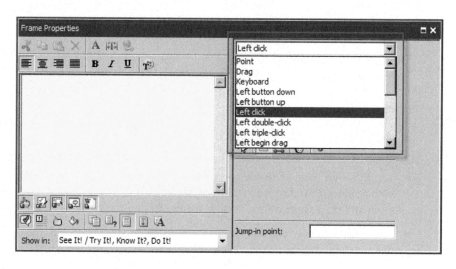

The default `<Events>` section is shown below:

```
<Events>
<Event Type="Move" ShiftKeyPrefix="true">Point</Event>
<Event Type="Drag">Drag</Event>
<Event Type="Key">Keyboard</Event>
<Event Type="LDown" ShiftKeyPrefix="true">Left button
    down</Event>
<Event Type="LUp">Left button up</Event>
<Event Type="LClick1" ShiftKeyPrefix="true">Left click</
    Event>
<Event Type="LClick2" ShiftKeyPrefix="true"> Left double-
    click</Event>
<Event Type="LClick3" ShiftKeyPrefix="true"> Left triple-
    click</Event>
<Event Type="LBeginDrag" ShiftKeyPrefix="true"> Left begin
    drag</Event>
<Event Type="RDown" ShiftKeyPrefix="true">Right button
    down</Event>
<Event Type="RUp">Right button down</Event>
<Event Type="RClick1" ShiftKeyPrefix="true">Right click</
    Event>
<Event Type="RClick2" ShiftKeyPrefix="true"> Right double-
    click</Event>
<Event Type="RClick3" ShiftKeyPrefix="true"> Right triple-
    click</Event>
<Event Type="RBeginDrag" ShiftKeyPrefix="true"> Right
    begin drag</Event>
```

```
<Event Type="MDown" ShiftKeyPrefix="true"> Middle button
    down</Event>
<Event Type="MUp">Middle button up</Event>
<Event Type="MClick1" ShiftKeyPrefix="true">Middle click</
    Event>
<Event Type="MClick2" ShiftKeyPrefix="true"> Middle
    double-click</Event>
<Event Type="MClick3" ShiftKeyPrefix="true"> Middle
    triple-click</Event>
<Event Type="MBeginDrag" ShiftKeyPrefix="true"> Middle
    begin drag</Event>
<Event Type="Wheel" ShiftKeyPrefix="true">Wheel</Event>
<Event Type="StringInput">String input</Event>
</Events>
```

The important things to note here are:

- `Event Type`: This ties in with the template context, which is explained below.

- `ShiftKeyPrefix`: This indicates whether the action can be combined with holding down the *SHIFT*, *CTRL*, or *ALT* keys. If this parameter is omitted, then a value of "`false`" is assumed.

- The actual text between the `<Event>` and `</Event>` tags is the text that is used in the drop-down list in the *Frame Properties* pane in the *Topic Editor*.

The <Classes> section

The next sections in the template file are the `<Class>` sections. There is one `<class>` statement for each Object Type that can be selected in the *Frame Properties* pane of the *Topic Editor*. The `<Class>` sections define template formats for specific types of objects that aren't covered in the `<Defaults>` section (which is described later). In fact, if you look at some of the definitions in the `<Class>` sections, you will see that some actions only have a comment indicating that the default template is used:

```
<Class Name="ROLE_SYSTEM_ROWHEADER" ListName="Row header"
    DisplayName="row header" Gender="neutral">
<!-- LClick1 handled by default -->
<!-- LClick2 handled by default -->
<!-- RClick1 handled by default -->
</Class>
```

As a more useful example, let's look at the template definitions for clicking on the Windows status bar.

```
<Class Name="ROLE_SYSTEM_STATUSBAR" ListName="Statusbar"
    DisplayName="statusbar" Gender="neutral">
<Template Context="LClick1">
<Text Sound="lclick14">Click the statusbar.</Text>
</Template>
<Template Context="LClick2">
```

```
<Text Sound="ldblclk8">Double-click the statusbar.</Text>
</Template>
<Template Context="Move">
<Text Sound="point4">Point to the statusbar.</Text>
</Template>
<Template Context="RClick1">
<Text Sound="rclick11">Right-click the statusbar.</Text>
</Template>
</Class>
```

The `<Class>` element itself includes four attributes. These are explained in the following list:

- Name: This specifies the type of object for which the `<Template>` elements within this `<Class>` will be applied). In the example above, the Name is set to ROLE_SYSTEM_STATUSBAR.

- ListName: This is the name of the element as it will be displayed in the **Object Type** drop-down in the *Frame Properties* pane.

- DisplayName: This is the name that will be used as the Object Type in the Bubble Text. Note that this is sometimes more of a phrase than a name. For example, for the **Titlebar button** object, the display name is "button in the title bar", because this gives a complete sentence of "Click on the `<Name>` button in the title bar.".

- Gender: This specifies the gender of the objects to which these `<Template>` definitions should apply. This may initially be confusing, but this is only because in the English language all objects are *neutral* (in terms of *masculine*, *feminine*, or *neutral*) so the same text can be used for all objects ("Click the XYZ button", "Press the XYZ key"). In some languages, *things* have a gender. For example, in French, a computer is male (*l'ordinateur*), whereas a key is female (*la clé*), and hence different template texts are provided for each gender.[1]

The `<Class>` element contains multiple `<Template>` elements. There will be one `<Template>` element for each type of action (`<context>`) that can be performed against the object specified in the `<Class>` element's Name attribute. Let's look at a single `<Template>` element.

```
<Template Context="LClick1">
<Text Sound="lclick14">Click the statusbar.</Text>
</Template>
```

At this level, the `<Template>` element used in a `<Class>` is the same as the `<Template>` element used in the `<Definitions>` section (which is described later). To save repeating ourselves, we will describe `<Template>` elements only once, in the section *The <Template> sections* on page 590, after we have looked at the `<Defaults>` section.

---

1 Thanks to Marc Wilms for the French lesson.

The \<Defaults\> section

Following the \<Classes\> section in the template file is the \<Defaults\> section. The \<Defaults\> section works in a very similar way to the \<Classes\> section, but whereas the \<Classes\> section is *object*-focused, containing a separate \<Class\> element for each object (which in turn contains a \<Template\> element for each action), the \<Defaults\> section is *action*-focused, containing a single \<Template\> element for each action, and has the actual object embedded within this \<Template\> element (as we shall see below).

A small extract of the \<Defaults\> section is shown below. Note that we have only included a single (and simple) \<Template\> element, just for the purposes of illustration.

```
<Defaults Gender="neutral">
<Template Context="LUp">
<!-- Example: Release the mouse button. -->
<Text Sound="lup">Release the mouse button.</Text>
</Template>
</Defaults>
```

The \<Defaults\> element takes a single attribute, Gender, which specifies the gender for which the text should be used. This works in exactly the same way as the Gender attribute on \<Class\> elements, but here, the attribute is specified at a higher level, and applies to all \<Template\> elements within the entire \<Defaults\> element. The implication of this is that for languages in which objects can have a specific gender, separate \<Defaults\> elements need to be defined, each with the appropriate Gender attribute value.

The \<Template\> sections

The \<Template\> sections contain the true core of the template file. They define the actual text that is to be displayed in the Bubble (and the sound that is to be played when this text is displayed).

As an example, let's look at the definition for a single Template Text (effectively, the content of a single Bubble). First, let's look at an example of a \<Template\> definition from the \<Defaults\> section of the template file.

```
<Template Context="LClick1">
<!-- Example: Click on the OK button. -->
<Text Sound="lclick">Click on the</Text>
<ObjectName />
<ObjectType />
<Text>.</Text>
</Template>
```

The \<Template\> element itself takes a single attribute. This is Context, which specifies the type of *action* (carried out against the object type defined in the \<Class\> element's Name attribute) to which this specific \<Template\>

definition applies. In the previous example, the `Context` attribute is set to `Lclick1`. The `Lclick1` action is a single-click on an object with the left mouse button. Therefore, this Template Text will be used for actions where the user left-clicks on a screen element.

The code within the `<Template>` and `</Template>` tags defines the actual Bubble Text, and any sound that should be played at the same time. In the example above, there are three distinct types of elements used (ignoring the comment, which is delimited by `<!--` and `-->`, in standard HTML form). These are:

Value	Meaning
`<Text>`	This defines static text that is to be displayed in the bubble. Note that in the example above there are two `<Text></Text>` pairs, because there are two pieces of static text: "**Click the**" and ".". You can have as many pieces of static text as you like in a single `<Template>` definition.
	The `<Text>` tag takes a single argument. This is `Sound`, which specifies the sound file that is to be played at the time that the text is displayed. In this example, the `Sound` argument is set to `lclick`, which means that the file `lclick.wav` (or other sound file format) will be played. UPK will look for this in a subfolder of the `Templates\en` folder called `Sound\Standard`, and if the file is not found, no sound will be played (but no error will be generated, either).
	Sound files are covered in more detail in *Chapter 11, Incorporating Sound Into Your Topics*.
`<ObjectName />`	This is a placeholder for the name of the object against which the Action was recorded. The XML transformation file will automatically substitute this with the actual Object Name.
`<ObjectType />`	Similar to `<ObjectName>`, this statement is a placeholder for the type of object against which the Action was recorded.

So much for the definition. Now let's look at what this does for us. Suppose we have recorded a left-click on the **Save** button. In this case, the **Frame Properties** pane will look similar to the example shown below:

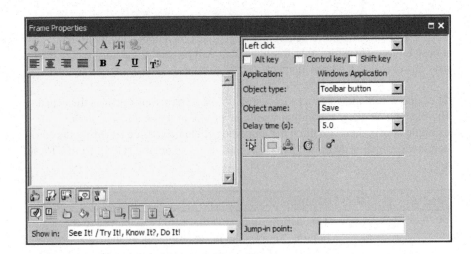

Specifically, note the **Object Type** (**Toolbar button**) and the **Object Name** (**Save**). Now let's look at what the template definition above will result in. This is shown in the following screenshot:

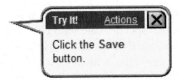

You should quite easily be able to correlate the template definition, the **Frame Properties**, and the elements in the Template. But to make sure that we are completely clear about what is happening, the following diagram pulls it all together:

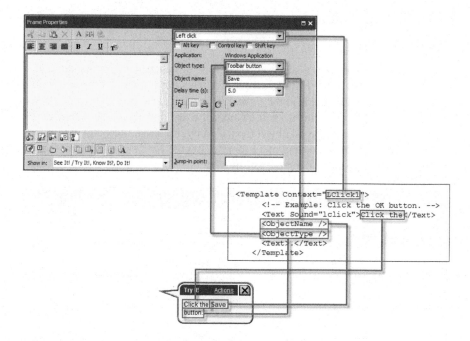

This is a simple example (String Input actions are a little more complicated), but it does clearly illustrate the relationship between the information in the *Frame Properties* pane, the Template, and the resulting Bubble Text.

The <Keynames> section

The <Keynames> section of the template file defines all of the names of the keyboard objects against which an action can be performed (that is, the keys on the keyboard).

An extract of the <KeyNames> element is shown below. Note that this has been truncated in the interests of brevity and there are actually many more keys than those listed here.

```
<KeyNames>
<Key Name="Alt">Alt</Key>
<Key Name="Control">Ctrl</Key>
<Key Name="Shift">Shift</Key>
<Key Name="Space">Space</Key>
<Key Name="Back">Backspace</Key>
<Key Name="Tab">Tab</Key>
<Key Name="Clear">Clear</Key>
<Key Name="Return">Enter</Key>
</KeyNames>
```

The <KeyNames> element itself is very simple. It does not take any attributes. This is largely because they are all the same type of object (keyboard keys) and there is only one action that can be performed against these objects, which is "**Press**".

The `<Key>` element takes a single attribute, `Name`, which specifies the name of the key, as captured by UPK during recording. This ties up with the key name in the **Key** and **Char key** fields in the *Frame Properties* pane for **Keyboard** actions. The `<Key>...</Key>` element itself contains the text that should be included in the bubble for the keyboard object (specified by the `Name` attribute). As an example, consider the recording of a user pressing the *ENTER* key. In this case, the *Frame Properties* pane will appear as follows:

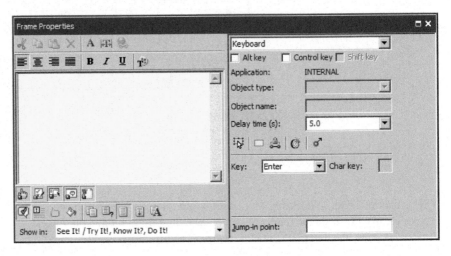

The resulting Bubble Text will be as shown in the following screenshot:

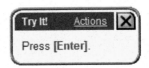

Again, let's see exactly how the Template, the *Frame Properties* pane and the Bubble Text all tie together:

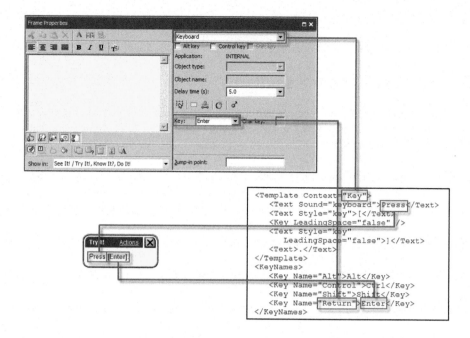

Note that only a portion of the <Keynames> section is also shown here—just enough to show where the text "Press" and the square brackets come from.

The <ShiftKeyPrefix> section

The <ShiftKeyPrefix> section defines the texts for multi-key keyboard actions (for example, pressing *CTRL+ALT+DELETE*).

```
<ShiftKeyPrefix>
  <Template Context="ShiftKeyPrefixSingle">
    <Text Sound="keybrd1">Press the</Text>
    <ShiftKey ShiftKey="Alt" Braces="true" />
    <ShiftKey ShiftKey="Control" Braces="true" />
    <ShiftKey ShiftKey="Shift" Braces="true" />
    <Text Sound="sngshift">key and</Text>
  </Template>
  <Template Context="ShiftKeyPrefixMulti">
    <Text Sound="keybrd1">Press the</Text>
    <ShiftKey ShiftKey="Alt" Braces="true" />
    <ShiftKeySeparator Type="First" Style="Text"
      LeadingSpace="false" ShiftKey="C" />
    <ShiftKey ShiftKey="Control" Braces="true" />
    <ShiftKeySeparator Type="Last" Style="Text"
      LeadingSpace="false" ShiftKey="S" />
    <ShiftKey ShiftKey="Shift" Braces="true" />
    <Text Sound="mltshift">keys and</Text>
  </Template>
  <Separator>+</Separator>
  <Separator1>,</Separator1>
  <Separator2> and</Separator2>
```

```
<UpperCase>ABCDEFGHIJKLMNOPQRSTUVWXYZ</UpperCase>
<LowerCase>abcdefghijklmnopqrstuvwxyz</LowerCase>
</ShiftKeyPrefix>
```

The <Instructions> section

The <Instructions> section contains all of the definitions for non-action-related text that is displayed, such as the static "Press Enter to continue" text that is displayed at the bottom of Explanation Frames.

The <Instructions> element itself does not take any attributes, and simply consists of a series of <Template> elements, as shown in the following example code:

```
<Instructions>
<Template Context="leadin">
  <Text Sound="leadin">Press [Enter] to </Text>
  <Text Style="Link" LeadingSpace="false"
    Link="javascript:HLink(0)"> start</Text>
  <Text>.</Text>
</Template>
</Instructions>
```

As before, note that this is a partial extract of the file. The actual <Instructions> section contains many more <Template> elements, one for each type (or use) of text. The following table lists all of the possible contexts (as specified in the Context attribute of the <Template> element) and describes their purpose.

Context	Purpose
leadin	The text that is displayed in the Start Frame, after any Custom Text, in *See It!*, *Try It!*, and *Do It!* modes.
leadout	The text that is displayed in the End Frame, after any Custom Text, in *See It!*, *Try It!*, and *Do It!* modes.
Continue	The text that is displayed in an Explanation Frame, after any Custom Text. This same text is used in *See It!* mode if the user has paused playback.
Pauselink	The Pause link that is displayed in *See It!* mode. Users can click on this link to pause playback.
knowit_leadin	The text that is displayed in the Start Frame in *Know It?* mode.
knowit_leadout	The text that is displayed in the End Frame in *Know It?* mode.
knowit_nextstep	The **Show Step** link that is displayed in *Know It?* mode if the user gives up.
knowit_explanation	The 'to continue' instructions displayed at the bottom of Explanation Frame.

Context	Purpose
leadin_score	The text that introduces the required score in *Know It?* mode.
knowit_warningL1	The text for the first level of remediation in *Know It?* mode.
knowit_warningL2	The text for the second level of remediation in *Know It?* mode.
knowit_warningL3_0	The text for the third level of remediation in *Know It?* mode, for non Action Area Actions.
knowit_warningL3_H	The text for the third level of remediation in *Know It?* mode, for Action Area Actions.
knowit_warningL4	The text for the fourth level of remediation in *Know It?* mode.
scoring	The table that shows the scoring information (target score, actual score, and so on) at the end of *Know It?* mode.
scoring_YES	The text that indicates that the user has passed the simulation in *Know It?* mode.
scoring_NO	The text that indicates that the user has not passed the simulation in *Know It?* mode.
knowit_continue	The text that is displayed if a step in *Know It?* mode is completed by UPK, asking the user to continue.
knowit_confirmdemo	The text that is displayed in *Know It?* mode if the user clicks the Show Step link, asking them to confirm that they want to see the step (and be marked down for it).
typingcomplete	The text that appears in the **Typing Complete** button for string input actions.
knowit_dragwarning	The text that tells the user that the action they are completing is a drag-and-drop action, and that the action will be completed for them.
knowit_finish_close	The text that is displayed when a user attempts to exit from a *Know It?* mode simulation before the end, asking them if they really want to exit.
strinp_suppress_example	This is not text that is displayed, but a parameter. If it is set to **0** then examples are included in the text for *Know It?* mode. If it is set to **1** then the examples are not included.
strinp_something_text	The text that is displayed for string input actions, if the (default) option is **Something**. (See the String input actions section of *Chapter 4, Editing a Topic* for more information on this.)

Context	Purpose
strinp_something_text_noexample	The text that is displayed for string input actions, if the (default) option is **Something**, but the 'suppress example' option has been selected (see strinp_suppress_example).
strinp_anything_text	The text that is displayed for string input actions, if the (default) option is **Anything**. (See the *String input actions* section of *Chapter 4, Editing a Topic* for more information on this.)
strinp_anything_text_noexample	The text that is displayed for string input actions, if the (default) option is **Anything**, but the 'suppress example' option has been selected (see strinp_suppress_example).
strinp_nothing	The text that is displayed for string input actions, if the user can leave the field empty. (See the section on *String input actions* in *Chapter 4, Editing a Topic* for more information on this.)
strinp_or	The text that is used to indicate that more than one string input option is possible.
strinp_formatter	This is not text that is displayed, but contains CSS styles that define the format of the input text.
decision_headline	The default text that is displayed above the decision paths on a decision frame. Note that this text can be overwritten by the author in the Topic file, in which case the Custom Text is used and not this Template Text.

Before delving deeper into the <Instructions> section, let's look at the simple example provided previously. As a refresher, this is:

```
<Template Context="leadin">
<Text Sound="leadin">Press [Enter] to </Text>
<Text Style="Link" LeadingSpace="false" Link="javascript:
HLink(0)">start</Text>
<Text>.</Text>
</Template>
```

This <Template> element is for the text that is displayed in the Start frame in *See It!*, *Try It!*, and *Do It!* modes. It contains three <Text> elements. You should already be familiar with basic <Text> elements, but the second <Text> element in this example introduces some additional specifications.

The first of these is the Style="Link" specification. This indicates that the text enclosed in the <Text> and </Text> elements is to be treated as a hyperlink. If you recall, in the lead-in text "**Press [Enter] to start**", the text "**start**" is a hyperlink.

The second new specification is the LeadingSpace attribute. This defines whether a space should be inserted before the text. If you look at the first

`<Text>` element above, there is already a space at the end of the preceding text, so the template does not need to include an additional one before this one. Therefore, this attribute is set to `False` (in this example).

Finally, this example includes a `Link` attribute, which has a value of `javascript:HLink(0)`. This attribute is used to define the target of the hyperlink. Each `HLink` specification contains a unique number, and this number ties up with an index maintained internally by UPK.

Now, let's look at a much more complicated example. The following example shows the `<Template>` definition for the 'level 4 remediation' warning that is displayed in *Know It*? mode if the user makes a mistake three times in a row (assuming that all three levels of remediation have been enabled).

```
<Template Context="knowit_warningL4">
<XHTMLText>
 <table xmlns="http://www.w3.org/1999/xhtml">
   <tr>
    <td valign="top" id="img_icon02"
        name="img_icon02" />
    <td>
      <a class="InstructText">
      <b>
      <font color="#000080">
        <div xmlns="http://www.w3.org/1999/xhtml">
            The action you have performed is incorrect.
        </div>
        <p>When you press OK, this step will be
           completed for you.</p>
        <p>When it is complete, you may continue with the
           next step.</p>
      </font>
      </b>
      </a>
      <input type="button" width="200" value="OK"
            onClick="HLink(10)" />
    </td>
  </tr>
 </table>
</XHTMLText>
</Template>
```

This example introduces a new pair of tags: `<XHTMLText>` and `</XHTMLText>`. These tags are used to indicate that the text between them is pure XHTML. Several of the following tags in the XHTML code have `xmlns` attributes. These specify the XML Namespaces that define what format the XHTML code can take. You do not need to worry too much about this. Everything else is standard (X)HTML, which in this example includes a table, several paragraphs, a hyperlink, and an input button.

■ The `<XHTMLText>` and `</XHTMLText>` tags are very useful indeed, as they allow you to include any kind of HTML code in your template (and therefore in your Bubbles).

Creating a custom template

OK, so far so good on the theory, but how do we actually *change* the Template Text? First, you need to decide whether your changes will apply to *all* simulations, or only to simulations for a specific set of exercises. For example, you may want to use separate templates for each product, project, or client (although I would hope that you strive for consistency). For our example, we will create a new template that applies only to the simulations that we will create for a specific client. We therefore want to take a copy of the existing template file, and then change this copy (and not the original). In fact, this is a very good practice, even if you intend on using your new template for *all* Topics; taking a copy will allow you to easily back out your changes (by reverting to the default template) if anything goes wrong.

Taking a copy of an existing template

To take a copy of a template, carry out the following steps:

1. Create a new folder for your new template. If you are creating a project-specific template, you might want to create a new folder within the project's existing folder structure in the Library. It is also a good practice to follow UPK's convention of having a separate sub-folder within this for each language that you will support. Even if you only plan on supporting (for example) English, it is a good idea to still create the language sub-folder—you never know what may happen in the future, and planning for it now could save you rework in the future. Plus, mirroring UPK's set-up will make it easier for future authors and administrators to understand which custom template relates to which original template. For our example, we will create a new folder of `Z_Templates\en\`.

   > ■ Using a prefix of "Z" is an old trick to ensure that the folder is listed toward the bottom of the Library folder list, out of the way of our actual content.

2. Locate the Package for the original template that you want to copy. This will be in the `\System\Templates\en\` (in our example) folder. You have a choice of basing your new template on the `Standard` template or the `Microsoft` template. For our exercise, we will use the `Standard - English` template as the basis for our new custom template.

3. Click on the template that you want to copy, hold down the *CTRL* key (to take a copy), and drag and drop the template onto your new folder (created in Step 1).

4. You will be asked if you want to take a copy or create a duplicate. Creating a duplicate will copy all related files, but in this case there are no related files, so you can select either option.

You now have a new copy of the Template Package in your `Z_Templates` folder. You can rename this Package to be anything that you like, although you should not use *exactly* the same name as the standard template, as this will make it difficult to determine which template a Topic uses when displaying the Topic's

Properties. Note that, as described earlier, the Template Package actually consists of three separate files. All three of these files will have been copied over.

Editing a custom template

You can edit your custom template directly from within the Template Package. Unfortunately, UPK does not include a native XML editor, so you will need to select the appropriate application on your PC to open this with. In the absence of anything better, Notepad works just fine.

To change your (copy of the default) template, follow these steps:

1. Navigate to the folder containing your custom Template Package.

2. Double-click on the Template Package to open it in the *Package Editor*. You will see the three files within the template.

3. Double-click on the file that you want to change (normally, the `template.xml` file), to open it.

4. The first time that you open this type of file you may be prompted to select the appropriate helper application. Select Notepad, or your preferred XML editor.

5. Make your changes as required (see the examples below).

6. Save the file, and close the helper application.

7. Save the Package and then close the *Package Editor*.

Customizing the Template Text

Assuming that you now have a working knowledge of the `template.xml` file (see the section *Understanding the template file* on page 585), let's now look at how to change the Template Text.

As an example, we will change the text that is displayed for string input actions. By default, this appears (in *See It!* and *Try It!* modes) as follows:

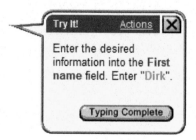

This always strikes me as a clumsy way of phrasing it. Plus, let's assume that our in-house documentation standards place field names in italics and user input in bold and black, and that we want our simulations to be consistent with this. So, we'll change the following:

1. Wording

2. Formatting of field names

3. Formatting of entered text

The first thing we need to do is find the section of the `template.xml` file that generates this Bubble Text. Search the `template.xml` file for `StringInput`, and you should find the following section of code:

```
<Template Context="StringInput">
  <!-- Example: Enter the desired information into the
Test field. Enter 123.-->
  <Text Sound="stginput">Enter the desired information
into the</Text>
  <ObjectName />
  <Text Sound="stginp2">field. Enter</Text>
  <StringInputExtension Type="anything" Sound="sivalid">a
valid value</StringInputExtension>
  <StringInputExtension Type="example"
Sound="siexample">e.g.</StringInputExtension>
  <Content />
  <StringInputExtension Type="blank" Sound="siblank">or
leave blank</StringInputExtension>
  <Text>.</Text>
</Template>
```

Update this code so that it looks like the following snippet. The changed code is shown in red.

● The `<StringInput Extension>` clauses relate to the string input options in the Topic Editor. `Type="example"` relates to string input option `<Something>` and requires the user to enter some valid text; `Type="anything"` relates to string input option `<Anything>` and requires the user to enter some valid text or leave the field blank); `Type="blank"`; relates to string input option `<Blank>`, and requires the user to enter a specific text or leave the field blank) options for input text. Refer to *Chapter 4, Editing a Topic* for more information on these options.

```
<Template Context="StringInput">
<!-- Example: Enter the desired information into the Test
field. Enter 123.-->
<Text Sound="stginput">Enter the appropriate value in
the</Text>
<ObjectName />
<Text Sound="stginp2">field. For this activity, you should
enter</Text>
<StringInputExtension Type="anything" Sound="sivalid">any
valid value</StringInputExtension>
<StringInputExtension Type="example" Sound="siexample">-
for example,</StringInputExtension>
<Content />
<StringInputExtension Type="blank" Sound="siblank">.
Alternatively, you can leave this field blank</
StringInputExtension>
<Text>.</Text>
</Template>
```

Now let's change the formatting of the field name and the value. This formatting is not defined in *this* section of the code, but you can see from this code that two placeholders are used: `<ObjectName />` and `<Content />`. So let's look for the definition of these objects in our template. Near the top of the file, you will see the following lines of code:

```
<Styles>
  <Style Name="Text" />
  <Style Name="ObjectName" Bold="true" Color="#000080" />
  <Style Name="ObjectType" />
  <Style Name="Content" Bold="true" Color="#ff0000" />
  <Style Name="Key" Bold="true" Color="#000080" />
  <Style Name="Link" Bold="true" Color="#0033cc" />
</Styles>
```

The <Styles> section defines the formatting of the placeholders used in our <Template> definition (along with some other examples not used in this example). Change these lines to be:

```
<Styles>
<Style Name="Text" />
<Style Name="ObjectName" Italic="true" Color="#000000" />
<Style Name="ObjectType" />
<Style Name="Content" Bold="true" Color="#000000" />
<Style Name="Key" Bold="true" Color="#000080" />
<Style Name="Link" Bold="true" Color="#0033cc" />
</Styles>
```

Save your changes and close your editor, and then save and close the Template Package. Once you have done this, go back into the exercise (to which this template has been assigned). The Bubble Text will now appear as follows:

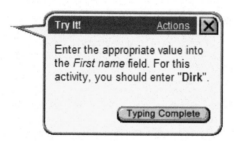

This has only been a simple, but hopefully this, along with the explanation of the template.xml file given earlier in this chapter has given you enough confidence to make further changes to your own templates, to better meet your (or your client's) needs.

Customizing the Template Text the easy way

Now that you have learned how to customize the Template Text by hand, it is time to let you into a little secret: UPK does in fact provide an editor that you can use for customizing the templates. This is called the *Template Editor* and is available from your **Start** menu. However, the *Template Editor* is not particularly straightforward, so it is wise to understand the logic behind it, before using it – hence my taking you through the manual approach first.

● Even if you register the Template Editor as the 'helper application' for XML files, double-clicking on the `template.xml` file in the Package will not open it in the *Template Editor*. You can't even right-click on the file in the Package and choose to 'open with' the Template Editor (the editor starts but the template is not opened within it). However, up until UPK 3.5 it was not even possible to edit any of the Template files from within the Package, so there is hope that Oracle will fully integrate the Template Editor into the Package Editor in a future release.

The *Template Editor* is an additional program installed along with UPK, and isn't really integrated into UPK itself (in that it cannot be invoked from within template Package) it is necessary to copy the `template.xml` file out of UPK and onto your local workstation before you can open it in the *Template Editor*.

To edit a template using the **Template Editor**, follow these steps:

1. Copy the template that you want to edit from the Template Package in the *Library*, and save it to your local workstation.

2. Start the *Template Editor* from the Windows **Start** menu.

3. From within the *Template Editor*, select menu option **File | Option**, and navigate to and select the `template.xml` file that you saved in Step 1.

4. The template will appear in the *Template Editor* as shown in the following screenshot:

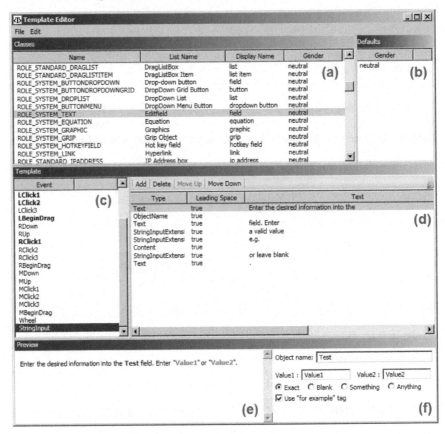

5. Select a class **(a)**, gender (if required) **(b)**, and event **(c)**, to display the template elements that are used to construct the Bubble Text **(d)** for this object/action in the rightmost side of the *Template* pane. You can see a preview of the text in the *Preview* pane **(e)**. You can also adjust the example data **(f)** for a more relevant example, if required.

6. To change the template text, double-click on the element that you want to change, in the rightmost side of the *Template* pane **(d)**, to display the *Element Properties* dialog box, shown in the following screenshot:

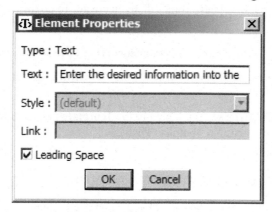

✚ Prior to UPK 11.x, the *Element Properties* pane included a *Sound* field, to allow you to choose the sound file to play for an element. This was removed in UPK 11.x, and replaced with the **Style** and **Link** fields. However, these two fields are disabled. Presumably they are 'for future expansion'., but as of UPK 12.1.0.1, we're still left guessing. If you *do* want to edit the sound associated with a template element then you need to manually edit the template, as described earlier in this chapter.

7. Change the options as required. Note that you can only change text elements, and add or remove the leading space. You cannot change the **Style** or **Link** fields.

8. Click **OK** to close the *Element Properties* dialog box.

9. Make any additional changes to the template by repeating the above steps.

10. When you have made all of your required changes, close the *Template Editor*, and then copy the `template.xml` file back into your custom Template Package in UPK.

The above instructions apply to changing the `<Classes>` section (including `<Template>` elements). You can also use the *Template Editor* to change the `<Instructions>`, `<ShiftKeyPrefix>`, `<Events>` and `<Keynames>` sections by selecting the appropriate option from the **Edit** menu. You cannot change the `<styles>` section via the *Template Editor* – to do that you need to manually edit the template, as described earlier in this chapter.

This has been a very brief introduction to the *Template Editor*. However, if you have followed through the explanation of the template file structure and contents above, you should have no problems with finding your way around the *Template Editor*.

Using your custom template

You now have your own template (regardless of whether you edited it directly or used the *Template Editor*), which you want to use for your exercises. So how do you tell UPK to use your template, instead of the default one? There are two considerations—using it for new exercises, and using it for any existing exercises. Let's look at both of these options.

Using a custom template as the default template

You can set up your custom template to be the default template, which means that it will be used for all new Topics that you create. To do this, follow the steps described below:

1. On the *Library* screen, select menu option **Tools | Options**.

2. In the *Options* dialog box, select the **Content Defaults | General** category.

3. Click the **Browse** button next to the **Template** field, and navigate to and select your custom Template Package.

4. Click on **Open**.

5. Back in the *Options* dialog box, click on **OK**.

The following screenshot shows the *Options* dialog box, with a custom template selected:

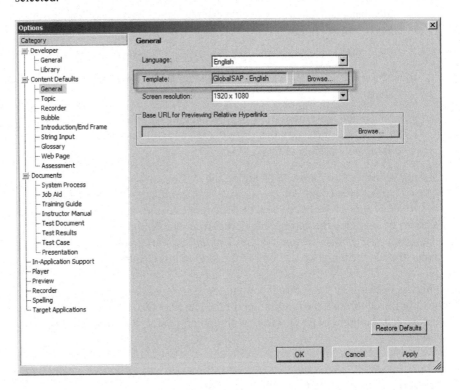

This custom template will now automatically be assigned to all new content objects that you create within your Library.

Assigning a custom template to existing Topics

Even if you have already created Topics using the standard template (or have imported Topics that do not use your custom template), you can still have these Topics use your new template. This is because the template is effectively applied at *display* time (whether this is when the Topic is being edited in the *Topic Editor*, when previewing from the *Outline Editor*, or during final publication). To assign a custom template to an existing Topic, carry out the following steps:

1. On the *Library* screen, select the Topic to which you want to apply the template.

2. Make sure that the *Properties* pane is displayed (click the **Properties** button (🖼) if it is not).

3. Make sure that the **Topic** category is expanded.

4. Click in the **Template** field.

5. Click on the 'ellipsis' button (⬚) on the far right of the Template field.

6. Navigate to and select your custom template, and then click **Open**.

An example of the *Properties* pane for a Topic, with a custom template selected, is shown in the following screenshot:

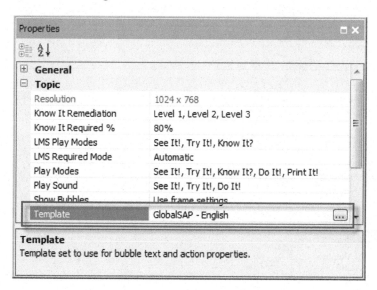

Defining a new object type

Appendix B, Object Types provides a list of all of the Object Types recognized by UPK, and the Template Text that is generated for each of them. Although you can customize the Template Text for any given object as described earlier in this chapter, in some cases it may be easier to just define your own Object Type. UPK will not 'capture' this Object Type during the recording, but authors will be able to select it from the Object Type field in the *Frame Properties* pane (see *Chapter 4, Editing a Topic*).

We will look at how to do this via a practical example. Users of OnDemand version 8.7 and below may recall that the *Frame Properties* pane contained a check-box that could be used with actual check-box Object Type, to indicate whether the check-box was currently selected or not on the captured screen. OnDemand would then use this field to determine whether the check-box would be selected or cleared by the Action, and generate an appropriate Template Text. This option disappeared around OnDemand 9.1, and now a single, generic Template Text is generated regardless of whether the action is setting or clearing the check-box, as shown in the two examples below. The first one shows the Template Text generated if the check-box is currently selected and needs to be cleared:

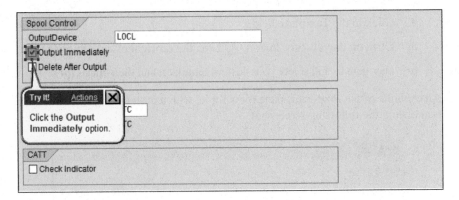

The next example shows the Template Text generated if the check-box is currently deselected and needs to be selected:

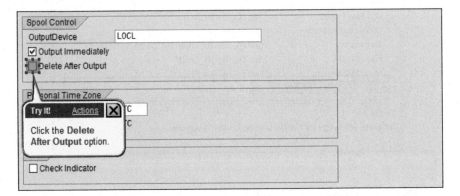

This isn't ideal, as although it is easy to infer the correct meaning in *See It!* mode or *Try It!* mode, in *Do It!* mode or any of the printed output documents, where the screenshot may not be visible, there is no indication of what the state of the check-box should be after the action has been completed. If the current state is selected, and the user follows this instruction, they will *clear* the check-box; but if it is currently deselected and the user follows the instruction, they will *select* the check-box. This could be catastrophic!

We will remove this ambiguity by defining two additional Object Types: **Checkbox - Selected** and **Checkbox - Deselected**. This will allow us to generate different Template Text for each of the check-box's possible states.

So let's look at how to do this. The first thing we need to do is to define our new Object Type. Open up your custom Template Package, and then open the file template.xml for editing, as described earlier in this chapter. Insert the following code into the <classes> section (anywhere you like – just not in the middle of another <class> definition):

● Note that in this case we will not change the built-in **Checkbox** Object Type, to make sure that we don't have any unintended impact on any existing Topics that happen to use this Object Type.

```xml
<Class Name="CHECKBOX_OFF"
    ListName="Checkbox - Deselected"
    DisplayName="checkbox"
    Gender="neutral">
    <Template Context="LClick1">
        <Text Sound="lclick1">Select the</Text>
        <ObjectName />
        <ObjectType />
        <Text>.</Text>
    </Template>
</Class>
<Class Name="CHECKBOX_ON"
    ListName="Checkbox - Selected"
    DisplayName="checkbox"
    Gender="neutral">
    <Template Context="LClick1">
        <Text Sound="lclick1">Clear the</Text>
        <ObjectName />
        <ObjectType />
        <Text>.</Text>
    </Template>
</Class>
```

Here, we are defining a new <Class> definition for each of our new Object Types. Let's look at the key information in these. The Name is the internal identifier of the Object Type. This can be anything you like, but it must be unique. ListName is the name that will appear in the **Object type** drop-down list in the **Frame Properties** pane, and the DisplayName specifies the text that will be substituted for <ObjectType /> in the template.

In this example, for the sake of brevity, we are only providing customized template texts for the Lclick1 action (a single left-click with the mouse), which means that all other actions (such as left double-click) will use the default text. In practice, you would probably want to provide customized template for all valid actions.

Save your updated template file, and then save and close your custom Template Package, as described earlier in this chapter. If you are currently editing a Topic in which you want to use this new Object type then close it, make sure that the

■ If you are providing your training content in additional languages then you will need to add your new Object Type to all of the language-specific templates as well.

■ Although the template text is built at display time, the Template association is retrieved when you open the Topic, so if you change the Template while the Topic is open, you will need to close and then re-open the Topic to pick up the latest changes to the Template.

updated template is assigned to it in the Topic's *Properties*, and then open the Topic in the *Topic Editor* again. Navigate to the Frame where you want to use this Object Type, and click on the drop-down list button for the **Object Type** field in the *Frame Properties* pane. You will now see that your new Object Type is available for selection (and that it is listed under the name specified by the `ListName` attribute in the template), as shown in the example below:

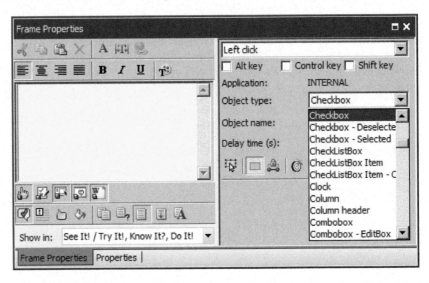

▲ It is important to note that UPK will not automatically identify this Object Type during the recording, but at least authors can select it in the *Topic Editor*.

We can now select the relevant Object Type, depending on whether the check-box is selected or not, and the relevant Template Text will be generated. If the check-box on the screen is currently selected, we can select the **Checkbox - Selected** Object Type, and the Template Text will appear as follows:

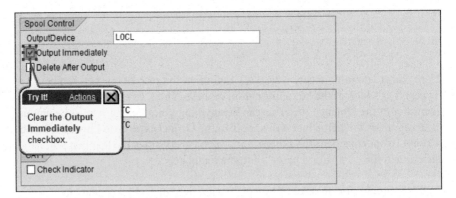

If the check-box is currently deselected, then we can select the **Checkbox - Deselected** Object Type, and the Template Text will appear as follows:

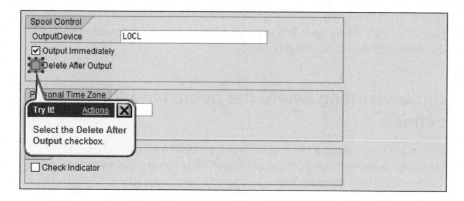

So there you have it. Brand new Object Types, available for selection in the *Topic Editor*, and with their own, unique Template Texts. And all of this with minimal effort.

You can find the Template that we just created in the sample `.odarc` file available from the author's website. It is named **GlobalSAP - English**.

Customizing the publishing formats

In the previous section, we configured the Template texts; these largely cover the Bubble Texts, plus a few other things (such as the *Know It?* mode remediation texts, and so on). However, this is only half of the story. When you publish a Topic, UPK generates all of the required Bubble Texts (using the template that we just configured), and then pushes this into the relevant format, depending on your publishing choices. Although for the most part, this book has been using the Player publishing format, you may recall from *Chapter 6, Publishing Your Content* that UPK allows you to publish to any or all of the following formats:

- Player and LMS
- HTML Web Site
- System Process
- Job Aid
- Training Guide
- Instructor Manual
- Test Document
- Test Results
- Test Case
- Presentation

With a little bit of effort, you can customize the style and format of these to meet your own needs. (You can even create your own format, if necessary, although that is beyond the scope of this book.)

Understanding where the publishing formats are defined

Each publishing format is defined in a separate **Deployment Package**. All of the Deployment Packages (one for each publishing format) are grouped together into a **publishing category**. When you publish your content, you first select the publishing category, and then select the specific publishing format(s) that you want to generate.

This approach means that you can have multiple publishing categories, in the same Library. For example, if you have multiple clients or projects, you can create a separate publishing category for each project, with each publishing category containing publishing formats specifically customized for that client or project (even if the customization is only a different logo). It also means that you can 're-use' content across clients by including (linking) it in the publishing Outline for those clients. When you publish a client's Outline, you simply select the appropriate publishing category, and all of the included content is automatically 'branded' for that client!

● There may be copyright or ethical considerations in doing this, but that's between you, your conscience, and the courts; UPK doesn't care.

As with the Templates, it is strongly recommended that you take a copy of a default publishing category and change the publishing formats only within the copy, rather than change any of the actual default publishing formats.

So how do we create our own publishing category? Well, the first thing to do is find out where the deployment categories are defined. A clue is given in the *Publishing Wizard*. If you don't skip the *Advanced Options* page, you will see the *Advanced Publishing Options*, as shown in the next screenshot. Note that the **Category** field is currently set to **User Productivity Kit** (which is the default publishing format). Click on the **Change** button to the right of this field, and the *Set Category and Language* dialog box, also shown in the following screenshot, is displayed.

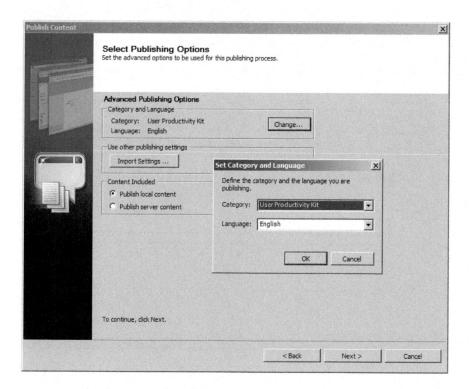

You can see here that it is possible to change the **Category** by selecting another value from the drop-down. However, there is currently only one option, **User Productivity Kit**. (This name may be different in earlier versions of UPK, or OnDemand before it, but there will still be only one in a new installation.) Cancel the wizard, and then go to the following folder in the Library: **System | Publishing | Styles**. You'll see the following:

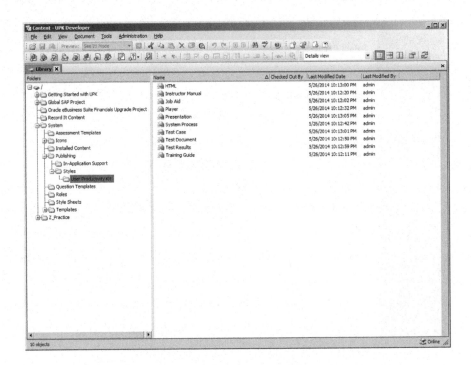

Note the name of the folder within the `Styles` folder: `User Productivity Kit`. This is the same name as we saw in the **Category** field on the *Advanced Publishing Options* screen. Now look at the list of packages contained within the `User Productivity Kit` folder. Compare this with the list of possible output types given at the start of this section. They're exactly the same! The `Styles` folder contains a sub-folder for each publishing category, and each Deployment Package within the sub-folder for a publishing category defines a specific publishing format.

Creating your own publishing category

As we saw in the previous section, the publishing categories that are selectable in the **Publishing Options** are controlled purely by the sub-folders in the `System/Publishing/Styles` folder. So to create a new, selectable publishing category, the first thing we need to do is to create a new sub-folder in this same folder. (It is always advisable to create your own custom copies of the standard objects, instead of directly editing them, in case you need to revert to—or just refer to—the originals.) We'll create a new sub-folder (use menu option **File | New | Folder**) for our new publishing style, and we'll call it **Global Training**.

● You must create the folder for your new publishing category within the existing `System/Publishing/Styles` folder, or UPK will not find it.

Next, copy *all* of the Deployment Packages for all of the various default publishing formats into your new custom publishing category folder. You can either copy and paste them, or drag and drop them, as you prefer.

It is important that you copy **all** of the Deployment Packages, even if you only want to customize one of these. Internally, UPK refers to the position of these options on the publishing menu, and if you remove all but one Package, and UPK normally positions this remaining Package as the seventh option, then you will get an "index error" when you try to publish your content, because there is no longer a seventh position.

We now have a copy of all of the standard Deployment Packages that we can work with, as shown in the following screenshot:

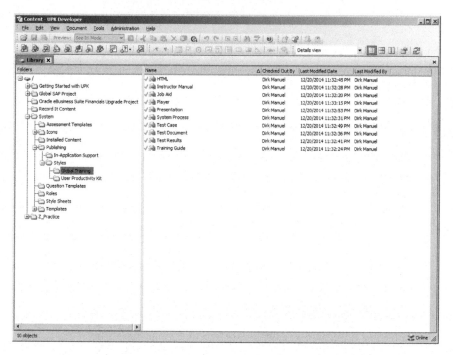

To prove that this simple copy works, open any existing Module or Section in the **Outline Editor**, and click the **Publish** button (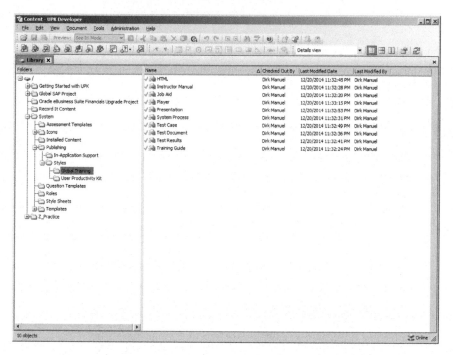) to launch the *Publishing Wizard*. Continue through to the *Advanced Publishing Options* screen, and click on the **Change** button in the **Category and Language** area. You will see that your custom publishing category is now selectable in the **Category** field, as shown in the next screenshot:

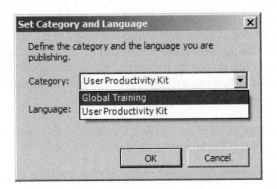

Click on **Cancel** to exit from the *Publishing Wizard*; we don't want to publish anything just yet as we were simply confirming that UPK can find our new Publishing Category.

Customizing the logo

Now that we have a new custom publishing category, we can customize it to our specific requirements. We will start by replacing the Oracle logo that appears in the publishing formats with our own company logo.

To customize the logo, carry out the following steps:

1. From the main *UPK Developer* screen, select menu option **Tools | Customize Logo**. The *Customize Logo* dialog box is displayed, as shown in the following screenshot:

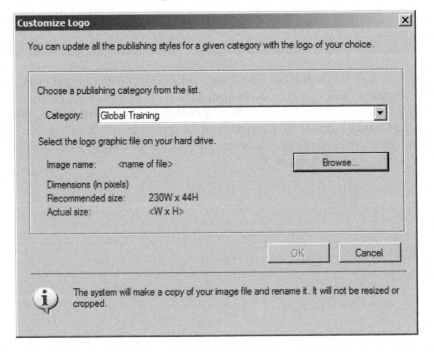

▲ Although you *could* perform all of your customization at the same time and then test it, it is always a good idea to perform one small change at a time, and test each change before moving on to the next thing that you want to change. This will make it much easier to resolve problems when they (inevitably) occur.

✦ The **Customize Logo** feature was introduced in UPK version 3.5. Prior to this, it was necessary to change each Deployment Format separately (which is sometimes still a better way to do it, as the Customize Logo feature down-samples the imported log image).

2. In the **Category** field, select the publishing category for which you want to change the logo. In our example, this will be our new custom publishing category, **Global Training**, as shown in the previous screenshot. Note that UPK will replace the logo in all of the publishing formats within the publishing category.

▲ Make sure that you select your custom deployment category and not the standard **User Productivity Kit** category, as there is no *undo* for this (although in a client/ server environment you can simply not check in your changed files—if you notice in time...).

3. Click on **Browse**, and navigate to and select your custom logo. Note that this should be 230 x 44 pixels for the best results. This does not need to have a specific name, as UPK will rename it (to `small_logo.gif`) when UPK imports it.

4. Click on **Open** to return to the *Customize Logo* dialog box.

5. Click on the **OK** button.

6. UPK will work its way through each of the publishing formats, replacing the logo in each of them. The following status bar will be displayed while the update is in progress:

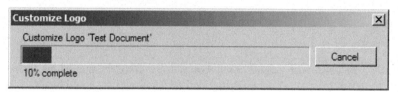

Once the update is complete, the following confirmation message is displayed:

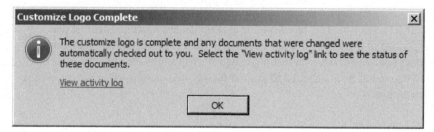

7. If you click the **View activity log** link, a list of all of the publishing formats that have been changed is displayed, as shown in the following screenshot:

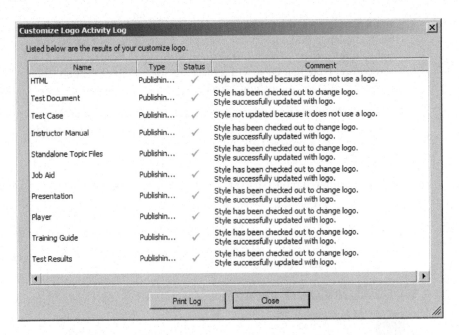

The Customize Logo Activity Log will list all of the publishing formats (or at least all of the ones that you copied...which should be all of them if you've followed my recommendations!).

8. Click on **Close** to close the *Customize Logo Activity Log* dialog box, and then click on **OK** to close the *Customize Logo Complete* message.

Now let's see what this has done for us. Publish any Outline Element (as explained in *Chapter 6, Publishing Your Content*, and make sure that you select your customized publishing category. You should see that the logo in the Player has been changed to your company logo, as shown in the following screenshot:

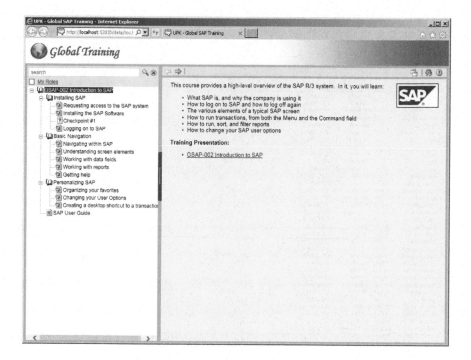

Note that UPK will down-sample the image wherever it needs a smaller image, which may then appear 'lossy' in some publishing formats. If you want to use a high-definition image, then you may want to replace the images one-by-one in the packages for the various Deployment Packages that you want to use, as described in *Customizing a publishing format* on page 619.

Customizing a publishing format

Changing the logo for an entire publishing category was an easy change. Now let's look at something a bit more challenging. The content of a Deployment Package, and how it can be customized, will vary depending on the publishing format that it defines, but in this section we will look at two of them, which should give us enough a grounding to be able to change any of the others. We will look at the Player, and a single (Word) document format.

Customizing the Player

In this section, we will make a small change to the Player publishing format. First, let's have a look at the content of the Deployment Package for this format. On the *Library* screen, navigate to your custom copy of the **Player** Deployment Package, and double-click on it to open it. The *Package Editor* opens in a new tab within the *UPK Developer* screen, as shown in the following screenshot:

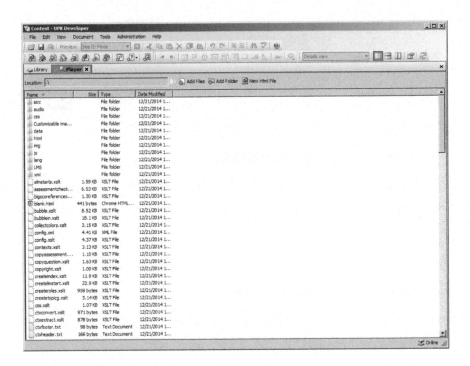

You can see that this Deployment Package, as with all packages in UPK, is simply a collection of files. Most of these files can be edited directly from within the *Package Editor*. For some file types, you may need to select the required helper application on your PC. For others you may need to copy the file out of the package and onto your PC, edit the file on your PC, and then copy the edited file back into the Package.

As we saw in *Chapter 4, Editing a Topic*, it is possible to add a small icon to any Bubble. We used this functionality to add an 'information' icon to Explanation Frames, as shown in the following example:

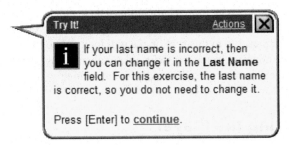

The icons that UPK provides are only black and white, in some cases obscure (some kind of a coughing dog??), and generally uninspiring. All of the available options are shown in the image below:

● These icons refer to image files in the Player deployment format package of `icon00.gif` through to `icon34.gif`, from top-left to bottom-right (excluding the 'no icon' square in the very upper-left).

For our custom Player, it would be nice to have a more visually appealing icon, like the one shown here:

Note that this is a relatively spurious example, and is intended just to illustrate the possibilities. You may want to consider using various customized icons to represent specific objects or activities (possibly that take place outside of the application being recorded) for your company, project, or system. For example, at one client I created UPK training simulations for forklift-mounted touch-screens in a warehouse, and used an image of a forklift as a customized icon, to indicate that the user should physically drive the forklift to a new location in the warehouse. Alternatively, you could use specific icons to represent the need to file a paper document, obtain supervisor approval, and so on.

To replace a standard bubble icon with a customized icon, carry out the following steps:

1. Open your custom Deployment Package for the **Player** publishing format.

2. Double-click on the `img` folder to open it (it is opened within the same tab).

3. Click on the **Add Files** button (🔲). The *Open* dialog box is displayed.

4. In the *Open* dialog box, navigate to and select the customized version of the file. It is important that the file has *exactly* the same name as the file that you are replacing. For our example, this is the file `icon01.gif`.

5. In response to the message that informs you that a file with the same name already exists in the package, choose to replace the existing file (remember, you still have a copy of the original file in the original package).

6. Save and then close the package.

Now, let's check that our changes have worked. Publish any Topic that uses the 'information' icon (make sure that you select your custom publishing category), and you should now see the following:

▲ Do not change the white exclamation mark icon (`icon02.gif`) as this is used by UPK itself in the remediation instructions for *Know It!* mode.

● As an alternative to Steps 3 and 4, you can also drag-and-drop (or copy-and-paste) the file from your local workstation, directly into the Package.

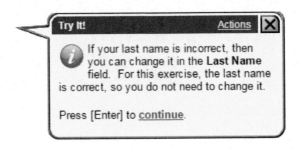

If your last name is incorrect, then you can change it in the **Last Name** field. For this exercise, the last name is correct, so you do not need to change it.

Press [Enter] to continue.

Great! Our changes work. However, there's one more thing we need to take care of—previews. There is an option to select the publishing category that should always be used for previews, and we need to change this to refer to our new publishing category (which contains our custom publishing format).

To set the publishing category to use for previews, carry out the following steps:

1. Select menu option **Tools | Options**.

2. Select the **Publishing Preview** category.

3. In the **Category** field, select your new custom publishing category.

4. Click **OK** to save your changes.

An example of the *Options* screen showing the selection of a custom publishing category is shown in the following screenshot:

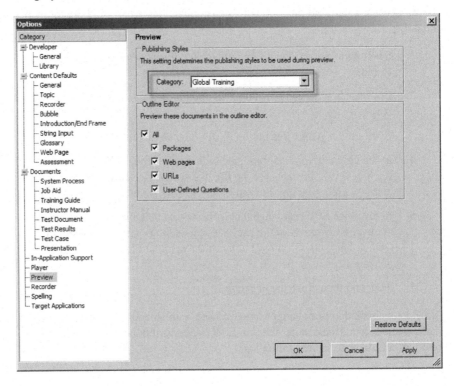

There is one more place where the old icon will appear, and this is within the *Topic Editor* itself (see the screenshot of the Bubble Icons earlier in this section). Unfortunately, there is no way to configure this, so if you do choose to customize these icons, you will need to provide your authors with a cheat-sheet showing which Bubble icon selection in the *Topic Editor* results in which icon in the Player.

Skinning the Player

The UPK Player is built as a combination of HTML, XML, CSS, and JavaScript files. All of these files are readily available in the Player publishing format Package, and can be changed in order to customize the appearance (and in some cases the behavior) of the Player.

Skins are a new feature in UPK 12. Prior to this version, any Player customization had to be done directly within the Player Publishing Package.

However, to provide maximum flexibility with minimum work, all of the visual elements (and a few functional elements) can be changed by way of a 'skin', which exists independently of a Player Deployment Package. Any customization should therefore be performed in a separate Skin, and not made to the Player publishing format within the publishing category (default or custom). There are a few very good reasons for this:

- Because the Skin is independent of the Deployment Package, you can use the same Skin in conjunction with different publishing categories, so you could (for example), use client-specific branding (logo, and so on) in the Deployment Category, and a different color scheme for each project via project-specific Skins.

- You choose the Skin at publishing time, which means that you can very easily switch the look and feel of the Player, while leaving the underlying branding (in the Player publishing format) the same, just by choosing a new Skin.

- You only need to include the specific elements that you want to change in your custom Skin - all other elements will use the definitions in the default Player publishing format. This is similar to how CSS works, although with UPK it is really just a two-level cascade: your custom Skin, and the default Player publishing format.

- Any changes made to the default publishing formats (within the User Productivity Kit publishing category) will be lost when you upgrade to a new version of UPK; Skins will not.

In the following sections, we will create a custom Skin for use with our Global SAP Project.

Creating a new Skin

A Skin is really just a type of Package. When you create a new Skin, UPK effectively creates a new Package for you, and copies into this three 'placeholder' files for your skin (these files are explained in the section *"Changing a Player Skin"*, below). You can then change these files as required, to format your new Skin.

To create a new Skin, carry out the steps explained below:

● UPK ships with an 'un-customized' skin called **Player Customization** that is located in the `System\Publishing\Styles` folder. You could take a copy of this to create your new skin, but as this is what UPK effectively does when you click on the **Create New Skin** button, there is little advantage in this approach.

● UPK also ships with a pre-defined skin called **Gray**. This is effectively an implementation of the **Modernized User Interface** that was provided in UPK 11.1.0.2.

1. On the Library screen, navigate to the folder in which you want to create your skin. You can store your Skin in any folder you like, but it may make sense to store it in the same folder as the publishing category for which it is designed (assuming that it is publishing category specific). Regardless of where you store it, it is recommended that you control access to the folder so that it is not accidentally changed by your authors. (See *Chapter 16, Customizing UPK* for information on securing folders.) For this example, we will store our custom in the `Templates` folder for our Global SAP Project.

2. On the *Library Toolbar*, click on the **Create New Skin** button (🏵). A new Skin Package is created, and opened in the standard *Package Editor*.

3. Change your Skin as explained in the section *"Changing a Player Skin"*, below.

4. Save the Skin Package under a suitable name (for this example, we will save our custom Skin as **Global SAP Project Skin**), and then close the *Package Editor*.

Changing a Player Skin

Assuming that you have created a new Skin, as explained above, you can now change this Skin to meet your specific requirements.

The Skin consists of (effectively) three files:

- `custom.css`: Use this file to change the appearance of the Player—such as changing the colors and fonts used, the spacing around elements, and so on.

- `config.xml`: Use this file to change the behavior and appearance of some Player elements.

- `resource.xml`: Use this file to change any of the textual elements used in the Player. Note that this file is (obviously) language-specific, so there are sub-folders per language within the Skin Package, and then a separate `resource.xml` file within the folder for each language.

These three files correspond to three files of the same names in the default Player Deployment Package, and initially contain minimal guideline entries. To customize any aspect of the Player, you simply locate the relevant element in appropriate file in the default Package, copy this element into the corresponding file in your custom Skin Package, and then change the element within your custom Skin as required.

You can also change any of the images used in the Player, by identifying the image that you want to change in the `img` folder of the default Player publishing format package, and then creating a new image with exactly the same name (and ideally the same dimensions) within the **root** of the Skin Package.

▲ It is worth emphasizing here that images are (inconsistently) stored in the root of the Skin Package, and not within an `img` folder.

Let's look at changing some of these elements, via our sample Skin. We will start by looking at the elements that are controlled by the `custom.css` file. The following illustration shows the main Player screen, and identifies the key components that can be customized via this file. The table below the image explains the purpose of each element and identifies the code element that controls it.

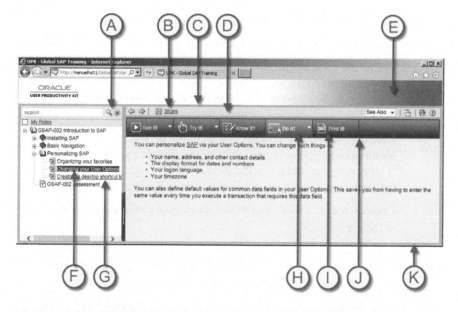

ID	Description	Code element
A	Search area background color	`.tocSearchColor`
B	Share link (font and color)	`.share_link:link`
C	Divider lines	`.Background`
D	Background color of 'toolbar'	`.HeaderDivBar`
E	Color of the rightmost side of the gradient-filled header bar; the left side is always white	`.HeaderTransparent`
F	Formatting of the selected Outline Element	`.tselected`
G	Formatting of an Outline Element when the cursor is hovered over it	`.thover`
H	Darkest color of the gradient fill for play mode buttons when the cursor is hovered over them	`.button`

➕ In earlier versions of UPK, the header bar used an image for coloring. That has been replaced by a gradient fill in UPK 12.

ID	Description	Code element
I	Darkest color of the gradient fill for play mode buttons when the play mode is selected	`.button:hover`
J	Color of the play mode buttons divider lines	`.dividerColor`
K	Color of the sides and bottom border of the overall Player window.	`.borderBackground`

Now that we know what we can change, let's change a few of these elements. Let's suppose that our client prefers a maroon-based palette to the default blue. First, we'll change the non-image elements

To customize the appearance of the main Player screen, carry out the steps shown below:

1. Open up the default Player publishing format Package.

2. Locate the `custom.css` file, and open it in a text editor

3. Locate the code for the element that you want to change, and copy it to the clipboard. Make sure that you capture the entire element (for CSS code, this is the element name, and everything from the opening brace immediately following it, to the corresponding closing brace.

   Note that you do not have to copy all of the default elements to your Skin Package; you only need to copy the ones that you want to change. If UPK does not find a specific element in your Skin Package, it will use the copy from the default publishing format Package instead.

4. Open up the `custom.css` file in your custom Skin Package, and paste in the copied code.

5. Change the code as required. Note that you will need some knowledge of CSS to do this (the O'Reilly book *Cascading Style Sheets - The Definitive Guide* is as good a reference as any other).

6. Save the file, then save and check in (if appropriate) the Skin Package.

As an example, the Skin for our sample exercise now looks like the example shown in the following code. All of this code was copied from the default `custom.css` file; changed values are shown in red. The 'Element' specifications in brackets relate to the identifiers in the prior table and image.

```
/* Blue shading (Element D) */
.headerDivbar
{
    height: 21px;
    background-color: #BDAEC6;
}
/* Divider lines (Element C) */
.background
{
    background-color: #9C8AA5;
```

```
        border-color: #9CA885;
}
/* border lines (Element K)*/
.borderBackground
{
        border-color: #732C7B;
        border-width: 5px;
}
.thover    /* (Element G) */
{
        color: #FFFFFF !important;
        background-color: #421C52;
        text-decoration: underline !important;
}
/* Selected outline item  (Element F) */
.tselected
{
        color: #FFFFFF !important;
        background-color: #732c7b;
}
/* Search background (Element A) */
.tocSearchColor
{
        background-color: #BDAEC6;
}
/* Header transparent color (Element K) */
.headerTransparent
{
        background-color: #421C52;
}
/*Mode button color (Element H) */
.button, .lastbutton, #playmodetable
{
        background-color: #9C8AA5;
        cursor: default;
        font-weight: normal;
}
.not-touch .button:hover   /* (Element I) */
{
        background-color: #BDAEC6;
        cursor: pointer;
        font-weight: bold;
}
/*Mode button line color (Element J) */
.dividerColor
{
        border-color: #421C52;
}
```

Let's look at how these changes have affected our Player:

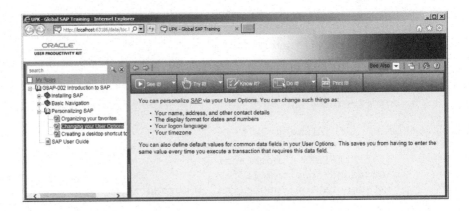

▲ Despite what the official Oracle documentation says, you cannot customize the main logo (in the upper-left corner of the screen) via the Skin. You can only customize it as described earlier in this chapter.

So far so good. Now, let's look at some of the images that we can change. The following table identifies the main images used on the main Player screen, and the associated image file for these. All images are contained in the `img\customizable` folder of the Player publishing format Package.

Icon	Description	Code element
	Search button	`searchbtn.gif`
	Cancel Search button	`clear.png`

	Previous Outline Element button	`previous.png`
		`previous_mouseover.png`
		`previous_disabled.png`

	Next Outline Element button	`next.png`
		`next_mouseover.png`
		`next_disabled.png`

	Share button	`share_link.gif`
	Open Concept in new tab button	`new_window_ios.gif`
	Preferences button	`prefs_button.gif`
	Help button	`help_button.gif`
	Open Module/Section icon	`module_o.gif`
	Closed Module/Section icon	`module_c.gif`
	Topic icon	`topic.gif`
	See It! mode button	`seeit.png`

● The 'mode' buttons are white images on a transparent background. They are shown here against a blue background for visibility.

Icon	Description	Code element
	Try It! mode button	tryit.png
	Know It! mode button	knowit.png
	Do It! mode button	doit.png
	Print It! mode button - Document	printitdoc.png
	Print It! mode button - HTML	printithtml.png
	Print It! mode button - PDF	printitpdf.png
	Test It! mode button	testit.png

Note that there are many more buttons than these that can be customized; the above table simply shows a representative selection of the more common ones:

To customize any of the Player images, follow the steps described below:

1. Open the default Player publishing format Package in the *Library*.

2. Navigate to the img/customizable folder within the Package.

3. Identify the specific file that you want to customize, and determine it's exact file name, and dimensions.

4. Use your preferred image editing software application to create a new image of the same type, and with exactly the same name and dimensions.

5. Open your customized Skin Package in the Library. Make sure you are at the root of this Package (and not in a subfolder).

6. Copy the image file you created in Step 4 into the Package. You can do this either by clicking on the **Add Files** button (🔲) and navigating and selecting your new image file, or by dragging the new image file from your PC into the package.

   Note that you do not have to copy all of the default images to your Skin Packages, only the ones that you want to change. If UPK does not find a required image in your Skin Package, it will use the copy from the default Package instead.

7. Save and close your Skin package, and check it in if necessary.

For our sample exercise, we will replace the **Previous Outline Element** and **Next Outline Element** buttons, to color them to be consistent with our new purple color theme. The contents of our Skin Package is now as follows:

■ You may find it helpful to copy the entire contents of the img/customizable folder to your PC, where you can use Windows Explorer to actually see the images; the image size will also be easily-visible in the Properties area of Windows Explorer when you select the image.

▲ Make sure that you select the correct image format, as Oracle have been gradually changing from .gif images to .png images, and in a few cases you will find identical files of both formats in the Package.

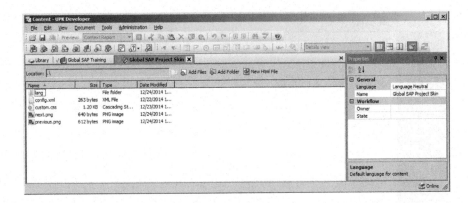

Our Player now looks like the example shown below. Note that the two buttons we changed are now shown. (In this example, I also changed the main logo, for consistency, but again, note that this must be changed in the `img` folder within the publishing format Package, and not in the Skin Package.)

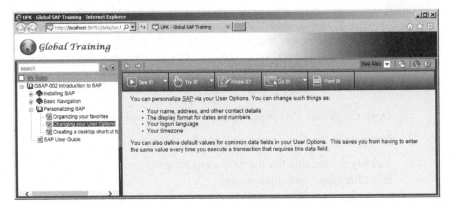

Finally, let's look at how to change some of the Player's text elements. Because these are language-specific, they are defined in a separate `resource.xml` file per language, which is contained in a language-specific sub-folder within both the default Player publishing format Package and the customized Skin Package. A sample extract from the English version of the default version of this file is shown below:

```xml
<?xml version="1.0" encoding="UTF-8"?>
<!--Copyright © 1998, 2014, Oracle and/or its affiliates.
All rights reserved.-->
<resources>
    <resource xml:id="R_interface_pause">"Pause"
            </resource>
    <resource xml:id="R_interface_resume">"Resume"
            </resource>
    <resource xml:id="R_bubble_closeondemand">"Close"
            </resource>
    <resource xml:id="R_menu_viewoutline">"View Outline"
            </resource>
```

```
<resource xml:id="R_menu_nextstep">"Next Step"
        </resource>
<resource xml:id="R_menu_prevstep">"Previous Step"
        </resource>
<resource xml:id="R_menu_play">"Play"
        </resource>
<resource xml:id="R_menu_start">"Restart Playback"
        </resource>
<resource xml:id="R_menu_alternatives">"Show next
        alternative action"</resource>
<resource xml:id="R_menu_concepts">"Display Concept"
        </resource>
<resource xml:id="R_menu_infoblocks">"Attachments"
        </resource>
<resource xml:id="R_menu_history">"History"</resource>
<resource xml:id="R_menu_preferences">"Preferences"
        </resource>
<resource xml:id="R_menu_share">"Share"</resource>
<resource xml:id="R_menu_help">"Help"</resource>
<resource xml:id="R_menu_Close">"Close Topic"
        </resource>
<resource xml:id="R_menu_Start">"Start"</resource>
<resource xml:id="R_menu_Finish">"Finish"</resource>
</resources>
```

To change any of the default texts, follow the steps shown below:

1. Open the default Player publishing format Package in the *Library*

2. Navigate to the `lang{code}/resource.xml` file (where `{code}` is the language code) within the Package, and open it in your preferred editor.

3. Locate the `<resource>` definition for the text that you want to change, and copy it to the clipboard.

4. Open your customized Skin Package, and navigate to the same language folder. Open the `resource.xml` file that you find there.

5. Paste the code that you copied from the default Package into the custom `resource.xml` file. Make sure that you paste this code within the `<resources>...</resources>` tags. The order of the individual `<resource>` definitions within this is not important.

   Note that you do not have to copy all of the `<resource>` definitions from the default Package to your custom Package, only the specific ones that you want to change. If UPK will does not find a required `<resource>` definition in your custom Skin Package, it will use the definition from the default Player Package instead.

6. Save and close your Skin package, and check it in if necessary.

For our sample exercise, we will change the names of the modes - not that I would normally recommend doing this, but in prior versions of UPK this was prohibitively difficult, and even now it is trickier than you'd think (as the

▲ Make sure that you use the `resource.xml` file, and not the `resources.xml` file. The latter is used for author / non-user-facing content.

definitions need to be changed in a couple of places), so this is a useful example to look at. Let's assume that we are working for a new client that subscribes to a 'show me', 'guide me', 'let me' training philosophy, and wants UPK to reinforce this. We would therefore have to copy the following `<resource>` definitions into our Skin (changed values are shown in red):

```xml
<?xml version="1.0" encoding="UTF-8"?>
<resources>
  <resource xml:id="R_mode_seeit">"Show Me"</resource>
  <resource xml:id="R_mode_tryit">"Let Me"</resource>
  <resource xml:id="R_mode_knowit">"Test Me"</resource>
  <resource xml:id="R_mode_doit">"Coach Me"</resource>
  <resource xml:id="R_mode_printit">"Print"</resource>
  <resource xml:id="R_mode_testit">"Evaluate"</resource>
  <resource xml:id="R_start_seeit">"Show Me"</resource>
  <resource xml:id="R_start_tryit">"Let Me"</resource>
  <resource xml:id="R_start_knowit">"Test Me"</resource>
  <resource xml:id="R_start_doit">"Coach Me"</resource>
  <resource xml:id="R_start_printit">"Print"</resource>
  <resource xml:id="R_start_testit">"Evaluate"</resource>
</resources>
```

Note that there are effectively two places where we have to change each of the mode names. The first set above (`R_mode_*`) defines the text that appears in the Bubble title bar during playback; the second set (`R_start_*`) defines the mode names as they appear on the play mode buttons on the Player main screen.

Again, there are many more texts that you can change, but the above example should at least give you enough confidence to tackle the remaining texts on your own.

Let's take a final look at our Player, now that we have changed the colors, images, and texts. Note that in this example, *Test It!* mode has been included, to show the complete scope of our changes.

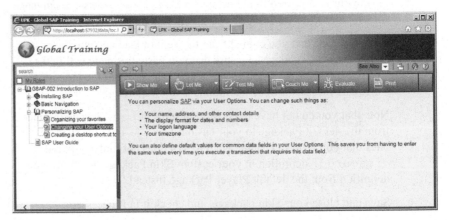

Compare this with the version we started with, on page 625. We've made quite a few changes, hopefully nearer to our client's wishes, and all without too much effort.

You can find the Skin that we just built in the sample `.odarc` file available from the author's website. It is named **Global SAP Project Skin**.

Using a Player Skin

Once you have created a custom Skin, using it is very simple. Publish as normal (see *Publishing Your Content* on page 215 for details of how to do this), and when you get to the last screen (the *Format Selection* screen), select the **Player and LMS** publishing format, then navigate to and select your custom Skin in the **Skin** field, as shown below:

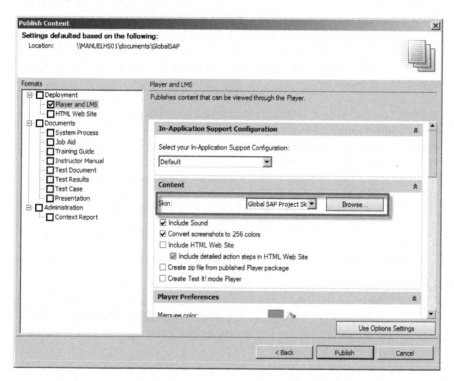

Note that this selection is independent of the publishing category chosen earlier in the Publishing Wizard. This means that you can re-use custom Skins across publishing categories.

Creating a new document format

Although UPK comes with several document publishing formats, you may find that none of these *completely* meet your requirements (or, more likely, you have a fussy client who wants things just a little bit different). If this is the case, then you can customize one of the existing document formats to more closely match your requirements. You can even create a brand new output document format, if necessary—although even then it is recommended that you take a copy of an existing format, and change the copy, as this is significantly easier than building a new document from a blank page.

In this section we will configure an existing document format to include some additional information. Because we still want to use the existing document format (on which we will base our new document) as-is, we will create a brand new document format for our purposes.

Older readers may recall a time when there was a **Context Report** available as a document format. This document included the Context ID for each screenshot within a Topic, and was useful for double-checking that things have been recorded correctly. For our example, we will re-create the Context Report, using the **System Process** document as our basis. This is perhaps a little simplistic (the Context ID is actually available in the Microsoft Excel format **Test Case** output), but the purpose is simply to show you how UPK's document formats work, and give you the confidence to consider customizing the document formats for your own clients or projects.

The first thing we will do is create a new **Publishing Package** that will hold our new document format. A Publishing Package is really just a special version of a standard **Package**, so we will create a new Package, and copy the contents of the System Process Publishing Package into our new Package. We *could* just copy the entire Publishing Package and rename it, but if we use a standard Package, it will have a different icon (see the next screenshot), which will be a convenient visual cue that this is a customized format—which may be useful when we upgrade.

To create a new Publishing Package, carry out the following steps:

1. In the *Library*, navigate to the `/System/Publishing/Styles` folder, and open the sub-folder for the publishing category that you want to change. For our purposes, we will use the **Global Training** category that we created earlier in this chapter (see *Creating your own publishing category* on page 614).

2. Create a new Package within this folder, by selecting menu option **File | New | Package**. The *Package Editor* is opened, and will show the Package as empty.

3. Navigate to the Publishing Package for the document type on which you want to base your new format (in our case, the **System Process** document), open it, and copy all of its contents

● As an alternative to Steps 3 and 4, you can display the *Library* in split-screen mode, and drag-and-drop the files between the two Packages.

4. Return to your new Package, and paste all of the copied files into it.

5. Save your new Package and give it an appropriate name (we will use a name of **Context Report** in our example).

The folder for your publishing category should now similar to the one in the following screenshot:

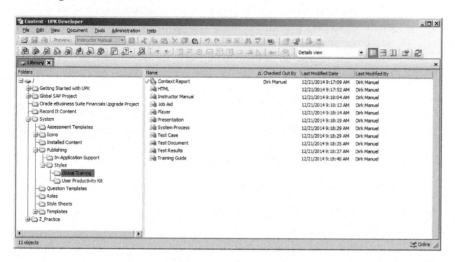

If you try to publish any content now, you will not see this document format in the *Publishing Wizard*. This is because UPK doesn't know where it should appear. Our next task is to include this document format in the *Publishing Wizard*.

There are a number of files that you need to change, within the Publishing Package, so that the new document format can be used correctly. These are:

- `style.xml`

- `style.resources.xml` (within the `lang/<code>` folder)

- `styleconfig.xml`

Changing each of these files is explained separately, below.

Step 1: Change style.xml

The first step in defining a new document format tis to change the `style.xml` file. Locate this file in the *Package Editor*, open it for editing, and change it as follows:

1. Locate the `<Category>` tag. The `CategoryOrder` parameter on this tag defines the publishing category in the *Publishing Wizard* within which the document format should appear. By default, UPK includes two categories: (1) **Deployment** and (2) **Documents** (see the example in *Publishing content—a generic approach* on page 224 for a reminder, if necessary). Change this to the sequential number of the category to which you want your new document format to be applied. For our purposes, we will create a new category. This will be the third category listed in the *Publishing Wizard*, so we will change the `CategoryOrder` to **3**.

2. The `StyleOrder` parameter on the `<Category>` tag defines the order of the publishing format within the category. Enter the appropriate value for this. If you are adding your new document format to an existing category then it is strongly recommended that you include the new document format after all of the existing formats—otherwise you will need to update all of the existing formats to reorder them. For our purposes, this will be the only document format in our new category, so we will set the `StyleOrder` parameter to **1**.

3. The `PreviewOrder` tag identifies the position within the Preview drop-down at which this new document style should appear. Change the value of this tag as required. By default, there are 11 built-in preview styles, so for our exercise, we will set this to **12**.

4. Save and close the `style.xml` file.

The relevant sections of the `style.xml` file should now appear a follows. The changed tags are shown in bold, with the new values in red.

▲ There are a number of additional tags that look as though you *should* change them here; don't. Any 'visible text' settings should be changed in the `style.resources.xml` file for the relevant language, instead.

```xml
<?xml version="1.0" encoding="UTF-8"?>
<!--Copyright © 1998, 2014, Oracle and/or its affiliates.
All rights reserved.-->
<Style xmlns:xlink="http://www.w3.org/1999/xlink"
xmlns:xi="http://www.w3.org/2003/XInclude">
 <Name ResId="StyleName">
 </Name>
 <NavBarGroups>
  <BarItem ResId="Content" Size="205">group43</BarItem>
  <BarItem ResId="Output" Size="140">group44</BarItem>
 </NavBarGroups>
 <Category CategoryOrder="3" StyleOrder="1"
           ResId="CategoryName">
 </Category>
 <Settings>
 <Setting>
  <Name>FeatureId</Name>
  <DefaultValue>Publishing_CR</DefaultValue>
 </Setting>
 <Setting>
  <Name>PreviewTitle</Name>
  <DefaultValue ResId="PreviewTitle"></DefaultValue>
 </Setting>
 <Setting>
  <Name>PreviewOrder</Name>
  <DefaultValue>12</DefaultValue>
 </Setting>
```

Step 2: Change style.resources.xml

Within the Publishing Package, open the `lang` folder, and then open the folder for the relevant language, within this. Locate the `style.resources.xml` file within the language folder, open it for editing, and change it as follows:

1. Locate the `StyleName` definition, and set this to the name of your new document format. This is the name that will appear in the **Formats** list in the *Publishing Wizard*. For our exercise, we will use **Context Report**.

2. If you are creating a new category, locate the `CategoryName` definition, and change this to the name of your new category. For our exercise, we will use **Administration**, so that developers know this is not an 'end-user facing' format.

3. Locate the `PreviewTitle` definition, and enter the name that should appear in the **Preview** drop-down for this document format. For our exercise, we will use **Context Report**.

4. Locate the `SubFolderName` definition, and update this to specify the folder in the published output to which documents in this format should be saved. For more information on these folders, refer to *Chapter 6, Publishing Your Content*. For this example, we will use a folder name of **CR** (for Context Report).

5. Locate the `LabelFormatDescriptionText` tag, and update this to provide a short description of the document format. This text appears on the last screen of the *Publishing Wizard*, when you select the document format.

The relevant sections of the `style.resources.xml` file should now appear as follows. The changed tags are shown in bold, with the new values in red.

```
<Resource xml:id="StyleName">Context Report</Resource>
<Resource xml:id="CategoryName">Administration</Resource>
<Resource xml:id="PreviewTitle">Context Report</Resource>
<Resource xml:id="SubFolderName">CR</Resource>
<Resource xml:id="labelFormatDescriptionText">Produces a
        document that lists the procedure steps,
        including the context IDs.</Resource>
```

Step 3: Change styleconfig.xml

Within the main (highest-level) folder of the Publishing Package for your new document format, locate the `styleconfig.xml` file, open it for editing, and change it as follows:,

1. Locate the `DocumentNamePrefix` tag, and change it to a short indicator for the document type. This is used in the filename of the saved document, if the **Use encoded folder and file names** option is not selected. For our exercise, we will use **CR** (for Context Report).

2. Locate the `DocumentNameRevisionPrefix` tag, and change it to a short indicator for the document type. This is used in the filename of the saved document, if the **Use encoded folder and file names** option is not selected. For our exercise, we will use **CR** (for Context Report).

Your `styleconfig.xml` file should now look similar to the example shown in the following screenshot. The changed tags are shown in bold, with the new values in red.

```
<PropertyGroup>
  <!-- Screenshot include method has the following
     values: Default, OncePerTopic, EveryFrame, None -->
  <ScreenshotInclusionMethod>Default
  </ScreenshotInclusionMethod>
  <ExcludeExplanation>false</ExcludeExplanation>
  <!-- DocumentType - single: create a doc for each
     topic; multi: create only one doc with all the topics
     in the selection; auto: If template has
     ForEachSection tags, it will behave like multi -->
  <DocumentType>single</DocumentType>
  <!-- DocumentNamePrefix - Appears in the output name
     (DocumentNamePrefix_docname.docx) -->
  <DocumentNamePrefix>CR</DocumentNamePrefix>
  <!-- DocumentNameRevisionPrefix - Appears in
     the output name, ONLY FOR SINGLETOPIC DOCUMENTS
     (DocumentNameRevisionPrefix_docname.docx)
     values - SPD: inserts SPD revision; JobAid: inserts
     JobAid revision; TestDoc: inserts TestDoc revision
     -->
  <DocumentNameRevisionPrefix>CR
  </DocumentNameRevisionPrefix>
</PropertyGroup>
```

Additional changes

All of the above changes will only give you a new document format that uses all of the same options as the document format on which it was based. There are many additional changes that you can make, by changing the relevant settings in the three files described above. However, for our purposes we have changed all that we need to, to make our new document format available, and additional changes are beyond the scope of this simple introduction.

For now, let's see how these changes appear in UPK. Firstly, the Preview list now appears as follows:

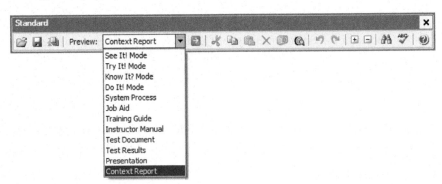

Here you can see that our new document format is listed, in **12th** place, as **Context Report**.

Now, let's check the Publishing Wizard:

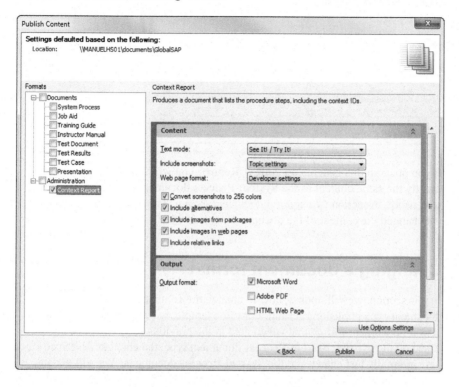

Here, you can see that we have a new category, of **Administration**, which contains our new document format, called **Context Report**. The description of this (in the upper-right portion of the screen) is as we specified, but all other options are exactly the same as for the standard **System Process** document, on which this new publication format was based.

To complete the review of our changes, the following screenshot shows the generated document, in a folder called **CR**, and with a suffix of **CR** in the file name:

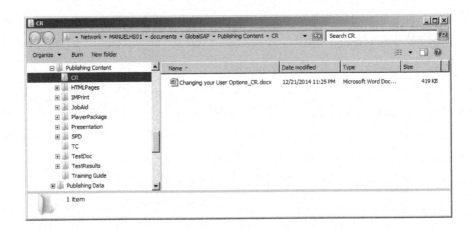

If you open up this generated **Context Report**, you will find that it generates exactly the same content as the **System Process** document (as shown in the next screenshot, in section *Changing a document format*. This is because we have not yet changed the content of the document—that is what we will do next.

Changing a document format

✦ The previous edition of this book, *Oracle UPK 11 Development* explained how to include the **Instructor Comments** into the **Instructor Manual** document, from which they were conspicuously absent. Oracle evidently took the hint and have now included the **Instructor Comments** in the default **Instructor Manual**. The example exercise used in this book has therefore been changed accordingly. Maybe in UPK 13 we'll see the **Context Report** re-instated...

In this section, we will look at how to change the content and layout of a document-type publishing format. For our example, we will work with **Context Report** document format that we created in the previous section, but as this was based on the existing **System Process** document type, the changes described here are really just changes to the **System Process** document. We will update this document to include the Context ID for each Frame. For the purpose of comparison, an excerpt of the current (default) contents of this document is provided below:

System·Process·Document¤
Changing·your·User·Options¤

Global Training

Step¤	Action¤	
3.¤	Click·the·Own·Data·menu.¶ Own Data	¤
4.¤	If·your·last·name·is·incorrect,·then·you·can·change·it·in·the·Last·Name·field.^For· this·exercise,·the·last·name·is·correct,·so·you·do·not·need·to·change·it.¤	¤

Step¤	Action¤	
5.¤	Click·in·the·First·name·field.¶ Dick	¤

The core component of any document format output is the
`PrintTemplate.docm` file (except, obviously, the Test Case format, which is
a Microsoft Excel Worksheet, and the Presentation format, which is a Microsoft
PowerPoint Presentation). The file type `.docm` indicates that this is a **Microsoft
Word Document with Macros**. It is the macros that do all the work. If you want
to change the content or format of a document, then this is the file to change.

To change the content of a document, carry out the following steps:

1. If you have not already done so, open the package for the document
   format, in the *Package Editor*.

2. Locate the file `lang\en\PrintTemplate.docm`, and double-click
   on it to open up this file in Word. Enable macros, if prompted.

3. You will see that the file contains a number of bookmarks. These are
   used as placeholders for the actual content, which is built separately by a
   series of `.xslt` files, and then dropped into this document. The **System
   Process** document (which we are changing in our example) is a single
   file that can contain multiple Modules, Sections, and Topics, all of which
   can contain Web Pages or Packages. The document may also contain a
   Glossary at the end. The basic processing logic for this document (as
   defined by the macros) is therefore:

▲ Be *very* careful
when editing the
`PrintTemplate.docm`
files; they are extremely
sensitive, and it is easy to
make a mistake. It is highly
recommended that you
make one small change,
test that this works, make
the next small change,
re-test, repeat, and so on.
In this way, you won't lose
too much work when it
inevitably breaks, as you
can easily revert to the 'last
working version'.

i.   Insert the name of the outline element being published, and the creation date, followed by a page break

ii.   Insert the copyright notice, followed by a page break

iii.   Insert the table of contents, followed by a page break

iv.   Repeat for each Module or Section in the Outline:

     a.   Insert the Module or Section name

     b.   Insert links to any websites provided via Packages

     c.   Insert any Web Pages attached to the Module or Section

     d.   Repeat for each Topic in the Module or Section:

          I.   Insert links to any websites provided via Packages

          II.   Insert any Web Pages attached to the Topic

          III.   Repeat for each Frame in the Topic:

              A.   Insert the screenshot

              B.   Insert the actions

              C.   Insert any attachments

          IV.   Loop

     e.   Loop

v.   Loop

vi.   Insert any Assessment

vii.   Insert the Glossary

4.   For our example, we want to insert the Context IDs for each screenshot. This is at Step iv.d.III.A in the outline given above. The relevant section of the document for this is:

ForEachFrame_Begin<Start of a repeating bookmark>]

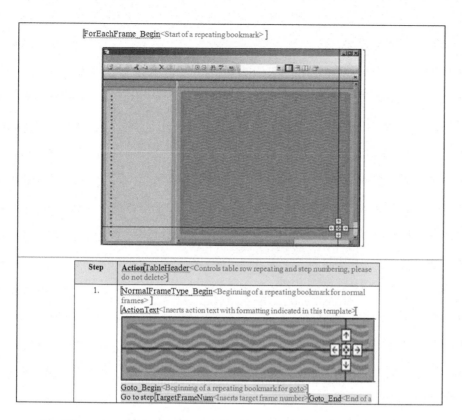

Step	Action TableHeader<Controls table row repeating and step numbering, please do not delete>
1.	NormalFrameType_Begin<Beginning of a repeating bookmark for normal frames>] [ActionText<Inserts action text with formatting indicated in this template>] Goto_Begin<Beginning of a repeating bookmark for goto> Go to step TargetFrameNum<Inserts target frame number> Goto_End<End of a

5. We want to insert the Context IDs, so we need to make space for this. Although we could simply add these below the screenshot, it would be cleaner (and more compact) if we could position these alongside the screenshot. To do this, we will use a two-column table: the leftmost column for the screenshot, and the rightmost column for the Context IDs. We have to reduce the size of the screenshot to fit this in, but as we are mainly concerned with the Context IDs, and the screenshot is just a visual check, this is acceptable.

Insert a table, and move the screenshot placeholder into the rightmost column of this. Be very careful, when moving the screenshot placeholder, that you also move the bookmark that surrounds this placeholder; it is not easy to see—even if you display the bookmarks—but it is there. You may find it easier to move the screenshot placeholder, and then select it and re-insert the bookmark (which is named **ScreenShotImage_1**).

The following screenshot shows the result of adding a table, and moving the screenshot placeholder into this:

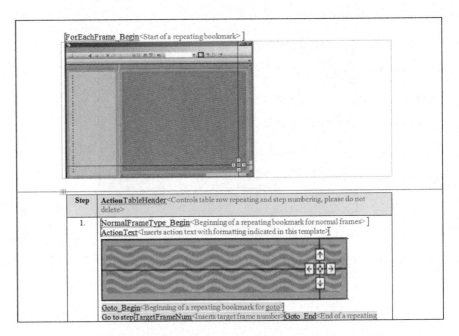

Note that the page margins have been adjusted to 1″ all round, and the Step/Action table resized to be 100% of the available width, to give us a bit more room (and because the default document just looks untidy and inconsistent by default).

6. We're now ready to insert our additional information (the Context IDs). To do this, we need to insert a placeholder that is wrapped in a specific bookmark. UPK provides a simple way of adding placeholder/bookmarks for several of the more common pieces of information: via an add-in (that's why the Word document is a .docm file). To access this add-in, click on the **Add-ins** tab within Word. Click on the point at which you want to insert the additional information in the document, and then select the relevant option from the menus available on the **Add-ins** ribbon.

Unfortunately, UPK does not include menu options for all possible bookmarks—and the Context IDs one is one of the missing ones. This means that we need to add it manually. Position the cursor in the rightmost column of our new table, and enter a suitable placeholder text (we will use **ContextIDs<Inserts context IDs>**). Then select all of this text, and insert a bookmark called **ContextIDs** around it.

■ If you want to apply specific formatting to the inserted information, then format this placeholder text as required; the substituted information will then be formatted in the same way.

Our Word template now looks like the example shown in the following screenshot. Note that we added a heading of "Context:" in front of the new placeholder/bookmark, just to keep things pretty. We also changed the document type, which is specified in the header.

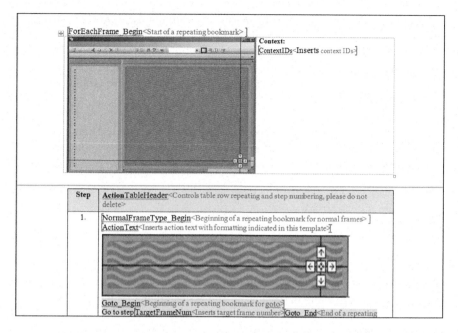

7. Once your `PrintTemplate.docm` file looks like the example above, save it, and close Word.

8. Back in the *Package Editor*, save and close the Package, and (if applicable) check it in.

Now let's see what this gives us. Publish (or Preview) any Topic, using your new **Context Report** publishing format. For our example, we now see the following

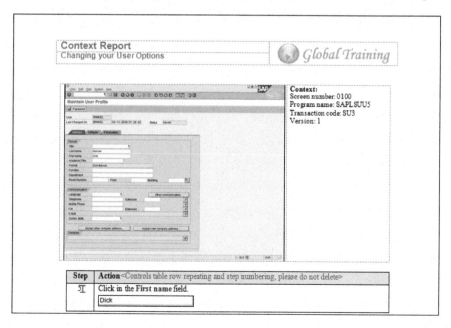

Compare this with the original version shown earlier in this section. You can see that our document has now been updated to include the Context IDs.

As noted at the start of this section, this is a fairly simple example, but it does at least introduce you to the concepts and possibilities available for UPK's output document formats.

You can find this new **Context Report** publishing format, inside a new publishing category called **Global Training**, in the sample `.odarc` file for this book, available from the author's website.

Summary

Out of the box, UPK contains everything that you need to create perfectly adequate training deliverables. But, for those of us not content (or unable) to stop at 'adequate', there are a number of things that can be done to configure UPK to produce exactly the output that we want, and in exactly the format that we want.

The default Bubble Text is controlled by the `template.xml` file. You can customize this file to change the text that is generated for each Object Type and Action combination. You can also define your own Object Types, to provide Bubble Text for elements that UPK does not natively recognize.

You can also change the format of the output generated by UPK. You can configure the on-line publishing formats, but most flexibility exists in changing the document formats, which you will more than likely want to do, to ensure that they meet your in-house styles, and contain specific information, in a specific format.

17
Localizing Your Content

UPK provides built-in support for several different languages, and has the ability to 'automatically' translate Topics recorded in one language into any of the other languages. Actually, it is far from automatic, but in its defense, it is much faster and simpler than calling in a translator and having them manually translate all of the text in a simulation. UPK provides built-in translations of its Template Text into 22 supported languages, and provides a relatively simple mechanism for facilitating the human translation of Custom Text. In this chapter, we'll look at both of these.

In this chapter you will learn:

- How to use a foreign-language template to translate Template Text
- How to use foreign languages in the deployment formats
- How to export Custom Text for translation, via either Word or XLIFF, and then import the translated content

Foreign-language templates

In *Chapter 4, Editing a Topic*, we looked at the default templates that ship with UPK. These templates specify the text that is to be used, by default, in the Bubbles, during playback. In *Chapter 16, Customizing UPK*, we looked at how to define our own Custom Template, and how to assign a Custom Template to a Module, Lesson, or Topic. Given this understanding of how templates in general work, it is not difficult to see how foreign-language templates would work. Essentially they work in exactly the same way.

When we created our own Custom Template, we took the existing (**Standard - English**) template from the system/templates/en folder. Observant readers

■ In this book, we use the term "foreign language" to refer to any language other than English (which is the language in which this book was originally written). If you are reading a translated version, you should make the appropriate mental adjustments.

will have noticed that the `system/templates` folder also contains several other folders, as shown in the following screenshot:

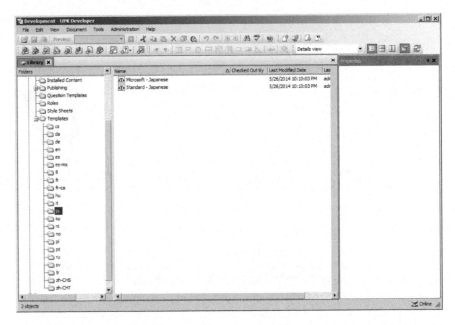

Each of these folders contains the same two Template Packages (**Microsoft** and **Standard**) as the /en folder, but in the language after which the folder is named. The folder names use the standard ISO two-character *language* (not country) code, plus a country/dialect suffix where necessary. So the /fr folder contains templates that define French-language text, and the /fr-ca directory contains templates for Canadian French.

Supported languages

✦ Support for Finnish, Turkish, Polish, Russian, Hungarian, Traditional Chinese, and Korean was added in UPK Version 3.5.

✦ Support for Czech was added in UPK 11.0.

UPK provides built-in support for the following languages:

- **cs**: Czech
- **da**: Danish
- **de**: German
- **en**: English
- **es**: Spanish
- **es-mx**: Mexican Spanish
- **fi**: Finnish
- **fr**: French
- **fr-ca**: French Canadian

- **hu**: Hungarian

- **it**: Italian

- **ja**: Japanese

- **ko**: Korean

- **nl**: Dutch

- **no**: Norwegian

- **pl**: Polish

- **pt**: Portuguese

- **ru**: Russian

- **sv**: Swedish

- **tr**: Turkish

- **zh-CHS**: Simplified Chinese

- **zh-CHT**: Traditional Chinese

So what do you do if you need to provide another language (other than the ones listed above)? Simple—you copy the directory for a currently supported language, (in exactly the same way as we created a custom (English) template in *Chapter 16, Customizing UPK*), rename it as appropriate, and then change all of the Template Text in the template(s) to the required language. (OK, so this last part might be a little time-consuming, but it is still faster than translating each individual Topic—and is reusable, too.)

▲ I'd advise against attempting to translate into Thai. Thai uses a 'byte-and-a-half' character set that is currently unsupported by UPK.

Foreign-language template format

The format and content of the foreign-language templates are exactly the same as the English-language templates, which were described in detail in *Chapter 16, Customizing UPK*. The code below an extract from the default Japanese-language template (/ja/Standard - Japanese), showing the Template Text for string input actions. The Japanese Template Text (as opposed to tags or comments, all of which are always in English) is shown in red, for emphasis (although I'm sure you'd be able to spot it, anyway).

```
<Template Context="StringInput">
  <!-- Example: Enter the desired information into the
Test field。 Enter 123。 -->
  <Text LeadingSpace="false" Sound="">[</Text>
  <ObjectName LeadingSpace="false" Sound="" />
  <Text Sound="stginp2-neutral" LeadingSpace="false">]フィ
ールドに目的の情報を入力します。</Text>
  <StringInputExtension Type="anything"
Sound="sivalid-neutral" LeadingSpace="false">有効な値</
StringInputExtension>
```

```
<StringInputExtension Type="example" Sound="siexample-
neutral" LeadingSpace="false">(例)</StringInputExtension>
  <Content LeadingSpace="false" Sound="" />
  <StringInputExtension Type="blank" Sound="siblank-
neutral" LeadingSpace="false">か、または空白</
StringInputExtension>
  <Text LeadingSpace="false" Sound="">にしてください。</
Text>
</Template>
```

Compare this with the English-language version from *Chapter 16, Configuring UPK*, which is repeated below, for your ease of reference. Again, the actual Template Text is shown in red, to simplify the comparison.

```
<Template Context="StringInput">
  <!-- Example: Enter the desired information into the
Test field. Enter 123.-->
  <Text Sound="stginput">Enter the desired information
into the</Text>
  <ObjectName />
  <Text Sound="stginp2">field. Enter</Text>
  <StringInputExtension Type="anything" Sound="sivalid">a
valid value</StringInputExtension>
  <StringInputExtension Type="example"
Sound="siexample">e.g.</StringInputExtension>
  <Content />
  <StringInputExtension Type="blank" Sound="siblank">or
leave blank</StringInputExtension>
  <Text>.</Text>
</Template>
```

Although there is not a *direct* match from English to Japanese (owing to the different sentence structures of the two languages), it is relatively easy to correlate one to the other. (It also helps that the tags and the comments are still in English!) While we're here, note that whereas the Sound settings in the English-language version are in the form "sivalid", the Japanese-language version is "sivalid-neutral". As explained in *Chapter 16, Configuring UPK*, this is because in some languages (Japanese in this case) *things* can be masculine, feminine, or neutral, and the words to use can change according to this. The example shown here considers the objects to be neutral. There are similar entries for masculine and feminine objects.

Providing existing content in a foreign language

In order to deliver existing content objects in a language other than the one in which they were originally developed, a number of specific steps need to be carried out. These are summarized below, and are explained fully in the next several sections of this document.

1. Take a copy of the existing content

2. Export the Custom Text and have it translated

3. Import the translated Custom Text

4. Select the appropriate foreign-language template, to translate the Template Text

5. Re-record the screenshots

6. Re-record any sound (if used)

7. Publish the content, using the appropriate deployment language

■ If you do not have any Custom Text, are not using sound, and will not be localizing the screenshots, then you could, in theory, simply change the template on the existing content (step 4), and publish to the appropriate foreign language (step 7), and then change the template back to the original language once you're done. However, few localization processes are this simple.

Taking a copy of the existing content

Before you 'localize' a content object, you should make a copy of that object. This is extremely important, and bears repeating: Make a copy of that object. Later in the translation process (step 2, in the list above) you will need to export this *copy*. If you export the original file, then when you import the translated text, you will overwrite the original! In contrast, if you take a copy of the document and export the copy for translation, then when you import the translation, it will update this copy, leaving the original document untouched and in the original language.

The fastest way to take a copy of a document is to select it on the *Library* screen, press *C$_{TRL}$+C* and then press *C$_{TRL}$+V*. This will take an exact copy, called exactly the same thing, and located in the same folder. You may want to rename it, or move it to another folder, to make sure that you do not select the wrong copy for export.

If you are going to translate a document and all of the documents related to it, you will need to take copies of all of these, and then link all of these copies to the copy of the original document that you made, so that the linked copies are also selected for translation, and not the originals.

■ If you copy the original Topic, then select **Paste Special** and choose the **Duplicate (selection and related)** this will also copy the 'related documents' for the selected Topic, and automatically link them (for example, it will copy the Concept Page from the original Topic, and then link the new Concept Page to the new Topic). However, use this with care as it will also copy any Glossary (including all glossary definitions) attached to the original Topic.

Using a foreign-language template

Once you have taken a copy of a content object (a Topic, in our example), the next step is to attach a foreign-language template to it.

Before we do that, let's see how the Topic looks (in the Player) when the English-language template is used.

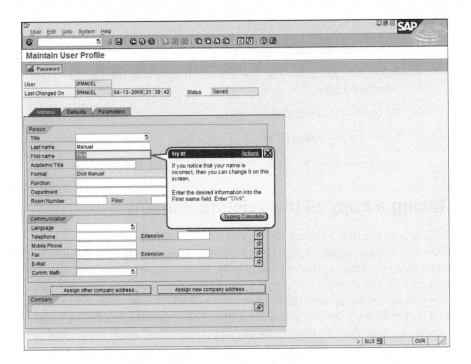

Now let's assign a foreign-language template to this Topic. How to do this was described in *Chapter 16, Customizing UPK*, but in summary, the steps are:

1. Select the Topic on the *Library* screen (or open it in the *Topic Editor*).

2. Display the **Properties** for the Topic by clicking on the **Properties** button (🔳).

3. Expand the **General** area.

4. In the **Template** field, navigate to, and select, the appropriate foreign-language template in the relevant language folder. In our example, this will be System/Templates/JA/Standard - Japanese.

Publish the exercise, and then run it. The Topic now appears as follows (again, this example is taken from the Player):

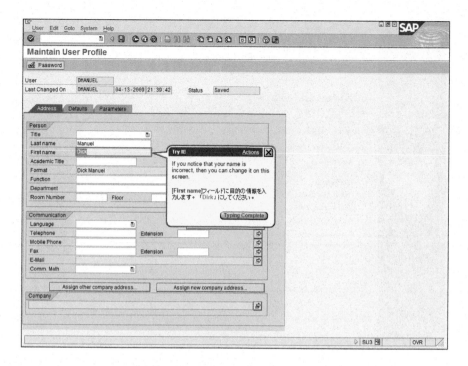

As you can see, the Template Text is now in Japanese. Success!

But wait! What about the custom text? For that matter, what about the **Typing Complete** button? And the **Actions** link? Fortunately, we can translate these, too, which is what we'll do in the following sections:

Using a foreign-language Deployment Package

What we have done so far is provide the Template Text in the foreign language. The other elements that you see in English above (excluding the Custom Text, which we'll look at in the next section) are tied to the Player (actually, they are tied to the *publishing format*, which just happens to be the Player in this example). So, how do we translate this text? Where is it defined? To answer the first question: we don't. UPK already ships with foreign-language versions of this text.

The answer to *where* the text is defined is simple. It is defined via the same **Publishing Options** that we looked at in *Chapter 16, Configuring UPK*. All you need to do is tell UPK which language to use when generating the output, and UPK will do the rest.

To use a foreign language in your published output, carry out the following steps:

1. Follow the steps given in *Chapter 6, Publishing Your Content*, until you reach the *Select Publishing Options* screen, shown in the following screenshot:

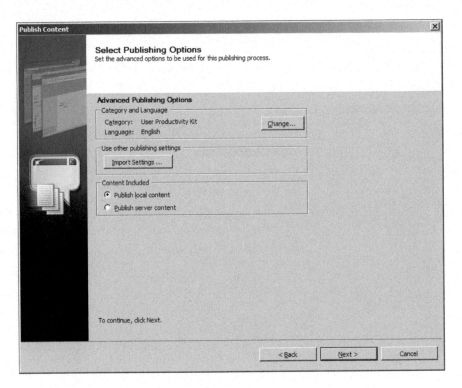

2. Note the **Advanced Publishing Options** section. This includes a specification of which language to use.

3. Click **Change**. The *Set Category and Language* dialog box is displayed. An example of this dialog box, with the **Language** list displayed, is shown below:

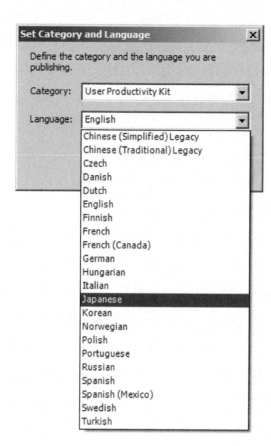

4. In the **Language** field, select the language in which you want the Player (in our case) to be generated—in our example, this is **Japanese**.

5. Click **OK** to return to the *Select Publishing Options* screen, and continue with publishing the Player (again, refer to *Chapter 6, Publishing Your Content* for additional guidance if necessary).

6. Once publication is complete (and the Player has been created), run it. The Topic will now be (almost) entirely in the foreign language (in our case Japanese), as shown in the next screenshot:

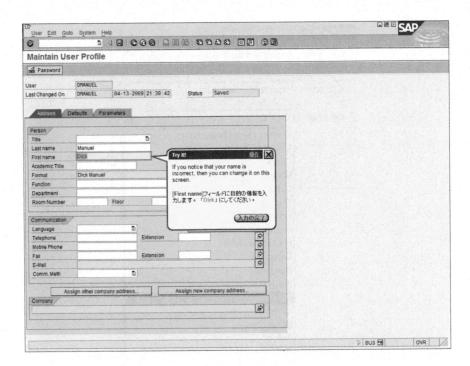

Note that the text **Try It!** in the Bubble title bar has not been translated. Apparently UPK's 'modes' are universally recognized, and require no translation! The only thing that remains untranslated now is the Custom Text, which you could forgive UPK for not managing to do. Next, we'll look at how to translate this.

Translating Custom Text

The steps described above apply to the Template Text. What if you have *Custom Text*? This text will also need translating, and no amount of fiddling around with templates or publishing options will do that for you. If you have Custom Text in your simulations—which will definitely be the case if you accept the recommendations of this book—then you will have to translate all of this text yourself (or at least arrange for the translation yourself). Fortunately, UPK provides a simple mechanism that allows you to export all of the Custom Text (only) to a Microsoft Word document (or XLIFF file) that you can then pass to a translator for translation. Once you receive the translated file back, UPK provides a way to import it again, overwriting (only) the Custom Text, creating a translated version of the content object(s).

Exporting content for translation

To export a content object for translation, carry out the steps described below:

■ If you really wanted to translate the mode names, you could do this via a custom Skin, as described in *Chapter 16, Configuring UPK.*

● An advantage of this approach is that the translator does not need to ever see UPK—they are working purely within Microsoft Word (or XLIFF file).

1. In the *Library*, click on the content object that you want to export for translation, to select it.

2. Select menu option **Tools | Export | Localization**. The *Export for Localization* dialog box is displayed, as shown in the following screenshot:

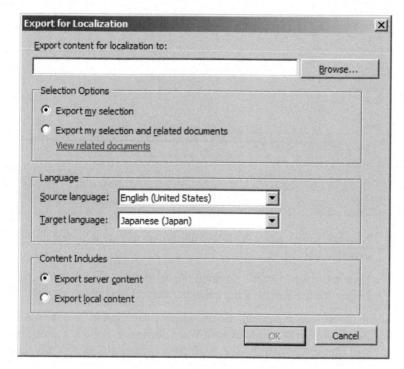

▲ You should export the content *before* changing the Language property for the content (in the content object's **Properties**) to specify the local language (this is described in the next section). This is because the currently-specified language will be used in the exported files, and should therefore specify the correct *source* language.

3. Click on the **Browse** button to the right of the **Export content for localization to:** field. The standard *Save As* dialog box is displayed, as shown below:

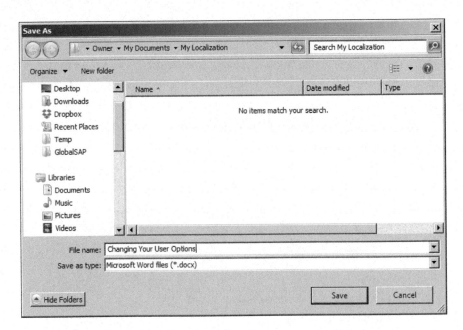

4. Navigate to and select the folder into which you want to save the exported file.

5. Enter a file name for the exported file in the **File name** field. This is largely for the benefit of the translator, so pick something sensible.

6. In the **Save as type** field, choose whether you want to save the file in XLIFF format or as a Microsoft Word document. For our exercise, we will export to **Word**; XLIFF is described separately, later in this chapter.

7. Click **Save** to close the *Save As* dialog box and return to the *Export for localization* dialog box.

8. Back in the *Export for Localization* dialog box, under **Selection Options**, select whether you want to export only the content that you selected (option **Export my selection**), or the selected content and all other related content, such as included Web Pages, and so on (option **Export my selection and related documents**). You would normally want to select the latter option.

If you are not sure which documents will be selected and exported, you can click the **View related documents** link, to display a list of them. Again, make sure that you are selecting the *copies* of the original-language content, unless you want to overwrite the originals.

9. In the **Source Language** field, select the current language of the content object (**English (United States)** in our case).

10. In the **Target Language** field, select the language into which the content object is to be translated (for this exercise, we will select **Japanese (Japan)**).

▲ If, when you took a copy of the Module, Section, or Topic, you manually copied the 'related documents' as well (instead of using **Paste Special | Duplicate**), then any Web Page(s) attached to the content object will be the **original** Web page. You should de-link these and then link in the **copies**, before exporting.

11. If you are working in a client/server environment, then choose whether you only want to export the version of the selected content objects that is on the server (option **Export server content**), or whether you want to include content that is checked out to your local repository (option **Export local content**). Note that if you select **Export local content** and the content object does not exist in your local repository, then the server version will be used.

12. Click on **OK**.

The custom text is extracted from the content object (in our example, a single Topic), and saved to a Word document. You can display this file in Microsoft Word (or compatible document editor), and the content will look as shown in the following extract:

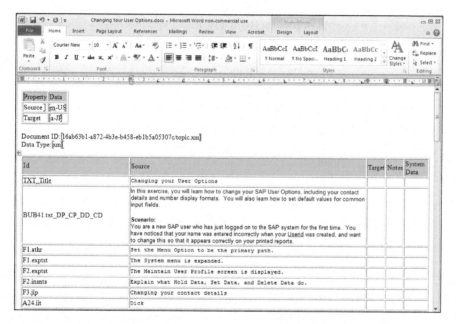

This document is extremely easy to understand. The first table in the document specifies the source and target languages. This is followed by two lines of code, and another table, for each content object being translated. The two lines of code provide the unique UPK identifier for the content object, and the document type of the content object. Both of these are only for UPK's internal use, and allow UPK to import the translated text into the correct place. This is why it is extremely important that you take a copy of the content that you want to translate, and then export the copy—the **Document ID** is the identifier of the document into which the translation will be imported.

✤ Prior to UPK 12, the source and target language specifications were provided via the 'source' and 'target' column headers in the content object tables. In UPK 12, this information has been moved to its own table at the top of the document, as shown here.

■ You can check the **Document ID** shown in the document heading with the **Document ID** shown for the content object on the Library (assuming that you are displaying the **Document ID** column) to confirm that you have indeed exported the copy and not the original of the content object.

The table below explains the content of each of the columns in the Word document:

Column	Contents
Id	The identifier of the text that is to be translated. As with the two lines of code above the table, this is internal to UPK, and allows UPK to import the translated text into the correct place. This typically includes characters identifying the source of the text. This is all purely internal information, but for the curious, some of the more common indicators are:

- `.txt`: Custom Bubble Text, or Web Page text
- `.jip`: A jump-in-point
- `.tt`: A ToolTip (typically, for a hyperlink)
- `.dhl`: A Decision Frame lead-in sentence
- `.dt`: A Decision Path
- `.iit`: Implicit text
- `.trm`: Glossary term
- `.athr`: Author Notes (preceded by Fn where n is the Frame number)
- `.exptst`: Expected Results (preceded by Fn where n is the Frame number)
- `.insnts`: Instructor Notes (preceded by Fn where n is the Frame number)

For Custom Bubble Text, the identifier includes a number of two-character pairs each preceded by an underscore (for example, **_DP,_CP,_DD,_CD** in the sample above). These determine the play mode in which the text will be used. The first character indicates the playback mode, as follows:

- D: Use in *See It!* and *Try It!* modes
- C: Use in *Do It!* mode
- A: Use in *Know It?* mode
- The second character indicates the output type, as follows:
- P: Use in the Player
- D: Use in printed output (that is, documents)

Column	Contents
Id (cont.)	So a code of **DP** indicates that the text is tagged for *See It!* and *Try It!* mode in the Player, and a code of **CD** indicates that the text is tagged for *Do It!* mode in printed output. As a single bubble text could have different portions tagged for different modes, you could have multiple rows in the translation table for the same bubble, but with different mode indicators. These need to be treated as separate translation units, despite any overlap in the texts. It is extremely important that the translator does not touch anything in this column, otherwise UPK will not be able to correctly re-import the file.
Source	This column contains the text in the source language. The translator should not change this text. If the translator is in the habit of over-typing the source-language text with the translated text then they should be advised to copy this column to the **<Target Language>** column, and over-type *that*, instead. Note that formatting is retained. This is useful for allowing the translator to match the format. Any formatting applied to the translated content will be retained when it is imported.
Target	This column is blank. The translator will enter their translation of the text in the **<Source Language>** column into this column. Note that the translator should format (bold, italics, and so on) the translated text to match the source text, as this text will be re-imported as formatted (and not as pure text).
Notes	You can enter any notes to the translator in this column (for example, telling them not to translate any screen elements!).
System Data	This column specifies other system-generated information required for translation (such as image properties). You will not normally need to change this information.

Enter any necessary notes, and then pass the Word document to the translator. The translator needs to translate everything in the second column, and place their translated text in the third column. Once you receive the translated file back, you can proceed to *Importing a translated file* on page 663.

Translating via XLIFF

XLIFF is an industry-standard format for exchanging files to be translated. It separates content from formatting, so that the translator can concentrate only on the text that needs to be translated. XLIFF also has the advantage that the translator does not need to have a copy of the software application used to create

● In addition to any Custom Text, the export file will also include all other related text that you have entered yourself, such as role names, Property values, and so on – basically anything that is not "UPK-generated" text.

✛ XLIFF support was introduced in OnDemand 9.1 (UPK 2.x).

the original source material (or even a copy of Microsoft Word)—they can use whatever XLIFF-compatible software they like.

XLIFF also works well with machine translation, because the translation software will understand the format of the file (assuming that it is XLIFF-compatible, which all good machine translation software will be).

For completeness, an extract of the .xlf file for the same section of the Topic as shown in the Word document earlier is given below. For clarity, the text to be translated is shown in red.

```xml
<?xml version="1.0" encoding="UTF-8"?>
<xliff version="1.1" xmlns="urn:oasis:names:tc:xliff:docu
ment:1.1">
 <file datatype="xml" original="6e8c8260-c281-443f-a975-
9adc081a0a87/topic.xml" source-language="en-US" target-
language="ja-JP">
  <body>
   <trans-unit id="TXT_Title">
    <source xml:lang="en-US">Changing your User Options</
source>
   </trans-unit>
   <trans-unit id="BUB41.txt_DP_CP_DD_CD">
    <source xml:lang="en-US" xmlns="urn:oasis:names:tc:xl
iff:document:1.1">
     <bpt id="1">&lt;p&gt;&lt;fmt font="Arial;10"&gt;</
bpt>In this exercise, you will learn how to change your
SAP User Options, including your contact details and
number display formats.  You will also learn how to set
default values for common input fields. <ept id="1">&lt;/
fmt&gt;&lt;/p&gt;</ept><bpt id="2">&lt;p&gt;&lt;fmt
font="Arial;10"&gt;</bpt><ept id="2">&lt;/fmt&gt;&lt;/
p&gt;</ept><bpt id="3">&lt;p&gt;&lt;fmt font="Arial;10"
sty="b"&gt;</bpt>Scenario:<ept id="3">&lt;/
fmt&gt;&lt;/p&gt;</ept><bpt id="4">&lt;p&gt;&lt;fmt
font="Arial;10"&gt;</bpt>You are a new SAP user who has
just logged on to the SAP system for the first time.  You
have noticed that your name was entered incorrectly when
your Userid was created, and want to change this so
that it appears correctly on your printed reports.<ept
id="4">&lt;/fmt&gt;&lt;/p&gt;</ept></source>
   </trans-unit>
   <trans-unit id="F1.athr">
    <source xml:lang="en-US">Set the Menu Option to be
the primary path.</source>
   </trans-unit>
   <trans-unit id="F1.exptst">
    <source xml:lang="en-US">The System menu is
expanded.</source>
   </trans-unit>
   <trans-unit id="F2.exptst">
    <source xml:lang="en-US">The Maintain User Profile
screen is displayed.</source>
```

```
      </trans-unit>
      <trans-unit id="F2.insnts">
       <source xml:lang="en-US">Explain what Hold Data, Set
Data, and Delete Data do.</source>
      </trans-unit>
      <trans-unit id="F3.jip">
       <source xml:lang="en-US">Changing your contact
details</source>
      </trans-unit>
      <trans-unit id="A24.iit">
       <source xml:lang="en-US">Dick</source>
      </trans-unit>
      <trans-unit id="TXT144">
       <source xml:lang="en-US">Dirk</source>
      </trans-unit>
      <trans-unit id="BUB47.txt_DP_CP_AP_DD_CD_AD">
       <source xml:lang="en-US" xmlns="urn:oasis:names:tc:xl
iff:document:1.1">
        <bpt id="5">&lt;p&gt;&lt;fmt font="Arial;10"&gt;</
bpt>If you notice that your name is incorrect, then
you can change it on this screen.<ept id="5">&lt;/
fmt&gt;&lt;/p&gt;</ept><bpt id="6">&lt;p&gt;&lt;fmt
font="Arial;10"&gt;</bpt><ept id="6">&lt;/fmt&gt;&lt;/
p&gt;</ept></source>
      </trans-unit>
      <trans-unit id="F4.exptst">
       <source xml:lang="en-US">Existing value can be
edited.</source>
      </trans-unit>
      <trans-unit id="F5.exptst">
       <source xml:lang="en-US">Function field becomes the
active field.</source>
      </trans-unit>
      <trans-unit id="TXT70">
       <source xml:lang="en-US">Training Analyst</source>
      </trans-unit>
```

Again, all of this is purely internal (it's referred to as a 'machine-readable' format for good reason) but for the adventurous reader, if you look into the code it's not really that difficult to follow. You can see the same identifiers as shown in the first column of the Word table in the `<trans-unit id>` tag, the source language is shown in the `<source>` tag, and so on. However, you shouldn't really need to interpret this file yourself. Just pass it to your translators, and when you receive it back, continue with *Importing a translated file*.

Importing a translated file

This section assumes that you have previously exported a Topic in Word format, sent this to your translator for translation, and have received the translated file back from the translator. The same steps apply to XLIFF files. For reference, an extract of the Word file that we have received back for our example Topic is shown below:

● The author takes no responsibility for the quality of the Japanese text in this example – it was obtained via `freetranslation. com`, and has not been verified by a Japanese speaker. It is provided solely for the purpose of illustration.

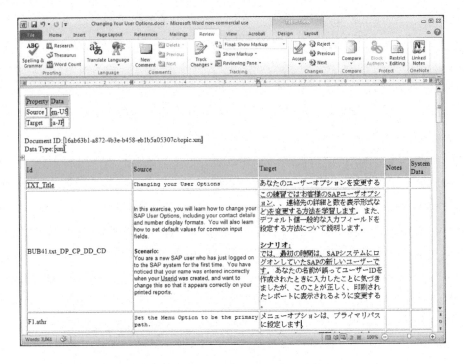

To import a file that has been translated, carry out the following steps:

1. From the *Library* screen, select menu option **Tools | Import | Localization**. You do not need to select the content object that you originally exported—UPK will use the **Document ID** in the translation file to locate the correct content objects(s) into which the translated text should be copied. The *Import for Localization* dialog box is displayed.

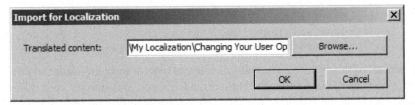

2. In the **Translated content** field, navigate to and select the file containing the translated text.

3. Click **OK**. You may see a *Security Warning* informing you that the `wordtoxliff.dot` file contains macros. If so, you need to **Enable Macros** (the import will not work without these macros). Eventually, the *Import Complete* dialog box is displayed, as shown in the following screenshot:

4. Click on the **View activity log** link. You should always display the Activity Log, as the *Import Complete* dialog box will not tell you if there have been any errors. The *Import Activity Log* dialog box for our example is shown in the next screenshot:

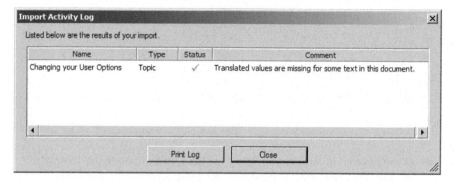

5. Check for any messages in the **Comment** column, to see if there were any problems with the import. If necessary, correct any errors in the input file, and then re-attempt the import. Note that you can re-import a single file as often as necessary; each import will overwrite the previous version (and not create a new copy).

6. Click **Close** to close the *Import Activity Log* dialog box, and then click **OK** to close the *Import Complete* dialog box.

● In this example, some values in the source file have not been translated; these were data fields that should not have been translated and were deliberately left blank. Where translated terms are not available, the source language text is retained.

Note that the import will *overwrite* the previous version of this content object. (Actually, it has overwritten only the text elements for this content object—the screenshots, Actions, and any links to or from the content object are retained.) This is why it is extremely important to take a copy of the object that you want to translate, and then export/translate/import this copy. The translated content object will be checked out to you if you are working in a client/server environment.

If you now display the content object (either in the Player or in Preview mode), you will see the translated version. For our example, we have translated a single Topic. The following screenshot shows a sample Frame taken from this Topic (this is the same Frame as shown in the original English version at the start of this chapter, if you want to compare).

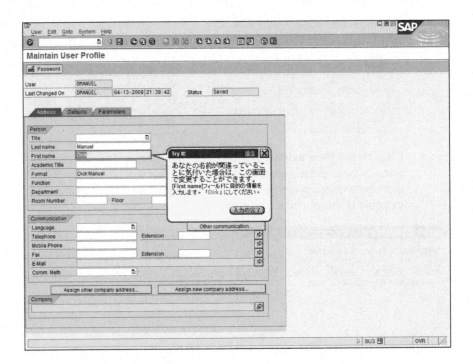

So now we have all of our Custom Text translated, in addition to the Template Text and the Player controls. If your users do not use a localized version of the application for which you are creating this training material, then you are finished. Otherwise, you still need to replace all of the screenshots. This is the subject of our next section.

Replacing screenshots with localized versions

We are now using a foreign-language template for all Template Text, and have translated all of our Custom Text. However, there is one more thing that may need to be translated: the screens themselves. Many applications (including Windows and SAP applications) allow users to select their language in order to have all of the screens displayed in that language. If you want your translated exercises to use screens for the relevant language (and in most cases you would—unless users are explicitly required to use English screens regardless of their native language) then you need to replace all of the screenshots in your simulation with the equivalent foreign-language versions. Although this may seem like a daunting prospect, UPK does provide a feature to simplify the rerecording of a topic.

When you re-record a topic, UPK will replace the screenshots in the recording with newly captured ones, and re-capture the Actions, but will leave all of the Custom Texts, and Explanation Frames intact. It will also retain any Alternative Paths and Branches, and any Alternative Actions recorded.

To re-record a Topic, carry out the following steps:

■ An alternative to using the Re-recorder function is to simply edit the Topic in the *Topic Editor*, and replace each screenshot individually, via menu option **Edit | Recapture | Screenshot**.

1. Start the application for which you want to replace the screens.

2. Switch to UPK, and open up the Topic in the *Topic Editor*.

3. Position yourself on the first frame for which you want to replace the screenshot (for translations, this will normally be the first frame in the recording).

4. From the menu bar, select menu option **Edit | Re-record Topic**. You are passed back to the application, and the *Rerecorder* panel is displayed in the upper-right corner of the screen, as shown in the following screenshot:

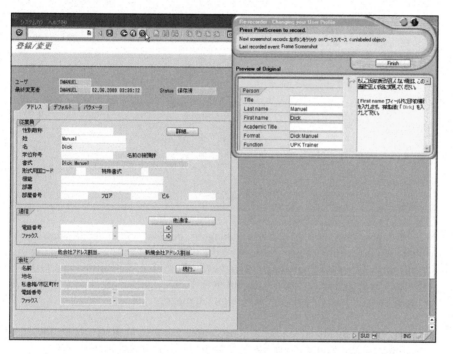

5. Note that the *Rerecorder* window contains a preview of the current (original language) screen (on the left) and the current (by now, translated) bubble text (on the right) so that you can confirm that you are capturing the correct screen.

6. Make sure that you are on the correct screen in the application, perform the required action, and then press the *PRINTSCREEN* key. The screenshot and action will be recaptured, and the recorder will automatically move on to the next frame. Repeat this step for all remaining frames in the current path.

7. If there are Alternative Paths or Branches in your simulation, then click on the next path in the path list, and return to Step 5.

8. Once you have recaptured all screenshots for all paths, click **Finish**. The *Rerecorder* window closes, and you are passed back into *Topic Editor*.

9. Save your changes, and close the *Topic Editor*.

■ If you only want to recapture the screenshots, and not the actions, then you can just press *PRINTSCREEN* and only the screenshot will be replaced. However, with some applications screen elements shift slightly to accommodate different languages, so you may want to recapture the actions as you go through the Topic, just to be thorough.

■ If you find it difficult to determine the correct action to perform for the Frame, you can replace the screenshots before importing the translated Custom Text (and/or before attaching the foreign-language template), so that you can read the current action in the source language. This will not be affected by the import of the translated text elements.

And that's it! Done! Our topic has now been completely translated, and appears in the Player as shown in the following screenshot:

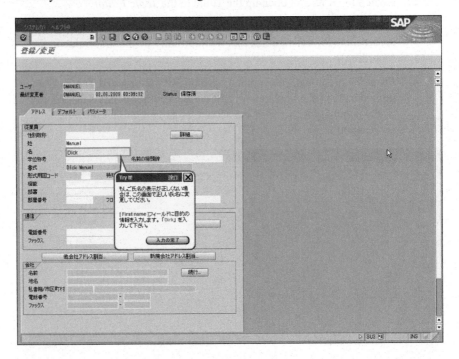

Nice job! Of course, the *difficult* part is making sure that you have the same data available in the local-language version of the system so that you can recapture the screenshots—otherwise you may also have to adjust all of the string input texts, references to screen data, and so on. But overall, it's significantly easier than recording a brand new Topic in the foreign language.

You can find the localized version of our sample exercise in the `.odarc` file available from the author's website. It is named **Changing your User Options (Chapter 17)**.

Re-recording the sound files

If you make use of sound in your Topics, then you will need to re-record the sound files, in the local language. The simplest way to do this is to re-record the sound files from within UPK, as explained in *Chapter 11, Incorporating Sound Into Your Topics*.

Alternatively, you may choose to export the existing sound files and pass these to the translator for re-recording, before importing them back into UPK. Again, how to do this is explained in *Chapter 11, Incorporating Sound Into Your Topics*.

Summary

Although UPK does not provide multi-language support from within a single Topic, it does make it relatively easy to provide a foreign-language version of an existing Topic. In its simplest form, assuming that you only use Template Texts and no Custom Texts, this is just a matter of attaching the relevant foreign-language template to a Topic, and publishing using the appropriate foreign-language deployment category.

If your Topic includes Custom Text (and most will), it is also necessary to translate this into the foreign language. UPK simplifies this, too, by allowing the Custom Text to be exported (in Microsoft Word or XLIFF format) for translation, and then re-imported into UPK once it has been translated.

To complete the localization process, it may be necessary to re-record any sound files, and recapture localized screenshots.

Once all of this has been done, you will have localized copies of your Topics, with (relatively) little effort.

Afterword

Congratulations, you have made it through to the end of this book. You are now well-equipped to begin developing quality training simulations using Oracle User Productivity Kit 12.

In this book you have learned not only what functionality UPK provides, but have also learned how to best make use of this functionality. You have seen practical examples of how to add value to your simulations, and how to make UPK generate the content that you want your trainees to see, rather than the default, 'vanilla' content.

You should now have a firm appreciation of what can be done with just a little extra effort. And you will no doubt have come to realize that if you do make the extra effort, your users, and your managers or clients, will undoubtedly thank you for it.

Happy developing!

A
Installing UPK

This Appendix explains how to install UPK 12. Why is this information hidden away at the back of the book in an Appendix? Surely, installing UPK is the first thing that you'll want to do? Well, no, not normally. UPK is an expensive piece of software, and is therefore almost solely the preserve of large corporations. These corporations are more likely than not either running a client/server environment which is installed and administered by a central IT group, or have a managed (and quite likely customized) installation process, possibly based on a push model, or automatic software base loading. In such cases, it is unlikely that a UPK author will install UPK themselves, and almost certainly not as a 'vanilla' install. In addition, even if you are installing UPK yourself, it is (hopefully!) a one-time activity, so there is no point in cluttering up the front of this book with information that you will use only once.

This Appendix explains how to install the **Developer Client** software, regardless of whether this is for a stand-alone (single user) environment or is for the client side of a client/server environment. (As mentioned above, in a multi-developer environment you are unlikely to be installing the server side yourself, and even if you are, that is beyond the scope of this book.) It also explains how to create a UPK Profile, which all authors will be required to do the first time they access UPK (or a new Library).

This Appendix assumes that you are in possession of the UPK installation files. If you are a paid-up license holder, you will know where to find these. If not, ask your company/client, or Oracle representative.

✛ Prior to UPK 11, a **Stand-alone Topic Player** could be installed separately. In UPK 11, this Player was automatically installed along with the client-side software. However, in UPK 12 Stand-alone Topics have been discontinued, so the Stand-alone Topic Player is no longer available for installation-- automatically or otherwise.

Installing the UPK Developer Client

To install the UPK Developer Client software, carry out the steps described below. Note that these steps are almost identical for both a stand-alone implementation and a client implementation (and the one step that is different is clearly identified as such).

1. Obtain the UPK installation pack, and then run the `setup.exe` file.

2. The following dialog box is displayed:

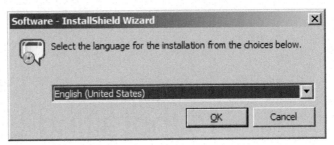

Select the language in which you want the installation instructions to be displayed, and then click on **OK**.

3. The following dialog box is displayed:

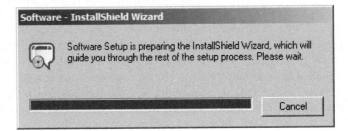

After a short while, the following screen is displayed:

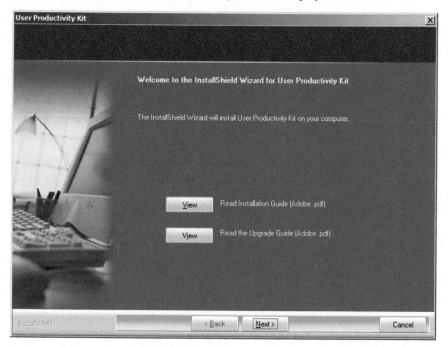

4. If you want to display the official *Oracle Installation Guide* and/or
   Upgrade Guide, then click on the relevant button. It is recommended
   that you display and print the relevant guide, before continuing. When
   you are ready to proceed with the installation, click **Next**.

5. The *Setup Type* screen is displayed, as shown below:

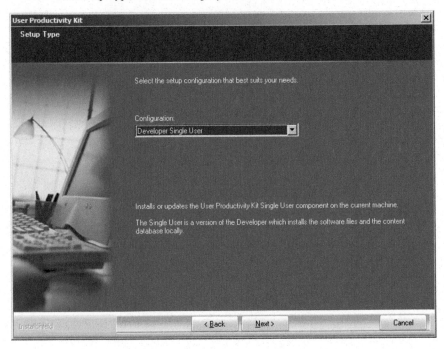

In the **Configuration** field, select the type of installation that you are performing. For our purposes, this will be one of:

- **Developer Client** for the client side of a client/server implementation (this will also install the Record It! Client)

- **Developer Record It! Client** if you only want to install the Record It! Wizard (typically you would only do this for a SME who will not be using may of UPK's features)

- **Developer Single User** for a stand-alone implementation

Once you have made your selection, click on **Next**.

✛ The ability to install the Record It! Client independently of the Developer Client is new in UPK 12. Previously, both clients would be installed by the Developer Client option.

6. The *Language Selection* screen is displayed, as shown below:

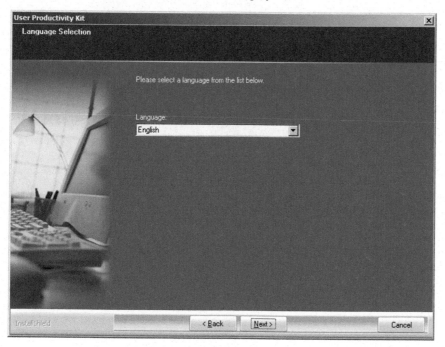

In the **Language** field, select the language in which you want UPK to be installed. This will determine in which language the *UPK Developer* screens will appear. If you are reading this book in English, then I'm guessing that you want to select **English**. Click **Next**.

7. UPK checks for the existence of a number of required programs on your PC. If any of them are missing, then the *Software Requirements* screen is displayed and you should continue with Step 8. Otherwise, continue with Step 10).

8. The *Software Requirements* screen is displayed, as shown below:

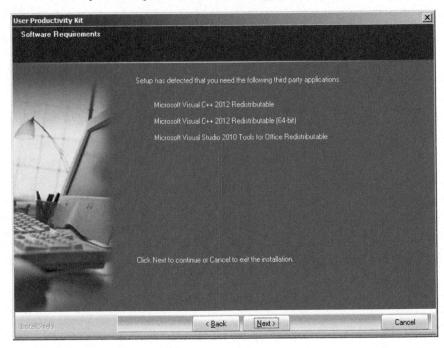

Click **Next**.

9. A dialog box similar to the following (depending upon the software component being installed) is displayed:

Once all of the prerequisite software is installed, continue with Step 10.

10. The *Select Program Folder* screen is displayed, as shown below:

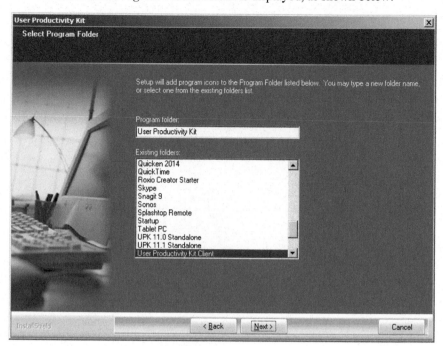

If necessary, you can change the name of the folder on the Start Menu into which the shortcuts for the installed UPK components will be placed. Generally, the default of **User Productivity Kit** should be sufficient. Click **Next**.

✦ For UPK 11 and earlier, you were presented with the option to install Start Menu shortcuts for the Record It! Client and/or the Developer Client, prior to Step 10. Now that you can install the Record It! Client independently of the Developer Client, both shortcuts will be installed for a Developer Client install, and only the *Record It! Wizard* shortcut will be installed for a Record It! Client install.

11. The *Choose Destination Location* screen is displayed, as shown below:

If necessary, you can change the folder into which the UPK executables will be installed. To do this, click on the **Change** button, and then navigate to and select the required folder. It is normally sufficient to accept the default path. Click **Next**.

12. The *Ready to Install the Program* screen is displayed, as shown below:

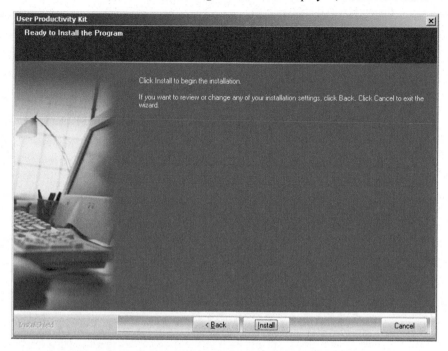

Click **Next**.

13. The *Setup Status* screen is displayed, as shown below. You can use the status bar to monitor the progress of the installation.

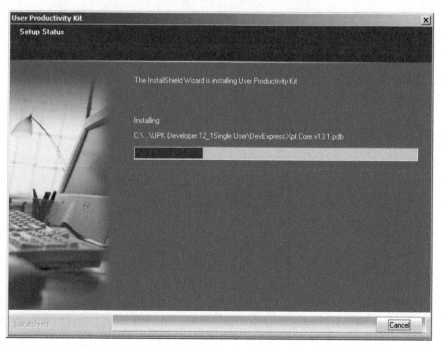

14. Once installation of the Developer application is complete, the following dialog box is displayed:

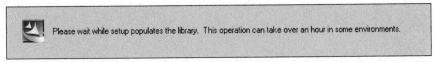

Please wait while setup populates the library. This operation can take over an hour in some environments.

During this step, all of the default Library files (the entire content of the System folder, and the sample files) are copied into the UPK database. This may take some time.

15. Once the Library has been fully populated, the following screen is displayed:

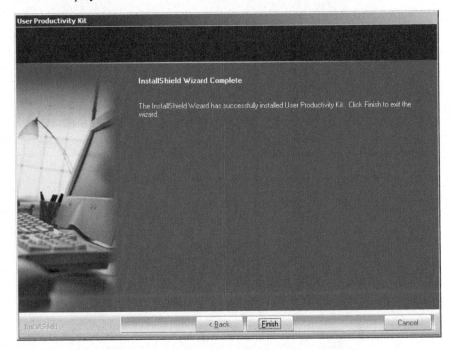

Click **Finish**.

UPK has now been installed and is ready for use.

Working with Profiles

In order to access the UPK Library (regardless of whether you are working in a stand-alone environment or a client/server environment) you need to create a Profile.

If you have access to multiple Libraries, then you will need to create multiple Profiles—one for each Library that you access. Interestingly, this, too, applies regardless of whether you are working in a stand-alone environment or a client/server environment. This means that even if you are a sole author working in your own installation of UPK, you can maintain entirely distinct libraries for separate clients or projects.

The first time that you access UPK you will be prompted to create a Profile. After that, each time that you access UPK you will be logged on with this (default) Profile. You can then crate additional profiles – and even set one of your additional Profiles as your new default profile. All of these options are described below.

Although the approach is basically the same in each type of environment, the exact information that you need to provide (when creating a Profile) will vary depending on whether you are accessing a stand-alone version of UPK, or logging onto a UPK client. These options are discussed separately below; refer to the one section that applies to your environment.

Creating a UPK profile in a stand-alone installation

To create a Profile in a stand-alone installation of UPK 12, carry out the steps described below.

1. How you start the Profile creation process depends on whether this is the first time you have accessed UPK or not.

    - If you are accessing UPK for the first time, then as soon as you select the UPK Developer Client from the Windows Start Menu, the *Profile Wizard* is displayed, and you should continue with Step 4.

    - If you have already accessed UPK and created a Profile (and are now creating an additional Profile for the same installation of UPK) then continue with Step 2.

2. Select menu option **Tools | Profiles**. The *Profile Manager* dialog box is displayed, as shown in the following example:

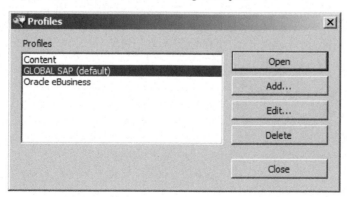

● In addition to creating a new Profile, you can also edit and delete Profiles from the *Profiles* dialog box. You also use this dialog box to log out of one Profile and log in to another (via the **Open** button).

In the *Profile Manager* dialog box, click on the **Add** button.

3. The *Welcome to the Profile Wizard* screen is displayed, as shown below.

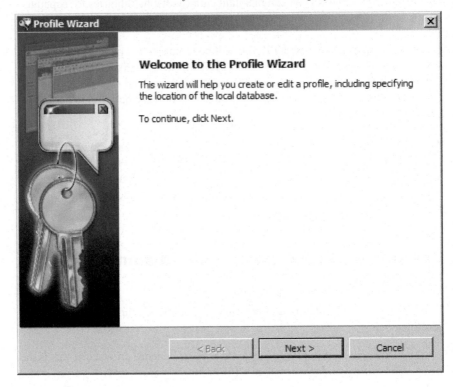

Click **Next**.

4. The *Profile Name* screen is displayed, as shown below:

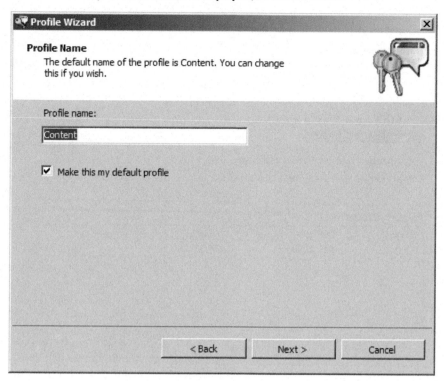

5. Enter a suitable name for this Profile, in the **Profile name** field. If you will be creating multiple profiles to provide separate libraries for different clients, projects, or for other reasons, you should make sure that this name is indicative of the content of the Library for this Profile.

6. If you want to log on to this Profile automatically when you start UPK, then select the **Make this my default profile** check-box. Note that if this is your first Profile then this check-box is automatically selected, and you cannot deselect it.

7. Click **Next**.

8. The *Data Storage Location* screen is displayed, as shown below:

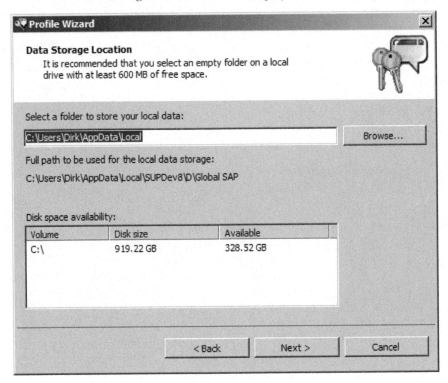

● All content objects that create, and any content objects that you 'check out' from the server, will be stored in your Local Repository until you check them in (again). It is recommended that this is a location on your local PC, and not a network location.

Confirm (or enter, or navigate to and select) the folder in which you want your UPK **Local Repository** to be stored. It is important that you choose a location that will not be accidentally modified, and that can easily be backed up.

9. Click **Next**.

10. The *Completing the Profile Wizard* screen is displayed, as shown below:

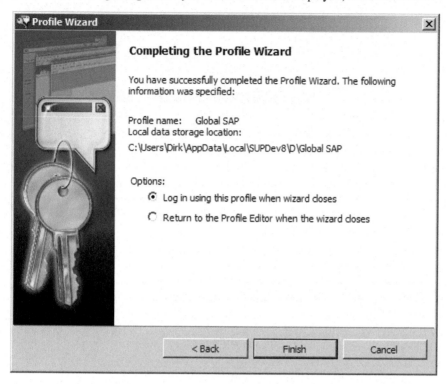

If you want access UPK, using the profile that you have just created, select **Log in using this profile when the wizard closes**. If you want to create another profile, select **Return to the Profile Editor**, and you will be returned to Step 2 after you click **Finish** in Step 11.

11. Click **Finish**. UPK will load all of the default files into the Library. This may take a while. During this load, you will see the following message:

Note that you will see this message (although it won't take as long) every time that you log on to UPK.

Once the Library has been loaded, the following message is displayed:

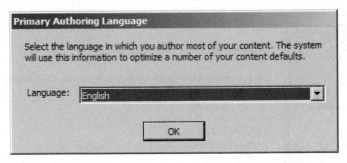

12. In the **Language** field, select the language in which you will be developing your content. This affects your default spellchecker, and the default templates that will be used. You can change all of these things for individual content objects, if required.

13. Click **OK**. The *Start Screen* is displayed, as shown in the following screenshot:

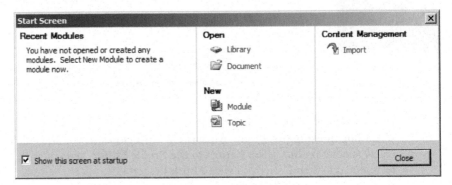

You have now set up your UPK profile, and successfully accessed UPK. Most of the steps above are a one-time setup; every subsequent time that you access UPK, you will start from the Start Screen shown above (unless you deselect the **Show this screen at startup** option).

Creating a UPK profile in a client/server environment

To create a new Profile in a client/server environment, carry out the steps described below:

1. How you start the Profile creation process depends on whether this is the first time you have accessed UPK or not.

   - If you are accessing UPK for the first time, then as soon as you select the **UPK Developer Client** or the **UPK Developer**

Record It! Client from the Windows Start menu, the profile Wizard is displayed, and you should continue with Step 4.

- If you have already accessed UPK and created a Profile (and are now creating an additional Profile for the same installation of UPK) then continue with Step 2.

2. Select menu option **Tools | Profiles**. The *Profiles* dialog box is displayed, as shown in the following example:

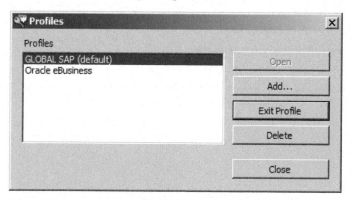

3. In the *Profiles* dialog box, click on the **Add** button. The *Welcome to the Profile Wizard* screen is displayed, as shown below.

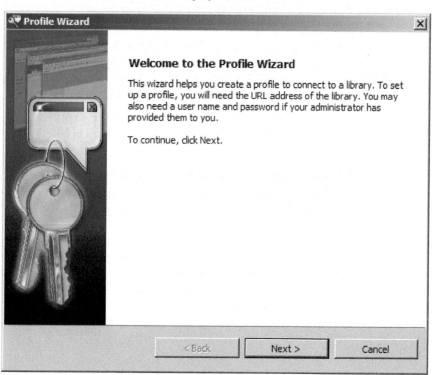

- In addition to creating a new Profile (as described below) you can also edit and delete Profiles from the *Profiles* dialog box. You also use this dialog box to log out of one Profile and log in to another (via the **Open** button).

4. Click **Next**. The *Library Location* screen is displayed, as shown below:

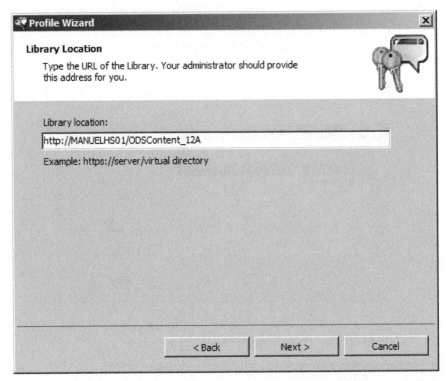

5. In the **Library location** field, enter the URL of the UPK Library that you will be accessing via this Profile. You should be given this by your UPK administrator (unless that's you, in which case you hopefully made a note of this when you installed UPK onto the server…).

6. Click **Next**. UPK will attempt to locate the Library via the URL specified. During this attempt, the following dialog box will be displayed:

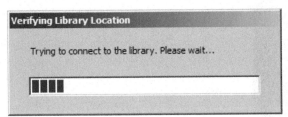

Once UPK has connected to the Library, the *Credentials* screen is displayed, as shown below:

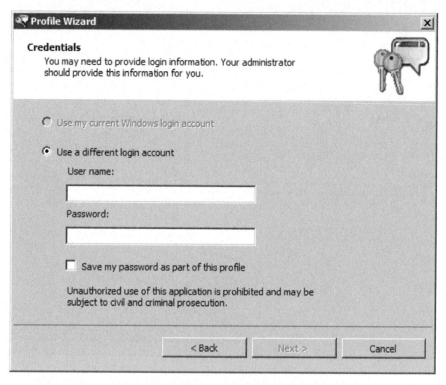

7. If UPK was set up to use Windows authorization, then select **Use my current Windows login account**. You will then be able to access the Library as long as you are logged in to your PC.

If UPK was set up to use 'standard' authorization, then select **Use a different login account option**, and then complete the following information:

i.   Enter your user name into the **User name** field.

ii. Enter your password into the **Password** field.

iii. If you want UPK to save your password in your Profile, then make sure that the **Save my password as part of this profile** check-box is selected. Otherwise, make sure that this check-box is cleared and you will be prompted to enter your password every time you try to access this Library.

● You should receive your user name and password from your UPK administrator.

■ You can change your password at any time via menu option **Tools | Change password**.

8. Click **Next**. The *Profile name* screen is displayed, as shown below:

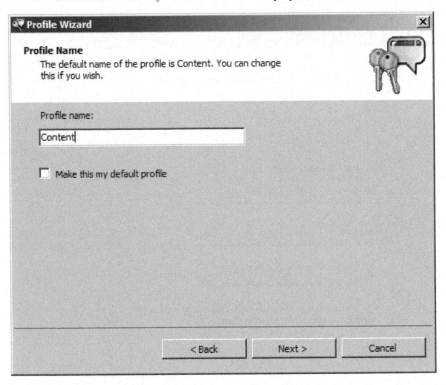

9. Enter a suitable name for this Profile, in the **Profile name** field. If you will be creating multiple profiles to provide separate libraries for different clients, projects, or for other reasons, you should make sure that this name is indicative of the content of the Library for this Profile.

10. If you want to log on to this Profile automatically when you start UPK, then select the **Make this my default profile** check-box. Note that if this is your first Profile then this check-box is automatically selected, and you cannot deselect it.

11. Click **Next**. The *Data Storage Location* screen is displayed:

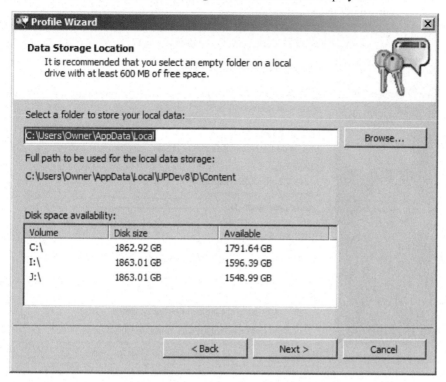

12. Confirm (or enter, or navigate to and select) the folder in which you want your UPK **Local Repository** to be stored. It is important that you choose a location that will not be accidentally modified, and that can easily be backed up.

■ If you edit your Profile at a later date and change the location of your Local Repository, then UPK will automatically move the current contents of this to the new location.

13. Click on **Next**. The *Completing the Profile Wizard* screen is displayed, as shown below:

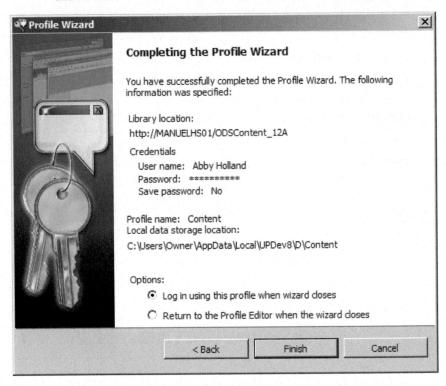

14. If you want to go directly to the Library, using the profile that you have just created, select **Log in using this profile when the wizard closes**. If you want to create another profile, select **Return to the Profile Editor when the wizard closes**, and return to Step 2 after you click **Finish** in Step 15.

15. Click **Finish**. The *Profile Wizard* dialog box is closed, and the *Primary Authoring Language* dialog box is displayed, as shown below:

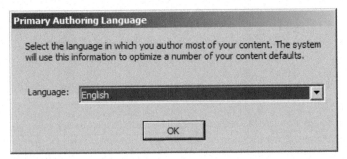

16. In the *Language* field, select the language in which you will be developing your content. This affects your default spell-checker, and the default templates that will be used. You can change all of these things for individual objects, if required.

17. Click **OK**. UPK will copy all of the necessary files from the Library on the server to your PC. This may take quite a while, depending on your network connection. During the transfer, the following progress bar is displayed:

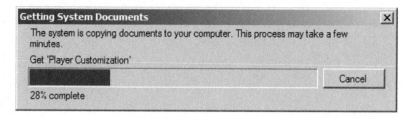

Once all required files have been downloaded, the *Start Screen* is displayed, as shown in the following screenshot:

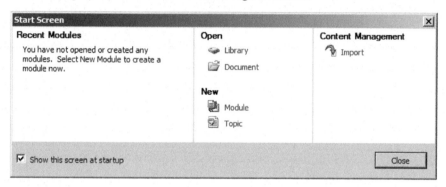

You have now set up your UPK profile, and successfully accessed UPK. Most of the steps above are a one-time setup; every subsequent time that you access UPK, you will start from the Start Screen shown above (unless you deselect the **Show this screen at startup** option).

Summary

This Appendix walked you through how to install the UPK 12.1 Developer Client software on your PC. It also explained how to create a Profile in order to access a Library.

B
User Options

This appendix provides a comprehensive explanation of all of the user option settings. All of these can be accessed via menu option **Tools | Options**. In addition, two categories - **Recorder** and **Documents > Test Case** are accessible via the **Set Options** link in Step 2 of the *Record It! Wizard*.

Developer category

The options in the **Developer** category control the developer's interactions with UPK.

General subcategory

The following table lists the options that are available in the **Developer | General** category, and describes their purpose:

Option	Description
Image Editor	This is the application that will be used for editing screenshots from within the **Topic Editor** (see the section *Editing screenshots* in *Chapter 4, Editing a Topic)*. This defaults to Microsoft Paint, but you can use the Browse button to navigate to and select the executable (`.exe` file) for any other image-editing application.

Option	Description
Package HTML Editor	This is the editor that will be used for editing HTML files contained in Packages. You have a choice of the following options:
	• **Use Developer's built-in HTML editor**: Selecting this option will result in UPK's own HTML editor being used. This editor is described in detail in *Chapter 9, Adding Value to Your Topics*.
	• **Use default HTML editor installed on your system**: Selecting this option will result in whichever application is associated with editing `.htm` and `.html` files being used.
	• **Select another HTML Editor**. Select this option if you want to use another HTML editor that is installed on your system. Click the **Browse** button and navigate to the executable for this editor.
Do Not Ask Again	Several dialog boxes that you will encounter as you use UPK will ask you to make a choice (for example, to check in only the document you selected, or check in the selected document and all related documents). Most of these dialog boxes also include a check-box labeled Do not ask me again. If you select this check-box, then UPK will remember your choice, and use this in future, instead of displaying the dialog box that asks you to make that choice. If you subsequently change your mind, you can click the **Reset Dialogs** button, and UPK will start asking you to make each choice again. Note that this will reset all dialog boxes.
Additional Help Links	If your organization has developed its own help system for UPK, then you can define up to two additional help menu options. Enter the name for the menu option, and the URL that this link should point to.

✛ The **Package HTML Editor** option was not available prior to UPK 12, as in prior releases it was only possible to use the built-in HTML editor.

✛ The **Additional Help Links** option was added in UPK 12.

Library subcategory

The following table lists the options that are available in the **Library** category, and describes their purpose:

Option	Description
Automatically save changes every...minutes	As you edit content objects in the Library, UPK will regularly save your changes to a temporary file. If there is a power cut, or UPK crashes (it has been known to...) or other disaster that takes place before you have the chance to save your changes yourself, UPK can revert to this temporary file, so that you do not lose (too much of) your work. If you are editing particularly large content objects, then the few seconds that UPK takes to save these documents may be disruptive to your work flow. In this case, you can deselect the **Automatically save changes every** check-box, and UPK will no longer perform these temporary saves. You can also change the frequency with which UPK saves your files, by adjusting the **minutes** field, as required.
Scan for Lost Documents	Documents can become 'lost' for a number of reasons – for example, if you have a document checked out to you, but another user deletes the Folder in the Library that contains it. If you think that this has happened to any of your documents, you can click on the **Scan for lost documents** button, to have UPK attempt to find them. Any 'found' documents will be visible in the *Lost Documents* view, from where you can restore them, if required. Refer to *Chapter 3, Working in the UPK Developer Client* for additional information on this functionality.
Available Disc Space*	When you create documents, check out documents, or 'get' documents (copy them from the server) they are stored in your Local Repository. This option allows you to change the amount of disc space that UPK reserves for your Local Repository. You should not normally need to change this.

Option	Description
Network Connection*	You can use the **Connection Speed** field to select the type of connection that you have to the network (where the Library is stored). This determines the amount of time UPK will wait for a response from the Library before deciding that there is a connection error.

* These options are applicable to a client/server environment only.

Content Defaults category

There are many formatting changes that you can make to your recordings so that they better meet your individual (or client/project) requirements. Thankfully, most of these can be defaulted through your **Content Defaults** options. Not all of them directly relate to the act of *recording*, but they all affect your recordings, so we will cover them all here.

General subcategory

The table below lists the options that are available in the **General** category, and explains their purpose:

Option	Description
Language	This option specifies the language against which your documents will be spell checked. This option is explained more fully in *Chapter 17, Localizing Your Content*.
Template	This option specifies the Template from which the Template Text will be taken (it is possible to have multiple templates for the same language; in fact, UPK ships with two separate Templates for each language). Templates are discussed in *Chapter 16, Customizing UPK*.
Base URL for Previewing Relative Hyperlinks	If you will use relative links for hyperlinks to non-UPK content that is on the same server as your published UPK Player, then specify the base URL that should be combined with the relative links so that the content can be previewed correctly within the UPK Developer. Refer to the section *"Using Relative URLs"* in *Chapter 9, Adding Value to Your Topics* for more information on using relative links.

Topic subcategory

The following table lists the options that are available in the **Topic** category, and describes their purpose.

Option	Description
Default Mode Settings	Use these check-boxes to select the modes that will be active in the Player and in the LMS, and select the modes in which sound will be played for the Topic. The values set here will be used as default settlings for the **LMS Play Modes**, **Play Modes**, and **Play Sound** Topic Properties, and can be changed there, if necessary,
LMS Required Mode	If your content will be accessed via an LMS, then by default, the mode that the user must complete a Topic in to be considered complete will be determined as the 'most restrictive' mode. If you want a specific mode to always be used, then you can set this as a default, here.
Frame delay	This field specifies the default amount of time for which UPK will wait, after completing the action, in *See It!* mode, before automatically advancing to the next screen. **5** seconds is a reasonable default. If any Frame has a significant amount of text, or information to see, you can change the delay for that individual Frame from within the *Topic Editor*. Setting a value of **0** will result in a much more 'movie-like' playback, but the downside is that Decision Frames and Explanation Frames (both of which are explained in later chapters of this book) will not be displayed at all, so you will want to manually adjust these.
Required Percentage	This option specifies the percentage that a user must achieve in *Know It?* mode to 'pass' the 'test'. 80% is not unreasonable (it allows for an occasional mis-click), but you should refer to your company's general practices for guidelines.
Remediation options	If a user makes a mistake in *Know It?* mode, they can be prompted with up to three levels of guidance on how to perform the action, with increasingly more help, before (at what is effectively Level 4) UPK takes over and performs the action for them. They will still be marked wrong, but these remediation levels provide them with the opportunity to try again. It is usually sensible to provide all three levels of remediation.

✛ The **Topic** category was introduced in UPK 12, although the **Frame Delay**, **Required Percentage** and **Remediation Options settings** were available under the **Content Defaults | General** category in earlier releases.

✛ In UPK 11 and earlier, the **Play Sound** options have their own subcategory, of **Sound**. In UPK 12, these options have been merged into the new **Topic** category.

✛ The **LMS Required Mode** setting was added to the User Options in UPK 12.1.0.1.

✛ Up to UPK 12.1.0.0, the **Screen Resolution** option was located under the **General** subcategory. It was moved to the **Topic** subcategory in UPK 12.1.0.1.

Option	Description
Screen resolution	As discussed earlier in this book, it is important that you record your simulations at exactly the same resolution that your users will use when playing back the recording. You can specify an exact resolution via this option. Note that you cannot change the resolution of a recording after it has been recorded, so you need to make sure it is correct before you record.

Recorder subcategory

The options under the **Recorder** subcategory of the **Content Defaults** category apply to what is captured during the recording process itself. Note that there is also a separate Recorder category (described in *Documents category* on page 709) which applies to how the developer records content.

The table below lists the options that are available in the **Recorder** category, and explains their purpose:

Option	Description
Automatically record keyboard shortcuts	If this option is selected (which is the default) then UPK will attempt to capture alternative actions during recording. This is often limited to keyboard shortcuts for menu options. For more information on alternative actions, refer to *Chapter 14, Allowing Alternatives*.
Enable automatic recording	If this option is selected, then UPK will *automatically* record drag-and-drop actions (even during manual recording). Otherwise, you will need to manually capture the mouse down and mouse up actions.
Distance between screenshots	When automatically recording drag-and-drop actions, UPK will capture additional screenshots as you drag. This setting specifies how far the cursor needs to move before UPK will capture a new screenshot.
Action area size in pixels	This setting specifies the size of the action area that UPK will capture during automatic recording of drag-and-drop activities. This is the area around the cursor when UPK captures the screenshot; the user must move the cursor into this area during playback.

Bubble subcategory

The options under the **Bubble** subcategory of the **Content Defaults** category allow you to define the defaults for your Bubbles (which are discussed more fully in *Chapter 4, Editing a Topic*).

The table below lists the options that are available in the **Bubble** category, and explains their purpose. Note that to set some of these options you need to click on the relevant button, and then select the required value in the pop-up window that is subsequently displayed.

Button	Name	Description
	Icon	Clicking on this button allows you to choose an icon to display in each Bubble. These icons are discussed in *Chapter 9, Adding Value to Your Topics*. It is not recommended that you have an icon in *every* Bubble (let alone the same icon in every Bubble—there are 35 to choose from), so you should not normally use this option.
	Pointer	Clicking on this button allows you to choose a default position for the pointer on a Bubble. Pointers are discussed in *Chapter 9, Adding Value to Your Topics*. Unless you choose not to have a pointer at all, it is unlikely that you will want to use a default for every Bubble. Just let UPK decide which position is best, based on the relative position of the Action Area.
	Fill	Clicking on this button allows you to choose the background color for the Bubble. The default light yellow is popular and widely-understood from other applications, but if the application that you are recording uses this color predominantly, you may want to choose another color. Whatever color you use, it should stand out from the application screen during playback. Note that you cannot change the color of the Bubble title bar (which is set to navy blue).
A	Font	Clicking on this button allows you to set the default font-family, size, and style (but not color) for your Bubble Text. This sets the default for both Template Text and Custom Text. You can change these individually for any given Bubble in the **Topic Editor**, although you would generally want to use the same for both.

Button	Name	Description
-	**Use Template Text**	By default, UPK will provide text to describe the recorded actions, based on the template selected in your **General** options. If you do not want to use this Template Text, then you can deselect this option. However, you will then need to provide Custom Text for all of your actions (or provide no text at all, which is unwise). Note that this only controls whether the Template Text is actually used. It is still available, and can be (re-)applied for an individual Frame within the *Topic Editor*.
-	**Show custom text first | Show template text first**	If you use Template Text then you can choose to have either the Template Text or the Custom Text displayed first. As discussed in *Chapter 9, Adding Value to Your Topics*, it is generally more useful to display the Custom Text first.

Introduction/End Frame subcategory

The options under the **Introduction/End Frame** subcategory of the **Content Defaults** category allow you to define the default background color and font for the Bubbles that are used on the Introduction (Start) Frame and the End Frame. Note that to set these options you need to click on the relevant button, and then select the required value in the pop-up window that is subsequently displayed.

The table below lists the options that are available in the **Introduction/End Frame** subcategory, and explains their purpose:

Button	Description
Fill	Clicking on this button allows you to choose the background color for the Start Frame and End Frame Bubbles. The default light yellow is popular and widely-understood from other applications, but if the application that you are recording uses this color predominantly, you may want to choose another color. Whatever color you use, it should stand out from the application screen during playback. Note that you cannot change the color of the Bubble title bar (which is set to navy blue).
Font	Clicking on this button allows you to set the default font-family, size, and style (but not color) for text in the Start Frame and the End Frame.

String Input subcategory

The options under the **String Input** subcategory of the **Content Defaults** category allow you to define the default background color and font for string input actions. Note that to set these options you need to click on the relevant button, and then select the required value in the pop-up window that is subsequently displayed:

The table below lists the options that are available in the **String Input** subcategory, and explains their purpose:

Button	Name	Description
	Fill	Clicking on this button allows you to choose the background color for the string input action area (that is, the area on the screen into which the user will type the text. By default, this is set to white.
	Font	Clicking on this button allows you to set the default font-family, size, and style (but not color) for your string input text. This defaults to Microsoft Sans Serif 8pt.

In order to better understand these options, it is worth considering how text input works. When UPK plays back a string input action, it overlays a text box onto the screenshot, at the point where the input field appears. This text box has a solid background. You may have expected this to be transparent, so that you could see the input field below it, but consider the case where the field contains an existing value that the user has to change—this would show through, too. You should therefore set the background of the text box to be exactly (and I cannot stress enough that this must be *exactly*) the same as the background color of the input fields in the application that you are recording. This is white in many applications, but (for example) SAP uses a deep yellow background for the active field, so

■ Refer to *Chapter 4, Editing a Topic* for more information on the background colors and fonts used in common applications.

when recording SAP, the background color of the string input field needs to be changed to match.

The same is true of the string input font. This must *exactly* match the font (family and size) that is used in your application for input fields. You may be able to find out this information from the application itself, or you may need to use trial and error to find the correct one.

Glossary subcategory

The options under the **Glossary sub**category of **Content Defaults** allow you to define the how Glossary links are added to your content:

The table below lists the options that are available in the **Glossary** category, and explains their purpose:

Option	Description
Create glossary links for...The first occurrence of the term in each location	If this option is selected then UPK will only create a Glossary Link for the first occurrence of the Glossary Term found in the Bubble or Web Page.
Create glossary links for...Every occurrence of the term	If this option is selected, then UPK will create a Glossary Link for every single occurrence of the Glossary Term—so if the term appears ten times in a single bubble, each of those ten occurrences will be turned into a hyperlink to the Glossary Definition.

For more information on Glossaries and generating Glossary Links, refer to *Chapter 9, Adding Value to Your Topics*.

Web Page subcategory

The options under the **Web Page** subcategory of the **Content Defaults** category allow you to define the default background color and font for Web Pages. Note that to set some of these options you need to click on the relevant button, and then select the required value in the pop-up window that is subsequently displayed.

The table below lists the options that are available in the **Web Page** subcategory, and explains their purpose:

Button	Name	Description
-	**Style Sheet**	If you want to control the format of text in your Web Pages via a Style Sheet, then select this option, and then click on the Browse button to navigate to and select the Style Sheet within your Library that you want to use.
-	**Content Defaults**	If you do not want to use a Style Sheet, then select this option, and then specify the default direct formatting for the text in your Web Pages via the following four options.
-	**Font Family**	Select the default font family for Web Page text.
-	**Font Size**	Select the default size and unit of measure for Web Page text.
	Text Color	Clicking on this button allows you to set the default color for text in Web Pages.
	Page Color	Clicking on this button allows you to choose the default background color for Web Pages. By default, this is set to white.

+ Style Sheets were introduced in UPK 12.

+ In UPK 11 and earlier, the **Font Family**, **Font Size**, and **Text Color** are set via the standard **Text** button. In UPK 12, these three attributes have their own dedicated fields.

● Although the **Text Color** icon is displayed as the standard **Fill** icon, it still works correctly. Most likely, this minor display error will be fixed in a future release.

Note that the **Style Sheet** and **Content Defaults** options are mutually exclusive - you can only select one or the other.

Web Pages are described in *Chapter 9, Adding Value to Your Topics*.

Assessment subcategory

The options under the **Assessment** subcategory of the **Content Defaults** category allow you to define the default settings for Assessments that you create.

The table below lists the options that are available in the **Assessment** category, and explains their purpose:

Option	Description
Passing score percentage	This option defines the default score that a user taking the assessment must achieve in order to 'pass' the assessment.

Option	Description
Question order	This option specifies the order in which the Questions included in the Assessment will be presented to the user. The choices are: • **As authored**: The Questions will be presented in the order in which they appear in the Assessment in the Assessment Editor. • **Random order**: The Questions will be presented in a random order that (effectively) changes each time that the Assessment is taken.
Answer order	This option specifies the order in which the answer choices are listed for a Question. The options are: • **As authored**: The answers will be presented in the order in which they appear in the Question in the Question Editor. • **Random order**: The answers will be presented in a random order that (effectively) changes each time that the Assessment is taken. Note that this option only applies to Question types that have multiple answers: Matching, Multiple Choice (Single Answer), and Multiple Choice (Many Answers).
Remediation	This option specifies the default level of remediation that should be provided to the user upon answering the Question. The options are available via the drop-down are: • **Results only**: The user sees only the text "Correct" or "Incorrect". • **User Asks**: The user sees the text "Correct" or "Incorrect", but this text is a hyperlink that the user can click on to see the correct answer and/or any remediation text specified for the question. • **Incorrect**: If the user specifies the correct answer, they see the text "Correct" (not hyperlinked). If they specify the incorrect answer, then the correct answer is displayed, along with any remediation text specified for the Question. • **Always**: The user sees the text "Correct" or "Incorrect", along with the correct answer and any remediation text specified for the Question.

Option	Description
Show Associated Content	If this option is selected, then if a user answers a Question incorrectly a link (named Show Associated Content) is provided in the feedback to allow the user to launch the content object to which this question has been associated (via the Question's Associated Content Property).
Display results summary after completing the assessment	If this option is selected then details of the user's score – including whether each Question was answered correctly or incorrectly, and their final score – are displayed when the user completes the Assessment. Otherwise, the user will only see a message informing them that they have completed the Assessment.

Assessments and Questions are described in *Chapter 12, Testing Your Users*.

Documents category

The options in the Documents category control the content of the printed output document types. All of these can be overridden at the time of publishing (refer to *Chapter 6, Publishing Your Content* for details).,

Word-based publishing formats

Most of the options in the Documents category are applicable to all of the 'Word-based' listed in the settings apply to all of the 'Word-based' publishing formats and are therefore listed together, below. These document formats are:

- **System Process**
- **Job Aid**
- **Training Guide**
- **Instructor Manual**
- **Test Document**
- **Test Results**

The table below lists the options that are available for the Word-based documents. Settings that do not apply to all document types are identified as such within the table.

Option	Description
Output format	Select the file type to be generated. This can be one or more of: • Microsoft Word document • Adobe PDF document • HTML Web Page
Screenshots | Include	Select whether or not screenshots should be included in the document, and how many should be included if they should. The available options are: • **Topic settings** – Use the settings in the Topic itself to decide which individual screenshots to include or not. Refer to *Chapter 4, Editing a Topic* for details of how to set this. • **One screenshot per topic** – Only include one screenshot per Topic. The first screenshot in the Topic will be used. • **One screenshot per frame** – Include a screenshot for every Frame in the Topic. **None** – Do not include any screenshots
Convert screenshots to 256 characters	Select this option to down-sample the screenshots to 256 colors. This can reduce the size of the generated file, especially for recordings of color-intensive applications.
Paper size	Select the paper size for the generated documents. You can choose **A4, Letter**, or **Print template** setting. This latter option will use whichever page size is configured in the associated deployment package template.
Text mode	Select the playback mode from which the text included in the document should be taken. Refer to *Chapter 4, Editing a Topic* for an explanation of text modes.
Web Page format	Choose whether Web Pages are formatted according to the Template (or direct formatting) applied to them, or according to the formatting applied to the publishing template itself (which will effectively override all individual Web Page formatting). The latter option will provide greater consistency, but you could lose 'exception' formatting that has been applied by the developer. This option does not apply to the **Job Aid, Test Document**, or **Test Results** formats.

✚ Older versions of UPK also allowed you to set the **Microsoft file type** (`.doc` or `.docx`). This option has been removed in UPK 12 - `.docx` is always used.

Option	Description
Use encoded folder and file names	If you select this option, then the file name under which each Topic will be saved will be UPK's internal 32-character object identifier for the Topic. Otherwise, the file name will be the Topic name. Using the 32-character object identifier is useful if links to Topics will be hard-coded in other sources (such as via an intranet site), as the link will not be broken if the name of the Topic is changed.
Include alternatives	By default, the document will include any alternative paths and alternative actions recorded in the Topic. If you want to exclude these, then deselect this option.
Include images from packages	Select this option if you want the document to include images contained in packages that have been linked to a Frame Bubble or the Web Page used as the Concept Page for the Topic. This option does not apply to the **Job Aid**, **Test Document**, or **Test Results** formats.
Include images in Web Pages	Select this option if you want the document to include images that have been inserted directly into a Web Page used as the Concept Page for the Topic. This option does not apply to the **Job Aid**, **Test Document**, or **Test Results** formats.
Include relative links	If you are using relative links in your content, then these links may not be useful in printed output formats (because they are designed to be *relative* to the location of the object containing the link, and if that object is a printed document (even if the document is being displayed on-line) the linking document does not have a 'location'. To avoid having incomplete URLs listed in your output document, by default, relative links are simply omitted from document output. If you decide that you *do* want to include the relative links, select the option **Include relative links**. Note that if you do this, you must be absolutely sure that your readers will be able to determine the full URL themselves, given the relative URL that will appear in the printed document.
Include assessments	By default, the **Training Guide** and **Instructor Guide** will include any Assessments available in the published Outline. If you want to exclude Assessments, then deselect this option. This option only applies to the **Training Guide** and **Instructor Guide** formats.

Option	Description
Include questions	By default, the **Training Guide** and **Instructor Guide** will include any inline Questions available in the published Outline. If you want to exclude inline Questions, then deselect this option. This option only applies to the **Training Guide** and **Instructor Guide** formats.

Excel-based documents

The **Test Case** is the only Excel-based output format, although there are four variations on this, as explained in the table below.

The table below lists the options that are available for the **Test Case** subcategory, and explains the purpose of each of these.

✛ Older versions of UPK also allowed you to set the **Microsoft file type** (.xls or .xlsx). This option has been removed in UPK 12 - .xlsx is always used.

Option	Description
Use encoded folder and file names	If you select this option, then the filename for the generated file will be the UPK 32-character object identifier for the selected Outline. Otherwise, the Outline name will be used as the filename.
Include alternatives	By default, the document will include any alternative paths recorded in the Topic. If you want to exclude these, then deselect this option.
Group actions by Context ID	When you record a simulation for certain targeted applications (see *Chapter 15, Integrating UPK with Other Applications*), UPK will capture the *context* of the action – the application, program, screen, and field acted upon). This context is included in the **Other** Test Case output file. By default, the rows in the file reflect the order the actions were carried out during recording. If you select this option, then all actions for a specific context are grouped together.
Text Mode	As we saw in *Chapter 4, Editing a Topic*, Bubble Text in Frames can be tagged to appear or not appear in different playback modes (**See It!/Try It!**, **Know It?**, and **Do It!**). This option allows you to choose which mode you want to use for the text in the document.

Option	Description
Format	Select the file type to be generated. This can be one or more of: • **Oracle Application Testing Suite** (this is the default) • **HP Quality Center** • **IBM Rational Quality Manager** • **Other** The **Other** option simply creates a spreadsheet containing **all** available information.

PowerPoint-based publishing formats

The **Presentation** is the only 'document' type published in Microsoft PowerPoint publishing format.

The following table lists the options that are available in the **Presentation** subcategory, and describes their purpose.

Option	Description
Convert screenshots to 256 characters	Select this option to down-sample the screenshots to 256 colors. This can reduce the size of the generated file, especially for recordings of color-intensive applications.
Include action areas	A screenshot is included in the Presentation for each Frame (tagged for inclusion in Print Mode). If you want the Action Area to be highlighted on this screenshot (as it is in the Player), then select this option, and use the Color button to select the color for the Action Area marquee.
Use encoded folder and file names	If you select this option, then the file name under which each Topic will be saved will be UPK's internal 32-character object identifier for the Topic. Otherwise, the file name will be the Topic name. Using the 32-character object identifier is useful if links to Topics will be hard-coded in other sources (such as via an intranet site), as the link will not be broken if the name of the Topic is changed.
Include alternatives	By default, the document will include any alternative paths and alternative actions recorded in the Topic. If you want to exclude these, then deselect this option.

Option	Description
Include relative links	If you are using relative links in your content, then these links may not be useful in printed output formats (because they are designed to be *relative* to the location of the object containing the link, and if that object is a printed document (even if the document is being displayed online) the linking document does not have a 'location'. To avoid having incomplete URLs listed in your output document, by default, relative links are simply omitted from document output. If you decide that you *do* want to include the relative links, select the option **Include relative links**. Note that if you do this, you must be absolutely sure that your readers will be able to determine the full URL themselves, given the relative URL that will appear in the printed document.
Text mode	Select the playback mode from which the text included in the document should be taken. Refer to *Chapter 4, Editing a Topic* for an explanation of text modes.

In-Application Support category

SmartHelp is UPK's way of providing in-application support for non-targeted applications. The options listed in the following table support this.

Option	Description
SmartHelp enabled	Select this check-box only if want to use SmartHelp for your application(s).
SmartHelp Installation URL	If you have chosen to use SmartHelp, then enter the URL of the location to which you saved UPK's SmartHelp installation files. If a user does not have SmartHelp installed, they will be prompted to install it from this URL.

For more information on installing and using SmartHelp, refer to the *Oracle UPK In-Application Support Guide* (E39857-01).

Player category

The options in the Player category control the format and content of the Player publishing format. They also allow you to define default settings for all of the player preferences that can be set by the user, from the Player **Preferences** button. These settings are also described in *Chapter 6, Publishing Your Content*. They are included again, below, for completeness of this Appendix.

Option	Description
Convert screenshots to 256 colors	Selecting this option will result in all screenshots being down-sampled to 256 colors, which will result in much smaller files. For most applications this is sufficient, but for simulations of graphics-intensive applications (such as photo-editing software) you may want to deselect this option.
Include HTML Web Site	If you select this option, then additional files will be generated to provide a 'pure HTML' index to the Player (that is, without the JavaScript-enabled hierarchical outline).
Include detailed action steps in HTML Web Site	If you chose to Include **HMTL Web Site** then you can use this option to control whether or not the HTML Web Site includes the full details of all actions, with images.
Create zip file from published Player package	You may find it easier to zip all of the Player files (which will typically run into the thousands of individual files) into a single file that you can distribute or load into a Learning Management System. UPK will create this zip file automatically if you select this option. The zip file will be saved to the `Player Package` folder in the publication directory.
Create Test It! mode Player	As explained in *Chapter 13, Using UPK for Application Testing*, UPK can provide a *Test It!* playback mode that guides testers through a task and captures the results of this test. If you select this option, an additional playback button (**Test It!**) is included in the Player. It is not recommended that this is enabled for user use.
Include Sound	If you want sound to be included in your Player, then select this option. The use of sound tends to significantly increase the overall size of the Player package, so if you know your users will not listen to the sound (perhaps their workstations do not have speakers attached to them) then you can deselect this option and exclude the sound files altogether. The use of sound is described in detail in *Chapter 11, Incorporating Sound Into Your Topics*.
Skin	If you have defined a custom Player **Skin**, then select this skin (use the **Browse** button to navigate to it and select it, if necessary). For information on creating your own Skin, refer to *Chapter 16, Configuring UPK*.

✛ Prior to UPK 12, you could select the sound frequency (to use), or "None". With UPK 12, sound is always published at a standard hard-coded frequency of 96kbps in ACC format (or .flv files for Windows 2008 SP2).

Option	Description
Format for Print It! mode	Select the type of document that you want to be provide via the **Print It!** button in the Player. You can choose from: • **System Process Document** • **Job Aid** • **Test Document** • **None** (No *Print It!* document is provided) Note that this selection is independent of any documents selected under **Documents** in the leftmost selection list. That is, you do not have to select **Job Aid** for publishing (on the left) to be able to provide the Job Aid via *Print It!*. In fact, even if you do publish the Job Aid, then if you choose **Job Aid** for *Print It!* mode, then UPK will generate a *separate* Job Aid document for use with *Print It!* (in a subfolder of the `PlayerPackage` folder).
Marquee color	This option defines the color of the rectangle that is shown around the action area during playback of the simulation. By default this is red, but if you need to (for example, if the application you are recording uses red prominently in its screens) then you can change this color by clicking on the **Fill** button (⬚) to the right of this option, and selecting the required color.
Play audio	This option allows you to specify which sounds should be played during playback. The choices are: • **None**: No sound will be played. • **Keyboard and mouse-clicks**: Only the sounds for keyboard presses and mouse-clicks will be played. Sounds for Bubble Text will not be played. • **All available sound**: All sound files used in the simulation will be played, including Bubble Text sound files. Note that the option **All available sound** is only relevant if the **Include sound** option under **Content** is selected. If you have chosen to not include sound files, then the **All available sound** option will have the same effect as the **Keyboard and mouse-clicks** option.
See It playback size	Use this option to select the default size for the (Windowed) *See It!* mode playback window (although it can be resized by the user).

✛ Full-screen *See It!* mode was discontinued in UPK 12.

Option	Description
Default playback mode	This option allows you to choose the mode in which the Topic will be launched when the user double-clicks on it in the Outline (as opposed to single-clicking on the Topic to select it and then clicking on the appropriate mode button). This defaults to *Try It!* mode.
Applicable outline display	If the Player is displayed in response to a context-sensitive help call, then you can choose whether the user initially sees a flat list of applicable content (**Applicable List**), or a filtered Outline (**Applicable Outline**). or the full Outline with the option to switch to the applicable Outline (**All**).
Show introduction text	By default, the Bubble Text specified on the Start Frame of the simulation will be displayed on the first screen of the Topic playback. If this option is deselected, then the entire Start Frame will be omitted from playback. You would normally only choose this option if you do not have Concept Pages attached to the Topics, in which case the contents of the Start Frame are shown in the Concept pane (so hiding the Start Frame during playback avoids seeing it twice). For more information on this option and the Start Frame, see *Chapter 9, Adding Value to Your Topics*.
Enable users to change their Player preferences	If this option is selected, then users will be able to change a number of Player options within the Player window itself. The options that they can change are: **Marquee color, Play audio, Show introduction text, Enable skipping in Try It! mode,** and **Key combination for advancing in Do It! mode.** I usually deselect this option, as I do not want users skipping in *Try It!* mode.

✛ The **Default playback mode** option was introduced in UPK 3.5.

✛ The **Applicable Outline** option was introduced in UPK 12.1. Previous versions displayed the flat list, with the option for the user to display the full Outline.

Option	Description
Enable skipping in Try It! mode	If this option is selected, then users can progress through the screens in *Try It!* mode simply by pressing the ENTER key on their keyboard. As the whole point of *Try It!* mode is that the users are trying it (!) allowing them to skip through the simulation is counter-productive. However, it can be useful when testing to be able to do this. I therefore always leave this option selected during development, and then deselect this option for the final publication. Note that this is just a default setting. If you deselect this option, but select **Enable users to change their Player preferences**, then although users will not initially be able to skip through a simulation, they will be able to go into their Preferences (assuming they know how to do so) and re-enable it. Therefore, if you deselect this option, you should also consider deselecting **Enable users to change their Player preferences**.
Enable Direct Do It!	If this option is selected, then if a user invokes context-sensitive help from within the application and only one Topic matches this context, then that Topic will automatically be launched in *Do It!* mode (versus being listed in the Player, for the user to select). This option applies only to targeted applications for which in-application performance support has been enabled (see *Chapter 15, Integrating UPK with Other Applications*).
Key combination for advancing in Do It! mode	In *Do It!* mode, the UPK window is displayed on top of the application with which the user is interacting. If the key combination specified by this option is pressed, then the instructions in the UPK window will advance to the next step (screen) in the UPK window, even though the application (and not UPK) is still the active window. (See *Chapter 1, An Introduction to Oracle User Productivity Kit* for a more detailed explanation of *Do It!* mode.) You can use any (one-, two-, or three-) key combination, but should choose one that is not used in the application to which the simulation applies. Note that you will have to educate your users on this key combination, especially if you deselect the **Enable users to change their Player preferences** option as the users will not even know that it exists.

✢ **Direct Do It!** was introduced in UPK 3.5.

Preview category

The following table lists the options that are available in the **Preview** category, and describes their purpose:

Option	Description
Publishing Styles	If you have defined a custom deployment format, then you can use the **Category** field to select the publishing format that should be used when you preview your content. Refer to *Chapter 16, Configuring UPK* for more information on custom deployment formats.
Outline Editor	When you select a Module, Section, or Topic in the Outline Editor, the attached **Concept Page** for that object will normally be displayed in the Concept pane. You can use the check-boxes in this section to enable or disable the automatic preview of the following types of files that can appear in the Concept pane: (files in) **Packages**, **Web pages**, **URLs**, and **User-Defined Questions**. If you deselect preview for any of these types of objects, then the Concept pane will simply display a message indicating that preview is disabled—although you can click on the **Preview** button (⬓) to override this setting and display the content object anyway.

✦ The ability to preview **User-Defined Questions** was added in UPK 12.1. Questions will appear in the Concept pane if you select a **Question** or an **Assessment** in the Outline.

Recorder category

The following table lists the options that are available in the **Recorder** category, and describes their purpose.

Option	Description
Screenshot capture	If you select **Manually record screenshots**, then you need to explicitly press the PrintScreen button (or other button - see the next option) whenever you want UPK to capture a screenshot (and action). If you select **Automatically record screenshots**, then UPK will automatically capture a screenshot every time that the screen changes, which is, in theory, every time that you perform an action.

Although I generally recommend manual recording, given that the Wizard is designed to simplify the recording process, **Automatically record screenshots** may be a better option for casual authors. |
| Time (in seconds) to hide recorder window before screen capture | This option defines the number of seconds that UPK will wait after you (the author) press PrintScreen before capturing the screenshot. |
| Screenshot Capture Key | This option specifies which key should be used to indicate to UPK that it should capture a screenshot (and the preceding action). By default, this is the PrintScreen key, but you can use the drop-down list and the check-boxes provided to select any other key combination. Whichever key combination you choose, you should make sure that this key combination is not used by the application that you are recording (specifically, make sure that you do not want to capture this key or key combination as an action).

If you use the **Automatically record screenshots** option then you still need to select a key, but this key is only used to start the recording and stop the recording. You cannot use a key combination for this (you can only use a single key). |
| Record sound with topic | The ability to record sound during the recording process was introduced in UPK version 3.6.1 (in which sound recording was completely re-vamped—see *Chapter 11, Incorporating Sound Into Your Topics* for full details).

If you select the **Record sound with topic** option, then sound is automatically captured via the computer's microphone during the recording of the simulation. Typically, this would be a 'narrative' that you want to include during playback, but a casual UPK user (such as an SME) could use the sound recording functionality to communicate their intentions or requirements to the author. |

Option	Description
Sound pause key	If you choose to capture sound during the recording of the simulation, sound is recorded constantly throughout the recording process. This may not always be desirable (for example, if you need to take a break, or are interrupted). You can therefore designate a key that the recorder can press to temporarily stop sound recording. This key is specified in the **Sound pause key** option, and defaults to the *PAUSE* key.
Open the Topic Editor	This setting is not available when recording via the Wizard, and editing is only possible at the end of recording. This setting is therefore disabled (but still visible) when accessed via the Wizard.

Spelling category

The following table lists the options that are available in the **Spelling** category, and describes their purpose.

● You can also access the **Spelling** options by clicking on the **Options** button from within the **Check Spelling** dialog box.

Option	Use
Ignore words in UPPERCASE	This is a fairly standard option in many spell-checkers, and simply tells the spell-checker to ignore all words that entirely in UPPERCASE (working on the assumption that these are acronyms or technical words).
Try to split compound words into two individual words	If you select this option then the spell-checker will suggest splitting compound words (words made up of two other words) into their component words. For example, it will suggest changing "spell-checker" to "spell checker". Some style guides recommend splitting compound words for clarity, although this may not always be what you want to do. This is a useful option as long as you review each suggestion rather than simply accepting them all.
Custom dictionary	This option can be used to specify the location of the user dictionary—that is, the dictionary to which non-standard words are added by the user when they click on the Add button in the **Check Spelling** dialog box (see earlier). By clicking on the **User Dictionaries** button, you can even specify multiple user dictionaries (for example, for multiple languages. You can also attach an existing dictionary (`.tlx` file), which is very useful if you have an in-house user dictionary that all authors should use.

Target Applications category

When you record actions performed in an application, UPK will attempt to capture the context of your actions. You can disable this automatic capture in some or all cases, by deselecting the relevant options in this section. The table below describes these options.

Option	Use
Both ExactMatch and SmartMatch	If this option is chosen then UPK will attempt to capture the context in all targeted applications, as well as in all other applications. You can choose which specific targeted applications the context is captured for under **ExactMatch Target Applications**.
SmartMatch Only	If this option is selected then UPK will not attempt to capture the context for targeted applications. In some circumstances, capturing the context in targeted applications can slow down the recording process; in others it may cause the recording process to 'hang'. Disabling ExactMatch may prevent these problems, but you will quite likely have to manually select or adjust the captured context (specifically, the **Object Type** and **Object Name** in the *Topic Editor*.
ExactMatch Target Applications	Make sure that the targeted applications for which UPK should attempt to capture the exact context of the recorded actions are selected; you can deselect the applications that you do not use.

C

Object Types

This chapter lists all of the Object Types that are recognized by UPK, and shows the Template Text that is generated for each type. The Template Text for both of the **Standard** template and the **Microsoft** template are shown in the following table. Where the **Microsoft** Template Text differs from the **Standard** Template Text, it is **highlighted**.

Object Type	Standard Template Text	Microsoft Template Text
ActiveX	Click the desired object.	Click the desired object.
Alert	Click the <ObjectName> alert.	Click the <ObjectName> alert.
Animation	Click the animation.	Click the animation.
Application	Click the <ObjectName> animation.	Click the <ObjectName> animation.
Balloon	Click the help balloon.	Click the help balloon.
Border	Click the <ObjectName> border.	Click the <ObjectName> border.
Calendar	Click the desired date.	Click the desired date.
Caret	Click the <ObjectName> caret.	Click the <ObjectName> caret.
Cartoon graphic	Click the <ObjectName> cartoon graphic.	Click the <ObjectName> cartoon graphic.
Chart	Click the <ObjectName> chart.	Click the <ObjectName> chart.
Checkbox	Click the <ObjectName> check box.	**Select the <ObjectName> option.**
CheckListBox	Select the desired item(s) in the <ObjectName> list.	Select the desired item(s) in the <ObjectName> list.
CheckListBox Item	Click the <ObjectName> list item.	Click the <ObjectName> list item.
CheckListBox Item - Checkbox	Select the box before the <ObjectName> item.	Select the check box before the <ObjectName> item.
Clock	Click the <ObjectName> clock.	Click the <ObjectName> clock.

Object Type	Standard Template Text	Microsoft Template Text
Column	Click an entry in the <ObjectName> column.	Click an entry in the <ObjectName> column.
Column Header	Click the <ObjectName> column header.	Click the <ObjectName> column header.
Combobox	Click the <ObjectName> list.	**Click the <ObjectName> box.**
Combobox - Editbox	Click in the edit field of the <ObjectName> combobox.	**Click the <ObjectName> box.**
Cursor	Click the <ObjectName> cursor.	Click the <ObjectName> cursor.
Date/Time box	Click the <ObjectName> date/time field.	**Click the <ObjectName> date/time box.**
Date/Time box - Down SpinButton	Click the <ObjectName> date/time box.	Click the <ObjectName> date/time box.
Date/Time box - Editbox	Click in the <ObjectName> field.	**Click in the <ObjectName> box.**
Date/Time box - Spinbox	Click the up or down arrow next to the <ObjectName> field.	Click the up or down arrow next to the <ObjectName> box.
Date/Time box - Up SpinButton	Click the <ObjectName> date/time box.	Click the <ObjectName> date/time box.
Diagram	Click the <ObjectName> diagram.	Click the <ObjectName> diagram.
Dial box	Click the <ObjectName> dial box.	Click the <ObjectName> dial box.
DragListBox	Click an entry in the list.	**Select an entry in the list.**
DragListBox Item	Click the <ObjectName> list item.	**Select the <ObjectName> list item.**
Drop-down button	Click the button to the right of the <ObjectName> field.	**Click the drop-down arrow to the right of the <ObjectName> box.**
DropDown Grid Button	Click the <ObjectName> button.	Click the <ObjectName> button.
DropDown List	Click an entry in the list.	Select an entry in the list.
DropDown Menu Button	Click the <ObjectName> dropdown button to activate the menu.	Click the <ObjectName> dropdown arrow to access the menu.
Editfield	Click in the <ObjectName> field.	**Click the <ObjectName> box.**
Equation	Click the <ObjectName> equation.	Click the <ObjectName> equation.
Graphics	Click the <ObjectName> graphic.	Click the <ObjectName> graphic.
Grip Object	Click the <ObjectName> grip.	Click the <ObjectName> grip.
Hot key field	Click the <ObjectName> hotkey field.	**Click the <ObjectName> keyboard shortcut box.**
Hyperlink	Click the <ObjectName> hyperlink.	**Click the <ObjectName> link.**

Object Type	Standard Template Text	Microsoft Template Text
IP Address box	Click in the <ObjectName> ip address.	**Click in the <ObjectName> Internet Protocol address.**
IP Address box - Editbox	Click in the <ObjectName> ip address field.	**Click in the <ObjectName> Internet Protocol address box.**
Listbox	Click an entry in the list.	**Select an entry in the list.**
Listbox item	Click the <ObjectName> list item.	Select the <ObjectName> list item.
Menu bar	Click the <ObjectName> menu bar.	Click the <ObjectName> menu bar.
Menu entry	Click the <ObjectName> menu.	**Click the <ObjectName> command.**
Object Group	Click the <ObjectName> object group.	Click the <ObjectName> object group.
Outline	Click the <ObjectName> tree control.	**Click an entry the <ObjectName> tree control.**
Outline item	Click the <ObjectName> tree item.	Click the <ObjectName> tree item.
Outline item button	Click the + button before the <ObjectName> tree item.	Click the plus sign before the <ObjectName> tree item.
Pager	Click the <ObjectName> arrow.	Click the <ObjectName> arrow.
Pager - Down Arrow	Click the <ObjectName> arrow.	Click the <ObjectName> arrow.
Pager - Horizontal	Click the <ObjectName> arrow.	Click the <ObjectName> arrow.
Pager - Left Arrow	Click the <ObjectName> arrow.	Click the <ObjectName> arrow.
Pager - Right Arrow	Click the <ObjectName> arrow.	Click the <ObjectName> arrow.
Pager - Up Arrow	Click the <ObjectName> arrow.	Click the <ObjectName> arrow.
Pager - Vertical	Click the <ObjectName> arrow.	Click the <ObjectName> arrow.
Pane	Click the <ObjectName> pane.	Click the <ObjectName> pane.
Pointer	Click the <ObjectName> pointer.	Click the <ObjectName> pointer.
Popup menu	Click the <ObjectName> menu.	**(Does not exist in Microsoft Template)**
Progress bar	Click the <ObjectName> progress bar.	Click the <ObjectName> progress bar.
Property page	Click the <ObjectName> property page.	Click the <ObjectName> property page.
Pushbutton	Click the <ObjectName> button.	Click the <ObjectName> button.
Radiobutton	Click the <ObjectName> option.	**Select the <ObjectName> option.**
RichEdit	Click the <ObjectName> field.	Click the <ObjectName> box.
Row	Click an entry in the <ObjectName> row.	Click an entry in the <ObjectName> row.
Row header	Click the <ObjectName> row header.	Click the <ObjectName> row header.
Ruler	Click the ruler.	Click the ruler.

Object Type	Standard Template Text	Microsoft Template Text
Ruler - Horizontal	Click the horizontal ruler.	Click the horizontal ruler.
Ruler - Vertical	Click the vertical ruler.	Click the vertical ruler.
Scrollbar	Click the <ObjectName> scrollbar.	Click the <ObjectName> scrollbar.
Scrollbar - Horizontal	Click the <ObjectName> scrollbar.	Click the <ObjectName> scrollbar.
Scrollbar - Vertical	Click the <ObjectName> scrollbar.	Click the <ObjectName> scrollbar.
Scrollbar box	Click the <ObjectName> scrollbar.	Click the <ObjectName> scrollbar.
Scrollbar box - Horizontal	Click the <ObjectName> scrollbar.	Click the <ObjectName> scrollbar.
Scrollbar box - vertical	Click the <ObjectName> scrollbar.	Click the <ObjectName> scrollbar.
Scrollbar button	Click the <ObjectName> button of the scrollbar.	**Click the <ObjectName> scroll arrow of the scrollbar.**
Scrollbar button - Down	Click the <ObjectName> button of the scrollbar.	**Click the <ObjectName> scroll arrow of the scrollbar.**
Scrollbar button - Horizontal	Click the <ObjectName> button of the scrollbar.	**Click the <ObjectName> scroll arrow of the scrollbar.**
Scrollbar button - Left	Click the <ObjectName> button of the scrollbar.	**Click the <ObjectName> scroll arrow of the scrollbar.**
Scrollbar button - PageDown	Click the <ObjectName> button of the scrollbar.	**Click the <ObjectName> scroll arrow of the scrollbar.**
Scrollbar button - PageLeft	Click the <ObjectName> button of the scrollbar.	**Click the <ObjectName> scroll arrow of the scrollbar.**
Scrollbar button - PageRight	Click the <ObjectName> button of the scrollbar.	**Click the <ObjectName> scroll arrow of the scrollbar.**
Scrollbar button - PageUp	Click the <ObjectName> button of the scrollbar.	**Click the <ObjectName> scroll arrow of the scrollbar.**
Scrollbar button - Right	Click the <ObjectName> button of the scrollbar.	**Click the <ObjectName> scroll arrow of the scrollbar.**
Scrollbar button - Up	Click the <ObjectName> button of the scrollbar.	**Click the <ObjectName> scroll arrow of the scrollbar.**
Scrollbar button - Vertical	Click the <ObjectName> button of the scrollbar.	**Click the <ObjectName> scroll arrow of the scrollbar.**
Separator	Click the <ObjectName> separator.	Click the <ObjectName> separator.
Slider	Click the <ObjectName> slider, and drag it to the desired level.	**Move the <ObjectName> slider to the desired level.**
Slider - Track	Click the <ObjectName> slider.	Click the <ObjectName> slider.
Sound	Click the <ObjectName> sound.	Click the <ObjectName> sound.
Spin box	Click the up or down arrow next to the <ObjectName> field.	**Click the up or down arrow next to the <ObjectName> box.**
Spin box - Down button	Click the down arrow next to the <ObjectName> field.	**Click the down arrow next to the <ObjectName> box.**

Object Type	Standard Template Text	Microsoft Template Text
Spin box - Up button	Click the up arrow next to the \<ObjectName> field.	**Click the up arrow next to the \<ObjectName> box.**
Static Text	Click in the \<ObjectName> field.	**Click the \<ObjectName> box.**
Statusbar	Click the statusbar.	**Click the status bar.**
Statusbar button	Click the \<ObjectName> button in the statusbar.	**Click the \<ObjectName> button on the statusbar.**
Tab	Click the \<ObjectName> tab.	Click the \<ObjectName> tab.
Tab - Horizontal	Click the \<ObjectName> horizontal tab.	Click the \<ObjectName> horizontal tab.
Tab - vertical	Click the \<ObjectName> vertical tab.	Click the \<ObjectName> vertical tab.
Tab list	Click the \<ObjectName> tab list.	Click the \<ObjectName> tab list.
Table	Click the \<ObjectName> table.	Click the \<ObjectName> table.
Table Cell	Click the \<ObjectName> cell.	Click the \<ObjectName> cell.
Titlebar	Click the titlebar.	Click the title bar.
Titlebar button	Click the \<ObjectName> button in the titlebar.	**Click the \<ObjectName> button on the titlebar.**
Toolbar	Click the \<ObjectName> toolbar.	Click the \<ObjectName> toolbar.
Toolbar button	Click the \<ObjectName> button.	Click the \<ObjectName> button.
Tooltip	Click the \<ObjectName> tooltip.	Click the \<ObjectName> tooltip.
Universal Object	Click the \<ObjectName> object.	Click the \<ObjectName> object.
Whitespace	Click the \<ObjectName> whitespace.	Click the \<ObjectName> whitespace.
Window	Click the \<ObjectName>.	Click the \<ObjectName>.
Workspace	Click the desired object.	Click the desired object.

D

Toolbar Buttons Quick Reference

Standard Toolbar

Button	Use	Shortcut	See Page
	Open a content object	$C_{TRL}+O$	
	Save the Outline Element or Topic (from within the relevant Editor)	$C_{TRL}+S$	
	Publish the currently-selected content object		*214*
	Preview the currently-selected Topic (select the required mode in the Preview field)		*211*
	Cut the currently-selected content object from the Library, Outline Element, or Assessment	$C_{TRL}+X$	
	Copy the currently-selected content object	$C_{TRL}+C$	
	Paste the content object on the clipboard into the selected folder or Outline Element	$C_{TRL}+V$	
	Delete the currently-selected content object or folder from the Library	D_{ELETE}	
	Record content for the currently-selected empty Topic		*197*
	Undo the last action	$C_{TRL}+Z$	*158*
	Redo the last action that you undid	$C_{TRL}+Y$	*159*
	Expand the currently-selected Outline Element and all of its children		

Button	Use	Shortcut	See Page
	Collapse the currently-selected Outline Element and all of its children		
	Search the content objects in the library for a specific text string, and optionally replace it	$C_{TRL}+F$	90
	Check the spelling in the currently-selected content object(s) (or objects within the currently-selected folder(s))	F7	206
	Help	F1	

Library Toolbar

Button	Use	Shortcut	See Page
	Create a new Module		189
	Create a new Section		189
	Create a new Topic		194
	Create a new Package		389
	Create a new Web Page		357
	Create a new Glossary		411
	Create a new Style Sheet		573
	Create a new Skin		624
	Create a new Assessment		477
	Create a new Question		463
	Create a new In-Application Configuration file		550

Recorder Panel

Button	Use	Shortcut	See Page
	Add or edit author notes		43
	Pause automatic recording / resume automatic recording		42
	Start capturing sound / stop capturing sound		40
	Open the sound tuning wizard		40
	Shows the current sound recording level		
	Discard the last capture		40

Versioning Toolbar

Button	Use	Shortcut	See Page
	Check in the currently-selected content object(s)		300
	Check in all content objects that are currently checked out to you		298
	Check out the currently-selected content object(s)		303
	Cancel the check-out of the currently-selected object(s)		304

View Toolbar

Button	Use	Shortcut	See Page
	Display the Library in a single pane		63
	Split the screen into two horizontal panes		63
	Split the screen into two vertical panes		63

Button	Use	Shortcut	See Page
	Show or hide the **Properties** pane	*F4*	*63*
	Refresh the Library (for example, to check for content objects recently checked in by other authors)	*F5*	*62*
-	Display the Related Documents pane	*C_{TRL}+D*	*69*
-	Display the Broken Links pane	*C_{TRL}+K*	*68*

Outline Editor Toolbar

Button	Use	Shortcut	See Page
	Create a new Module and link it into the currently-selected Outline Element	*C_{TRL}+M*	*193*
	Create a new Section and link it into the currently-selected Outline Element	*C_{TRL}+E*	*193*
	Create an empty Topic and link it into the currently-selected Outline Element	*C_{TRL}+T*	*196*
	Create a new Assessment and link it into the currently-selected Outline Element	*C_{TRL}+N*	
	Create a new Question and link it into the currently-selected Outline Element (select the required Question type from the drop-down)		
	Remove the currently-selected object from the Outline Element	*D_{ELETE}*	*203*
	Move the selected object up one position in its container Outline Element	*C_{TRL}+U*	*203*
	Move the selected object down one position in its container Outline Element	*C_{TRL}+W*	*203*

Topic Editing Toolbar

Button	Use	Shortcut	See Page
	Display or edit the Context ID for the current Frame	*A_{LT}+E,I*	*541*
	Search for additional content objects in the Library that contain the same context as the currently-selected Frame.	*A_{LT}+E,F*	*95*

Button	Use	Shortcut	See Page
	Insert a Frame or Path into the Topic immediately after the currently-selected Frame (select the required type of Frame or Path from the button's drop-down menu):	ALT+I	
	Record one or more additional Frames	ALT+I,M	162
	Record an Alternative Action	ALT+I,A	321
	Record an Alternative Path	ALT+I,P	325
	Insert a Decision Frame	ALT+I,D	329
	Record a Decision Path	ALT+I,E	331
	Insert an Explanation Frame	ALT+I,F	349
	Insert a Blank Frame	ALT+I+B	165
	Insert a No-Context Frame	ALT+I,N	164
	Delete the currently-displayed/selected Action, Path, or Frame (select the Action or Path type from the button's drop-down menu):	ALT+D ALT+L	
	Delete the current Alternative Action	ALT+D,A	
	Delete the currently-selected Path	ALT+D,P	335
	Delete the current Frame	ALT+D,F ALT+L,F	174
	Delete the currently-selected Decision Frame	ALT+D,D ALT+L,D	
-	Delete the currently-selected Decision Path	ALT+D,E ALT+L,D	328
	Recapture the current Action or Screenshot:	ALT+E,R	
	Re-record the Action for the current Frame	ALT+E,R,A	119
	Re-capture the screenshot for the current Frame	ALT+E,R,S	166
	Copy the selected Frame(s) to the clipboard	ALT+E,F	355

● If you open the Topic from the Library then the shortcut *ALT+D* activates the **Delete** menu; if you open the Topic from an Outline Element then *ALT+L* does.

Button	Use	Shortcut	See Page
	Paste the frame(s) currently on the clipboard into the Topic immediately following the currently-selected Frame	$ALT+E,E$	355
	Edit the screenshot for the currently-selected Frame	$ALT+E,E$	171
	Allow UPK to decide whether to include or exclude the current Frame's screenshot in printed output (icon indicates included or excluded, respectively)		172
	Force inclusion of the current Frame's screenshot in printed output		172
	Force exclusion of the current Frame's screenshot from printed output		171
	Create overlays for one or more screenshots in the Topic		175
	Edit the overlays currently defined for the Topic		178
	Remove all overlays from the Topic	$ALT+E,O$	179

Topic Navigation and View Toolbar

Button	Use	Shortcut	See Page
	Go to the Topic's Start Frame		105
	Go to the previous Frame in the Topic	$ALT+LEFT$	105
	Go to the next Frame in the Topic		105
	Go to the Topic's End Frame (use the button's drop-down menu to select the Path, if Branches exist)	$ALT+G,L$ then select	106
	Go to a specific Frame within the Topic (enter the Frame number when prompted)		106
	Go to the previous Action for the Frame	$ALT+UP$	324
	Go to the next Action for the Frame		324
	Toggle between showing and hiding the Action Area on the screen	$ALT+V,O,A$	101

Button	Use	Shortcut	See Page
	Toggle between showing and hiding the Print Area on the screen	*Alt+V,O,P*	*101*

Frame Properties Pane

Button	Use	Shortcut	See Page
	Cut the currently-selected Custom Text to the clipboard	*Ctrl+X*	
	Copy the currently-selected Custom Text to the clipboard	*Ctrl+C*	
	Paste the contents of the clipboard into the Custom Text input area	*Ctrl+V*	
	Delete the currently-selected Custom Text	*Delete*	
	Select the font for the currently-selected Custom Text		*153*
	Set the currently-selected Custom Text as non-breaking		*153*
	Create a hyperlink from the currently-selected Custom Text		*383*
	Left-align the Bubble Text		
	Center the Bubble Text		
	Right-align the Bubble Text		
	Set the Bubble Text as fully-justified		
	Set the currently-selected Custom Text in bold	*Ctrl+B*	
	Set the currently-selected Custom Text in italics	*Ctrl+I*	
	Set the currently-selected Custom Text underlined	*Ctrl+U*	
	Change the color of the currently-selected Custom Text		
	Set the currently-selected Custom Text as visible in See It! and Try It! modes		*155*
	Set the currently-selected Custom Text as visible in Know It? mode		*155*

Button	Use	Shortcut	See Page
	Set the currently-selected Custom Text as visible in *Do It!* mode		*155*
	Set the currently-selected Custom Text as visible in on-line output		*155*
	Set the currently-selected Custom Text as visible in printed output		*155*
	Toggle the Bubble between being displayed and hidden in *See It!* and *Try It!* modes		*141*
	Insert an icon into the current Bubble (select the icon from the pop-up box)		*141*
	Select the position on the Bubble from which the bubble pointer extends		*139*
	Set the background color of the Bubble		
	Insert the Template Text as custom Text for the current Frame		*150*
	Toggle between displaying and hiding the Template Text for the current Frame in Know It? mode		*151*
	Toggle between showing and hiding the Template Text for the current Frame in all modes		*151*
	Toggle between showing the Custom Text before any Template Text in the Bubble, and showing it after any Template Text		*152*
	Select the font in which Template Text should be displayed		
	Modify the Action Area or Print Area:		
	Create a new Action Area		*113*
	Delete the selected Action Area		*113*
	Copy the Action Area for this Frame from the previous Frame		*113*
	Create a Print Area (separate from the Action Area)		*114*
	Delete the Print Area and revert to using the Action Area as the Print Area		*115*
	Toggle between showing and hiding the Action Area during playback		*101*

Button	Use	Shortcut	See Page
	Display the Bubble Text for the current Frame and the next Frame in the same step in *Do It!* mode		*145*
	Toggle between ignoring and using context for the Frame (if context is ignored, Template Text will not be used)		*117*
	Move the end-point of the current path		*327*

FOR DECISION FRAMES:

Button	Use	Shortcut	See Page
	Record a new Decision Path (must have the Decision Frame selected)		*331*
	Rename the selected Decision Path (first select the Path in the Path List)		*329*
	Delete the selected Decision Path (first select the Path in the Path List)		*335*

FOR STRING INPUT ACTIONS:

Button	Use	Shortcut	See Page
A	Select the font for the input text		*128*
	Change the background color of the string input action area		*126*
Aa	Make the string input case sensitive		*137*
...	Make the input field a password field (input will be masked)		*137*
+/-	Change the string input options:		
T	Provide another text that the trainee can enter in *Know It?* mode		*130*
	Change the captured input text		*131*
	Allow the trainee to enter any value or leave the field blank		*131*
	Allow the trainee to enter any value (but they must enter something)		*131*
	Allow the trainee to enter any of the specified texts or leave the field blank		*131*
	Delete the currently-selected input text		*136*
	Set the currently-selected input text to be the default input value		*137*
	Remove all options except the explicitly-specified input texts		*136*

Concept Pane Toolbar

Button	Use	Shortcut	See Page
	Link a content object as the Concept Page for the selected Module, Section, or Topic		*381*
	Create a new Web Page to use as the Concept Page for the selected Module, Section, or Topic		*382*
	Create a new Package and use a file within this as the Concept Page for the selected Module, Section, or Topic		*405*
	Edit the document currently linked as the Concept Page		
	Remove the currently-linked content object from the Concept Pane		
	Preview the content object that is currently linked as the Concept Page (assuming that it is not set to auto-preview in the *Concept* pane – see **Tools** | **Options** | **Preview**)		
	Play or pause the sound file for the content object linked as the Concept Page		
	Stop sound playback		

Web Page Editor - Appearance Toolbar

Button	Use	Shortcut	See Page
	Change the color of the currently-selected text		
	Change the background color of the currently-selected text		
	Strike through the selected text		
	Set the currently-selected text in subscript		
	Set the currently-selected text in superscript		
	Clear all directly-applied formatting from the selected text		
	Format the selected text as a bulleted list		

Button	Use	Shortcut	See Page
	Format the selected text as a numbered list		
	Decrease indentation for the selected paragraphs		
	Indent the selected paragraphs		
	Format the selected paragraphs as a block quote		
	Click on this button to display a dialog box that allows you to set the spacing before and after the selected paragraphs		
-	Display the HTML source for the Web page	$C_{TRL}+$ $S_{HIFT}+L$	

Web Page Editor - Font and Formatting Toolbar

Button	Use	Shortcut	See Page
B	Set the currently-selected text in bold	$C_{TRL}+B$	
I	Set the currently-selected text in italics	$C_{TRL}+I$	
U	Set the currently-selected text underlined	$C_{TRL}+U$	
	Left-align the currently-selected paragraph(s)		
	Center the currently-selected paragraph(s)		
	Right-align the currently-selected paragraph(s)	$C_{TRL}+R$	
	Set the currently-selected paragraph(s) as fully-justified	$C_{TRL}+J$	

Web Page Editor - Package Toolbar

Button	Use	Shortcut	See Page
▸¶	Format the selected text for left-to-right reading (this is the default).		

Button	Use	Shortcut	See Page
¶◄	Format the selected text for right-to-left reading.		
	Insert a form.		
☑	Insert a checkbox form element into the form		
◎	Insert an option button (a.k.a. a radio button) form element into the form		
abl	Insert an edit field into the form		
ab cd	Insert a text input box into the form		
	Insert a selection field form element into the form		
▢	Insert a button form element into the form		
	Insert an image		
	Insert a hidden field		
<div>	Insert a HTML DIV container		
	Toggle between showing the HTML source for the page and the WYSIWYG view		

Web Page Editor - Tools Toolbar

Button	Use	Shortcut	See Page
	Search for a specific string within the current Web Page		
ab ↓ac	Search for a specific string on within the current Web Page and replace it with another specified string		
	Display boundaries for block-level elements		*371*
-	Select the preview mode for the Web Page (Player or Print)		
	Open the Web Page in the browser, formatted for the selected mode		*372*

Sound Editor Toolbar

Button	Use	Shortcut	See Page
	Import sound: Import a sound file from your PC into this Frame		*456*
	Export sound: Export the current sound for the Frame		*455*
	Record sound: Record new sound for the Frame		*452*
	Insert sound: Record new sound and insert it at the current cursor position		
	Play / Pause: Play the section of sound currently selected in the timeline, and pause the currently-playing sound, respectively.		
	Stop: Stop the sound playback.		
	Cut: Cut the currently-selected portion of sound.		
	Copy: Copy the currently-selected portion of sound.		
	Paste: Paste the section of sound currently on the sound clipboard into the timeline at the current cursor position		
	Delete: Delete the currently-selected portion of sound		
	Select frame: Select all of the sound for the current frame.		
	Deselect all: Cancel any current selection.		
	Select start of frame sound: Extend the current selection backwards to the start of sound for the current Frame.		
	Select end of frame sound: Extend the current selection forwards to the end of sound for the current Frame.		
	Crop to selection: Crop the sound for the Frame so that it consists of only the current selection		
	Zoom: Change the scope of the timeline so that it includes specific sound		*448*
	Modify length or amplitude: Change the duration or amplification of a portion of sound		*449*

Button	Use	Shortcut	See Page
	Sound Tuning Wizard: Launch the *Sound Tuning Wizard*		*453*
Sound Recorder:			
	Restart: Return to the start of the sound clip		*453*
	Go to previous Frame: Go to the previous Frame		
	Go to next Frame: Go to the next Frame		
	Pause / Restart: Pause sound recording, and restart sound recording		*453*

Package Editor Toolbar

Button	Use	Shortcut	See Page
	Upload a file from your PC into the Package		*390*
	Upload a folder and all of its contents from your PC into the Package		*390*
	Create a new HTML file and include it in the Package		*406*

Style Editor - Styles Toolbar

Button	Use	Shortcut	See Page
	Add a new style definition to the Style Sheet.		*574*
	Delete the selected style definition.		*574*
	Make the currently-selected style definition the default for the element type.		*575*
	Add a print variant for the currently-selected style.		*576*
	Add a language variant for the currently-selected style.		*576*

Style Editor - Text/Paragraph Toolbar

Button	Use	Shortcut	See Page
	Set the text color for the element		
	Set the background (fill) color of the element		
B	Format the element text in bold		
I	Format the element text in italics		
<u>U</u>	Underline the element text		
abc	Strike through the element text		
	Set the element text as left-aligned		
	Set the element text as centered		
	Set the element text as right-aligned		
	Set the element text as fully justified		
	Define the margin (amount of space) that should be provided outside of the container for the element text		*579*
	Define a border (color and width) around the text element		*579*
	Set the width and/or height of an image element		*580*
	Define the padding (amount of space) that should be provided within the text container on each side of the contents.		*580*

Style Editor - Table and List Toolbar

Button	Use	Shortcut	See Page
	Align text within selected table element to the top of the cell		
	Align text within selected table element to the center of the cell		

Button	Use	Shortcut	See Page
	Align text within selected table element to the bottom of the cell		
	Align text within selected table element to the element baseline		*581*
	Position the table caption above the table		
	Position the table caption below the table		

Index

I

IAS
  Application Instances, 554
  Global settings, 555
  Sources, 550
IAS Information
  At the end of Publishing, 558
IAS Profile
  Creating, 550
  Selecting during publishing, 556
IBM Rational Quality Manager, 21, 515, 713
Icon
  Option, 703
Icons
  Customizing, 621
IIS server, 566
Image Editor
  Option, 697
Images
  In Web Pages, 376
  Using in Web Pages, 376
Implicit text, 122
Implicit Text, 31
Import
  Content defaults, 37, 55
  Content objects, 312
  For localization, 663
  Selective, 315
  Selective imports, 315
  Sound files, 456
In Application Support, 549
In-Application Support
  Publishing options for, 225
Include action areas
  Option, 713
Include alternatives
  Option, 711, 712, 713
Include assessments
  Option, 711
Include detailed action steps in HTML Web Site
  Option, 715
Include images from packages
  Option, 711
Include images in Web Pages
  Option, 711
Include questions
  Option, 712
Include relative links

Option, 711, 714
Infoblocks, 356, 388
Instructor Manual, 261
  Description of, 20
  Example, 265
Instructor Notes
  In the Topic Editor, 179
Introduction Frame, 342
Introduction pane, 196
Introduction text
  Publishing option, 228, 717
iTutor, 10

J

Job Aid, 249
  Description of, 20
  Example, 253
Jump-in Points, 431
  Defining, 431
  In the Player, 432

K

Keep checked out, 52, 302
Keyboard
  Actions, 118
Keyboard Actions
  Action properties vs. the Template, 595
Keyword Index
  For HTML Web Site, 237
Keywords, 434
  Property, 435
Know It? mode
  Considerations for Decision Frames, 335
  Description of, 18
  In Assessments, 481
  Template text in, 151
  Testing, 212
Know It Remediation, 223
Know It Required %, 223
Know It? Required Percentage
  Option, 701
Knowledge Center, 233, 556, 563
  Publishing to, 233
Knowledge Pathways, 563
Knowledge Verification, 18
kp.html, 505, 563

P

X

C2360.2